Iran's Nowruz Revolution

#Nowruz

AMIR FASSIHI, M.D.

Copyright © 2012 Amir Fassihi
All rights reserved.
Cover Design by Ali Nouri
ISBN-13:
978-1478344087
ISBN-10:
1478344083

For a Free and Prosperous Iran

CONTENTS

CONTENTS 2
ACKNOWLEDGMENTS 6
INTRODUCTION 8

PART I – Legacy of Violence

CHAPTER 1 - Fear, Trauma and Post Traumatic Stress Disorder. 24

Living with fear in Iran - Historical review and understanding of trauma and Post Traumatic Stress Disorder in humans and its effect on societies - Complex PTSD in Iranian society and its psychological manifestations -The unique Iranian experience with fear, trauma and terror and its repercussions during and after the revolution, the Iran-Iraq war, the political repression and killings of the 1990's, and up until present day Iran and its current state of psychological crisis.

Chapter 2- 100 Generation Legacy of Violence- Part I: War in the Age of Empires. 56

War as a way of life for Iranians - From the first generation in 550BCE during the rise of the Persian Empire to Alexander's conquest of Iran (10th generation) to the 25 generation long Persian-Roman wars, to the persecution and massacre of Iranian Christians, Manichaests and Mazdakites to the Byzantium and civil wars of the 47th-48th generation, the last conquest of Jerusalem and Egypt by Iranians followed by immediate retreat and chaos in the Persian Empire.

CHAPTER 3 – 100 Generation Legacy of Violence- Part II: Islamic Centuries of Conquest and Bloodshed 106

Violence and bloodshed from the Islamic invasion of Iran in Battle of Qadisiya to schism in Islam, 200 years of civil war against Islamic Caliphate rule in Iran- Islamic invasions into today's Afghanistan, Central Asia and India - Creation of Turkic slave trade, rise of Turkic Sultans and continued Turkic civil wars in Iran.

CHAPTER 4 –100 Generation Legacy of Violence- Part III: The Genocides and Violence of Tribal Centuries 150

The great Mongolian Genocide and its aftermath – Tamerlane – Safavids and the resurrection of Iran as a nation - Persecution of Sunnis to wars against the Ottoman Empire -The golden 87th generation -Iran's demise and occupation by Afghan Warlords - Nader Shah – Continued foreign and civil wars in the 18th and 19th century - Rise of military dictatorships in 20th century and the acceptance of violence as political fait accompli in 1979 Islamic Revolution during the 102nd generation's lifetime.

Chapter 5 - Violence as fait accompli of human beings 220

Evidence of violence since the dawn of agricultural era 10,000 years ago – Violence in contemporary hunter-gatherer societies – Violence in prehistoric and pre-agricultural societies – Violence in Homo Sapiens' closest relative, the chimpanzee – Violence as *fait accompli* of human beings – Expectation and assumption of Iranians that violence is the only practical instrument for political change.

PART II – Promise of Nonviolence

Chapter 6 - The Beginnings of Nonviolence 232

Introduction to study of nonviolence from Henry David Thoreau and his essay on Civil Disobedience to Leo Tolstoy and his influence on Gandhi to Gandhi's first jail term and successful application of civil disobedience in South Africa.

Chapter 7 – Civil Disobedience in India 264

Development of nonviolence as an instrument for social change in India from Gandhi's struggles for equality for untouchables and the failed attempts at civil disobedience in 1920's to nationwide civil disobedience against the British instituted Salt Act to the eventual independence, partition and civil war in India.

Chapter 8 - Nonviolence is reborn in America......................318

Development of Martin Luther King's nonviolent movement in America from Rosa Parks and the Montgomery Bus Boycott to James Lawson and nonviolent resistance at the lunch counters in Nashville to the Freedom Ride - Letter from the Birmingham Jail - King's stance on Vietnam - King's campaign to help the poor and to his assassination.

Chapter 9 Nonviolence As Science 364

Scientific theory of nonviolent struggle by Gene Sharp in 1973 - The birth of leaderless revolution in Philippines– Development of the framework and model for Truth and Reconciliation Commission in South Africa.

PART III – Celebrations as Civil Disobedience

Chapter 10 – Rituals and Celebrations through anthropologic and psychological views..420

Introduction to Clyde Kluckhohn's study of rituals and celebrations in Navajos to Milan Psychiatric group and study of rituals for psychological healing to Van der Hart and use of rituals in psychotherapy to Judith Herman's stages of recovering from trauma.

Chapter 11 –Celebrations of Resistance against Winter......432

Introduction to Iranian celebrations, their significance, traditions, myths and folklore - Yalda Celebration (December 21st), the start of winter, variations in food and customs and folklore of Yalda - Portrayal of Sadeh, the fortieth and coldest night of winter (January 30th) - Esfandgan (February 26th), the ancient celebration for women and the month long celebration of women's rights in Esfand as civil disobedience - Description of Souri, the Festival of Fire on last Tuesday of winter and Souri Celebration as civil disobedience.

Chapter 12 - Celebrations of Rebirth and Renewal in Spring 466

Celebrations of Spring from Nowruz, the start of New Year and its significance on shaping the Iranian identity and spirit of resistance to *'Sizdah bedar'* the celebration of nature on the 13th day of Spring - *'Farvardegan'* celebration as memorial celebration on the 19th day of Spring - *'Ordibeheshtgan'* (Earth Day) Celebration on April 23rd as civil disobedience - *'Khordadgan'* as Lover's Day Celebration on May 27th.

Chapter 13 –Summer and Autumn Celebrations and the Cycle of Life 486

Tirgan (July 4th), the ancient celebration of peace and its mythological roots – Celebration of *Tirgan* with neighbors – Water games on *Tirgan* as civil disobedience – *Amordadgan* (July 29th), Celebration of the elderly – *Shahrivargan* (August 26th) Veteran's Day Celebration – The grand harvest festival of *Mehregan* as civil disobedience (October 8th) – The historical and mythological roots of *Mehregan* Celebration – *Abangan* (November 1st) Mother's Day Celebration –

Azargan (November 30th) Celebrating enlightenment, spirituality and freedom of consciousness – *Bahmangan* (January 22nd) as celebration of kindness to animals- Father's Day celebration on Ferdowsi's birthday.

Epilogue **512**

Nowruz Revolution in this game of *Shogi*.

Bibliography/References **537**

ACKNOWLEDGMENTS

This book would not have been possible without the love, support and encouragement of my wife. Through all the years of writing and rewriting this text, she was the pillar of stability in my life as well as the source of love and strength.

I began the manuscript shortly after my daughter's first birthday. She is almost eight years old as I write this and my second daughter is nearing four. Throughout this project, they were cradles of joy, energy, hope as well as constant reminders of humanity's innocence and its potential for the future. May they one day grow to read this manuscript and may their generation one day live in an Iran where every day is Nowruz.

I must thank my mother and father for their love and support. Through the revolution, war and constant moving from one country to another, they gave their all to keep the family together and placed our education at the highest priority, always seeking to enroll us in the best schools possible and with the best teachers. I am a product of those schools and those teachers.

I have to thank Ms. Partow Nooriala whose relentless feedback and critical focus were a source of constant improvement and reflection. In addition, as my mother-in-law, her delicious cooking was the source of energy for me and my family and we hope to continue enjoying her advice and cooking for many years to come.

I am grateful to James O'Shea Wade (Jim Wade) whose four decades of experience as an editor were instrumental and necessary for the massive task of editing and polishing this manuscript. I am forever indebted to his patience, knowledge and wisdom.

I also like to thank Barbara De Santis whose twenty five years of experience in book publishing were critical in making the final adjustments and additions to the manuscript.

I like to thank Elham Gheytanchi who patiently reviewed the manuscript and gave constructive feedback and insight and also Dr. Esmail Nooriala who reviewed the manuscript at the beginnings of the project and provided valuable advice. Also, a special thank you to Ali Nouri for the beautiful cover design.

To all my friends and family who through these years patiently encouraged and supported this project, thank you.

May we all one day experience an Iran where every day is Nowruz.

INTRODUCTION

"There are only two invincible forces in the twentieth century: the Atom Bomb and Nonviolence."

-Bishop Leonidas Proano of Ecuador, Latin American activist of 20th century referred to as the 'Bishop of the poor'.[1]

PTSD

Before starting my residency in radiology, I had to spend a year doing an internship in general medicine at any hospital in the United States. I had done two rotations at the VA hospital in San Francisco and I enjoyed having veterans as my patients. Thus, I chose Veterans Hospital in West Los Angeles. On an otherwise unremarkable night, I was called by the ER to admit one of my five patients for the shift. I was happy to find that the patient was a straightforward case of pneumonia. I ordered his medications and scheduled a follow-up chest x-ray for the morning. I asked him if he was taking any other medications. He said no. I asked him if he was depressed or if he had any psychiatric issues. He said no to that as well. I asked him about alcohol and drugs, and he said he smoked a pack of cigarettes a day. He was an African American in his fifties and had served in Vietnam as a young soldier. I told him he needed to quit smoking and that I could refer him to our smoking cessation clinic. But he didn't have the patience for a conversation and responded, "Just give me my antibiotics."

For the next few days, he was just a name on my list. I would order a chest x-ray for each morning and a blood test to see if his white blood cell count was coming down. I would visit him very briefly at 6:30 am during my morning rush, wake him in bed, do a quick physical exam and move on to see my other patients. Given his impatience upon admission, I made a conscious decision to just treat his pneumonia and let him leave as soon as he felt better.

On the third morning after his admission, I went to see him. He was sitting up in his bed and was clearly in great discomfort. He was holding his neck and his face was wet with tears. I asked him, "What's wrong?" The way he was holding his neck was evidence of some sort of pain in his neck or lower face. It took a few minutes for him to gather his composure and answer me. As I waited, fear began overtaking me. I knew this man was in great pain and in need of urgent attention, but I didn't know why. He had been

INTRODUCTION

completely fine the night before and I couldn't imagine what could have happened. I will never forget what he finally told me, while tears streamed down his face: "I tried to hang myself early this morning. I couldn't. I think I hurt my neck."

There are moments in your life that your concern about the modern world and its problems simply stops. In that instant, you don't care anymore about your meetings, your obligations, or your schedule. Tomorrow doesn't matter anymore and you don't care if you have lunch or not. In those moments, someone else's pain becomes yours, your heart beats with their rhythm and their sorrow engulfs you.

We have very few such moments in our lives. Some call them 'paradigm shifts', moments when you wake up and you realize you've been in a deep sleep and that playing the role of a mouse running round and round on a wheel was just a dream. Then reality sets in and you see the world through different eyes. You realize you had been just looking at and talking to someone's shadow and that now you are really seeing that person. And in such moments, if you manage to remain in this altered state of awareness, you may be able to see yourself.

After a long day of evaluating him for physical injury to the cervical spine and a series of evaluations by our psychiatrist, the patient was diagnosed with Post Traumatic Stress Disorder caused by experiences decades ago. After dealing with this patient, PTSD slowly began to take on a new meaning for me.

Looking back in my life, I can now recognize psychological illness in countless individuals I have known. Most had relatively successful lives with relatively successful children; but underneath the surface there were problems. Yet, despite my schoolbook training on psychological disorders and my interest in the human mind, it wasn't until I encountered this patient during my internship that I gained a deeper understanding of the true pain of mental illness.

For people who have worked with veterans of wars or patients who have experienced violence, PTSD is as common as hypertension. There are countless conferences, lectures, and clinics devoted to it in VA hospitals. Most charts on veterans of war have these letters written somewhere in them, and even if not, you can nearly always find some symptoms associated with it. Veterans have a high incidence of PTSD, which, if severe enough, can affect every facet of their lives.

In addition, the effects on those suffering from trauma are not confined to the individual; they impact his or her family and set the tone for the household and the personality of the family. In a core family of five, it is often not the actions of the majority that influence a family's overall psychological well-being. One person in a family suffering from depression or anxiety will cause the family to function ineffectively and, at times, in ways similar to that of the directly affected individual. Thus ten individuals suffering from a psychological disorder can often be regarded as the cause of suffering for ten families.

This thought made me wonder—what if the number of those suffering from trauma is not just in the thousands, but hundreds of thousands or millions. Would we not then have hundreds of thousands or millions of families dealing with this psychological illness? What effect would this have on a society? Would that society behave differently than a psychologically healthy population? If a sufficiently large number of families in a nation are impacted by PTSD, will that nation manifest the underlying psychological traits of its population?

Sometime after this incident, I picked up a copy of 'Trauma and Recovery' by Dr. Judith Herman of Harvard University. I wanted to gain a deeper understanding of PTSD in patients, but to my great surprise, in addition to having a deeper understanding for trauma and PTSD in patients, the book profoundly influenced my thoughts on trauma, fear and terror on those living under totalitarian states and dictatorships. I had spent my childhood in a totalitarian state and through this book, I gained a much deeper understanding of the deliberate use of terror in totalitarian states and particularly the use of fear in such states, an understanding which I thought would be of great benefit for Iranians in their struggle for democracy. Thus this new insight and focus on the deliberate infliction of terror and trauma by despotic regimes and, specifically by the rulers of the Islamic Republic of Iran, played a major role in inspiring me to write this book.

But there were several other pieces that came together, elements that ultimately influenced the form and content of the book.

Chuka

On the main highway linking Iran's Gilan province in the north to the capital city of Tehran lies a small town called Loshan. On a late misty and dark night in October 1996, an incident occurred there that has had profound

INTRODUCTION

influence on my life. Much of the inspiration for this book may be related to events that led up to this night.

Standing at a checkpoint within this mountainous region, through which vehicles were usually allowed to travel freely to Tehran, was a young *basiji* armed with a machine gun, making every car slow down to a near stop before letting them pass. While steadying his machine gun in one hand, he occasionally glanced at a piece of paper he was holding in his other. Late that night, upon seeing a white Toyota Land Cruiser approaching the checkpoint, he motioned the car to pull over. Checking the piece of paper once again to make sure that he had identified the car's license plate correctly, he ordered the driver to get out of the car.

The Land Cruiser was the third in a convoy of white Land Cruisers leaving Gilan province that evening and heading for the capital along the twisting, mountainous highway. In the first vehicle were three representatives of the feared Intelligence Ministry; in the second vehicle, three representatives of the Ministry of Industry. These six individuals had been selected by Iran's then-president, Ali Akbar Hashemi Rafsanjani, as a jury to settle a four-year-long dispute between the two ministries on charges brought about by Ministry of Intelligence against the passenger in the 3rd Land Cruiser.

The passenger in the third vehicle was Chairman of the Board and CEO of Chuka, one of the largest paper manufacturing companies in the Middle East employing more than 3,000 workers in mid 1990s. The car was driven by his first deputy. After 48 hours of non-stop meetings and interviews with local and regional officials, including the governor and the chief of police of Gilan province and workers in the factory, the six-man jury had judged the management of Chuka and the Minister of Industry to be innocent on nearly three dozen trumped up charges including charges of un-Islamic behavior, western tendencies and even corruption and bribery. The jury, after 72 hours of investigation, had cleared the management of Chuka of any wrongdoing and had taken the side of the Ministry of Industry on this issue.

The passenger, exhausted after two days of meetings, was asleep at the time but when the car was stopped, he was urgently awakened by his deputy. Upon the driver's inquiring as to why they were being stopped, the young Basiji informed them of a dispatch about a hit and run incident with a description of the car involved and its license plate—the one on their vehicle. He was told they had hit another vehicle on their way and were responsible for the deaths of five people, a hit and run crime which could easily land one in prison for life. He had been ordered to hold the passengers in his jailhouse until authorities arrived from Tehran to take custody of them. The passenger and the driver were led along the dark highway to a large jail room in a building on the side of the road and put in a cell. On the other side of its iron bars was a single desk with a telephone and a small transistor radio. On the bare walls were pictures of Ayatollah Khamenei and Ayatollah Khomeini, the current and previous Supreme Leaders of Iran. A single wire hung from the ceiling holding a naked light bulb that provided the only light in the place, which was enshrouded in the dark and misty air of Loshan.

In the jail cell, the deputy driving the vehicle, now in tears, curled himself in the corner, holding his head and rocking back and forth. The CEO of Chuka, standing by the bars, occasionally would turn to his deputy and old friend to console him and remind him that "this is not about you!" Yet, his deputy and friend who was always in a cheerful mood and loved to play tennis could not be calmed. He knew very well that this was not about him, but he also knew that forces of violence beyond his control were now dictating his fate.

For four years now, his boss, with the backing of Dr. Mohammad Reza Nematzadeh, the Minister of Industry, had fought Ali Fallahian, the feared Minister of Intelligence and one of the most powerful men in Iran. For two years, there had been arguments in Rafsanjani's cabinet between Nematzadeh and Fallahian. Quarrel was over security at Iranian factories and specifically the issue of security at Chuka, Iran's largest paper manufacturer. The man Nematzadeh had chosen to run Iran's major paper manufacturing facility was known as a brilliant manager who had returned to Iran after years of living in the United States. He had come back to help rebuild a country devastated by the war with Iraq. The enterprise he had been assigned to manage was a chronically ill company founded by Canadians in the 1970's. A money losing and nearly bankrupt enterprise dependent on state subsidies, the operation had never achieved more than 20% of its production capacity.

Expensive pulp was imported for this industry from Scandinavian countries which was more expensive than the sale price of finished cardboard boxes made by Chuka. In addition, tens of thousands of acres of pristine Iranian forests in the north had been decimated to supply the long-fiber pulp needed for manufacturing. Chuka's thousands of workers were underpaid and unhappy and the company as a whole was a money-losing entity that required millions of dollars in state subsidy each year to maintain minimal production.

Within his first two years, the man standing behind the iron bars and staring at the basiji had put an end to this pointless environmental destruction

INTRODUCTION

carried out to harvest the few trees with appropriate fiber and turned over the previously assigned acres of forest to the Department of Forestry and Ministry of Agriculture. A paper-making operation, he had notified the Ministry of Industry, had a responsibility to make sure that thousands of appropriate trees, which would serve as the long-fiber source of pulp, were planted in the same forests to replace those cut down. To eliminate the need for importing expensive pulp from abroad, the man now in custody had set up the most comprehensive recycling system in the Middle East, with thousands of small and large entrepreneurs setting up paper pressing machines in towns and cities across Iran. Even some small villages had obtained paper presses and were hunting everywhere for used cardboard boxes, magazines and newspapers. These recycled paper products were purchased by Chuka at a nationwide fixed price per kilo and used to make pulp for manufacturing paper and cardboard. In his first year, the head of Chuka had instituted salary bonus incentives for workers, tied to the company's productivity and also additional bonuses for ideas which were put forth by workers and implemented in the factory. Chuka, which had been producing only a fraction of its output capacity for nearly twenty years, had managed through incentives and restructuring to increase production to 120% of previously thought limit of output while eliminating the importation of expensive pulp and unsustainable deforestation. The previously bankrupt company was now making millions of dollars in profit and had become an interest for many in the Ministry of Intelligence hoping to make themselves or their family rich.

The additional salaries of thousands of workers had led to spending and consumption that had sparked economic growth in the city of Talesh and nearby towns in Gilan, creating a regional economic boom for thousands of businesses that prospered as a result of Chuka's success. Aditionally, some of the proceeds were used to build a local college and a division II soccer team. The governor of Gilan had become one of the CEO's strongest supporters. The local clerics held him in high regard, particularly after they had learned he was the nephew of Grand Ayatollah Khonsari, one of the leading scholars and teachers of Islam in Qom, a holy city that was the center of theological studies in Iran.

A petroleum engineer by training, he had come to United States in 1968 to post graduate work in Computer Sciences, a field relatively new at the time. He had immediately returned to Iran and was on the team that had set up Iran's first computer, the size of a room for Tehran's municipality. He was then hired by IBM, working and learning in the most innovating and progressive company of 1970's ,where he had been sent to places as diverse as Kenya, Italy, and Harvard University for the latest management courses and seminars. Never interested in politics, he had initially stayed in Iran after the 1979 revolution, continuing his work as an engineer and a consultant. Shortly later, the war and the stress of living in a revolutionary country had forced him to take his family to the United States. In 1992, he had returned to his native country hoping to help rebuild a devastated economy. Local artists, environmentalists, businessmen, mayors, and community leaders had befriended him, hoping to learn from his experience consulting and leading some of the largest companies in Iran. Yet to his sadness he had learned that it was not rational business decisions that determined the fate of his workers and Iranians in general, but sources of violence.

Within six months after taking the helm of Chuka, with the backing of the Minister of Industry, Chuka's CEO had removed the Intelligence Ministry's representative for *'herasat'* who had intervened in a management decision on how to run the company; an intervention with implications of personal gain for the officer. *'Herasat'* — the security service's operatives— served as the Intelligence Ministry's eyes, ears and influence in every factory, university and institution throughout Iran. In addition, *herasat* officers were in charge of recruiting *basijis* from factories and universities; and along with the Revolutionary Guards, served as the repressive and violent agents of enforcement for the clerics who were, and still are, in control of the Islamic Republic.

In 1990's, the powerful intelligence ministry, in the name of privatization, was helping to sell large and valuable Iranian enterprises very cheap to families of revolutionary guard commanders and leading clerics in Iran. The *herasat* officers in each factory were often the first to take advantage of such exploitation. Yet not all intelligence and *herasat* officers were corrupt and to replace the fired *'herasat'* officer, and in order not to completely alienate the Intelligence Ministry, he had brought in another intelligence officer sympathetic to the company's ambitions and the needs of the local population.

The exchange of *'herasat'* officers by factory management had tremendous security implications for the Islamic Republic. In the mid 1990's, *herasat* was at the heart of the security apparatus of the regime and in particular, the feared Intelligence Ministry and Fallahian, its minister. The ability to fire a *herasat* representative from an institution in Iran, even if another officer was brought

INTRODUCTION

in, meant that the institution could potentially be free of surveillance and interference by the security forces. Knowing the implications of this case, many technocrats in various industries had supported Chuka's CEO, hoping it was a precedent that would allow them to do the same thing. This action had also been supported by Nematzadeh, Rafsanjani's Minister of Industry, but strongly opposed by Fallahian, the Minster of Intelligence and head of the Islamic Republic's security apparatus. For four years, the battle had been waged between the two ministries, which often plunged the two ministers into contentious and intense debates in meetings of Rafsanjani's cabinet over this issue of *herasat's* interference with industry. More than four dozen trumped up charges ranging from financial corruption to un-Islamic behavior were fabricated against management of Chuka and each was fought and defeated.

In addition to the insult of the removal of his chosen *herasat* representative, Fallahian bitterly resented the popularity of Chuka's chief executive amongst the several thousand factory workers. On several occasions, after he learned that local leaders and Friday Prayer Imam's had encouraged the CEO to become a candidate for election to *majles* [parliament] and represent Talesh, he had sent armed plain-clothes security forces to the factory and threatened Chuka's leader, warning him to abandon any thought of a political career.

In October of 1996, a week before the incident, the dispute between the two ministries finally came to a boil. On a routine morning visit to the factory, the CEO of Chuka was flagged down on the highway by a dozen sympathetic workers who notified him of several dozen plain clothes militia with machine guns taking over the factory. On the walls were spray painted 'Death to Nematzadeh', the minister of Industry and death to management of Chuka. The matter had been immediately reported to President Rafsanjani who was on an official state visit to South Africa. Rafsanjani had ordered back 1) a complete media silence on the matter and 2) a six man jury with three representatives from Ministry of Intelligence and three from Ministry of Industry to come up with a verdict and resolve the issue once and for all. The six man jury, after three days of investigation and interviews with factory workers and regional leaders including the governor and chief of police of Gilan, had voted in favor of the management of Chuka, clearing the CEO of wrongdoing and backing him on the replacement of the corrupt *herasat* officer.

That night, locked in a cell and pondering his fate, he realized that he had won many battles but had lost the war against the forces of violence. Fallahian, who was responsible for several hundred kidnappings and deaths in 1990's, probably had a team on his way from Tehran's Intelligence headquarters to dispose of this threat to the system.

Those who govern the Islamic Republic know very well that only violence can ultimately guarantee their survival and power. Their fate, and the fate of this generation of Iranians, is determined by and through the use of repression and terror.

Ultimately, the struggle of modern Iran is the struggle between those who believe decisions for managing the country should be made using logic, reason, dialogue, and free choice versus those who believe decisions should be made by those wielding the gun. It is the struggle between democracy and despotism manifesting itself in factories, schools, streets, ministries and even through proxy wars in other countries. My generation of Iranians is the victim of this political culture of violence dominating Iran. Yet, the generation before us, because of the Islamic Revolution of 1979, also had its fate determined through violence. My grandparents' generation in 1953 also had its political differences settled through violence. The generation before, during Reza Shah's time, also used military power to determine politically decisions.

The struggle in Iran is ultimately the struggle against violence. It manifests itself through ordinary citizens coming together to lessen the pain and fear of violence while generation after generation gets consumed as their fate is shaped through violence.

Knowing he had lost the struggle, the chief executive of Chuka knew he had to find a way to save his life. Turning to his deputy, he signaled him to just go along with his story and then, turning to the *basiji*, he told the kid that he was merely a hitchhiker picked up for the ride to Tehran and had been asleep throughout the ride. The *basiji*, not knowing why the two men were being detained and reasoning that only the driver should be held responsible for a hit-and-run, began to feel uneasy when the driver of the Land Cruiser assured him that he did not even know his passenger. The 'hitchhiker' convinced the young *basiji* to allow him to a make a phone call to his wife in Tehran and let her know he would be home late. When he got on the phone, he called his second deputy, and awakened him late at night. "Grab a pen and listen carefully," he ordered. He then provided the necessary phone numbers and instructed his deputy to first call the chief of police of Gilan and then the

INTRODUCTION

governor of Gilan at their homes to tell them he is being held in the Loshan jail at the checkpoint. His second deputy was then to call Nematzadeh, the Minister of Industry, at his home and inform him of the situation. He was then to try calling the two-vehicle convoy in the mountains every five minutes until they reached a location with cell phone reception.

Within minutes, orders came down the line. It was the chief of police of Gilan who came to the rescue. He telephoned the *basiji*, and angrily ordered him to release the two prisoners immediately. The two men left the jail, and disappeared into the darkness.

Over the following three days, the Minister of Industry would repeatedly accuse Fallahian of another kidnapping and murder, this time a technocrat, while Fallahian and the intelligence ministry denied any involvement. The young *basiji* swore that the two men had been released at the order of the Chief of Police of Gilan prior to arrival of intelligence units from Tehran. Repeated searches of the canyons in the Alborz Mountains turned up no trace of the two men or their vehicle.

That man who disappeared that evening along with his deputy was my father and the events that led up to this incident, even though they were a world apart from the relative peace of my medical school in San Francisco, were a series of 'paradigm shifts' for me.

As soon as he and his deputy had left the jail, my father, after removing the batteries from their cell phones, fled and took refuge in a friend's empty villa along the Caspian Coast. For three days, disconnected from everyone, he tried to find some relief by taking in the beauty and tranquility of the sea while knowing that his disappearance might have unpredictable consequences. Sitting on the beach, my father came to the same conclusion that millions of others in his generation had reached. He told himself, "It's not worth it!" The system is too fundamentally flawed for individuals to make changes for the country. As long as Iran is ruled by violence, any achievement is a short-term endeavor doomed to eventual failure.

The story of my father is emblematic of the experience of my parents' generation. They fought to make their country a better place, but were ultimately defeated by the forces of violence and, at one point, most told themselves, "It's not worth it!" They gave up on their ideals and principles and focused on trying to survive under the repression of the Islamic Republic.

They were traumatized by violence and concluded the rule of violence would be their collective destiny. They would compulsively anticipate the horrors and risks that would accompany whatever successor regime might come to power. They believed that without the defeat of the forces of violence, any attempt at democracy, economic prosperity, and human rights would be a short-term endeavor, leading to a resurgence of even more unbearable despotism, war, and strife.

A superficial look at violence in today's world may lead the reader to blame circumstances, evil personalities, or misunderstandings as the root cause of violence in humanity. Yet if one studies violence in generation after generation of human beings, one can quickly realize that the political culture of violence itself creates the circumstances, evil personalities, and misunderstandings leading to further violence. The fate of each generation is ultimately determined by the culture of the people and, if the adopted and accepted political culture of a generation is the culture of violence, then the fate of the generation will be decided by violence.

***

I thought of the concept for this book near the end of winter in 2004. The previous 12 months had been especially turbulent and chaotic for Iranians. The United States had invaded Iraq in the west. The Taliban had fallen in the east. Spontaneous demonstrations on the anniversary of the June student uprising were severely crushed by the regime; women were becoming bolder and crossing red lines. The yearly march for, and celebrations of, International Women's Rights on March 8th was harshly suppressed by the regime. As I watched the events from a distance, I came across more and more blogs, emails, and the pronouncements of pundits encouraging Iranians to come into the streets on the Festival of Fire—the Souri Festival— at the end of winter and make that celebration a symbol of their hopes and desires. In response, I heard revolutionary guard commanders making greater threats against people's participation on that night. Iranian state television began a campaign of fear, reminding people of potential injury and even death as a result of playing with fire and firecrackers on this evening. Videos of clerics calling participants of this festival 'pagans', 'devil-worshipers', 'fire-worshipers' and 'ignorant' were broadcast on state TV.

The festival of fire on the evening before the last Wednesday of winter is one of the grand celebrations of Iran. It is the last celebration of the year before Nowruz. Every Iranian can recall holding their parents' and grandparents' hands as a child while jumping over fires and singing the traditional song of this night. As I waited for this night to come in 2004, I kept remembering the sense of boldness I experienced as a child on this night

INTRODUCTION

as boys and girls mingled with each other, played music, danced and turned neighborhood after neighborhood of Tehran into the sites of countless celebrations of fire in the streets.

How would the regime react this year? More importantly, how would people react to the regime's threats? Would they stay at home, hoping to come out the next year? Would they not sing? Would girls and boys not hold hands on this night as they had boldly done in those early years of revolution and war that I remembered?

For the 24 hours preceding and during the celebration in 2004 I was glued to the Internet, checking blogs, chatting with friends, family, and acquaintances, and making occasional phone calls to relatives asking about the celebrations in their neighborhood. I was pleasantly surprised to find that tens of millions had come into the streets in nearly every city in Iran to jump over the fire and participate in the tradition I remembered so vividly. Occasionally, some of those in the security forces who were far from the celebrations in their hometowns were seen jumping over the fires as well. It was as if, for one night, all of Iran had decided that this celebration was bigger than politics, bigger than the revolutionary guards, bigger than their animosities and even their fears.

Yet, the next day, it was all over. The Islamic Republic was back in business as usual. Music was banned, celebrations in the streets again not tolerated, women segregated, and the same totalitarian regime remained in power. It was as if people had celebrated the end of winter, only to find out this winter continues in perpetual darkness and cold.

I thought to myself, how powerful and beautiful it was that night, when Iranians collectively made a statement of joy. Yet I lamented that the celebration was only one night of freedom, freedom eclipsed by 364 nights of gloom. How powerful it would be if this celebration were to take place every night, once a week, or once a month, not just as a celebration but as expression of discontent and act of civil disobedience.

***

Iranians are well aware of the monthly celebrations of ancient Iran, most of which were functions and rituals of the Zoroastrian religion and pre-Zoroastrian traditions and beliefs and were mostly forgotten by everyone except the few Zoroastrians as Iranians converted their religion to Islam. Yet, during the Islamization of Iran more than a thousand years ago, many of the celebrations survived as Iranians continued to celebrate some of the more important ones as national celebrations. This allowed those few celebrations, like the Souri Festival of Fire and Nowruz, which celebrated the beginning of spring and the New Year, to survive and function until today for my generation. Religious beliefs of Yalda were eliminated from that celebration as well, thus allowing it to prosper and function as a national celebration for the people of my generation. But nearly all the other monthly celebrations were forgotten because Iranians had failed to look at them as national celebrations.

What if my generation could reinterpret the ancient monthly celebrations of Iran national celebrations? What if we could make sense out of these rituals for the needs of my generation, my children's generation and the 21st century Iranian society? How could celebrations be used not only as acts of civil disobedience against the Islamic Republic, but also to raise awareness on the environment, women's rights, rights of the elderly, the rights of religious minorities, the right to play music and dance, and the freedom for the pursuit of happiness?

Yet, what can be the role of these celebrations for this generation's struggle for freedom? How can they become tools against the sword and the whip? How are celebrations relevant to the use of violence in despotism?

I realized the answer a year later as I was talking to a friend who visited Shiraz during the Nowruz celebrations. He told me how he witnessed several hundred families take a day trip on Nowruz of that year to the sprouting plains of Pasargad, one of the powerful symbols of Iranian past. Prior to this celebration, callers had announced on Persian satellite television that this was their symbolic act for democracy and freedom. In response, the regime had sent several busloads of basijis and revolutionary guards to the same site. I anticipated that there would be violence at this relatively minor event, which, apart from a few blogs, did not get coverage in the media. Afterwards, I asked my friend "Did the soldiers use violence against the people?"

"Of course not!" he replied in a matter of fact way. "It's Nowruz. Who's going to use violence?" He implied that I should have known better than to ask that question. He was right, I thought to myself. It's Nowruz— why would there be violence?

The families gathering to celebrate Nowruz in Pasargad and next to ruins of the tomb of Cyrus and of the ancient palace structures, in the kind and loving manner required of this day, had offered the soldiers food and sweets, treating the young men as if they were their own children. The soldiers, who were away from their families on this Nowruz, had decided to enjoy the celebration in the same way they had done all their lives, while allowing this celebration to proceed without interference.

This was when I realized that the principles of kindness and humanity in nonviolence so desperately needed for a long-term nonviolent Iranian struggle for democracy are the same principles every Iranian learns to practice as a child on Nowruz. These principles are the same principles which guide civil disobedience movements for democracy and human rights. My generation's challenge is to apply these principles to every Iranian celebration throughout the year, while bringing less known celebrations back to life based on the same principles of nonviolence. Having a celebration of civil disobedience every month, shaped on the principles of nonviolence seen in Nowruz, I thought, could be a tremendous cultural treasure, one that my generation cannot fail to ignore.

In addition to the legacy of violence in Iran, this book is also a study of the philosophy and practice of nonviolence advocated by some of the great teachers of 20th century and how these lessons apply to the Iranian struggle for a nonviolent revolution. It outlines how the principles of nonviolence which every Iranian learns during their celebration of Nowruz are the same principles of humanity taught and practiced by inspiring figures like Gandhi and Martin Luther King. Yet ultimately, this book is a review of the potential of Iranian celebrations as acts of civil disobedience.

Iranians are desperately looking for additional means and methods to further their campaign against the terror that has become so prevalent in their society. Since 2009, collectively, children and grandmothers have risen from the depth of fear to announce to the world that freedom "is worth it!" Their 21st century struggle against one of the most ruthless religious totalitarian states still in existence will test the philosophy and theory of nonviolence and will be written about for generations to come.

There is an ancient Iranian wish repeated every year on Nowruz throughout homes of Iran: "May your everyday be Nowruz." May the ancient celebrations of Iran be additional tools for this generation's hopes for freedom and may they serve to advance the cause of democracy and implant the culture of nonviolence in the hearts and minds of human beings.

May Iranians finally overcome the politics of terror and may they live in a country where every day is Nowruz.

"And so, to the end of history, murder shall breed murder, always in the name of right and honor and peace, until the gods are tired of blood and create a race that can understand.

~George Bernard Shaw, "Caesar and Cleopatra"

PART I

Legacy of Violence

CHAPTER 1 - Fear, Trauma and Post Traumatic Stress Disorder.

"You never forget horror!"

An Iranian childhood

You never forget horror. It stays with you, reminding you of its presence, eating away at your sense of self, wounding your body, mind and spirit. It can turn a peaceful moment into a reoccurring nightmare, an ordinary day into an unforgettable one.

It should have been a normal afternoon. My cousins, grandparents, aunts and uncles were over our house. The adults were playing cards and backgammon, and we children were amusing ourselves with games. Our front door bell rang, and I left the younger kids, rushed past the adults at the tables, across the marble courtyard, and through the pool garden of yellow jasmine and old trees. The other guests were overdue and I hurried to open the door.

I never expected to find a revolutionary guard brandishing a machine gun. In his twenties, his youth obscured by an overgrown beard, the young man acted more like my friend, than foe. Behind him stood other soldiers, around the same age, shouldering their guns. I knew why they were there. A sixteen-year-old family member, the closest to an older sister to me, had an arrest warrant for belonging to a leftist political group. A death warrant had been issued in her absence for her role in repeated distribution of anti-government literature. In the past I had often overheard the adults reassure the soldiers that she had escaped through the Turkish border and was now a refugee in some European country. But we children knew better.

As the half dozen soldiers marched through the garden, I could see the adults scrambling to hide the playing cards, rushing to flush the homemade beers down the kitchen sink, the women hurrying to don their headscarves, at least, to give the appearance they were friends of the revolution. Some of the guards remained with the adults, and one asked me, the eldest of the children, to follow him to one of the bedrooms. I was frightened and robotically did as I was told. I glanced over my shoulder to the parents watching nervously, and saw the guard who greeted me at the door, rounding up all the other children, no more than six-years-old, and leading them into another room.

In the bedroom facing the garden, I stood frozen, uncertain what to expect. He then asked me to sit on the bed. Outside I heard a dog barking incessantly. The scent of jasmine drifted in from an open window. Was this guard going to hurt me? But he was acting strange, as if we were old friends. He told me of the wonder and contributions of the revolution and how it was making Iran a better place, and then asked me about the missing girl. I told him what my relatives repeated so often; she was a refugee in Europe.

In the other room, my little brother, too young and unaware of the horrors outside our house and trying to be as helpful as always had volunteered to help the friendly soldier. He told him what we all knew: she was in hiding, in fact, staying at Mr. K,'s, a close friend of my father's. The guard had smiled and exited to the living room. From the hallway I watched the guards screaming 'traitors' at the adults, 'enemies of the revolution,' singling out my father, whose friend had provided the safe house. I will never forget the horror I saw that afternoon on my mother's face. I will never forget that day.

From then on, the details of my cousin's whereabouts were hidden from us children. I don't know how she escaped Mr. K's place. But somehow, before the soldiers arrived, she did. For months after that, her hideaway was a bedroom in the house of an old woman, the mother of another of my father's friends. Only my father was aware of her whereabouts, keeping it secret from even my mother.

Later we would learn of my cousin's escape to Turkey and to safety. My father's friend had paid a sheep-herder to smuggle her across the border. It was a joyous moment and a relief for the entire family to know that she was unharmed, but the scars from the fear and trauma of that episode would never go away completely. The horror of that incident and the everyday fear and uncertainty of living in the Islamic Republic shook my mother's foundation of well-being and security. Over months and years the emotional burden would take its toll. Her heightened sense of fear and anxiety translated into hyper-vigilance and infiltrated everyday life. Even years later in the United States, fearful for my safety, she would beg me to avoid all political groups and rallies. She hated discussions on politics and avoided politically-oriented television programs and commentaries, anything that might threaten the stability and safety of our lives.

She was not alone. In nearly every Iranian family, someone will ask you to change the channel if the program is about human rights and democracy. Slowly the Iranian culture changed. As the revolution unfolded and more and more citizens where horrified and shocked by the dire consequences of political activity, gatherings and parties became increasingly devoid of political discourse, focusing instead, on the lighter aspects of Iranian life, *kabab* and music and playing cards. Self-censorship became a routine part of Iranian life.

When I came to America, I noticed the same pattern of behavior in Iranian-Americans who had each fled their native country for a variety of reasons. Even the Iranian Student Group in UCLA where I was a student prohibited any political discussion or use of political symbols. I saw similar bans in nearly every other Iranian-American student group in universities across the United States, places which should have been bastions of free speech. Many non-profit Iranian-American groups, societies and foundations were created in America with the same culture of self-censorship. Each proudly promoted themselves as 'non-political'* which really meant no discussions of human rights or democracy, nothing that would recall the horrors of the past.

Who could blame them? Politics had not just torn Iran apart but their families too. In nearly every Iranian family, you can find an Islamist, a leftist, a monarchist or, at the very least, someone with a strong political opinion. During the revolution, siblings and cousins turned on each other and political discussion often led to insults and threats, sometimes even fights.

As a child, I remember a politicized society far different during the revolution and I recall many family gatherings and parties during those revolutionary days where discussion on politics would dominate. Unfortunately, I also remember many occasions when seemingly friendly, political discussions would turn angry. To diffuse a heated argument or to distract themselves and avoid confrontation, an adult would often turn to a child in the room and ask a non-related question. Political discussions intrigued me and I was usually the only child remaining in the room. The questions were usually generic, asking the name of my school or what grade I was in. Many times I was asked, "What do you want to be when you grow up?" My answer was always the same. "A doctor."

---

* The proper term used for student organizations, foundations and non-profit artistic and cultural organizations in Europe, America and much of the free world who do not engage in political advocacy is 'non-partisan'.

"Wonderful," they would inevitably say, habitually suggesting a specialty in psychiatry. Often I would hear: "I can send you many crazy family and friends as referrals and you'll have a full practice!" Of course it was said in jest and meant to cool down the heated debate in the room. But after hearing this a few times, I thought maybe there was something more to it. Maybe there was truth in what they were saying. This particular response has recently been the focus of my attention and of much interest to me.

Psychological Trauma

At the heart of nearly every culture there are taboos. Openly discussing psychological disorders in families is one of those taboos prevalent across the world, and it certainly was in the Iranian culture of my childhood. Yet the desire of human beings to break away from this cultural self-censorship requires them to bring out the truth in nonconventional ways. On a personal level, such truths sometimes appear in our dreams or manifest themselves in our behaviors. In societies, such truths are sometimes expressed in music, literature, theatre, art and, today, in film. In every-day life, they are often expressed through humor. A simple comment at a party meant to diffuse a tense situation is frequently an opportunity to comment on an otherwise taboo subject.

I take a look at my own family, and at the families of friends and those around me. Every Iranian family has or knows of someone struggling with depression, anxiety or anger. Addiction to alcohol or drugs is a major problem among Iranians. Insomnia and mood swings are common complaints. Some Iranians have emotionally detached themselves from their families; others have been abandoned.

One can assume the proportion of people with genetically associated psychiatric disorders to be relatively equal in a peace loving country such as Sweden versus a terrified, traumatized society such as the one in Iraq today. But it would be a gross mistake to think that the psychological state of Iraqis suffering from daily terror is comparable, in severity and extent, to a European country or even the Iraq of 1970s. Trauma in the form of violence and terror has a definite effect on the body, mind, and spirit. Trauma can manifest itself as anxiety, depression, addiction, anger, mood swings, insomnia, even suicide. It can even take its toll on the body, expressing itself as high cholesterol, hypertension, diabetes, or chronic pain.

In general, if you look at a family, you can get a sense of the general personality of the family. Some families are more relaxed and some are rather tense. Some are angry and some are exhausted. Families have a personality that is the product of the collective interaction between their individual members. In addition, often a single member's psychological issues influence the state of mind of the entire family. An angry mother affects the anxiety level of her children. A depressed father sets the mood in the house. A troubled child exacerbates the parents' anxiety.

The personality of a family will also dictate its interaction with other families. In a community, how we behave and socialize is the collective result of family and individual behaviors. If enough families are depressed or fearful, then the community manifests those depressive or anxious traits. A depressed community cares less about its schools, hospitals, roads, culture, and arts which impacts its culture, politics, and economic production. And, just like the case within a family, it doesn't take the majority of families suffering from a psychological disorder to influence the community. A social gathering that includes only a single angry family can soon turn into an angry affair, in turn influencing other families. Just like in a family, where just one member can dictate or influence the psychological health of an entire family, a small minority of families can dictate the psychological health of a community.

The mood and the personality of a country is eventually a product of the collective behavior of its many communities. If you have a series of communities that are depressed, afraid and traumatized, then you will have a country that is psychologically afraid, depressed and traumatized.

Of course, not every single person in this country will be affected. What we are talking about is the collective psychological state of a society, not its individuals. You may be an Iranian reading this and saying to yourself that my family is ok. We are doing quite well and don't live in fear, but the actions of the entire country are generally not a reflection of the majority of its silent citizens, but the powerful influence of a vocal minority united by their pain.

If the mood of a country can be the sum of the collective moods of a minority united in psychological pain and suffering, then what is the mood of Iran? Is the national psychological state of Iran one of depression or anxiety? Is the psychological state of Iran relaxed? Euphoric? Is Iran fearful or insecure? Is it angry?

What is really the psychological state of Iranians? How can a minority in power imprison an entire nation? What kind of psychological weapon do they have to use against them?

CHAPTER 2

How did the revolution affect Iranians? What about the imprisonments, tortures, arrests, murders, kidnappings, and mass executions? How did the war with Iraq, the bombings of cities, and the Scud missiles affect them? What was the psychological effect of the crushing of the nonviolent uprising in June of 2009?

When you talk to the young generation in Iran, nearly all can tell stories of being detained, slapped, beaten, and even whipped for simple pleasures such as attending a party, holding hands, or drinking alcohol. And the beating and humiliation is not just carried out by the security forces; the culture of public beatings and humiliation permeates Iranian society. Women and children are routinely humiliated and physically punished at home, in the streets, at work or in schools. Workers who attempt to go on strike are beaten and debased, their leaders imprisoned and tortured. Parents are addicted, depressed, angry and anxious, and their children suffer the consequences.

Immediately after the revolution, when Iranian women marched to protest the forceful wearing of the Islamic *hijab*, supporters of the Islamic Republic rushed to the streets shouting *"ya roo sari- ya tou-sari,"* "either *hijab*, or beating." After public floggings and beatings, every terrorized woman was forced to wear the Islamic *hijab*.

Possession of alcohol carries punishment of flogging, sometimes in public with up to 100 lashes. Adultery, if proven through a witness, carries the horrific punishment of stoning, the accused blindfolded, and a ring of people hurling stones until the accused dies.

A teenage boy and girl holding hands in public can be arrested and fined, or sentenced to either prison or flogging. Even walking together can result in detention. On her visit to Iran, my sister, a teenager at the time, was walking with a male cousin when security officers arrested them. After years of living abroad or due to fear, my sister was unable to recall our cousin's last name and was taken into custody for suspicion of unlawful and out-of-wedlock relationship with a boy. To avoid punishment, documents had to be provided by our family to prove they were cousins and innocent.

Such stories are routine for Iranians. Every family has a story of a teenaged daughter or son picked up by soldiers, or arrested in their homes during a party, along with their guests, with the alcohol and music confiscated as evidence.

Punishments against ethnic or religious minorities are even more horrifying. In January 2008, five robbers in the southeastern province of Sistan-Baluchestan had "the right hand and left foot cut off, making it difficult, if not impossible, for the condemned to walk, even with a cane or crutches."[2] Kurds, who are mostly Sunnis, were the most courageous ethnic group against the Islamic Republic and suffered the worst consequences with more Kurds tortured, killed or executed than any other ethnic group. Baha'i children, a religious minority in Iran, are banned from schools or employment unless they denounce their religious beliefs. Their parents are imprisoned and their community and religious leaders killed. There is a concerted system-wide effort by Islamic Republic to eliminate Baha'is from Iranian society not unlike the Nazis' attempts to eliminate Jews from German society.

The Islamic Republic wants total control over every aspect of its citizens' lives and will employ any form of punishment to terrorize their citizens into submission.

One thing is certain. Nearly all Iranians since 1979 have been victims of or witness to actual or threat of violence, thereby creating a form of psychological trauma.

Dealing with the Iranian dilemma of violence cannot take place without understanding the psychological effect of violence and the long-term effects of trauma on a human being. But before we examine the culture and politics of violence, our journey and story must begin with the study of fear and trauma, how Post Traumatic Stress Disorder came about as a diagnosis in the 20th century, the effect of trauma on human beings, families and society and the evaluation of the psychological state of Iran.

Once we understand the extent the psychological manifestation of fear and trauma and the reactions of some in the form of Post-Traumatic Stress Disorder, then we can begin to understand the magnitude of its prevalence in Iranian society. And only then can we think about how to treat such an immense problem.

Jean-Martin Charcot and the Study of Hysteria

During the latter part of the 19th century in France, notably after the founding of the Third Republic in 1870, the struggle between religion and secularism, particularly faith as opposed to science, led prominent figures in science and medicine to speak out and educate their fellow citizens on how the light and reason of science could dispel the darkness of myths and superstition. Doctors felt a responsibility to improve both public health in general and medical treatment of all types. They were acting in the ancient tradition of the great Greek physician Hippocrates, the first physician to advocate secularism in medicine, the separation of the ministrations of medicine from religion and freeing medical practice from religious laws and beliefs.

Jean-Martin Charcot was one such physician. He was a renowned neurologist and pathologist, and, at heart, a secularist. For thirty years, he was the director of the Salpetriere, an enormous old hospital in Paris that was home to patients with various illnesses and problems. Through a number of important contributions to the field of medicine, he had established himself as one of the premiere physicians of modern Europe; but it was his study of the strange madness in women then called 'hysteria' that was most controversial and is most relevant to our story.

'Hysteria' had been described since ancient times and considered a disease afflicting only women. Hysteria was thought to originate in the uterus ('hyster' in Greek), and from there proceeded to drive the patient mad. When Charcot first turned his attention to this disease, the Salpetriere was an asylum for beggars, prostitutes and the insane. Many patients were diagnosed as suffering from hysteria, which Charcot called the 'Great Neurosis'. He emphasized observation, classification, and description, and exhaustively documented the symptoms of this illness. By 1880 he had conclusively demonstrated that hysteria was an illness whose symptoms could be induced and relieved artificially through hypnosis, which indicated that it was not due to possession by the devil (the 'treatment' offered by religion was exorcism). His Tuesday lectures on hysteria, where he demonstrated his patients' symptoms and his use of hypnosis were famous, drawing physicians and interested non-physicians from all over Europe.[3] Yet despite his own discoveries, he was unable to acknowledge the psychological roots of hysteria and rejected any notion of trauma or violence as having anything to do with this disorder. His demonstrations included showing women becoming more hysterical upon touching the region of ovaries on the abdomen. But he never considered talking to their patients, and the stories his patients told were of no consequence to him. Although Charcot was important in establishing hysteria as pathology and in separating it from the superstitious beliefs of ancient times, he did not take the next step and attempt to determine its true nature.

But he did inspire some of his students to do just that. One of them, Pierre Janet, believed that trauma was a cause of hysteria and investigated it. In a study of 591 patients with hysteria, he found that 257 of the patients had a traumatic origin to their psychopathology.[4] However, the most controversial early work on trauma was not done by Janet, but by a young medical student visiting the Salpetriere from Vienna, Sigmund Freud. While working with Charcot, he learned a great deal about hysteria in women. He absorbed what Charcot and Janet had learned, and upon returning to Vienna continued his work, becoming famous and controversial a few years later.[5]

Sigmund Freud's Early Work with Hysteria

Unlike Charcot, Freud had immense curiosity and the patience required for listening. He started talking to his patients and spent hours upon hours listening to them. What he heard was outrageous. His hysterical female patients repeatedly told of sexual abuse, rape and violence in their childhood, inflicted on them by their fathers, uncles, brothers and family friends. The extent of such violence against women included horror stories of fathers being paid to have their daughters play the role of sexual toys at orgies.

Freud delved into the memories of these patients. After a while, he came to the conclusion that beneath the more minor traumas of adulthood that had triggered the onset of hysterical symptoms were major traumatic events, including sexual trauma and violence, in childhood. By 1896, Freud thought he had found the cause of hysteria and published a report on 18 cases entitled *The Aetiology of Hysteria*. He believed he was on the cusp of a major discovery and that this report would bring him fame. But his *Aetiology of Hysteria* received a cold reception from academicians and the public.[6]

To Europe's bourgeois and upper classes of the late 19th century, what Freud was suggesting was simply unacceptable. Hysteria was a very common illness in Vienna and throughout Europe. Some of Freud's patients were the daughters of well-known aristocratic families, and if what he was saying was true, then sexual abuse and violence against children were very common, including those within the elite class of Europe. According to Freud's theory, women suffering from this disorder were not patients afflicted with physiologically induced madness from a pathologic state of the uterus, but victims of violence manifesting itself as a psychological illness.

Such suggestions were simply too outrageous for the European elite. Freud was subjected to such strong criticism that within a year he slowly began changing his mind about hysteria and started doubting the stories he was told. Soon, he insisted the stories of his hysterical patients were more the expressions of sexual desires and fantasies than actual memories of genuine violence and trauma. Instead of listening to his patients as he used to, he began arguing with them. By the first decade of the 20th century, without ever giving a fully satisfactory reason, Freud had abandoned his earlier claims of childhood sexual trauma and violence as the cause of hysteria.[7]

Dr. Judith Herman writes:
"Out of the ruins of his theory for hysteria, trauma and violence, Freud eventually developed 'psychoanalysis' influencing thousands of psychologists and psychiatrists of the 20th century. The most dominant psychological theory of the 20th century and a household word, [psychoanalysis] was founded and developed on rejecting women's stories of violence and trauma and attributing them to desires and fantasies."[8]

By 1910, what had begun as an important contribution to women's rights had become a tool used by the patriarchal elite of Europe to deny their abuse. The study of trauma and violence and its effects on human beings was virtually abandoned, and nearly forgotten, until the extraordinary circumstances that arose in Europe in 1914.

History of PTSD during the 20th Century

The story of humanity is a mixture of tragedy and comedy. Just as some of our greatest literary works are built on tragic events, some of our greatest scientific discoveries were made in the most tragic of times.

Such was the case during the Great War of 1914-1918. In World War I, humanity experienced trauma unlike any in the past. The magnitude of the war was staggering; 9 million soldiers died, 12.5 million civilians were killed, 24 million people wounded and 10 million lost their homes and became refugees.

Most horrifying were the new modern methods of warfare. Although ancient warfare was just as horrific, the brutality was limited compared to the new weapons of the 20th century. World War I fundamentally changed how wars were fought. Machine guns, invented in 1889, had widespread use for the first-time in World War I. It was the first time bombs were dropped from planes upon civilians and their homes. In 1916, the British invented the tank as a new weapon of warfare. The Germans soon followed and developed their own tanks. Other new weapons such as poison gas, heavy long range artillery and submarines were also developed and used for the first time.

World War I marks the first modern war of attrition and exhaustion. The psychological effects on soldiers of these new weapons and methods were also new. Both armies soon began to witness significant numbers of previously healthy men developing the symptoms of women's hysteria. Both armies requested help from their physicians and medical community. According to one estimate, mental breakdown represented 40% of British battle casualties.[9] A British psychologist named Charles Myers thought such psychological symptoms were the result of exploding shells that damaged the brain, and labeled this disorder 'shell shock'.[10]

Despite the violence of the war, some traditional physicians and early psychiatrists claimed that many of the symptoms were due to laziness and cowardice, blaming the individuals rather than the war itself. Many soldiers were beaten, threatened and punished if they did not go back to the battlefront. A psychiatrist named Yealland reported a soldier was so traumatized he could not speak. The soldier was strapped to a chair and electric shocks repeatedly applied to his throat for hours until the patient spoke.[11] Upon success, the doctor administering the electric shocks, told the patient: "Remember, you must behave as the hero I expect you to be... A man who has gone through so many battles should have better control of himself!"[12]

But a few were bold enough to champion a new philosophy and approach. One of them, Dr. W.H.R. Rivers, a professor of neurophysiology, psychology and anthropology, advocated humane treatment and the use of psychiatric advances such as psychoanalysis. His research and success with the new methods were instrumental in establishing the use of psychological methods to heal trauma, and later in developing more effective treatments for Americans in the next world war.

Two fundamental principles and conclusions came out of his studies of patients suffering from trauma and violence in World War I. The first was that psychological trauma and overwhelming fear can cause mental and physical dysfunction in even the bravest soldier and can affect someone with a healthy childhood. Anyone was at risk, but younger soldiers were more vulnerable than older ones. The second conclusion was that the most effective motivations to overcome fear were not abstract principles of fighting for freedom, patriotism or hatred of the enemy. It was the love of soldiers for one another[13]. Much of the knowledge gained in World War I was used in the Second World War but to limited extent.

The systematic large-scale study of effects of trauma on the brain, however, did not really occur until the Vietnam War. Soldiers returning from war began having community meetings to discuss the war and their terrifying experiences. By mid-1970s hundreds of these groups across the United States attracted the attention of psychiatrists. Eventually, the U.S. Veterans Administration commissioned a comprehensive study of the psychological effects of trauma on returning soldiers, resulting in a five volume publication describing the syndrome and symptoms of Post-Traumatic Stress Disorder and demonstrating beyond any question its direct relationship to the trauma and violence experienced in combat.[14]

In 1980, for the first-time, the American Psychiatric Association made this disorder an 'official' mental illness, and included a new category, 'Post Traumatic Stress Disorder', in its third edition of its manual, the Diagnostic and Statistical Manual of Mental Disorders (DSM). Now psychologists and psychiatrists could gather statistical information and descriptions of the symptoms and make the appropriate diagnosis of Post-Traumatic Stress Disorder in their patients.

To the amazement of American psychologists, the majority of people expressing symptoms of trauma and newly diagnosed with PTSD had never been to Vietnam. With the new diagnostic tools in hand, it became clear that in addition to former soldiers, many women also exhibited the symptoms of PTSD. This was nearly 100 years from the time Freud first suggested and then vehemently denied that sexual trauma and violence could be the cause of mental disorder.

The new awareness gained through the struggles for women's rights during the 1970s and 1980s provided an atmosphere in which women could once again discuss their sexual trauma. And, just like a hundred years before, the results were as shocking. The experiences that Freud had labeled fantasies a century before were now shown to be real. One study picked 900 randomly selected women from American cities and interviewed them in depth about their experiences and their past. The result was devastating. One in four women had been raped. One in three reported sexual molestation in childhood.[15] Later more comprehensive studies on rape showed rape to be less prevalent but still a horrifying 7.3% of women and 1.3% of men reported histories of sexual assault.[16]

Before this time, rape was not discussed in polite society. Women were taught to be ashamed for being sexually molested. Psychologists dismissed children's stories of abuse as fantasies. Teenagers and young women raped in schools and outside their homes were blamed for instigating the act. Families, communities and society as a whole preferred to look away and ignore the issue rather than punish those responsible. One American feminist, Betty Friedan, called the issue of sexual violence against women the "problem without a name."[17] The situation could have been brushed under the rug just as it had been in Freud's time. PTSD could have been labeled as the diagnosis for a disorder caused only by war. But this time the world was different as was the status of women in society.

It was soon realized that PTSD could be caused by any psychological trauma. The common instigators were found to be feelings of intense fear, helplessness, loss of control, and the threat of annihilation.[18] Most significantly, the types of psychological trauma found to cause this disorder were not just violence from sexual trauma or violence and trauma from war, but every day common events.

Physical assaults and violence inflicted on both men and women were found to cause illness in large number of patients. But it was not just experiencing and witnessing violence and assault that caused the disorder. PTSD was found in ambulance drivers, police officers, and emergency-room doctors at higher rates than in the regular population. A witness to an accident could be just as traumatized as the victim. Learning of the sudden death of a loved one could be traumatic, as could simply learning of the violence, assaults, torture or pain inflicted on a loved one.

Humiliation can be traumatic. Losing one's job, home, car or any other important elements of one's life can be traumatic. Surgery can be traumatic. There are patients who for various reasons when undergoing surgery suddenly wake from the anesthesia; 56% of these patients were found to develop PTSD.[19]

PTSD strikes far and wide. In another study, 48.4% of women reporting a history of rape were diagnosed with PTSD. 10.7% of men witnessing death or serious injury developed PTSD.[20] A study of 10,000 patients with histories of being severely maltreated as children had 4 to 12 times a greater risk of developing alcoholism, engaging in drug abuse, becoming depressed or attempting suicide.[21] One study diagnosed PTSD in 20% of children who had experienced or witnessed domestic violence.[22] In another study, 34.5% of children involved in traffic accidents developed PTSD.[23] In another study, 1.5% of women met the criteria for PTSD six months after childbirth.[24] In a study of ex-prisoners of war from World War II, 56% of the soldiers continued to have PTSD forty years after their trauma. The National Comorbidity Survey reported that the overall estimated lifetime prevalence of PTSD among adult Americans was 7.8%.[25] Overall, the many studies done on the effects of psychological trauma on people demonstrated that approximately 20% of people experiencing trauma later develop the signs and symptoms of PTSD.[26]

This is the data found in the United States. One can easily realize that during the last 30 years Iranians have experienced trauma that cannot be imagined by the average American. Iranians have lived through devastating violence, either experiencing it themselves or witnessing it, and, subsequently numbed by it. Being humiliated or beaten by security forces are everyday occurrences for my generation. My parents' generation experienced even more trauma and violence. Executions, tortures, confiscation of property and humiliations were front-page events and everyday incidents in their lives.

While unaware of the science behind PTSD, the Islamic Republic realized that public beatings and torture were more effective in numbing the population into submission. They understood the traumatic effects of public hangings, and the power of executions performed after the families were told of their loved ones' torture and rape. Fearful children behave much more in accord with the demands of the regime, which is why physical abuse by teachers in classrooms was and is tolerated. I witnessed many beatings of classmates by teachers and principals during my elementary school years in Iran.

Although its victims do not realize it, the Islamic Republic's incompetence in managing the Iranian economy and unemployment has become a source of not only stress but also trauma in many Iranian families. The regime's incompetence in maintaining adequate infrastructure and safe highways has resulted in Iran having one of the world's highest rates of automobile accidents and deaths. The evidence of psychological trauma can be found everywhere in the Iranian society. Even the most fortunate Iranians have not been spared.

The Brain and its Structures

So what is it that happens to a body in the event of violence and psychological trauma? In order to better understand the answer, one needs to understand both the physiological effects on the body as well as the consequent psychological symptoms.

To think of the brain in simple terms, make your right hand into a fist. Your forearm will act as the spinal cord, a highway of information. The spinal cord takes sensory messages from the body to the brain, and relays them to your muscles and to your organs. Your wrist represents the part of the brain on top of your spine called the midbrain, sometimes referred to as the 'reptilian' brain. The midbrain is an area responsible for sending all instructions necessary for daily survival of us as organisms. These are the basic instructions about your heart rate, respiration, digestion, blood pressure, and your awake and alert cycle. An organism cannot survive with damage to the midbrain. The fingers on your wrist represent the portions of the brain we call the limbic system and are involved in the formation of emotions such as anger, fear and pleasure. It also functions as traffic signals directing the appropriate creation of memory in various parts of the cortex. If you take your left hand and place it on your right fist, your left hand will be the cortex, a gigantic storage facility for memory and processing of information. In simplified terms, think of it as a giant computer hard drive and a computer processor in one.

There are two important structures in the limbic system called the amygdala and hippocampus. The amygdala serves much like a traffic signal, directing and facilitating the storage of emotions and the organism's reaction to emotionally charged events. The memory of this emotion is stored in the cortex. The hippocampus is a traffic signal that stores the memory of the time and place of an event. Thus, for example, if one experiences their house on fire, the amygdala directs the storage of the emotional memory of fear in a particular part of brain, while the hippocampus directs storage of the details of how and when the fire occurred in another part of the cortex.

'Fight' or 'flight'? – The Functioning of the Limbic System

When an organism is confronted with sudden or threatening events, the reaction of the body is called 'startled response'. An example of this is jumping when someone suddenly startles us. All vertebrate organisms have this reaction. Human infants also possess this physiological reaction. It is the most basic survival skill of any organism. This reaction is also purely reflexive. There are no thought processes involved. In other words we are startled before we know what is happening.[27]

After this initial reaction, there is evaluation of the environment. The cortex starts processing the sensory information received. A message is then formed and sent to the limbic system. The limbic system processes the message and forms the proper emotion such as fear or anger. In order to process the proper emotion, the limbic system needs to check back with the cortex and access all of the memories appropriate for this incident. So, if someone has a stored memory of a loud sound associated with witnessing someone getting shot, the association of loud sound and gunshots is relayed to the limbic system. From this memory, the limbic system then forms a new emotion of fear. But if the memory of a loud sound is associated with an annoying friend playing a prank, the limbic system will then send instructions to either laugh or be angry.

In addition, the limbic system is also in control of what is called the autonomic nervous system which regulates the general sense of the body. It is called autonomic because it is not under the direct control of the cortex and thus is not consciously controlled. There are two components to the autonomic nervous system, the sympathetic and parasympathetic systems. The sympathetic system is sometimes referred to as the 'fight' or 'flight' system.

Anger and fear are emotions important to survival and can prepare the body for fight or can help the body prepare for fleeing. Such survival mechanisms are essential to mammals. In the prehistoric wilderness, witnessing a threatening animal required the body to prepare itself for a fight, or provide the energy needed for running. If a prehistoric human being was confronted with a tiger, his or her body would want to be ready for either a fight or flight. This is true for nearly every animal.

When an organism is placed in sympathetic mode, reaction to events is emotionally motivated through anger or fear. Reason and dialogue are absent in an individual's decision making, elements that require calmness and peace. In the face of danger or stress, human beings typically do not respond as rational beings capable of analyzing and making reasoned decisions about a complicated environment. They are emotional animals ready for a physical and emotional struggle.

An individual experiencing fear is now prime for this 'fight' or 'flight.' If a family experiences fear, violence or trauma, this 'fight' or 'flight' reaction or 'sympathetic mode' will also be the initial reaction of the family. The family on heightened alert is then ready for the challenge ahead without much need for the cortex, reason or calm. Similarly, a community or a society responds in the same fashion. After all, a society is the collective sum of human beings physiologically and biologically responding to its environment. A society experiencing fear, violence or terrorism is immediately placed on alert or the 'sympathetic mode,' ready for 'fight' or 'flight.'

Even though they are not acting on a basis derived from what is known about the science or psychology of fear, many despotic governments have realized that by instilling fear on the population, individuals are placed in the sympathetic mode. In other words, they go on alert. This is very helpful for governments as a tool for mobilizing large portions of the population to serve their needs. Often, since the need of an autocratic regime is continued war, the internal use of fear and terrorism is used to place the population on alert and ready for war. The population is then ready to serve the army and 'fight' or is ready to escape persecution and flee the country. Use of fear and internal terrorism by the Nazis is a prime example of a regime placing the population on this sympathetic or alert mode for eventual war.

Great acts of violence and fear arousing the society's sympathetic mode can also be brought about by foreign-sponsored acts of terror which place the population in 'fight' or 'flight' mode. Iraq's invasion of Iran in 1980 caused a 'fight' reaction in Iranians, and the country responded more forcefully than Saddam Hussein had anticipated. Osama Bin Laden's attack on the United States on September 11th also placed the American public in the sympathetic mode, readying them for a 'fight'. This societal psychological reaction by Americans in the form of 'fight' led to the quick invasion of Afghanistan, followed by the invasion of Iraq, despite lack of Iraqi involvement in 9/11. Such wars could not have taken place without the population being in such state of alert or 'sympathetic mode.'

In adulthood, when a person undergoes intense fear, both the amygdala and hippocampus are there to store the memories of the event both emotionally and spatially. There is reason to believe that if both of these mechanisms are functioning properly, then that individual can overcome the experience of trauma and heal himself properly. Such individuals can describe and talk about the traumatic events as events with proper time and place and as events in one's past. These events are perceived to be part of the history of that individual and are no longer deemed to be threatening to that individual. But those whose hippocampus does not appropriately store the traumatic event have a well-established memory of fear without properly processing where that fear arises. This fear of an unknown leads to a form of anxiety.[28] PTSD is a particular type of anxiety disorder. This malfunction in how a memory is processed and stored in some individuals at time of intense fear and trauma is perhaps the root cause of PTSD.

CHAPTER 2

Manifestations of PTSD in Individuals and Societies

There are three manifestations of disease seen in those who develop PTSD. The first one is called hyperarousal. These are the people who we describe as "on the edge" and who react irritably to small provocations. This is most often seen as bursts of anger directed at children by parents who suffer from this disorder, where small mistakes by children can be the cause of anger out of proportion to the cause. Hyperaroused individuals are hyperalert and sleep poorly, and focus on the return of danger both consciously in their daily lives as well as unconsciously through dreams.

Hyperaroused people also frequently complain of psychosomatic pains. These are actual physical pains or aches in the body that originate from mental and emotional causes. In the old days, people referred to such pains as symptoms "in your head". Today it is known that such symptoms in people suffering from PTSD do start in the brain but the pain is real and these patients do suffer. There is an emotional pain that manifests itself as pain in the joints, muscles, back and abdomen.

A number of studies have shown that patients with this disorder suffer from a combination of generalized anxiety symptoms and specific fears. Their bodies are not in a relaxed mode, but are always on the alert for danger. They have intense reactions to the stimuli associated with the traumatic event, such as the smell of fire or the sound of gunshots. In a study, sounds of combat were played for individuals who had never been to war. There was no specific reaction from these people. The same sounds were then played for soldiers who had gone to Vietnam. The soldiers showed an increase in heart rate and blood pressure. Some were agitated, others angry. And a few were so hurt and disturbed by these sounds that they asked the examiner to stop.

People with PTSD take longer to fall asleep and are more sensitive to noise. They awaken more frequently during the night and, in general, have numerous types of sleep disturbances. These reactions comprise the first set of symptoms called hyperarousal states.[29]

Then there are the second types of symptoms that some people develop called intrusions. These patients have a difficult time resuming the normal activities of life because of recurrent thoughts of the traumatic event. The traumatic events become an abnormal form of recurring memory in which the person repeatedly sees the images of horrifying moments, both while awake and, more often, as nightmares. The images, sounds and even smells associated with those events can immediately bring back memories of previous trauma. And when these patients do remember the trauma, they experience it with the same sense of horror with which they had initially experienced the event. When both awake and asleep, their heart rate and blood pressure increase. These patients also do not return to normal, relaxed levels because of the constant reminders of the traumatic event.[30]

In Iran, much of the trauma that people experienced was the result of the revolution, the war, and the violent acts of the Islamic Republic against the population. Even though much of this experience was many years in the past, Iranians get constant reminders of the beatings and torture on radio and television. In my experience many Iranians choose not to watch politically inclined television stations that show reminders of such traumas. Not only do they choose not to watch such programming, they *insist* on not watching them. A substantial number of such Iranians watch only entertainment oriented stations, and, to the best of their ability, avoid not only the television shows reminiscent of their trauma but any music and books associated with the event and even locations where political activities have taken place. Any discussion regarding political events, political prisoners, and violence in the form of war, beatings, tortures and human rights violations is unacceptable to people engaged in a strategy of avoidance. They quickly attempt to change the subject.

Intrusions and hyperarousals create exaggerated and abnormal forms of defense mechanisms. The symptoms are messages sent to the body to avoid all situations where previous trauma arose. Then there are the third types of symptoms called constriction. In these symptoms, the defense mechanisms shut down and the person goes into a state of surrender. These people do not try to avoid reminders of trauma and violence. Instead, they alter their state of consciousness. The symptoms are sometimes called 'numbing'. In such people situations of danger and repeated trauma not only do not bring about episodes of anger or rage, they invoke a detached form of unusual calm.[31]

Traumatic events continue to plague them, but it's as though their bodies do not feel it. This is another defense mechanism, but one built to reduce pain in an environment where the person realizes there is no escape. A woman who was raped asks, "Did you ever see a rabbit stuck in the glare of your headlights when you're going down the road at night? Transfixed. It's as though the animal knew it was going to get it but the rabbit did not show any emotion."[32] People who are tortured report reaching a point where they don't feel pain anymore. Their thoughts wander and the beatings are looked upon as if being done to another person's body. It's as though the person feels the beating is not happening to them and they are just watching it being inflicted on someone else.

In PTSD, these symptoms are followed by feelings of indifference and emotional detachment. The victims of the disorder become passive and relinquish all forms of struggle. A veteran of World War II described it: "Like most others in my unit, I was numb… we called it the two-thousand-year-old-stare… the wide, hollowed eyes of a man who no longer cares… I felt as if I hadn't actually been in battle."[33]

Another interesting observation about such people is their inability to plan for the future. These persons lose confidence in their own abilities and rely more and on superstition and magical thinking. Such patients frequently resort to using lucky charms and other devices designed to deflect bad omens. A study of schoolchildren who were kidnapped showed that, years after the incident, they often looked for signs and omens to protect them and guide their behavior.

Complex PTSD as a Result of Chronic Trauma

But what happens when a trauma is not a one-time event, but an everyday occurrence? What happens to a teenager beaten at a park for holding hands with his girlfriend and who subsequently runs into the security forces repeatedly while walking in the streets or in the parks? In Iran, security forces can rush into one's home, take the host and his guests as prisoners while beating and insulting them for holding a can of beer. What happens to a person psychologically when such events are constant and the threat of such repetition is felt every evening? What happens to a woman after repeated beatings and threats by her husband, or a child who repeatedly experiences abuse and neglect by those delegated to protect her?

These are no longer cases of PTSD from a one-time trauma. These people develop symptoms of the same type of complex form of post-traumatic stress disorder that is found in captivity. The Islamic Republic of Iran is a form of political captivity; the threat and use of repeated violence is a tool for numbing the population into a type of PTSD described by Dr. Judith Herman as Complex PTSD. But in Iran, the regime is not the only source of captivity and violence. Much violence also occurs in people's homes and is not only limited to countries like Iran. Dr. Herman, when speaking of such captivity in today's modern society writes:

"Women and children are not ordinarily chained, even though this occurs more often than one might think. The barriers to escape are generally invisible. They are nonetheless extremely powerful. Children are rendered captive by their condition of dependency. Women are rendered captive by economic, social, psychological, and legal subordination, as well as by physical force."[34]

Much like such women described by Dr. Herman above, the majority of Iranians are not chained like political prisoners; Iranians are rendered captive by "economic, social, psychological, and legal subordination, as well as physical force".[35] In captivity, the perpetrator uses 'coercive control' to become the most powerful person in the victim's life. In return, the "psychology of the victim is shaped by the actions and beliefs of the perpetrator."[36] In the setting of captivity, people sometimes find themselves becoming defenders of their own captivity and end up associating their own needs with the need of their captor. This is frequently seen by rational individuals defending the actions of Islamic Republic, or more often seen in women defending patriarchy, their captivity at home, and the right of their husbands to rule over them.

The ultimate goal of the Islamic Republic and any totalitarian regime is total submission of the individual to the regime. This is not an easy process, but as long as a significant minority of individuals suffers from complex PTSD and another proportion of the population suffers from trauma and its manifestation as PTSD, the regime can maintain relative control over the entire population. In such a setting, the regime does not need to repetitively use violence. The method involves a great act of trauma in the form of violence against individuals and the use of that initial violence as a continued threat to others.

In the case of the Islamic Republic, torture of political prisoners serves as a threat and reminder for the general public. The terrorizing circumstance in which a student or women's rights activist is detained and beaten is deliberately publicized to serve as a threat against others. In such a setting, while a small minority of Iranians call for women's rights, democracy and secularism, a great number of people discourage, ridicule and demand their silence to avoid further retaliation by the regime. The regime uses fear, trauma and terror to create a population with PTSD and complex PTSD, and people who discourage any step towards their freedom.

CHAPTER 2

Terror

In the post-Communist era, perhaps no international issue is more acute than the threat of terrorism and use of terror. Yet, as acute as the problem is, and as much as Iranians have suffered from terrorism, many Iranians may not know exactly what terror means.

Although the word terror has been incorporated into the Persian language in the same form as in English, its meaning and its use in Iran has evolved to represent an act different from the one labeled terror in English. In English, the word terror means "a state of intense fear," or "violence used in order to intimidate a population into granting their demands." In Persian, the word terror means "to assassinate", particularly for political reasons.

Thus it's important for Iranians to learn that 'terrorism' is any intentional act to cause intense fear. Such an act could be blowing up an airplane, flying an airplane into a building, or blowing up a city bus or train. It could also be acts planned by an army such as the invasion of a country with the deliberate creation of intense fear in the form of 'Shock and Awe'. These are the more common acts of terror shown in the media. But the majority of terrorist activities are often ignored. Such acts could be a teacher beating a student into silence to control the whole classroom, a father beating his child to instill fear, a husband beating his wife to submission, or a security officer beating or lashing out at someone for improper conduct.

The definition of psychological trauma is wider than that of terror, and even events that are, seemingly, less threatening can be traumatic for a person. The American Psychiatric Association, in its latest Diagnostic and Statistical Manual (DSM IV), states that PTSD can develop in an individual in response to three types of events:

1) Incidents that are or are perceived to be threatening to one's own life or bodily integrity;

2) Being a witness to acts of violence to others; or

3) Hearing of violence to or the unexpected or violent death of close associates.

According to DSM IV, events that qualify as traumatic to both adults and children include combat, sexual and physical assault, being held hostage or imprisoned, terrorism, torture, natural and man-made disasters, accidents, and receiving a diagnosis of a life-threatening illness.

Revolution and Violence in Khomeini's Iran – Trauma and Societal Sympathetic Reaction

The causes and events of the Iranian revolution are too vast and beyond the scope and purpose of this book, but an overview of the traumatic, terrorizing and violent events that have led to the current traumatized state of Iranians is necessary.

Ayatollah Ruhollah Khomeini was a product of a culture of violence perhaps as old as humanity itself. Traumatic and violent events were tools available to him during his years of turmoil and terror after the Islamic Revolution. Those experiencing or witnessing traumatic events could then activate the stress hormones of their families, then their communities, and eventually the entire society. In other words, through the use of terror and creation of fear, they created a society in sympathetic mode; a society whose heart rate, like an individual in sympathetic mode, is beating at a higher rate, whose respiration is deeper, and blood pressure higher. A society ready to 'fight' or 'flight', just like a threatened individual.

Before 1978, Khomeini was mostly unsuccessful in arousing the sympathetic response of society. In 1960's and 70's, there were minor petty acts of arson and violence by both followers of Khomeini and various Leftist and Marxist groups. For the first half of 1978 there were minor demonstrations, minor threats and a few other acts of arson. But these events were not traumatic enough to raise the sympathetic reaction of the nation. On August 19th, 1978 Khomeini was finally able to activate the sympathetic nervous system of society and create a society in the 'fight' or 'flight' mode and instill fear in the hearts of everyone.

On a smoldering summer afternoon in Abadan, where the temperature can easily reach over 110 degrees, the first great act of terror took place. Thugs thought to be followers of Khomeini placed chains around the exit doors of a popular movie theater called Cinema Rex. The movie theater was sold-out with a crowd of 377, including children enjoying their summer vacation. The theater was set on fire and burnt to the ground, women and children screaming, struggling to open the chained exit doors. This was the first great, albeit horrific act of terrorism that reverberated in form of anger or fear in hearts of Iranians. An entire country felt the horror of Cinema Rex and as mentioned before, being a witness to such an event can be as terrorizing and traumatic as experiencing it.

CHAPTER 2

Immediately the sympathetic reaction was activated in millions and from that day on, Iranian society was placed in the 'fight' or 'flight' mode. Khomeini spread the rumor that the Shah's intelligence service, SAVAK, was responsible for Cinema Rex and many believed him. Khomeini sensed the heightened emotional state of the nation and planned a street demonstration two weeks after the Cinema Rex incident on the religious occasion of Eid-e-Fitr.

On that day, while in 'fight' mode, thousands of protesters took to the streets of Tehran and other cities. This was repeated days later on September 8th in Tehran's Jaleh Square. With the country in 'fight' mode from a high sympathetic response, violence broke out, the army opened fire on the demonstrators, and as the result of the violence, the sympathetic mode was reactivated in millions more Iranians. During the autumn of 1978, the society was on alert, reacting to events much like an individual reacting to trauma. Large numbers of people were ready for 'fight' and another group of people were preparing for 'flight'.

Until the Cinema Rex horror, Khomeini had not realized what a powerful psychological weapon terrorism is, and how a society placed in fear can respond in 'fight' or 'flight'. Once he learned of this weapon, he used it more and more. His arrival to Tehran on January 16th, 1979 from exile in France was followed days later by public executions, which helped maintain a state of alert and fear for a population in sympathetic mode. This was followed by confiscations of property, beatings and more executions. Without the use of terror, violence and fear, the population would eventually calm itself from the 'alert' mode. Such calmness is a necessary tool for free speech and democracy. But these end-results were not the ultimate goal of Khomeini and the regime in power. Khomeini needed a population acting out of emotion rather than reason.

The significant point about psychological trauma to keep in mind, and one discussed earlier, is that witnessing violence can be just as traumatic as experiencing violence. Khomeini's regime used this principle very effectively. From the earliest days of the revolution, executions and beatings were not done in silence or in secret but openly. Newspapers were given direct access to print the photos of those executed on the front pages. The regime also made the conscious decision to be as visible as possible on every street corner and to publicize its violence in the media. Martial law was declared. Cars and individuals were searched in public view. People's belongings and property were confiscated and widely reported in the media.

As long as the danger of violence was imminent, society would not get the chance to calm itself. Violence was needed to drive the society away from reason, dialogue and democracy and toward an emotional response, anger and acceptance of autocracy. In 1979, the confiscation of properties, the execution of Shah's supporters and generals, forcing *hejab* on women through the use of violence, and public lashings of citizens for possession of alcohol and western music were only a few of the instruments used to create a state of terror and fear. In November 1979 through the hostage crisis, Khomeini and the newly established regime were able to intensify the state of terror and fear in society. They successfully promoted the U.S. as the 'Great Satan,' using it as a continued reminder of violence, fear and terror, and a signal for people to stay on 'alert' or in sympathetic mode.

The 'fight' response in a society placed in sympathetic mode without a distinct outside enemy will ultimately turn against itself. One way to diffuse this tense psychological state is to turn the attention of society to a foreign threat. Khomeini needed a foreign enemy. Picking a fight with the United States through the hostage crisis did not end in violence. The Americans were exhausted from the Vietnam War and did not want to begin a war with another emotionally charged nation. Khomeini then attempted to export the revolution to neighboring Arab states and instigate violence in neighboring countries.

Shortly later, a 'cultural revolution' was initiated by Khomeini. They first closed all of the universities and began purging all faculty and students not willing to conform to Islamic law. As if everything else was not traumatic enough, destroying the hopes and dreams of hundreds of thousands of young people attempting to get an education was meant to complete the campaign of psychological trauma.

None of these attempts were conscious decisions made with knowledge of human and societal psychological response to violence and trauma. Khomeini did not have psychologists advising him. It was all done through trial and error. Acts of terrorism were performed and the reaction of population gauged. When the voice of reason was heard in newspapers and speeches, another act of terror, violence or international crisis was created to again place the society into the psychological 'sympathetic' mode once more. There was a need for a more serious enemy and a more serious state of terror in the country.

CHAPTER 2

Saddam's Bloody War

Our house in Gheytarieh, in the northeast of Tehran, was at the foot of the majestic Alborz Mountains, which climb several thousand feet in less than a few miles creating a fortress-like wall north of Tehran. Each year in autumn, snow on the tips of those mountains heralds the coming of winter. In September of 1980, I was seven years old, looking outside our window aimlessly at the skyline of Tehran, perhaps like hundreds of thousands of other children. I'm not sure if I could appreciate the smog-free blue sky of the Tehran of my childhood or the thousands of gardens and ancient trees in the northern section of the city, in Shemiran, now destroyed. Like any other child, I was just staring outside when I saw an incredible spectacle in the sky, which, to my surprise, few adults now remember. In the horizon appeared a dual-rotor military transport helicopter. As I was watching, I noticed another coming over the horizon, and then another and another. What appeared like a parade of military helicopters was followed by a spectacle of Phantoms and other fighter jets, then one military transport plane after another. It was a majestic procession of military hardware. I had no idea what this meant at the time.

We live in an era where young boys are taught that violence is routine, heroic and necessary. For me, this fly-over, which lasted more than an hour, was mesmerizing. Like American children collecting baseball cards of their favorite players, my generation of little boys witnessing the incredible military shopping spree of the Shah would collect cards with pictures of fighter jets, helicopters, tanks and artillery. Instead of baseball stats, these cards contained the weight, price and destructive powers of each toy. I thought what I was witnessing was majestic and beautiful. I no longer think it is beautiful. I no longer believe it is heroic, routine, or necessary.

I'm not sure if these hundreds of military aircraft were going west to east, fleeing what was happening on the western border, or going east to west in aid of the extraordinary circumstances that had taken place. I do not know what those pilots where thinking, what my mother was doing or how my father's day was spent at work. But I do know that that September morning, which could have been an otherwise beautiful autumn morning, was the most tragic day for people of my generation.

Khomeini's attempts to direct the societal 'adrenaline rush' at a threat posed by a foreign enemy finally paid off. While instigating conflicts with the Shi'ites in southern Iraq and starting small-scale skirmishes along the border, he found another master of terror in Saddam. A fellow lunatic, Saddam, was also well aware that to survive he, too, needed to inflict fear, trauma and anxiety on the people in his country. This internal Iraqi terror also needed to be turned against a foreign enemy before it was turned on himself. In the chaos next door he found his opportunity. The Iran-Iraq war was an opportunity for a long-term state of violence, fear, terror and trauma between two masters of violence. Throughout the war, Iranians (and Iraqis) would maintain a high emotionally charged psychological state without the opportunity for calm, dialogue and reason.

For the invasion, Saddam had stockpiled 2,500 tanks, 1,400 artillery pieces and 340 fighter jets. On September 22nd 1980, he hurled 9 Iraqi divisions into western Iran, together with an air campaign involving up to 100 fighter planes, which met little resistance.[37] Saddam's invasion and its great use of violence came immediately on the heels of another major trauma against the Iranian Armed Forces. Shortly after the Revolution, many of the Iranian military leaders were executed and up to 7,500 purged from the Armed Forces. After three failed coup attempts in the summer of 1980 the number of purged officers totaled 12,000. Because of the purging and execution of so many Iranian officers, the army and air force operational units were in shambles, with less than 500 operational tanks and 100 operable aircraft.[38] Saddam's attack began one of the bloodiest wars Iranians had seen in centuries.

The invasion of Iran by Saddam's army sparked a societal sympathetic mode in the form of 'fight' unseen in many generations. Hundreds of thousands volunteered for the war, and the economy was placed on a fast track to supply the needs of war and counteract the international isolation. The societal 'sympathetic' rush was so great that a foreign war did not diffuse all the energy gathered in the 'fight' mode of the population. There was still too much adrenaline in society despite the great societal rush to war. In 1981 the MEK [Mujahidin-e-Khalq], together with a minority branch called Fadayian-Khalq, began a violent confrontation with Khomeini and the regime on the streets of cities and towns across Iran. Executions, street battles and firing squads became everyday events. The population was nearly all in the 'fight' or 'flight' mode, with many different factions relying on violence for their survival. The government began a terror campaign of crackdown, mass arrests and tortures. In one day in September 1981 alone, 149 people were either hung or shot by firing squads. During the fall of that same year, up to

7,700 people were killed in the streets, in public view or by firing squads. Those imprisoned numbered in the tens of thousands.[39]

In September of 1982, two years after the start of the war, and after the pushback of all Iraqi units from Iranian territory, in fear of Khomeini's expansionism, the Saudis offered $70 billion dollars to the Iranian regime in exchange for peace.[40] But the regime, which needed a continued source of trauma, tension and adrenaline for its survival, refused the offer and chose further violence, promising to march first to Karbala and then to Jerusalem.

The 1980s was a decade Iranians would rather forget. The Iraq war dragged on for eight years, eventually costing more than 500,000 Iranian and Iraqi lives. Those injured, displaced or those who lost fathers, brothers or uncles, numbered in the millions. By 1983 Saddam had stockpiled enough mustard gas to start using chemical warfare against both the Iranian troops and the restive Iraqi Kurds in Northern Iraq. Other chemical agents soon followed such as phosgene, tabun, soman and sarin. During the course of war about 50,000 Iranians died as a result of chemical warfare. In addition countless Iranian and Iraqi Kurds were the victims of such trauma-inducing weaponry, and continue to suffer the devastating health consequences of such weapons to this day.[41]

War of the Cities – Terrorizing the Population into Defeat

On February 7th 1984, another front was opened in the Iraqi war called the 'War of the Cities'. The people of Tehran, Isfahan and other major cities, relatively spared from the war until then, were now involved. For millions of already traumatized Iranians, a nightmare of nighttime bombings began.

I distinctly remember the first night of the bombings. It was a school night. What started with a red alert at two in the morning was followed by the deafening and constant sound of anti-air batteries firing. After scrambling around in the dark and not knowing what to do, my family gathered in the safest point of the house. In the pitch black and horrifying dark, as my three – year-old sister was screaming in fear, we listened to the thunderous bombardment of antiaircraft machine guns, each barrage lasting for 30 to 45 minutes. The sky was lit up with thousands of bullets and missiles aiming to shoot down the aircraft. What followed was the sound of a bomb exploding, the loudest sound I had ever heard. Our house shook as if an earthquake had struck. -

In the morning there was a frantic effort to find out where the bomb had fallen. It turned out that the Iraqis could not afford to send multiple planes to Tehran. In addition, the 600-mile journey from Iraq and back did not allow the plane to carry multiple bombs. Thus each night one or two planes would fly to Tehran, Isfahan, Tabriz or another major city, and would start a psychological campaign specifically designed to frighten and traumatize the population into defeat. The routine of red alerts in the early morning hours, accompanied by the deafening sounds of anti-aircraft artillery, was followed each night by the horrific sound of a bomb randomly killing a family. The sound of the bomb would shake the entire city, breaking all the windows in the neighborhood where the bomb fell. This scenario was repeated night after night for weeks. What began as a traumatic experience soon became routine, and many were soon numbed by the endless trauma.

The psychological trauma from the 'War of the Cities' became even more intensified in 1988. Iraq was able to modify its Scud missiles to fly more than twice their normal range, finally enabling them to hit Tehran. On February 28th, 1988, Iraq launched the first five of what it called its new 'Al-Hussein' missiles.[42] Unlike the nighttime bombing campaigns, these missiles offered no warning. They would come at any time during the day or night, and the explosive force of the missile's warhead and its impact on the demolished house and neighborhood were worse than the bombs dropped by a plane. The sound, force, and psychological effects were beyond horrifying. Its unpredictability also added another dimension of fear not seen during the first 'War of the Cities' campaign. In addition, rumors were spread in the cities that Saddam might place a chemical warhead on a missile. During February, March and April, the Iraqis fired over 200 of these missiles, most of which targeted Tehran.[43]

By later 1980's, what began as a societal fear creating a 'fight' or 'flight' reaction had turned into chronic trauma and societal anxiety. In 1988, this societal anxiety was turned into panic. Millions fled Tehran as the result of the missiles. Tehran's streets on some days looked deserted, with the population in a trance. By mid-1988, the constant state of fear and terror had created a depleted and traumatized society suffering from Complex PTSD.

A Permanent State of Crisis and Chain Killings

Those in power sensed the psychological exhaustion not only in the volunteer army fighting Saddam, but also within the Revolutionary Guards protecting the interests of the regime. With the population numbed and no longer able to react, the regime had to remove any remaining threats against its existence to better secure its future.

In August of 1988, orders were drafted and signed by Khomeini to execute all political prisoners who were still not psychologically or physiologically broken and remained threats to the regime. Within days and weeks, in an otherwise beautiful hot and dry summer, in Iranian cities where the shade of trees and sounds of mountain streams can create a heavenly atmosphere, thousands of political prisoners who continued to believe in their political rights were suddenly executed and their bodies placed in unmarked mass graves. Within days, hundreds of thousands of Iranians in cities across the world learned of a loved one executed overnight. There was no more psychological energy for a fight. The nation placed in sympathetic mode for eight years was no longer able to wield a response. Iranian society was psychologically exhausted and broken.

The extent of violence and trauma in society did not end in the summer of 1988. Islamic Republic continued its policy of fear and terror with the flogging of people, the stoning of women, the humiliation of mothers, fathers and grandparents, raids into people's homes at nights and detention of women displaying too much of their hair. Fallahian, Rafsanjani's minister of Intelligence, planned and carried out the murder of more than 150 activists, intellectuals, writers and business leaders in 1990's in what became famously known as the 'Chain Killings'. Some of the murders happened in gruesome manner in the homes of activists and opposition leaders in European countries. Other were kidnapped and never heard of again and very few were lucky to escape intelligent ministry's wrath like my father. In 1990's the 'Chain Killings' were a source of terror for anyone contemplating political activity.

In July of 1998, after tens of thousands of students at Tehran University marched into the streets to protest the ruthless killing of a classmate in his dorm room, they were beaten, jailed, tortured and up to 19 lost their lives. The security officers called them thugs and the reformist President Khatami, in a speech in Hamedan, called the protesting students 'anarchists'.

Again, when millions marched into the streets in the summer and autumn of 2009, after the disputed elections, the population was terrorized into submission through beatings, rapes, tortures and killings.

The Islamic Republic survives as long as it has the means to instill fear, to psychologically traumatize its population through violence, and induce sympathetic exhaustion in large number of those suffering from PTSD. Under these circumstances, society will express the same symptoms and behavior patterns as an individual with PTSD. The actions of such a nation and its inability to heal itself, to rise up and create a healthy future, are no different from that of a war veteran or an abused child or a rape victim with PTSD who is placed in an environment with repeated reminders of the violence and trauma. What we call psychological defeat is, in fact, the placement of a large minority of the population in Post-Traumatic Stress, Complex PTSD and the exhaustion of the sympathetic mode, a large enough percentage of the population sufficient to paralyze the entire society.

Conclusion

I have no doubt that millions of Iranians suffer from post-traumatic stress disorder. I strongly believe that Iranian psychological paralysis makes it extremely difficult to hear the saner voices attempting to call attention to the true state of the country.

Violence is the tool for such repression and fundamental threat to democracy and human rights. It is the tool needed to create fear. Without the use of violence and the presence of fear, the leadership of the Islamic Republic is no more than a collection of individuals forced to accept the will of the people. Without the threat of violence and use of fear, women cannot be consigned to second-class status, and minorities cannot be treated as aliens in their own country. Without fear, no form of government can take shape other than through reason and dialogue. Without fear and violence, no form of government other than democracy is possible. Such a task may seem impossible in a society that has suffered immensely from violence and one which is in a traumatized and fearful state.

But fear can be overcome, phobias can be treated and a person afflicted with PTSD can be made well again. However, treating a nation suffering from fear, anxiety and trauma is different than treating an individual. One cannot expect to place an entire nation on medication or to prescribe therapy for millions of individuals. Societal psychological illnesses need societal solutions.

This form of societal therapy cannot be a quick fix solution, just as the treatment of an individual does not have a magic pill. An Iranian solution cannot be short-term, suitable only for a superficial problem but an attempt to reach the unconscious mind of a nation that has lost its heroes, identity, celebrations, pride and confidence. It must include the awakening of that unconscious mind that can see beyond fear, beyond violence and beyond punishment and revenge. The Iranian solution must be a societal effort at healing and therapy for a societal, psychological problem brought about by violence. It must understand violence as the root cause of today's predicament and must focus on overcoming fear and ultimately the defeat of fear as the central goal of a psychological, political, and societal transformation

CHAPTER 2- 100 GENERATION LEGACY OF VIOLENCE- PART I: WAR IN THE AGE OF EMPIRES.

"Few nations in the world present more of a justification for the study of history than Iran."

~ Richard Nelson Frye

I once read that the native Mi'Kmaq tribe in eastern Canada believes that wisdom for important decision-makings for the people should take into account the fate of 15 generations, the memory, knowledge and advice of the previous seven generations, the struggle, experience and wisdom of the current generation and the hopes and desires of the next seven generations.[44] If Iranians are to use their knowledge, wisdom and experience with violence to make an important decision about their current struggle against despotism, how many generations of memories and knowledge on violence can they gather? If the story of each human generation is roughly 25 years, what can humanity learn of violence through the experience of more than 2,500 years of recorded Iranian history, one of the longest stories of humanity? How many of the more than 100 generations lived 25 years free of violence and fear without having their fate determined through foreign wars, civil wars or military coups? If we are to find out how many of the 100 generations had their fate determined through reason and peace as opposed to violence, that could be of tremendous value in evaluating the challenge to nonviolence and peace for this generation of Iranians and the next 25 years of Iran.

Once we have a more detailed account of violence and peace of more than 100 generations of Iranians, we can better understand who Iranians are, how they have struggled against violence in the past and how they will likely react against violence today. So the path to understanding nonviolence in Iran must begin with understanding the culture and legacy of violence, particularly through the experience of Iranians.

Cyrus the Great

Archaeologists have unearthed tremendous evidence of culture and civilization in Middle East that spans nearly 10,000 years. Civilizations such as Sumer, Babylon, Elam and Assyria are important foundations for today's Western civilization and important historical footsteps for humanity. But amongst Iranians, the names and locations of such kingdoms do not play an important role in creating their cultural identity. These ancient cultures and civilizations are historical facts relevant to scholars but as removed from the Iranian culture as they are from the European culture.

For Iranians, their history and thus an important source of cultural symbolism begins in 6th century BCE with the man the world calls Cyrus the Great. Coincidently, their mythology ends with Cyrus as well. He is one of the most important symbols of Iranian cultural and national identity. In Cyrus, Iranians see that rare figure in history whose life takes on mythological proportions, yet lives on in the minds of scholars as a historical figure. If Iranians are to move toward a culture where their fate is not determined through violence, the appropriate place of such important historical figures and symbols needs to be defined and explained to children.

The story of the life of Cyrus the Great, which an Iranian child learns is the story which Herodotus wrote three generations after Cyrus's death, basing it on the accounts he gathered on his travels within the empire created by Cyrus and writing the first great anthropological and historical work.

According to Herodotus, the story of Cyrus begins in the Mede kingdom, with its capital in Ekbatana, which is today's city of Hamedan, situated in the Zagros Mountains in western Iran. Herodotus tells us that those mountains were covered with dense forests at the time. Amongst these green mountains lived a king named Astyagos. His daughter Mandana was married to a Persian and lived amongst the Persian tribes in the hills and valleys surrounding Pasargad in central Iran.

King Astyagos dreamed one night of a vine coming out of his daughter's belly, which got bigger and bigger until it engulfed all of Asia. This dream frightened him, and he called the astrologers, priests and dream readers of his kingdom to interpret this vision for him. He was told that his daughter would bring a child into this world who would overtake, first his kingdom, and then all of Asia. Fearful of such a grandchild, when his daughter gave birth, he ordered her to come to his palace with the child. There, Astyagos took the child away, handed him to his minister Harpagos, and ordered him to kill the child and bury him.[45]

This culture of kill or be killed is a fundamental aspect of violence. Whether that threat is by rebels, a foreign army or an unborn child is irrelevant to a despot or a government that must rely on violence to survive. This need for violence against a perceived existential threat is perhaps one of the root causes of violence in human history.

The minister, who did not have the heart for such a task, ordered a herdsman to his palace. He handed the child to him and ordered to take the child into the forest and leave him there for wild beasts. The story tells us that when the herdsman returned to his village, his wife informed him that their child had been stillborn. Not having the heart to kill the infant prince, he took the gold and fine clothing from the newborn, dressed his dead child in them, showed the tiny body to Harpagos, and proceeded to raise Cyrus as his own child without telling the minister.[46]

Whether this story is true or a myth, it forms the backbone of one of the most important symbols of Iranian culture. The person who Iranians consider the founder of their country lived despite an attempt at violence against him and because of the kindness of a humble individual.

When Cyrus was ten years old, an event took place that altered the child's destiny. The children of the village played a game in which they created a make-believe kingdom, and Cyrus was chosen as the king. This, perhaps, is the first hint that this ten-year-old had a certain charisma and intellect that earned him the high regard of his peers. But one child, the son of a minister, refused to take orders from this herdsman's son. Cyrus, getting carried away in the game, ordered his royal guards to tie the child up and beat him as punishment for his refusal to take orders from a king.[47]

When the father of the beaten child heard of this, he took Cyrus to Astyagos and demanded justice from him. The King, while questioning the child, found a strange resemblance between the child and himself. When he inquired about the age of Cyrus, and realized it was near his own grandson's age if he had lived, his suspicion grew. He ordered the herdsman to his palace and, after torturing him, found out the true story. Having discovered an affinity for this child, he decided to let him live, sent him to Pasargad to live with his mother, and decided to punish his minister who had betrayed him.[48]

The king then invited Harpagos, his minister, and some guests for dinner, and ordered his soldiers to take the minister's thirteen-year-old son, kill him, and make a stew with the child's flesh. He served the food to the minister, and asked Harpagos if he had enjoyed his meal. His guards then brought forth the remaining parts of the child's body, including his head and arms. The devastated minister held himself together in order to save his own life, yet conceived an imperishable hatred for the King.[49]

Conquest of Medes

Years later, the same minister heard that Cyrus had turned into a fine young prince amongst the Persians and had won the respect and admiration of his peers. In a secret letter, Harpagos told Cyrus that if he put together an army of Persians and headed toward the Mede kingdom, King Astyagos would likely name Harpagos as the general of his army. In such an event, he would abandon the King and surrender the army to Cyrus, leaving the door open for Cyrus to take Ekbatana and the Mede kingdom.[50]

Historians believe that, despite the betrayal of Astyagos by Harpagos, the path to victory for Cyrus was not easy. Nicolaus of Damascus tells us of a fierce battle between the Mede and Persian armies in the fields around Pasargad. Pulianus tells us that Cyrus was defeated three times by the Mede army. The fourth battle was in Pasargad itself, which was home to the women and children of the Persian rebel army. In this fourth battle, the women and children were on the hilltop watching the violence below.[51]

With the defeat of the Mede army in Pasargad, the Persians, together with Harpagos marched to Ekbatana, the Mede capital and seat of Astyagos. The norms of warfare at the time were for the winning army to either slaughter or take the King and his family as slaves. Such an act would cement their victory and prevent the people from using the royal family as symbols for an uprising. In addition, it was customary for the winning army to take the religious statues of the gods of those defeated to their own lands as hostages. The priests of the vanquished country were also killed or taken as slaves in order to diminish the risk of uprising. The citizens were also the property of the new king, and could be taken as slaves as needed. A defeated population expected this; it was the price of living in the culture of war and violence.

But, when Cyrus reached Ekbatana, he performed an act so extraordinary that it changed the course of Iranian and perhaps human history. People's homes, properties, and temples were respected. The priests, who now had to pray for the new king, were also allowed to pray for the old king. Not only did he not torture, enslave or kill Astyagos[52], he allowed him to live as a king amongst the Medes.[53] Cyrus, in turn, placed himself as the King over

Astyagos, which meant he was now the king of a king. The treasury of the former king was taken as plunder of war from Ekbatana to Pasargad, which allowed Cyrus for the first time to raise and train a professional army.[54]

Conquest of Lydia

At the time, the ancient Middle East was divided into three major powers. In the far southwest was the four thousand-year-old civilization of ancient Egypt, with its pharaohs ruling the cities and towns along the Nile. Anatolia (today's Turkey), was dominated by Lydia, a Greek city-state ruled by King Croesus in his wealthy capital, Sardis. In the Fertile Crescent, Babylon's influence extended from the shores of the Persian Gulf to the Mediterranean Sea. The change in the balance of power in Mede presented an opportunity for change in the balance of power between these three powers. When violence rules, any change in balance of powers will lead to renewed warfare until a new balance of power is formed. Croesus, King of Lydia, likely regarded Cyrus as a vulnerable and inexperienced Persian ruling over Medes. According to Herodotus, it was Croesus, expecting help from the Spartans who decided to take advantage of the situation and began to march his army east toward Medes. But the impatient Croesus marched east before the Spartan army could prepare and march to his aid.[55]

The armies of Croesus and Cyrus met in Pteria, in Eastern Anatolia, during the winter months of 546 BCE and engaged in a battle from which both sides retreated; neither could claim victory. Croesus decided to take the remainder of his army back to Sardis, wait for fresh troops, as well as the Spartan army to arrive, and then to attack again in the spring.

The mountains of Anatolia are an inhospitable place in wintertime. A modern army with tanks and armored vehicles using 20th century roads would have a difficult time marching across these mountains in wintertime, much less an army of foot soldiers trekking along the mountains without roads. Thus, Croesus was assured that Cyrus would have to go back to Pasargad and prepare for another battle in spring.

But Cyrus must have been well in tuned to the psyche of his time. He knew that Croesus would go back to his own kingdom, and could raise as large an army as needed, while he, as the new Persian king, now in control of Medes, had to raise an army from a population perhaps foreign to him. Thus, he decided to do the unthinkable and march west across the winter snows of Anatolia in a surprise attack upon the unsuspecting Lydian army.[56] The dispersed Lydian soldiers were on their way back to their towns and villages for the winter's rest when the Persian army caught up with them.[57] The remnant of Croesus' army that survived the attack retreated to Sardis but was defeated after a short siege of the city. Cyrus entered Sardis in 546 BCE.

Upon entering Sardis, Cyrus treated his adversary, the King of Lydia, with respect. This action has immense symbolic value for Iranians and serves as one of the important justifications for the culture of benevolent despotism so prevalent in Iranian culture. Citizens were respected and people were not taken as slaves. The temples were respected, and priests were allowed to continue the practice of their Greek religion. Cyrus wanted Croesus to maintain the same lifestyle and position of respect as before, but was afraid that if he were left in Sardis, he would raise an army and rebel against his rule. Accordingly, Croesus was given a city in Mede and allowed to take his family and court there as their king.[58] The rich treasury of Sardis was taken as bounty and sent to the rapidly growing and developing capital of Persians in Pasargad (Persepolis). Harpagos, the minister whom Herodotus tells us had saved his life as a child, was made the King of Sardis and Lydia. Thus Cyrus was now the King of Anshan, where his home city in Pasargad lay, King of Mede, and the King of Lydia. From this point on, he was acknowledged as the King of Kings.

For the first time in human history, a state's borders extended far beyond the king's capital. For the first time, a king was ruling over lands with different religions, languages and cultures where each state, ruled by its despotic king, was also the subject of a foreign power. Thus in the early moments in their history, the first generation of Iranians, through a new system of power and rule over far off lands which the world today knows as imperialism created the world's first empire famously known as the Persian Empire.

Each city-state conquered by Cyrus was now called a *satrap*, or a state within the larger empire. The citizens of a *satrap* spoke their own language, prayed to their own gods, built their own temples, baths and schools. This arrangement, however, should not be regarded as an ideal system with 20th century standards of freedom and democracy. The political system was despotic; citizens had no say in the affairs of state. They were subjects of the King, but subjects whose religion, language and culture was respected under the rule of a benevolent despot. Thus, one of the most important symbolic stories of the Iranian culture, which every Iranian learns as a child, begins with the creation of a benevolent empire ruled by a benevolent despot. Here, in a symbolic story of Iranian culture, seemingly unrelated to the violence of Islamic Republic, lies one of justifications of despotism in Iranian culture. Accordingly, one of the recurring themes of Iranian culture and history is the search for the benevolent despot whose employment of violence is justified by his embodiment of the virtues of justice, righteousness and truthfulness.

Cyrus is believed to have gone east after the defeat of Sardis into Central Asia. After these conquests, Cyrus now controlled territories extending from the shores of the Mediterranean Sea in western Anatolia to the Oxus and Jaxartes rivers in Central Asia. Yet, he still did not have control over the most powerful and richest city in the world, Babylon.

Conquest of Babylon

Olmstead tells us that, at this time, Babylon was 'in chaos'. The reforms of the Babylonian king had alienated the priesthood. In addition, those enslaved and suffering under the Babylonian king had heard of Cyrus's tolerance for other cultures and religions. The enslaved Jews in Babylon were "hailing Cyrus as the Lord's anointed who would grant return to Zion."[59] In addition, Dandameyev suggests that merchants were also disgruntled at the situation in Babylon and the blocking of trade routes.[60] In the lands under Cyrus's rule, merchants saw the opportunity for relatively safe travel and trade across many states without fear of crossing borders from one kingdom to another. This gigantic political and economic revolution of humanity created by the first generation of Iranians perhaps can be seen as humanity's first form of globalization, extending free trade and travel throughout the lands ruled by Cyrus.

Around this time, Babylon's governor for the lands east of the Tigris, defected to Cyrus. Herodotus tells us of the siege of Babylon. In his version of story, the Persian troops were stopped outside the impenetrable gates of this ancient city. Cyrus then ordered his troops to divert the great Euphrates River, which went through the center of the city. When the waters of the Euphrates fell below waist level, the Persian troops entered the city by way of the riverbed and opened the gates. In autumn of 539 BCE, the Persian army is thought to have entered Babylon, the center of ancient human civilization.[61]

Upon entering the city, Cyrus continued his rule of benevolent despotism, proclaiming peace to the city and all its citizens. Cyrus tells us on a clay cylinder that records the history of his reign:

"...My numerous troops marched peacefully into Babylon. In all Sumer and Akkad I permitted no unfriendly treatment..."[62]

The religious images, statues and symbols of all the ancient gods captured and taken as hostage in Babylon under the previous king were returned to their temples. With these gods went instructions for rebuilding of temples. [63] Bricks at a temple in Uruk have the inscription, "Cyrus, builder of Esagila and Ezida..."[64] All the god-symbols captured by the Babylonian king in the lands of Assyria and Babylonia were returned to their people. The inhabitants of those cities who had been brought to Babylon as slaves were also collected and restored to their homes. [65]

The Jews, who had been taken as slaves to Babylon decades before were also freed. Because they had no statues, images or symbols of their God taken by the Babylonian king, the items looted from their temple in Jerusalem were collected and taken back. A decree was then made by Cyrus for the great temple of Jerusalem to be rebuilt.[66]

Cyrus placed such importance on his belief of benevolence in the form of freedom of religion and cultural practices that he ordered a record of his practice inscribed on a clay cylinder; it included his message of tolerance for peoples' religions and beliefs. This cylinder with the written message, today resting in the British Museum, must have been on display in Babylon for the population. His statement on the rights of citizens to peace, the decree commanding his soldiers not to harm the population and to respect populations' properties are considered some of humanity's oldest statements concerning human rights and important symbolic achievements in human history.

Few people in history are universally accorded the title 'Great'. Such individuals often forever altered, not just the course of their people's history, but also the course of human history. During his reign and for the first time in human history, the people of various religions and cultures were gathered under the same political and military system. This new form of nation was a country with many languages, religions, gods and cultures. Through conquest, he founded the first empire-state, yet the greatness of Cyrus lies not in his military success but in his benevolence and the creation of humanity's first pluralistic state.

1st Generation of Iranians

The first generation of human beings with whom Iranians identify as their direct cultural and historical ancestors, guided by the charismatic leader whom they called the King of Kings, witnessed the birth of an empire from the conquest of many states. The qualities of kindness and righteousness much heralded in Iranian mythology as qualities of a benevolent king are seen in Cyrus.

Cyrus was born into a culture of militarism and violence and achieved his success through his army's superior use of violence. In return, the use of violence for benevolence was institutionalized and justified within the Iranian culture. This institutionalized use of violence for the despot under the names of Kings, Sultans, Caliphs and Supreme Leaders in turn has justified the raising of armies, the crushing of dissent and rebellion and invasion of foreign lands repeatedly in Iranian history.

In the simplistic world where symbolic figures are held up to children as exemplars of good or evil, Iranians are often forced to label Cyrus as one of the two.

In seminars and conferences on human rights and democracy, I often meet individuals falling into one of the above two categories. Like an intern attempting to pass along a 30-second bit of advice, I often find myself trying to show the limitations in labeling such Iranian symbols as good or evil while explaining that *actions* intended to cause harm or instill fear should be labeled as wrong and virtues such as kindness labeled as good.

Cambyses and the Conquest of Egypt

Cyrus the Great died during a battle in central Asia in the year 530 BCE. According to Herodotus, Cyrus had a dream in which he saw the eldest son of his eastern general Hystapes growing wings on his shoulders. One wing of the eagle overshadowed Asia, and the other, Europe. Hystapes's son was about twenty years old at this time and not participating in battle in the east.

Herodotus tells us that Cyrus, troubled by this dream, summoned his general and told him, "Your son has been found plotting against me and against my throne." He ordered him to go back to Pasargad (Persepolis) as quickly as he could and bring this 20-year- old boy back for examination. The general then left in order to question his young son. That young man's name was Darius, and he was to play the most important role in the destiny of not just the Persian Empire but perhaps also Iranian civilization. Cyrus continued east, crossing over the Araxes River where he was soon killed in a battle.[67] His body was sent back to Pasargad (Persepolis) to be placed in a tomb built during his lifetime. Prior to his death, Cyrus had followed the tribal hereditary tradition of leadership selection and picked his son Cambyses to lead the empire he had built.

Cambyses followed in the footsteps of his father, and soon began preparations for further invasion and conquest. From this second generation of Iranians, young men, perhaps not unlike the young American boys I saw volunteer for the war with Saddam, were recruited from cities and villages across the Persian Empire. They were taught how to carry a sword, how to shoot an arrow, and to hurl a javelin. They left behind their lovers, mothers, and fathers for the invasion of Egypt, the oldest and the richest civilization at the time.

The pharaohs had ruled Egypt for thousands of years, using their powers to create some of the greatest monuments celebrating their absolute rule over their people. In addition, Egypt was the gateway to the rich natural resources and exotic plants and animals of Africa. Cyrus had dreamt of conquering Egypt, but died in battle without realizing that dream. His son, born into a culture of war, where wealth was achieved often through conquest, set out to realize that dream. Over 50,000 soldiers were gathered and the largest army the world had ever seen crossed the Sinai Desert conquering Egypt in 525 BCE. With this conquest, 3,000 years of Egyptian culture, history, tradition and way of life was threatened.

Cambyses initially continued in the tradition of benevolent despot as his father. He respected the leadership of the Egyptian pharaoh and kept their tradition alive. He allowed Egyptians to continue practicing their religion and to maintain their ancient culture just as his father had done with the cultures he had conquered.

After the conquest of Egypt, Cambyses made plans and preparations to use his immense army for conquest of all known nations of Africa from Carthage to Ethiopia. No army in history had the power of violence Cambyses possessed. No city or king could withstand the force of this advancing army. Yet, as history repeatedly shows, no army is as powerful as the force of nature, often determining the course of history.

In one of the great violent acts of nature, as the Persian Empire's great army was marching across the desert in Africa, a sandstorm approached, and nearly 50,000 soldiers vanished on their way to conquer the rest of Africa. This lost Persian army was hidden for 2,500 years until 20th century when a geological team from Helwan University searching for petroleum came across well-preserved remains of human bones, textiles and weapons thought to be their remains.[68]

When the news reached Cambyses back in Egypt, he lost control of himself. He blamed the Egyptians and their magical religion for this act of nature.[69] With the hatred brewing, the great tradition of benevolence of Cyrus and his respect for other religions and cultures no longer prevailed. On his return to Memphis, Cambyses vented his anger on the Egyptian gods, temples and priests, and blamed them for the sandstorm that had engulfed his army. The Egyptian temples were burnt and their valuables looted.[70] Cambyses's madness, anger, hatred, and violence soon involved his brother Bardia, his pregnant sister, and his governor/king of Lydia. He also ordered twelve Persian aristocrats buried alive.[71]

Soon, news reached Cambyses that people in and around his capital in Pasargad (Persepolis) had rebelled against his rule. Thus, in the spring of 522 BC, Cambyses left Egypt to take control of his capital and crush the rebellion. While in Syria, on his way back to Persia, Cambyses died suddenly.[72] With his death, the first and largest empire humanity had seen was in chaos. Cyrus's other son, Bardia, had been killed earlier by Cambyses but there were a few people back in the capital who claimed to be Bardia.

One of these claimants, Gaumata, who had taken control of the throne, announced a three-year exemption from taxes in every Satrap.[73] Yet this was an empire dependent on the taxes it collected from its conquered provinces. In addition, nearly every satrap and territory which Cyrus and Cambyses had conquered was in rebellion and in danger of disintegration.

The fate of the second generation of Iranians was in the balance. The empire built through violence a generation before was about to fall apart. Only a military and strategic genius could have saved this vast empire at this critical moment. Fortunately, a genius was found— the son of Cyrus's general, the now twenty-seven-year old Darius who Herodotus tells us Cyrus had dreamt about.

Darius – The Great King

Seven aristocratic families back in Pasargad (Persepolis) united themselves politically and chose Darius as the King of Kings. While we do not know the circumstances surrounding him being chosen, it is noteworthy that this young and inexperienced man was selected during a time of great uncertainty and fear. Darius was picked as the King of Kings over all generals and elders including his father, an unprecedented decision indicating the incredible capability and potential seen in him by the elders.

Upon taking power, Darius was immediately faced with disaster. He first canceled the tax forgiveness, which sent the country into frenzy. He then systematically took control of his inherited empire one satrap at a time. During the first two years of his rule, he was constantly fighting citizen rebellions and crushing them throughout the empire. He first defeated the rebellion in Elam, and then Babylon.[74] His army then marched across the empire and suppressed every rebellion one city at a time. From account of the name of cities known to have rebelled, one quickly comes to the realization that nearly every major city from the Mediterranean coast and Egypt to the plains of central Asia was in rebellion. Professor Pierre Bryant estimates that 100,000 people of this second generation of Iranians may have died during these rebellions.[75] Once again, the fate of human beings was settled through violence.

The techniques of punishment by Darius also reverted back to the ancient Middle Eastern practices common in Assyria and Babylonia. On Darius's instructions, the rebel leaders in Babylon and 49 others were nailed to city walls to serve as examples for others. Many other rebel leaders were executed. In Medes, he ordered two rebel leaders to have "their nose, tongue and ears cut off, one eye taken out, and the prisoners chained to the wall at his palace for everyone to see." As for the commanders, Darius proudly boasted, "I ordered them to be skinned alive and then their skins be filled with straw and the bodies hung for display."[76] According to Pierre Bryant, such punishment was common in the ancient Middle East, especially in Assyria.[77]

Through the systemic use of violence to crush rebellions, Darius successfully established peace, stability and security across the empire. For empires built on violence, security and stability is achieved only after such complete victory through violence. It was during these decades of relative peace that Darius made the achievements for which Iranians now label him as 'The Great King'. It is important for Iranians today to realize that these great historical achievements were accomplished in a time of peace rather than war. It was a momentary peace, however, that came on the heels of violence.

The great palaces and structures of Persepolis were built. A great winter palace was also built in Susa, as well as a palace in Babylon for the King's son. Magical walled gardens and palaces called 'paradis' were built in his capital. Darius undertook the construction of a massive transportation infrastructure on a scale unheard of in human history. Roads were built across the empire. The most famous was the royal road linking Susa in today's southwestern Iran to Sardis, the western capital of the empire in today's western Turkey. Garrisons for security were placed at various points along the highways and the entire empire from India to Europe was safe for trade and travel.

During his reign, it was not unusual for small parties to travel the empire in safety. Even when an imperial party was transporting silver for the treasury, it was guarded by a small group of soldiers, often not numbering more than ten.[78] Along the roads, inns for travelers were built. The postal system was put in place with way-stations at carefully spaced intervals, where messengers could change horses. Mail was taken across the country twenty-four hours a day without stop. Herodotus tells us that nothing mortal traveled faster than these messengers. "Neither snow, nor rain, nor heat, nor darkness of night prevents them from accomplishing…the task…with the very utmost speed."[79] Information that previously took months to be carried across the empire now took days.

During his visits to provinces in India, Darius realized the potential of trade between India and the Mediterranean ports and ordered a canal built linking the Nile to the Red Sea, a great engineering and human achievement not repeated until the building of Suez Canal in the modern era. The canal was a great achievement, not just for Persians, but also for humanity, linking the waterways of the Persian Gulf, the Red Sea and Indian Ocean to the Mediterranean Sea. Herodotus describes the canal as about 80 feet wide, enough for two war galleys to pass through side by side. He describes the length of the voyage as four days.[80] In addition, Darius fixed the currency and introduced the standardized gold coin of Daric.

Despite the massive rebellions and ensuing violence, he attempted to win back the good will of his people through promotion of local cultures and religions and promotion of economy. The temple in Jerusalem which was authorized to be rebuilt during the time of Cyrus was completed during his reign. Darius' name appears on Egyptian temples built in Memphis, Edfu and Great Oasis. He ordered the high priest Sais to build the first known medical school, a great 'house of life' at the temple. Weights and measures were standardized, elements which are fundamental in the story of humanity's growth. Government administration and taxation were organized. And, like other Persian kings, he maintained a no-slave policy throughout the empire.

Yet, despite his efforts on establishing trade, security and administrative bureaucracy, Darius, while leading the 2nd and 3rd generation of Iranians, had to maintain the culture of war and conquest inherited from the past. In that tradition, Darius first took his armies east to India. The established *satrap* in northwest India became one of the most fruitful conquests, providing a yearly tax in gold, while all other *satraps* were paying in silver. After India, Darius armies traveled west and crossed the Bosporus into Europe and then marched north to the Danube River. Upon crossing the Danube, the Persian army continued to march north, conquering one tribe after another without much resistance. It is not clear how far north Darius marched, but somewhere along the way he gave up on the unknown and endless European lands inhabited by mostly nomadic tribes.

With this last conquest taking him to Eastern Europe, the extent of the Achaemenid expansion begun under Cyrus reached its zenith. For nearly three generations, the empire had been in a constant state of war. The spoils of wars financed a professional standing army unmatched at the time in history and essential for suppression of constant uprisings and rebellions against taxes and against the empire.

Despite Darius's economic and military accomplishments, the continued ancient despotic rule led to another series of wars, rebellions and struggles. The third generation of Iranians, who lived during the later years of Darius's reign also had violence determine their fate, participating as soldiers in another series of rebellions and foreign wars. Their grandfathers had fought as soldiers during Cyrus's campaign and their fathers were either part of the army which conquered Egypt or participated as rebels against taxes and the empire.

Rebellions began to take place in cities of Asia Minor in 499 BCE. In response, the central government placed tyrants in charge of those cities, with freedom to use any form of violence necessary to maintain order. One such tyrant, named Aristagoras, witnessed the great unhappiness and resentment generated by Persian rule and saw opportunity in rebellion. He went across to Greece to request aid for his insurgency. The Spartans refused aid, but the Athenians provided him with twenty ships for his military campaign.

With the help of the Athenians, rebels conquered and burned the great city of Sardis in 498 BCE, known as the western capital of the Persian Empire, and former capital of Lydia. After the sacking of Sardis, other Greek cities in Asia Minor joined in the rebellion. As he had done before, Darius sent his army to take control of the rebel cities, and by 495 BCE, four years after the start of the rebellions, all of Asia Minor was again under the Persian Empire's control. In response to the Athenian aid to the insurgency, Darius decided to send a relatively small force of 25,000 soldiers to attack and punish Athenians for their support of rebellions. This force was met and defeated by a Greek army of 10,000 to 15,000 at Marathon; Herodotus writes that approximately 4,000 Persian soldiers perished in the battle. The Persian defeat at Marathon ensured the continued independence of Athens from Persian rule and marked an epochal event in Greek history.

The news of defeat in battle reached Darius while he was in Egypt putting down another outbreak of rebellion against his rule. Plans for vengeful attack on Athens were interrupted by continued rebellion in Egypt and the sudden death of the sixty four year old 'Great King' who had been chosen to lead an empire at the age of twenty seven.

For Iranians, the remains of Darius's great palace built by him in Pasargad (Persepolis) are one of the most important symbols of their identity. Yet Iranians give scant attention to the constant insurgency and violent counter-insurgency that marred his rule. This violence was ultimately the method that determined the fate of the second and third generation of Iranians. In despotic systems, public projects, economic growth, education, and infrastructure are luxuries enjoyed only after the greater part of resources are devoted to maintaining forces that impose an 'armed peace'. In democratic cultures, however, internal resentment is voiced through reason in the form of dialogue, articles, speeches, books and, ultimately, through ballot boxes. National resources are not spent on suppressing dissent, but on creating wealth and maintaining justice.

Had Darius become chosen as a leader in a hypothetical, non-violent (and highly unlikely) democratic world in 500 BC, he would be considered one of humanity's great benefactors. But like all other rulers of those ancient times, his legacy is stained by violence. I believe my generation of Iranians struggling for democracy and human rights in Iran has an obligation to teach the Iranian children of tomorrow about the great economic, artistic, and infrastructure achievement of Darius's time. However, violence, empire building, and warfare should be thought of as symbols of a cultural past unfit for the modern democratic world.

Xerxes

After Darius, his son Xerxes took control of the empire. In order to prevent Athenian aid to further rebellions and insurgencies in Asia Minor, he spent four years planning the conquest of Greece through one of the greatest military expedition in history. He built an army of 200-300,000 soldiers in Asia Minor, together with 1,200 ships. The resources of an empire, instead of being spent on infrastructure, trade, economy, art and education, were spent on weapons, ships and supplies for another war.

Athenians, who did not see any potential for victory against the army, abandoned their city and fled west. The army reached Athens, already abandoned, and burnt their temples and their city. For Xerxes, this act of violence was justified by Athenian aid to rebels who had burned Sardis a few years before. A lesson from violence throughout history is the constant justification of violence as a response to earlier acts of violence in the form of revenge or punishment.

The Persian army occupying the burnt city of Athens sent its ships west to capture the Athenians fleeing from their homes. The Persian navy, in search of Athenian citizens, faced the Greek navy in the battle of Salamis and was defeated, during which the majority of the Persian ships, unable to maneuver in narrow and rough Aegean waters, sank, many as a result of colliding with each other.

After the defeat of his navy in September of 480 BCE, Xerxes took half of his army back to Mesopotamia, where he had heard the news of another major rebellion in Babylon. The remaining Persian army in Greece was to camp and spend the winter there, but many soldiers, disillusioned by the lack of reward, abandoned the army. The remaining soldiers now with low morale, faced a Greek army fighting for their survival and their land. During the battle against the Greeks, the Persian commander Mardonius was killed and the remaining army defeated.

Meanwhile, Xerxes crushed the Babylonian rebellion. But the King, who had promised treasures and wealth from Greece in his failed expedition, ordered the city of Babylon looted and the temples burnt. In less than four generations since Cyrus had commanded his army to respect the properties and temples of conquered people, the despotism of the empire had allowed the elimination of the religious tolerance and respect for people's property. The fifth generation of Iranians led by Xerxes, like every generation before witnessed its resources and energy spent on acts of violence through the failed expedition to Greece or counter-insurgency against rebellions.

During the lifetime of the sixth generation of Iranians, Xerxes was murdered and upon his death, many *satraps* rebelled once again. Xerxes son, Artaxerxes, first fought wars and rebellions in the northeast province of Bactria.[81] He was then confronted with a major rebellion in Egypt.[82] In an effort to aid the Egyptians against war with Persians, the Greeks entered the war and resumed fighting with the Persians leading to the Battle of Cyprus in 450 BCE.

In 405 BCE, in the lifetime of the seventh generation, another popular uprising took place in Egypt. Egyptian rebels, gaining independence for a short six years, formed alliances with other rebels in Cyprus and cities in Greek Hellas.[83] Most famous of these conflicts was the attempt by Cyrus, the brother to King Artaxerxes II, who amassed an army of 100,000, including 10,000 Greek mercenaries to dethrone the king and take power. The army of Artaxerxes II numbered at least twice as many and defeated Cyrus's rebel army in a battle near Babylon in 401BCE. Soon, other rebellions took place in Asia Minor and Cyprus, followed by a rebellion by Cadusians in what is today Gilan on southwestern shore of the Caspian Sea.[84] This generation of boys and young men were again pulled from their farms and villages to settle the dispute over who should rule the empire through war and violence.

The army raised by Artaxerxes II to crush rebellions in the spring of 374BCE is thought by some estimates to have numbered 200,000 Asiatic troops and 20,000 troops from Greece, with the support of 200 ships.[85] I cannot just read through these numbers and fail to see the immense wealth and human life wasted on decisions which, in a democracy, would be settled through the deliberations of those elected by their fellow citizens. Hundreds of thousands of human beings were taken from their farms, homes and villages, and given swords, javelins and bows to crush rebellions, not unlike the hundreds of thousands of *basijis* and revolutionary guards recruited from towns and villages in Iran to crush the rebellions of today. Instead of building canals, schools, libraries, and monuments, the despot's subjects were forced to beat and kill other human beings. Money, which could have been used for agriculture and arts, was used to transport and feed an army for war in Egypt. The decline of empires, countries, and civilizations occurs when investments are made in building up forces to employ violence rather than undertaking prospects that will make life better for ordinary people.

With the death of Artaxerxes II in 358 BCE, which occurred during the lifetime of the 9th generation, nearly every satrap rose up in rebellion again. Quarrels between the sons over who should be the king took place, leading to murder within the family until Artaxerxes III took power.[86] Egyptians once again rebelled against the Persians, but this time the continued decline of the empire led to defeat of its army at the hands of Egyptian rebels. Consequently, rebellions took place in Syria, Asia Minor, and Cyprus.

Rebellion by the Phoenicians led to the burning of the royal palace in Lebanon.[87] The Persian King was again forced to use his resources to build a great army in order to march across the empire, killing insurgents and burning towns and villages aiding rebel soldiers. Another Egyptian uprising was crushed in 342 BCE, after which the Persian King, in attempting to teach the Egyptians a lesson in violence, not only killed Apis, the sacred Egyptian cow, but had it cooked and served at a banquet. He looted temples, burnt and destroyed cities, and killed thousands of Egyptians.[88]

If there is one recurring lesson from the study of Iranian history, it's that those who come to power through violence must maintain their power with violence and ultimately will perish through violence. Such was the case with Artaxerxes III. After spending his life fighting others in order for him and his family to stay in power, he was murdered in 338 BCE. Most of his sons, except for the youngest, were also killed along with their father. That youngest son, referred to as Artaxerxes IV, was also murdered less than two years after securing the throne. An empire created through the use of violence and maintained through the creation of unbelievable armies and near constant war and rebellions, was now so decayed that nearly everyone in the royal family capable of rule had perished. With no capable leader in the immediate royal family, a distant relation of the family named Darius, who had gained a reputation for putting down rebellions by Cadusian tribesman, and who had been given the governorship of Armenia, was chosen as the king and named Darius III.

Since the creation of the Persian Empire by Cyrus, nine generations had their lives and destiny determined through violence. The infrastructure and trade had been decaying for more than a century due to lack of planning; many of the *satraps* were intermittently autonomous and frequently in open rebellion against the central government. The citizens must have been unhappy.

For the people of my generation, actively witnessing or participating in democracies in Europe and America, it is almost second nature for us to realize that no matter how peaceful and respectful a leader is toward his people and their beliefs, there will always be dissent against leadership. Without democratic institutions, people are forced to rebel and use violence to oust a leader. That leader will have one of two options. The first is to abdicate. The second is to initiate bloodshed, mass killing, and the systemic use of terror in order to stay in power. Such dissent in cultures of violence leads to instability and uncertainty which are great enemies for the advancement of any civilization. During times of instability, fear spreads, the economy does not grow, schools are not built, philosophers are not born, and the arts wither. In such times, cultures decay and civilizations crumble.

Alexander

The decay of the Persian Empire from within left it vulnerable to any foreign leader who could amass an army and plunder its substantial riches. Such a foreign threat could have come from the unification of Turkic tribes in the northeast, the Mongolian tribes farther east, the Arabian tribes in the southwest, the Egyptians, or the Greeks.

At this point in Iranian history, it was the Greeks who were united under a powerful Macedonian king named Philip II. During Philip II's war against Athens and Thebes, his young son Alexander led the cavalry on the left wing of his father's army, which successfully annihilated his enemies. After the murder of his father in 336 BCE, Alexander, at the age of twenty, became the king of Macedonia and Greece and faced many challengers to his rule.

In order to solidify his position, Alexander marched his army north into the Balkans. While there, rumors spread in Greece that Alexander had died. This led the citizens of Athens and Thebes to revolt against Alexander and besiege the Macedonian Garrison in Greece. Alexander attacked the Greek city of Thebes, killing 6,000 and taking 30,000 prisoners. With the exception of its temples, the city was destroyed, the population enslaved, and Thebes wiped off the ancient map of Greece.[89] This severe punishment sent shockwaves through the remaining Greek cities, subduing the Athenians and sending the message that this young monarch had the will and the resources for violence as his disposal.

Having subdued the hostile Greek city-states, Alexander took the greatest gamble in history, enticing his soldiers with the treasures of Sardis, Babylon, Susa and Persepolis. The army was experienced in battle from the Balkan and Greek military victories. Its morale was also high, as was its belief in the genius of its now twenty-one year old leader.

In an otherwise splendid spring of 334 BCE, the 10th generation of what Iranians consider their cultural ancestors received the news, spreading from city to city, that the young Macedonian king had crossed the Hellespont with an army of 30,000 infantry and 5,000 cavalry, using 160 triremes. The Macedonian infantry employed a virtually unstoppable formation of troops organized as a phalanx, which is thought to have been created in the early

Greco-Persian wars to overcome the superior effectiveness of Persian archers, and which had been perfected by Phillip II and Alexander.

This unit, acting in disciplined concert and with almost invincible inertial movement forward, would either force the enemy infantry to retreat or compel enemy soldiers to fall to the ground where they were massacred. This formation was vulnerable to attacks on its flanks or its rear but Phillip and Alexander used their cavalry to interdict such assaults.

Upon crossing into Asia, Alexander's army faced the Persian Empire's army on the opposite eastern shore of the Granicus River. Persians placed their 20,000 cavalry in the front, with their Greek mercenary infantry of 20,000 fighting for Persians in the back and to the sides. Alexander crossed the river, his cavalry engaging and overcoming the Persians, while his phalanxes attacked through the center of the enemy force. Once it broke through the central enemy rank, Alexander's heavy infantry forced the Persians cavalry to flee, leaving the hired Greek mercenaries unsupported. Abandoned by those who had hired them, over 18,000 were slaughtered by the Greeks and Macedonians. Thus was the fate of the first of three battles deciding not just the course of Iranian history and civilization, but the course of world history and western civilization.

With this defeat, the fabulously wealthy Sardis, the western capital of what was then the Persian Empire, surrendered. Alexander then marched along the Mediterranean coast, taking possession of the cities along his path and adding thousands of soldiers to his ranks. Faced by this grave threat, Darius III personally led the main Persian army and made camp for battle approximately two days march east of the Syrian Gates, in southwestern corner of what is present day Turkey.

Mistakenly thinking Alexander was reluctant to join in battle against his large force, Darius deployed his forces to the north of Alexander's position and then turned south to meet Alexander's army on the battlefield along a two mile stretch of land between hills on the east and the Mediterranean sea on the west for a battle that would also alter world history.

The size of the Persian army is thought to have numbered 100,000, twice as large as Alexander's army. But, once again demonstrating his military genius, Alexander out-maneuvered the enemy forces. The resulting slaughter was horrific. As the Persian army and its 10,000 Greek mercenaries were overwhelmed, Darius, fearing injury or possible death, threw aside his shield, abandoned his chariot, mounted a horse and, in full view of his entire army, fled the battle scene. Tens of thousands of Persian soldiers witnessed their abandonment by their fleeing king, an act that would repeat itself several other times in Iranian history. After their ruler escaped, Persian soldiers began to flee in order to save their own lives and were then hunted down by the Macedonians and slaughtered on the hilltops and in the fields around the battlefield. The Battle of Issus marked the crumbling of the Persian Empire. Alexander, after the battle, proclaimed himself the king of Asia.

Unopposed, Alexander marched his army south, capturing Tyre and Gaza, and then marched into Egypt where he laid the foundations for the building of the city of Alexandria. He then marched back to Assyria, crossing the Euphrates over a bridge built with boats. About 70 miles north of Arbela, in Gaugamela, Alexander saw a Persian army awaiting battle. This third violent conflict would become known as the Battle of Gaugamela.

The size of the Persian army is uncertain, with estimates ranging from 50,000 to 100,000, mostly cavalry and infantry recruited from the eastern provinces of Iran. The cavalry was again placed on the flanks, with Darius's royal chariot in the center among the infantry. Darius, at this time, had chosen a plain as the site of battle in order to better maneuver his large army. Alexander, after receiving intelligence about his adversary, rested his army for four days while the two armies were camped seven miles apart.

When the two armies joined battle, Alexander once again outmaneuvered Darius and inflicted a crushing defeat to his enemy.

Arrian, describing the climactic moment of the battle writes: "all things together appeared full of terror to Darius, who had already long been in a state of fear, so that he was the first to turn and flee."[90]

Again, tens of thousands of soldiers recruited from across Iranian plateau, and even some from India, seeing their king flee for his own safety, also chose to flee in order to save their own lives, and perhaps find their way back to their homes, children and lovers. A great massacre took place as young boys were desperately running away from the battlefield, while getting chased down and killed by the Macedonian cavalry. Alexander himself took a cavalry unit and chased Darius as far as Arbela, now Irbil in Iraq's Kurdistan. With this defeat, the great empire, once thought invincible, crumbled to the ground. Its treasuries, palaces, cities and people were now the property of another king, one who had outperformed the empire in his use of violence

Alexander then marched to the great and ancient city of Babylon. There, he paid respect to Babylonian religion in the same manner as Cyrus had. As a youth, Alexander had studied Xenophon's classic Cyropaedia, "The

CHAPTER 2

Education of Cyrus"[91] and highly respected Cyrus for the concept of benevolent despotism which Alexander himself had adopted.

From Babylon, Alexander marched for twenty days to Susa, the winter capital of Iran, and captured enormous treasures unheard of in the ancient world. Forty thousand talents of gold and silver and nine thousand gold Darics were captured in the palace, making each of Alexander's soldiers one of the richest men in the world.[92] But this was only part of the Persian Empire's riches. The bulk of the treasure was in the main palace in Persepolis built two hundred years before, by the Great King, Darius I.

Knowing of the treasure in the capital, Alexander rushed to get to it before the possible looting by the population. On his way, his army was ambushed by the remaining Persian soldiers led by Ario Barzan, inflicting heavy casualty on Alexander's troops. Alexander managed to outflank Ario Barzan's troops which led to the massacre of the last remaining Persian soldiers. After this last victory, Alexander made a rapid nighttime march toward the capital in order to secure the largest treasure ever collected in one place.

In the palace and the adjacent treasury, Alexander and his soldiers found 120,000 talents of gold and silver,[93] an incredible amount by any standard equivalent to some 3,960 tons in weight. Combining the treasures of Susa and Persepolis, Alexander had amassed 180,000 talents of gold and silver, marking one of the greatest sudden transfers of wealth from one people to another in human history.[94]

Part of the treasure was moved to Ecbatana on the back of 20,000 mules and horses and 5,000 camels.[95] The troops were given the freedom to ransack and pillage the capital city and the palaces, taking whatever possessions they chose.[96] Alexander spent four months in the capital, living in the grand palaces of the former empire. Finally, in a drunken act of vengeance, the conqueror set fire to the main palace structures built by Darius, known to Iranians today as the 'Seat of Jamshid' and to Europeans as the remains of Persepolis. This destruction was revenge for the burning of Athens by Xerxes. The ruins of this complex of palaces are considered by Iranians as symbols of their history and past and one of the most important symbols of Iranian identity.

Alexander next marched to Khurasan, and then as far east as Tajikistan, founding several cities along the way, all named Alexandria, including one which was later renamed Kandahar. In the province of Bactria, he married the Persian noble Roxana. There, he dispensed with his Macedonian clothing and adopted the Persian royal robes and styles in emulation of the former kings. He then went south, across into the northwest provinces of India, where he defeated an Indian army of 30,000 cavalry, 38,000 infantry and 30 elephants.

Alexander continued marching east in northern India until his army refused to march any longer, forcing him to go back. On his return, he learned that many of his newly acquired satraps or provinces were in rebellion. Some of his soldiers were also rebelling for a number of reasons, amongst which was Alexander's decision to adopt Persian costumes, clothing, and culture. He executed the ringleaders of the mutiny, and then, in a mass ceremony, wedded ninety-one senior officers to Persian noblewomen in an Iranian wedding ceremony lasting five days.[97] This was an effort by Alexander to force the Persian style, customs, and culture upon his army. Upon reaching Babylon, one month short of his 33rd birthday, Alexander suddenly died of an unknown sickness following a drinking party. Thus, the historical symbol which the Europeans refer to as Alexander the Great, who in twelve years rewrote the history of humanity, suddenly died without a designated successor. His empire would not outlive him for long.

Seleucids

The sudden collapse of the Persian political system and the destruction of its symbols of government must have been a major traumatic event. The empire, which for more than two hundred years had given structure to the lives of its people, was suddenly no more. New non-Persian leaders were now in charge. But, just as destabilizing was the sudden death of Alexander with no designated heirs left to rule. The chaos of the disintegrating empire was further intensified by the inevitable conflict among Alexander's generals for power. Once again, another generation was to have its fate determined through violence.

Through a series of battles against other generals, Seleucus eventually captured and took power in Babylon while throughout the fragmented empire, every member of Alexander's family and possible heir was killed.[98] Over the next few decades, there was near constant violence and war as Seleucus marched eastward, conquering one city and satrap after another until reaching the Jaxartes River.[99] Bloody conflict between the former generals of Alexander continued throughout the lives of the 11th generation of Iranians until Seleucus was assassinated in 281 BCE— forty-two years after the death of Alexander.

CHAPTER 2

The new generation of Iranians living after Seleucus's assassination was the 12th after Cyrus and was once again heir to the legacy of violence. Wars over dominance continued for another generation. The Seleucid family now in charge of the Iranian plateau built their capital of Seleucia outside the ancient and decaying city of Babylon. In 250 BCE, during the lifetime of the 13th generation, in the far northeast corner of Iran, the Parthians, who, like the Persians, were an Iranian ethnic group began to gather strength. Over the next several generations, they would recapture all of the Iranian plateau and mark a new era in Iranian history.

***

Ashkanians (Parthians)

Although much of the 500 years of Parthian history has been lost in the mists of time, enough of it survives to create a panorama of virtually continuous warfare. The founder of the Parthian dynasty, Arsaces, known to Persians as Ashkan, rose to power by revolting against the Seleucid king. He reigned only for two years before he died. Nevertheless, he was the first in a succession of kings who would remain in power for more than 20 generations, longer than any other succession of rulers in Iranian history.

Initially, war was waged primarily by Parthians against the Seleucid kings for control of the Iranian plateau. This war and rebellion first consumed the lives of the 13th generation of Iranians. War between these two sides then continued during the lifetime of the 14th generation. The Parthian children of the 14th generation took control of the lands in the northeast while there was chaos, war and rebellion in Seleucia, Babylon, Asia Minor and Egypt. The 15th generation, led by Arsaces III, marched as far west as Ekbatana, where Anahita's great temple and Cyrus's grandfather's palace were said to have been still standing, yet stripped of all gold, silver and valuables. As war continued, their army was once again defeated by the Seleucid king marching all the way to northeast and capturing the Parthian capital. This was followed by Iranians of this generation engaging in guerilla warfare against the Seleucid king. Warfare, rebellion and insurrection continued during the lifetime of the 16th generation, this time led by Mithridates I against Antiochus IV. Finally, through a series of military victories, Iranians managed for the first time to conquer the lands extending from the Oxus River in northeast, to the Euphrates in the west, and from the Caspian Sea in the north to Persian Gulf in the south. This was more than 150 years, or six generations, after the conquest of Iran by Alexander and the ensuing state of nearly continuous conflict.

War continued and plagued another generation of human beings living in Iranian plateau, this time the 18th generation against the remaining descendants of the Seleucid dynasty. Iranians marched west and captured Judea with its prosperous capital of Jerusalem but were defeated in subsequent battle, with the cities of Babylon and Media being plundered and changing hands.[100] In the ensuing violence, Parthians dealt a devastating blow to the last Seleucid king.[101] They then continued west and severely punished the people of Seleucia. The remnant of the Seleucid army was taken as slaves.[102] With the death of this last Seleucid king in 129 BCE, the two hundred year history of conflict between the Iranians led by the Parthians, and the successor generations of Macedonian generals came to an end. The Parthian king created a new city, Ctesiphon, outside the city of Seleucia on the eastern banks of the Tigris River. This city was to play a central role in the next thousand years of Iranian history.

Ordinarily, with the defeat of the last remaining Seleucid claimant for power, the Parthian king and the Iranian people should have experienced a period of relative calm and peace, a period of peace due to the lack of a formidable enemy. Yet Phraates II, leading this generation of Iranians, learned of nomadic tribes ransacking and looting the northeast cities and towns around the Jaxartes (Syr Darya) and Oxus (Amu Darya) Rivers. He was forced to dispatch his forces to the east, again conscripting young boys and fathers from their farms and villages for another series of wars.[103]

The Parthian Army was decisively defeated by the nomadic tribes. Phraates' army was dispersed and the King was killed. Mithridates II, who then took power, was a much more capable general than his predecessor. He raised an army and decimated the nomadic tribes in Bactria and Central Asia, slaughtering and massacring the nomadic soldiers and even their families.[104]

But even after Mithridates' victories, he faced a rebellion in Babylon, led by his own appointed governor, which he crushed.[105] War and violence continued as he directed his army north and conquered Armenia in 100 BCE followed by continued war with the capable Armenian king, Tigranes.[106] The succession of wars dominated the lives of this 20th generation of Iranians.

Meanwhile, the rising power of Rome had found an ingenious general in Pompey, who had successfully countered all threats to Rome in Africa and Spain. The ruling class in Roman culture, one also built on violence, sent the Roman Republic's armies east into Asia. In 66 BCE, Pompey marched into

CHAPTER 2

Armenia and defeated Tigranes. The Parthians and the Romans, now in direct contact, engaged in warfare almost immediately. The Persian-Roman wars, lasting centuries, were to become one of the longest series of wars in human history. The 21st generation of Iranians witnessed the Roman army with seven legions and support of 4,000 cavalry, totaling 42,000 soldiers advancing east where they were severely crushed by the Parthian cavalry in north of what is today Syria. Of the 40,000 Roman soldiers, more than half were killed. Ten thousand of them were able to cross the Euphrates River and escape. Another 10,000 were taken as prisoners and sent to the city of Merv in today's Afghanistan, where they eventually settled and intermarried with the local population[107].

Yet, only ten years since the last major battle, the army of Orodes, the Parthian king, again resumed war with Rome and marched across Syria and went as far as Judea, overwhelming the Roman garrisons. Within two years however, during a Roman counterattack, his forces were repulsed. The Parthian king's son was killed on this expedition and the depressed king yielded his throne to his other son. Phraates IV, upon taking the throne murdered all political rivals, including his father and his brothers, demonstrating how violence ruled this 22nd generation's fate.

About the same time, Marc Anthony, ruling over Rome's eastern provinces and bent on exploiting the internal strife in the Parthian leadership, gathered 16 to 18 Roman legions totaling about 60,000 soldiers for a grand invasion. In addition, 10,000 Gallic and Iberian cavalry, and 30,000 auxiliary horse and infantry were recruited.[108]

Marc Anthony's army of more than 100,000 left Egypt in the hot summer of 36 BCE, and soon reached the western banks of the Euphrates. Unable to cross the river with such a vast army, Marc Anthony marched north into Armenia but was surprised by an agile Parthian cavalry, which carried out a strategy of sharp attacks and tactical withdrawals. After losing his siege units and unable to breech city gates, he went as far as today's city of Tabriz, but retreated as he was sharply attacked in a hit and run battle which raged for nineteen days, resulting in horrendous casualties for his forces. During the following winter, even more Roman troops died. Marc Anthony eventually managed to escape from this debacle and fled back to Egypt and into the arms of his lover, Cleopatra.

The 23rd generation of Iranians was on the cusp of another series of wars against Rome when suddenly their king, Phraates IV, was murdered by his son. This led to civil war between different factions of Parthian family which continued for decades and consumed the talents and resources of the 24th generation. Eventually, Artabanus of the Parthian family gained control. The civil war in Iran continued during the life of the 25th generation as members of Parthian nobility presented another family member as their king. Artabanus was forced to flee west where he was to raise another army for another series of wars.

The continued civil war and chaos continued across the lands, including a seven-year insurrection in Seleucia. When the new Parthian king managed to gain control, he marched into Armenia where he found valleys of death, disease and famine.[109] The Roman army followed the Parthian army and marched into Armenia, ravaging the countryside, but once again the Parthians defeated them on the battlefield.

The Parthians' defeat of the Romans in Armenia resulted, after 63 CE, in 40 years of peace between Iranians and Romans, the longest period of peace between the two contending powers, with Armenia remaining under Parthian domination. Yet peace with Rome did not put an end to violence for Iranians. In 75 CE, nine years after the peace treaty with Rome, a nomadic people called the Alani tribe from the north poured into the country, ravaging the land. They marched across Iran and then headed up the mountains of Zagros into Media, and finally into Armenia. Then the nomads crossed back east, taking large amount of booty and headed back to their original lands in the north.

In 77 CE, with the death of the Parthian king, the 26th Iranian generation found itself once again in a state of turmoil and instability, with up to four kings at one time claiming to be the 'King of Kings'.[110] The 27th generation lived through renewed conflict with Rome, which was now at the height of its power. The supremely confident and gifted Roman Emperor, Trajan, having led a brilliantly successful campaign of conquest in Romania, led his war-tested army across the northern Euphrates in the spring of 113 CE and continued east into Armenia, where the Armenian king was dethroned and killed. Trajan then marched south into Mesopotamia and reached Babylon, encountering little resistance from a devastated and exhausted Parthian army of an Iranian population that had been eviscerated by war, violence, and political turmoil.

Encountering no resistance in Babylon, Trajan's army marched to the nearby city of Seleucia and then into Ctesiphon and captured the capital of the Parthian empire. The Romans continued their march southeast into Susa, and for the first time, Roman soldiers stood on the shores of the Persian

Gulf.[111] But only a year after his triumph, the Roman Emperor died suddenly and the Parthian king reappeared in Ctesiphon and successfully took back his capital.[112]

Trajan's successor, Hadrian, realizing that an over-extended Rome could not maintain control over Mesopotamia, decided to retreat and signed a peace treaty with the Parthian king in 122 CE.[113] The treaty gave the 28th generation of Iranians a brief period of peace—until the nomadic tribes once again invaded, only to be repelled and forced back to their northern territories. Aside from war with nomadic tribes, the lives of this generation were expended in civil war between two members of a Parthian family in the east and the west, each one claiming to be king.

The 29th generation of Iranians again engaged in battle with the Romans yet again, initially devastating the enemy force and marching across the Euphrates and into Syria.[114] Within two years, however, the Roman army invaded Syria and decisively defeated the Parthian army. The Romans continued their march into Armenia, destroying the Armenian city of Artaxata (Artashat), then invaded Babylon and captured and plundered the city of Seleucia. This was followed by another capture of Ctesiphon. The royal palace in Ctesiphon was burnt to the ground. Roman forces then thrust into Media and took the city of Ekbatana, the ancient capital of the Mede kingdom.[115] There, they found themselves in a once fruitful land that had endured so many generations of strife that its people had been reduced to a state bordering on starvation. As is often the case in human history, after prolonged series of wars and violence, during which not just human beings, but animals, plants and the environment are victims of destruction, epidemics of disease and sickness spread across the countryside. Once again, history shows that the violent pursuit of conquest and power takes a dreadful toll on the viability of humanity and the natural world that sustains it. In such settings, as both mythology and history warn us, the force of nature, in turn, has its revenge on mankind.

The 29th generation of Iranians was a victim of this wrath of nature. They witnessed their families and neighbors, as well as the Roman soldiers who had successfully conquered the eastern lands, struck down by a virulent plague, which the Romans brought back to Italy. This plague spread from the ruins of Iranian cities to Italy and decimated the Gaelic and Germanic people of northern Europe and brought death to nearly every flourishing town in Italy. As many as 2,000 people per day were in Rome alone. It is estimated that what became known as the Antonine Plague (thought to be a pandemic of smallpox) incubated in the ruins of Iranian cities, killed a total of five million people worldwide. Those in the 30th generation of Iranians were the children of those who managed to survive this implacable wrath of nature.

After an internal struggle for the Parthian throne, Rome once again seized the opportunity to invade Iran, forcing the 31st generation of Iranians to witness horrors similar to those experienced by their grandparents. Romans marched into Ctesiphon, plundering the city and taking thousands of Iranians as slaves. But again, as in previous conflicts, the Romans were confronted with an insurgency that threatened their lines of supply and, after a massacre of outlying detachments of their garrisons, were compelled to retreat.[116] Soon, civil war broke out in what was left of Iran. This was followed by another invasion only four years later by the Roman emperor. With the death of the Iranian king in 208 CE, civil war broke out yet again between his sons. The 32nd generation of Iranians was caught up in unremitting civil war and violence engulfing the country. Yet another army was raised for another war with Rome.[117] This war in 217 CE was the last war fought between Rome and an Iran ruled by the Parthian family of dynasts. By now, the savage conflict with Rome and near constant war and violence had lasted for more than ten generations.

In 220 CE, only three years after the last Parthian war with Rome, Ardeshir of Sassanid family, the governor/king of central provinces that formerly included the Achaemenid capital of Pasargad (Persepolis), revolted against the last Parthian king and demanded an end to chaos and instability and a return to Iranian traditions and religion. Ardeshir, the son of a Zoroastrian priest, used religion as a tool for war and a symbol to unite the people. After a series of bloody confrontations, which included three major battles, the last Parthian king was defeated and killed on the plains of Hormuz, a few miles east of today's Ahvaz. Thus ended more than five hundred years of rule by a single family in Iran, the longest of any other dynasty in Iranian history. Ardeshir of the Sassanid family was now the powerful general and monarch extending his control over Iranian plateau and beginning an era in Iranian history in which religion would be employed to justify rule and conquest. [118]

***

CHAPTER 2

Sassanid

Generations of unrelenting foreign wars and near constant civil war between various family members had created a country decaying morally, spiritually, and materially. Little had been done to support economic development or build infrastructure under a succession of rulers fighting for power.

The Achaemenid kings had lived twenty generations prior to the rise of Sassanid family during an era past, which must have seemed to Iranians of the thirty-first generation more like legend and mythology than history. While people searched for a moral and political solution for a more stable system of government, they believed the Parthians had deviated from their Iranian culture and had become enamored of the Hellenistic culture of the West. The Sassanid's rallying cry was the imperative to restore Iranian culture to its Iranian roots. In this movement, people believed that it was not just poor leadership that had resulted in generations of violence and decay, but also lack of moral and spiritual standards. People were convinced that upholding the tenets of Zoroastrianism and the incorporation of its religious laws and values into politics and government was the solution needed to overcome the moral decay of their period.

For this new movement, a religious and cultural return to Iranian roots under the slogan of "good thoughts, good words and good deeds" was the imperative which was perhaps the religious inspiration the country needed in the time of Parthian moral decay. Ardeshir was using the ancient Zoroastrianism religion of Iran as a unifying symbol for the new generation of Iranians.

Upon conquest of Ctesiphon by Ardeshir, members of his Sassanid family were dispatched throughout Iran to remove the Parthian family members still ruling over the provinces. Within two years, Ardeshir had crushed all resistance to his rule. Yet he had come to power on the promise of Iran's return to glory, wealth, and empire. In such a culture, Achaemenid conquests in Europe and Egypt were symbols of achievements and a culture whose symbols of greatness are those of conquest will ultimately embark on the same path to war. As soon as he achieved internal stability, Ardeshir waged war against Rome by crossing the Euphrates in 229 CE. This resulted in several bloody battles that led to the plundering of Media by the Roman army.

Finally, Ardeshir took over Armenia and peace with Rome was concluded in 232 CE.[119] Unfortunately this peace with Rome did not bring peace for the people. Armenians rose up against their new king in an armed struggle which was violently crushed. Armenia was relatively quiet for eight years, until the death of Ardeshir in 240 CE and the advent of the 33rd generation of Iranians. But, once again, Ardeshir's son and successor, Shapur, was faced with general revolt in Armenia and portions of Mesopotamia. The new king, after putting down all internal rebellions in his first year, declared war against Rome.

Shapur's army crossed the Euphrates and marched all the way to the Mediterranean Sea, plundering and destroying farms and villages on his way. Unlike the Achaemenid kings, who placed local governors in charge of taxation and administration, this Sassanid king, like his Parthian predecessor, mostly carried out large-scale raids and looting, and had no plans for permanent occupations or administration.[120]

The Romans caught up with Shapur and defeated the Iranian army west of the Euphrates. Shapur spent the next fourteen years suppressing internal rebellions as far east as Balkh, and raising an army for another war with Rome. In 258 CE, Shapur again marched his army across the Euphrates, looting towns and villages on his way to Antioch. However his army was again defeated by the Roman emperor Valerian. But in a subsequent battle, the Roman army was surrounded and overwhelmed. Emperor Valerian was taken prisoner by Shapur in one of the most significant episodes of Sassanid history. The young empire, built from ground up only one generation before, had not only defeated the Romans, but also captured their emperor, a significant moral victory that would boost the confidence and morale of the members of the Sassanid family, who would rule Iran for more than 400 years. The capture of Valerian sent shockwaves throughout Asia and Europe. The Roman emperor, in chains, was taken in a humiliating triumph across Iran from town to town as evidence of the victory over the Romans.

Valerian's son carried on Rome's war with Iran. The lands between the Euphrates and the Mediterranean Sea, including Syria, were repeatedly ravaged by armies marching east and west. Even after Iranian withdrawal, war and violence continued, with a local leader west of the Euphrates rising to power and sending his army east, capturing Mesopotamia in 263 CE before being assassinated.[121]

The last seven years of Shapur's rule were spent in peace. During this time, Shapur built the city of *Gondi-Shapur* in Khuzestan which became the intellectual center of ancient Iran, housing Iran's first university, as well as Iran's first teaching hospital and medical school. Its library would later become one of the centers of knowledge for medicine and the sciences. Shapur also built the city of Nishapur in Khurasan. Centuries later, the city became home to some of Iran's most extensive libraries. Some of the greatest Iranian thinkers, including Omar Khayyam and Attar Nishapuri, were products of this city. The city of Bishapur was also built on the road linking Istakhr to Susa. Today, the great reliefs carved into the rocks alongside the cliffs near this city, called Naqsh-e-Rostam, are some of the most important remaining symbols of the Sassanid era and of the Iranian past.

Another of Shapur's achievements was building the dam on the Karun River in Shushtar. Constructed by tens of thousands of Romans taken as slaves with Valerian, it was built to eliminate the recurring flooding of Khuzestan by this great river. It is of utmost important for the Iranians of my generation to realize that these great achievements of ancient Persians, which most Iranians take pride in, were not the result of violence or conquest; they were isolated events occurring in short spans of peace within generations of war. Shapur I died in 270 CE.

Under the Sassanid regime, the *magis* or priests across Iran were united in implementing governmental policies. During this time, this religious class grew in numbers, and developed its own hierarchy with the creation of the position called *Mobedan-e-Mobed*, similar to today's Supreme Leader or the Pope.[122] *Mobedan-e-Mobed* also functioned as the religious adviser to the King.[123] The country's laws were adopted and written by them, thus making legislation part of the religious establishment's function. In addition, they also served as judges and thus the judiciary branch was under their control.

The priests obtained a position of power in every part of society. Aside from dictating the laws, executions, and punishments, they officiated during births, wedding ceremonies, and burial services, as well as national celebrations. Prayers and rituals were ordained for virtually every part of life.[124] Young priests were sent to distant towns and villages to preach,[125] playing a role similar to that of today's young clergy finishing their schooling in Qom. Education was also entirely in the hands of members of this religious class, who considered science and philosophy as extensions of religion.[126] With the religious establishment's influence in every aspect of life, this class soon became one of the most powerful and richest classes in Iran, similar to the position the clergy have attained in Iran since the advent of the Islamic Republic.[127]

In Ardeshir's time, old scattered Zoroastrian books and material were gathered to create a standard text of Avesta. Scientific, mathematical, and astronomical texts from India and Greece were also collected during Shapur's time and added to religious texts. The committee in charge of this task created what is referred to as the Sassanid Avesta, a collection of 21 books containing accumulated knowledge, which included books on medicine, astronomy, philosophy, mythology and legend. It was a collection of knowledge more similar to an encyclopedia than a religious text.[128] Much of this text was later destroyed and is lost today.

The religious revolution during the Sassanid era was not unlike the change which took place in Iran with the arrival of Khomeini and the Islamic Republic. With the incorporation of religious institutions into government, a new culture of religious intolerance was born. It is a historical certainty that whenever a country declares an official state religion as Iran did, sooner or later this state religion will be used as a weapon to first delegitimize other religions and then to instigate persecution. Carved in stone and, known as *Kertir's Inscription*, the Sassanid religious class proudly documented and celebrated their role in persecuting Christians, Manichaeists, Brahmans, Shamans, Nestorians, and Buddhists. Other documents from his time recount the persecution of Jews and those converting to Christianity. Zoroastrianism, which had flourished independent of government as a religion of "good thoughts, good words and good deeds," was now incorporated as an official institution within the government and was now a tool for violence and persecution.

Mani

In the same year that Shapur came to power in 242 CE, Mani is said to have delivered his first speech.[129] Mani was a physician born in Babylon during the end of the Parthian era. It is said that he spent his youth amongst the Christians in Babylon and later traveled through much of the world, including India. In 242 CE, he presented a new view and philosophy of dualism founded on Gnosticism. He preached that salvation was possible through education, self-denial, vegetarianism, fasting and chastity. He believed there was an eternal conflict between the spirit and the material world, and considered everything spiritual as good and the material world as evil. His philosophy was born from the multi-cultural and multi-religious world of Babylon, and he used many concepts derived from various religions.

He had a set of followers who translated his work into many different languages.

His philosophy had immense influence on Iranians. His six religious books, translated into many languages, soon became influential in lands as far east as China. Several Turkic tribes and kingdoms of Central Asia were converts to Manichaeism. The religion also had tremendous followings and influence in Europe, influencing early Christian thinkers such as St. Augustine before it was pronounced a heresy by the Catholic Church. Its influence reached its height in the seventh century; followers of Manichaeism continued to exist until the sixteenth century.

Mani plays an important role in understanding the Sassanid view toward religious minorities. He was given relative freedom under Shapur I to preach his philosophy and religion throughout Iran. But, with the rise in power of religious class during the reign of Bahram I, tolerance for other religions also came to an end. It is said that his visit to Gondi-Shapur, which was the center of medicine at that time, caused an uproar amongst the religious priests. The new shah, under pressure, ordered that Mani be executed. After his death, his followers were viciously persecuted and forced into hiding, more evidence that religion can be a source of violence when incorporated into the government of a state.

Sassanid Wars Continued

Within the monarchial system of government the death of a king is often followed by an heir to the throne coming to power solely because of his familial relationship to the late king. This form of leadership selection often brings to power a random leader without the necessary talent to lead the nation. Such ill-equipped and weak leaders would in turn cause the decay of economic productivity and trade. The 34th generation of Iranians witnessed the death of their great King Shapur, who had defeated Emperor Valerian and who undertook an unprecedented nation building project through the construction of cities and canals.

For the next 40 years, an entire generation witnessed one short lived, weak and unsuccessful king replaced by another. Shapur was followed by Hormizd I, who ruled for one year. He was followed by Bahram I, who ruled for five years. His son, Bahram II, was in power for seven years. He spent most of those years ferociously suppressing rebellions in the east, until news arrived that the Roman army was heading to Ctesiphon.

The Iranian capital was sacked and plundered in 283 CE, with Armenia being taken by the Romans again. Bahram II's successor ruled for only four months before being deposed. A struggle then ensued within the royal family between the two younger sons of Shapur I, with Narseh finally taking power in 296 CE. He resumed attacking Rome and engaged in two inconclusive battles. In a third, waged in northern Syria, the Roman army was defeated, and the Emperor Galerius was forced to swim across the northern Euphrates for safety. The following winter, Galerius launched a surprise attack and annihilated Narseh's forces. Five provinces in the west were handed over to the Romans and the Tigris River was set as the boundary between the two nations. Narseh abdicated the throne in 301 CE. His son, and successor, spent his seven years on the throne suppressing revolts and rebellions in Sistan and Kushan before being killed. This continued political turmoil and uncertainty, followed by rebellions and war, blighted the lives of the 35th generation of Iranians. Thus another generation spent its resources and talents on violence.

The political turmoil led to economic and military decay, followed by insurgencies across the country. The nomadic Arabic tribes south of the Persian Gulf began attacking the southern cities, ravaging and plundering the countryside and cities located in places as distant as the Fars province. Meanwhile, the nobles in the capital, facing the chaos of failed leadership, killed the king's oldest son, blinded the second, and imprisoned the third. Without a leader and any heir to the throne, the fetus the queen was carrying was named the king, and the crown was placed on his mother.

Shapur II

Iran was ruled by the nobles until the child, Shapur II, was of proper age to lead. In a rare turn of good fortune for Iranians, the child became an adept leader who reigned as king for 70 years, longer than any other monarch in Iranian history. Nearly three generations lived under his rule. He was the contemporary of ten Roman emperors. In the first 28 years of his life, there were no major wars with Rome, but this generation of Iranians suffered under violence of nomadic Arabic tribes pillaging southern Iranian towns and cities. Rebellions also broke out in Mesopotamia. These rebellions were followed by a war with Rome that was waged for 13 years. The war ended after tens of thousands of deaths on both sides. Immediately after the war, the Persian army was rushed to northeastern Iran to put down rebellions by Turkic tribes. The Roman army was recalled to Europe to fight in their own civil war.

It was during the reign of Shapur II, when Romans adopted Christianity as their state religion. After the series of wars with Rome by the middle-aged Shapur, the Christians in Iran were looked upon as sympathizers and supporters of Iran's implacable enemy, the Romans. Christians living in Iran were now persecuted for their religious beliefs, forced to pay double tax, and not allowed to personally serve in the war. After a Christian bishop refused to collect the tax, claiming that his people were too poor, he was arrested and, together with 100 priests, executed in Susa.[130] This execution was followed by 40 years of the slaughter of Christians across the country and destruction of Christian churches. In intervals between his initial battles with Rome, Shapur spent his years fighting Hun invaders from the northeast, as well as the rebellion of Gilani tribes in the north.[131] This was followed by another major war with Rome.

In this war, Shapur II first crossed the Tigris with a large army and marched west, plundering several cities and causing thousands of deaths. This provoked a response by the Roman Emperor who raised a grand army of more than 100,000. The large Roman army was split into two. Some 30,000 were sent to Armenia with orders to join the larger contingent later near Ctesiphon. The emperor himself loaded his remaining forces onto 1,100 ships on the Euphrates for a voyage south to the Iranian capital. He faced no serious threats to his grand army, yet his army was unable to subdue the well-fortified cities in Mesopotamia.

It is easy to read about these numbers and descriptions of vast armies and forget the immense human, societal, and economic costs associated with such wars. Raising an army of 100,000 soldiers, whether Roman or Iranian, is a tremendous economic strain on an ancient population far smaller than today's. As was and is the case in all other wars, it is forgotten how such wars would force mothers and daughters to take on enormous additional responsibilities while the most productive men were sent to their deaths in faraway lands.

The large Roman army continued down the Euphrates until it reached the royal canal built to link the two great rivers, the Tigris and the Euphrates. In a battle that began at dawn, bloody fighting lasted for 12 hours, after which the Iranians fled back to their capital in Ctesiphon, with the Romans pursuing them to the city gates. Thousands of young soldiers were killed on both sides.

The more than 60,000 soldiers of the Roman army outside the gates of Ctesiphon were faced with a fortified city that the Romans found impregnable. Unable to penetrate the city's defenses, the Roman Emperor Julian decided to retreat. During the retreat, Julian was hit by a javelin in the breast and soon died. The Roman army, facing either death or enslavement, fought with all its might, exacting a heavy toll of Iranian casualties, and then attempted to hasten its retreat. During the next four days, the Romans repeatedly came under attack, suffering heavy losses, and were able to move only 18 miles. Some soldiers swam across the Tigris for safety.

The panicked Romans accepted the Iranian terms of peace, which included the return of five provinces in Mesopotamia lost by Shapur's grandfather, Narseh, 65 years before.[132] The great king, who had been accorded the crown while still a fetus, upon dying at the age of 70, left his empire in the most powerful position Iran had enjoyed since the Achaemenid era. He had continued on the path of Shapur I in the building of cities and infrastructure across the country during the short intervals of peace. Much of the grandeur of the Sassanid dynasty and much of Iranian civilization is the result of these infrastructure-building projects during these short intervals of peace.

Yazdegered I and Bahram Gur

The death of Shapur II occurred in the lifetime of the 38th generation of Iranians. This generation's parents and grandparents had also lived during his long reign. The death of the old king gave rise to a sense of anxiety and uncertainty throughout the country. His successor ruled for four years before he was deposed, and the king after that was in place for five years before he died. During these nine years, there was an expedition against an Arab rebellion in the southwest. This was followed by murder and instability in the Armenian court, which led the Iranian king to send a 10,000-man occupying force. The Armenian king, fearing his capture, attacked and annihilated the entire Iranian garrison. This act meant the resumption of war with Armenia and her Roman allies after only seven years of peace. The Romans, who had been severely weakened from a major defeat at the hands of the Goths, could not summon the strength for another war with Iran, and were forced to sue for peace, granting a great deal of Armenian territory to the Iranians.

The next Sassanid king who came to power ruled for 11 years before being murdered by his own soldiers in a mutiny. The 39th generation of

Iranians were burdened with this sense of anxiety and uncertainty; their kings were being assassinated and replaced in a game of political maneuvering and violence in the upper aristocratic class. These events led to the rise in power of Yazdegerd I in 399 CE.

During Yazdegerd's 21 years of rule, the 'eternal city' of Rome was sacked by nomadic invaders in 410 CE leading to a time of relative peace between Iranians and Romans. All eastern Roman territories formerly under Achaemenid rule were open for conquest, yet Yazdegerd, perhaps a rarity, did not have the stomach for more war and chose peace.

He allowed the Christians, who had been severely persecuted during the long reign of Shapur II, to practice their religion freely. Yazdegerd was said to have been cured of a malady by a Christian bishop who gained considerable influence over him. During his reign, the Christians were allowed to rebuild their churches destroyed generations before. Yazdegerd, at this time, was said to have even contemplated being baptized, and went as far as persecuting Zoroastrian Magis.

Yet, in a state built on institutions of religion, such relative religious freedom to minorities will ultimately become a threat to the system. Under pressure, Yazdegerd abandoned his interest in and tolerance of Christianity and authorized the destruction of the Christian sect, which resulted in five years of cruel and terrible persecution and death of Christians in Iran. Even after his death, which occurred under unknown circumstances, his successor, Bahram Gur, continued the persecution of the Christians. So fierce was the persecution that a large number of refugees crossed the western borders into Roman territories.[133] Bahram Gur demanded the Romans return his Christian subjects, and when the Romans refused, he declared war. Thus, the 40th generation of Iranians, whose grandparents had fought the last major war against the Romans, were again to become victims of another war waged by their leaders.

Only three years after this war, panic spread from city to city across Iran as the frightened citizens began telling stories of 'White Huns' crossing the Oxus River in central Asia, and ravaging the countryside and cities in the northeast. Bahram Gur was again forced to raise an army for war and subsequently defeated the Huns which brought about a period of peace for Iranians lasting 15 years. As was the case for previous generations during such brief moments of peace, architectural, cultural and infrastructure developments helped create some of the enduring foundations of Iranian civilization.

Interestingly, Bahram Gur took a trip to India where he commissioned 4,000-5,000 musicians and dancers to come to Iran. These traveling artists were the gypsies of the Iranian past, and roamed the streets of the country's towns and cities providing music and entertainment for the citizens. It is very likely that the subsequent immense growth of Iranian music during the latter Sassanid era may have been due to the introduction of such a musical culture into the Iranian society.

Bahram Gur died in 440 CE after a 20-year reign, 15 years of which was in peace. His son, Yazdegerd II, came to power and immediately declared war on Rome.

Yazdegerd II

The pattern repeats itself over and over again. After gaining the throne through violence, keeping it entails the use of violence in internal repression and making war to legitimize the king's rule. Yazdegerd II, like every other king of Iran, had to start a war because of the culture he lived in. However, to label such individuals as inherently violent, or the people of Iran as violent and responsible for repeated wars is a misunderstanding of the political culture of violence in which they lived and which guided them.

The Romans, who had been devastated by repeated plunder and sacking of their cities by nomadic tribes, did not have the strength for another war, and chose to pay Iran an annual sum of money. Yazdegerd II then engaged in eight years of struggle in the east with the nomadic tribes of central Asia. With stability and security achieved on the eastern front, Yazdegerd II plunged into a series of wars in Armenia, which ultimately led to the defeat of the Armenians and the persecution and murder of their leaders. The Armenian religious patriarch Joseph was murdered. The persecution was then extended to the city of Karka in Mesopotamia, where the leader of the Christian sect, John the Metropolitan, was killed, along with thousands of other Christians. The city of Karka, now called Kirkuk, was, until recently, the site of an annual gathering of Christians in an ancient church on the city's hilltop to commemorate that massacre.

For a thousand years of Zoroastrian history during the Achaemenid and Parthian era when religious institutions were separate from the government (a form that today we call 'secular' states) there are no known instances of persecution, violence, or massacre in the name of Zoroastrianism. Yet, once religion was injected into the government in the Sassanid era, one sees the rise of violence and persecution in the name of religion. Iranians struggling for human rights and democracy must help others understand that a state's 'official' religion, which empowers rule by a theocracy, is unable to serve the spiritual goal of religion. Only through the separation of church and state, and the elimination of violence from religious teachings and practices, can religion fulfill its true spiritual function. This is the greatest challenge for Islam today across the Middle East.

Yazdegerd II who ruled during the lifetime of the 41st generation, died after 17 years of rule. After a two year bloody struggle between his sons, he was ultimately succeeded by his elder son, Pirooz. Like rulers in every generation before, he was immediately faced with the threat of war, this time from the White Huns on the eastern borders. The series of wars with the Huns marred his 27-year rule from 457 CE to 484 CE. These wars continued until a crushing defeat of the Iranian troops. This defeat created the opportunity for a major rebellion in Armenia, where the citizens were severely persecuted for their religious beliefs and forced to accept Zoroastrianism. Thus, this generation of Iranians, their sons, brothers, and fathers fought in wars and rebellions simultaneously on the eastern and western borders. Pirooz, who desperately needed a major victory, was defeated and killed by the Huns. By the end of his reign, 42 generations of Iranians had their lives plagued and fates determined by war and violence.

Pirooz was succeeded by his brother Balash, who was forced to pay a tribute to the king of the White Huns for peace. In order to find stability on the western border, the new king signed a declaration granting rights of worship for Christians in Armenia and an edict of toleration.[134] Meanwhile, the former King Pirooz's son, Kobad, had taken refuge amongst the White Huns, and when the Iranian king stopped making tribute after two years, Kobad was given an army by the Huns and marched into Iran to fight against his uncle. His uncle, who had lost support of Zoroastrian priests because of his tolerance for Christians was blinded and killed before the arrival of his nephew.

Kobad

Though Kobad's accession to power did not trigger a civil war, it did not mean that Iranians could live in peace. The new king had to immediately begin a campaign to annihilate the Khazars from the north, nomads who had invaded the Kur Valley in today's Azerbaijan and Georgia, plundering the countryside in their campaign. The Khazars were easily defeated by Kobad's large army, in a struggle that left countless dead and yielded large amounts of treasure captured by the Iranian king.

Meanwhile, throughout Iran, the ever-growing gap between the rich and the poor, and the stratification of society into various classes were creating the need for a new social revolution to overthrow the aristocracy and religious classes that exploited the labor of the poor. At this critical moment, the philosopher Mazdak asserted that people should not live in a class-ridden society, that "all are born equal and have the right to maintain their equality through life".[135] In his worldview, capital did not belong to an elite few but would be held in common by the society at large. He also believed women were not the property of men and should live in common amongst men in communes. He was preaching an early form of communism in the highly stratified society of the late 5th century CE Iran. His message was so powerful that tens of thousands of citizens across the country began to heed him. So convincing was he that even the King of Iran, Kobad, is known to have become a disciple. Soon, communes were built across the country with thousands of women, including many from the aristocratic families, flooding to countryside to live as equals amongst others.

Mazdak's revolution, spreading across Iran with an unbelievable energy and threatening both the religious and aristocratic rule, had to be eliminated by the ruling elite who had gained legitimacy and power through violence. But first they had to depose the king, who had become a disciple. Thus, in 498 CE, 12 years after Kobad came to power, the clergy, the nobles, and the army mounted a coup. After Kobad was arrested and imprisoned, his brother Zamasp was placed on the throne, and the persecution of Mazdakites was initiated. Kobad's wife, however, was able to help her husband escape from prison and take refuge amongst the White Huns in the northeast. Just as he had done 15 years before, he marched to Iran with an army and regained the throne. In the process of seeking the support of the nobility, he officially withdrew his support for Mazdak, but there is some evidence that he privately continued to court Mazdakite adherents.

At the same time, like every other king who needed to employ violence to maintain his autocratic rule, he was forced to resume making war. He could not attack the White Huns, who had twice provided him with an army to take the crown, and had sheltered him as a guest during his years of exile. Accordingly, Kobad resumed war with Rome after nearly 80 years of peace between the two sides, the longest period of peace between these two foes.

He overwhelmed Rome's forces in Armenia. Then Kobad received news that the White Huns were on a rampage in the northeast, and was forced to engage in another series of wars. The Romans quickly reoccupied their lost territory and a truce was reached which lasted seven years. This was followed by ten years of war and violence during which Kobad utterly crushed the White Huns, who would never again pose a serious threat to Iran.[136] This was followed by a massacre of the Mazdakites, who had continued to attract supporters across the country. This internal crushing of dissent was followed by a crushing of a rebellion in Georgia after the policy of toleration for the Christians was revoked by the local governor. This was followed by renewed warfare against the Romans, who had slowly built up their military strength in the Middle East during the 10 years of war between the Iranians and the Huns.

During his war with the Huns in the east and in order to delay further war with Rome, Kobad proposed that the Roman emperor adopt and raise his favorite son, Khosrow, who was later known as 'Anushirwan', or 'The Immortal Soul', and would become one of the famous kings in Iranian history. The Roman emperor declined and war followed.

The Roman army marched into Armenia in 526 CE and was defeated by the Iranians. Romans were again defeated in a subsequent battle in 528 CE. Another Roman force was put together which defeated Iranians in three successive battles. These battles were followed three years later by another Iranian attempt at invading Syria.[137] Afterwards, Kobad, the old king who had ruled for over 40 years, and whose reign was marred by continuous wars against the Romans, the White Huns, and the extirpation of Mazdak's communism, died of natural causes.

Khosrow - Anushirvan

Decades of Kobad's benevolent tolerance of the Mazdakite had led to the creation of thousands of communes across the country with hundreds of thousands of followers, which threatened the power of the aristocracy and religious regime. The next king had to use brute force to maintain the status quo. Within the nobility and the clergy, disagreements arose on who was most suitable to take the crown. Kobad, on a visit to Nishapur, had sexual relations with a peasant's daughter who gave birth to a son named Khosrow. Kobad, who adored this son, had suggested to the Roman emperor to adopt him as a sign of goodwill. After the king's death, many of the nobility and the clergy supported him as the new king. Upon taking power, in order to solidify his position, Khosrow murdered all his brothers and to ensure that he would face no significant further challenge to his rule, he also murdered all his brothers' male offspring.[138]

Khosrow 'Anushirvan' —meaning 'the immortal soul'— then began the extermination of Mazdak and his followers, on a scale not seen previously in Iranian history. Mazdak, who had survived the previous massacre, was killed, together with close to 100,000 of his followers.[139] So draconian were the measures taken that the Mazdakites never again threatened the Sassanid rule over Iran. In order to carry out internal crushing of dissent, Khosrow 'Anushirvan' made peace with Eastern Roman Empire in 533 CE. Amongst the provisions of the treaty, Byzantium and Iran were to be allies 'forever'.[140] This treaty, *Pax Perpetuum* was to create the 'eternal peace' between two empires in near constant war with each other for centuries.

For the 45th generation who witnessed the obliteration of the Mazdakite movement, the 'eternal peace' with Rome may have been some consolation, just as the end of the Iraq-Iran war was a great relief for people in my generation. And, in another historical parallel, the crushing of the Mazdakites was not unlike the violence the Islamic Republic inflicted on political dissidents in the 1980s, which ultimately led to the execution of thousands of political prisoners. In any country poisoned by political violence, when political leadership in power is maintained through savage repression and whose neighboring countries also live in the same culture of violence, such moments of peace are a surcease from ongoing wars—but only for a short time. The 'eternal peace' with Rome lasted seven years.

Khosrow 'Anushirvan', while witnessing the Eastern Roman military successes in Africa and Italy, decided to break the peace treaty in 540 CE and, in a surprise attack, ensure the safety of his western borders. Instead of spending his resources in efforts to capture forts and cities in Mesopotamia and Armenia, Khosrow ordered his army to cross the Euphrates and head straight for the heart of Roman power on the eastern banks of the Mediterranean Sea, the city of Antioch. When he reached Antioch, he destroyed every house and building whose owners refused to hand over their possessions voluntarily.[141] On his march back east through a northern route, he again plundered the cities in his path and extorted contributions from them.[142] War with Rome was then diverted instead to the Caucuses, as Anushirvan's army marched north to Lazica (in today's Georgia) on the shores of the Black Sea. Thus began the bloody Lazic Wars or the Great Wars of Egrisi between Iran and Byzantium, lasting twenty years.

The balance of power, which had shifted in favor of Iranians, was even more solidified after this war. Iran and Byzantium signed yet another peace treaty. Upon making peace, Anushirvan continued battles against the Huns in today's Afghanistan followed by attacks against the Khazars in the north. At the same time, news reached Iran that the Christian nation of Abyssinia (Ethiopia) had invaded Yemen, making it an Abyssinian province and building Christian churches. Anushirvan used this opportunity to strengthen his navy. His ships sailed from the Persian Gulf across to Arabia for a distance of 2,000 miles and successfully captured Yemen, placing it under Iranian rule for the first time.[143]

The Eastern Roman emperor, alarmed by Anushirvan's ever-growing military power resumed war after only nine years of relative peace.[144] By the time the third war with Byzantium broke out, Khosrow-Anushirvan was more than seventy years old and had been in power for more than forty years. But the old man, despite his age, led his army once again as they defeated the Romans. The Eastern Roman emperor was deposed after his defeats, and Byzantium was forced to pay 45,000 gold pieces to secure peace.

During his time, Ctesiphon, a city built during the Parthian era on the eastern bank of Tigris River, became one of the most populous cities of its time. It was the largest of a group of seven adjacent cities on the two sides of Tigris, extending to the Euphrates. These cities, among them the ancient cities of Babylon and Seleucia, became the center of commerce and trade, as well as the heart of the Iranian economy. They were connected by a series of farms and gardens, as well as bridges over the Tigris. Many of them had cobblestone streets and an endless number of palaces, home to a huge aristocratic class made up of the clergy and the royal retainers. Arabs later called this region 'Mada-in', which meant 'the cities'.[145] A large bazaar existed there, with a Jewish population very active in trade. Christians were extended freedoms because of a peace treaty with Byzantium. Many churches were built during this time, including the two famous churches of St. Mary's and St. Serge.[146]

Important tax reforms took place. Khosrow Anushirvan was deeply interested in agriculture, realizing the importance of farming as the basis of economic production. His long reign was distinguished by many projects for reclaiming wastelands into farmland including the building of dams and canals as well as *qanats* (artificial underground canals), considered great innovative achievement of ancient Persians. During his era, Iran had the most productive economy in its history since the Achaemenid time. Like Darius, the 'Great King', Khosrow relied on the importance of communication within the empire, restoring the postal and the highway systems. Bridges and roads were built across the country, and the existing roads were repaired and improved. In addition, safety and security were ensured, thus promoting trade and economic growth. For the first time in history, this monarch encouraged visitors and travelers from abroad, showing great hospitality to foreigners. Many philosophers and scientists escaping persecution by the Romans came to Iran during his time, including seven Neo-Platonic philosophers the Roman emperor had expelled from its territory. During his reign, the works of Aristotle and Plato were translated into the Pahlavi language and made available to Iranians. Anushirvan himself is said to have read the Persian translations of these great philosophers. He greatly expanded the teaching institutions in Gundishapur, which influenced the growth of philosophy, medicine, physics, poetry, rhetoric, and astronomy in Sassanid Iran, and provided the pillars of intellectual renaissance in science and philosophy several centuries later in the Islamic era.

'Khudhay-Namak' or 'The Book of the Kings', which included all the known legends, mythology and history of Iran was written in this period. During his time, books on philosophy and literature were brought in from India and translated into Persian. The game of chess was also imported from India. For the first time, Iranian entrepreneurs brought silkworms from Khotan and established the silk industry.

Architecture had an important revival during his reign with the most important architectural achievement being the grand palace of Kasra in Ctesiphon whose grand archway is still standing today. At 80feet in width and 110feet high, it is considered the largest brick archway ever made. Much of the structure survived until the 19th century, when the flooding of 1888 destroyed a third of the ruins. Even Saddam Hussein respected the grandeur of Anushirvan's palace in Ctesiphon, and, in cooperation with the University of Chicago attempted to rebuild the structure when the 1991 war halted this endeavor. The Ctesiphon palace was sited in the center of a grand garden 6,000 meters wide, bordered by a wall 6-1/2 meters (21 feet) tall, portions of which still stand today. A thousand years later, the arched mosques of Iran were inspired by the buildings and architecture of this era.[147]

The main audience hall of the palace, measuring 80 feet wide, 160 feet long, and 110 feet high was the largest single chamber built in the history of

Iran. Two rings were placed on the ceiling above his seat hanging the crown, which weighed 91 kilograms, and too heavy for any person to wear. The shah would sit underneath the crown, and for the visitors coming from afar it would appear that he was wearing the crown. The two rings from which this massive crown was suspended were still present in 1888, prior to collapse of the ceiling.[148]

The great 'Baharestan' rug in the throne room was considered the grandest and most expensive rug ever made. Measuring approximately 70 feet in length by 60 feet in width, "it represented a garden, the ground wrought in gold, and the walks in silver; meadows of emerald, and rivulets of pearls; trees, flowers and fruits of sparkling diamonds, rubies and other precious stones".[149] It depicted the image of a vast garden with ponds and streams and was meant as a place in which the shah could stand in the middle of winter and feel the presence of spring.

Iranian art during this era achieved its pinnacle and its second renaissance after the empire building era of Darius. Hundreds of mansions were built in Ctesiphon from the immense wealth acquired through victories in foreign wars, as well as economic and tax reforms. Each of these mansions, together with the grand palace, was filled with murals of Iranian legend, mythology and heroes. Artists were commissioned to paint portraits of nobility. The greatest painter was commissioned to paint the Sassanid king for a collection of family dynasty portraits housed in Ctesiphon. Many works of literature were first written in this era, and were later rewritten in the Islamic era. The colorful rugs, tapestry and clothing marked the economic prosperity of the citizens, as well as the immense economic power of a country now turned one of the richest in the world. Iranian clothing and textiles were the fashion in lands as far as Egypt and China.[150]

During his reign, polo was a favorite pastime of the nobility; players included the Queen and other women of society. Music was highly valued and thousands of musicians lived in Iranian cities. An orchestra would accompany the king on his hunting expeditions and in nearly every Iranian city, music was played both at dawn and at sunset.

Anushirvan's great place in Iranian history however, is not due to his military campaigns against the Romans, his crushing defeat of the Huns in the east, his naval conquest of Yemen, or the massacre of tens of thousands of Mazdakites. Although the 45th generation of Iranians, like every generation before, had its political fate settled with violence, it was in peace and an enriched culture that this 45th generation achieved its greatness.

Turmoil after Khosrow's Death and The Demise of the Sassanid Regime

The 46th generation of Iranians whose parents had successfully defeated their western and eastern enemies, and provided security and peace, followed by the richest economic and artistic expansion in Iranian history, were told in 579 CE that the old king 'Anushirvan' has died after 48 years of reign. His son, Hormizd IV, succeeded the throne.

War with Byzantium was immediately resumed, followed by a series of violent expeditions and battles lasting ten years, without clear winners. At the same time, news reached Ctesiphon of the invasion of the northeast provinces by Turkic tribes. There, a brilliant military general, Bahram Choubin, soundly defeated the Turks. Wars in central Asia were followed by successful campaigns in the Caucasus against the Khazar tribes. Bahram was named the commander of the Iranian forces in the west, and continued his successful campaigns against Byzantium in Georgia. There, after a minor defeat, the Iranian king fearing his popularity, removed Bahram from his position. This led to rebellion in the military and an army headed by Bahram marched on Ctesiphon.

The King, who had imprisoned many nobles and clergy, was unpopular in the country and politically isolated. He was blinded by the rebels, and his son Khosrow-Parviz was placed on the throne. Khosrow-Parviz, after being defeated by his father's general, refused to take orders from Bahram and took refuge in Byzantium. War, violence, and uncertainty continued as Khosrow Parviz was given an army by the Byzantine emperor to use in the march back to Iran. Bahram, with inferior forces, was able to inflict massive casualties on Khosrow's army and forced him to withdraw to Azarbaijan. In a subsequent battle however, Bahram's army was defeated, and he was assassinated a year later as he fled to central Asia.[151] Civil war over control of Iran between this general and Khosrow Parviz was the fate of the 46th generation of Iranians.

Only twelve years after marching to Iran with a Byzantine army, war between Khosrow Parviz and Byzantium resumed in 603 CE. Like his grandfather, Khosrow Anushirvan, Khosrow Parviz, or the 'Victorious', led one successful military campaign after another against Byzantium. Within four years, he had crossed the Euphrates and captured Armenia, pillaging villages and farms as he marched across the lands. For the first time the inhabitants of Constantinople saw the burning of villages outside their city as the Iranian army marched closer.[152] From there, he sent an army composed of both Persian and Arab units south to fight the Arab rebellions of Hira on the western shores of the Euphrates. There, the Arab units deserted the army, and the remaining Iranian soldiers were annihilated.[153] This battle of Dhu Qar was significant, because for the first time it demonstrated that the Arabs, when united, were a force to be reckoned with, and signaled the vulnerability of the Iranian western flank and its capital. It was around this time that an otherwise ordinary man named Mohammad, while sitting alone in a cave near Mecca, as he had done most of his life, heard a series of messages that was later to change the course of Iranian and world history.

Meanwhile, Byzantium was going through a period of anarchy and disarray, with all its territories open to conquest by foreigners. Khosrow-Parviz, unable to breech the massive walls of Constantinople, marched his army south and captured Syria, including Damascus and Antioch, on the shores of the Mediterranean Sea. This was followed by the sacking of Jerusalem, where the true cross, the most sacred treasure of Christianity, which the Christians believed to have been used for Jesus, was taken back to Ctesiphon as booty.[154] Then the Iranian army marched across the Sinai Desert into Egypt, which was occupied by the Iranian forces for the last time in history. Meanwhile, Byzantium's forces defeated the Iranian forces in Armenia, thus expelling Iranian troops from Asia Minor and outflanking the army units spread across Egypt and the west.[155]

While in Asia Minor, a Byzantine general united his forces with the Khazars of the north and marched across Azarbaijan, Urumia, and northern Mesopotamia, pillaging farms and villages in his path. There he defeated the Iranian army, which forced Khosrow to flee to his capital. The Byzantium army, while chasing the King, captured Dastgird, a residence of the King 70 miles north of Ctesiphon, where they found enormous treasures. Khosrow blamed his generals for the destruction and defeat of his army, and planned to execute them, but a rebellion broke out and the King was murdered.

Khosrow-Parviz's reign was marred by greed, paranoia, instability, and violence. At one point, he ordered the execution of some 36,000 political and religious prisoners, but this atrocity was averted after the head of the guards reportedly begged the King to revoke the order.[156] The army commanders defeated in their battles were killed as punishment for failure.[157] The clergy meanwhile was hostile to Khosrow because the king had developed an interest in Christianity after his stay in Byzantium.

Iran's treasury was greatly diminished after his senseless wars against Byzantium and in Egypt. From more than 486 million mesghals (a unit of measurement close to five grams) of gold, the treasury was reduced to 150 million. Khosrow-Parviz's wealth was estimated to be 800 million mesghals of gold at its height.[158]

The king's son, Kavad II, who had conspired to murder his father, assumed the crown. Lacking sufficient military resources, he made peace with Byzantium and returned the true cross to the Christian emperor.[159] Both empires had been devastated by generations of war. Kavad II died after a year, and was succeeded by his infant son Ardeshir III. His general, Shahrbaraz, with the help of the Byzantium army, marched into Ctesiphon, killed the infant and his family, but retained power only for two years before he in turn was murdered. The remnants of Iran's forces were once again defeated in the north by the Khazars, who invaded Armenia.[160] A man pretending to be the nephew of Khosrow in eastern Iran was killed on his way to Ctesiphon. Every male offspring of the royal family had been murdered. The situation was so volatile that the nobility in Iran's rigidly patriarchal society was forced to put Khosrow's daughter Boran on the throne. This first woman in Iranian history to wear the crown survived for only a year, after which a succession of men and women held the crown briefly and died violently. In the midst of this anarchy, the country declined into impoverishment and disorder. After all the bloodshed, no member of the royal family survived to assume the crown. The Sassanid family, which had ruled Iran for more than 17 generations, was virtually extinct.

In order to save the country, a grandson of Khosrow was persuaded to assume the crown but the country remained in disarray from the time of his death in 628 CE, until the coming of power of a distant Sassanid relative from Istakhr named Yazdegerd III in 632 CE. In the interim four years, ten shahs came to power and were killed or deposed. The lifetime of Iran's 48th generation was scarred by the ill-fated invasion of Egypt, the defeat in Asia Minor, and the internal violence and turmoil that ensued.

Once again the conquest of an enfeebled Iran was inevitable—but the next invasion would be mounted by forces that, unlike Alexander's, came not just for plunder but also sought to inculcate a new religion and a new philosophy. The invaders' messages of 'brotherhood', 'classless society', 'unity with God', and 'self-sacrifice', may have resonated with many Iranians, whose parents, grandparents and ancestors, going back 15 generations, had heeded similar messages from Mani and Mazdak. They were perhaps ready for a new guiding principle for their lives, delivered by a new force in world history, but perhaps unaware of the incredible threat and potential violence of continued religious government.

48 generations of Iranians had their fate determined through violence. Yet, the violence of new religious laws enforced on them by an occupying force whose language and customs they did not understand was beyond any trauma and violence that they could imagine; trauma and violence which continue to pain them today and of which they are constantly reminded by another religious regime that imposes religious laws, restrictions and ideology on society.

Yet many Iranians, having seen the corruption of the once sacred Zoroastrian religion, were now apathetic about their religion and perhaps more importantly, because of the chaos, instability and corruption in the once powerful Sassanid family, apathetic on who should govern and rule over them. It was at this time that Iranians encountered a new force in world history—Islam.

CHAPTER 3 – 100 GENERATION LEGACY OF VIOLENCE- PART II: ISLAMIC CENTURIES OF CONQUEST AND BLOODSHED

"These events and the use of violence in the name of Islam are painful to hear for most Muslims, but are deep cultural wounds that resurface constantly as forms of fundamentalisms through the likes of Khomeini or the Taliban, who continuously attempt to recreate the totalitarian state of this period."

The message of Islam unified the tribes on the Arabian Peninsula. It's prophet, during the 23 years of his life after the revelation of tenets of Islam, had sent letters to the courts of Iran and Byzantium, yet on his deathbed, Islam had not spread beyond the Arabian Peninsula. After his death in 632CE, Abu Bakr, a well-respected elderly statesman, an early convert to Islam and a confidant of the prophet, was chosen by the community elders as Islam's first Caliph.

Abu Bakr became not only Islam's spiritual leader, but like the prophet, its political leader. Early in his reign, he concluded that the time was ripe to send an Islamic army north to cities on western shore of Euphrates and outside the military domain of Ctesiphon. The predominantly Christian Arabs of the region agreed to pay a yearly tax called *jizyah* in return for their security and their right to practice their religions. The Muslims in return employed these citizens to serve as spies and gather intelligence on the Sassanid regime. The booty captured from these cities was sent to Medina and distributed amongst the Muslims, the first of many such remittances to come.

The same culture of violence prevalent worldwide in ancient times, which had consumed the resources of more than 48 generations of Iranians, would also consume the resources of generations of Arabs. Thus, Islam, was adopted and infected by the same political violence prevalent in Arabian culture— just as Christianity had been infused with the Roman Empire's political violence. In effect, Islam became not just the source of spiritual guidance, but also a tool for political and material gains, forced to employ and justify further violence.

Similar to ancient customs of conquest and imperialism, men conquered by Islamic armies either had to pay *jizyah* or, if they refused, were either arrested or enslaved and sent to Medina.[161] The alternative was for a person to declare himself a Muslim and aid the conquering army. In return for denouncing his community and family's religion, that person was often rewarded with material gain, positions of power, and exemption from being enslaved or paying the *jizyah*, a particularly heavy burden for the poor.

Abu Bakr's reign was short, lasting a little more than two years before he died of natural causes. Two years later, Omar, the second caliph of Islam, ordered a new commander, Abu Abid, to take lead of the Arab forces and prepare for crossing of the Euphrates.

In 635CE, the 13th year after the start of the Islamic calendar, Abu Abid's army crossed Euphrates into the land between the two great rivers, where it was met by an Iranian force. Abu Abid, his brothers, and his nephews who had accompanied him to this battle were killed. The Arab army was routed and destroyed. When Omar learned of this debacle, he became depressed and did not mention the campaign for a year. Meanwhile, because of political chaos, turmoil and instability, Iranians failed to make investments in rebuilding their military or preparing for any future attacks.

Qadisiya

After a year, intelligence about the disarray of Iran and its forces was again relayed to Omar, who ordered a second invasion by an Islamic army led by his veteran commander, Sa'd. In response, Yazdegerd III, the last Sassanid King of Iran crowned in the chaotic atmosphere of the time, ordered an army of twelve thousand led by Mehran, to stand on the eastern banks of Euphrates and repel the Arabs. Upon crossing the river, Mehran and his army were defeated and his soldiers dispersed. Towns and villages on the Eastern banks of Euphrates were conquered by the Islamic army. Omar's army reached the great river of Tigris to the East and went as far as Basra to the south.

North of this area, along the banks of Tigris, were the seven cities interconnected by farms and gardens and collectively referred to by Arabs as Mada-in. The jewel of these cities was the capital city of Ctesiphon on the eastern shore of Tigris. From his palace there, a terrified Yazdegerd III ordered his general in Khurasan, Rostam (Farrokh Hormozd) to come west and gather an army to repel the invading force.

A total of 30,000 of Rostam's forces camped a few miles from an equally numerous Arabian army in an area between the two great rivers called Qadisiya. The battle in Qadisiya between these two forces not only was to determine the destiny of Iran for centuries to come, but would become one of the most important battles in history, turning Islam into a tool for imperialism and affirming its status as a world power.[162] For four months, the two armies stood apart and stared each other down.[163] Then, in June of 637CE, fighting began, the outcome of which would depend on the ability of one of these two armies to use superior violence to annihilate the other and thereby dictate what faith would be embraced by millions in years to come.

After three days of skirmish, the dust kicked up by the two armies was swirled into a sandstorm, blinding both sides and turning the battle into a confused melee of hand-to-hand combat.[164] A group of Arab soldiers made their way through the center of Iranian lines, fighting their way through to Rostam's tent. He fled but was caught and killed which demoralized and routed his forces. The supplies and treasure captured by the Muslims exceeded anything they had seen before. Thousands of Iranian captives were sent to the bazaar of Medina to be sold as slaves. Each victorious Arab soldier was given hundreds and sometimes thousands of pieces of gold, making him one of the richest men of the time.[165] The battle of Qadisiyyah ended in utter defeat for the Iranians.

For centuries after, Qadisiya became a symbol of conquest for Muslims. Even in the 20th century, Saddam Hussein used Qadisiya repeatedly as a symbol for his wars and violence against Iran and later the United States. The area in Baghdad in which Saddam built all his government ministries was named Qadisiya. In 1986, when he needed to raise money through government bonds for his continued war and violence, he named the bonds Qadisiya bonds. The Iraqi media, prior to the 2003 invasion by forces of the United States (and its 'coalition of the willing') repeatedly referred to the upcoming war as Saddam's Qadisiya.[166] Cultures are built around symbols. If symbols creating a culture are those of violence, war, and conquest, then the ensuing culture is one of war, violence, and conquest. Thus, the birth of Qadisiya in many ways symbolically marks the dawn of the culture of Islamic imperialism. For Iranians, Qadisiya is a symbol of defeat and the opening for centuries of further violence in the name of Islam. This symbol of defeat has left Iranians bitter, often nurturing anger, hatred and violence against Islam itself.

CHAPTER 3

After the battle, Sa'd's army marched to Babylon, one of the seven interconnected cities collectively known as Mada'in. There the remnants of the Iranian army under the leadership of their three remaining commanders Mehran, Firuzan, and Hormozan continued to struggle. In Babylon, fighting continued on the central ruins of what was then regarded as the Tower of Babel until all Iranian soldiers and their commanders were either killed or had fled. After the battle, Mehran retreated to the capital city of Ctesiphon to continue his fight; Firuzan went to Western-Central Iran in Nahavand, where in the final battle to come, he would determine the destiny of not just his forces, but destiny of Iranians altogether. Hormozan went to the southwestern province of today's Khuzestan, where he would continue to fight and, upon being taken as prisoner-slave, would become involved in the Iranian planned assassination of Islam's second Caliph in Medina, an assassination that reverberates and exacerbates tensions in Islam until today.[167]

In order to slow the path of the invading army, during their escape east, Iranians destroyed every bridge across the Tigris River. The city of Seleucia, another of the seven cities of Mada'in, centuries-old at the time and built by the descendants of the soldiers in Alexander's army was then sacked. Unable to advance further, the Muslim army camped across the river Tigris from Ctesiphon and remained there for months.

Built at the end of the Parthian era, Ctesiphon had served as the capital of nearly 30 generations of Iranians. Its many palaces were filled with murals of Iranian mythology, portraits of its residents, statues and artwork of Sassanid era. The royal family was in possession of collection of paintings of Sassanid family and kings dating back generations. The city had libraries that contained the accumulated, contemporary knowledge of science, religion, and mythology which Iranians had gathered over centuries. Amongst the palaces, the most famous was the Palace of Abiz, built during the Parthian era and the grand Palace of Kasra, the seat of Sassanid King.

After Qadisiya

Unable to cross the Tigris, the army of Sa'd swelled to 50,000 from the infusion of new soldiers in search of treasure and justifying their use of violence in the name of Islam. The pillaging and sacking of towns caused a shortage of food in Mesopotamia followed by famine. The lack of food was so severe that the people of nearby towns and cities were forced to eat the stray dogs and cats in order to survive. Meanwhile across the river, fear and panic had caused a mass escape of Iranians east from Ctesiphon, leaving the capital deserted.[168]

Yazdegerd III, who was still in Ctesiphon, also decided to desert the city. He left a small force of one thousand to defend the walls and prevent looting in case of eventual Iranian victory. The people in between the two rivers who were now desperate for food approached Sa'd's army and announced their friendship and peaceful intentions. In return for peace, they showed the Muslim army a stretch of Tigris up north that was shallow enough for soldiers to cross on horseback.[169] Upon crossing the river, the remaining defenders fled Ctesiphon at night through its eastern gates and left the capital open for conquest.

When the 50,000 strong Sa'ad's army came into the city, the capital was virtually abandoned. Hundreds of empty palaces, and thousands of empty homes, gardens, schools, and libraries were left to the invaders. According to one account, Iranians were able to carry and escape with only half the incredible amount of gold in the treasury.[170] Part of the looted gold was put aside to be sent to Medina; the rest was divided between the soldiers who had sacked Ctesiphon.[171] The rug of 'Baharestan', in the main auditorium of the king's palace, known to Iranians as the most spectacular handmade rug ever created, was sent to Medina. There, unable to find a building large enough to accommodate the rug, Omar ordered the rug to be cut into little pieces and each piece be sold in the bazaar.[172]

The next battle occurred in an area on western edge of Zagros Mountains, in a place called Jalulah. Arab chroniclers say that when the Iranians were escaping from Ctesiphon, from this place, each had to go his own separate way. Some were going to Azarbaijan, others to Khuzestan, Fars, and Khurasan. Before separating they gathered once again and built defensive lines.

The entire country was now plunged into fear and panic. The 49th generation of Iranians was experiencing a disaster unlike any endured by their ancestors. Seeing the fall of the central government, many states and regions declared their independence from the Sassanid regime. Yazdegerd III was going from city to city trying to gather troops. The veteran Arab army finally marched east to Jalulah. The defensive lines were no match for the veteran Arabian army and it was another defeat for the Iranians.[173] After this battle, many Iranian military units having lost all hope in the Sassanid family joined the Muslim forces.[174]

During the next four years (637-641CE), the Arab army slowly conquered the towns and cities in today's South-Western Iran, including the ancient city of Susa. The city of Gondi-Shapur, with its famous university and medical school, was also sacked. Hormozan, one of the remaining Iranian commanders went inside the fortified city of Tustar (Shushtar) and readied for battle. Without proper siege equipment needed to break down city gates, the Arabian army was forced to wait outside the city walls and starve the Iranians out.

For weeks, the army was stationed outside until one day an Iranian citizen from the city approached the Arabian army and asked to see their commander. He told the commander of a secret passage across the wall to his house within the city. He proposed to show the passageway in return for sparing of his life and that of his family.[175] Later that evening, several Arabian soldiers accompanied the man through the passageway into the city, wearing Iranian clothing given to them by this man. As they walked to the center of the city, they came upon the central citadel in which Hormozan was stationed and, looking up, they saw the Iranian commander speaking to some of his soldiers. That evening, two hundred soldiers stealthily entered the city and attacked the guards at the main gate. Upon opening the gates, the Arab army flooded in and conquered the city. Hormozan and some of his followers in the citadel surrendered after they received assurances that their lives would be spared. Hormozan was sent to Medina to have Omar, Islam's second caliph, decide his fate.[176] But as chance would have it, it was Hormozan who was to later decide on the fate of Omar and thereby send a great shockwave across the Islamic world.

Within a year the central province of Fars, the heart of Iranian civilization was conquered.

Nahavand

Meanwhile terror had spread across Iran. Everywhere, Iranians were seen fleeing eastward to mountains of Afghanistan, central Asia, India and even China, where the Sassanid royal family ultimately found refuge. Hundreds of thousands who fled to India were to freely continue practicing their Zoroastrian religion and formed the Parsi minority population of India.

With the defeat and collapse of all of Iran at hand, Yazdegerd III pulled together volunteers for one last Iranian army. These new soldiers, the largest army Iran had gathered for decades, camped near Hamedan (Ecbatana) in an area called Nahavand for the fateful last battle and the last hope for the survival of a way of life.[177] The commander of the Arabian army sent a letter to Omar in Medina asking for help, stating that he faced an enemy army of 150,000.[178] Omar made an important speech, saying that up to now "Islam and God have been on our side to defeat the infidels. But now infidels are gathering an army to darken the light of God. Our commander in Kufa has sent me a letter telling me that infidels from the lands of Tous, Tabarestan, Damavand, Gorgan, Rey, Isfahan, Qom, Hamedan, Mahin and Masbezan are gathered to defeat your brothers in Kufa and Basra."[179]

Islamic forces called from every quarter in Middle East, camped across from the Iranian army in Nahavand in western Iran. As the Iranian force grew larger from the arrival of new volunteers, the commanders of the outnumbered Muslim army decided to avoid conflict and retreat in order to retain Mesopotamia. They falsely informed their troops that the great Caliph of Islam, Omar, was dead in Medina, which made the pullback to Kufa necessary. But the Iranians attacked the withdrawing Muslim army and the adversaries engaged in a hand-to-hand battle. The battle raged for two days until the Iranians retired back to their fortified lines and were defeated on the third day of battle. 30,000 were left on the field and were captured. More than 80,000 were killed in the battle or in nearby hills as they were escaping the battle.[180]

Muslims call the victory at Nahavand fought in the spring of 642CE as 'Fath-ol-Fotouh', the 'victory of all victories'.[181] After this, there was no centralized resistance by the Sassanid regime, but local fighting continued in nearly every city. The Arabian army conquered Qom and Kashan. Upon reaching Rey, in today's southern Tehran, an army of soldiers from the Caspian coast led by Isfandyar fought another battle but was defeated.[182] Within a year, Ekbatana (Hamedan) and later portions of Azarbaijan were conquered.[183] Kerman, Sistan and Khurasan were next.[184]

In each conquered city, citizens agreed to pay the *jizyah* tax in order to peacefully retain their religion, but in many cities including Isfahan, Qom, and Istakhr, rebellions ensued. Citizens of Istakhr forced the Muslim army to withdraw. Upon the death of his predecessor, the new general conquering Istakhr took a horrific revenge.[185] The Islamic chronicler, Ibn Balkhi estimates the number of those killed in crushing of this rebellion at 40,000.[186]

The state of Khurasan in northeast rebelled in the year 650 CE, only a few years after being conquered. The Islamic army had to return and retake the territories in the northeast, including the states of Tabarestan (Mazandaran) and Gorgan.[187] Sistan in Southeast was conquered during the reign of the third Islamic Caliph, Uthman, but upon the death of the Caliph, the people rebelled and forced his governor to flee the region.[188] Similarly in Azarbaijan, rebellion and insurgency continued, with Omar forced to change his commanders and governors in the region in order to successfully crush the insurgency.[189]

For forty-eight generations, Iranians had been relentlessly subjected to war and violence, sometimes in victory, other times in defeat. Yet this generation's defeat was far different and more traumatic than any other. After this defeat, Iranians were occupied by people speaking foreign tongues and unfamiliar with their culture. Uncomfortable in the confines of the cities of Ctesiphon, Seleucia, and Babylon, Omar ordered the building of new cities of Kufa and Basra to house the tens of thousands of Arab citizens pouring into the region in search of the spoils of conquest. The deserted cities of Babylon, Seleucia and Ctesiphon, once the centers of Iranian, and at times even human civilization, soon crumbled into ruins.

In pre-Islamic Arabian society, images of gods in forms of statues and rocks were housed in Mecca and worshipped by the Arabian tribes. The prophet of Islam strictly forbade this practice, which Muslims referred to as idol worshipping. Upon coming to Iran, the new soldiers of Islam encountered many paintings and statues, often depicting myths and legends. Afraid that such images may be worshiped by Iranians, murals and portraits everywhere were destroyed and Iranians were forbidden to paint or make statues or any other artistic image or symbol. This was a mortal blow to the artistic heritage of Iranian culture. Music was also banned by foreign occupiers attempting to eliminate another vital part of Iranian culture that they considered threatening to their rule. Books and libraries were destroyed by the conquerors. This resulted in the destruction of countless works of knowledge and literature, which are often the fundamental pillars of a culture.[190] Most of the books surviving were the texts, mostly religious, saved by the remaining faithful Zoroastrians in their homes.

As Muslim power and reach expanded, more and more people from across the Middle East left their belongings, cultures and religion to join this army in order to get their share of the riches taken from nonbelievers. While many converts to Islam sought unity with God, peace, brotherhood, and a classless society, others waged a religious war in search of power and wealth. Such continues to be the case in the politicized Iran of today.

What the 49th generation of Iranians experienced was not unlike the repressive and blindly destructive rule of the Taliban in Afghanistan or the rule of Islamic Republic in Iran. In fact, countless regimes to come would emulate the violence of this era in their attempts to recreate the imagined (and imaginary) utopian society of the early Islamic period.

Killing of Omar

The violence whirling across Iran was not just a traumatic experience in the lives of the 49th generation of Iranians, but a traumatic ordeal for the Islamic world, one which continues to foment anger, hatred, and violence until today. As the violence of further conquest and occupation continued throughout a defeated Iran, Iranians taken as slaves to Medina planned and carried out the assassination of Omar, sending shockwaves across the conquered lands.

The assassin was an Iranian Christian carpenter slave named Firuzan, known in Medina as Abu Lolo. After the final Iranian defeat in Nahavand and upon the arrival of the captured Iranian slaves in Medina, he is said to have been deeply moved, approaching the children in the slave caravan entering the city, and kissing them on their foreheads. Not long after, during a noontime prayer led by Omar, Abu Lolo attacked the Islamic caliph, stabbing him six times with a dagger. He then stabbed himself to death.

The dagger had been seen a few days prior in the possession of Hormozan, the Iranian general now also a slave in Medina. Thus the governor of Khuzestan who had fought in Qadisiyyah and later in Tustar and who was brought to Medina was amongst the Iranian conspirators who were put to death.[191] Rebellions ensued in nearly every Iranian province against occupying forces as the news of the assassination reached Iranian towns. The killing of Omar remains the cause of smoldering, anger and hatred that continues to plague the Islamic world.

In towns and villages of Iran, there is a celebration that is still sometimes practiced called '*Omar-koshi*' or 'Omar-killing'. During this celebration, effigies of Omar are made out of cloth. As the effigy is paraded in main town streets and squares, people sing and dance while hurling insults at the symbol of Islam's second caliph, one of the closest friends and allies of the Prophet and the father of one the Prophet's favorite wives. The effigy is then burnt before a cheering crowd.

My mother and other family members recall this celebration in Tehran. She remembers that a great uncle would throw a party every year in honor and memory of *'Omar Khoshi'*. She recalls family members, who were ignoring each other over personal animosities, overcoming their differences and attending this party filled with music and illumination. My father recalls many such *'Omar Koshi'* celebrations as a child growing up in the city of Arak. He remembers women becoming ecstatic with the dancing and singing. In these celebrations, children would sing:

Abu Lolo, chera ranget parideh
Abu Lolo, why so pale

Mageh khikeh Omar kheili darideh
Was tearing Omar's fat belly overdone

The celebration of Omar-killing is no doubt the remnant of hatred ingrained in society that glorifies revenge and violence. One can see how violence from events fourteen century before can create a cycle of anger and hatred justifying further violence, to the extent that the assassination of Islam's second caliph is not only justified but celebrated by devout Iranian Muslims. Violence bequeaths a bitter legacy.

Uthman

The wounds afflicted on Omar did not immediately kill the caliph. The piercing of Omar's abdomen proved to be fatal, but it took several days for the caliph to die. As his life drained away, he appointed a council of six to elect the next leader of Islamic world within three days. In this council, Uthman from the Umayyad family and Ali from the Hashemite family were most qualified for the position. Uthman was an elderly figure over seventy years of age. He was the widowed husband of the prophet's daughter, Rokeiya. Upon her death, he had married the prophet's other daughter Um Kulthum, who had also passed away. The prophet used to say he loved Uthman "so dearly that, if another daughter had yet remained, he would have given her to him."[192] But he was from the Umayyad family, whose members were fierce enemies of the prophet and Islam during the early years. Their family was responsible for the prophet's persecution, intimidation and ridicule in Mecca followed by his near death and escape from Mecca to Medina. Ali, from the Hashemite family, was younger, about 50 years of age. He was the prophet's nephew and devout follower from the very first revelations of Islam. He was the husband of the prophet's daughter, Fatemeh, and the father of prophet's only two grandchildren, Hassan and Hussein.

After two days of deliberation, there was no consensus. Ultimately, Abdul Rahman, empowered to choose the next caliph, held repeated, long, private discussions with Uthman and Ali. Finally, on November 7, 644AD, the first day of the Arabian new year and the 24th year since the Hijra of the prophet and the initial date of the Islamic Calendar, Abdul Rahman stood in a crowded mosque, raised the hand of Uthman, and proclaimed him the third Caliph of Islam.

Within weeks, as the news that Iranian conspirators had murdered Omar reached towns and cities across Iran, several thousand Arabian soldiers stationed in each city as occupiers and tax collectors were forced to brutally crush the uprisings. Uthman, the new caliph of Islam ordered the Governor of Basra, Ibn Amir, to set about exterminating every insurgency encountered as he marched his army all the way to the Oxus River. 40,000 were taken captive during this campaign.[193] His subordinate commanders marched south and violently suppressed and massacred the insurgents in Kerman and Sistan. Others were dispatched to the region that is today's Afghanistan to crush the rebellions in Kabul, Herat, and Ghazna. In the eastern regions of Sistan and Kabul, these forces destroyed statues thought to be of Buddha; one Muslim general gave the fragments of one to traumatized local worshipers, who were told "these are thine: this I did only to let thee know that this thing can neither hurt thee nor can it do thee good."[194] For many years to come, these outlying provinces would continuously rebel only to be confronted and crushed by the superior Muslim forces.

Meanwhile, in the eighth year of Uthman's rule, Yazdgerd III persisted in attempts to lead a rebellion against the occupying forces. But the defeat of nearly every city and province meant there were no allies on which the former king could depend.

None of the remaining independent yet subordinate regional governors, alarmed at the risk posed by his presence, wanted him to stay in their domains and one even sent a group of soldiers one to assassinate him. Yazdegerd fled and sought shelter from a miller but was murdered in the middle of the night in the year 651CE after unsuccessfully spending fifteen years leading rebellions and insurgencies across Iran. [195]

His son Pyruz continued the struggle against the occupation of Islamic forces. He took refuge in China and for nearly 30 years continued to lobby the Chinese government while his sister became wife to the Chinese emperor. With the help of the Chinese, he came back to Sistan in the year 658CE and formed a government that lasted for five years. He died in China, where his tombstone still lies. His son Narsieh, Yazdegerd's grandson, carried on the struggle and attempted to raise an army. He died in 710CE after spending much of his life trying to win back Iran. The last prominent survivor of the Sassanid dynasty was the son of Narsieh named Khosrow, who attacked again with the help of Turks and failed to defeat the Muslims. With him lies the last attempt by a known Sassanid family member who spent his life in the attempt to reclaim the family's empire.

Mu'awiyah

Meanwhile, Mu'awiya, a relative of Uthman, a member of Umayyad family, and the governor of Damascus, had taken complete control of nearby provinces in Syria and created a powerful political and military force. His armies pillaged Armenia and marched through Azarbaijan and then to Tabarestan (today's Mazandaran) on the southeastern shore of the Caspian Sea. They then pushed on as far north as Georgia and reached the Black Sea, bringing many new provinces under his and Islamic army's control.

What began as a relative period of cooperation and unity between the Umayyad and Hashemite families in Uthman's initial years as caliph soon soured into distrust and open criticism. Reports were pouring in from the provinces of tyranny, terror, corruption, and favoritism by local authorities, who lived luxuriously in Damascus, Kufa, Basra, and in Egypt. Ibn Amir, who was the governor of Basra and had put down much of the rebellion in Iran, had placed his uncles, brothers, cousins, and family members in charge of various towns and cities under his domain.[196] The governor of Kufa, facing criticism of the path Islam had taken, called out for "crushing [the] sedition and arrogance of the men of Kufa with a rod of iron."[197] The governor employed violent measures like those used in suppressing the rebellions in Iran as a means of keeping the citizens of Kufa in check.

People in Medina were increasingly critical of the old caliph who, after twelve years of rule, was more than 80 years old and appeared ineffectual in confronting corruption and violence by subordinates. The cries of demands for a 'classless society', 'brotherhood', 'peace and unity with God', the pillars on which Islam was founded, seemed forgotten by many who were questioning his leadership. Reports of extravagant lifestyles outraged many Muslims. Al Zubeir, one of the prophet's closest companions and a member of the Council that had elected Uthman, possessed 1,000 slaves, both male and female, as well as 1,000 horses. In every city under the military domain of the caliph, he owned a palace, including a grand palace in Basra. Similar accounts about other high-ranking leaders of Islam were known throughout the Islamic world. Uthman's palace in Medina, in addition to its vast treasures, contained "marble pillars, walls of costly stucco, grand gates and gardens."[198] Uthman's house in Medina was run by 400 slaves brought from Iran, Egypt and Byzantium.[199]

The growing criticism created an underground conspiracy in the cities of Kufa, Basra, and in Egypt. In the 12th year of Uthman's rule, several thousand conspirators from Basra, Kufa and Egypt marched to Medina. Unable to force Uthman out of office, they turned to violence, surrounding his house and attempting to force their way in. Uthman's slaves, together with several thousand citizens of Medina, his companions and associates, including Ali from the Hashemite family and Hassan and Hussein, the prophet's grandsons, successfully defended Uthman's gate and prevented the rebels from entering, but some swarmed over the walls and fell upon the old Caliph, raining down mortal blows on his head. Violence, which had poisoned the purpose and culture of Islam through foreign wars and through continued incorporation of religion into politics, had now infiltrated the heart of Islam, causing Muslims to fight and murder other Muslims.

Ali, the fourth Caliphate of Islam and the first Shi'ite Imam

Within days of Uthman's burial in July 656CE, Ali, from the Hashemite family, was elected as the fourth caliph of Islam. Yet the murder of Uthman by the rebels and the subsequent support of the rebels for Ali had created a schism in the Islamic world, justifying further violence. The Umayyad family together with Ayesha, the Prophet's widow, did not support Ali. In addition, Ali lacked the power to punish the rebels who had murdered the caliph, which created great animosity between the Umayyad and Hashemite families. Thus began one of the most turbulent years in Iran's Islamic period and events that forever divided Muslims into Shi'ites and Sunnis.

When he came to power, Ali promised to return Islam to its true roots. He replaced the governors in Basra and Kufa with trusted companions. This

CHAPTER 3

change proved popular for those Iranians who had accepted Islam but were troubled by the tyranny, corruption, and violence afflicting the religion. But Mu'awiyah, Governor of Syria and a member of Umayyad family, refused to submit to the new caliph's rule. In order to maintain tighter control over the provinces, Ali transferred his capital from Medina to Kufa, the new garrison city built in Iraq adjacent to the abandoned cities of Babylon, Seleucia and Ctesiphon.

Meanwhile, Al-Zubair and Ayesha moved and occupied Basra in order to gather supplies and supporters for the eventual civil war against Ali. In the battle that ensued, Ali was victorious. But soon he was challenged by Mu'awiyah, cousin of Uthman and the leading member of Umayyad family in Syria. The armies of Mu'awiyah and Ali met at Siffin. After 110 days of repeated attempts at negotiations, a bloody battle ensued, lasting for three days. Fearing defeat, in a brilliant move which has become one of the most retold stories of early Islamic period, Mu'awiyah, ordered his soldiers to place pages from the Quran on their swords and demand arbitration and an end to fighting. Upon seeing the impalement of the pages of the Quran, Ali's soldiers ceased fighting and forced arbitration upon their leader.

The eight months of arbitration that followed did not resolve the issue of leadership for the Islamic world. Mu'awiyah continued to rule from Damascus and Ali sited his headquarters in Kufa. In another blow to Hashemite family in Kufa, 12,000 of Ali's soldiers rebelled and left the army to create a new sect, one separate from those we know as Sunni's and Shi'ites. Calling themselves Kharijites (dissenters), they refused to accept either Ali or Mu'awiyah as caliphs, asserting that the caliphate was not solely the right of the Umayyad or Hashemite family but open to any Muslim qualified to become the leader of Islamic world.

These dissenters created a fundamentalist and extremist view of religion where they regarded only themselves as the people of God and true followers of Islam fighting against those wandering from the path. Ali personally went to their camp outside of Kufa and offered their leaders the governorship of the rich province of Isfahan in Iran if they would accept his leadership.[200]

The struggle between Ali and the rebels went on until, in 661AD, the fifth year of Ali's turbulent reign as Caliph, during which the Islamic world was torn repeatedly by violence, the Kharijites met and swore to murder not only Ali in Kufa but also Mu'awiyah in Damascus and Amr, the governor of Egypt. As the conspirators swore their allegiance, they each dipped their swords in poison and went their separate ways. In Egypt, Amr survived the assassination attempt but his deputy was killed. Mu'awiyah in Damascus was wounded by a conspirator's sword and fell gravely ill. His physician had nearly lost hope until Mu'awiyah rallied and recovered.

In the mosque in Kufa, as Ali was leading the congregation in prayer, the assassin struck him with his sword. The wound was not immediately fatal. But the poison from the sword ultimately killed the sixty-year-old nephew of the Prophet.

Hassan and Hussein

Upon Ali's death, Mu'awiyah, who had control over Syria and Egypt, saw the opportunity to expand his empire to include Iraq and Iran. Ali's older son Hassan, known to Shi'ites as their second Imam after Ali, was Umayyad family's main rival; he had at his disposal an army of 40,000 inherited from his father. But Hassan, instead of leading his army to war against Mu'awiyah, chose to send an expeditionary force of 12,000 to oppose the army of his rival while he remained in the Sassanid palaces of Ecbatana and awaited word of the outcome. There he received news that his force had been defeated by his enemy. He was forced to negotiate with Mu'awiyah and retired to Medina, where shortly later he was poisoned and killed by one of his wives in his harem.

Umayyad family now had at their disposal an empire stretching from the Atlantic coast in Morocco to the Oxus River in central Asia. Unlike the first four Islamic caliphs, who were elected to their position by a committee, Mu'awiyah assumed his power through his unrivaled military force, which stretched from northeastern provinces of Iran and Central Asia to Spain. Most submitted to his rule out of fear of brutality and persecution.

Before his death after 19 years of rule as Islamic caliph in Damascus, he proclaimed his son Yezid as his heir and called for representatives from each city in his empire to pledge their allegiance to his son.[201] There were several other candidates in Medina who possessed the family ties that qualified them to be the caliph. The most prominent candidate who today serves as an incredibly important symbol for Iranians and is considered one of the pillars of Shi'ism was Hussein, the younger son of Ali and the only surviving grandchild of the prophet.

Yezid was immediately faced with discontent of Muslims in Kufa where there was a strong allegiance to Ali and the Hashemite family. Later, supporters of Hashemite family became known as Shi'ites. Letters were sent

CHAPTER 3

to Hussein in Mecca by citizens of Kufa asserting their support for the prophet's grandson and inviting him to lead a war against Yezid. Ignoring the warning signs and threat to his life, Hussein, together with his family and seventy of his companions, left Mecca for Kufa in order to incite a revolt against the Umayyad rule. After crossing the great Arabian Desert and nearing Kufa, messengers warned him to head back to Mecca but he went on with his journey, still hoping to inspire an insurrection. As he approached Kufa with his family and companions, each new traveler brought increasingly dire news from Kufa. The poet Al-Farazdak, who crossed paths with him in the desert, told him "The heart of the city is with thee ; but its sword against thee."[202]

Despite the warnings, Hussein continued on his fateful journey to Kufa. The anniversary of events that followed is commemorated as the mourning of Ashura for the Shi'ites. On this day today, hundreds of thousands of Shi'ites throughout Iran, southern Iraq, and Lebanon participate in a ritual of sacrifice. It is considered the greatest day of mourning in the Shi'ite calendar. The story that follows is one that every child in Iran learns and is as important a part of the Iranian culture today as the death of Jesus is for Christian cultures.

Nearing Kufa, Hussein, his family, and companions approached the city along the western shore of Euphrates as 4000 strong Umayyad cavalry followed and watched his every move. Refusing to take orders to surrender or head back to Mecca, Hussein pitched his camp 25 miles from Kufa in a field called Karbala, which today is considered one of the holiest sites in Shi'ite Islam. Fearing that his commander would not take the necessary action against the prophet's grandson, the governor in Kufa ordered a tyrannical commander and violent man named Shimr to go to Karbala and to bring Hussein to Kufa either dead or alive. As a reward for ridding the Umayyad family of its greatest threat, Shimr was promised the governorship and revenues of the Rey province in Iran.[203]

On the 8th of Moharram, as the new commander approached the fields of Karbala, Hussein, along with his family and companions stood their ground and refused to submit. What followed was just another version of the age-old human tragedy in which leadership is attained through bloodshed rather than reason, dialogue, and the will of the people as expressed in free elections. It is the same story repeated in today's Iran where the tyrannical regime, proclaiming itself the bearer of Hussein's flag, employs the same means of violent oppression against the people, students, journalists, and activists who question its rule.

On the 9th of Moharram, anticipating the great violence that was to be inflicted on his family, Hussein asked for a day of respite, during which his family could be taken away to safety. He offered his family members and companions the opportunity to leave him and take safe passage back to Mecca. No one was willing to leave. His companions now cut off from the water of the river formed their tents and encampment into a circular barricade against the several thousand cavalry surrounding them. That evening, Hussein's sister Zeinab came into Hussein's tent wild in grief and inconsolable. Hussein's son Ali was suffering from a fever as a result of the weeks of harsh travel across the desert and the abrupt denial of access to water. The deprivation of water to succor the sick is regarded by Shi'ites as a symbolic, unforgiveable act against the prophet's sick great grandson, a gesture of cruelty that continues to burden and fracture the unity of the Islamic world.

I grew up watching the Shi'ite processions of *Moharram* marking this day. Like my parents and grandparents, I have watched grown men weep as this story was repeated in increasingly emotional contexts. Yet it seems the lessons of violence are lost and the same culture of political violence has reshaped itself with new names, new heroes, new cries and new hopes. Those who hold the sword today are armed with more advanced weaponry and have modern tools of propaganda at their disposal. Yet, the same rules of violence that determined the fate of this generation determine my generation's fate as well.

On the morning of the 10th in the month of *Moharram*, Hussein repeated his demand to be taken to the caliph for a private audience but was again refused. Finally, stepping forth with his companions, he walked forward, sword in hand, accepting his destiny. There was a moment of stillness that was followed by a single arrow shot by one of the men in the encircling cavalry. Then came a shower of arrows, which fell on the women and children of Hussein's family. Kazim, nephew of Hussein, ten years of age, was one of the first to die, pierced by an arrow while in his uncle's arms. All around them, cousins and nephews of Hussein were falling from the onslaught of arrows. The scene became even more horrifying as the reeds around the camp were set on fire and the flames spread to the tents. Hussein, who had been separated from his family, was shot by an arrow. Shimr, who led the attack on Hussein, trampled his body with his horse and then cut off his head with his sword. Hussein's head, together with those of seventy of his companions, were then taken to Kufa and paraded through its streets.

CHAPTER 3

In the palace of Kufa, as governor turned the head of Hussein with a staff for a closer look, an aged voice from the onlookers was heard crying "Gently ! It is the prophet's grandson. By the Lord! I have seen these very lips kissed by the blessed mouth of the prophet"[204] Hussein's sister, Hussein's feverish and sick son Ali (known as the 4th Shi'ite Imam), and his two daughters were the only survivors of the massacre and along with the grisly trophy of Hussein's head were sent to Yezid in Damascus. Accounts of the horror and terror at Karbala were related by the few survivors and spread by word of mouth through the cities of Medina, Mecca, and Kufa. Today, images of this symbolic mourning are broadcast by CNN and the BBC as hundreds of thousands of Shi'ite men and women beat their breasts in processions on Ashura while crying "Hussein, Hussein, Hussein!" It is a powerful symbolic religious reminder of the extent of sacrifice made by Hussein and it helps create the culture of self-sacrifice and martyrdom seen today in Shi'ism.

Yet Hussein, who stood up against the Umayyad regime and became a symbol of resistance to tyrannical regimes, has today been used by just such a tyrannical regime to shore up its legitimacy and justify the violence it freely employs to retain power. The continued exploitation of this important cultural symbol by the current regime will gravely injure and distort the meaning and interpretation of Shi'ism for generations of Iranians to come and can threaten the elimination of such cultural symbols— and ultimately the Shi'ite religion itself— from Iranian culture. Iranians who are aware of this power of symbols must remind others that Shi'ism is threatened— and not by Europe, the United States, or the Sunnis— but by the regime that continues to use religion as a political tool and as an instrument of terror and violence.

The Umayyad decades after the death of Hussein are known as the dark ages of Iranian history where most acts which could symbolize the Iranian culture were deemed un-Islamic by the regime and censored or destroyed. Prior to this, 49 generations of Iranians had experienced war, rebellion, and violence without a single generation living continuously in peace. For the 50th, 51st and 52nd generation of Iranians living under the Umayyad regime, violence included foreign occupation by people speaking a different tongue, rulers who were bent on proselytizing their religion yet perhaps with the real motive for wealth and power. The occupation required the prohibition of any symbolic act deemed un-Islamic or threatening to oppressive regime in power acts, thus music, dance, painting, sculpture, and celebrations were banned.

A new classed society emerged with the Arab governors, their families and soldiers occupying towns and cities across Iran as the ruling elite. Iranians who accepted Islam had lesser rights in society and were called *mawali* (plural of *maula*). They were not allowed to hold positions in the bureaucracy and when they walked on the streets, they were required to walk a few steps behind their Arab superiors. Those who remained committed to their Zoroastrian, Christian, and Jewish faiths were third-class citizens, with even fewer rights, forced to pay *jaziya* tax, and tolerated in society. Then there were the Buddhists, Manichaean, and Mazdakites who were systematically extirpated as idol worshipers and the faithful of unaccepted faiths.

Tens of thousands of Iranians were held as slaves within palaces of Damascus, Kufa, Basra, and Medina. In each town and city of Iran, an Arab governor called *amir* was placed in power with several hundred soldiers as the military occupying force and in charge of crushing dissent and local rebellions. A *qazi* was assigned as a judge enforcing Islamic law on all citizens. A man was placed in charge of tax collection and referred to as *dehqan*. This position which required the ability to speak Iranian tongues was often held by an Iranian convert to Islam. Governors of Basra and Kufa each placed sent their sons, cousins and uncles in charge as governors of various Iranian provinces. In many towns and villages of Iran, one still finds mausoleums called *Imamzadeh*, which are respected by Iranians as tombs of the Hashemite family members, though they are more likely the tombs of Umayyad governors and *amirs* sent to these regions as the officials in charge of the provinces.

Umayyad regime was also not content with the size of the empire and would repeatedly order further military expeditions justifying further violence in the name of Islam. Islamic forces crossed the Oxus River and captured Bukhara during the Umayyad rule. Samarkand was captured shortly later.[205] During this further expansion, violence against newly acquired people was just as horrifying as before. Yazid ibn Muhallab, in his expedition to expand Islamic rule in Khwarazm in Central Asia removed the clothing from his prisoners and kept them in the fields outside the city until they froze to death.[206] Qutaiba's son, another Umayyad general, in the year 708CE, crucified thousands of inhabitants of Taleqan. Despite the iron hand of Umayyad rule, rebellions were common, signifying the popular hatred for the Muslim occupation, especially in the far eastern provinces. In the southeastern province of Sistan, Muslims were called followers of *Ahriman* (the devil), which inspired constant local rebellions, fighting, and violence.[207] In Qom, when the local population rose up against the occupiers, the heads of members of prominent Zoroastrian families were cut off.[208] Slave markets flourished in Kufa, Basra, Balkh, and Merv as thousands of new slaves arrived with every Islamic victory and crushing of rebellion.[209]

These events and the use of violence in the name of Islam are painful to hear for most Muslims, but are deep cultural wounds that resurface constantly as forms of fundamentalisms through the likes of Khomeini or the Taliban, who continuously attempt to recreate the totalitarian state of this period. Most Ayatollahs in Iran favor the banning of music, dancing, and the arts, in imitation of similar prohibitions in early years of Islam. The fear of western culture amongst many Muslims is also a contemporary version of the Umayyad regime's fear of infection by non-Arab and non-Islamic cultures. In that era, it was Iranian music and arts that were suppressed through violence. Today, versions of European, American, and other cultures of the West are those attacked and suppressed on the streets of Iran.

Just as the Umayyad period, those in power through violence use totalitarian means to force the population into submission. Such fundamentalist views, attempting to recreate the culture of early period in Islam, fuel anger and hatred which in turn, often get directed towards Islam itself and the spiritual beliefs of Muslims. Thus the battle for freedom gets mistakenly directed against religion rather than violence. The struggle for democracy and human rights in Iran is the struggle to realize that the underlying source of despotism, totalitarianism, corruption, injustice, and inequality is violence itself.

Over a period of 89 years, Yezid was succeeded by his son, Mu'awiyah II, who was succeeded by others of the Umayyad family, all of whom continued to hold power through the use of violence. Three generations lived in the dark decades of Umayyad rule. In order to overcome this era in their history, Iranians united around a young leader who picked up a symbolic black flag as his banner of defiance. The young leader was named Abu Muslim and within several years of raising his flag, hundreds of thousands of Iranians, mostly from the Khurasan province in the northeast joined him to rid Iranians of caliphate's rule in Damascus.

Abu Muslim Khurasani

Not much is known of Abu Muslim's childhood. He was a *malawi*, an Iranian convert to Islam considered a second class citizen by the Umayyad regime. Some sources speak of him learning the trade of saddle-making as a youth.[210] Some claim he was from Merv, others speculate he was from Isfahan. Countless retelling of his story generation after generation from grandparent to grandchild would redefine his life not as a historical figure, but as an important Iranian symbol, which within Iranian culture would attain mythological levels. Centuries later, in Iranian taverns and teahouses, the legendary tales of *Abu Muslim nameh*, inspired by his life, would become the most popular recited Iranian narrative, surpassed only by the epic tales of Ferdowsi's *Shahnameh*. He continues to be an incredibly popular figure in today's Iran with even the popular soccer team of Khurasan named Abu Muslim.

During his lifetime, there were numerous attempts at dethroning the royal family in Damascus. Within the Arab world, the main opposition to Umayyad family rule came from members of the prophet's Hashemite family, many of whom continued to favor the rule of Ali's descendants and would ultimately form the Shi'ite faction of Islam. But within the Hashemite family, opposition to Umayyad rule also came from another branch of the family, those who were the descendants of the prophet's uncle, Abbas.

Abu Muslim, nineteen years old at the time, is said to have been discovered and recruited in a prison in Kufa by members of Al Abbas family. It is not known why he was imprisoned or how he was released. From prison, he was taken to Imam Ebrahim, the underground leader of the Abbas family and then, along with the funds made available to him, sent to Khurasan to take advantage of anti-Umayyad sentiments there and to recruit soldiers for an insurrection against the regime.[211]

Abu Muslim traveled from city to city in Khurasan calling on people to rise and fight against the Umayyad rule. He asked his supporters to wear black as a symbol of their struggle and soon displaying black became a symbolic gesture whereby an ordinary citizen could proclaim his or her allegiance for the uprising.

Letters were sent to various cities of Khurasan calling on people to wear black, place black parchments on the walls and windows of houses, and prepare to celebrate the advent of Umayyad regime's demise.[212] Soon, people began to join Abu Muslim from many cities. Nearly all the opponents of the Umayyad regime in Khurasan joined him in his call including the powerful Zoroastrian families and youths. At one point, fighters were pouring into Abu Muslim's camp from 60 different towns and cities.[213] Within seven years after his call for an uprising, he had created an army of black-clad soldiers who were prepared for war.[214]

Soon, the Muslim world was divided into those who wore black signifying support for the Hashemite and Abbas family versus the supporters of Umayyad family, who continued to use the green color of Islam as their symbol. This separation of Islam signified by colors continues to this day. One can still easily identify the black flags, headgear, and hejab across the Shi'ite world extending from northeast Iran to southern Iraq and amongst the followers of Hezbollah in Lebanon.

Abu Muslim's army soon took over Merv, one of the largest cities of Khurasan and a military stronghold. Then, one by one, all the cities in Khurasan were out of Umayyad hands and, for the first time in a century, in the hands of Iranians.[215] The young general then ordered his army to march toward the seat of the Umayyad caliphate. In Kufa, the two armies met and the Umayyad's army of 100,000 was defeated. Most of the defeated soldiers were killed as they fled. After the defeat, the Umayyad caliph first fled to Damascus and then to Egypt, where he was killed. The members of his family throughout the empire where either killed or fled to Spain where they established the caliphate of Cordoba lasting until 1031CE. Thus ended the Umayyad era, perhaps one of the most divisive periods in the history of Middle East.

After the defeat of the Umayyad army in 749CE, Abu Muslim, leading the largest Muslim army of his time, installed Abu Abbas Safah, the heir of the Al Abbas family, as the Caliph in Kufa while Abu Muslim stayed in Khurasan to govern the Iranian provinces.[216] The brother of the new Caliph in Kufa, Mansour, suspecting that Abu Muslim would eventually use his power to install himself as Caliph, warned his brother many times of Abu Muslim's powers and popularity, but his brother ignored him.[217] Five years later, Mansour himself became Caliph of the Islamic world and was determined to rid himself of the threat of his popular general and governor in Khurasan. After repeated invitations, Abu Muslim finally agreed to leave his stronghold in Khurasan and come to Kufa as the guest of the new Caliph. Unaware that a plan to murder him had been set in motion, Abu Muslim spent his first night as the Caliph's guest without incident. In a story that has been immortalized in Iranian culture, it was on the second night of his stay when Mansour instructed ten of his guards to hide inside the host's chamber. There, while visiting the military leader, Mansour asked Abu Muslim if he could see his sword. The moment sword was handed it over, signal was given and Caliph's men fell upon Abu Muslim and stabbed him to death thus ending the Iranian threat to Islamic Caliphate rule.[218]

Abbasids

The rise to power of Mansour of the Abbasid family occurred during the lifetime of the 53rd generation of Iranians. Damascus, which was the seat of power during the reign of the Umayyad family, was not suitable as a capital for the Abbasid Empire because of the strong Umayyad influence in the city. In addition, having the seat of government in Damascus made it more difficult to keep control of Iranian provinces of Fars, Azarbaijan, Khurasan and Sistan in addition to Central Asia, which was the battleground for the advancement of Islam. Thus Kufa, in Iraq, was made the capital. Yet Kufa did not have the infrastructure required to house the vast bureaucracy needed to govern an empire extending from Morocco to Central Asia.

Mansour was advised to build a new capital and situate it capital in a place between the two great rivers of Euphrates and Tigris. These rivers could serve as defensive barriers and the location was a more suitable one than Damascus as a center for control. Mansour personally picked a site near a Sassanid village, the name of which for Iranians meant 'God-given'. He was assured by the Iranian villagers that the area enjoyed cool, pleasant nights and was not infested by mosquitoes, a real problem elsewhere in the Fertile Crescent. The land chosen for the site of the new capital was across the river, thirty miles from the abandoned grand city of Ctesiphon.

Drawing on his incredible wealth, the new Caliph oversaw the creation of a new city and infrastructure, one suited as the capital of an empire, unlike any previously seen. Over 100,000 craftsmen were employed from across the empire.[219] The grand palace of Khosrow in Ctesiphon, with the largest brick dome ever built, together with the smaller palace of Qasr-e-Shirin in Iran inspired the Caliph to have his palaces and mosques built in the architectural style of brick dome, one of the grand achievements of Iranian architecture perfected in the building of Ctesiphon.[220] Thus the dome, a favored design of Sassanid architects, was introduced as the predominant feature of the palaces and mosques of the new city and ultimately those throughout the new Islamic Empire.

The grand city was to be called Medina-al-Salam or the City of Peace. Unlike most ancient cities built in a square pattern, the new city was built as a circle with concentric palaces and buildings moving closer and closer to the center. In the center of the city, the palace of the Caliph was to be built with a grand green dome serving as a landmark for any traveler who came in sight of the city. Atop the dome, the statue of a horseman was placed. The grand mosque was built next to the palace. Without access to adequate quarries, hundreds of thousands of large bricks were made, some weighing as much as two hundred pounds. The outer defensive wall of this grand, circular city was built 90 feet high with a 75 feet wide base narrowing to 37 feet at the top.[221] Up to 160,000 giant bricks were used on each course of the wall, some weighing as much as 200 pounds. Huge iron gates were brought in or forged for the four main gates of the city. One of the iron gates was brought from Damascus and was thought to have had Pharaonic origins. Another was brought by barges from a nearby ruined city in Mada'in. The workers were told by the natives that it had been made during the time of King Solomon.[222] A water moat was built around the impenetrable 90 feet high walls of the city with underground canals supplying the water from the river.

Within the Medina-al-Salam or City of Peace, grand buildings for each ministry was to be built modeled on the structure of the previous Sassanid bureaucracy.[223] Unlike the previous Umayyad regime, the new Abbasid regime changed its policy on the status of Iranians and Iranian culture. For the first time since the birth of Islam, Iranian converts to Islam were allowed to work as ministers. Sassanid ministerial procedures, bookkeeping and traditions were resurrected and Persian aristocratic families were employed for the day-to-day running of the empire. Most notable of these were the Barmakites, who were brought in from Khurasan and would serve as ministers and prime-ministers of the Caliph for generations, helping to resurrect the grandeur of the Sassanid court under an Abbasid name. In addition, Iranian music, dance, arts, and wine banned for four generations under the previous fundamentalist Umayyad regime, were once again allowed by the new Caliph who was creating a grand capital of an empire in which a mixture of the best of Arabic and Iranian cultures would form the basis of a new Middle Eastern culture.

The city of Medina-al-Salam or City of Peace was to mark the birth of a new civilization in which the knowledge of the world was to be collected in its libraries and taught in its universities. Translators were hired to convert the texts of every available book from Latin, Greek, Hebrew, Pahlavi, and Sanskrit into Arabic. Arabic, as the official language of the empire, became a vital means of communication between scholars and scientists as far away as Central Asia and Spain. Formerly persecuted Jewish and Christian physicians, scholars, and scientists were allowed to work and publish in the new city, thus attracting much of the intellectual wealth of western civilization. Publishing houses were created where books were read aloud while dozens of scribes copied the originals and mass produced books on mathematics, engineering, architecture, astronomy, medicine, literature, philosophy, religion and mysticism. Books from this city were to be exported across the empire and into libraries as far as Spain and Bukhara.

Bridges were built across the Tigris and Euphrates to ensure easy passage for the thousands of caravans bringing goods from east and west. The stories told in hundreds of inns and taverns by travelers from India and China to Europe were collected and published as books of fairytales and travels, the most famous of which were the eighteen volumes of collected ancient Iranian accounts, as well as Arabic and Middle Eastern stories and fairytales told by Scheherazade (Shahrzad) the story teller.

Even before the completion of its outer walls, vast fertile lands in the suburbs of the city were purchased by the citizens and aristocratic families of the empire who were populating this grand capital, helping to create one of the largest and most populous cities in the world of the Middle Ages and the capital of new Islam. The city was constructed from scratch on a scale greater than anything in human history.

Prayers were read by the Caliph while the great city was ordained with its official name of Medina-al-Salam. Yet the tens of thousands of builders, architects, and workers (who were mostly Iranians) never referred to it by its official name, always referring to it as Baghdad, the Persian name of the nearby Sassanid village meaning God-given.[224]

Thus the city of One Thousand and One Nights was born.

Violence continues in Abbasid Era

The building of Baghdad by the new rulers of the Islamic Empire did bring about an intellectual and cultural renaissance, but it did not usher in a new period of tranquility and peace. The assassinated Abu Muslim became a symbol of valor for Iranians as others trying to fill his shoes fought again and again in Khurasan to avenge his death and reclaim their independence from the Islamic Caliphate. Khurasan was humming with rumors that Abu Muslim was alive and hidden in the Alborz Mountains waiting to return on the day of judgment, all of which fueled further Iranian rebellions against the Caliph. Sinbad, a Zoroastrian and a close personal friend of Abu Muslim, as well as many other associates and supporters, were intent on reviving Iranian independence from the Islamic caliphate. Sinbad's followers and their families, who together numbered 60,000, defeated the governor of Ray south of today's Tehran and took over the local governor's arsenal.

Soon, volunteers and fighters began pouring in from Mazandaran across the Alborz Mountains and along the coast of Caspian Sea as well as cities in Khurasan, swelling his army to 100,000. On the fields outside the city of Ray, Sinbad's army met the army of Mansour of the Abbasid family and suffered such a crushing defeat that the bones and remains of Sinbad's soldiers were still visible, according to a historian in the Islamic year 300, nearly two hundred years after the slaughter. The women and children of the men in Sinbad's defeated army were taken as slaves.[225]

Another rebellion was led by a man named Ostad Asis, a Zoroastrian who some claimed as a prophet. His supporters in Khurasan were said to have numbered 300,000 citizens.[226] In his battle against the Abbasid armies, over seventy thousand of his followers were killed and another fourteen thousands were taken as slaves.[227] In Mazandaran, a vast, violent uprising broke out against Arab occupiers with so much hatred and anger fueling it that it led to the slaughter of many Arabs settlers in the region as well as many Iranian converts to Islam. Some women forced to marry Arabs against their wishes were seen handing their husbands over to be killed.

Yet the rebellions were defeated one by one including those led by Vendidad Hormoz and Shervin. Caliphate's commander, Yezid ibn Mohleb, who crushed the rebellions was then given the governorship of Gorgan as his prize. To quell the uprising, he had promised to shed a river of blood in Mazandaran so great that it could turn the waterwheel of a mill. It is said that he did just what he vowed.[228] A man named Maghneh, who claimed to be a prophet, led a violent rebellion in Khurasan.[229] Ravandian was a movement aimed specifically at killing Mansour and avenging death of Abu Muslim. Violent uprisings in Damavand and Taleqan were more violently crushed around the same time.[230]

Prior to his death, Abu Muslim proudly claimed that his soldiers were responsible for the death of more than 100,000 of his enemies. The total of those killed in the numerous uprisings in the generation after Abu Muslim's assassination far surpassed that. Thus the 53rd and 54th generation of Iranians endured one of the most traumatic periods in Iranian history, more violent than what their grandparents and great grandparents had experienced under the dark rule of the Umayyad regime.

55th Generation of Iranians

This generation, whose grandparents lived during the rise of Abu Muslim, grew up hearing stories about the courage of the young Khurasani leader. During their years however, another courageous, symbolic hero would come to the fore and become a mythological figure for Iranians. When he was executed in public, legend has it that when one of his hands was cut off, he used the other hand to wipe his blood off his face and defiantly stated that he did not want to see his face hung on the city gates 'yellowed in fear'. For twenty years, the insurgency led by him exploited the mountainous terrain of Azarbaijan to wage guerrilla warfare and annihilate soldiers in one Abbasid garrison after another. When cornered, his followers would ascend to the safety of their fort atop the Qaradaq Mountain in eastern Azarbaijan where the Abbasid soldiers could not withstand the cold winters and were repeatedly forced to retreat.

A thousand years later, in the struggle for democracy and human rights in today's Islamic Republic, on the anniversary of this legendary figure's birthday on June 29th, hundreds of young and old Azarbaijanis leave their towns and villages and climb to the peak of the mountain where his fortress stands and where his legend of resistance endures.

Every year, security forces of the Islamic Republic also converge at the foot of this mountain and attempt to disrupt this pilgrimage— but the power of a cultural symbol prevails and people overcome their fears to climb to the summit, a place UNESCO has recognized as a world heritage site. The power of this cultural symbol inspires resistance and resilience, even in the face of vicious repression, and, each year, revives a culture of courage and strength for Iranians.

Those who make this perilous pilgrimage relive the experience of 50 generations before them. The pilgrims find, when they reach the ruins of the fort high in the green mountains of Azarbaijan, that the legend of Babak, the hero of the 55th generation of Iranians comes alive.

Babak

Even prior to the collapse of the Sassanid Empire, those in Azarbaijan who called themselves *Khorramdinan* had been fighting to maintain their distinctive culture and the freedom to practice their religion. *Khorramdinan* or followers of 'joyous religion' believed in Mazdak's revolutionary ideas of communal life, which had been suppressed by the previous Sassanid regime.

After the Arab invasion, these followers continued their struggle to resurrect Mazdak's philosophy and blend it with the old Zoroastrian traditions to create a neo-Mazdakite *khorramdin* religion.[231] Even before the rise of Babak, two Arab chroniclers spoke of the rise of *khorramdin* followers in the more central cities of Rey (Southern Tehran) and Hamedan (formerly Ecbatana). Abu'l-Ma'ali and Mas'udi mention 100,000 and 200,000 supporters of *Khorramdin*, indicating the tremendous following and strength Babak later enjoyed during his rebellion.[232] Historians consider Babak not as the founder of this movement, but its last adopted leader.

The *Khorramdin* fighters were called the Red Warriors. This symbolic color played an important communicative role just like the color black used by Abu Muslim. Here again is a reminder of the importance of symbolism for a successful movement or struggle. Symbols such as a color help with communication and their relative ease of reproduction allows people to easily express themselves and their allegiance.

During Babak's rise to power within the *Khoramdin* movement, his followers began taking control of cities and villages in Azarbaijan and freed these regions from Islamic Caliphate rule. These insurgents used the mountains and the geography of Azarbaijan to their advantage against the Caliphate armies who were more accustomed to fighting on the plains or in the desert. Thus, the repeated attempts of Caliphate armies to fight the insurgency and guerrilla warfare of Babak produced defeated armies who failed to take control of Azarbaijan for Muslims.

For 20 years, the Abbasid Caliphate kept sending garrisons and armies to Azarbaijan and each time they were defeated and forced to withdraw. Massoudi tells us that over the 20 years of rebellion by Babak, over 200,000 of Abbasid soldiers and government officials were killed.[233] This figure, which appears difficult to believe, nevertheless reflects the immense threat of the Azarbaijani insurgency to Abbasid Caliph during the lifetime of the 55th generation of Iranians.

In the year 836CE, the Caliph sent an army to put an end to Babak's rebellion, one led by an Iranian commander named Afshin who had allied himself with the Abbasid Caliphate. Afshin managed to surround Babak in his mountain fort. Despite the horrifying winters of Azarbaijan, for two years Afshin persisted in his pursuit, while the Abbasid Caliphate kept sending reinforcements of soldiers and supplies. Babak's besieged followers and soldiers kept fighting, even while suffering from the shortage of food and the cold. The constant stream of reinforcements finally forced Babak and 50 of his men to flee one night to Armenia in an attempt to reach Byzantium. In Armenia, Babak was caught and sent back to the Caliph. It is said that the Caliph was ecstatic on finally seeing him in chains. He ordered his two hands to be cut off in public before his execution. His feet were cut off next and his body was displayed hanging from a gibbet in Samara. Later, his head was toured around the Islamic empire for show. The legend maintains that Babak was calm and defiant when his hands were cut off in public. It was here that he announced when his dead body was put on display be did not want people "to see the yellowed color of a man in fear, but Babak wearing red in pride."[234]

Abbasid Caliphate in Baghdad - Continued

While the insurgency in Azarbaijan swirled around those of the 55th generation, the rest of the Islamic Empire was also in turmoil.

Mansour's son Mahdi became the heir to the Caliphate in the year 774CE. During the eleven years of his reign a genocidal campaign led to the complete expulsion and extermination of the Iranian Manicheasts. Manichaeism was soon completely wiped off the map of Middle East. His reign was followed by Harun al-Rashid, the fifth Abbasid Caliphate and perhaps the most famous of all in this period. He is well known for the intellectual and artistic flowering that took place during his reign, including the building of the Bayt al-hikma library (House of Wisdom). He lived luxuriously in a court distinguished by a galaxy of musicians, poets and scholars. Yet he used religion extensively as a political tool and called for a military Jihad nearly once a year. During his reign, his wars in the name of his Islamic Empire reached the Bosporus and Cyprus. He had a deep hatred for the Shi'ites and is famous for bringing Imam Mousa Kazem, the Shi'ites' seventh Imam to Baghdad, where he died as a prisoner of the Caliph. Towards the end of his rule, rebellions broke out in the northeast provinces of Khurasan; they were not quelled until after his death. [235]

Harun's twenty three years of reign, known for prosperity in Baghdad, ended in 809CE, and his chosen younger son, Al-Amin, became Caliph and the governor of western lands that include today's Iraq. His older son, Al-Ma'mun, born to an Iranian concubine, was named the governor of all eastern lands, which included Iran. Iranians soon accepted Al-Ma'mun as one of their own and gave him the title of the 'son of our sister'.

Ma'mun was also chosen by Harun to be the heir to the Caliphate after Al-Amin's death. But the struggle for power between the two brothers, balanced on the heels of violence, soon gave way to fraternal bloodshed. Al-Amin denied his brothers right to the Caliphate and ordered the Friday prayer leaders to praise his sons rather than his brother. Finally, Al-Amin, in control of Baghdad, ordered his brother to relinquish control of the Iranian provinces. Upon Ma'mun's refusal, Al-Amin named his son heir-apparent to the Caliphate and ordered his general to march to Khurasan.[236] Al-Ma'mun, due to the loyalty of his brilliant Iranian general, Taher, had successive victories over Al-Amin and captured the city of Baghdad, in the course of which the Caliph was killed.

In 821CE, during the lifetime of the 56th generation of Iranians, after the 20-year civil war in Abbasid lands, Taher became the governor of all Caliphate lands east of Iraq, thus serving as the governor of Iran. This powerful Khurasani governor and general effectively handed the throne to Al-Ma'mun of the Abbasid family, a transfer of power similar to that carried out by Abu Muslim several generations before. Upon return to Khurasan, Taher began leaving the name of Ma'mun, the Caliphate of Islam, out of the Friday prayer. In 821CE, he even minted coins that did not bear the Caliph's name, a virtual declaration of independence of Iran from Baghdad and Abbasid rule.[237] But such acts could not be tolerated by Baghdad and the general died within a year, most believe of poisoning.[238]

Despite his death, Taher's governorship over Khurasan was a pivotal point in Abbasid and Iranian history. From this point on, the Caliphate in Baghdad allowed the Iranian Taherid family to rule over Iran, but only while its members continued to acknowledge the Caliph in Baghdad as the legitimate religious leader of Islam.[239]

The political violence continued in Iran during the 56th generation of Iranians and the reign of Taher's son, Talha. In the South East province of Sistan, rebellions by Kharijates were put down by the Tahirids. Upon Talha's death, the Islamic armies crossed the Oxus River into central Asia against a local ruler, Afshin Kawus, in lands that were still only partially Islamized.[240]

Over the next few decades, Taharid's armies went farther into Central Asia than any other previous Muslim force in order to forcibly convert the mostly pagan Turks. Thousands of Turkic captives were taken to the cities of Bukhara and Samarkand and sold. From the wholesale slave markets of these cities, they were sent to Baghdad and other cities to serve the wealthy class in charge of the Islamic Empire. In the ninth century, the heavy demand for slaves caused prices to rise across the region. In this early phase of the biggest slave trade in history of Middle East and the second largest in human history after the African trade during the colonial era, the Tahirid family was in control of the traffic. The expansion into Central Asia and institutionalization of slave trade is the legacy of violence for the 56th generation of Iranians.

The year 839CE, just one year after the execution of Babak, also marks the birth of another generation of Iranians. During the lifetime of this 57th generation, Mazyar, a recent convert to Islam and the local ruler of Tabarestan (Mazandaran), the province on the southeastern shore of the Caspian Sea, refused to pay tribute to Tahirid family in Khurasan, thus causing another civil war.[241] Mazyar allied himself with Afshin Haydar, the general famous for his capture of Babak and his battles against Byzantium. The Tahirid family was forced to send an army to the Caspian coast to put down the Iranian rebellion and capture Mazyar.

Mazyar and Afshin were sent to Samarra for a trial and accused of sympathy for the un-Islamic religions of Manichaeists, Buddhists and pagans in Central Asia. They were accused of the desire to see "the Arabs and Turks abased and the ancient glories of Persia restored."[242] They were executed and their bodies hung from the same gate on which Babak's mutilated corpse had been displayed two years previously. [243]

In the 25 years of life of the 57th generation, insurgency, uncertainty, and turmoil ruled the region as the Tahirid family and the Abbasid family relied on the sword to claim legitimacy for their rule and to enforce stability in their domain. Aside from the nationalist Iranian inspired insurgencies such as those of Babak, Mazyar, and Afshin, other insurgencies were instigated by Shi'ites, the most significant of which was the rebellion of the Zaid family along the Caspian coast. Rebellions also took place in Qazvin and Zanjan. Tahirid tax collectors were expelled from Gorgan and the city of Ray was held briefly by the insurgents.[244] Thus the fate of another generation of Iranians, the 57th, was determined by strife and violence.

Yaqub

The 58th generation of Iranians continued to live in the same turmoil as all the generations that came before.

In the southeastern province of Sistan, a charismatic soldier and a military commander named Yaqub Leis or Yaqub 'the lion' won a string of victories against Caliphate forces and attracted enough followers to encroach on the Tahirid stronghold of Khurasan. In 873CE, after 50 years, or two generations of Tahirid rule in Khurasan, Yaqub managed to capture Nishapur and expel the Tahirid king from the city.[245] Prior to becoming a soldier, Yaqub had been a copper-smith and since copper in Arabic is called *saffar*, Yaqub's family ruling over southeastern Iran was referred to as the Saffarids.

The employment of Islam as a political tool for attacking and plundering non-Islamic lands continued under Yaqub in the mountainous region of today's Afghanistan and Pakistan. Yaqub spent a decade fighting native non-Islamic rulers and for the first time successfully expanded Islam into this mountainous region all the way to the borders of India.[246] Again, violence in the name of Islam justified the looting of gold and silver from Buddhist and Hindu temples in towns and cities of the region. The spread of Islam east was popular throughout the Abbasid lands as spoils of war were sent as presents to the Caliphate in Baghdad. On one occasion, fifty gold and silver statues were collected from temples in Kabul and sent to the Caliph in Baghdad, who in turn sent them to Mecca.[247] The exotic looted statues of Hindu gods brought to Baghdad were cause for great excitement for the people which helped popularize further wars and conquests.

By 875CE, Yaqub had control of Sistan and Kerman in the southeast, portions of Afghanistan in the east, Khurasan in the northeast and had extended his control to southwestern city of Gundishapur, thus frightening the Caliph, who tried to appease Yaqub by granting him dominion over all lands formerly held by the Tahirid family and vowing that his name would resound in the prayers of the faithful in Medina and Mecca.[248] Yet Yaqub, who, unlike the Tahirids, for the first time made Persian the language of his court and refused to be addressed in Arabic, marched on to Baghdad. Along the Tigris River, 50 miles from the capital, he was dealt his first major defeat, thus saving Baghdad from capture. After the battle, the rich central province of Fars, in addition to the eastern provinces, remained within the Saffarid control. Yaqub died three years later from an illness in 879CE.

Unlike the Tahirid family, the Yaqub and later Saffarids were completely independent of Baghdad. His resurrection of the Persian language in his court is considered a vital step in the eventual preservation of Iranian identity and later the resurrection of Iran as a country. Though Yaqub's decision represented a victory for Iranian culture, his struggle for power meant that Iranians of the 58th generation, like those in generations past, lived out their lives in a climate of violence.

Over the next several decades, unremitting violence and war continued between the Saffarid family, the Zaid family in Tabarestan (Mazandaran), the remnants of the Tahirid family, the new rising power in Transoxania, the

Samanid family and the forces of Abbasid caliphate in Baghdad. There was not a single year during the lifetime of this generation in which an army was not seen marching across Iran, fighting another for control of the population and resources. Those decades were filled with numerous battles, plunder, rebellions, and insurgencies.[249]

After 22 years of near constant fighting, in an attempt to capture the land of Khwarazm, east of the Caspian Sea and northeast of Iran, Amr of the Saffarid family was decisively defeated by the Samanid forces. He was captured and sent to Baghdad as a prisoner where he was killed in 902CE. With his death, the Saffarid family, after 40 years of rule, faded from Iran. Khurasan was captured by members of the Samanid family, which would maintain control over its population and resources for generations. Fars was later captured by the Abbasid forces of Baghdad. Members of Saffarid family retained control of Sistan for several more decades until those provinces were also taken by the Samanid family.

Thus the 59th generation of Iranians, like every generation that came before, spent their lives and much of their resources attempting to determine their fate through violence.

Samanids/Ziyarids/Buyids

The Samanids, who first rose to power in Transoxania and later made Khurasan their center of power, claimed to be descendants of the aristocratic family of the great Sassanid general, Bahram Chubin.[250] During the tumultuous century of warfare between Tahirids, Saffarids, Ziarids and Abbasids, the Samanids planted the seed of their growth in the lands of Khwarazm, its capital of Gurganj near the Aral Sea and the cities of Samarkand and Bukhara in Transoxania. The Samanids greatly extended their frontiers into Central Asia, becoming one of the main players in the trade slave of Turks across the Middle East and at the same time securing their cities from the raids of Turkic tribes in Central Asia.

The Samanid rise to power took place during the lifetime of the 59th generation of Iranians and their children in the 60th generation. In addition to lands in the northeast, the Samanid family also took control of Tabarestan (Mazandaran), Ray and Isfahan.[251] Within a few years, Zaidi Shi'ite revolts broke out in Tabarestan and Gorgan, continuing the course of violence engrained in the culture. In 914CE, the murder of the Samanid ruler brought to power his eight-year-old son, who was advised by a capable and learned vizier, Abd-Allah Jaihani. The family was thrown into turmoil. Civil war broke out between the forces loyal to the child against forces allied with his uncle, with the child emerging victorious. Many provinces, including Ray and Tabarestan, had to be reconquered.

Jaihani was deposed as minister eight years later after being accused of Shi'ite sympathies and Manichaean dualistic tendencies. In part due to the efforts of this learned vizier, Jaihani, and his successor, Abu'l Fadl Bal'ami, Bukhara became famous as a center of learning throughout the Islamic world. Among the most notable of those who brought it into such prominence was the great poet Rudaki. For the first time, the Persian language was written in Arabic script by this generation of Iranians, giving rise to the formal structure of the language still used today in Iran. Books written in the city together with those collected from across the Islamic world were gathered in the impressive library of Bukhara. The literary rise of the Persian language began with the efforts of this 59th generation living under the Samanid rule.

The 60th generation of Iranians, entering the world in 915CE enjoyed the fruits of the artistic, scientific and religious renaissance that their parents had helped foment. But for them, their legacy was also of violence. In 930CE, Mardavich Ziyarid, a descendent of a royal family in Gilan that traced its ancestry back to the Sassanid era, defeated the warlord in control of Qazvin and later conquered Ray, Zanjan, Abhar, Qum and Karaj. [252] He was murdered as he was making preparations to conquer Baghdad with the intention of crowning himself king in the former Iranian capital of Ctesiphon and resurrecting the Sassanid Empire. [253] After his death, a peace treaty with the Samanid court was nullified and fighting resumed in the northern and northeast territories of Iran. This conflict between the Ziyarid family of Mardavich and the Samanid went on for decades.

Mardavich's Ziyarid family was also a patron of the arts and sciences. Their court, like the Samanid, attracted famous poets and scholars from all across Iran, including two of the greatest Iranian scholars and thinkers, Ibn Sina (Avicenna) and Biruni. Much of the grandeur of what some consider a golden era was due to the patronage in arts and science during Ziyarid and Samanid rule. Like the Samanids, the members of Ziyarids were also Sunnis who did not allow religious freedom for Shi'ites. [254]

While Samanids were occupying Khurasan and Transoxania, and Ziyarids remained in charge of northern and central provinces, the Buyids, another Iranian family and adherents of the Shiite sect, managed to take possession of the South.[255] The Buyid's rise to power came after several attacks on the still Khorramite population of Azerbaijan, during which a number of fortresses and valuable spoils of war were taken.[256] The proceeds from plundering enabled them to hire a larger mercenary army, which eventually led to their capture of Baghdad. While allowing the Abbasid Caliph to retain his title, the Buyids took complete control of Baghdad and the Abbasid Empire.

Thus with Samanids in the northeast, Ziyarids in the north and central provinces and Buyids in the south and in Baghdad, Iranians for the first time were occupying the seats of power in all territories formerly of Sassanid dominion. The Buyids revived old royal Sassanid traditions and for the first time, referred to themselves as *Shahanshah*, or king of kings, the title given to Achaemenid and Sassanid kings. Those in the 60th, 61st, and 62nd generations, considered the golden age of Iran in terms of the arts and sciences, lived in a time of continuous civil war between these various Iranian families. This golden age was not the result of violence, but, incredibly, took place despite internecine strife. These wars between autonomous warlords and kings ended with the rise to power of a Turkic family in Ghazni (in today's Afghanistan) during the lifetime of the 63rd generation of Iranians.

***

The slave trade of 'infidel' Turks from Central Asia also reached its zenith in this era. While skin color was used to justify enslavement and slave trafficking during the colonial era, the proselytizing of Islam was used as a tool for the despicable enslavement of human beings. Army after army marched into Central Asia with the stated intent of islamicizing the Turkic people, who were Buddhists, Manichaests or practitioners of more primitive and ancient tribal religions. Turkic men, women, and children were then separated from their families and sold in the slave bazaars of Bukhara and Samarkand where wholesalers would often buy a number of slaves for transit to the slave bazaar of Baghdad. Everything was taxed, even the costs of transporting slaves.

Those enslaved served in roles ranging from domestic servants, concubines, and administrators to soldiers. Books were written on how to determine which slaves from which Turkic tribe would be suitable for such different roles. The most desirable slaves were those deemed capable of serving as administrators or soldiers. Enslaved Turkic children were sent to special schools to be taught either administrative or military skills; this schooling would allow them to eventually dominate the Samanid society, attaining the highest positions in the government and military. In the mid-10th century, a Turkic military leader named Abu Mansour Sabuktagin, whose parents were raised as slaves, became powerful enough to appoint himself the governor of Khurasan. Several years later, he was forced to leave his position after the splintering of Turkish factions within the government. He left for the city of Ghazni in what is today eastern Afghanistan. His son Mahmud, upon coming to power overthrew the Samanids and established the first Turkic dynasty ruling over Iran.

Shahnameh

It is important to pause for a moment and discuss an event that was to influence every generation of Iranians hereafter. This event was not a war or an assassination. It was the creation of a great work of literature. It was the fulfillment of the dream of many Iranian scholars who attempted to gather the scattered pieces of Iranian mythology and epics into a single volume called *Shahnameh*. It was the most important cultural project in the 2,500-year history of Iran and it took place during this Samanid era of artistic and scholarly renaissance.

The revival of Persian language in its new form during the Samanid era created an intense thirst for learning about pre-Islamic Iranian history and mythology. The *dehqan* class, who were the land owning aristocrats of the time, were still preserving the memory of the Iranian legends, history, cultural celebrations and mythology. But this class of Iranians was quickly withering away. Fewer and fewer children were able to read the Pahlavi script of the Persian language and, in the absence of a systemic effort, Iranian oral history and epics that stretched over time from the mythological creation of the world to the end of the Sassanid dynasty, were fast fading from memory. Khurasan was the historic center where the bulk of material about Iranian legend, mythology and history was still present. Hamza al-Isfahani in the beginning of the 10th century wrote:

"As regards the Persians, their dispersed [historical] accounts and reports and their scattered stories concerning lovers, were turned into verse for their kings, registered in books and permanently deposited in storehouses which were libraries. The number of these books assembled was so large that it cannot be specified. Most of them were lost when their kingdom disappeared, though remnants of them survived, the number of which exceeds 10,000 sheets written in their Persian script."[257]

The most important of these epic accounts was a compilation written at the end of the Sassanid era called 'Khwaday-namag', the 'Book of Kings'. This book was translated into Arabic at the time but has since been lost. [258] With the development of the new Arabic script for the Persian language couple of generations before, books and stories written in the old script were disappearing. With the renaissance and renewed interest in Iranian culture during the Samanid era, however, there was a rush to keep such stories, considered by Iranians as pillars of their culture, alive. Abu-al-Muayyad Balkhi was one of the first to write a *'Shahnameh'*, the story of Iranian mythology. Only fragments of his book, written in prose, have survived. Another *Shahnameh*, written by the scholar Abu Ali, has also been lost. We have only a record of its existence at the time. The governor of Tus commissioned another *Shahnameh*. Only the preface of this work remains, declaring that the full text was written by four Zoroastrian scholars who pulled together many sources to make a concordance of the work. All of these works were in prose.

In an effort to ensure survival of the material, the Samanid court commissioned a gigantic project to write the entire Iranian mythology in verse. This task was assigned to a poet named Abu Mansur ibn Daqiqi. But he was killed unexpectedly after completing only 1,000 verses of the story. Yet the work was not left unfinished. The same year which Daqiqi was killed, a young *dehqan* named Ferdowsi from the city of Tus in Khurasan began what was to become the most important of the four great works of Iranian literature.

By the time this young *dehqan* completed some 50,000 couplets, he was more than 80 years old, the Samanid regime had passed from the scene, and the new Ghaznavid regime of Sultan Mahmud, who was of Turkic origin, was not interested in the mythological epic of Iranians. Ferdowsi died in poverty and with a broken heart, but his daughter kept the work alive, and his *Shahnameh* became the standard of Iranian language and literature, influencing every poet and scholar of Iranian culture thereafter. This immense work of Iranian mythology is the single most important text that has standardized and kept the written and spoken Persian language constant over 1000 years, a linguistic phenomenon unmatched in any other language. Ferdowsi, when describing his own era and time in Iranian history, spoke of it as a time of never ending wars and violence. Thus, perhaps it was only fitting for him to create a masterpiece lamenting the tragedy of war and violence where at the climax of the Iranian epic, Rostam the hero, upon killing his arch enemy, realizes that his enemy was his long lost son.

CHAPTER 3

Ghaznavids

By the end of the golden 10th century, violence had caused a decline in the state of agriculture and the condition of the countryside across the Samanid state. Land owning aristocrats or '*dehqan*' were impoverished. Mass migrations had occurred from the rural to the urban areas centered around the cities of Bukhara, Samarkand and particularly Nishapur, making them overcrowded metropolises with suboptimal infrastructure for the large influx of peasants looking for work. In order to fund the continuous military campaigns and their bureaucracies, the Samanids were forced to confiscate lands in lieu of taxes, thus reducing the number of taxable lands in their domain.[259]

The nearly bankrupt government and dissatisfaction of the population made conditions ripe for a new political system to rise to power. Mahmud, the son of a Samanid Turkic general who was a former Turkic slave working as a soldier, settled in the city of Ghazni. After a series of battles, he took control of the lands of Transoxania and Khurasan, thus pushing the Samanid family off the political stage. Mahmud made the city of Ghazni, in today's eastern Afghanistan, his capital, which is why his dynasty was later referred to as Ghaznavids.

His thirty-two years of reign, overlapping the lifetimes of the 63rd and 64th generation of Iranians was one continuous campaign of warfare and plundering. He conquered territories stretching from Western mountains of Kurdistan and Azerbaijan to the province of Khwarazm adjacent to the Aral Sea in the north and Ganges Valley of India in the south. As opposed to the Iranian Samanid and Taherid families who plundered and devastated the Turkic population of Central Asia for slavery and wealth, Mahmud, who was Turkic, found unmatched sources of gold and treasure in the Buddhist and Hindu temples of India, giving rise to his title as the great *qazi* (warrior of the faith) and hammer of the infidel Hindus.[260] He was the first ruler to call himself a Sultan, signifying complete independence from Baghdad. He saw himself not only as a Muslim crusader but also as a Sunni crusader, using religion to march against the Shi'ite Buyid family in control of today's southern Iran and Iraq.[261]

His initial conquest of Khurasan provided him with rich farmland and centers of commerce, allowing him to further fund his military campaigns. During his subsequent campaign to India, the Qarakhanid Turkic tribe of Transoxania invaded his province of Khurasan, occupying the cities of Balkh and Nishapur. Mahmud was forced to march back from India to purge his territories of the invaders and extend his domain further north and into Transoxania.

In his conquests, he is most famous for his horrendous military campaigns in India. Every winter, his armies would march south into India, plundering the countryside and searching for temples filled with golden treasures. Soldiers rampaged through homes and captured the 'infidel' Hindus to be sold as slaves. One by one, the Indian kingdoms were overrun. Mahmud's campaign in 1025CE was perhaps the most devastating where he led his army across the Thar Desert of India to the Somnat peninsula along the shores of Indian Ocean. There he discovered the great and famous temple of the Moon-God Mah-a-deva. The building was more than a thousand years old at the time and one of the great centers of pilgrimage for Hindus. It was endowed with income from 10,000 villages and unsurpassed in the amount of treasure it contained. An Islamic chronicler wrote:

"December 1025... The Indians made a desperate resistance. They would go weeping and crying for help into the temple and then issue forth to battle and fight [to the death]. The number of slain exceeded 50,000. The king looked upon the idols with wonder and gave orders for seizing the spoils and appropriating the treasures."[262]

News of the Sultan Mahmud's triumphs made him a hero of Islam; news of his conquests spread to Baghdad and beyond. All in all there were seventeen invasions of India by Mahmud. The gold and silver plundered from India provided extra currency for circulation within the Islamic world, thus stimulating trade across Iran. Splendid buildings were built in Ghazna. In addition, tens of thousands of Indian slaves flooded the Islamic slave markets of the Middle East. In one expedition alone in 1018CE, 53,000 Indian enslaved captives were brought back and sold in Ghazna.[263] After each return from India, slave merchants from all across the Muslim world would gather in Ghazna to purchase slaves for sale throughout their provinces.

The violence of warfare and conquest by Sultan Mahmud of Ghaznavid was the legacy of the 63rd and 64th generation of Iranians. His son Masud, who came to power in 1030CE, was also a soldier. He continued his father's campaigning in India, leading expeditions to previously untouched provinces. Meanwhile his hold on Khurasan was weakening due to the rise of the Seljuqs, a new, powerful Turkic military force in Transoxania. Masud attempted to rid himself of the Seljuq threat through execution of many of their leaders in 1033CE. However this turned Seljuqs into bitter enemies of

Ghaznavids leading to several Seljuq military victories and finally to the defeat of the Ghaznavid army in the battle of Dandanaqan in 1040CE near Merv which ended the Ghaznavid rule in Khurasan.[264]

By 1054CE, Seljuq forces were advancing into Anatolia and a year later Sunni Seljuq armies captured Baghdad, ending the Shi'ite Buyid dominance of the Caliphate. For the first time since the Sassanid era, the territories extending from the Oxus River in central Asia to Tigris River were under a single ruler. Warfare and violence continued as Seljuqs marched into Armenia and Georgia, plundering the cities and countryside as well as the rich province of Cappadocia, home to St Basil's Church in today's Turkey. In 1068CE, Byzantium was invaded and the cycle of violence and warfare continued.

In 1094CE, the grand Seljuq Empire disintegrated into several pieces and in the following year the first Christian crusade took place. The 65th and 66th generations of Iranians lived during chaotic times as civil war raged within the Seljuq family over control of territories in today's Iran, Iraq and provinces in Anatolia.

The breakdown of central authority by the Seljuqs meant turmoil and anarchy in cities and towns across Iran. When describing the lives of this generation, "Page after page of the work of the historian Ibn-al-Athir," writes Richard Frye, "are filled with accounts of bloodshed and rapine."[265]

In 1156CE, upon the death of Seljuq ruler in Khurasan, a new Turkic power in Khwarazm in Central Asia took control of Khurasan. In 1194CE, the ruler of Khwarazm, known as Khwarazm-Shah, defeated the last Seljuq Sultan of Hamedan. The last Seljuq Sultan of Kerman abandoned his throne after his province was overrun by Ghuzz Turks. By 1212CE, the Khwarazm rulers filled the void left across the region by conquering provinces that were near the Tigris River. Five generations of Iranians, the 67th, 68th, 69th, 70th and 71st lived during these times of unending civil war. Violence, as always, was inseparable from politics. The political fate of every Iranian generation until now had been determined by the sword.

The Mongol Invasion

In the 13th century, Europe had just passed through the centuries known as the Dark Ages. Much of the immense heritage of Greek and Roman science and philosophy had largely passed into oblivion or been lost in Europe through centuries of warfare and religious intolerance. Yet in the Middle East, despite its never-ending cycles of violence, human beings had managed to reach a new peak of development in the arts and economic systems. Hundreds of great libraries were sited across the region. Many schools and hospitals were built in these centuries. Perhaps one of the greatest of all places on earth at the time in diversity of knowledge, particularly in science and philosophy, were the lands northeast of today's Iran, in today's countries of Turkmenistan, Tajikistan, and Uzbekistan. Over 200 towns and cities existed in this region, notably the cities of Samarkand, Bukhara, and the capital of Khwarazm at Gorang (Urgench), each with populations of hundreds of thousands.

The European crusades in 12th century had greatly changed trade across the world. In was no longer safe for the great caravans of China and India to travel to the Mediterranean Sea. Thus the caravan route was diverted north through Russia and Ukraine and traders had to travel through the kingdom of Khwarazm. These caravans, which often numbered up to 5,000 camels together with 2,000 merchants, would leave China for the long journey west to the cities of Bukhara and Samarkand, where they were met by similar caravans from the South bringing Indian goods and caravans from the southwest bringing goods from Iran and the Middle East. Goods would be unloaded at the great bazaars of Bukhara and Samarkand and new ones loaded onto the camels. Before heading to Europe, all the caravans would converge on the Khwarazm capital of Gorganj (Urgench) adjacent to the Aral Sea as their last great stop before Russia.

There are several undisputed lessons of history, one of which is that where trade prospers, civilizations flourish. These cities experienced tremendous growth and a renaissance thanks to the merchants coming from all points of the compass. The taverns and teahouses were lively and filled with wealthy merchants during their sojourns. They enjoyed ample entertainment, food, and wine and exchanged information on safe routes, bandits, and political changes in lands as far as away as Korea and the British Isles. The great cities of Tus, Nishapur, Merv, and Herat in Khurasan had also flourished, becoming industrial and agricultural centers providing goods for the merchants who made their way along the 'Silk Road'. Ray and Shiraz in central Iran had each undergone a renaissance in the arts and sciences as well.

In the year 1199, during the lifetime of the 71st generation of Iranians, the Sultan of Khwarazm died and his power was handed down to his son Mohammad as was the usual custom of Iranian monarchy. Upon taking power, he continued in the same tradition of his forefathers, ruling as a despot and waging war on neighboring states. Violent rebellions against his

CHAPTER 3

rule also continued in the same fashion as before, including one in the city of Samarkand where rebels began killing members of Khwarazm family. It is said that after the rebellion was crushed, 10,000 people suspected of being rebels were killed.[266] Within 10 years of taking power, Sultan Mohammad employed brute force to take control of Mazandaran and Kerman in addition to Khurasan. He led a military campaign west to the Zagros Mountains and was preparing for an attack against Baghdad while even dreaming of conquering China. He was the most powerful of all kings in the region and, as is often seen in history, with his power came the culture of self-worship typical of such leaders.

In the lands east of Khwarazm, vast plains spread out all the way to China in the East, Siberia to the North, and the Himalayan Mountains in the South. These great plains were dotted by tens of thousands of nomadic tribes, most of them Turkic in the West and Mongolian in East.

In the winter of 1215CE, Sultan Mohammad Khwarazm-Shah had taken his army on an expedition to the land of today's Kyrgyzstan to attack several Turkic tribes living there.[267] In this campaign, he came across an army headed by a Mongolian named Jooji who was chasing bands of Tatars. Upon seeing the Iranian king and his forces, Jooji sent Khwarazm-Shah a message saying that he had no ill intentions towards them. He told them that he had been given orders by his Khan only to chase and wipe out certain bands of fighters. Khwarazm-Shah, who was drunk with power, sent a reply to Jooji that all non-Muslims are '*koffar*' or infidels and he did not discriminate or give special privileges to one 'koffar' tribe over another. Thus he ordered his army to attack Jooji's forces as he watched from a distance.

The battle had no clear winners. Jooji's Mongolian army disbanded and escaped back to the East. But how these Mongolians fought the battle made a strong impression on the Shah. It is said that for weeks he was preoccupied with this battle, often speaking of the great skills Mongolians had shown in archery, swordsmanship, and horseback riding.

Within a year, news reached Iranians that the Mongolian tribes have been united under a Khan called Genghis, who has led the Mongols in the conquest of Tibet and Beijing, the capital of China.[268] In order to confirm this news, Khwarazm Shah sent a delegation to China to see firsthand what had happened and who was in control. One of the members of the delegation wrote in his journal that upon reaching the first city in China, they saw a great mound in the distance from a far. As they drew near it, they kept wondering what it was. When they reached it, they found that it was composed of human skeletons.

On reaching the capital of China, they came across a path soiled and blackened repeatedly from what they thought at first as some sort of oil, only to find out later it was human blood. For three days they walked along this path until they reached the capital. In the city, they witnessed a mount of skeletons on the side of a tall building and were told that the Chinese hurled 20,000 of their women and children from this building to prevent them from becoming slaves for the Mongolians.

Genghis Khan respectfully accepted the delegation and sent a message to the Shah that he wanted them to be partners in peace. "Say ye unto the Khwarazm-Shah," Genghis Khan told the delegation, "that I am the sovereign of sunrise, and thou the sovereign of the sunset. Let there be between us a firm treaty of friendship, amity and peace, and let traders and caravans on both sides come and go."[269] He told the delegation that he had secured the routes along the 'Silk Road' and wanted his caravans to head west and engage in trade. Khwarazm-Shah, filled with a self-worshipping sense of his power and majesty, responded contemptuously to Genghis Khan's message. His delegates had been dispatched to collect intelligence only and not to establish trade relationships.

Shortly after this exchange, 450 Mongolian traders started on their journey west with goods ready for trade. With them they brought gold, silver, silk and other luxury goods. On crossing the great Mongolian plains, the first Iranian city they came across on the eastern edge of Khwarazm kingdom was the city of Otrar. There, the Amir of the city ordered the goods confiscated and the merchants killed. Only one merchant made his way back to China, bearing the horrible news of his companions' fate to Genghis Khan. The Great Khan sent another delegation, this time to Khwarazm-Shah himself, asking him to turn over the Amir of Otrar for the crime he had committed. Khwarazm-Shah refused and killed the members of the new delegation. With this outrage, the violence which the 72nd generation would experience would be unlike any other in human history and not repeated at such a scale until Hitler in the 20th century. With this act, a chapter in Iran's long history closes and a new one begins.

CHAPTER 4 –100 GENERATION LEGACY OF VIOLENCE- PART III: THE GENOCIDES AND VIOLENCE OF TRIBAL CENTURIES

> *"Of the seven Turkic tribes that supported the young Ismail, the Qajar tribe would continue to dominate Iranian politics into 20th century."*

Genghis Khan

In 1219 CE Genghis Khan began his march west from Mongolia with an estimated army of 150,000-200,000 men.[270,271] It is thought that at the time there were an estimated 600,000 soldiers scattered across hundreds of cities and towns on Iranian plateaus. In addition, if needed to deal with a desperate situation, an additional 2 million young men and boys could have been recruited from the cities, villages, and farms across the region.

In his campaign to overwhelm and control all the Mongolian tribes and conquer China, Genghis Khan had perfected the use of violence. In preparation for the invasion of China, he had inspected thousands of Mongolian camps. In each one, women were busy manufacturing arrows while the men performed military drills on horseback. His heavy cavalry wore armor created from four layers of specially woven silk and leather making it impenetrable to light weapons. The outer layer was lacquered for protection against rain. Each soldier was equipped with a curved sword for close combat and a lance to attack enemy cavalry. The light cavalry carried two bows and a javelin, one bow used while on horseback and the other on foot when greater precision over a longer distance was required. Each soldier carried three quivers filled with arrows; one was filled with arrows specially designed for piercing armor. Each soldier also carried a kettle, a ration of dried meat, and a water-tight bag. With them they also had a change of clothes, which could be inflated and used in crossing of rivers. Each Mongolian soldier, in addition to his own horse would at times take 2-3 other horses on the journey to carry supplies and increase the speed of movement forward. Occasionally some of the horses were slaughtered for their meat. [272]

In addition to the perfection of tactics, the defeat of China had led to the development of valuable siege technology by the Mongolians. Among the most effective were battering rams, scaling ladders, and four-wheeled mobile shields. They also had with them counterweight trebuchets able to sling objects (such as boulders) weighing up to 140kg over the walls and into enemy cities, a device later used by the Mongolians to sling plague infested corpses into besieged cities, the first form of biological warfare. From China they also acquired flame-throwing tubes, and huge double and triple siege bows that could punch holes in city walls from hundreds of yards away. Such weapons were carried on wagons and on camels for the 1,500- mile journey across Asia. [273]

Genghis Khan made sure that each Mongol soldier was fully aware of the murder of the 450 merchants and hungering for revenge. The Mongolians' rallying cry was, predictably, "Let us ride out against the Islamic people, to gain vengeance!"[274]

Before an army could be assembled, Khwarazm Shah who had little in the way of talent in military matters and who had ascended to the throne merely by virtue of birth and his family's use of brute force, fled west with his retinue of servants, slaves, and the women totaling 20,000 persons and abandoned his provinces, leaving them without leadership.

Genghis Khan and his army arrived and first captured the city of Otrar, the same city whose Emir (or governor) had killed the men in his delegation. Despite the immense strength of the Mongolians and their siege weapons, the citizens of the city held off the siege outside their walls for five long months.[275] Mongolians were finally able to breach the city's defenses after a senior commander attempted to flee from a side gate. After he was caught and killed, the Mongolians broke in through that same gate. The Emir fled to the central citadel and fought for another month with several hundred of his guards, until all were out of arrows and killed. The governor then fled to upper levels of citadel where he and others trapped there began throwing tiles and bricks at the Mongolian soldiers.[276] After his capture, he had molten silver poured into his eyes and ears and was then tortured to death. The citizens of Otrar were either killed or taken as slaves. The city was flattened into rubble and rediscovered by archeologists 800 years later.[277] Genghis Khan's armies were then divided and sent with instructions to plunder and destroy towns and villages in the region.[278] The Khan, accompanied by Tooli, another of his sons, took the main portion of the army and headed towards Bukhara, one of the two jewels of Central Asia.

Bukhara rivaled Baghdad in splendor. With a population of hundreds of thousands, it was called the 'dome of Islam in the East'. Its scholars, writing in both Arabic and Persian, made this city, along with Samarkand, centers of commerce, knowledge, philosophy and the arts in Central Asia. Its royal library housed 45,000 books, with each room devoted to a different discipline. A traveler and historian who had visited the city called it the "meeting-place of the most unique intellects of the age."[279] Students and scholars would flock to the city from all over the Middle East to study in its colleges.

In between the near constant cycle of violence, the citizens of the city had managed to build wide city streets paved with stone.[280] The great mosque of the city was an architectural masterpiece with a minaret 47 meters tall. Given the numerous earthquakes in the region, the structure was built on an inverted pyramid foundation made of cement 10 meters deep and allowed to harden for three years. A layer of reed was then placed atop the foundation as shock absorber. Created by master architect Bako, it was the only building to survive the Mongolians and remained the tallest building in Central Asia for seven hundred years.[281] Legend has it that upon seeing the great minaret of the mosque, Genghis Khan announced: 'This structure is the first thing I've ever bowed to.'"[282]

For three days, the Mongolian army surrounded the city. Faced with choice of starvation or possible escape, the city's garrison of an estimated 20,000 attacked the Mongolians but was soundly defeated and slaughtered to the last man. Without further hope, the citizens surrendered and opened the gates to their vast city for the invaders.

The city's storehouses were opened to feed the Mongolian warriors and their horses. The Khan then asked the citizens to identify and bring him the richest men. Two hundred and eighty were sent forth and for each, the Khan assigned a bodyguard in order to ensure they were robbed by the Khan or his generals and not by the ordinary Mongolian troopers.[283] The buildings in the city, most built of wood, were then set ablaze. In the end, one of the only structures that remained standing was the main city mosque, which was made of stone. Genghis Khan then had the men in the city separated and forced tens of thousands of them to follow the Mongolian army on foot as slaves. As they were separated, the men were forced to watch as Mongolian soldiers, who had been without their women for months, raped or enslaved their wives, and children. "Deeds were done there which baffle description. Every possible outrage was enacted before those to whom it was most dreadful to be present."[284] Except for those who could serve as slaves, the remaining citizens were then systematically slaughtered.

Bukhara's libraries and universities, housing countless handwritten books, products of a civilization's achievement in science, literature, and philosophy, were destroyed overnight, along with hospitals, bazaars, palaces, and infrastructure. The few surviving citizens had nothing left except the clothes on their backs. Many managed to flee this carnage. One of them who arrived at Khurasan was asked what has happened. He replied using five Persian words meaning "they came, they destroyed, they burnt, they killed, and they left". [285] For Iranians, these five words describe the Mongolian horror more succinctly and more completely than any other words.

Genghis Khan and his army did not conquer and occupy cities; they destroyed cities and killed or enslaved their citizens. The entire population of a city was usually escorted into the plains outside city walls and either killed or taken as slaves. Mongolians had no use for cities as they felt uncomfortable within the confines of a building.

The Khan next headed toward the city of Samarkand. A jewel and pride of Iranian history, Samarkand was built like many other ancient Iranian cities with an inner citadel and an outer suburb. The city encompassed an area of forty-four square miles enclosed by a wall measuring twenty-seven miles long.[286] Fresh water was supplied to its citizens via eight canals branching into 680 channels, with the flow of water in each regulated by a gate.[287] This abundant supply of water allowed virtually every house to have a garden with fruit trees and roses. The cypresses and elms of the city were famous throughout Iran. [288]

There were over 100,000 households in the city, making an estimated population of more than 500,000. Aside from being a major stopping point for caravans, Samarkand was also an industrial center. Famous silk and cotton textiles were made in the nearby valleys. Arms and metal work were important exports from workshops near adjacent coal mines. But the city was most famous for its production of paper, supplying the great thirst for books flourishing in Iran and making its way west all the way to Europe and east as far as Korea.

In the waning months of the winter of 1220 CE, just prior to the new year celebration of Nowruz, the Mongolian army could be seen approaching Samarkand. When they neared the city, Genghis Khan ordered the slaves on foot to stay behind and sent only a portion of his cavalry forward. The soldiers garrisoned to defend the city were estimated between 50,000 to 100,000 soldiers. Upon seeing the much smaller force of Mongolian cavalry nearing the gates, tens of thousands of infantrymen streamed through the city's gates to attack. Genghis Khan ordered the cavalry to withdraw until the

CHAPTER 5

Samarkand soldiers were well away from the city. He then ordered the remainder of his army to attack the rear. The entire Samarkand garrison was massacred as hundreds of thousands of absolutely horrified citizens of the city watched from across the city's walls.[289] The great city of Samarkand was now defenseless. After surrounding the city for some five to ten days, the Mongolians were able to force their way in.

The destruction at Bukhara was repeated. Nearly the entire city was burnt. Its citizens were ordered to leave and go into the plains outside the city. From the citizens, 30,000 men were separated to serve again as additional slaves and to provide labor for siege warfare and diversion of rivers for future attacks. Fifty thousand were permitted to go back to their ruined city after paying two hundred thousand gold pieces to the invaders. The rest were slaughtered in the plains.[290] Several hundred managed to survive by hiding underneath the thousands of corpses strewn over the plains.

Genghis Khan's sons were then each ordered to go from city to city and town to town on the northeastern Iranian plateau and in Central Asia and unleash a tornado of destruction and massacre, the likes of which the world had never seen before. Another unit of 30,000 was ordered to hunt and kill the Shah. Within a year, cities and states that were unique in the 13th century in terms of population, knowledge, sciences, and economy were no more than ruins dotted with millions of corpses of the 72nd generation of Iranians.[291] It was an immense, desolate landscape of burnt villages, and destroyed farms and gardens.

The Mongolian unit chasing the Shah arrived in Balkh and then in Herat, two of the major four cities in Khurasan. Upon reaching the city of Balkh, the terrified citizens brought gifts and presents to the invaders and asked to be spared. Upon reaching the city of Zaveh, the population closed all gates and refused to provide food for the invaders.[292] Having instructions only to capture the Shah, the Mongolian unit was about to head west again, leaving the city intact when the cheering population of the city was seen climbing the walls and beating their drums. This angered the Mongolians, who momentarily abandoned their pursuit of the Shah in order to devastate the city. It was stormed and every single citizen killed. The Mongolians took whatever they were able to carry and left the city in burning ruins.[293]

Upon hearing that the Mongolians were in Khurasan, the Shah fled from Nishapur to the city of Rey, just south of today's Tehran. There he was met by an Iranian force of 30,000 ready for battle. The Shah was told there are enough resources to raise an army and crush the pursuing Mongolians. In addition, the ruler of Lorestan invited the Shah to come to his mountainous area where he had an army of 100,000 familiar with the terrain and able to outmaneuver and defeat any Mongolian army.[294] Yet the panicking Shah was also paranoid and feared that the ruler of Lorestan intended to take his place as the most powerful Shah in the region. Thus he refused his help.[295] At this time news came that the Mongolian army had reached Rey, massacred its citizens, and destroyed the city.[296]

Nearly all of the 20,000 people in Shah's entourage were killed as the Mongolians caught up with them. The Shah survived and fled to the mountains with a few of his remaining followers. The Mongolians, thinking he was escaping to Baghdad, searched that route for days. But the Shah headed north and found his way to the shores of the Caspian Sea. When the Mongolian army reached him there, he boarded a boat with his companions and sailed to a small, isolated island where he soon after died alone with his servant.[297]

The Mongolian army chasing the Shah pushed ahead with its destruction and massacres, rampaging through Azerbaijan, Armenia, and Georgia and circling the Caspian Sea north on the way back east, the only army to ever accomplish this task. Another Mongolian army reached Urgench, the prosperous former capital of the Shah along the Aral Sea with a population of hundreds of thousands.

The Shah's mother, who was still in control of the city, decided to leave and, before doing so, ordered all the political prisoners and imprisoned members of the royal family killed so they could not claim the throne once the Mongolians had destroyed the city.[298] The Mongolian army, thought to have numbered more than 100,000, entered the city after an incredible six months of siege and numerous attempts to destroy the city walls. The fertile soils of the province did not have sufficient rocks to supply the catapults of the Mongolian army, so the Mongolians had to hurl mulberry trees at city walls. Unable to breach the defenses, they turned to hurling burning naphtha into the city and diverting the river to force the citizens out from thirst. Finally, upon breaching the walls, savage combat between the Mongolians and the city's citizens ensued neighborhood to neighborhood for seven days and seven nights. Scenes of violence and fighting were seen on the streets, on rooftops, in people's yards, and in their living rooms. Since the Mongolians were unable to gain control of the entire city, they built a dam upstream and diverted the river to flood the city. After days of fighting and flooding, there were only three neighborhoods of the former capital remaining intact. The entire city was ultimately destroyed and the exhausted survivors forced to surrender.

The Mongolians separated thousands of craftsmen, blacksmiths, architects and artisans and sent them as slaves on foot to Mongolia and China to help build their towns and cities. The rest of the city's inhabitants were taken into the surrounding plains and massacred. The number of citizens killed is unknown, but the death toll certainly must have added up to hundreds of thousands. All were killed in little more than a week. After the massacre of those outside the city, the Mongolians then went back to the city and destroyed all remaining structures. Today the ruins of Urgench found in the desert are all that remains of the once thriving city and are now protected by UNESCO as a world heritage site.

While he was razing the capital, news reached Genghis Khan that the people of Khurasan were rebelling and fighting the Mongolians. He sent one of his sons to devastate the province. He himself went to Balkh and then to the city of Merv where 80 Mongolian soldiers had been captured by the local governor and paraded through the city. By the time he reached the city, he was furious at the population's resistance.

Merv was another of the jewels of Khurasan. Its ten libraries are thought to have contained 150,000 books. It was in the city's observatory that Omar Khayyam did much of his work on astronomy and where he resurrected Iranian solar calendar. The city measured 100 square kilometers. Within the city, each house had a garden and each garden was supplied with water from underground tunnels supplied from a reservoir created by a nearby dam across the River Murgab.[299] It was described as a city of mosques and mansions. The glittering dome of Sultan Sanjar's mausoleum, covered with turquoise tiles, could be seen by travelers one day's march away. [300]

Tens of thousands of refugees fleeing the destruction of their towns and villages had taken refuge within the city and were living in the streets. Upon its capture and as he had done with many other cities, the Khan ordered the terrified and psychologically paralyzed citizens to leave through the city gates and gather in nearby plains. In the cold February of 1221, it took four days for the hundreds of thousands of citizens to leave. Then the killing began. The wealthy were tortured to make them reveal where their treasures were hidden and killed once the treasures were found. Except for 400 artisans taken as slaves, Mongolians ordered every single person killed, including children. Some 500 people avoided being killed by hiding underneath the corpses and ruins for days.

When the Mongolians left, a cleric and few other citizens who had survived the massacre began examining the aftermath. Juvaini tells us:

"He now together with some other persons passed 13 days and nights counting the people slain within the city. Taking into account only those that were plain to see and leaving aside those that had been killed in holes and cavities and in the villages and deserts, they arrived at a figure of more than one million three hundred thousand."[301]

Western historians hesitantly quote this figure and regard it as improbable. Even if the number of those killed totaled a fraction of the figures given by Juvaini, the massacres in each city in Khwarazm or Khurasan alone would make it one of the most horrific acts of violence in history, only rivaled by equivalent acts using modern technology and weapons in the 20th century. Today's city of Merv is built thirty miles from the ruins of the former city.

Of all the massacres, the one taken place in Nishapur in Khurasan is the most infamous. Known for its rose gardens and heavenly climate, Nishapur, since its foundation by King Shapur during the Sassanid era, had become a prosperous city and province. Ralph Fox writes: "Every day the caravans brought in great stores of merchandise for its wealthy merchants and, as a manufacturing center, it was without a rival in the Muslim world."[302] Genghis Khan gave one of his armies an order to capture the city. In the battle that ensued, the citizens refused to surrender and fought off the Mongolians. An arrow from soldiers defending the walls successfully reached its target and killed the Mongolian who was not only the general of that particular army, but also Genghis Khan's son-in-law. His pregnant wife, Genghis's daughter was enraged when she heard about her husband's death.

The Khan's daughter ordered the Mongolian army not to leave any living creatures in the city, including animals, and to so thoroughly obliterate it that travelers would never know that a city had previously existed at the site. The Mongolians attacked all sides of the city at once. Fighting continued all day, into the night and until the next morning. After nearly thirty-six hours, there were seventy breaches in the city's walls and ten thousand Mongolian troops within the city.[303] It took Mongolians four days to kill every living being in Nishapur.

Having heard that 500 people had survived the massacre at Merv by hiding underneath corpses, the Mongolian general ordered his troops to cut off the heads of every citizen. Three great pyramids were created of citizens' heads: one of the men, the second of the women, and the third of their

CHAPTER 5

children.[304] The Mongolian army then diverted the river and flooded the ruins until there were no visible remnants of the historical city. Four hundred Mongolians stayed behind to kill anyone who had hidden in the rubble and survived. The Nishapur massacre and destruction today, in the collective memory of Iranians, vividly represents the horror, trauma and destruction of the Mongolian invasion.

After much of Khurasan and Central Asia had been destroyed, Genghis Khan was informed that the citizens of Herat who had previously surrendered to his rule and were spared by one of his sons, had rebelled against the new, harsh conditions imposed by the conquerors. After learning how many of his soldiers had died, Genghis screamed at his sons "If you had massacred everyone in that city like other cities, this wouldn't have happened."[305] He ordered that not a single person be left alive in Herat. The citizens of Herat fought hard, holding back the besieging Mongolians for six months and seventeen days.[306] But starvation ultimately allowed the conquerors to overcome the population. Hundreds of thousands were massacred in Herat. Several days after the massacre, more than two thousand people who had hid in basements and in ruins gathered in the bazaar when the Mongolians sent 3,000 men back into the ruins to kill anyone left alive. A total of sixteen people survived out of a population of hundreds of thousands by hiding for many days in a place adjacent to a steep cliff. Over the next several weeks, twenty-four others from nearby villages who had survived joined them. Forty survivors of the genocide in Herat lived in the ruins of their former city for fifteen years, surviving first by eating human flesh or wheat and barley found in ruined basements and warehouses. After the destruction of Herat, Khurasan, the economic, artistic and agricultural heart of Iran since mythological times, lost its glorious place as one of the centers of Iranian economic production and culture.

Genghis Khan then headed south and destroyed towns and cities in Sistan, Kerman and southeastern areas of Iran. Next, he ventured into Northwestern India and continued his destruction. There, messengers brought him the news that people in Tibet and Northern China had rebelled against him. Because he felt he would not live for many more years, he began to return to Mongolia and ordered all his sons and their armies, still engaged in destroying towns and villages across Iranian plateau, to also head back to Mongolia. He decreed that the countless slaves who had helped him besiege and capture city after city be killed.[307] On his way back to Mongolia, as he passed the city of Balkh, he ordered that all refugees gathered in the ruined city also be killed.[308]

The 72nd generation of Iranians did not experience the usual violence from wars, rebellions, or military suppression inflicted on 71 previous generations. They experienced the almost unimaginable Mongolian genocide, one of the greatest acts of violence in human history and one of the greatest crimes ever committed. Genghis Khan ranks next to 20th century's Hitler, as one of the horrific killers in human history. With the return of Genghis Khan and his sons to Mongolia, the initial campaign of destruction ended with the eastern and northern halves of Iran in ruins. The central cities, the southwestern province of today's Khuzestan and much of the towns and cities within the Zagros Mountains as well as Baghdad, the seat of the Abbasid caliphate, survived the initial destruction.

Genghis Khan died on August 26th, 1227 while fighting a rebellion in northwestern China. He chose his third son, Ogtay to become the Khan of Mongolia and to manage his vast empire extending from the Pacific coast of China to eastern Iran and portions of India. No other general in history had mastered the use of violence quite like him and no other leader before or after was able to create an empire as vast as his.

Ogtay and Hulago

The lifetime of the 73rd generation of Iranians, the children of those who experienced Genghis Khan's genocide, coincided with the lifetime of the children of Genghis Khan. The political violence of the Khan was adopted by his son, who sent a second Iranian expedition to complete Khan's unfinished business. After wreaking havoc in Kabul, Zabolestan (in Afghanistan), Tabarestan(Mazandaran) and Gilan, Ogtay's army had the mission to conquer the 500–year-old seat of the Abbasid Caliphate and one of the remaining wealthy cities of the 13th century.[309]

At the same time, Ogtay Khan sent other armies across different regions of the world. The Mongolians conquered all of northern China and Korea. An army of 150,000 was sent to Europe leaving behind a trail of death and destruction. The Mongolians invaded Russia and Ukraine and managed to go as far west as Germany in the north and Hungary to the south, ultimately reaching the coast of the Adriatic Sea. They were in position to destroy western and southern Europe when suddenly, after making a 6,000-mile journey from Central Asia, a messenger brought news that Ogtay Khan had died. All the Mongolian armies were ordered to head back to Mongolia as soon as possible, including the army that was on the way to Baghdad. Thus Baghdad and much of the Middle East, as well as Western and Southern Europe, escaped this second Mongolian destruction.

Twenty years later, the next generation of Mongolians continued on their violent rampage. Southern China was conquered and an army of 120,000 was sent to the Middle East, led by Genghis' grandson Hulago, to capture Baghdad and finish the business of his grandfather in the Middle East.[310] As the Mongolians neared Baghdad, hundreds of thousands of terrorized citizens fled their farms, villages and towns to take refuge in the capital. After the defeat of the caliphate army in Iraq, the siege of Baghdad around its once impenetrable walls took three weeks, during which the palm trees in the region were cut down and their trunks turned into lethal missiles. Gunpowder technology was also improved and used to fire metal cases filled with shrapnel. The Mongolian army entered the suburbs of the great city, which was overflowing with refugees, and began destroying houses and buildings block by city block, working its way to the city center. For six straight days and nights, Mongolians destroyed buildings and massacred citizens. Mosques, libraries, palaces, parks, and ministries were leveled . The 37th and the last Abbasid caliph, together with 3,000 of his associates, surrendered unconditionally. The key to the 520-year-old Abbasid treasury was handed over to Hulago. Upon seeing the vast treasures of Baghdad and Abbasid family, Hulago asked one of the legendary questions in Iranian history.

After three days of imprisoning the Caliph without food or water, Hulago ordered him to start eating the gold in the treasury. The starving caliph looked at him in surprise and said that gold is not for eating. Hulago then asked him, "Then why did you hold on to this treasure when you could have spent on armies to defeat me and why didn't you use the steel in your palace doors to make weapons for your army and why didn't you prevent me from crossing the Oxus river when I couldn't cross the river?" The Caliph replied, "It was the will of God," Hulago then tells him "Then what is about to happen to you and your family is also the will of your God".[311] The last Abbasid caliph was then rolled up in a rug and trampled to death.

The massacres, destruction, and burning of Baghdad went on for seventeen days. Anyone who had any relationship to the Abbasid family was eventually found and killed. The Abbasid family line was obliterated. After days and nights of horror, the stench and foul air present from hundreds of thousands of corpses and burnt buildings was so strong that it forced the

Mongolian army to leave the city. The estimated number of people killed in that one week in Baghdad is as high as eight hundred thousand people.[312]

Hulago next captured Damascus and left a 10,000- man force to defend the city.[313] The Mongolians then decided to conquer Egypt. Egyptians under the rule of Mamluks had been busy fighting the French in the Crusades for decades, but were forced to divert their armies to fight the Mongolians. In the battle that ensued, the combat-tested veteran Mamluk army of the crusades defeated the Mongolians. It is perhaps the only time a Mongolian army was defeated on the battlefield since the coming to power of Hulago's grandfather, Genghis Khan. Thus Egypt survived the invasion.

Another country that survived the Mongolian invasion, massacres, and genocide was Japan. After the conquest of Korea, the Mongolians boarded Korean and Chinese ships, but a typhoon destroyed much of the fleet. The Japanese, for centuries, referred to this storm that saved Japan from the Mongols as the 'divine wind', or 'Kami-Kaze'. Centuries later, in World War II, Japanese suicide aircraft were also referred to as divine winds or Kamikazes.

The Aftermath of Mongol Invasion

The Mongolian expeditions of Genghis Khan and his sons Ogtay and Hulago were a fatal blow to the desires and dreams of the 72nd, 73rd and 74th generation of Iranians. After the Mongolian invasions, Iranians continued to experience rule of the Mongolian descendants through violence, brutality and cultural disregard for human life. Known as the rule of the Il-Khans, the Mongolian warlords each in possession of a ruined city or town in Iran passed on their rule to their children and later grandchildren. The 75th, 76th, and 77th generation of Iranians lived under the rule of these Mongolian and later Turkic warlords, often under terrorizing conditions. The Il-Khans adopted Islam with a very fundamentalist and extremist view and applied Islamic *Sharia* law, often in terrorizing and Taliban-like manner. These warlords were often at war with each other and jockeying for power. In such circumstances, an ingenious and powerful warlord has the opportunity to triumph over all the others and consolidate the powers of violence under one grand army. Such genius came about in the 78th generation and set the standards for political terror which still continues to horrify Iranians.

***

CHAPTER 5

Tamerlane – 78th and 79th Generation of Iranians

Perhaps nothing in the world is more complex, more intriguing, and more incredible than the human mind. Even more fascinating is the birth of a child whose mind is so exceptional he or she baffles science. When given opportunity and resources, these talented children have the potential to become the Mozarts, Picassos, and Einsteins of the world, and can make an enduring impact on humankind. Yet the benevolent contribution of such human minds to humanity is not a certainty.

A talented child born into a family and culture of peace, may become a Sufi mystic, while another born into a culture of violence, reading the same Quranic text may decide to hijack a plane into a building. Those teaching and instigating such children also each have read the same text yet are nurtured differently and preach different world philosophies. In their ancient Zoroastrian tradition, Iranians believed the universe to be a constant struggle between forces of good and evil. As human beings, they believed our ingenuity and talents can be employed by either of such forces and that ingenuity does not equate benevolence. Each child they believed, depending on the circumstances, can learn to service the forces of either good or evil in the world.

For the 73rd-78th generation of Iranians living in the aftermath of the Mongolian genocide, the destruction of their civilization left them and their descendants with little hope of becoming their society's future engineers, architects, physicians, or philosophers. At a very young age, children were often sent to *madrasas* and taught to read the Quran as the first and sometimes the only instrument for learning.

Amongst the children of the 78th generation of Iranians, two very young children of distinction would surface with the ability to learn the Quran more quickly and more comprehensively than any others. These two extraordinary individuals were not just able to answer Quranic questions, they were able to recite the entire holy book of Quran, page by page, word for word, from beginning to end. Known as '*Hafez*,' (memorizers), these two incredible children would shape the destiny of not just their generation's fate, but the destiny of Iranians for centuries to come.

Born in Shiraz in 1320 C.E., the first of this generation's two '*Hafez*' was Shams al-Din. His father, who is thought to have been a merchant, died at a young age leaving the family impoverished. Shams al-Din did menial tasks to survive as a young boy, later working as dough maker and copyist of manuscripts.[314] As an adult Shams al-Din turned his back on organized religion and devoted his time to the study and worship of love expressed in words. Each of his poems, odes known metrically as *'ghazals'*, display his impressive facility with language and offer a melodic, impressionistic and surrealistic expression of life and love.

> I
> Have
> Learned
> So much from God
> That I can no longer
> Call
> Myself
>
> A Christian, a Hindu, a Muslim
> A Buddhist, a Jew.
>
> The Truth has shared so much of itself
> With me
>
> That I can no longer call myself
> A man, a woman, an angel
> Or even pure
> Soul.
>
> Love has
> Befriended Hafez so completely
> It has turned to ash
> And freed
> Me
>
> Of every concept and image
> My mind has ever known.[315]

Generation after generation, Iranians would learn to recite his words, studying his imagery, and symbolism, using his poems as instruments to shape their culture and outlook on life. He became known as Hafez, and as Iranians believe, wrote of 'life as love'. His denunciation of violence and his impact on Iranians are matched by few. Even during his own lifetime his poems became symbols of an Iranian culture that rejected religious and political fear and violence. His collected works, known as *'divan,'* is the single most influential work of Iranian literature and culture. Today, in homes throughout the towns and villages of Iran, his *'divan'* is often placed in a position of honor next to the family's holy text and read on both celebratory and sorrowful occasions. During his lifetime, travelers and merchants from lands as far away as India brought his verses back with them for those hungry for such impressive literature.

Within a few years of the birth of the first *'Hafez'* a second was born near the historic city of Samarkand. Prior to his birth, his father, a tribal leader and a descendant of Genghis Khan, dreamt one evening of a boy offering him a curved sword. He accepted the strange gift, and swinging it in the air, saw the world illuminated. When he asked his Sheik the meaning of his dream the Sheik replied: "A son will be born to you who, with the might of his sword, will conquer the whole world, converting all men to Islam, and cleansing the earth from the darkness of innovations and error".[316] On April 9th 1336, his son was born and named Timur, meaning 'Steel'.[317]

Timur who also became a *'Hafez'* of Quran as a child, would turn his incredible intellect not as Shams al-Din did, to the study of language and love, but to war and conquest. Timur redefined the culture of terror and violence for Iranians, elevating the use of fear for political rule, and creating horrific means of terrorizing and subduing human beings. His incredibly ingenious forms for instilling fear are widely known today in Iranian society and continue to set the standard on how far a ruler is willing to terrorize and kill to maintain power. He created one of the world's first feared intelligence services with spies infiltrating towns and cities across his territories and was unparalleled in his imagination to invent methods of torture. There is no doubt that the *'divan'* of the first *'Hafez'* and its celebration of love influences the world philosophy of millions of Iranians today, just as it did the 78th generation of Iranians. But it was the philosophy and ingenious use of terror by the second *'hafez'* who instituted the benchmark for the culture of terror still gripping modern Iran and much of the Middle East.

***

In his youth, Timur became known for his prowess as a mighty hunter and fighter. Later he gained prominence as a mercenary. While leading a hired mercenary unit of one thousand in Sistan, he suffered severe injuries and lost use of his right arm and leg. Iranians referred to him as 'Timur-Lang', or Timur the Lame. The name was adopted into European languages as Timurlane and later, Tamerlane.

Tamerlane spent many of his early years gathering fellow fighters to gain control over a town or a province. He was a shrewd and ingenious politician and a master at turning his enemies against each other. After repeated attempts in his quest to fulfill the prophecy of his birth, he captured, with the help of two hundred and forty soldiers, the town of Qarshi in today's southern Uzbekistan, by scaling the city walls in a surprise overnight raid.[318] Not long after, with the help of an ally, he was to capture Samarkand.[319] This was followed by a string of victories against nearby towns and warlords including the conquest of Balkh, where he killed his former ally who had betrayed him in battle, plundered and pillaged the city of its wealth and in a signal of how he was intending to rule through terror, razed the city to the ground.[320] After each victory, the riches and rewards of looting and raping attracted more and more mercenaries and soldiers to his camp.

Even when outnumbered, he used his brilliant mind to overcome or manipulate his enemies into defeat. At times to instill fear in the opposition, he would order his army to light hundreds of campfires across the hills surrounding his larger enemies. Upon the enemy's retreat, his cavalry tied branches from their horses raising dust when they gave chase, creating the perception a larger force was in pursuit.[321]

Through the terror and later conquest of all cities in Central Asia and defeat of all his local rival warlords, Tamerlane's army grew to 100,000 soldiers, sustained by the plunder of cities and provinces. He spent ten years resting in his beloved Samarkand, building a court fit for a king and his army. He summoned the most skilled artisans to his capital, rebuilding and beautifying the city, which was to be his grand possession and jewel.

Like any other conqueror who rose to power through violence, Tamerlane was forced to continue to employ violence to feed his troops. Having overwhelmed the provinces of Central Asia, his next great conquest lay in the capture of the provinces in today's Iran. As leader of an immense and powerful army, he rallied his soldiers. "Now is the time of festival for warriors. You know that a hero's place of rejoicing is the battlefield, that the songs one sings there are war-cries, and that the wine one drinks is the blood of the foe."[322]

CHAPTER 5

Herat in western Afghanistan with its nearby garrison town of Fushanj, was the first large city his 100,000 strong army came across. Upon breaching the walls of Fushanj outside of Herat, he massacred every single person. Rivers of blood flowed through the streets.[323] The previous Mongolian destruction of Herat had occurred during the lifetime of the citizens' great, great, great grandparents, six generations before. But the memory of that destruction must have lingered. When news of Fushanj's massacre reached Herat along with Tamerlane's message that he would raze the walls to the ground and annihilate the entire population unless they surrendered, the citizens submitted without resistance and offered their wealth and treasures to the invader.[324] Systematically and with discipline, the soldiers robbed each home in the city, torturing family members suspected of hiding coins or jewels.

"It is remarkable that there were in this city all sorts of treasures, as silver money, unpolished precious stones, the richest thrones, crowns of gold, silver vessels, gold and silver brocades, and curiosities of all kinds"[325], wrote the court historian Sharaf ad-din Ali Yazdi. Everything was placed on camels and carried away. Scholars, architects, craftsmen and artists were then rounded up and sent to the conqueror's beloved capital of Samarkand.[326] Sarbedaran, an Iranian Shi'ite ruling clan that had rebelled against the Mongols in Khurasan and was the ruling warlords of the region, immediately surrendered to Tamerlane as his vast army marched into their plains.

Tamerlane advanced his army to Mazandaran, along the Caspian Sea, plundering the countryside and further enriching his 100,000 man army. One by one, the people in cities and towns fell to their knees, handing the fruits of a lifetime of economic production and achievement to the plunderers. When the city of Isfizar rebelled against his rule, instead of killing its citizens, he constructed a tower of doom, sentencing them to a terrifying death. Two thousand of Isfizar's citizens were cemented into bricks and mortars of the walls while still alive.[327]

Tamerlane proceeded with his 100,000 strong army to the south-eastern province of Sistan where he had been wounded as a youth and had lost use of his right arm and leg.[328] The region's prosperous capital, Zaranj, mounted a courageous defense where the conqueror's horse was shot from under him and killed. Tamerlane who already harbored a hatred for the city responsible for his injuries during his youth, became enraged, showing no mercy with the enemy. "He then laid the city waste, leaving in it not a tree or a wall and destroyed it utterly, no mark or trace of it remaining." Windmills, agricultural lands, dykes, irrigation canals and mills were destroyed. Everyone was killed wrote the court historian Sharaf ad-din Ali Yazdi, "from persons of a hundred years old, to infants in the cradle."[329] The once green, prosperous and agricultural valleys of Sistan, the lands of Iranian mythology and heroes, were destroyed and to this day are deserts and poverty stricken regions. Kandahar fell to him in 1384CE.[330]

In Spring of 1386CE, Tamerlane learned that a 90,000 strong army of Golden Horde, the Mongol descendants ruling southern Russian and Ukraine, sacked the splendid and prosperous city of Tabriz in northwestern Iran. They "pillaged the place and exercised all imaginable cruelties and abominations... and all the riches, treasures, and rarities which had been amassed there during a great many years were consumed in less than six days".[331] Tamerlane directed his army toward the city and captured Tabriz, one of the greatest cities of the region at the time. A huge ransom was placed on the citizens and like he had done in the other great cities he conquered, craftsmen, artists, and architects were rounded and sent to his beloved Samarkand to help the conqueror build more palaces and treasures.

Samarkand was Tamerlane's grand achievement in life. Any violence or terror was justified for beautifying it. He placed as much attention in building the palaces, mosques and public squares of the city as he did on his conquests and killings. Every architect's plans were inspected by him personally and the architects had to adhere to strict construction schedules. He expected the same degree of perfection from them in the building of Samarkand as he expected from his soldiers on the battlefield.

After Tabriz, he attacked the Christian lands of Georgia where he declared he was waging Holy War for the faith of the Prophet[332] and told his troops that it pleased Allah to annihilate the infidels and the unbelievers.[333] After a courageous defense by the Georgians in their capital of Tiflis (Tbilisi), he heavily punished the people of the region through starvation, enslavement and cruel tortures. Those who were killed in Georgia were said to outnumber those still alive.[334]

From Georgia, he marched west, "seeping into Asia Minor like poison."[335] Upon capture of the citadel in Van, those who survived his sword were tied and thrown a thousand feet down a cliff to their horrifying deaths.[336]

On his return through Iran, Tamerlane turned his attention to the most fertile and prosperous province of Fars in today's central Iran where the cities of Isfahan, Shiraz, Kerman and Yazd lay.

CHAPTER 5

The province of Fars, with its capital of Shiraz, was ruled by Shah Shoja of Muzaffarid dynasty, an Iranian family who had served in the Il-Khan's court and who had managed to overtake the Il-khanate rule in Fars province. Upon seizing power, Shah Shoja had blinded and imprisoned his cruel and tyrannical father. Shah Shoja had made peace with Tamerlane, but upon Shah Shoja's death, there was now need for violence to determine rule.

At a furiously fast pace, Tamerlane brought his army of 70,000 outside the gates of Isfahan and levied an incredibly heavy tax followed by events and actions which still today horrify Iranians. Today, every Iranian child knows the story of Isfahan and has learned of the sequence of events which followed. From the Supreme Leader of Iran to every opposition activist, the precedence of the extent of horror and terror for rule exemplified in Isfahan is known. The events from that day serve as a reminder that if a dictator that is willing to use any level of violence to gain obedience is in power, freedom 'is not worth it!' For Iranians, the cruelty of Tamerlane in Isfahan has become the symbol of mankind's cruelty and willingness to rule with terror.

The terrified citizens of Isfahan had agreed to the heavy tax and Tamerlane rode through the city inspecting the buildings, bazaars and palaces of his latest conquest. That evening, his soldiers guarded the city and Tamerlane joined his larger army outside the gates. In the middle of the night, the sound of drums of a blacksmith was heard calling on the people of Isfahan to attack Tamerlane's garrison and free themselves of his wrath. Soon, angry citizens responded, thirsting for freedom, and attacked the soldiers and in less than an hour, 3000 of Tamerlane's soldiers were killed followed by huge celebrations by the people. Yet the celebratory mood shifted and gave way to fear. In the middle of the night, captive in their large city with its dozen gates, the citizens realized Tamerlane would retaliate with incredible terror.

When news reached the conqueror of the people's attack on his soldiers, he "drew the sword of his wrath and took arrows from the quiver of his tyranny and advanced to the city, roaring, overthrowing, like a dog or a lion or leopard; and when he came in sight of the city, he ordered bloodshed and sacrilege, slaughter and plunder, devastation of crops, women's breasts to be cut off, infants to be destroyed, bodies dismembered, honor to be insulted."[337] In anger, Tamerlane ordered each of his seventy thousand soldiers, upon entering the city, to bring him the severed head of an Isfahan citizen. Otherwise, they would be beheaded.

The killing was so difficult that some soldiers were paying up to 20 dinars to others to carry out the task. But as the day went on and the slaughter continued, the price for each severed head was reduced to half the amount.[338] Those who escaped the city were hunted down by cavalry in the snow of the plains and slaughtered. Twenty eight towers of skulls were erected around the city, each containing several thousand heads. These towers of skulls forever memorialized in Iranian culture were warnings to any Iranian in any city who refused to accept Tamerlane's rule. (The number of those killed in just a day in Isfahan matches the number of those killed by the atomic bomb in Hiroshima.) When word of this massacre reached the terrified citizens of Shiraz, not a single citizen voiced opposition and the citizens completely emptied their coffers and handed ten million dinars of silver to Tamerlane.[339]

While he was in Fars province, Tamerlane was informed that a messenger had arrived from his beloved Samarkand; a 100,000 strong force of the Golden Horde, the Mongolian descendants of Genghis Khan then ruling Russia and Ukraine, were plundering the Transoxanian countryside and positioning itself to destroy Samarkand. The citizens of Khwarazm had also risen up and rebelled against his rule. Tamerlane rushed his entire army of 70,000 north at such a speed that it is said that along the way to Transoxania lay corpses of horses that had died of exhaustion. Before any of his enemies could get near Samarkand, he arrived, surprising everyone.

The 100,000 Golden Horde army, stunned and in disarray, fled north. Tamerlane pursued his enemy in what was to become one of the most difficult military undertakings in history, taking his men to the northern reaches of Russia to a land where the "sun did not set" and where his Muslim army had to obtain new instructions on how to perform the five daily prayers without benefit of the usual sunrise and sunset.

Months of trekking north and then west took him through forests and over muddy, difficult terrain where both Napoleon and Hitler's armies were later to fail. When Tamerlane met his enemy, his soldiers, exhausted from enduring hunger and cold were forced to battle a larger army, and one more accustomed to the frigid steppes of Russia. There, the now fifty-five year-old military genius outmaneuvered the superior enemy force, proclaiming his rights as one of the greatest generals in history. The remnants of his enemy's army were pursued to Volga; along the way lay 100,000 slaughtered soldiers, their wives and children taken as slaves.

The treasure collected from the rich Golden Horde army was incredibly large. Tamerlane destroyed Sarai on the Volga River, an extremely rich and prosperous city along the silk route, linking the Italian merchants of the Black Sea to the trans-Asiatic route north of the Caspian. With the destruction of Sarai and the previous destruction of Urgench in Khwarazm by Genghis Khan, the northern silk route was now destroyed.

Tamerlane, with the vast treasures he had collected, began massive building across much of his conquered lands and particularly in Samarkand. - Each town had to build at least one mosque, one school, a public bath, and one *caravanserai* (roadside inns for merchants and travelers). After decades of destruction and terror under his rule, he turned his genius to rebuilding the country. He understood the importance of agriculture and trade, and saw to the creation of canals, bridges, orchards, and workshops. He offered premiums to ruined merchants and sent letters to all the kings in Europe urging them to send their merchants to trade. Unlike the Mongolians, who were more comfortable living in tents, he preferred palaces and built grand structures that chroniclers called some of the loveliest ever constructed. The greatest architects and masons gathered from his empire created his magical structures in Samarkand.

It is a symptom of a culture sickened by violence when its citizens learn to overlook the violence of a conqueror, a king, a Sultan, or a Supreme Leader in favor of the services they have provided for the people. In my interaction with Iranians, I found it puzzling how some spoke highly of Tamerlane, citing the artistic and cultural renaissance in Samarkand during his reign. Now I realize that the same culture causes Iranians to overlook the violence of the Islamic Republic in favor of its (questionable) economic accomplishments or its mastering of nuclear technology. Such defense of a violent regime is a symptom of a culture that justifies and overlooks terror.

The current green movement in Iran is up against an ingrained culture of political violence learned through generations. Within this culture, there is no other way to rule except than through killings and terror. What differentiates one rule from the other is the perceived number of those killed to maintain rule, which means the ruler who kills the least to stay in power is perceived the best. If that ruler also has some grand achievements, he is deemed wonderful. An Iranian ruling culture sickened from generation after generation of violence has learned to numb itself to violence and terror, justifying it as *fait accompli*. Iranians quickly realize violence is the inevitable fate of the people and the price for stability and security. For many Iranians, the ends of artistic achievement and economic prosperity justify the use of terror and killings.

After his long stay in Samarkand and the rebuilding of the city, Tamerlane turned his attention to the riches and gold of India subjecting that country to one of the most horrific and terrorizing campaigns in its history. He raised the flag of Islam and commanded his army to destroy the land of 'idol-worshipers' and 'infidels'. While marching across India, he devastated towns and villages. In Punjab, "the land was laid waste, stripped bare; men, women and children were carried off as slaves". In many towns and cities, the stench of death was so strong that no one dared to return. So much wealth and treasure was taken from Punjab during the march to Delhi that Tamerlane's army forced 100,000 Indian slaves to follow and carry the spoils of conquest for them. Upon reaching Delhi, Tamerlane's army was outnumbered by the slaves and he ordered every one of his soldiers and companions to immediately kill all their slaves or else face punishments. Nearly 100,000 were killed on that day outside the city of Delhi.

On December 17th, 1398, the Indian army with its war elephants left the gates of Delhi and met Tamerlane on the plains outside the city. As the two armies were about to meet, the conqueror watching the procession from the hilltop, threw himself to the ground and asked Allah for his blessing and his aid against the 'infidels.'[340] The bloody battle ended with full retreat by Indians and their slaughter as they were reaching the gates of Delhi. "So great were the heaps of corpses that the battlefield resembled a dark mountain and rivers of blood rushed across it in mighty waves," wrote Ghiyat ad-din Ali, the diarist of the Indian campaign.[341] Tamerlane had just accomplished conquering one of the richest cities in the world, a task both Alexander and Genghis Khan had failed to achieve.

The conqueror wanted the city to be systematically looted, yet in an unclear chain of events, the ordered pillaging turned into incredible massacre, "so terrible that some streets were blocked by the heaps of the dead."[342] In his memoirs, Tamerlane, who had been responsible for so much destruction and murder during his life, wrote "never has anyone heard of such murders and such despair." [343]

Women were raped in the streets and in their homes. Some soldiers walked away from Delhi with as many as many as 100 to 150 slaves, carrying looted treasures and valuables from their own homes.[344] Except for the Muslim neighborhoods, much of Delhi was torched and left in ruins. Muslim slaves were separated and spared. Ninety elephants were required to carry just the personal treasures, precious stones and jewels of Tamerlane back to Samarkand. It took 150 years before Delhi would regain its place as the seat of government. Tamerlane extended his senseless killing and destruction east across the Ganges, killing as many as a hundred thousand more as he marched east. In all, it is estimated that approximately one million Indians were slaughtered in the Indian campaign.[345]

Upon his return from India, Tamerlane invaded Syria, raping, looting and plundering towns and cities. When the garrison in Damascus fired upon his soldiers, he massacred its citizens and burned the city. Treasure gathered from Damascus was so great that they could not find enough mules and camels to carry the loads.[346] In June of 1401CE he marched to Baghdad where the citizens closed the city gates and refused to surrender. After 40 days of constant barrage against city walls, Tamerlane's soldiers forced their way into the city. He ordered each soldier to bring him two severed heads of citizens, and across town, 120 pyramids where built, composed of 90,000 human heads. "Not a house in the town was to be left standing-nor any buildings except mosques, schools and hospitals."[347]

He then marched his army toward the Ottomans and defeated the Turkish army, which was preparing for the siege and capture of Constantinople. After the battle of Ankara in 1402CE, as punishment for the people's support of the Ottomans, "he ordered women and children to be taken to a plain outside the city, and ordered the children less than seven years of age to be placed apart, and ordered his people to ride over these same children."[348] Mothers fell to their knees and his soldiers initially hesitated. Yet Tamerlane mounted his horse and trampled the children shouting "Now I should like to see who will not ride after us?" Seven thousand children were killed on that day in view of their screaming mothers.[349]

He returned to his beloved Samarkand for the nineteenth time to continue his building projects, now using architects and stonemasons brought from Delhi and Damascus. With poor eyesight, the frail and elderly ruler, no longer able to ride a horse would inspect every element of his buildings, mosques and palaces and severely punish architects for delays and mistakes. A little later, the elderly 'Hafez' fell ill and on February 18, 1405, as the imams recited the required prayers from Quran to help him find his way to paradise, the 'Ruler of the World' passed away during his seventieth year of life. The low estimate of those killed during his reign numbers 7 million human beings.[350] The high estimate reaches 20 million.[351] Tamerlane ranks behind Genghis Khan and Hitler and is comparable to Stalin, and Pol Pot as one of the most horrific killers in human history. Two generations of Iranians, the 78th and 79th, experienced his terror and rule. Yet the cultural memory of those pyramids of skull outside the gates of Isfahan continues to disturb Iranians like the memory of a horrific event haunting a traumatized patient. His willingness to employ any level of violence in order to maintain power has set the gold standard which continues to serve as a guide for despots in today's Middle East from the streets of Damascus to the back alleys of Tehran.

Following the Death of Tamerlane

As expected, after the death of Tamerlane, a violent struggle for power broke out across his lands. In the chaos and power vacuum that ensued, the most powerful symbol unifying fighters and their warlords was their association with a tribe. Within two years after Tamerlane's death, a Turkoman tribe known as the 'Black Sheep' (Qara-Qoyunlu) and led by Jahan Shah took control of the flourishing city of Tabriz while Tamerlane's grandson maintained control of northeast.

As was the custom for rule, Jahan Shah was brutal. On one occasion, citizens in Isfahan, whose grandparents and great grandparents had seen the beheadings of Tamerlane, rebelled against the injustice inflicted on them. Jahan Shah crushed the insurgency, the predictable response of a despot. On his way back to Tabriz, word reached him that the citizens of Isfahan had once more rebelled against his garrison. It is not known how many thousands of his warriors were sent to crush the recurrent rebellion. But we do know of the tragedy experienced by the citizens of Isfahan because of a Venetian chronicler who was visiting with Jahan Shah's army in Iran at the time.

"Jahan-Shah… sent his army to the city and ordered for his soldiers to plunder it. Soldiers were ordered to burn down the city's buildings and each soldier who left the city was ordered to bring with him the severed head of one male citizen of Isfahan. The soldiers upon hunting down all the men of the city could not find any more male citizens and in order to fulfill their duty as a soldier, they began severing the heads of women and shaving their hair… after this, nearly all of Isfahan lay in ruins."[352]

Soon another Turkmen tribe known as the 'White Sheep' (Aq-Qoyunlu) and led by Uzun Hassan (Hassan Beig) rose to power and defeated Jahan Shah and shortly after defeated an army from the east commanded by Tamerlane's grandson. The rise of Uzun Hassan, during the life of the 82nd generation, marks a new era in Iranian history. Uzun Hassan was benevolent to his people and promoted the arts and architecture. He enjoyed the company of poets, musicians, and artists. Because of him, his capital city, Tabriz, flourished in a way far greater than it had in any previous era.[353] Uzun Hassan allowed religious freedom and was married to a Christian Byzantine princess from the Trebizond kingdom. His Queen, Theodora, was famous in Iran as Despina Khatun or Lady Despina. She plays an immense symbolic role in Iranian history as her daughter Martha was the mother of Ismail Safavid, the founder of the Safavid Dynasty, which made her the maternal grandmother of Shah Ismail I.

Meanwhile, war and violence continued for Iranians. In 1471CE, only four years after his defeat of Jahan Shah's army, Uzun Hassan and his wife received an ambassador from Venice, Caterino Zeno, whose wife was the niece of Despina Khatun. Zeno urged Uzun Hassan to send an army against the Ottomans and stop them from continuing their march across the Balkans, into Europe and, quite possibly, into Venice. He was authorized to commit support of 100 Venetian warships against the Ottomans.

War with the Ottomans required a grand army and upon agreeing to the plan, Uzun Hassan diverted the talents of 100,000 men and boys for the next chapter of violence in Iranian history. Most of the 100,000 soldiers were on foot and accompanied by approximately 20,000 cavalry. The grand Ottoman army had five divisions of 15,000 to 30,000 each. Two of the divisions were cavalry. In addition there was another Ottoman cavalry division, an advance force that marched 12 miles ahead of the main army, securing a supply of food for the army.[354] Uzun Hassan's army marched west and in the land that is today's northern Syria the two armies met. The Ottomans were initially defeated. But in the third battle, they prevailed and decimated Uzun Hassan's army.[355] The Ottomans, however, instead of chasing the Iranians and capturing Tabriz, decided to head back to their capital of Istanbul (formerly Constantinople) and celebrate their victory.

After Uzun Hassan's retreat to Tabriz, his regime collapsed into turmoil and further violence consumed the lives of this generation of Iranians. Rebellions broke out in Shiraz and the defeated King was forced to brutally use his remaining units against the insurgency. Uzun Hassan died of an unspecified illness only three years after he violently suppressed the rebellion in Shiraz.

***

Safavids

Meanwhile, in his court in Tabriz, relations were made that would reshape the history of Iranians and ultimately resurrect Iran as a nation after eight centuries of absence. Uzun Hassan and Despina Khatun's daughter was married to a man named Heydar, who was a descendent of Sheikh Safi al Din, the great Sufi leader from Ardebil who was greatly loved by his disciples. Sheikh Safi al Din was a follower of the Shafei branch of Sunni Islam, and famous throughout Azerbaijan. His descendants, however, had adopted the Twelve Imam Shi'ism branch of Islam and were devout Shi'ites. Heydar, as descendant of Sheikh Safi, was considered by the people as a religious leader while at the same time was given an official position in the government as governor of Ardebil.

It is a recurring theme of Iranian and world history that when a religion is institutionalized and incorporated into government, it is poisoned by power and violence. In turn, God and spirituality is replaced by rulers who claim to rule by divine right. While serving as the governor of Ardebil, Heydar's 10,000 religious followers, who wore red caps as symbols of their faith, marched north into Caucuses in what is today's Republic of Azerbaijan and, after massacring some of the population, accumulated a great amount of wealth through plunder.[356] In the course of Heydar's war, now justified as holy conquest, 6,000 slaves were brought back to Ardebil. This wealth attracted several thousand new recruits to his army of red caps, thus providing him with the means to make even greater conquests.[357] Heydar and his religious Shi'ite fanatical followers were particularly intent on annihilating Christians in the Caucuses.[358]

Shortly after his religious 'Jihad' to the Caucuses, Heydar asked the Turkmen 'White Sheep' king for permission for a second Jihad, this time an invasion of the province of Shirvan in today's Republic of Azerbaijan. Upon the destruction and plundering of Shirvan, Yaghoub, son of Uzun Hassan, fearful of Heydar's rise in power, sent a 50,000 strong army to defeat Heydar's 12,000 fanatical religious soldiers. The two armies met in the mountains of Alborz and, after an extremely bloody battle, Heydar was killed. His wife, Martha and her three children, including the one-year-old Ismail Safavid were put in a prison in the ruined city of Istakhr near Shiraz.

The Boy King

For four years, Ismail, as well as his mother and two brothers, were imprisoned in a place distant from their stronghold of Ardebil in Azerbaijan. Upon the death of the king (who had slain his father), they were freed and received a warm welcome in Ardebil from the religious followers of his father. Soon, news of the children's arrival spread through towns and villages of Azerbaijan. People from nearby towns and villages would flock to their home to get a glimpse of the descendants of their spiritual Sufi leader, including the young Ismail. But as the children's' popularity grew, their threat to the new king also increased.

The King's army was sent to Azerbaijan with instructions to either imprison or kill the descendants of Sheikh Safi. The children learned of the plan and fled in the middle of the night along with 300 followers. As they were passing through the mountains, Ismail's older brother performed a ritual for then 12-year-old Ismail and named him '*morshed-e-kamel*' or the 'perfected' or 'supreme' religious and spiritual leader, the highest religious position within the Sufi sect. The older brother, supported by his 300 followers, then hurled themselves against the army of several thousand and, in a courageous move to spare the lives of his mother and younger brothers, attacked them head on. He and his followers were killed to the last man.[359] But this allowed the family to escape. The children were given refuge within homes of their followers across Azerbaijan. This event could have been merely a footnote in the 2,500 year history of Iran, an insignificant episode in which a 12-year-old was given a title far beyond his years and capability. But this was not an ordinary 12-year-old; by the time he turned 15, he created and commanded the most powerful army in the region and, after 800 years of absence from the world stage, resurrected the country of Iran, an entity that Iranians, by this time in history, remembered only as ancient history and mythology.

Shah Ismail I

In the political and societal chaos of this tribal era, the leaders of seven major Turkic tribes found in Ismail a great opportunity for consolidation of power against their enemies, including the Ottoman Empire in the west. Of these seven Turkic tribes that supported the young Ismail, the Qajar tribe would continue to dominate Iranian politics into 20th century, well after the demise of the Safavid family.

While in hiding, Ismail managed to gather 1,500 followers and marched them into Ardebil, the stronghold of his ancestors, where they received a hero's welcome. The people thought of Ismail as divine and soon the child also believed in his divine destiny. From Ardebil, the now 13-year-old Ismail organized his followers for an attack against the governor of Shirvan and his strategic fort of Golestan in the Caucuses. Ismail's fanatical Shi'ite followers, who firmly believed in their leader's divine capabilities, refused to use any form of firearms or cannons previously employed by Uzun Hassan and solely relied on their power of faith and their willingness for self-sacrifice. Thus Ismail was able to create a Shiite army with soldiers ready to die as a religious duty. Ismail's victory in Shirvan was followed by capture of Baku and provinces extending to Georgia. This was followed by a victorious battle against the 'White Sheep' army after which the fifteen-year-old leader, marched into Tabriz, the capital of the former king, for the coronation of the new king.

Immediately after crowning himself, Ismail, who knew his powers depended on him being the religious leader of the country, demanded that Shi'ism be designated the official religion of country. His followers in court reminded the young Shi'ite king that in the city of Tabriz alone, with its population of 300,000, two-thirds of the people were Sunnis. If there were to be public prayers in the main mosque of the city blessing the name of the twelve Shi'ite Imams and cursing the first three Islamic caliphs, it might well result in rioting in the city and undermine the new King's position. But he was a Shi'ite religious leader who needed his subjects to worship him as divine. In addition, the Ottomans were using Sunni Islam for political gains and considered their Sultan as the leader of the Sunni Islamic world. In order to solidify his powers in Iran, Ismail had to ensure that the population of the country was Shi'ite and felt no loyalty to the Ottomans.

In reaction to threat of riots in Tabriz, the young Shah replied, "I've been chosen for this task by God himself and the holy Imams are at my side and I take no one's thoughts and advice on such matters. With the will of God, if the public speaks against it, I will use the sword and will not leave one person alive."[360] As expected, the public prayers performed in the name of the Twelve Shi'ite Imams and cursing of the first three Caliphs of Islam sparked an uprising by the majority Sunni population of Tabriz, which was suppressed as Ismail's battled-hardened red cap followers lashed out with a ferocity that far exceeded that of the disorganized mob of citizens.

CHAPTER 5

Bloody confrontations ensued in all neighborhoods until every citizen venturing in the streets, out of fear of violent repercussions, was seen wearing or carrying a red symbol. It is estimated that in the waves of violence, nearly 20,000 citizens of Tabriz were slaughtered in the name of Shi'ism. [361]

In the following eight years, the teenage Shah of Iran marched on with his Sufi Shi'ite army in league with armies of the powerful Turkic tribes of Iran, capturing city after city and extending his rule from the northwest province of Azerbaijan to the city of Baghdad in the west, to the province of Kerman in southeast and the city of Herat in the northeast. In plundering cities, Ismail was known to take only a modest share for himself and was exceptionally generous in dividing the spoils amongst his soldiers. In addition to the material gain, his soldiers believed that there would be spiritual rewards for inflicting violence in the name of religion. In different towns and cities, Sunni prayer leaders and Imams who refused to convert to Shi'ism or refused to swear an oath of loyalty to Ismail Shah were swiftly put to death.

Meanwhile, the Ottomans, fearful of the rise of Ismail and Shi'ism, began their own ruthless and violent persecution of Shi'ites in Anatolia. Within the Ottoman provinces, those who had shown any loyalty to Shi'ites and Safavid family were tortured in public and killed. Shi'ites were branded on their foreheads so that they could easily be singled out as members of the religious sect not tolerated by the Sunni Sultan. Later, in Istanbul, the Sunni leaders issued a fatwa stating that the Shi'ite preachings were considered *'kufr'* or blasphemy and a believer responsible for the righteous killing of one Shi'ite would be more rewarded in Heaven than for killing of seventy Christians.[362] After this fatwa, the murder of Shi'ites in Anatolia dramatically accelerated; it is estimated by one chronicler that 40,000 Shi'ites were massacred. Tens of thousands of others fled east into safety behind Iran's borders. In return tens of thousands of Sunnis in Iran fled west to relocate within the Ottoman borders. In threatening and insulting letters exchanged between the Ottoman Sultan and Shah Ismail, both would repeatedly call each other the 'Zahhak' of their time, the mythological evil king of Iran with serpents coiled on his shoulders. [363]

It was inevitable that two regimes created through violence would go to war. But before the war against the Ottomans, Shah Ismail had to deal with a new threat in the east. In the lands of Khwarazm and today's Afghanistan, a new Uzbek warlord called Shibak Khan had risen to power. Within 10 years, he had conquered all the provinces extending from the Aral Sea to Khurasan and was threatening the eastern provinces of Iran.[364] The Uzbek king claimed

Genghis Khan was his great, great, great, great grandfather 11 generations removed.

In a battle outside the city of Merv, Safavids defeated the forces of Shibak Khan. When the Uzbek leader was dragged to Shah Ismail, still bleeding from his wounds, the twenty four year old king ordered his fanatical Sufi Shi'ite followers to get on their knees and to tear his body apart using their teeth and to eat his flesh while others watched. His scalp was then filled with hay and sent to the Ottoman Sultan, a vivid warning of what lay in store for him if he dared to make war with Iran. Shibak's skull was gilded with gold and used as a wine goblet by the Shah. One arm was sent to the governor of Mazandaran, who had shown signs of friendship with the Uzbek king.

Chaldiran

Meanwhile the Ottomans with their artillery and army were marching through the Balkans and southeastern Europe without encountering any formidable challenger. Sultan Selim I, also called Selim Yavuz and known to Europeans as Selim 'the Grim', had recently ascended the throne and strangled his two brothers and his five orphan nephews. As a reward for his massacre of 40,000 Shi'ites in Anatolia, he had given himself the title of 'the Just'. [365]

The Ottoman and Safavid armies finally met in 1514 on the plains of Chaldiran near today's border between Iran and Turkey for a battle that would determine the destiny of a 'divine' king cherished by his followers.[366] The Ottomans had brought with them 300 cannons used to devastate one European army after another. The number of troops on each side in this battle between the two armies is not certain, but most agree that Shah Ismail's troops were outnumbered somewhere between two to one and four to one.[367] In addition, Shah Ismail's troops refused to use cannons or gunpowder, on the grounds that such weapons were dishonorable and only used by cowards. Shah Ismail's fanatical followers had such a deep belief in the divine powers of their leader that their courage on the battlefield was limitless, to the point of being suicidal.

Outnumbered and outgunned on the battlefield, Shah Ismail's fearless troops relying on faith, made a charge against the much larger veteran army of the Ottomans and their cannons. Profoundly shocked, the entire Ottoman army fell into disarray. Ottoman units that were taken aback by the charge began to retreat when their generals ordered the cannons to bombard the battlefield where both the Ottoman and Safavid units were in a hand-to-hand battle. The Safavid horses, never having seen canons, were terrorized by the artillery fire and began to run in every direction without regard for their riders. In addition, Shah Ismail was injured in the battle, which forced him to withdraw from the battlefield, thus turning the tide and forever altering the fate of the young king.

Iranian army made up of mostly cavalry was far more agile than the Ottomans carrying artillery. Their agility allowed them the opportunity to carry out a 'scorched earth' practice on their retreat, denying supplies to the Ottomans. Any source of food in towns and farms of Azerbaijan in their path was burnt and destroyed. When the Ottomans finally reached the capital, they were hungry, exhausted, and disappointed. Shah Ismail, having fled to the mountains of Azerbaijan, attempted to lure the Ottomans into a dangerous game of cat and mouse. Not having the will to fight and fearing the imminent harsh Azerbaijani winter, Ottoman soldiers mutinied against their king and forced him to retreat after only a week's stay in Tabriz. Appreciating the beautiful buildings and works of art in the capital, Sultan Selim gathered the city's one thousand craftsmen, artisans, and architects, the architectural and artistic talents of that Iranian generation and marched them back to Istanbul to help him build the jewel that it is today.

Shah Ismail, who had endured his first defeat, was embarrassed because his 'divinity' had proved less than omnipotent. He began drinking and was so brokenhearted that he spent much of the remaining 10 years of his life drunk and depressed. He died at the age of 37, probably from complications brought on by alcoholism. His 24 years of rule coincided with the lifetime of the 83rd generation of Iranians, who once again, like every generation before them, experienced war, rebellion, and violence as the only practical method for political gain.

Upon Shah Ismail's death, with no regard for governing ability, the throne and thus the powers for national decision-making and management fell into the hands of his son, Tahmasb, who was 10 years and three month old at the time.

Tahmasb

After the ascendency of the child monarch, *qizilbash* religious chiefs began a ferocious campaign to ensure that they would have a major role in government affairs. This quickly plunged the country into a devastating civil war. With violence prevailing within Iran and the crumbling of Iran's institutions, the Uzbek armies in the east, seizing the opportunity to attack, took the cities of Tus and Astarabad and, for months, besieged the city of Herat. On one occasion, an attempt by a Takalu tribesman to abduct the king led the Shah to order the execution and elimination of all Takalu members. After this massacre, the Takalu tribe was wiped off the political map of Iran.[368]

Internal conflicts consumed 10 years of this 84th generation of Iranians until Shah Tahmasb was at the age when he was able to take political control. Yet the continued violence had devastated the region's economy, infrastructure, and army. Aside from the yearly raids and plundering of what was now the wasteland of Khurasan in the northeast, there were five major invasions by the Uzbeks, who further devastated a region already reduced to ruins by nearly three hundred years of plunder and destruction since the time of Genghis Khan.

In 1533CE, the Uzbeks' siege of the city of Herat lasted 18 months, during which the citizens were forced to eat the stray cats and dogs of the city in order to survive.[369] Shortly after, news was spread from town to town that a 90,000-man army of King Suleiman 'the magnificent' was marching east toward Iran. This was just 19 years after the battle of Chaldiran. With much of Iran in ruins and Iranians having lost their fervor for a Sufi Shi'ite 'divine king', Shah Tahmasb could not gather an army greater than 7,000. But while he was unable to take the Ottomans head-on, he had learned a great lesson from the 'scorched earth' policy of his father. Once again, farms, wells, canals, gardens, trees, bushes, and grasslands were burnt and destroyed. This time, the destruction was done on a much greater scale comprising an 800 km path west of Tabriz. The destruction was 250 miles wide. It extended far to the south and was inflicted on northern Mesopotamia and the rich farmlands north of Baghdad.

This devastation was not only a logistical nightmare for the Ottomans, it also destroyed what villagers and farmers had painstakingly created and nurtured for a lifetime, making them, once again, the real victims of violence. For those in the 84th generation of Iranians, nearly all of their country lay in ruins. Trade had also come to a standstill as a consequence of decades-long Ottoman wars. Iran had been reduced to one of the lowest economic and military levels in its history.

By the time the 90,000 soldiers in the Ottoman army reached Tabriz, many of the army's animals had died along the way from starvation. King Suleiman's army was far from its supply lines. To make matters worse, upon reaching the capital, the Ottomans encountered a heavy fall of snow, one seldom seen by the elders of the city.[370] The desperate Ottoman army was forced to flee the city and head south to Baghdad.

The Ottomans again attempted a massive invasion of Iran 15 years later in 1548. Again not a single blade of grass was left in the provinces separating Tabriz from the Ottoman frontiers. The citizens of Tabriz filled every canal, *qanat**, and well with dirt to deny drinking water to the enemy.[371] Once again, the Ottomans occupied Tabriz and once again, as their pack animals began to die, they were forced to retreat.

Only five years after this devastation, in 1553 King Suleiman attempted another grand invasion of Iran and again was met with scorched earth policy of Shah Tahmasb. Once more Suleiman occupied Tabriz and again was forced to retreat. After this final retreat, a peace treaty was signed between the two kings in 1555, this time on much better terms for the Iranians. Tabriz and the northwest province of Azerbaijan were to be part of Iran, while Baghdad and Mesopotamia were to become Ottoman provinces.

In 1574 the Shah fell ill and, after two years of struggling with illness, the Safavid king, now sixty-two years old and holder of the crown for more than 50 years, died on May 14th of 1576. He had nine sons and no anointed successor. Predictably, in a political system ruled by violence, the country was plunged into political turmoil, giving way to a deadly game in which the man with the greatest capacity for killing and unrestricted mayhem would become king.

One of the Shah's sons was crowned king but killed immediately by the guards at the coronation.[372] 30,000 people assembled and freed the Shah's brilliant but now opium addicted son, who had been imprisoned for twenty years because his father feared he would mount a coup. This son was then crowned but soon began murdering all the supporters of his rival brother and anyone who had held an important office under his father. He systematically executed or blinded any family member who could possibly challenge him, but his sister managed to have him killed. She was supported by the same soldiers who had freed him and given their allegiance to him.[373] Finally, the nearly blind son of Tahmasb, his only remaining heir, was crowned king. For eleven years, until his son Abbas Mirza took the helm, this generation of Iranians lived in political turmoil and violence. Meanwhile, the traditional

---

* Underground canals dug at base of mountains for fresh water.

enemies of Safavids, the Uzbeks in the east and Ottomans in the west, once again began devastating the countryside, its citizens, and infrastructure.

After a nine-month siege of Herat, the city fell into the hands of the Uzbeks. They also swept through Mashhad, plundering the city. The shrine of Imam Reza, the Shi'ite's 8th Imam, was stripped of all ornaments, gold, and silver. The chandeliers, carpets, and anything of value were plundered. The only thing remaining was the railing around the tomb.[374] The news of the bankrupt king and his empty treasury also reached the Ottomans, who decided to break their peace treaty and occupied Tabriz. This time, the occupation would last twenty years.

Once the richest and most beautiful city in Iran, Tabriz, the capital of Shah Ismail, had been abandoned because of its proximity to the Ottoman border and the capital had been relocated to the more central city of Qazvin. Tens of thousands of Tabriz's citizens fled upon the Ottoman invasion. Thousands of craftsmen and artisans also left for their safety. Ottomans banned the Safavid red caps and any clothing suggestive of Safavid culture. By the time the occupation ended, Tabriz was in ruins.[375] Meanwhile, within Iran, various tribes were jockeying for power. In this turmoil, the Ustajlu tribe managed to outwit the others and take possession of Shah's son, Abbas Mirza, then 14 years of age. Using the fourteen year old as bait, the head of Ustajlu tribe came to Qazvin and, with support of other *qizilbash* leaders, successfully pulled off a coup, crowning the young Abbas Mirza as Shah but making the tribal leader the *de facto* ruler of Iran.

In the undemocratic tradition of monarchy where the son of the king is placed on the throne regardless of talent and capability, centuries can pass before someone intelligent, and worthy of managing the country comes to power. Amongst this random chance, every thousand years, a leader comes to power who truly deserves to be given the challenge of leading a country. Such leaders have the potential not only to change the fate of their generation, but at times the fate of a civilization. In the worst circumstances possible, in which Iran was about to be overrun from east and west, this young boy came on the scene and changed the course of history for Iranians. Abbas Mirza, upon coming to power was named Shah Abbas, but towards the end of his rule and immediately after, Iranians as well as the European travelers and chroniclers spontaneously began referring to him as Shah Abbas the Great.

***

CHAPTER 5

Shah Abbas the Great

When he was named King, he was 17 years old, powerless and merely a puppet king brought to power by the *qizilbash* chief, Murshid Quli Khan. In theory, as the Safavid king, like his great-grandfather Shah Ismail, he was still considered *murshid-e-kamel* or the supreme religious leader. But devotion to a religious leader had much diminished since the time of his great grandfather. The *qizilbash* chiefs, once devout followers of his family, were each jockeying for position and power with little regard for religion or the Safavid king.

In order to first solidify his position in Iran, the Shah signed a humiliating peace treaty with Ottomans giving them control of Azerbaijan, Kurdistan, Lorestan and Georgia. Internally, Shah Abbas had to overcome the influence of his *qizilbash* chiefs, especially Murshed Quli Khan who had carried out the coup against his father, named the young boy king and had called himself *vakil* or the guardian of the king. The young king's opportunity came only few months after his coronation. When a plot by rival chiefs to assassinate Murshid Quli Khan was discovered, the 17-year-old Shah Abbas made a brilliant tactical move. First he had the conspirators killed as punishment and then he had Murshed Quli Khan assassinated, which eliminated all serious internal threats to his rule and gave him a complete monopoly of political power.[376] He spent the next 10 years creating and training his army. When sufficiently powerful, he marched to today's Afghanistan and inflicted a crushing defeat on the Uzbeks in 1598 and took possession of the city of Herat. Shortly after this victory, he transferred his capital from Qazvin to the more central city of Isfahan.

Having secured the eastern borders and restored internal security, the Shah's thoughts turned to Tabriz and Azerbaijan. After making a feint to the north with his army, he led his troops on a blazingly fast forced march west, reaching Tabriz in six days. When his troops were 12 miles from the city, cheering broke out throughout the city and everyone who possessed any remaining symbolic red Safavid head gear or symbol brought it out of hiding in a show of support. The Ottoman commander with 5,000 of his soldiers was unprepared and outside Tabriz on the surprise march and was handily defeated.

The Ottoman army counterattacked but in a decisive battle on November 6th, 1605, near the city of Tabriz, Shah Abbas, showing great tactical leadership defeated the Ottoman army and forced all Ottoman soldiers to retreat from Iranian territory.[377] Once more the Ottomans attempted to invade Iran in 1613, but were again defeated and forced to retreat. In 1623, Shah Abbas captured Baghdad, which had been taken from his grandfather.

As a young man, Shah Abbas had been forced to accept a humiliating agreement handing over some of the richest provinces to the Ottomans in exchange for peace. By the end of his reign, the Ottomans no longer could count on easy conquests along their eastern borders. Shah Abbas's forty-one years of rule, although marred by violence, was unlike the violence experienced through much of Iranian history.

For the first 86 generations of Iranians, violence determining their fate was largely destructive. Yet Shah Abbas, through his success on the battlefield, was able to reduce the violence experienced by merchants, villagers and average people. In addition, once he defeated his enemies to east and west, instead of further costly military campaigns, he focused on economic and cultural growth. He monopolized the use of violence and made strict rules on his soldiers. There were still severe punishments for those who broke the law and, later, for his sons, who were suspected of plots against him. Yet victories on the battlefield and elimination of internal political threats allowed average citizens to flourish economically and culturally in an atmosphere of relative peace. Iranians had not experienced such economic and political security for centuries. It was during this generation of relative peace and security that Iranian culture flourished unlike any other time in its history.

If we are to learn of violence in every generation, how each generation's dreams, like my parent's generation's dreams, were destroyed and what was not accomplished as generation after generation's talent was wasted over struggles for power, it is also relevant to appreciate what one generation was able to accomplish when the threat of foreign and domestic violence was to a large extent eliminated for only a few decades without rebellions, major wars and the sacrifice of a generation's talent.

I often think about the 87th generation that lived during the time of Shah Abbas and think about what my generation could accomplish in the next twenty five years if violence were to a large extent eliminated from Iranian culture and politics and our talents were allowed to flourish.

Economic and Artistic Renaissance – The Golden 87th Generation of Iranians

Shah Abbas' decision of 1598 to move his capital to the newly rebuilt Isfahan outside the more ancient city was made in order to represent his nation's new status in the world. Outside the ancient city of Isfahan, four large vineyards or gardens (*chahar-baghs*) were bought by the king, which allowed the creation of the main boulevards named for these four gardens. Plans were also made for the central square built around a giant polo field. While the city was being built, Shah Abbas attended to the promotion of trade, the economy, and the arts throughout Iran.

Under his guidance, this generation turned carpet weaving from a cottage industry producing tribal patterns to a fine art and an important source of export to Europe, China and India.

During and for some time after his rule, Iranian textile and silk were renowned in European markets for quality and design. In the bazaar of Isfahan alone, there were stalls for 25,000 textile workers and "the chief of the textile guild was one of the most powerful men in the country. Even the governor feared him."[378] Velvet production was also turned into a thriving industry during this time.

Shah Abbas encouraged 300 Chinese potters and their families to settle in Iran and soon, high quality ceramics with Persian designs, rivaling the Chinese, was produced across the country and exported to European markets.[379] The production of glazed ceramic tiles, named *kashi* also reached its peak during Shah Abbas's time.[380] Colors on these tiles were nearly all made of mineral elements such as cobalt, manganese, lead and copper, thus providing the material necessary to produce highly prized works of art which have withstood the scorching Iranian sun for centuries without fading.[381] Iranian fine art and painting as well as the 'art of the book', which included illustration, manuscript illumination, and calligraphy also reached its peak during this generation's relative peace.[382]

All kinds of fruits and vegetables were produced in Iran and consumed within thousands of towns and villages and, in particular, within the city of Isfahan. High quality grapes were grown in abundance, particularly in Shiraz, to meet the demand for the wine industry of Iran. The Islamic prohibition of wine was only "occasionally and capriciously" enforced during the Safavid era.[383] Shah Abbas was a deeply religious man, yet extremely cautious of the influence of religion on state and would boast that "his reign was free from the destructive dissensions between rival religious officials and from their aspirations to political power."[384] Large quantities of wine were consumed at the court and in taverns across Iran. Even the members of the clerical class were seen consuming wine. The French traveler Travernier speaks of a meeting with "a rich Mullah outside Kerman who invited me to his house and gave me some excellent wine."[385] Wine was regularly served and consumed at state banquets and national celebrations.

In every town a *kalantar* was appointed; his function was to protect the people against injustice and harassment by local governors.[386] In each town, a *kad-khuda* who functioned as the official of the common-law administration, was chosen through consensus by the community itself.[387] A system of 'meritocracy' was established to ensure that officials were selected on the basis of capability rather than birth.[388] On one occasion, the Shah was out hunting and came across a shepherd boy playing the flute. The boy gave such thoughtful and intelligent answers in reply to the Shah's questioning that he was taken to the Royal Court and given education and training. He eventually became superintendent of the royal workshops and ultimately the Shah's ambassador to the Mogul court in India.[389] On another occasion, Muhammad Beg, a tailor in Tabriz, was recognized for his intellect and promoted, ultimately achieving the post of a *vizier* (minister).

Securing safe passage and resting places for merchants and caravans was also an important priority for the Shah. On every route, facilities called *caravanserai* were built which in addition for rest were designed so that merchants could display some of their wares and conduct business even while in route. European travelers spoke of the sudden transition to safety of travel once inside Persia.

In order to further facilitate trade, Shah Abbas drove the Portuguese navy who had established heavy tax on trade in the Persian Gulf out of Bahrain, later dislodging them from their stronghold on the Strait of Hormuz and then establishing the city of Bandar Abbas on the Strait of Hormuz as a strategic strongpoint.

During his time, the European nations as well as the East India Company each had to negotiate terms of trade on equal footing with Iranians as opposed to the later system of colonialism under which the terms of trade were imposed upon the Asian nations. Consequently, the Safavid state obtained much profit derived from these freely negotiated and favorable terms.[390]

In order to circumvent the Ottomans, who were almost constantly at war with the Safavid and the European states, Shah Abbas established the trade route through Gilan on the Caspian Coast to Astrakhan, up the Volga and across Ukraine. This route of Gilan-Astrakhan-Southern Russia became a major thoroughfare for trade, with caravans carrying large variety of products such as brocades (richly decorative shuttle woven fabrics mostly using silk), tafettas (crisp smooth woven fabric made from silk), shagreens (roughened untanned leather often of horse), moroccan leather (made of sheep skin) and velour (plush knitted fabric made of cotton). But the most important product by far coming from Iran to Europe was silk. Silk production in Iran reached its zenith in his time and in 1660s, decades after the death of Shah Abbas, a year's production of silk in Iran was 1,670,000 pounds, most of which was made for export to Europe.[391]

But perhaps the greatest achievement of Shah Abbas and what continues to inspire and enrich Iranians today was the building of his beloved capital of Isfahan.

Isfahan - *Nisf-e-Jahan*

If you ever get to visit Iran as a tourist, without a doubt you'll be taken to the central city of Isfahan. While sitting in a taxicab, shopping at its bazaar or having tea at one of its coffeehouses, you will hear the words 'Isfahan, *nisf-e-jahan*' uttered proudly by its citizens. '*nisf-e-jahan*' is not an expression referring to the meaning of the word Isfahan. '*nisf-e-jahan*' or 'half-the-world' is a label given by European travelers at the time and a reference to Isfahan's grandeur during the time of relative peace, security and prosperity of Shah Abbas.

Prior to the building of the city, Shah Abbas and his master planner, Sheikh Bahai, devised a grand agricultural plan for the city through the building of a comprehensive system of irrigation.[392] Water for this agricultural growth was diverted from Isfahan's famous river Zayandeh-Rud (River-that-gives-Life). The two main foci of city planning in the capital were the main boulevards of *Chahar-Bagh* (four-gardens) and the main city square of *Maydan-Naqsh-e-Jahan* (Exemplar of the World).

The majestic upper and lower boulevards were the main arteries of the city. Forty eight meters wide, the upper boulevard started near the grounds of Chihil-Sutoon Palace and ran south for about a mile to the river. Nearly the entire length of Chahar-Bagh Blvd, approximately two and half miles, was lined with gardens. On the east side of the boulevard were the Nightingale

Garden, the Mulberry Garden and the Garden of the Dervishes; on the west, The Vineyard, the Throne garden and the Octagonal Garden. Roger Savory writes:

"The lattice work of walls of the gardens which bordered on the Chahar Bagh feed views of the animated scene in the avenue to those within the gardens, and glimpses of the gardens to those promenading in the avenue."[393]

Four parallel rows of Plane Trees [*chenar*], spanned the entire 2 1/2 miles of the boulevard north and south of the river while "water conducted in stone channels, ran down the center, falling in miniature cascades from terrace to terrace, and was occasionally collected in great square or octagonal basins, when crossroads cut the avenue."[394]

Across the river was built the magnificent Allahverdi Khan Bridge. Named after Shah Abbas's Georgian commander, the bridge is more popularly known today for its thirty-three arches giving rise to its current name of *si-o-seh-pol*. Nine meters wide and almost a quarter mile long, it was built with both an upper and a lower promenade. The lower promenade was built as a vaulted passageway cut through the central piers of the bridge and raised only slightly above water. On either side of the upper promenade, there was a covered arcade 76 cm wide pierced by 90 archways giving access to the central road as well as views of the river. "One would hardly expect," wrote Lord Curzon, "to have to travel to Persia to see what may, in all probability, be termed the stateliest bridge in the world."[395]

South of the bridge, the boulevard continued for another mile and a half to the immense gardens of Hezar-jarib. In the center of the garden was a large pool with twelve equal sections and naturally pressurized fountains flowing in every section of the pool.[396,397] In the southern end of the boulevard were also several non-Muslim neighborhoods, most importantly the Armenian neighborhood of New Julfa. The other main ethnic minority groups in Isfahan were the Indians who mostly worked as brokers for foreign traders and as moneylenders. The capital also had a sizeable Jewish population and a considerable Zoroastrian population known as *gabrs* who lived in the neighborhood known at the time as *gabrestan*. Various Christian and Catholic sects invited by the Shah also lived in the capital. The Augustinians, Carmelites and Capuchins lived in the main commercial center of the city itself, while the Jesuits and Dominicans lived in the suburbs of Julfa.[398] There were craftsmen and artisans from all over Europe and Asia, including Swiss watchmakers and Chinese master potters, living and working in the capital.[399]

Chardin, who wrote one of the most comprehensive accounts of the city, states that the circumference of the city was 24 mile. He states that the city had 12 gates, 162 mosques, 48 *madrasas* (schools), 1,802 *caravanserais* (traveler's inn), 273 public baths and 12 cemeteries. Within 30 miles of the city, there were hundreds of villages providing food and wine for the estimated 600,000-1,100,000 inhabitants.[400]

Naqsh-e-Jahan Square

The main attraction of the city known as Maydan Naqsh-e-Jahan (Exemplar of the World) was the grand royal square, 507 meters in length and 158 meters in width. At the southern end of the expansive plaza was commissioned a public mosque which is considered today one of the grand achievements of Iranian architecture. The arched entrance, 27 meters high was the largest arched structure built in Iran since the building of Kasra's palace in Ctesiphon in the Sassanid era. Rich and colorful polychrome (*haft-rang*) tiles with the superb calligraphy of Ali Reza were used for the decoration. Speaking of the entrance, Arthur Pope writes : "one of the most beautiful and imposing ever erected in Persia, indeed one of the most dramatic and satisfying anywhere."[401] In the eastern wall of the square was built a private mosque for the royalty and King using the finest material and craftsmen of the time. On the Western wall of the square was built 'Ali Qapu' or 'Sublime Porte' which was "once a lodging, a grandstand, and audience chamber, and a state gateway leading to the palace grounds".[402]

But the grand achievement was Qaysariyya or the Royal Bazaar, the economic heart of Iran, built on the northern end of Maydan and extending all the way to the old city. Atop its main entrance was a gallery where musicians would play and sing from sunrise to sunset whenever the Shah was in the capital. To the right of the main gate was the Royal Mint followed by endless repeating linked structures consisting of shops, booths, public baths, mosques, *caravanserais* and *madrasas*. Thousands of caravans bringing products from Europe, China and India through the city's twelve gates would converge upon the grand bazaar where the products were received, weighed and assessed. Each section of the bazaar was devoted to a different trade with its own trade guild administering its section and serving as arbitrator in disputes. Each section of the bazaar had its own gate, its own security, and its own fire guards. Water flowing through the bazaar and gathering at pools in central courtyards kept the air cool and the atmosphere pleasant. The Royal Bazaar of Isfahan covered total area of 11.5 square miles.[403]

All around the edge of the Great Square or Maydan ran a waterway 3 1/2 meters wide and 2 meters deep lined on each side with plane [*chenar*] trees providing a shade for the strollers within the square. The theme and emphasis on commerce continued within the Great Maydan [Great Square] with two-story row of continuous shops around the square, interrupted only by the Maydan's four principal buildings. At any one time, one could see people from many parts of the world: "English, Dutch, Portuguese, Arabians, Turkes, Jewes, Armenians, Muscovians and Indians," wrote the chroniclers.[404]

All around the great square, within the grand bazaar and along the great avenues of the city were countless coffeehouses, winehouses, and drinking parlors(*kooknar-khaneh*) serving concoctions of opiates and even hallucinogenic drinks. The coffeehouses, wine houses and drinking parlors (*kooknar-khaneh*) were often linked to each other from the inside so that one could walk from one place to another as if walking through decorated and eventful caverns. Their floors were covered with rugs and the walls generally decorated with murals of lovers, musicians or heroic and mythological scenes from Shahnameh. Walking from one coffeehouse and wine house to another, one would come across musical ensembles, entertainers and singers attracting customers by reciting poetry and stories by classical poets, as well as wrestling shows, jesters and comedians and, one of the most popular of them all, the reciting and singing of Iranian mythological stories of Shahnameh.

Some of the places were largely dedicated to games such as chess, backgammon, and cards, while others were simply meeting places for artists and entertainers.[405] Business was brisk throughout the day but as sunset neared, the coffee houses and taverns were buzzing with crowds and the grand square was filled with mummers, jugglers, puppet-players, acrobats, storytellers, dervishes, and prostitutes.[406] Prostitution was legalized and taxed and prostitutes like all other merchants were under protection of the state and subject to regulations.[407]

Around sunset, hundreds of thousands of Isfahanis, after the day's work would embark on the ritual of *havakhori* [catching air] along the main boulevards of the city, atop its bridges and within its numerous gardens. As John Fryer wrote: "Night drawing on, all the Pride of Spahaun[Isfahan] was met in Chaurbaug [Chahar-Bagh], and the grandees were airing themselves, prancing about with their numerous trains, striving to outvie each other in pomp and generosity."[408]

Shah Abbas was often seen amongst the crowd in simple and informal clothing enjoying the entertainment.[409] He was most fond of productions of Ferdowsi's Shahnameh and one of his favorite hangouts was a coffeehouse named Baba Shams on the Chahar Bagh Boulevard.[410]

The great Safavid king is a reminder of the extent of prosperity and joy a country and culture is capable of realizing, if led by a responsible government focused on the needs of the population, economic growth, domestic and international security, and the arts. It is the tragedy of Iranian history that the number of generations who had the privilege of living under such governments during the 2,500 year history of Iran can be counted on the fingers of one hand, in contrast to the continuity of regularly elected governments in democratic systems. Shah Abbas's reign is not a symbol of the success of despotic systems of government; instead it exemplifies the potential of human beings if given talented, caring, and ingenious leaders and managers concerned for the welfare of citizens rather than their own self-interests. Shah Abbas was proud of his elimination of the influence of religious institutions from his rule and he often boasted about his elimination of the power of *qizilbashs* and the clergy from government. If one looks back at the atmosphere and the culture of Isfahan during Shah Abbas's era, one can imagine the cultural and economic potential of a secular and democratic Iran of the 21st-century built on the principles of human rights and led by responsible and capable governments freely elected by the people.

The cultural and economic demise of Iran subsequent to the reign of Shah Abbas is also a reminder that cultural and economic accomplishments do sometimes take place in despotic regimes, but they always turn to ruins as the violent culture that had brought the despotic ruler to power resurfaces one or two generations down the line in the form of incapable and irresponsible governments run by those who care more about themselves and their survival than the welfare of the citizens.

Shah Abbas - Death -Demise of Safavids

The era of Shah Abbas may be considered one of the more peaceful and secure times in Iranian history, but such peace did not mean the elimination of political violence. It merely meant its containment on the international scene through a series of military victories and the elimination of violent rebellions across the country through economic prosperity. Yet violence continued to dominate the political climate of the time.

Shah Abbas clearly remembered how as a 14-year-old, he was used as a pawn, by the *qizilbash* chiefs who united against the rule of his father. Thus he was most terrified of his sons for similar reasons. In February of 1615, acting on rumors that his eldest son would be used as a puppet in a plot against him, Shah Abbas had his son, Mohammad Baqir, assassinated. Six years later, when the Shah fell gravely ill, his third son who thought he would gain the crown, prematurely celebrated his father's death. When Shah Abbas recovered, he had this son blinded. Similarly, he blinded his fifth son with hot iron rods. His second and fourth sons died as boys before becoming serious threats to his rule.[411]

On August 30, 1621, Sheikh Bahai, the scholar, architect and engineer who was Shah Abbas's right-hand man in designing the capital passed away. In the day of mourning in Isfahan, "despite the size of the square, men were pressed tightly against one another, and the pall-bearer could only with difficulty make progress through the crowd."[412]

Eight years later, in 1629, the main architect of Iran's prosperity and security, the 'Great' king who had consolidated his powers at the age of 17 and who had engineered Iran's artistic, economic, and intellectual renaissance died in Kashan while on a trip to his favorite province of Mazandaran. When the news spread throughout the country, there was a mood of gloom and uncertainty that overpowered any sense of hope. Iranian prosperity had not been due to elimination of political violence, but merely its suppression for a few decades, and now that the great king had died, the return of violence was inevitable. Perhaps no other sentence more concisely summarized the fate of Iranians after the death of Shah Abbas than when Chardin, the most celebrated of Safavid chroniclers wrote: "When this great prince ceased to live, Persia ceased to prosper!"[413]

Iran after Shah Abbas the Great

Having disposed of his remaining sons, the 19-year-old grandson of Shah Abbas was named King and became known as Shah Safi. He lacked the talent and intelligence required to govern a country and was raised as a virtual prisoner together with his mother in the haram. Lack of proper leadership or a system for power sharing led to the rapid economic and military disintegration of the country. Within nine years after the death of Shah Abbas, the Ottomans renewed their war with Iran and recaptured Baghdad and the provinces of Iraq. In the same year, the key strategic city of Qandahar was captured by the Mughal ruler of India. Shah Safi, who was known to be an opium addict, was often prescribed alcohol by his physician to counteract the evil effects of his addiction.[414] His rule was described by one European chronicler as "tis certain there has not been in Persia a more cruel and bloody reign than his" and as "…one continued series of cruelties". Another European chronicler described it as "frequent instances of barbarity which stained his reign with blood."[415]

The combined negative effects of opium and alcohol brought Shah Safi to his death at the young age of 32. He was replaced by his eight-and-a-half year-old son Abbas, the great grandson of Shah Abbas I, who became known as Shah Abbas II. The turmoil and political uncertainty continued in Iran and led to further deterioration of the Iranian economy and infrastructure. When Abbas II was 12, his chief vizier was assassinated. A few days later he ordered the execution of all the conspirators. Merely in the position of power due to hereditary rule of monarchy, he had also become an alcoholic as a child during his virtual imprisonment in the haram. During his reign, like his great-grandfather he was tolerant of Christians, but at one point he ordered all Jews within Iran to make public conversions to Islam. Up to 100,000 Jews were forced to outwardly embrace Islam while continuing to practice their religion in secret and in their homes.[416] This king also died at the young age of 32, likely due to complications of alcoholism. An entire generation of Iranians, the 89th generation, lived during his 24-year rule of violence and watched the slow economic and military decay of the country. During his reign, he managed to recover Kandahar from the Mughal emperor and to repulse three subsequent attempts to recapture the city.[417]

The military and economic decline of Iran continued when the next incapable and untalented member of the Safavid family, Suleiman I, the son of Abbas II, was crowned king. Suleiman I had also spent all his life in his father's haram prior to becoming king and was also an alcoholic. His 28-year rule during the lifetime of the 90th generation of Iranians saw the continued decay of Iranian economy and infrastructure and the squandering of much of the talents of another entire generation. During the lifetime of this 90th generation, violence continued as Iranians witnessed plundering of northeastern provinces of Damghan, Semnan, and Astarabad by members of the Turcoman tribes, who killed many of the citizens in these provinces.[418] The western provinces of Iran, however avoided another war because of the major defeat of the Ottoman army in the Battle of Vienna in 1683. Suleiman I also died of the complications of alcoholism. During his reign, members of the religious class, especially powerful figures like Mohammad Baqir Majlisi, once again gained power over the affairs of the state and with this resurgence, another round of religious persecutions, this time against the spiritual Sufi sect, began in Iran. The Sufis were called the "this foul and hellish growth" and Sufi garment and dance (*sama*) was banned and all Sufi sects "from the point of view of the Shi'ite faith, were to be rejected and renounced."[419,420]

After the death of Suleiman I from complications of alcoholism, a son known as Shah Sultan Hussein, also an alcoholic from being raised in the haram, was brought forth. During his reign, Iran saw the continued decay of its infrastructure and economy. Corruption within provincial governments was rampant. Travelers were often robbed by the very officials charged with protecting them. The 91st generation of Iranians lived at a time in history when violence and anarchy penetrated more and more of society. So complete was the breakdown of the military that in 1698 a band of Baluchi tribesmen raided and plundered the province of Kerman in the southeast, nearly reached the city of Yazd and threatened Bandar Abbas.[421] Unable to even fend off a band of thieves, Shah Sultan Hussein was forced to hire a Georgian prince to defeat the invaders.[422]

In 1709, Afghan tribes captured Qandahar and Herat.[423] Iran was now in complete disintegration in every corner. In the south, the island of Bahrain was captured by the Sultanate of Oman, thus ending the Iranian influence in the southern Persian Gulf. In the west, the Ottomans were eyeing the northwest Iranian provinces and in the north, Russia's Peter the Great was planning the invasion of Iran. In 1715, the Russian ambassador to Iran, Artemii Petrovich Volynsky, in a report to the Tsar described the complete disintegration of Persia's society, military, and economy. He reported the general situation in Iran "so disturbed, and the army so demoralized and inefficient, that the country could be easily conquered by a small Russian army."[424] In 1721, the Tsar of Russia decided to proceed and to begin the invasion of Iran. In order to justify his action for invasion, he ordered his consul in Rasht to report to Isfahan to protest the mistreatment of two Russian nationals in Iran. When the consul reached Isfahan to deliver the message about Russia's anger and its declaration of war, he was surprised to find the city besieged by an Afghan warlord with a force consisting of a mere 20,000 troops.

***

CHAPTER 5

Beginning in October 1721, Mahmud, the warlord of Ghilzai Afghans had embarked on a military and looting expedition across Iran's southeastern regions. In March 1722 he marched his army to the capital of Isfahan. Not having a proper army for defense, the Safavid Shah gathered several thousand citizens, among them merchants, farmers, and artisans, and ordered them to march out the city and attack the Afghan army. This hastily gathered force was defeated on March 8th, in Gulnabad, 18 miles from the city gates. Mahmud could have forced his way into the city that same day, but he assumed that there must be a large Iranian army within the city, so he decided to starve the population into submission.[425]

The citizens of Isfahan, a city built as the jewel of Iran by their great-grandparents 100 years earlier, clearly knew of the terrifying events when the 79th generation of Isfahanis, 12 generations before them, had shut their city gates against Tamerlane who later beheaded more than 70,000 of their great-great-grandparents. They probably also were aware that nine generations before, after their great, great grandparents had again rebelled against Jahan Shah of the Black Sheep Turcoman tribe, he had ordered each soldier in his army to bring him a severed head of an Isfahani man. This time, Isfahani citizens decided to keep their city gates shut and die of starvation rather than face another terrorizing round of horrors. Thus, the New Year celebration of Nowruz in 1722 took place under terrifying circumstances of fear and hunger.

The Shah, besieged in Isfahan, decided to crown his eldest son as the heir to the throne and sneak him out of the city to Azerbaijan in order to raise some troops. Sultan Mahmud Mirza who had rarely left the haram was brought forth and named heir to the throne. During the ceremony, Mahmud Mirza became very nervous and ran down into the *andarun*, the private section of the haram and locked himself in. This was an embarrassing moment for the nobles and the king; their capital was under siege and they were in a life or death situation. Thus they brought the Shah's second son forward for his coronation ceremony. But after several days, he too was found to be unsuitable. Finally, the Shah's third son, the 18 year old Tahmasb, was brought forth. Along with 200 companions, he managed to flee past the enemy lines to reach Qazvin. But there, instead of raising an army, he also began drinking. Thus, no serious help came for the hundreds of thousands of embattled Isfahanis who had their city gates shut from the inside.

Soon after the Nowruz celebrations, merely a month since the siege started, food supplies began running short and the poor were left starving. That spring may be considered one of the most difficult in Isfahan's history.

By the beginning of summer the city was almost completely void of food, even for the wealthy. Citizens were seen in the streets hunting down stray cats and dogs in order to feed their children. By the end of summer, citizens of Isfahan began eating the surviving mice and rats. Meanwhile the number of those dying of starvation and disease was beyond counting. Unable to bury their dead, Isfahan's inhabitants left corpses littering the boulevards, parks, squares and bazaars of the city. Finally in autumn, those who had the strength to live began feeding on human flesh in order to survive. Unable to withstand the starvation any longer, the Safavid King surrendered the city unconditionally to Mahmud on October 22nd 1722. At least 80,000 Isfahanis are estimated to have died from starvation and disease during the seven-month siege.[426] Fearing an uprising, Mahmud executed 3,000 Iranian officials, nobles, and guards.[427] Three years later, in 1725, fearing another attempt at dethroning him, Mahmud ordered the general massacre of anyone left from the Safavid family. In the same year, Mahmud was seen acting oddly and displaying behavior and symptoms that historians believe indicated an advanced stage of tertiary syphilis involving his brain. He was overthrown by his cousin Ashraf and died at the age of 26.[428]

The 92nd generation of Iranians experienced the anarchy and disintegration of Iran followed by the sacking of the capital. The country, in nearly complete disarray prior to the capture of Isfahan, was now in a state bordering on total chaos consuming the lives of another generation living in violence. The northwestern provinces of Iran were partitioned by the Ottomans and the Russians in the Russo-Ottoman Treaty of 1724. Six Russian battalions landed in Gilan and another Russian force captured Baku.

As luck would have it, the death of Peter the Great halted any further Russian expansion into Iran. An even greater stroke of luck, which prevented the complete disintegration of the country, was the rise to power of Nader, one of the most talented military geniuses in Iranian history. Nader would crown himself Nader Shah and was later known across European courts as the "last great conqueror of Asia" and celebrated as the "Napoleon of Iran". At the point he was discovered, Isfahan was under occupation by Afghan warlords and Nader was the leader of a band of fighters in Khurasan.

Nader created a professional army from scratch and never ceased to lead his soldiers at the head of his army. He was an incredibly powerful warrior and an ingenious general who had that rare belief in himself and that even rarer ability to make those around him believe in him as well. He was born into a life of violence, lived a life of violence, led the entire nation through continuous wars of violence, and finally died in violence. The 93rd generation of Iranians lived during his time of wars and conquests.

***

Nader Shah - Defeating the Afghans

When Isfahan surrendered, Tahmasb, the crowned king now residing in Qazvin, proclaimed himself the king but soon fled the city as Mahmud sent troops for his capture. While in forests of Mazandaran, he learned of a feared band of soldiers from the Afshar tribe pillaging and robbing the towns and villages of Khurasan led by Nader.[429] Shah Tahmasb sent an envoy and requested his cooperation against the Afghans. Nader accepted the offer and marched into the Shah's camp leading a force of 2,000 Kurds and Afshars.

Nader's father, variously described as a shepherd, skinner, peasant, and camel-driver by historians, died when he was young. During the Uzbek raid and the pillaging of Khurasan, he and his mother were taken as slaves. As a child, he had managed to escape captivity while his mother died in captivity. Thereafter he had joined a band of Afshar horsemen and soon became their leader. He joined Tahmasb's army in a siege of Mashhad against a local warlord and upon the successful capture of the city, he was given authority to lead the army. Shortly after, he captured Herat where he was seen at the head of his army on the battlefield, cutting down one of the Afghan leaders with his own sword.[430]

After the victory of Herat, Nader marched west and after a bloody battle defeated the Afghans north of Isfahan. Upon their retreat to Isfahan, Afghans massacred more than 3,000 of the *ulama* (religious scholars) and set the magnificent bazaar of Isfahan on fire. They then collected all available animals in the city and, along with the treasures they could gather, fled to Shiraz. Nader marched into the city of Isfahan on November 16th, 1729.[431] This was seven and half years after the siege and sacking of the former grand capital.

Tahmasb was overjoyed at going back to his father's palaces and the haram in which he was raised. But upon entering the city, his joy was turned into grief as Isfahan "was, indeed, only a shadow of its former self."[432] Sheikh Hazin who entered the city soon after Nader wrote: "I... beheld that great city... in utter ruin and desertion. Of all that population and of my friends scarcely anyone remained."[433] Of Tahmasb's father's palace, only naked walls remained. When the Safavid king walked into the former haram, an old woman dressed as a slave threw her arms around his neck. The worn out lady turned out to be his mother; she had survived the massacre by disguising herself as a slave.

Nader Shah of Afshar

The joy occasioned by the return of Safavid king to Isfahan was short lived. Nader ordered the plundering of homes to pay his soldiers, even selling some of city's prisoners as slaves for additional booty.[434] Several weeks later, Nader marched south to Shiraz where he found Afghans waiting for him with a force of 20,000.[435] Nader's brilliant military tactics again won the day; 10,000 Afghans were captured during the battle.[436] With the defeat of Abdali and Ghilzai Afghan armies, the first of Nader's major enemies was destroyed. A greater task now awaited him in the West. The professional army of Ottoman Empire was occupying the western provinces of Georgia, Armenia, Azarbaijan, Daghistan, Shirvan, most of Iraq, Kurdistan, Hamedan and Kermanshah.[437] Their defeat and expulsion from Iranian soil was Nader's next military task.

He spent several months in Shiraz, where much of the town and all its gardens had been destroyed during the Afghan occupation and war.[438] Then he made a night's march to Nahavand where, after defeating the Ottoman garrison, he recaptured Sanandaj in Kurdistan, as well as Malayer and Hamedan.[439] He then defeated the remaining Ottoman forces in Azerbaijan and captured the cities of Tabriz and Ardabil.[440] While in Azerbaijan, he learned of a mutiny against his rule by the Abdali Afghans of Herat, who had surrendered to him a few years earlier. He also was informed that they were marching on Mashhad. He marched east with his army through Mazandaran and, after ten months of fighting and a siege of Herat, defeated the Abdali Afghans.[441]

While in the east, Nader heard the news that Shah Tahmasb, after several months of drinking and partying, had foolishly attacked the Ottomans with a force of 18,000 in order to capture Yerevan. He was not only soundly defeated but he also lost all the provinces previously captured. Despite the defeat, back in Isfahan, the Safavid king had again engaged in pleasures and festivities to such an extent that "one would say no defeat had occurred."[442] In all, he had lost more territories than Nader had gained. Afterwards, he was forced to sign a peace treaty with the Ottomans that allowed the Ottomans to retain all territories now in their possession, except for Tabriz. This made Nader furious. He rejected the peace treaty and swore to win back all the provinces through his superior military capabilities. In a letter to all "headsmen, peoples and nobles of the kingdom," Nader wrote "Verily this peace is, in the eyes of wisdom, naught but a picture upon water and a mere mirage..."[443]

From the east, he marched straight to Isfahan and invited the Shah to a reception at the Hezar-jarib garden of the city. There, after three days of festivities and while the king was fully intoxicated, he gathered all *qizilbash* chiefs, nobles of the country, and prominent religious figures and let them observe the embarrassingly drunken Shah Tahmasb. He then proclaimed that Shah Tahmasb should step down and his infant son be made king.[444] The infant Shah Abbas III was eight months old when, during the coronation ceremony, Nader placed a sword and a shield next to the child's cradle and ordered that drums be beaten for seven days in celebration.[445] Nader had effectively made himself the most powerful figure in the country and the de facto king. He then declared war against the Ottomans and began the siege of Baghdad.

The siege consisted of building 2,700 towers around the city, each spaced a musket shot apart. In order to save the province of Iraq, the Ottomans recalled 80,000 soldiers from their European provinces and marched them to Baghdad. Nader left 12,000 men to carry on the siege and took the rest along with him for the battle against the oncoming Ottoman army. The two forces met, along the banks of Tigris, thirty leagues from Baghdad.

Battle began at 8am where Nader, at the head of his army of 50,000, charged at the Ottomans and managed to capture their artillery. A reserve force of 20,000 Ottomans were able to push back and recapture the cannons. Nader's horse was wounded and fell, but Nader quickly grabbed another horse and continued to lead his men. The battle continued until the afternoon, when the July heat left much of Nader's Army exhausted and struggling from thirst. The Ottomans, with their backs to the river, were positioned to cut off the supply of water to Nader's army. The afternoon wind also hindered Nader's efforts as the dust from more than 100,000 soldiers battling each other was suspended in the air, causing near zero visibility. Amongst the chaos, Nader's second horse was shot and killed, throwing Nader to the ground. Panic ensued within his army when many soldiers thought their leader had been killed. Nader's army soon began its retreat, losing all of their artillery and baggage. Over 30,000 of Nader's soldiers were killed in the retreat and another 3,000 captured.[446] Victory for the Ottomans, however, was not complete, since Nader survived the battle.

After the victory, as the Ottomans marched into Baghdad, it seemed to them that they were marching into a tomb rather than a town. Thousands were suffering from hunger and disease and corpses were piled up all over the city. An estimated 110,000 people died while Nader besieged the city.[447] The devastation of the countryside around Baghdad was so extensive that the Ottoman army, facing starvation, was forced to retreat to Kirkuk.[448]

Nader led his remaining soldiers, mostly on foot and many naked, back to Iran and gave them leave to return to their homes and recover from their ordeal. He then sent instructions across the country for undertaking the production of arms and equipment and manufacturing artillery and munitions of better quality and greater quantity than before.[449] In an incredible two months, Nader reconstituted his army and marched west to fight the Ottomans. There, in a series of battles, he defeated all Ottoman forces in the region, putting those remaining in flight back to Istanbul. Nader then occupied Hilla, Najaf, and Karbala. The remaining Ottoman governor in Baghdad then surrendered to Nader and agreed to hand back to Iran all provinces captured by the Ottomans in the last ten years and retreat to the frontiers agreed on in the Turko-Persian Treaty of 1639. In return, Baghdad was left under Ottoman rule.[450] Nader spent the next several years in one violent campaign after another against opponents ranging from Georgians in the northwest to Baluchi tribes in the southeast. By 1735 all Russian forces had been forced to withdraw from Iranian territories. Having recovered all territories lost over the last 100 years, Nader decided it was time to crown himself king.

He sent orders to all cities and towns across the country that all nobles, qazi's (judges), *ulama* (religious scholars) were to assemble on the Mughan plains for a national council. This gathering was given the responsibility of conferring the crown upon the person who the council considered most worthy. Twelve thousand temporary structures, as well as mosques, rest houses, bazaars, and baths were erected for this occasion. Twenty thousand delegates together with servants and slaves, numbering 100,000 were present when on March 8th 1736, Nader Khan was crowned as Nader Shah of the Afshar dynasty, bringing to end more than 200 years of Safavid family rule in Iran. For three days and three nights musicians were ordered to play without pause.[451] After the coronation and the Nowruz celebration of the new year, Nader made plans for conquests in the east, beginning with the capture of Qandahar.

CHAPTER 5

Conquest of India

At the head of 80,000 men, Nader marched to Qandahar via Kerman and Sistan. Qandahar's defensive positions were destroyed and its inhabitants were moved to the nearby newly erected city of Nader-Abad. His soldiers were given the spoils of the city and were free to take whatever possessions they chose from people's homes.[452] He stayed in Nader-Abad for two months, where he made preparations for his next military campaign. He was now the king with no major enemies within or along the borders of Iran. But he was a general and generals in power need wars. In addition, he had created a large professional army that needed to be paid. The country lacked the resources to support the army's increasingly heavy demands. Accordingly, preparations were made for the invasion of the rich provinces of India.

Within weeks, his army of 80,000 captured Kabul, followed by Ghazni, then Lahore and then Kashmir. He continued his march east across northern India looting towns, villages, and homes. He appointed governors as he pleased while marching onto the wealthy capital of Mughal India in Delhi. Seventy miles north of Delhi, he met the Indian army at the battle of Karnal. In the battle, the Mughal Indian army had an advance force of war elephants with blades on their trunks. It was expected that these fearsome war elephants would wreak havoc in the enemy lines.

The evening before the battle, Nader Shah ordered his troops to mount camels laden with pots of oil. On the morning of the battle, these camels were placed on the front lines of Nader Shah's grand army. When the Mughal Indian army, preceded by their elephants charged, Nader Shah ordered his troops to dismount and then set the pots of oil ablaze. Thousands of terrorized camels with burning oil on their backs began screaming and then running full speed towards the war elephants and the Mughal army. The elephants seeing camelbacks of fire coming at them were in turn terrorized and turned on their own army, which plunged the entire Mughal force into disarray and panic.

Nader Shah then ordered the charge of his army and, within three hours, defeated Mohammad Shah, the Mughal King of India and took him hostage. Over 20,000 Indian soldiers were killed in the Battle of Karnal. He then marched into the wealthy capital of Delhi, just as Tamerlane had done several centuries before.

In Delhi the defeated population, having lost 20,000 of their citizen soldiers in the Battle of Karnal, were now told they would have to pay a large tribute to the invader. Most of the population was passive, but anger was in the air. Shortly after, rumors were spread across the city that Nader Shah has been killed by one of Mohammad Shah's haram guards. Anger of Delhi citizens turned to riots. Nader Shah's dispersed soldiers were walking through the city in ones and twos, when the city's furious inhabitants fell upon them and killed many in neighborhood after neighborhood.

In response, Nader Shah sent a thousand guards to restore order but soon learned that they had been fired on and more reinforcements were needed. Together with some guards, he rode from the palace to Rowshan-o-Dowleh Mosque. On his way, stones and rocks were thrown from balconies and one of his guards was killed while riding beside him. These events drove Nader Shah into a murderous rage. At the mosque, he climbed to the Golden Dome and issued orders for his troops to kill every citizen in districts in which his soldiers had been attacked. He then raised his sword in the air in a signal for the massacre to begin.[453] The killings of the citizens of Delhi began at nine in the morning.

Thousands of Nader's soldiers rushed into houses and shops slaughtering innocent and guilty alike in revenge. Houses were burnt after being looted. Many women, fearing rape, threw themselves into city wells. In other families, fathers would kill their children and wives before committing suicide.[454] The killing and pillaging continued into the afternoon while enormous amounts of wealth were taken from peoples' homes. The jewelry district of the city was hit the hardest. Thousands of homes were in flames and corpses were piling up in the streets. Finally, Mohammad Shah sent an envoy begging Nader Shah to stop the killings. At three in the afternoon, six hours after the pillaging and massacre began, Nader Shah ordered "let their lives be spared."[455] Estimated 20,000-30,000 citizens of Delhi were killed in the six hours of massacre.

Ascending the Peacock Throne

Nader Shah then ordered tributes to be collected from Delhi and the adjacent provinces. He ordered the province of Punjab to pay 7 crore or 70 million rupees of gold. The governor of the province upon hearing the request joked that a string of wagons from Bengal to Delhi would be needed to carry it. For his comments, he was severely beaten and punished, after which he committed suicide.[456] The total amount of gold and treasure collected from Mohammad Shah, the nobles, the merchant, the peasants, artisans and soldiers of India by Nader Shah is estimated to be an incredible

70 crore of gold or 700 million rupees, equivalent to 90 billion sterling pounds or $135 billion dollars of gold today.[457] It is one of the largest sudden transfers of wealth from one nation to another in human history and it involved most of the wealth which India had gathered since the invasion of Tamerlane.

The amount of treasure was so large that Nader Shah sent an order to Iran that every Iranian citizen would be exempt from paying taxes for three years, an incredible forgiving of tax never previously done in Iranian history and one not repeated until the petroleum era of the 20th century. Amongst the treasures collected was the famous Peacock Throne, which continued to be used by Iranian monarchy and served until the 1979 revolution as the symbol of Iranian royalty. The Throne was a golden platform and seat of the King decorated with diamonds, pearls, 108 large rubies and 116 emeralds. Amongst the treasures brought back were also Kooh-e-Noor (Mountain of Light) and Darya-e-Noor (Sea of Light) diamonds. The Kooh-e-Noor or Mountain of Light was a 186 1/16 carat diamond, one of the largest diamonds ever found in the world. Its history dated back to the era of myth; legend had it that whoever owned this diamond would rule the world. The stone was later acquired by the British in the 19th century where it was cut down to its current size and placed upon the British crown and is amongst the crown jewels in the Tower of London. Nader Shah also acquired the Darya-e-Noor diamond, a 182 carat pale pink diamond which continued to be the centerpiece of Iranian crown in the Qajar and Pahlavi era until the 1979 revolution, during which it fell, along with the remainder of royal jewels, into the hands of the revolutionaries and now is part of the collection of Pahlavi crowns and jewels in Tehran.

While his troops were collecting the gold and treasure of India, Nader Shah wed his son to the Indian Mughal king's niece. According to the protocol for marriage, the officials had to investigate and report the groom's seven generation of ancestry, which meant they had to document Nader Shah's ancestors six generations back. "Tell them", Nader Shah screamed at them in anger, "that the prince is the son of Nader Shah, the son of the sword, the grandson of the sword; and so on, till they have a descent of seventy instead of seven generations."[458] Here, on this accidental inquiry of an Iranian ruler's ancestry, Nader Shah instinctively tells us that he is the descendant of seventy generations of the sword and his rank, title and privilege is through the sword. But in fact, by this time in Iranian history, Nader Shah was the descendant of at least 92 generations of the sword.

Nader Shah Is Killed

Upon returning from India and with the capital acquired, Nader Shah built a navy, captured Bahrain and Oman. Shortly after, he captured territories across Oxus River (Amu Darya River) in Central Asia and in the Caucuses, bringing province after province under his rule. Yet soon he began showing symptoms of what has been described as a "disorder of the mind". He was becoming more and more paranoid, lashing out at his generals, his guards, and his son. After a near miss assassination attempt against him, he accused his son of conspiracy and in a fit of rage, ordered his son to be blinded. Afterwards, he regretted his act and ordered all the nobles who watched him blind his son executed. Over the following months, his paranoia increased to the point that he ordered the summary execution of anyone he suspected of being an enemy, including generals and nobles.

In order to feed his army of 150,000, he imposed crippling taxation on and confiscated the wealth of the citizens under his rule. He contemplated the invasion of Russia and then considered invading the Ottoman Empire and sacking Istanbul.[459] He saw himself as the next Genghis Khan and Tamerlane. He crushed rebellions on his way through Kerman and Yazd and left towers of skulls as a memory of his last attempt at squeezing the population through taxes.[460] He had become obsessed with hoarding treasures and collecting revenue and regarded his guards and commanders with increasing paranoia.

In the morning of June 30, 1747, the Shah's paranoia turned to panic and he contemplated fleeing from his army alone. His guards begged him not to leave the grand army in chaos and swore to protect him. As evening came he could not control his paranoia and called his Afghan generals to his royal tent. There, he told them of his suspicions about his Persian guards and ordered the Afghans to arrest all Persian officers in the morning and kill anyone who resisted arrest. This order was overheard by a Persian guardsman who informed the Persian officers. Plans were made for his assassination that evening.[461] In early hours of the morning of July 1st, sixteen conspirators entered his tent. The legendary warrior was able to grab hold of his sword and decapitated first two conspirators before tripping on the ropes in the tent and was stabbed to death.

CHAPTER 5

Chaos after Nader Shah's Death

The news of his death spread through the camp amongst tens of thousands of his troops like wildfire. His army disbanded and splintered into many different factions while looting his mythical treasures. Within Nader Shah's army, the Afghans, under the leadership of their commander, Ahmad Khan Abdali, fought their way clear and free with vast amount of treasure including the *Kooh-e-Noor* diamond. They then seized the eastern half of Nader's empire, calling it the Kingdom of Afghanistan. The bulk of the remnants of the army gathered around Nader Shah's nephew Adil, who took possession of Mashhad in the northeast.

Karim Khan of the Zand tribe managed to take control of western-central Iran. Azad Khan, a Ghilzai Afghan, exploited the anarchy to seize control of Azerbaijan in the northwest, while the Qajar tribe, managed to secure Mazandaran and Gilan along the Caspian coast. The civil war over power and control continued as Azad Khan fought the Qajars in Mazandaran while engaging in continuous battles against Karim Khan. Over the next ten years, Isfahan would repeatedly be captured, looted and then recaptured by various forces. At one point, Isfahan and nearby provinces were so devastated that the famine stricken city could hardly support its own populace, much less an occupying army.

The Qajars were finally routed and defeated by Karim Khan in February of 1759. In order to eliminate the future Qajar threats against him, he took the oldest son of Qajar tribe hostage and kept him at his court in Shiraz. The son, Mohammad, had been castrated by Nader Shah's nephew, Adil Shah, at the age of six, in order to prevent him from taking leadership of Qajar tribe. Thus, he was referred to as 'agha', -- eunuch.

Realizing the potential threat of Afghans within his provinces, Karim Khan ordered a general massacre of Afghans across northern Iran. Nine thousand Afghans were massacred in what at the time was the small town of Tehran.[462] Survivors were chased down as far as the city of Yazd in the south.[463] A few years later in 1763, Karim Khan was able to occupy Tabriz and Urmia in Azerbaijan province, making him the most powerful ruler of Iran in post-Nader era, a man who never allowed himself to be called the Shah, always insisting to be called *vakil* or 'representative'. [464]

***

In the culture of rule through any means necessary, the supreme military leader, whether called the Shah, Sultan, Caliph, Khan or, as in the case today, Supreme Leader, is allowed to use whatever cruelty is necessary to maintain power over the people. Any questioning of the leader's decision or position in society is severely and punitively dealt with in order to secure the status quo of institutions in power. Often, the despotic leader, in power through violence, will know little, if anything, about the economy, trade, or the arts and will care little about the welfare of those living under his rule. A despotic ruler must rely purely on the sword and the whip to maintain power, which often entails more and more beatings and massacres against discontent. Meanwhile, the economy and culture is neglected and the people become increasingly impoverished. The impoverishment of the population continues until the despotic regime, relying on ever dwindling tax revenue, can no longer maintain a disciplined and well-ordered army. Thus the despotic regime will either start a foreign war in the hopes of plunder and looting to pay for his military and lifestyle or will be overthrown by a rising military force within the country, feeding on the discontent of the people. If neither of these scenarios take place, then a leader of a foreign army, taking advantage of the crumbling military capabilities of the regime, will invade in order to loot and plunder and pay for his own military.

Iranian culture has a concept of benevolent despotism where an unwritten 'social contract' exists that requires the despot to rule with '*farr-e-izadi*' or 'the spirit of God'. Yet absolute power's corrosive and corrupting effects creates only a handful of such 'social contracts' every 1000 years. Such despotic rulers realize that investment in the economy, infrastructure, and trade will ultimately reduce uprisings, rebellions, and the number of dissidents against their rule. The despotic ruler will create a kinder, gentler image of himself by focusing his efforts on encouraging growth in agriculture, trade, and the arts.

The reign of Shah Abbas the Great is an example of such an intelligent and benevolent despotic ruler eliminating the need for rebellions and uprisings. Karim Khan of Zand was another of those benevolent despotic rulers who focused on the economy, trade, and the arts and who ruled over the population by gaining their respect, rather than employing ever increasing violence. Karim Khan had risen to power through use of the sword and crushed all rebellions against his rule. These suppressions of uprisings include one of his last major internal campaigns, in which, after he defeated rebel forces defending two fortresses in Bihbahan, he erected towers of rebels' skulls as a warning to others.[465] Afterwards, Karim Khan who always insisted to be called '*vakil*' meaning representative, entered his capital of Shiraz and did not leave the capital again for the remaining fourteen years of his life. These fourteen years represent another one of those rare instances in Iranian history where a despotic ruler had the intellectual skills to manage the country and that rarer insight to use the power of violence in his hand for the welfare of the citizens while focusing his resources on economy, trade, and the arts, creating a kinder, gentler attitude towards the citizens.

***

Karim Khan of Zand

During Karim Khan's reign, many of the clergy who had fled to Najaf and Karbala to escape the violence in Iran returned. In addition, many dervishes returned to Iran as well but were again attacked and persecuted by the ulama, or the clergy.[466] Tribal groups that had also fled their homeland were once again welcomed in the country.[467] Karim Khan attempted to repopulate and rebuild the devastated and ruined country of Iran, which had been suffering from virtually continuous disintegration since the time of Shah Abbas the Great. He sent official invitations to Jews and Christians to resettle in Shiraz to help the city prosper. One caravan of refugees returning to Iran from Baghdad in 1763 numbered 10,000 citizens. He also he reached out to merchants and bankers to encourage them to move to Shiraz. During his reign, complete villages around Isfahan and Shiraz were given to Armenians to encourage their settlement. Shiraz during his reign became the largest Jewish center in Iran.[468]

During times of drought and famine, funds from the treasury were used to purchase grain from distant provinces to be sold to suffering citizens at below cost. In Shiraz, he rebuilt the city walls, which included eighty towers. The *arg* or citadel and palace complex of the city were also built. In addition, mosques, baths, and *caravanserais* were built in the city under his guidance. He renovated some of the city's most sacred structures, which included the tomb or shrines of Hafez, Sa'adi, and Shah Shoja.[469] By design, his treasury was always left empty and any funds arriving were immediately spent on buildings, amenities, wages, pensions, and security.[470]

But such rebuilding in central Iran could not compensate for the unbelievable devastation the country had experienced since the reign of Shah Abbas. The estimated population of Isfahan during Karim Khan's reign cited by European travelers was 20,000-50,000, evidence of astounding depopulation and devastation. Isfahan during the reign of Shah Abbas had between 600,000-1,000,000 inhabitants. In effect, Karim Khan was in charge of a wasteland destroyed through generations of violence.

In addition, during his reign of benevolent despotism, Iranian politics was not free of war. Nine years after coming to power, Karim Khan went to war with the Ottoman Turks on two fronts, one in the south near Basra and a second in the region of Kurdistan. In 1775, a 30,000-man army led by Karim Khan's general, Sadiq Khan, marched to Basra and managed to blockade the city for over a year. After an Ottoman relief force from Baghdad was defeated, the blockade continued until the starving people of Basra submitted. Capture of Basra quickly devolved into looting and senseless slaughter. Throughout the city women were abducted and raped. The city, already void of food, was looted until there was nothing of value left. The soldiers then turned to the countryside, robbing the nearby Arabian tribes.[471] After these events, Basra "bled of all wealth, depopulated by plague, siege, and occupation…lost its commercial importance… and was no longer of use even as a bargaining-point in negotiations…"[472]

Shortly later, Karim Khan, now in his seventies, died after a six-month illness. Immediately, everything fell into chaos and civil war. His Qajar hostage, Agha Mohammad, who was allowed to go hunting and was on horseback at the time, kept on riding his horse north to Mazandaran. One of Karim Khan's commanders took over Isfahan.[473]

Karim Khan's general, Sadiq Khan, who had led the war in Basra, attacked Shiraz and, after an eight month siege, took the city but was murdered along with all of his sons. Nearly every town and city was occupied by a warlord controlling the population through cruelty. It was a matter of time until a vicious warlord capable of outdoing all others in inflicting terror would emerge victorious. It didn't take long. Mohammad Khan of Qajar tribe, whose family possessed the rich province of Mazandaran, and who had been castrated as a child and thus called '*agha**', serving as hostage most of his adult life, had enough sense for brutality to outdo all others and take control of his generation's fate.

***

---

* Meaning 'eunich' and with different spelling in Persian than the word '*agha*' meaning 'gentleman'.

CHAPTER 5

Agha Mohammad Khan

The Qajar tribal leader in Mazandaran had nine sons. His eldest, Agha Mohammad Khan managed to consolidate his family through politics. Not having a son, he favored his nephew, Fath Ali, who was to become the Shah after his rule.[474] He led a civil war against the Zand tribe which led to a Qajar victory in a battle south of Alborz Mountains. This was followed by plundering of Simnan, Damghan, Shahrud and Bistam which generated a rich reward for his soldiers and his numerous brothers.[475] A year later he invaded Gilan, the other rich tropic province of Iran, on the south-western shores of the Caspian Sea. The plundering of Rasht in Gilan provided him with further rewards keeping his soldiers content.[476] His army soon followed up this victory by crossing the Alborz mountains and capturing the cities of Qazvin and Zanjan.[477]

Another Zand army from the south forced the Qajars to flee to Astarabad and close the city gates. The Zands besieged the city, but the surrounding countryside had been so devastated that their horses and soldiers were soon out of supplies. In addition, the Zand's supply lines to Mazandaran were constantly harassed and destroyed by the Qajar horsemen. Soon, the Zand army dispersed and was completely defeated by the Qajars. The Qajar forces then marched south and after defeating the remaining Zand army near Kashan, managed to capture Isfahan.[478] The plundering of Isfahan by Qajar soldiers brought them more wealth than they had acquired through the plundering of cities in the north.

In order to maintain his military rule over Isfahan and central Iran and at the same time maintain control over his tropical provinces of Gilan and Mazandaran, Agha Mohammad Khan needed to have a capital more centrally located between these two regions. Along the southern steppes of Alborz mountains, in between the cities of Simnan in the east and Qazvin to the west and north of the historical city of Ray, lay a town where streams of melting snow from the Alborz Mountains had carved underground streams and rivers linking the basements of one house to another. The cool air from these underground streams was used for cooling of homes and the water used for cooking. My father recalls as a child visiting some homes that continued to have access to these underground rivers and caverns and recalls children catching small fish in these underground waters. This town, which had been nearly absent from Iranian history, was at times home to gangs of thieves and robbers who could easily hide in these underground caverns from any army chasing them. In the devastated wasteland of Iran experiencing 94 generations of violence, nearly every city and region in ruins, this oasis on the foot of Alborz Mountains had managed to retain its environment and its ancient gardens. In March 1786, after the capture of Isfahan, Agha Mohammad Khan walked into the oasis town of Tehran and named it his capital, symbolically creating a new era in Iranian history.

In the years that followed, the Zands and Agha Mohammad Khan's Qajars continued the civil war and struggle for supremacy, a contest that saw cities repeatedly taken by one faction and retaken by the other. This resulted in the reduction of Iranian civilization and society to a state of abject misery. After a 6 month siege in the city of Kerman, Lutf Ali Khan, the last Zand ruler, surrendered to Agha Mohammad Khan.

Angered at the popular support of Kerman for the Zand family, Agha Mohammad Khan ordered every eyeball of the male citizen in the city removed and brought to him. In a horrific scene which forever will be memorialized by Iranian cultural psyche in infamy, 20,000 pairs of eyeballs from all the men in the city were brought forth to the new king and poured in front of him. As far as women and children, 20,000 were taken as slaves and sent to Tehran. Over the next 90 days, Kerman was systematically looted and plundered of any value. On Agha Mohammad Khan's orders, Lutf Ali Khan, the last Zand ruler, was raped by slaves. He was then blinded, tortured, and finally died under torture.[479] Kerman was devastated and left as a wasteland.

After Kerman, Agha Mohammad Khan decided to invade and plunder Georgia in search of more wealth and prestige. With more than 40,000 horsemen, he defeated the Georgian army outside its capital of Tbilisi. The city was systematically plundered neighborhood by neighborhood, city block by city block, and house by house. Fifteen thousand Georgian women and children were taken as slaves and sent to Iran. This was followed by a massacre of the remaining population. An eyewitness who visited the city shortly after the destruction wrote:

"In traversing the city to the gate of Handshu, I found not a living creature but two infirm old men, whom the enemy had treated with great cruelty, to make them confess where they had concealed their money and treasures. The city was almost entirely consumed, and still continued to smoke in different places; and the stench from the putrefying bodies, together with the heat which prevailed, was intolerable…"[480]

Agha Mohammad Khan then marched to the northeast province of Khurasan, a wasteland by this time in Iranian history with each town and city ruled by a warlord brutality subjugating the people. Nader Shah's grandson Shahrukh, sixty-three and still in charge of Mashhad, was tortured until he gave up the remaining treasures of his grandfather.[481]

Violence by this time had become so predominant in the Iranian politics that when Agha Mohammad Khan asked his nephew's six-year-old son what his first action would be if he were to become the king, the child replied, "To have you strangled!". Only the intervention from the child's mother, father, and family prevented him from being executed on the spot.[482]

Agha Mohammad Khan then returned to Tehran, where he contemplated marching on Herat and the Durrani kingdom of Afghanistan, and even an invasion that would take him to Bukhara in the northeast. But news soon reached him that Russia's Catherine II had sent an expedition into the southeastern Caucasus, which forced the Shah to make preparations for another invasion of the Caucuses. Upon crossing the river Aras in the northwest, while resting in a town named Shusha one evening, he was disturbed by a quarrel between two servants over a melon. Angry at their disrespect, he ordered their immediate execution. A Kurdish tribal leader visiting the Shah begged him to forgive the servants. When the Shah refused, he begged him to only execute them at dawn. The Shah obliged, but left the two servants free for the evening. When the Shah was asleep, the two condemned men, together with another servant stabbed the eunuch king and the founder of Qajar dynasty to death.[483] As is expected, his sudden death sent the country into political turmoil.

The Kurdish leader besieged Qazvin, attempting to become the king, while the former king's brother marched from Azerbaijan to Tehran in order to take power. When he saw Tehran's gates closed to him, he went west to Karaj and proclaimed himself the king. Meanwhile, the former king's nephew and heir apparent, Fath Ali, marched onto Tehran and, after two battles west of the city, defeated his uncle and the Kurdish leader and on Nowruz of 1798, in the Gulistan palace of Tehran, proclaimed himself the second king from the Qajar family.[484] His thirty-seven-year rule coincided with the lifetime of the 95th and 96th generation of Iranians.

Fath Ali Shah

In 1804, only six years after Fath Ali came to power and after several years of minor military campaigns against the Ottomans and Afghans in the east and west, Iran was again involved in a major war with a neighbor, this time with the Russians to the north.

In 1813, a well-trained modern army of Russians numbering 2,260 soldiers routed a 30,000-man Qajar army during a two day battle in which 1,200 Iranians were killed and 537 taken prisoners compared to 127 dead and wounded Russians. The peace treaty that was signed in the village of Gulistan was humiliating to Iranians. In the treaty, Russia annexed the provinces of Georgia, Baku, Qarabagh, Ganja and Shirvan, the Republics of Georgia and Azerbaijan today. In addition, from then on, only Russians were allowed to have warships on Caspian Sea. The humiliation and ill-treatment of Muslims in the Caucuses over the next few years forced tens of thousands to flee to Iran. The situation also created strong anti-Russian sentiments in Iran, culminating in the religious class calling for jihad against the Russians. In June 1826, the Iranian clergy issued a fatwa declaring that opposing Jihad against the infidel Russians was a sign of disbelief in Islam.[485] Thus, another war was waged with Russia followed by another humiliating defeat at the hands of the modern Russian army. A peace treaty was signed at Turkmanchai. The provinces of Erivan and Nakhchivan were also annexed by Russia and Iran was forced to pay 20,000,000 rubles to Russians, a tremendous sum of money for a country largely reduced to a wasteland by generations of war and violence.[486] Russians were also entitled to approve of the heir to the Iranian throne. Thus began a neo-colonial relationship between Iran and the European powers that lasted until the latter half of the twentieth century.

After thirty-seven years of rule and two failed and humiliating military campaigns, Fath Ali Shah died in 1834. His grandson Muhammad Mirza was crowned as king, but the country fell into political turmoil as Ali Mirza Farmanfarma in Shiraz arranged to proclaim himself king. The provinces in the west and southwest were in anarchy and open rebellion, led by the Lur and Bakhtiari tribes. Revolts against the Qajars were eventually and brutally crushed.[487]

With the encouragement of Russia, Iran in 1836 instigated another war against the Durrani Kingdom of Afghanistan for the city of Herat, the last war initiated by Iran. After several months of unsuccessful siege and political pressure by Great Britain, this campaign was abandoned.[488] Over the next few years, the southern half of Iran was frequently in a state of rebellion and turmoil. The reign of Muhammad Shah lasted 14 years and coincided with the earlier years in the lifetime of the 97th generation of Iranians.

By this time in history, Iran was virtually a failed state. Frequent terrorizing cross-border raids by the Uzbeks for the slave trade were experienced in the northeast provinces of Khurasan and Gurgan. The slaves captured were sent to the flourishing slave markets of Khiva, Bukhara and other towns within Uzbek territory.[489] Raids were made even on larger cities of Mashhad and Astarabad. Caravans, if they dared to travel through this area, were even more in harm's way since they provided both merchandise and slaves for the raiding parties.[490]

The insecurity, instability and violence encountered on highways created a state in which food and other commodities could not be moved over very long distances. Thus local and regional crop failures and droughts triggered sudden episodes of starvation and famine. Cities like Mashhad that attracted pilgrims from across Iran were often hosts to many suffering from contagious diseases, making the pilgrim cities particularly vulnerable to sudden epidemics. Pilgrims traveling to holy shrines in search of cures for their diseases often mingled with other travelers in the cities' bazaars and caravanserais, spreading their disease to the local population. Kermanshah and Hamedan in the West, which were Iran's gateway to the holy cities of Najaf and Karbala were particularly vulnerable to epidemics of disease. In the 1830s, cholera and plague spread from Eastern Ottoman provinces across Iran, extending to the northeastern province of Gurgan, depopulating towns and villages, and disrupting commercial activity.

Iran Violence in 19th and 20th century

The broken, bankrupt and disillusioned Iran of mid-nineteenth century no longer had an appetite for war, especially since the enemies in west, north and south were the grand empires of the Ottomans, Russia and Great Britain. There was not even the strength of will for the rebellions that had been endemic throughout Iranian history.

Watching the events in Europe from afar, the Iranian intellectuals of the 1840's attempted to achieve similar prosperity for Iranians through the creation of intellectual, economic and artistic civil institutions much like those of the Europeans. The person who led this effort came from the most unexpected place within the Iranian society. The Qajar king's Prime Minister had a cook whose young son showed great intellectual potential as a child. The boy, named Mirza Taqi, was educated and rose to prominence within the Iranian political establishment, eventually becoming known as Mirza Taqi

Khan. In 1848 he was named the Prime Minster of the country and began a series of economic and political reforms, the likes of which had not been seen since the era of Shah Abbas the Great. He founded *Darolfonoon*, the first European style university in Iran, which later paved the way for the establishment of University of Tehran. He helped set up the first newspaper in the country. He also helped entrepreneurs and government agencies establish the textile, weaponry, sugar, glass, tea, and ceramic industries. He slashed unnecessary expenditures and created a national budget while separating the royal treasury from the public treasury and placing the Shah on a salary. He disciplined the army and made plans for the establishment of a navy.

Tariff was established to help ailing Iranian industries compete against the British and Russian imports. He instituted quarantines against contagious diseases and carried out the first national inoculation program against small pox based on a method called variolation. With tremendous changes taking place throughout Iran in a matter of less than a decade, people began to refer to their Prime Minister as Amir Kabir (Great).

Yet 96 generations of violence infiltrating the culture of the country could not be eliminated through such reforms and the establishment of few civil institutions. The 97th generation of Iranians, unlike the previous ones, did not experience war, violence and destruction, but their fate was again determined by violence. Fearing the Prime Minister's popularity, Mirza Taghi Khan, known as Amir Kabir was dismissed by the Shah and exiled from Tehran. Soon after, the Shah with the encouragement of his mother and his family, ordered the assassination of Amir Kabir, which took place in a public bath in the city of Kashan.

The next two generations of Iranians, the 98th and 99th, lived in a time free of foreign wars and major rebellions. Iran experienced fifty years of relative calm during the reign of Nasser-al-Din Shah (1848-1896) while the country played the pawn in a great game between the two military powers of Russia and Great Britain. It was during the relative peace of these two generations that many Iranians began to realize that their prosperity did not depend merely on the creation of intellectual, economic and military institutions but something more. For the first time in Iranian history, words such as 'democracy', 'citizen's rights', 'rule of law', and 'court of law' were introduced into the Iranian intellectual vocabulary. The continued efforts of the 99th generation of Iranians for justice led to the 'Constitutional Revolution' in 1906, considered by many as one of the greatest events in Iranian history. It

CHAPTER 5

took place in an atmosphere free of violence and without massacre of the royal family and public executions of anti-revolutionaries, an incredible achievement for Iranians after one hundred generations of violence and 2,500 years of history.

After the elections, the first freely elected Iranian parliament, known as the *majles*, convened to represent the citizens of the country and make national decisions for their prosperity. Yet, is it any surprise that the legacy of nearly one hundred generations of violence could not be put to rest. Within two years after the democratic election of first Iranian parliament, Mohammad Ali Shah of Qajar resorted to military force, using his canons for the bombard of the parliament building, once again placing the fate of another generation of Iranians in the hands of violence. Freedom fighters from the cities of Tabriz, Isfahan, Qazvin, and Rasht took up arms against the Qajar king and forced him to flee the country, reinforcing the belief that even a struggle for democracy must involve the use of guns and cannons.

Yet even after the victory of freedom fighters and return of the constitutional government in Iran, it wasn't long before use of violence would settle the next generation's political fate. Reza Shah who was an ingenious soldier who had risen within the ranks of the military to become the Minister of the Army and later the Prime Minister, carried out a successful coup. Well versed in political violence, he knew that he had to eliminate his enemies through force or get eliminated himself. Accordingly, he forced the last Qajar Shah to abdicate the throne and named himself Reza Shah of Pahlavi. Intellectuals and opponents to his rule persecuted, imprisoned, and a few executed. Some fled to Europe. Others retired from politics for duration of his rule, including Mohammad Mossadeq, who would later become a democratically elected prime minister of Iran. The fate of the 100th generation of Iranians, the generation of my great grandparents was also determined by violence, but Reza Shah was also an ingenious visionary who had a grand strategic vision on how to manage and build a country.

Reza Shah's sixteen years of military rule brought significant prosperity to a nation that had largely been in ruins since the 18th century. His economic and cultural vision and drive were no less than that of Amir Kabir or Shah Abbas and Iranians benefited just as greatly. He built the infrastructure of the country's capital, Tehran, in an effort not unlike the building of Isfahan by Shah Abbas. He rebuilt and disciplined the army and imposed security throughout the Iranian provinces, much as Shah Abbas had done during his lifetime. Tehran University was built, paving the way for the education and intellectual growth of my parents' generation. Modern factories were built, industry and trade was encouraged as well as music and the arts. Yet his ingenious manner of resurrecting the Iranian economy, military and infrastructure once again taught the Iranians the wrong lessons, ones that justify political violence and military rule

During the second great World War, the allied occupiers of Iran forced Reza Shah's army to disband. After the war, the absence of a powerful military rule over Iran gave rise to one of the most incredible events in Iranian history, the resurrection of democracy and the democratic election of Mohammad Mossadeq as the Prime Minister of Iran. But as Iranians sadly learned in the summer of 1953, without the elimination of the culture of violence from politics, democracy is only a short-term experiment awaiting the upheaval of a new violent force determined to rule through its military.

The Americans, aware of the threat of a communist takeover of Iran and aware of the incredible geopolitical importance of Iranian oil, gave way to British demands for a military coup. President Eisenhower ordered the CIA to plan and carry out the establishment of a military rule sympathetic to the west. In what became Operation Ajax, suitcases filled with cash were taken to Iran by CIA operatives and disbursed to the inner city *luti's* or thugs, sympathetic military officers and leading politicians sympathetic to the military coup, including Ayatollah Kashani, the most influential cleric of his generation. Mohammad Mossadeq was imprisoned and eventually died under house arrest. His Foreign Minister, Hossein Fatemi, only 37 years old was executed. Thousands of communist and nationalist sympathizers were imprisoned, press was strictly censored and a state of military rule was again established in Iran. The 1953 coup sealed the fate of my grandparents' generation, or the 101st generation of Iranians through the force of violence.

The last Shah of Iran ruled using his military and use of political violence much like every generation before. He created SAVAK, the infamous ministry of intelligence. The Evin prison was built, a place that continues to strike fear in the hearts of my generation. The Shah banned all political activities except those loyal to himself and in a famous television appearance in 1976, he announced that those not in favor of his single party system can obtain passports and leave the country. Keenly aware of the historical inevitability of war and violence for Iranians, he spent billions buying the most sophisticated weaponry available. Yet like his father, he also had a vision for building the country that brought tremendous cultural, social and economic prosperity to Iranians. Again teaching the wrong lesson to some

CHAPTER 5

that use of political violence is the most optimal solution for settling political fate.

Twenty-five years after Shah's military coup, my parent's generation or the 102nd generation, once again chose violence as the tool necessary for determining their fate. In the autumn of 1978, tens of thousands, followed by hundreds of thousands of Iranians began to shout *"Marg bar Shah"* (Death to Shah) from rooftops and sidewalks, thus legitimizing the use of violence against the Shah and his family and also paving the way for the eventual execution of many of the Shah's generals and supporters.

Later, the same political culture of violence was resurrected by those shouting *"Marg bar Amrica"* (Death to America), leading to the attack on the American Embassy in Tehran followed by decades of animosity and near war. Shouts of "death to anti-revolutionaries" became more and more used as an order and eventually led those with guns to execute thousands of political prisoners in the 1980's. *"Marg bar Israel"* (Death to Israel), became a constant slogan in our morning chants in elementary school, watched over by the *nazem** of the school, ruler in hand and ready to punish anyone merely lip-syncing our morning requirements. Political violence infiltrated every facet of my generation's life and without a doubt was the most influential determinant in the fate of my generation of Iranians.

As a child, playing soccer using pink striped plastic balls and placing bricks as goal posts in the streets of Tehran, I, along with the rest of the 103rd generation of Iranians, watched the events of the revolution and ensuing war unfold around us. My street was filled with refugee children and families fleeing the death and destruction of their homes in Ahvaz and Abadan. Death to Saddam became a rallying cry for nearly everyone. I witnessed bombings by Iraqi aircraft, and learned that chemical weapons were being used against children not much older than me in a war that took the lives of more than half a million people on both sides and left millions more physically or psychologically wounded.

As expected, political violence continued after the war through harassment and threats against those questioning the legitimacy of the revolutionary regime. Over 300 intellectuals, artists, political activists and writers were abducted and assassinated in the 1990's, many killed in shocking manners, intended to instill more fear in the population. The regime's violent actions and killings extended even to France, Germany and Austria, where

---

* School superintendent

Iranian political activists were murdered in their homes and on the streets. Attacks against teenagers and adults in the parks and on the sidewalks of Iran were meant as a demonstration of the regime's determination to go to any length to crush dissent by employing the repressive violence at its disposal. Violence against women was tolerated in order to suppress the threat of disobedience by half of Iran's population. Homes, private parties, and weddings were routinely raided to maintain the condition of a traumatized population living in fear. Iranians were routinely reminded of a possible military confrontation with the United States or Israel. When a relative opening of society took place during the reform movement after 1997, intellectuals, journalists, and student activists were imprisoned and tortured. Newspapers were shut down and their publishers threatened with violence.

And finally, after the contentious elections of 2009, when millions went into the streets to protest against the disputed election results peacefully, they were beaten and killed on the streets. Many who were arrested were taken to detention centers where they were raped and tortured by the security officers. Iranians who continue to dare to speak are beaten, killed or sent to prison.

It is violence, after all, that has always determined and continues to determine the fate of Iranians.

CHAPTER 5 - VIOLENCE AS *FAIT ACCOMPLI* OF HUMAN BEINGS

"The story of human race is war. Except for brief and precarious interludes, there has never been peace in the world; and long before history began, murderous strife was universal and unending."

~Winston Churchill

Political violence engulfing Iran is not a new phenomenon. It was not created by Khomeini or Khamenei. It was, and is, not the product of Islam or Shi'ism. It is not a response to the Arab-Israeli conflict, American imperialism or war in Iraq. The Taliban in Afghanistan did not invent political violence. It has always been political violence itself that has created all of the above and through continuous creation of circumstances continues to blight the lives of generations of human beings.

It was adoption of political culture of violence that gave rise to Khomeini, taught Khalkhali to kill, took Americans as hostages, murdered thousands of political prisoners, and imprisoned student activists. It is political violence that dictates how a supreme leader should kill, imprison, and torture. It will create the next Supreme Leader, Shah, Sultan or President and will dictate how that leader should terrorize its people. The culture of political violence bent on its own survival will brew hatred between the Sunnis and the Shi'ites. If unsuccessful at achieving that goal, it will brew hatred between Muslims and Jews or Muslims and Christians. Political violence will lead to the compulsory drafting of the next generations of Iranians into its military and will teach them to use guns. In order to advance its cause, it will teach them to hate. Those who learn to kill and terrorize will be rewarded by politics of violence with privileged position and wealth. Those persecuted will wait until they, in turn, can employ violence to their advantage.

We can assume that a small percentage of human beings are inherently violent. The American Psychiatric Association has a category of psychiatric disorder named anti-social personality disorder characterized by "pervasive pattern of disregard for and violation of the rights of others" and which manifests itself before the age of 15. One of the hallmarks of this personality disorder is a "lack of remorse, as indicated by being indifferent to or rationalizing having hurt, mistreated, or stolen from another." Lack of empathy is an important element of this disorder. We can safely assume that a small percentage of human beings throughout history who committed some of the great acts of violence had elements of this disorder. We can also safely assume that a small percentage of human beings will continue to manifest elements of this disorder in the future. Yet the vast majority of human beings who are not genetically inclined or predisposed to this disorder are the ones who murder, torture and rape in war and are responsible for much of humanity's acts of violence. Ordinary people are forced to become soldiers in armies, are thought to hate another set of human beings labeled as enemy, are then sent to faraway lands where they are forced to and at times commit rape and torture from the enraged hatred which they had learned to adopt. In inner cities, the same ordinary boys become members of gangs and are thought to use violence as a duty. Thus violence that manifests itself in society is often not driven by genetics (except in the minority of cases described above), but through learned behavior.

Iranians have struggled with the culture of political violence for more than one hundred generations. But this culture is not unique to Iranians. The 2,500 years of Iranian history is just one of many vivid panoramas of violence. A review of 2,500 years of British, Greek or Italian history will yield similar panoramas of violence. I am certain that a review of Baltic, Germanic, and French history will yield a similar story as well. Indians, Chinese, Japanese, Koreans, Mongolians will likely tell you the same story of violence going as far back as they can recall.

Every generation of Americans will also tell you the same story of violence. Millions of Americans came into the streets in March of 2003 and unsuccessfully protested against the most powerful military in history sending a generation to Iraq for war. They failed and the political culture of violence again prevailed. The American generation before was conscripted and sent to Vietnam while American political leaders were assassinated at home. Their parents were sent to the Koreas and fought in World War II. Their grandparents were forced to fight in the Great First World War. The generation before them was forced into the Spanish-American war and the wars against Native Americans west of the Mississippi. Their parents fought and died in Civil War, the bloodiest war in American history. Generation before was sent to the Mexican-American war of 1948 and the Second Seminole War (1835–1842) in Florida. The second generation of Americans fought the war of 1812 and the Creek War of 1813 against Native Americans and the first generation fought the American Revolution. Generation before generation prior to the American Revolution fought in wars for the British Empire.

In every culture and throughout human history, violence has had the most important role in determining the fate of each generation.

A glance at any pre-historic city-state farming society will also reveal the widespread use of violence and terror. Material left from the ruins of Babylon, Sumer, or ancient Egypt provides a wealth of evidence of violence just as horrifying as its use in the 20th century. Centuries of slavery led to building of grand pyramids as tombs for pharaohs. Wars between city-states of Babylon and her neighbors were just as numerous as wars in the modern era. The earliest Egyptian hieroglyphs record the victorious war of Egypt's first pharaoh. The oldest Sumerian story is the epic of warrior king Gilgamesh. Ancient Chinese texts are filled with stories of wars and violence and much of the Mayan text is devoted to the victorious wars of the Mayan kings.

Violence in Prehistoric Society

One study of the remains of early farmers in Britain dating to early Neolithic period, about 4,000 BCE found hundreds of flint arrowheads, especially at the gates of their compound.[491] Contemporary with the archery attacks were evidence of fires and destruction at these camps. Skeletal remains of one adult, beneath burnt rubble at the bottom of a ditch, showed "the young man had been shot in the back by a flint-tipped arrow and was carrying an infant in his arms who had been 'crushed beneath him when he fell."[492]

In one study of warfare in fifty primitive hunter gatherer societies, only five were found to have engaged "infrequently or never" in any type of offensive or defensive war, and four of these five apparently peaceful groups were recently driven by warfare into isolated refuges, protecting them from further conflict. Thus these 'pacifist' groups were, in effect, defeated populations, unable to carry out further war.[493]

In another study of war in ninety primitive societies, twelve were found to engage in warfare "rarely or never". Yet, most of these twelve groups were either living in isolation, like the Tikopia islanders of Polynesia and the Cayapa tribe of Ecuador, or were living under the protection of a modern state, like the Gonds of India or the Lapps in Scandinavia. Of the ninety societies studied only three groups did not engage in warfare and were not either under state protection or living in isolation and those were the Mbuti of

Zaire, the Semang of Malaysia, and the Copper Eskimo of arctic Canada.[494] Another study of 157 North American tribes found that only seven of them had not engaged in any type of warfare or raiding.[495] Even many isolated hunter-gatherers of Australian Aboriginals, living in the deserts, were found to have participated in raids.[496]

In a study of homicide rate amongst hunter-gatherer Kung San (Bushmen) of the Kalahari Desert, formerly described as 'peaceful', the rate of murder per capita within the population from 1920-1955 was higher than the murder rate in the United States.[497] In a study of one Copper Eskimo camp in early twentieth century, *every* adult male in the fifteen families reported being involved in a homicide sometime in their life.[498] The Copper Eskimos, one of the ninety societies found not to engage in warfare, had such high rates of homicide that the Royal Canadian Mounted Police was forced to impose sanctions against killings within the tribe.[499] Amongst the Netsilik Eskimos, the murder rate was four times the murder rate in the United States and fifteen to forty times higher than the rate in modern European countries.[500] In a study of primitive hunter-gatherer Gebusi tribe of New Guinea, individuals were routinely killed when they were suspected of engaging in witchcraft and sorcery, Bruce Knauft writes: "Only the most extreme instances of modern mass slaughter would equal or surpass the Gebusi homicide rate over a period of several decades."[501]

In addition, the frequency of warfare was also greater in primitive societies. In the previously mentioned study of ninety societies, about 75% went to war "at least once every two years before they were pacified or incorporated by more dominant societies."[502] During five and a half month study of the Dugum Dani tribe in New Guinea, tribesmen were observed to participate in seven battles and nine raids. In another study of a Yanamamo village in South America, the villagers were raided twenty five times in a fifteen month period. [503]

Douglas Bamborth[504] reports on archeological digs in the North American Great Plains showing native tribal farming groups who lived near Missouri river prior to arrival of Europeans invested substantial amount of time and energy in building defensive walls and fortifications. Along the Crow Creek, near the Missouri River floodplains, archeological digs showed a community of 50 houses surrounded by two fortification ditches.[505] Radiocarbon examination of the remains of this settlement showed natives were living there around 1325 CE, well before the arrival of Europeans.[506] In 1978, erosion of earth at the site revealed the skeletal remains of 478 individuals. Nearly 40% of these individuals showed evidence of blows to the head and skull fractures as the cause of death. Some skulls had up to five blows to the head.[507] Nearly a quarter showed the breakage of teeth at the gum line indicating sharp blows to the mouth. Ninety percent of the skulls showed evidence of scalping in the form of cut marks circling the skull with victims as young as one year old. Some had their hands and feet cut off, while in other cases noses had been slit or tongues had been severed and removed through a cut in the throat. The bodies had been left in the open for some time, since there was evidence of carnivores feeding on the corpses before someone placed them all in a ditch for burial. All in all, the archeological site paints a vivid picture of a massacre of an entire village, except for the relative underrepresentation of young women amongst the dead, an indication that young girls had been taken as prisoners or slaves by the invading party.[508] Remains of the houses and fortifications indicate that the structures had been burned down at the time of the massacre.

***

Prehistoric Human Violence

Human beings have struggled and lived with violence for a long time, perhaps far longer than the advent of farming and civilization 400 generations or 10,000 years ago. Violence has perhaps been a part of humanity dating back to its birth nearly 200,000 years or 8000 generations ago. Evidence of violent death can be seen in the oldest burial remains scattered across the world. In the Ofnet Cave in Germany dating to around 10,000 years ago, a cache of thirty-four trophy skulls was found; it included heads of women and children killed with multiple holes made on the skull by stone axes.[509] In Taleheim in Germany, bodies of eighteen adults and sixteen children were found in a pit dating to 7,500 BCE. The remains on the skeletons showed the victims were killed by blows by six different stone axes.[510] In the remains of fifty nine individuals which include women and children in an Egyptian cemetery dating from 14,000-12,000 years ago, 40 percent were buried with stone projectiles within or associated with their skeleton.[511] Wounds on the remains of children were all on head and neck suggesting execution style killing. One adult skeleton showed evidence of as many as twenty wounds. All in all, more than fifty percent of the remains in this pre-historic Egyptian burial ground were determined to have died of violence.[512] Thirty thousand year old burials in the Czech Republic show evidence of trauma from weapons, especially cranial fractures.[513] Other remains in Southern France from the same era (circa 36,000-24,000 years ago), shows cut marks on the forehead suggesting scalping of the individual.[514] I am sure as older remains are found reaching to dawn of modern human beings (homo sapiens), there would continue to be ample evidence of violence on their remains.

***

Violence in Chimpanzees

What if we go even further and look at violence in our closest animal relative? If violence can be traced to the birth of humanity, then perhaps we are predetermined to be violent. If so, a look at violence in our closest genetic relative, the Chimpanzees, may be of value as well. Our genes and the genes of the Chimpanzee are very similar with the most important difference being the much greater brain volume in human beings.

Chimpanzees may look peaceful when compared to horrors of wars, the atom bomb, genocides, or crimes in modern prisons at the hand of human beings. But because we don't see Chimpanzees develop a bow and arrow or learn to use an AK-47 does not mean the capacity and potential for violence is absent.

In early 1970's Jane Goodall was studying the Kasakela chimp community in Gombe Stream. In the previous ten years, tremendous changes had taken place in the area she was studying. Because of farming, the forest in which these chimpanzees lived, previously sixty miles in extent, was reduced to two miles in length, severely limiting the terrority in which several chimp communities lived perhaps placing them under societal stress, not unlike human beings whose foliage or farming lands' extent has been reduced by forces outside their control.

The chimps were often seen patrolling their territory smiliar to human beings protecting their land. On one occasion, Jane Goodall witnessed some chimpanzees viciously attack a mother and her child from another Chimpanzee community. The child was taken from the mother, killed, and parts of her eaten by the attacking chimps.[515] The mother's 'crime' was perhaps not unlike the crime of a human mother and child attacked and killed by members of an enemy tribe or country. Similar attacks against mothers and their infants of other chimp communities were seen a few more times in the same chimp colony.[516] The crime of the mothers may have been as simple as accidental passage into a neighboring colony's territory.

CHAPTER 5

Around the same time as these incidents, the Kasakela chimpanzee colony was divided into two groups. As is typical of chimpanzees holding their territories, the groups of males, often accompanied by females, would spend their time patrolling their territories. At times, when the two groups came upon each other, there were scenes of charging displays, but, generally, no violence. By 1974, threatening displays turned into violent confrontations. Violent raids were undertaken by the northern community into the southern territory with brutal attacks on members of the southern group. By 1977, all the male members of the southern community were either killed or presumed dead. They had managed to wipe out the male members of an enemy tribe, not unlike the massacring of one nation's army by another. "If they had firearms and had been taught to use them," Jane Goodall later wrote, "I suspect they would have used them to kill."[517]

After eliminating their southern neighboring community, the victorious chimpanzee tribe was then bordered by another southern tribe larger than themselves. The bigger group began a series of confrontations with the victorious group, eventually driving them away from their conquered teritory.[518]

"The human-like complexities found in chimpanzee politics are truly impressive," writes Paul Ehrlich, author of 'Human Natures: Genes, Cultures and the Human Prospect'. "Machiavelli would be proud of them." The ethologist, Frans de Waal, who studied a colony of chimpanzees in Arnhem Zoo in the Netherlands, tells the story of Yeroen, Nikkie and Luit and their ultimate fate determined by violence.

Twenty three chimpanzees lived in the Arnhem zoo within a large and pleasant park-like enclosure. The most dominant male within the group was Nikkie, who would maintain power through the help of his ally, Yoroen. Yet, there was a third powerful and muscular chimp named Luit who could beat either Nikkie or Yoroen in a one-on-one contest. But Luit was helpless as long as Nikkie and Yoroen were allies, fighting alongside each other.[519] Whenever there was a falling out between Nikkie and Yoroen, Luit would make a move carrying out stone and branch hurling displays of strength.

This struggle for leadership often led to tense engagements between the chimps with slight injuries. A few months later, Nikkie and Yoroen finally made their move against Luit in middle of the night. The next day, zookeepers found Luit badly injured. His toes were bitten off. His testicles were cut off and missing and he had so many wounds in his chest that he died later that day.[520]

We know of one hundred generations of violence in human history until the twentieth century. We know of perhaps four hundred generations of violence since the birth of farming and civilization and 8000 generations of violence since the birth of human species 200,000 years ago. Animals naturally use violence in self-defense or in hunt, but out of millions of animal species and more than five thousand mammals, only two species, us and the chimpanzees are known to carry out acts of violence not related to self-defense or hunt and in such gruesome manners.[521]

Does this mean we are violent as a species and hopeless in creating a nonviolent society?

Winston Churchill who wrote the 1,000 year history of Great Britain prior to becoming Prime Minister later concluded:

"The story of human race is war. Except for brief and precarious interludes, there has never been peace in the world; and long before history began, murderous strife was universal and unending."

Our story tells us that my generation of Iranians, the 103rd generation should have its fate determined by violence, either through a bloody foreign war or a massively violent internal rebellion followed by another group, either from within Iran or a foreign force holding the gun.

Conclusion to Violence

How many more generations will experience the horrors of violence? What kinds of violence will the ingenious human mind invent in the 21st and 22nd centuries? What stories will there be in the next several centuries of continued genocide and war, now with weapons such as the AK-47 and the atom bomb? What evils or dark eras will humans experience in the next 1000 years or 2500 years of humanity? Are we doomed to live in the cycle of violence and war repeated since the dawn of human beings? Are we doomed because we are human beings?

Or should we be hopeful *because* we are human beings?

We must be conscious that a human being is just another organism trying to survive like all other species. Moreover, while not necessarily more violent than other species, due to exceptional brain size and intelligence, humans are incredibly gifted and creative in use of violence against perceived threats. Our incredible brain allows us to be the only animal capable of sharpening a piece of rock, placing it on a wooden stick, and shooting it at another animal or human being. We're the only animal capable of building an AK-47 and the white phosphorus bomb.

But further than this, we are the only organism capable of using violence as a tool for the survival of abstract concepts such as our nation, religion, ideology or tribe, concepts which are only possible because of our brain's incredible capacity to create symbols for such abstract concepts. Incredible violence in effect is then used by human beings for the survival of symbols such as ideology and religion as opposed to only physical survival seen in other animals.

The incredible growth of our brain size and intelligence has created an organism that when the perceived survival of its ideology, religion, nationality or tribe is at stake, is capable of any form of violence. We're the only animal capable of creating a symbol for an enemy and teach our children to hate the symbol and be willing to kill anyone associated with that symbol.

Yet we cannot assume that human beings are more violent than other species because of our incredible ingenuity for violence. We cannot forget that our ability to create a symbol, teach that symbol to our children through words, images and acts is not limited to creation of symbols of hate and violence. Our incredible brain has also allowed us to be the only animal capable of creating symbolic words, images or acts signifying kindness and compassion. Unlike animals trapped in the predetermined rule of their genes, using violence for physical survival, we are free to create a culture, teach our children that culture, and have that culture be represented as anything we wish. Because of our ability for creating the symbols of peace, friendship, rights and laws, we're the only animal capable of creating cultures built on symbolic words, acts and images representing human rights and democracy.

Perhaps, after all, we're not doomed to be trapped in the abyss of violence because we are human beings, but perhaps we are blessed *because* we are human beings.

The creation of a culture free of violence requires the elimination of violent words, images and acts from homes, schools, streets, and most importantly, the religion, ideologies and politics of the country. This elimination requires the elimination of undemocratic political institutions that are in power through violence and instituting free elections of officials without fear or threat of violence. Elimination of violence from religion requires the separation of all religious institutions from levers of power in the government and the elimination of violence from politics through the adoption of the principles of human rights in the constitution of the country protecting every human being from the threat or use of violence.

But this task of purging violence from cultures and societies has a formidable opponent— violence itself.

How do you defeat powerful human inventions, ingenuities and advancements in violence without using this powerful weapon of violence itself?

Those who see our salvation in a human being's capacity for learning, reason, empathy and compassion know of the extraordinary weapon of nonviolence that was created in the 20th century which was the missing tool for going to battle against violence without the use of violence itself.

Through nonviolence, human beings created and invented the methods and mechanisms of struggle to free themselves of political terror, enslavement, oppression, and fear to match the greatest weapons of violence. For the first time, human beings were able to create the ideas and concepts on how to defeat the incredible powers of violence without resorting to violence itself; an incredible achievement which brought to life the hopes and dreams of countless human philosophers of kindness and compassion. Many believe there were two invincible forces created in the 20th century against those holding the gun. One was the atom bomb, the second was nonviolence. If there is any hope for humanity, it is not in the creation of the first as deterrence against violence, but the use of the second in the elimination of violence. And if Iranians are to find peace and security in the most volatile region in the world, home to cross-roads of civilizations, it will not be through the creation of an atom bomb, but through the successful use of nonviolence and the elimination of forces of violence from their politics, religion and perhaps from the region.

The philosophy of nonviolence and the methods and mechanisms of nonviolent struggle against violence may perhaps be one of the greatest discoveries of human beings, a discovery which many nations, who successfully applied it against horrifying and brutal regimes, call as invincible as the atom bomb.

Yet most Iranians so well versed in methods and tactics of violence wonder how one can challenge a ruthless, violent system with nonviolence? If violence itself is a tool, how can nonviolence, or the refusal to resort to violence, be used as a mechanism and not for pacifism? What is a nonviolent struggle and what is <u>nonviolence</u>?

"Hours before his death, Margaret Bourke White, a U.S. journalist asked Gandhi 'How would you meet the Atom Bomb ... With nonviolence?' and Gandhi replied:
I will not go underground. I will not go into shelter. I will come out in the open and let the pilot see I have not a trace of evil against him. The pilot will not see our faces from his great height, I know. But that longing in our hearts – that he will not come to harm – would reach up to him and his eyes would be opened."

~ from Gandhi on War and Peace

PART II

Promise of Nonviolence

CHAPTER 6 - THE BEGINNINGS OF NONVIOLENCE

"Others... serve the State chiefly with their heads; and, as they rarely make any moral distinctions, they are as likely to serve the devil, without intending it, as God."

~Henry David Thoreau

Nonviolence as a Modern Phenomenon

A European or American reader looking at the 100-generation cycle of violence in Iran and the brutality of the Islamic Republic may falsely assume that an Iranian today knows nothing but violence. Yet, when the same reader travels to Iran and looks beyond the politics of terror, he or she sees a culture far different than the one read about in history books or seen in media. Peering into the bookshelves in an Iranian home, the visitor will find many books on practice and the philosophy of kindness and compassion, starting with perhaps the first and most important Iranian philosopher and teacher, Zoroaster. Then the Western visitor will see the advice of kindness, humanity and justice in Sa'adi and the practice, adoration and worship of love and pleasure in Hafez, two other pillars of Iranian culture. Looking around the bookshelf, one comes to *Shahnameh*, the great gathering of Iranian mythology by Ferdowsi and perhaps the most important pillar of Iranian culture where the visitor finds lessons in tragedy of violence and war. The wealth of books and literature on love expands to include great Iranian philosophers in the Sufi tradition such as Sohrevardi, Attar Nishapuri and of course another of the pillars of Iranian literature and culture, Jallaledin Rumi.

Aside from their literature, the Iranian host will also remind the Westerner of the proud and ancient heritage of national celebrations of seasons, particularly Nowruz, when anger, fighting and hatred between family and siblings are inhibited and where kindness and charity predominates family and societal life.

Yet, when the visitor asks the host how the culture of love and kindness can be used against the incredible violence of Islamic Republic and its leaders' grip on power, the Iranian host is speechless. Suddenly, the Iranian literature and heritage of celebrations are looked upon as great humane ways of life more appropriate for advice, pleasure and as poetry and art than having any real significance in politics.

What the host and the visitor soon realize is that although this immense culture of kindness and love is present in Iranian homes and culture, such philosophy is only appropriate for individuals and useless against the swords of soldiers and so unless it can be turned into practical steps against violence, such philosophies of love and kindness will be good only as advice for individual transformation for the foreseeable future.

Use of such philosophy of love and kindness, as instruments only for personal growth and irrelevant as societal tools against the sword and the gun would have been the fate of human beings except for the incredible transformation of the philosophy of love into philosophy, methods and practice of nonviolence in the 20th century. This transformation first occurred through visionary works on nonviolence in 19th century and application of those ideas and theories by philosophers, scholars, activists and great leaders of the 20th century.

If one is to understand the use of nonviolence as a method for societal as opposed to individual change, then one must begin with the roots of this incredible vision in the 19th century. If one were to plan a strategy for a conventional military war, one would need to study the tactics and strategies of ingenious generals in history. One would need to study the principles of warfare and the mechanisms and methods available for war and destruction. Throughout the study of military history, one must learn about the overall strategy, the importance of soldiers' morale, decision-making at the command level, and leadership in war. Regardless of the earliest and the contemporary versions and effectiveness of weaponry, technology, and tactics used in warfare, the study of history is of utmost importance when attempting to fight a new war.

In a nonviolent struggle in which one side employs violence and the other refrains from its use, those who adhere to the principles of nonviolence need to include as much strategy, planning, and discipline as those who wage a war using the power of violence. We cannot understand the importance of strategy and discipline in a nonviolent struggle without carefully studying the story, philosophy and history of nonviolence. Only then we can study the societal and cultural tools available to this generation for their next epic battle in Iranian history.

CHAPTER 6

The Roots of Nonviolence - Henry David Thoreau

Henry David Thoreau's essay published in 1849, *On [the?] Duty of Civil Disobedience*, is considered one of the first and most important philosophical works on nonviolence. Here, for the first time, a philosopher argues succinctly for civil disobedience or the intentional disobeying of unjust laws.

Born in 1817 in Massachusetts, Thoreau attended Harvard University and graduated in 1837, but became disenchanted with people's blind acceptance of unjust laws and human detachment from nature. He withdrew to the shore of Walden Pond, where in isolation from civilized and industrial world, he built a cabin and lived amongst the animals and plants. During his life, he urged that individuals should listen to their conscience and consciously disobey all unjust laws.

In his attempt to listen to his conscience, he refused to pay tax to a Massachusetts government that indirectly continued to support slavery through trade with the south. While in seclusion in the forest, he wrote his famous book, *Walden*, which is now considered one of the great works of American literature. But for those in search of nonviolence, it was his essay 'Civil Disobedience' which was far more influential.

His essay was first published in 1849 with the title '*Resistance to Civil Government*'. It was only after his death when it was reprinted with its new title 'On Duty of Civil Disobedience' or simply 'Civil Disobedience', titles never used by Thoreau during his lifetime.[522] In his essay, he was most critical of people's undue respect for the law. He despised people who bowed before the laws of the government without questioning them and without using their conscience to decide what was right. He wrote: "A common and natural result of an undue respect for law is, that you may see a file of soldiers, colonel, captain, corporal, privates, powder-monkeys and all, marching in admirable order over hill and dale to the wars, against their wills, aye, against their common sense and conscience… The mass of men serve the state thus, not as men mainly, but as machines, with their bodies." "Others, as most legislators, politicians, lawyers, ministers, and office-holders, serve the State chiefly with their heads; and, as they rarely make any moral distinctions, they are as likely to serve the devil, without intending it, as God."[523]

He was most critical of his government's support for an "immoral war against Mexico" and the US government's acceptance of the evil of slavery. He wrote: "I cannot for an instance recognize that political organization as my government which is the *slave's* government also." And then, in his essay, he continues: "when a sixth of the population of a nation which has undertaken to be the refuge of liberty are slaves, and a whole country is unjustly overrun and conquered by a foreign army, and subjected to military law, I think that it is not too soon for honest men to rebel and revolutionize."[524]

Thoreau's most significant contribution was the notion that unjust laws, laws against humanity and laws which go against the truth and conscience of a human being must not only be ignored, but they must also be disobeyed intentionally. Later, because of his work and works of many other activists, Massachusetts would become the center of anti-slavery sentiment and do exactly what Thoreau advocated—many of its citizens refused to recognize the validity of the Fugitive Slave Law (which compelled local governments in non-slave-owning states to forcibly return runaway slaves to their Southern masters) and actively resisted the US government's attempt to enforce it. His important contribution that unjust laws must be intentionally disobeyed as basis of a nonviolent struggle is an important work of philosophy much needed in the struggle for democracy in today's Iran.

Unlike the concept of civil disobedience advocated by Thoreau, with the coming of Khatami to power in Iran in 1997, the reformists in Iran adopted *mobarezeh-madani* meaning (civil-struggle) as central to their strategy as opposed to *nafarmani-madani* (civil-disobedience). Thus reformists, instead of advocating disobedience to the unjust laws and institutions of the Islamic Republic, continuously would advocate adherence to such laws and struggle within the civil institutions of the Islamic Republic and within the frameworks of unjust constitution of Islamic Republic. Thoreau directly confronts this Iranian reformist philosophy that the laws of Islamic Republic must be obeyed and change should come through legal pathways in the struggle for justice. As opposed to misunderstood notion of 'civil disobedience' advocated by the Iranian reformists, Thoreau tells us that 'civil disobedience' is the *intentional* disobedience of a law. In addition, he emphasized that violence employed to strike down such unjust laws can be as unjust and immoral as the imposition of those laws.

As if writing against Khatami, the reformists and the reform strategy through *civil-struggle*, Thoreau wrote: "Those who, while they disapprove of the character and measures of a government, yield to it their allegiance and support, are undoubtedly its most conscientious supporters, and so frequently the most serious obstacles to reform."[525] He then continues: "Unjust laws exist: shall we be content to obey them, or shall we endeavor to amend them, and obey them until we have succeeded, or shall we transgress them at once?

Men generally, under such a government as this, think that they ought to wait until they have persuaded the majority to alter them. They think that, if they should resist, the remedy would be worse than the evil. But it is the fault of the government itself that the remedy is worse than the evil. It makes it worse".[526]

Finally, when speaking of responsibility of public officers and tax collectors of his time and those who make the machinery of political terror in Islamic Republic possible, he wrote: "If you really wish to do anything, resign your office. When the subject has refused allegiance, and the officer has resigned his office, then the revolution is accomplished."[527]

***

Leo Tolstoy

To learn of the next great philosopher of nonviolence in 19th century, one is transported from the serene Walden Pond in America to the vast plains of Russia.

This great next philosopher and contributor to nonviolence was born in a wealthy and aristocratic family from the military caste in Russia. Many poor peasants in Russia making a pilgrimage to Russian Orthodox holy shrines had to pass through his grand estate[528]. He was born into a religious family, but in a culture that believed that religion was more of a concern for women, children and the poor than for men like him. In his adolescent years, despite his religious upbringing, his brothers encouraged him to have sex with a prostitute and begin a life of debauchery. "… and this is how I spent those ten years of my life."[529]

Upon marrying, he changed his lifestyle and moved with his wife to his family estate of Yasnaya Polyana in Tula region of Russia, approximately 200km from Moscow. [530] There he lived an ideal of a couple who marry for love and live in the country and devote themselves to their children and pleasures of art: "…. As a nature worshipper, he celebrated the flowing rivers, the melting ice, the singing birds, the mowing of the peasants. The apple orchards of [his estate] Yasnaya Polyana were famous."

There, with the help of his wife he wrote his first literary work. It was a novel, but he referred to it as an "epic in prose". His masterpiece, "*War and Peace*" was immediately hailed as one of the greatest novels ever written and Leo Tolstoy immediately became one of the most celebrated and highly regarded writers of the 19th century. With its publication, he was no longer just a wealthy Russian aristocrat, but one of the most famous Russians in the world.

In the first twenty years of marriage, while living at his estate and with the help of his wife he also completed his second novel "Anna Karenina". With the publication of the second book, he was accorded the respect, fame, and fortune given to the greatest novelists of 19th century, the kind very few attained in their lifetime.

Yet, at the peak of his fame and wealth, Tolstoy gave his entire fortune and estate to his wife and began a life of simplicity much like that of the peasants of Russia. His lasting philosophical contributions to nonviolence began a bit little later. In 1881, when he was 53 years old, he wrote a letter to Tsar Alexander III asking him to pardon the assassins of Alexander II on the grounds that it was the proper Christian thing to do. After this letter, he began to devote himself to persuading his fellow human beings that love had to overcome the evil of violence. Based on his religion beliefs, he concluded that a true Christian could never harm another person or hate him or her.

He believed that the sermon of Jesus on the Mount spoke to the core of Christianity but that Christianity had lost sight of that essential truth. During that sermon, Jesus had preached: ".... Love your enemies and pray for those who persecute you... ".[531]

He believed the Christian Church, in its approval and justification of wars, violence, and murder had drifted away from the true message of Christ. In 1881-1882, he wrote a *"Critique of Dogmatic Theology"* in which he examined a series of Church documents and concluded that they were more blasphemous than any of the works of Voltaire.[532] After studying those documents, he wrote, "I had intended to go to God and I found my way into a sinking bog, which evokes in me only those feelings of which I am most afraid; disgust, malice and indignation."[533]

In a later pamphlet *"Church and State"* (1882), attacking the union of church and state, he condemned the term Christian-State as paradoxical and nonsensical as "hot ice; either such a state is no state, or, more likely, its Christianity is no Christianity." In reading this passage, one can instantaneously imagine him not talking about the 19th century church and state in Russia, but seeing the present as an Iranian living in Iran discussing the conflation of Islam and the State.

Later, in his work "My Religion" written in 1884, he built and developed his philosophy of nonviolence based on what Jesus said during his sermon on the Mount—"Resist, not evil".[534] Tolstoy wrote: "I was taught to judge and punish. Then I was taught to make war; that is, to resist evil men with murder, and the military caste, of which I was a member, was called the Christ-loving military, and their activity was sanctified by a Christian blessing"

The Kingdom of God…

His most important work however for the philosophy of nonviolence was written in 1894 and called "The Kingdom of God is Within You". In this book, Tolstoy expressed his rejection of violence in the most succinct way and further developed the Christian concept of non-resistance as the antidote to the evil of violence and injustice of his era.

Again, Tolstoy's philosophy relied on the Sermon on the Mount. It was in this direct, simple yet profound sermon that Jesus, before he was crucified presented many important concepts of Christianity: "Judge not that ye shall be judged… ", "Love thy enemy" and "Resist, not evil".

For Tolstoy, the message of Jesus was clear: Do not submit to evil, when faced with evil. Do not commit violence and murder in order to prevent violence. He considered these imperatives as important pillars of Christianity, which Tolstoy claimed the amalgam of church and state has ignored and suppressed. Jesus's message: "Resist, not evil" was a clear indication for Tolstoy that Christians, by committing murder through wars and injustice by enslaving those in conquered nations are implicated in the sin and evil that Jesus preached against.

In "The Kingdom of God…", Tolstoy spent a considerable amount of time addressing those who reject the philosophy of non-violence and continue to advocate the use of violence. The first of those advocates he mentioned are European Christians who claim that use of violence is "not opposed by the teachings of Christ; that it is permitted and even enjoined, on the Christians by the Old and New Testaments."[535] "According to these people" he states, "a Christian government is not in the least bound to be guided by the spirit of peace, forgiveness of injuries, and love for enemies."[536] These people, he believed, have completely misunderstood Christianity and claimed that if people were to fully understand the teachings of the Church that "professes to believe in a Christ of punishment and warfare, not of forgiveness, no one would believe in the Church."[537]

Then he addresses the second proponents of violence, those who believe the world is filled with evil and violent individuals and if "these wicked men were not restrained by force, the whole world and all good men would come to ruin through them."[538] This he also believed to be against his Christian religious values according to which we are "all equals and brothers, as sons of one Father in heaven."[539]

Tolstoy was very critical of the preachers who adamantly objected to the breaking of any of the Ten Commandments, but when it comes to nonviolence they "openly teach that we must not understand it too literally, but that there are conditions and circumstances in which we must do the direct opposite, that is, go to law, fight, and punish."[540] He then addresses the most common and most frequently used arguments for the use of violence. He claims that this group's acceptance of violence is based on belief "that this question is one which has long ago been decided perfectly, clearly and satisfactory, and that it is not worthwhile to talk about."[541] This faction, he believed, are those who believe violence has always been a part of human history and will always be a part of human history.

Tolstoy divides the proponents of violence and his critics into two groups of people. Those conservatives who maintain the status quo governments and regimes built on violence and who need violence in order to suppress, persecute, and punish their opponents— in particular, the revolutionaries. The second group he labels as the revolutionaries who believe that violence is necessary to fight the status quo regimes and overthrow the government.[542] He claims that his critics believe the concept of nonviolence "would turn mankind aside out of the path of civilization along which is moving," a path he believed was deeply rooted in violence.[543]

Miraculous Life of Christ

Tolstoy believed that for one to understand the message of religion, one does not need to believe in miracles or elaborate symbolic stories of the past. One only needs to realize the truth in the message of love and the need for love in humanity and its application in the path toward perfection. For Tolstoy, forgiveness, love for all, especially for the enemy, and nonresistance to evil were the pillars of religion without which one cannot understand the essence of God. For him, religion was not a set of rules to follow blindly, but rational tools given to us by some of the great mystics of the world. Through meditation, nature and love, he himself had set upon this path. He eventually spent most of his life preaching the philosophy of love.

Tolstoy believed that along the path of finding individual inward perfection, truth, and love as preached by mystics and philosophers, human beings could also set out on the journey of perfection in society through the application of nonviolence as a societal and cultural philosophy. This renunciation of violence in society and the elimination of violence in society, he believed, would lead humans to the "kingdom of God, when all men will cease to learn to make war, when all shall be taught of God and united in love, and the lion will lie down with the lamb."[544]

But like thousands of other philosophers of love before him, Tolstoy did not provide a detailed plan on how to eliminate violence from society. He only believed that if everyone followed this path of nonresistance to evil, then evil in the form of violence could be eliminated. Yet he failed to realize that one can never have a society where every single individual finds the path of love. If you have a community of 1,000 individuals and 999 of them has accepted the philosophy of love, even if one person decides to use violence and pick up a gun, that person can soon enslave others through violence. The modern solution of humanity to this ancient problem has been to reserve the power of violence through a police force taking orders from democratically elected officials of the people. In the police force, the task of maintaining order is granted through lawful punishment, the actual use of violence, or the threat of violence against citizens who break the law and who resort to violence. Yet, as it often happens, if a society moves toward a more undemocratic structure, this lawful use of violence by the police becomes a tool for the government to serve its own needs and to maintain power for itself.

We can safely assume that a police force will always be needed in any society and there will always be individuals or groups who will make every effort to use violence for material gain or to enslave others. A mystic like Tolstoy may have had the ability to see love in the heart of every single individual, yet without concrete steps through which this love can be expressed and practiced, hatred will have as great a chance of infecting the heart of humanity as love does.

In addition, humanity is well acquainted with the language of violence, which is easily taught to others. Yet, in practice, the language of love and the culture of love is unfamiliar and more difficult to spread. At the time of his writings, political violence had been inflicted on humanity for thousands of years through organized institutions of monarchy and church, accumulating vast wealth and gaining complete control over the will of the majority. The response to this culture of hatred and violence needed not just the philosophy of love but concrete, specific, practical steps and methods requisite for its success. That was something Tolstoy was unable to accomplish during his lifetime. His attempt to spread the culture of love fell short in Russia; the powers of the regime and the elite were spreading hatred and violence far beyond his ambit.

Tolstoy did provide two specific ways to go about translating nonviolence into action which were revolutionary at the time. The first was the elimination of compulsory military service, which at the time was prevalent not only in Russia but throughout much of human history. Tolstoy called for the elimination of this practice as an important step toward the elimination of violence in society. This is an important concept that Iranians must also collectively advocate for the democratic Iran of tomorrow. Compulsory military service takes young Iranian men and women away from their family, careers, and education during the most fruitful and important years of their lives and through threat of punishment, this age-old conscription teaches them the use of guns and violence and destroys the free spirit these individuals had nurtured in their childhood. The second practical step Tolstoy proposed was for Russians to refuse service in the military and thus resist supporting Russia's wars of imperialism. This preaching of nonparticipation against foreign wars was already in practice by a Christian sect in Russia called the Dukhobors. These Christians were much like the Quakers in America who refused to engage in violence as a fundamental tenant of their religion. Dukhobors rejected the institution of governmentally authorized church and priesthood and promoted a communal and democratic way of life. They were fiercely persecuted by the Tsarist regime. In 1840, because of their refusal to serve in the military for a foreign war, their lands were taken from them and they were settled near the Sea of Azov by the Black Sea. Near the end of 19th century, the Russian government again began persecuting them and required them to again participate in a war. Depleted of their resources, they no longer had the funds to emigrate and escape from the grasp of the Tsar. At that time, Tolstoy no longer had his wealth and estate to help with their cause. It had been a long time since he had left all his wealth to his wife and had a life of simplicity much like the peasants of Russia. He cleaned his own room, made his own shoes, and grew his own food. But in order to help the cause of those believers of nonviolence, he rapidly completed his final novel *'Resurrection'* and with the immense royalty income from his book he helped 12,000 Dukhobors immigrate to Canada.

Tolstoy spent the rest of his life preaching nonresistance to evil and the philosophy of forgiveness and love. His book "The Kingdom of God is

Within You" did not pass the censors in Czarist Russia and was banned. Yet because of his fame, the book was soon translated into many different languages, including English, and was widely published in Europe. A copy of this book in English was obtained by a Quaker in South Africa which history famously knows as Mr. Coates. This person who at the time was also practicing the philosophy of nonresistance to evil had befriended a young Hindu lawyer who had been sent on a one-year mission to South Africa for a legal case. Amongst the books given to this young Hindu in order to acquaint him with the concept of love in Christianity was a copy of Tolstoy's "Kingdom of God...". The young Hindu later wrote: "Tolstoy's *The Kingdom of God is within you* overwhelmed me. It left an abiding impression on me. Before the independent thinking, profound morality, and the truthfulness of this book, all the books given me by Mr. Coates seemed to pale into insignificance."[545]

'A Letter to a Hindu'

In 1908, in response to a request from the editor of 'Free Hindustan' newspaper, Tolstoy, now an old mystic and philosopher of love, wrote an immensely important letter to the people of India, 'A Letter to a Hindu'. The letter was addressed to Tarak Nas Das, an anti-British revolutionary leader of Indian movement for independence. Yet its message of nonviolence was rejected by Nas Das and other Indians struggling against British imperialism because they believed Tolstoy was advocating the adoption of a passive tactical approach. The letter, printed in *Free Hindustan* Newspaper, was passed along from person to person until it came into the hands of that same young Hindu lawyer in South Africa. He was asked whether this letter was worth publishing in his South African newspaper. He replied: "To me, as the humble follower of that great teacher [Tolstoy] whom I have long looked upon as one of my guides, it is a matter of honor to be connected with the publication of this letter, such especially as the one which is now being given to the world."[546]. He volunteered to translate it into Hindu and encouraged various Indian newspapers to publish it.

Written with his usual eloquence, Tolstoy's letter was a response to an Indian culture that had used the age-old methods of violence in the struggle against British oppression. The old Russian mystic succinctly laid out the philosophy of love and encouraged Indians to search their hearts and find the truth of love within them. In the letter, Tolstoy begins "The oppression of a majority by a minority, and the demoralization inevitably resulting from it, is a phenomenon that has always occupied me and has done so most particularly of late...The reason for the astonishing fact that a majority of working people submit to a handful of idlers who control their labor and their very lives is always and everywhere the same—whether the oppressors and oppressed are of one race or whether, as in India and elsewhere, the oppressors are of a different nation."

The letter reads as if Tolstoy was addressing the Iranians of today and not the Indians from a century before. His letter continues to define love as the nature of God and points out that God's love cannot be present in political religion, which is certainly the case of those in Iran who are in power today and don't hesitate to terrorize and murder in the name of God.

In his 'A Letter to a Hindu', which today reads as if he were writing 'A Letter to an Iranian', he criticized those who, in the name of religion, use violence to alter and obscure the message of love and perhaps the true message of religion. He believed in the overwhelming power of love and its ability to overcome tyranny and repression. "Thus the truth that this life should be directed by the spiritual element which is its basis, which manifests itself as love, and which is so natural to man ... had to struggle not merely against the obscurity with which it was expressed and the intentional and unintentional distortions surrounding it, but also against deliberate violence, which by means of persecutions and punishments sought to compel men to accept religious laws authorized by the rulers and conflicting with the truth. Such a hindrance and misrepresentation of the truth...occurred everywhere: in Confucianism and Taoism, in Buddhism and in Christianity, in Mohammedanism and in your Brahmanism."

Tolstoy told Hindu readers in his letter that "love represents the highest morality" and "this truth was so interwoven everywhere with all kinds of falsehoods which distorted it, that finally nothing of it remained but words. It was thought that this highest morality was only applicable to private life for home use, but that in public life all forms of violence such as imprisonment, executions, and wars might be used for the protection of the majority against a minority of evildoers... such a teaching, despite its inner contradiction, was so firmly established that the very people who recognize love as a virtue accept as lawful at the same time an order of life based on violence and allowing men not merely to torture but even to kill one another."

We look at India and its 20th century nonviolent struggle against the British as the model and inspiration for much of nonviolent movements throughout 20th century, yet we fail to realize that India fought the British for generations by relying on violence before adopting nonviolence. Indians who read Tolstoy's letter, ridiculed such talk of love and nonviolence and regarded it as weakness. 'Free Hindustan', the newspaper that received this letter had the motto: "Resistance to aggression is not simply justifiable but imperative, nonresistance hurts both Altruism and Egotism." What Tolstoy was telling the people of India was in direct opposition to what they believed. Thus, India's belief in violence caused Tolstoy's letter to be ignored and, if it were not for the young Hindu lawyer in South Africa, it might well have been forgotten.

In 1909, the young Hindu lawyer wrote to Tolstoy. In his diary Tolstoy writes that he has received "a pleasant letter from a Hindu of the Transvaal [South Africa]". Tolstoy may, as some mystics do, have sensed the immense importance of this individual to humanity. Tolstoy may have sensed that this young man would become one of the most important and influential figures of the 20th-century. That in 50 years, people would regard him as not only as the greatest philosopher of nonviolence but also one of the greatest generals leading a non-violent army into battle for human rights. This young man would influence nonviolent struggle against oppression in countries as far distant as the Philippines and the United States. Albert Einstein later would write of this young Hindu: "Generations to come will scarce believe that such a one as this ever in flesh and blood walked upon this earth."

Letters were later exchanged between the young Hindu and the aged Tolstoy, who was nearing the end of his long life. In 1910, the young man sent Tolstoy a copy of his manifesto for nonviolence, 'Indian Home Rule' and informed Tolstoy of the influence of the belief that 'Kingdom of God is Within You' had upon him. Perhaps at this time Tolstoy knew that this man was to follow in his footstep and carry the torch for the message of love.

In 1909, when he received the letter from the young Hindu, Tolstoy was 81 years old, but he continued to travel and wander through Russia. On a journey to a convent in Astapovo, where his sister was the mother superior, he fell gravely ill and was housed in the railroad stationmaster's dwelling. On a cold evening on November 7th, 1910, Leo Nikolayevich Tolstoy died in his sleep. His longtime friend and companion Vladimir Chertkov wrote : "Leo Tolstoy's actual death was so quiet and so peaceful that I felt a certain sense of relief." He wrote that on the evening before, Tolstoy, who was in a state of semi-consciousness, "all of a sudden - as if arguing with himself - broke out in a loud voice: 'We all re [-veal]... our manifestations... This manifestation is over... That's all..." [547]

When the great Russian mystic and perhaps one of the greatest Russians of all time died, Russia grieved. A young student visiting the Duma [parliament] that day wrote: "I found everyone there in an anxious, agitated mood. Everyone was waiting for something extraordinary and immense to happen: Something as extraordinary and as immense as Tolstoy's death."[548] The speaker of Duma, standing in the chamber filled to capacity proposed that everyone stand in honor of Tolstoy's memory. This was met with opposition from rightist members of Duma who refused to honor the memory of the man who defied both the Church and the Crown. But their opposition fell on deaf ears and the Duma adjourned in honor of Tolstoy's death.

Meetings and memorials were held throughout Russia, triggering violent reaction by the Cossack's. Another student wrote :

He is dead! For us what a deep loss!
Cold he lies, cold in the frozen ground.
The flame that burned away our dross
Is quenched forever, without a sound.

Quenched. . . now all is empty and cold
My heart aches, and I feel within a pain.
I cannot believe, though it must be told
And I want to weep but all in vain.

Farewell, our Tolstoy, our native sun,
Sooner or later, we must yield to fate.
Farewell! Thanks for deeds well done,
For sacred words that have no date.

You've taught us much, you've left us
As much as life can ever leave.
Your Gospel, your works, shall bless us,
We've much to learn, much to grieve. [549]

Leo Tolstoy was buried in a simple grave 500 meters from his home on his estate, Yasnaya Polyana, where he had written his novels 'War and Peace' and 'Anna Karenina'. Thousands of peasants lined up to visit his grave. A month before he died, Tolstoy sent his very last long letter to that young Hindu lawyer who would take his place as the leading apostle of nonviolence and one of the greatest teachers of humanity in the 20th century—Mohandas Karamchand Gandhi.[550]

Gandhi

Born in the western city of Porbandar on October 2, 1869, Mohandas K. Gandhi was the youngest of four children. His father was a civil servant much like his grandfather. Gandhi described his father as one who did not have any ambition to accumulate wealth. He described his mother as a saint. She was deeply religious and never deviated from her religious vows.[551] Gandhi recalled that when he was a child in school, "It was with some difficulty that I got through the multiplication tables. The fact that I recollect nothing more of those days than having learnt, in company of other boys, to call our teacher all kinds of names, would strongly suggest that my intellect must have been sluggish, and my memory raw."[552]

When he was 13, his parents arranged for his marriage, as was the custom in India, to a girl of the same age. She was the family's third choice as the bride; the first two died before they reached the age of 13. Gandhi bitterly resented such arranged marriages and wrote a great deal in later life criticizing them. In later years he also voiced opposition to elaborate Indian weddings that imposed heavy burdens and unnecessary stress on the parents and the family.

In high school, he was confronted with his first moral test. He developed a close friendship with a boy who soon confessed that there was a clandestine meat eating movement (contrary to Hindu practice); it included many other boys in school as well as teachers. Meat eating may sound trivial to a Westerner today, but to Gandhi and the Hindu culture he was from, such an act was considered sacrilege. In order to understand the importance of this secret society and its meaning in the Indian world, one must bear in mind India's plight at the end of 19th century.

A proud country with a rich and diverse culture dating back four thousand years, India had finally been driven to its knees after centuries of violence. A paralyzed and broken nation of two hundred million had endured centuries of violence, an experience not unlike that of the people of Iran, but with one main difference. The geographic situation of Iran and the rivalry of the great Russian and British empires had spared Iran from becoming a colony, while in India, a commercial company with the help of the British government, with no rivals from Russia, had managed to enslave the entire defeated nation. The East India company was disbanded in the mid- 19th century and India, with its wealth, people, culture and history was handed to the Queen of England. She had become "Empress of India" and that huge nation became "the jewel in the crown" of the British Empire. The English were masters in someone else's home. They ruled India as, in effect, the owners of India.

As can be expected in any enslaved nation, numerous underground and open societies and opposition groups to British rule had sprung up across India with the intent of obtaining 'swaraj', or freedom. The philosophy of those activists in the 19th century was not unlike the philosophy of many Iranian activists of the 20th century. Observing the situation, Indians blamed their culture as an important element of their subjection. In order to overcome the British, these freedom fighters of India had to first overcome restraints imposed by their own culture, which they believed was the reason that their efforts were futile, and adopt elements of British culture. In the fight against the British, they believed the only way to move forward was to resort to violence, and in order to be violent they had to be as strong as the British. Thus, against the precepts of their religion, many Hindus would eat meat in secrecy, acting on their belief that this would make them physically stronger in their eventual violent struggle against British rule. Gandhi was introduced to one such a group and, for a year, met with members in a secluded spot near a riverbank and then at the State House. He ate meat to get stronger for the eventual fight against the British. This was done in secrecy, without the knowledge of his parents and in violation of the rules of his religion and his culture. [553]

After that year, Gandhi decided to cease eating meat because he feared that this forbidden practice, if he were caught doing it, would devastate his deeply religious mother. This was crucial in determining the future of the young Gandhi. Such incidents in childhood, which seem trivial to others, are often life-changing experiences. When he was 18, Gandhi, with the help of his older brother, was sent to England to become a barrister. [Under the British legal system, then as now, a barrister would argue cases in court and be "instructed" by another lawyer—a solicitor—who would also act on behalf of a client.] But before he left, another incident occurred, which was far more than trivial.

The Hindus have a caste system that assigns a person to a particular category in society according to their ancestry and dictates that individual's

CHAPTER 6

role, in life and work. It is a form of cultural predestination. Before he was to set sail to England, the elders in Gandhi's caste summoned him to a meeting and informed him that it was against their caste and religion to allow Gandhi to go to England. In England, they said, it is impossible to live and eat amongst the British without jeopardizing one's religion. Gandhi replied that he has sworn an oath to his mother to not touch meat and that he saw nothing in his religion that forbid him going to England.

In the face of Gandhi's defiance, the elders declared him an outcaste. Everyone in his caste was obligated to cut all ties with him. Gandhi's family members, in-laws, and friends in his caste were split—some supported his position; others opposed him going to England. In the years to come, Gandhi did not condemn those who opposed his decision to go and always treated them with kindness. According to the rules of his faith, none of his relatives, including members of his wife's family, were allowed to entertain him. Gandhi refrained from even drinking a glass of water in their homes in order not to offend them and jeopardize their standing in Hindu society.

This may have been a formative experience in helping Gandhi develop his later principles. Gandhi spent the rest of his life trying to persuade his fellow Indians to abolish the caste system and played a central role in granting full freedom and citizenship to members of the fifth and the lowest caste known as the 'untouchables'. He loved India and deeply loved the Hindu culture, yet he fought throughout his life against those Hindu cultural practices he considered malevolent. He was a very religious man, truly a man of God, but he fought against superstition within his religion.

After 3 years of study in England, he passed the bar exam and became a barrister. On his return to India, he learned of his mother's death. He had regarded her as an angel in his life. With the help of his brother, he set up a law practice in India, yet he was not successful. After nearly two years of legal drudgery, he was told about a case in South Africa. It involved a dispute between two Indian merchants and he was offered the opportunity to go there for one year, for a salary of 105 pounds, and assist in resolving the dispute. Given his poor prospects for finding work in India, he decided to leave his wife and family once again and go to South Africa.

Prior to getting to his destination in Pretoria, Gandhi was insulted at court by the judge for wearing a turban and later beaten on the stagecoach by its driver. In the following year, Gandhi was introduced to Mr. Baker and Mr. Coates, two Englishmen who tried to convert him to Christianity by talking to him about the Bible and lending him various Christian books. One of them was Tolstoy's "Kingdom of God...". At the same time, Abdullah Sheth was introducing him to Islam and "always had something to say about its beauty", Gandhi wrote.[554] He purchased an English translation of Quran and studied the doctrine of Islam.

On his last day of stay in South Africa, Abdullah Sheth held a farewell party for Gandhi. During the gathering, Gandhi happened to look at a newspaper sitting on the table where he noticed in a paragraph in the corner of the paper a few lines about a bill before the legislature which would deprive Indians of their right to elect members to legislative assembly. He started asking around and found that no one was aware of this bill. Gandhi focused on returning home to his family and simply announced that this bill "if it passes into law, will make our lot extremely difficult. It is the first nail into our coffin. It strikes at the root of self-respect."[555] Hearing this, the crowd began to ask Gandhi to stay a month longer in order to lobby against this bill. Gandhi accepted, but refused to accept any payment for such public service. This seemingly accidental glimpse of the newspaper article, and the request by the guests for Gandhi to stay an additional month was the page that ended Gandhi's chapter as a private lawyer and began the chapter in his life as a public servant and a hero in South Africa.

Within two weeks, Gandhi organized an army of volunteers to gather a huge number of signatures on a petition to be sent to the legislature. Eventually, 10,000 signatures were secured, a considerable percentage of the 40,000 Indians living in South Africa. Gandhi then saw the need to create an organization that he named the Natal Indian Congress to defend the rights of Indians. For Gandhi, the practice of law was no more than a means to pay his bills. His real passion was now public service and the defense of Indian self-respect. His one month postponement in South Africa eventually turned into three years, after which he asked for a six month leave to go to India and bring his wife and two sons to South Africa.

When he returned to India, Gandhi wrote a pamphlet describing the conditions of Indians in South Africa and the prevalence of racism and injustice against them. Soon word reached the British in South Africa of Gandhi's public relations campaign, his pamphlet, and his activism against discrimination. In retaliation, on his arrival back to South Africa, Gandhi's ship was quarantined for 23 days with 800 passengers inside. In the ship, passengers asked him what he would do with his 'nonviolence' if he were to be attacked. For the passengers and India, the 'nonviolence' that this young lawyer was advocating was still ridiculed as ineffective and weak. He replied,

CHAPTER 6

"I hope God will give me the courage and the sense to forgive them and to refrain from bringing them to law. I have no anger against them. I am only sorry for their ignorance and their narrowness. I know that they sincerely believe that what they are doing today is right and proper. I have no reason therefore to be angry with them."[556] The passengers were then allowed to land, but word reached Gandhi from officials in the government who recommended him leaving the ship at night and in secrecy for his protection.

Gandhi refused to enter South Africa like a 'thief'. He sent his family ahead and came ashore with a few companions. As soon as he was spotted, white settlers surrounded him and separated him from his companions. They then began beating him with punches, kicks, rocks and brickbats. His turban was snatched away and the crowd began to punch and kick him in the face. Gandhi fell to the ground, semiconscious, and grabbed a railing. In that desperate encounter that almost surely could have cost him his life, he looked up and, as if seeing an angel, he saw the wife of the police superintendent walking down the street. She was familiar with Gandhi and came to his side. The white settlers, who were taught not to use violence in presence of a lady, were forced to stop. They began shouting "Hang Gandhi, Hang Gandhi". Eventually, with the lady's help and, later, with the help of the superintendent himself, Gandhi was saved.

Once Gandhi was safe in the police station, the public prosecutor asked Gandhi to identify his assailants for their arrest. Gandhi replied: "...I do not hold the assailants to blame... I do not want to bring anyone to book. I am sure that, when the truth becomes known, they will be sorry for their conduct." Gandhi was 28 years old at the time of this incident and, without knowing, he was helping write the principles of non-violence that would be published 100 years later in textbooks. In his autobiography, he names the chapter recounting this incident the 'Test'. Gandhi was tested not to learn whether he could survive the beating: he was tested to see if he could forgive his assailants. And it wasn't just Gandhi being tested. Principles of nonviolence were being tested. For the ability to forgive is the ability to heal one's soul and forgiveness serves as an important principle in nonviolence. Forgiveness is one of the most powerful and important characteristics of a human being and the most important tool for purging hatred and anger from a person.

In the culture of violence, a child is taught from his or her earliest years that punishment is the consequence of wrong-doing. Punishment in the culture of violence is supposed to lead to rehabilitation. Today, many have learned the ill effects of such methods when used on children. Yet, in most societies, physical punishment is replaced by other forms of psychological and emotional punishments, particularly in prisons. The principles of reward and punishment that govern rules of violence continue to be the most prevalent principles governing the world today. Society punishes adolescents who do not perform well by not allowing them to attend good universities and obtain a good education. If a teenager is unfortunate enough to be raised in a family full of stress, if that individual suffers from psychological or emotional trauma during school years or suffers psychological illnesses such as depression or anxiety, if he or she is introduced to the wrong crowd of friends, we label that child as troublesome, not smart or capable, and will forever punish that child by labeling him or her as deviant. As adults, those who have psychological illnesses such as depression, anxiety disorders, or addictions learn how limited is society's tolerance for such illnesses. Society punishes them through termination of their jobs, and their families punish them by isolating them.

Then there is revenge, which is the other aspect of the philosophy of violence and goes hand in hand with punishment. Revenge is a form of rough justice meant as vengeance for an action or injury. In the cultures of violence, while punishment is meant as a tool for reformation, revenge is a tool for personal and societal vengeance and satisfaction. And such justice is meted out in many societies today, under the sanction of tribal or traditional justification. We are not just satisfied with punishment; we also seek revenge on criminals. A person who commits murder is then murdered by the state, not only as punishment, but as a form of revenge for the family of the victim. And in many cultures, even if the victim's family refuses, for moral reasons, to approve of revenge, the murderer is still murdered by the state in order to satisfy the society's desire for revenge. One who commits rape is placed in a prison and in circumstances in which he himself is raped. And the response of a society that believes in culture of violence to such barbaric treatment of a criminal is: 'They' deserve it.

'They' are all too often innocent children who, throughout their lives, were victims of psychological, emotional, and physical abuse. Under these circumstances, these children attend schools that punish them for misbehaving and as punishment deprive them of opportunities to obtain education. As young adults, they learn to use violence in the same manner in which they had learned as children and seen used around them. These grown children, adopting methods of violence are then punished for their learned behavior, which does nothing for their education and healing, but only delays further acts of violence.

This cycle of revenge and punishment is one of the pillars of the justice system in dealing with criminals throughout the world. It was manifest in one of the first written laws in human history, dating to 1780 BCE in Babylon when, Hammurabi, promulgated a total of 282 laws inflicting punishment and revenge. These laws, and those that followed in various societies were modified to varying degrees over time, but the principles of punishment and revenge are still the prevalent form of justice in much of the world. The most famous of Hammurabi's laws, one which has come to symbolize every other law, was number 196 which stated: "If a man put out the eye of another man, his eye shall be put out." This law of revenge known as an eye for an eye is the cornerstone for political and state use of violence prevalent throughout most of the world.

When Gandhi was asked to identify his assailants and help file charges, he replied that his assailants were not to blame, but the government that fueled their hatred by justifying racism was to blame. When they were children, they were taught to hate the Indians; why then, Gandhi had replied, can we blame them and punish them for acting out their hatred. They were taught to use violence as a right or even an obligation.

Yet, Gandhi was able to forgive but as he explored the path to nonviolence, he did not figure out how societies can learn to forgive. How can a nation forgive military and intelligence services that systematically torture and kill thousands over decades? Although Gandhi had begun to suggest the difficult act of forgiveness, many questions regarding forgiveness were not answered until nearly a century later and, ironically, it was again in South Africa where many such difficult questions were addressed.

Gandhi spent the next ten years in South Africa on the path towards self-transformation. Aside from his activism, he built a successful law practice in which he earned as much as five thousand pounds a year, a considerable sum for an Indian in South Africa in those years. He never accepted money for his public service and returned gifts that were not related to his law practice. In 1903 he was given a copy of the book 'Unto This Last' by John Ruskin. The book made such a strong impression on him that he later called it "the turning point in my life." After reading the book, he decided to change his life according to certain ideals. The teachings of this book he later summarized in his autobiography as :

1) The good of the individual is contained in the good of all.

2) A lawyer's work has the same value as the barber's, inasmuch as all have the same right to earn their livelihoods from their work.

3) A life of labor, i.e., the life of a tiller of the soil and the craftsman, is a life eminently worth living.

The lessons in the book inspired him to lead a life that brought him closer to nature. With the help of some wealthy individuals, he purchased a 100 acre piece of land in nearby town of Phoenix and set up his newspaper press on the farm. He spent the next few years traveling back and forth from the farm to Johannesburg, where his law office was located. Events after 1906, however, changed Gandhi from a lawyer interested in public service to a fulltime servant of his people and justice.

1906

In that year the South African government passed a law requiring all Indian men, women, and children to register with the authorities, submit to fingerprinting, and accept a certificate which they were to carry with them at all times. Failure to do this made Indians subject to fines, imprisonment, or deportation. In addition, the ordinance allowed a white police officer to accost an Indian woman on the street or enter her home and demand that she produce a certificate of registration. Gandhi declared that if this ordinance were to be adopted, it would result in the "absolute ruin for the Indians of South Africa... Better to die than submit to such a law."[557]

A meeting was called at the Imperial Theatre in Johannesburg, where on September 11, 1906, nearly three thousand Indians packed the theatre in order to decide what to do. The angry audience listened to speech after speech renouncing the ordinance, until Sheth Haji Habib asked those present to take an oath before God as their witness. This strongly resonated with Gandhi. He was a firm believer in God and thought that such pledges were not to be taken lightly. So when it was his time to speak, he was in a state of great inspiration and emotion. He began by explaining to the audience, which included Muslims, Hindus and Parsis, the significance of a pledge with God as witness as opposed to a regular pledge. He then told them:

CHAPTER 6

"Resolutions of this nature cannot be passed by a majority vote. Only those who take the pledge can be bound by it... Everyone must only search his own heart, and if the inner voice assures him that he has the requisite strength to carry him through, then only should he pledge himself and then only would his pledge bear fruit...if on the one hand [he] who takes a pledge must be a robust optimist, on the other hand he must be prepared for the worst... Imagine that all of us present here, numbering 3,000 at the most, pledge themselves. Imagine again that the remaining 10,000 Indians [in South Africa] take no such pledge. We will only provoke ridicule in the beginning. Again, it is quite possible that in spite of the present warning some or many of those who pledge themselves might weaken at the very first trial. We might have to go to jail, where we might be insulted. We might have to go hungry and suffer extreme heat or cold. Hard labor might be imposed upon us. We might be flogged by rude warders. We might be fined heavily and our property might be attached and held up to auction if there are only a few resisters left. Opulent today, we might be reduced to abject poverty tomorrow. We might be deported. Suffering from starvation and similar hardship in jail, some of us might fall ill and even die... But I can boldly declare, and with certainty, that so long as there is even a handful of men true to their pledge, there can only be only one end to the struggle, and that is victory..."[558]

After Gandhi spoke, he sat down. The 3,000 people present in the theatre listened to his words in perfect silence. Others spoke after him about their responsibilities and the responsibility of the audience. The president of the meeting then read a resolution of noncompliance that Gandhi had helped prepare. The resolution was passed and an oath in the name of God was taken by everyone present.

After the collective vow, Gandhi more and more realized his dislike for the term 'passive-resistance' often used at the time for nonviolent resistance and began to search for a better term to describe his method of nonviolent struggle. The word 'Satyagraha' was then chosen as the symbol for their struggle. Satya - meaning 'truth' also means 'soul' and 'agraha' means firmness or force. 'Satyagraha' thus meant truth-force or soul-force. For Gandhi, Satyagraha was not a physical force but a force achieved through the human heart. From this point on, Gandhi's movement was not led by Gandhi himself, but by the principles of Satyagraha. With the principle-led leadership of Satyagraha, Gandhi would follow what he believed was the path of truth, love, and God and he would ask every other Indian to follow in the same path of Satyagraha. Gandhi described Satyagraha as "the vindication of truth not by infliction of suffering on the opponent but on one's self." The Satyagraha force achieves victory when the opponent is "weaned from error by patience and sympathy." He believed the force of a Satyagrahi came not from the strength of his arm but from inner strength.

Gandhi later said: "Satyagraha is the exact opposite of an-eye-for-an-eye-for-an-eye-for-an-eye which ends in making everybody blind. You cannot inject new ideas into a man's head by chopping it off; neither will you infuse a new spirit into his heart by piercing it with a dagger. Acts of violence create bitterness in the survivors and brutality in the destroyers; Satyagraha aims to exalt both sides."[559]

On July 31, 1907, the Transvaal government in South Africa adopted the Asiatic Registration Act. Indians called it the 'Black Act'. Gandhi announced that Indians would offer Satyagraha in return. Some Indians registered as the law required, but most of those who had made their pledge in the theatre did not. A number of Indians including Gandhi were called before a magistrate. Gandhi announced that as their leader, he merited the heaviest punishment. He was given two months of jail without hard labor. This was Gandhi's first jail term.

In prison, Gandhi would read the Hindu holy scriptures of the Bhagavad Gita in the morning, an English translation of the Koran at noon, and would read the Bible to a Chinese Christian convert in the afternoon. He also reread Tolstoy's books on nonviolence. While he was in prison, a visitor one day interrupted his readings with a message from General Jan Christaan Smuts offering a compromise to Gandhi. Smuts stated that the 'Black Act' would be repealed only after all the Indians voluntarily registered. Gandhi accepted the compromise, trusted the General's promise, and was soon released from prison.

Back in Johannesburg, he was faced with angry responses from his fellow Indians. Why would Gandhi agree to such a compromise? Why wouldn't the law be repealed first? Indians saw this compromise as a trick by General Smuts to make them register and did not believe he was sincere about repealing the laws. In a meeting, an Indian angrily addressed Gandhi stating "We have heard that you have betrayed the community and sold it to General Smuts for a sum of fifteen thousand pounds. We will never give the fingerprints or allow others to do so. I swear with Allah as my witness that I will kill the man who takes the lead in applying for registration."[560] Gandhi replied that it was in the nature of a compromise to give something to

CHAPTER 6

General Smuts in order to achieve a gain. As far as a trick by General Smuts he said : "A Satyagrahi bids goodbye to fear. He is therefore never afraid of trusting his opponent. Even if the opponent plays him false twenty times, the Satyagrahi is ready to trust him for the twenty-first time - for an implicit trust in human nature is the very essence of his creed."[561]

Gandhi arranged to be the first to register on February 10th. He was accompanied to the registration office by several companions, including a friend named Mir Alam. On the way there, Mir Alam stopped and again asked Gandhi what he was doing. Gandhi replied "I propose to take out a certificate of registration" Before he could hear a response, he was knocked unconscious by a heavy blow to his head. Kicks and beatings followed. Gandhi was taken to a nearby house. When he gained consciousness, the first question he asked was "Where is Mir Alam?" He has been arrested with others, he was told. Gandhi replied "They should be released...they thought they were doing right, and I have no desire to prosecute them."[562].

The philosophy of Gandhi was for those harmed, injured or hurt by an enemy to love that enemy as a human being and not allow hate to enter the heart. This he could only achieve through forgiveness of the actions of the enemy. It was his courage and a firm belief in the goodness of humanity and the power of nonviolence that gave him the strength to forgive. He believed in truth, justice, and love which he thought eventually would overcome his enemies and supporters of violence. Those who practiced violence, he believed, were misguided and educated in such methods. We cannot punish them or harm them for their ignorance. We must only attempt to educate them and show them the path of love.

Gandhi asked the registration office to bring him the registration material in order to be the first to register. Eventually, many Indians in South Africa registered even though they did not agree with Gandhi in trusting General Smuts completely. Smuts, by offering this compromise, had certainly been successful in destroying the cohesiveness of the Indian community. So we can imagine how embarrassed Gandhi must have felt when, not long after the voluntary registration, General Smuts went back on his word and announced that the 'Black Act' would not be repealed. Yet Gandhi was not a person to be broken this easily. His belief in Satyagraha did not come through reason or experience. It was a belief derived from his deep religious convictions and his profound belief in God. Such beliefs are not easily extinguished.

Gandhi continued to campaign against the registration act, but the resistance had taken its toll on him. More and more people were giving up hope and abandoning the movement. In addition, funds were running short. At this time, Herman Kallenbach, a wealthy German-Jewish architect in South Africa, an admirer of Gandhi and one of his close associates, purchased a 1,100 acre land outside of Johannesburg and in 1910 offered it to Gandhi and the Satyagrahis, free of charge. Kallenbach, along with Henry Polak, were Gandhi's most intimate associates, supporting him and lobbying the British on behalf of Gandhi's cause. Gandhi soon moved his Satyagrahis to the new ashram and set up his newspaper press there. In honor of that old Russian mystic who had written so much on nonviolence and love, Gandhi named this second ashram 'Leo Tolstoy Farm'.

Gandhi soon resumed the nonviolent struggle against the 'Black Act'. On August 16, 1908, a large number of Indians gathered in the Hamidia Mosque in Johannesburg. After a succession of speeches, over 2,000 registration cards were thrown into a huge bonfire in center of the mosque and as those cards burned, a huge cheer went up from the crowd. The nonviolent struggle of the Indians in South Africa for their rights had again begun. Gandhi began to gather volunteers in order to approach the police and notify them that they did not have a registration card. Volunteers lined up and soon Gandhi and 75 of his companions were sent to prison.

While in prison this second time, Gandhi found a copy of Henry David Thoreau's 'Civil Disobedience' in the prison library. As he was sitting in prison, he read the remarks of that mystic in Massachusetts who had found love for humanity while searching for humanity's soul alone by the shore of Walden Pond. Gandhi read Thoreau's essay with great care. Gandhi later told that the following paragraph written by Thoreau while in prison for civil disobedience greatly affected Gandhi since he had also been imprisoned for civil disobedience. Thoreau had written:

"I saw, that if there was a wall of stone between me and my townsmen, there was a still more difficult one to climb or break through before they could get to be as free as I was. I did not feel for a moment confined, and the walls seemed a great waste of stone and mortar... as they could not reach me, they had resolved to punish the body... I saw that the state was half-witted... and that it did not know its friends from its foes, and I lost all my remaining respect for it and pitied it."[563]

As he read these words, the soul of that Massachusetts philosopher must have directly reached his heart. He began to use the term 'Civil Disobedience' when trying to explain Satyagraha to the English, yet even as these words did not completely convey his struggle, he began more and more to just use Satyagraha, even while speaking or writing in English.

This following paragraph from Thoreau also greatly influenced Gandhi and helped shape his strategy in his struggle for the rest of his life. This paragraph expresses one of the important principles of a nonviolent struggle.

Thoreau wrote: "I know this well, that if one thousand, if one hundred, if ten men whom I could name - if ten *honest* men only - ay, if one HONEST man, in this state of Massachusetts, *ceasing to hold slaves,* were actually withdraw from this copartnership, and be locked up in the county jail therefore, it would be the abolition of slavery in America. For it does not matter how small the beginning may seem to be: What is once well done is done forever."[564]

These were powerful and important words written by one of 19th centuries great philosophers of nonviolence. Nonviolent resistance is the struggle that comes from the soul. In such a struggle, a single soul has the ability to be as large and powerful as an army of ten thousand and to awaken the consciousness of an entire society.

In a way, nonviolent struggle can be more similar to warfare related in mythology. In mythology, and in particular in Iranian mythology, you have hero-figures who symbolize the soul of the nation. Their strength is as much as an army of ten thousand. Their every word and every deed is symbolic of the entire struggle. Such is the potential of a nonviolent movement where the soul of one individual can ignite a fire in the hearts of millions. The great 20th-century scholar of mythology, Joseph Campbell, had said that myths show us the potential of humanity. Gandhi was now showing the world the potential of nonviolence for humanity. With his philosophy, new hero-figures and acts of courage were to be created to match the greatest hero-figures of mythology; heroes with the courage to stand for principles and to fight injustice on behalf of tens of thousands against guns, tanks and terror.

In 1912, Gopal Krishna Gokhale, professor of English and Economics in India and one of the leaders of Indian liberation movement came for a visit to South Africa and was greatly impressed with the work of then 43- year- old Gandhi. During Gokhale's tour of South Africa, British generals in the country promised him that that the registration act, as well as the three-pound tax on indentured Indian laborers would be annulled. Having won an apparent victory, he notified Gandhi of the pledge and asked Gandhi to come to India within a year. When told of the pledge to repeal the act, Gandhi replied "I doubt it very much. You do not know the Ministers as I do." In a town hall meeting of Indians, Gokhale announced, "Gandhi has in him the marvelous spiritual power to turn ordinary men around him into heroes and martyrs." He went on to say that in Gandhi's presence, "one is ashamed to do anything unworthy, in fact, one is afraid of thinking anything unworthy."[565]

As Gandhi had predicted, General Smuts went back on his word again and announced that the European settlers who were the original employers of indentured laborers would not agree to lift the three pound tax. In response, Gandhi announced that negotiations had failed, closed the Tolstoy farm and began preparations for a major battle ahead. "The fight this time must be for altering the spirit of the Government and the European population of South Africa. And the result can only be attained by prolonged and bitter suffering that must melt the hearts alike of the Government and the predominant partner."[566] Gandhi sent a letter to Gokhale in India saying that he was about to throw his 'all' into it. In reply, Gokhale believing Gandhi has the backing of large number of Indians in South Africa inquired about the number of soldiers in this 'army of peace'. Gandhi wrote him that for his army of nonviolence, he could count of between sixteen at the very least and a maximum of sixty-six. Gokhale, a seasoned veteran of the Indian struggle in India was amused by these numbers and must have immediately written off the struggle. But Gokhale did not understand one of the principles of nonviolence. Nonviolence is not about the quantity and size of armies. It is fought with the power of the soul. The strength is not in the numbers of those who follow the principles of nonviolence, but in their hearts.

As the battle between the forces of nonviolence and violence was approaching, redress of a third grievance was added to the Indian demands. On March 14, 1913, a justice of the Cape Colony Supreme Court ruled that only Christian marriages were legal in South Africa. This ruling invalidated all Hindu, Muslim, and Parsi (Indians of Zoroastrian heritage) marriages, thus making married Indian women no more than concubines without any marital rights. Up until now, the meetings of Satyagrahis were mostly comprised of Indian men. But now the tide was about to change. For the first time, large numbers of women began to join the movement. Kasturba, Gandhi's wife also joined the struggle. In the battle ahead, women were now going to take the lead in civil disobedience and breaking of law.

Plans were made for a group of Indian women from Natal to cross the border into Transvaal without registration, an illegal act under the South African law. At the same time, another group of Indian women, this time from Transvaal, were to cross the border into Natal. If they were not arrested, they were to walk to Newcastle coal mines and lobby the miners to go on strike. Upon the illegal crossing of the borders, those entering Transvaal were arrested, but the women entering Natal managed to walk to the mines. By the time the authorities arrested those women, they had convinced the Indian indentured miners to go on strike. Over 5,000 miners, inspired by the women, left their work and went on strike. Gandhi who did not know what to do with all these miners decided that if the authorities did not arrest them, they would march for eight days, with Tolstoy Farm as their final destination.

Gandhi informed the strikers of the principles of nonviolence and the hardship ahead. He told them about the ordeal of prison in its worst form and urged them to go back if they were unable to handle what they would face. He could provide a ration of a pound and a half of bread and an ounce of sugar per person per day for the journey. The strikers were to sleep under the open sky and conduct themselves in a moral and peaceful way. If arrested, they were to submit without any resistance. European settlers along the way had threatened to shoot the Indians like rabbits as they proceeded through various towns and villages. The miners were instructed not to return violence with violence under any circumstances. Before he and the miners crossed the border, Gandhi called General Smuts on telephone. Within minutes, he received a response from General Smuts' secretary: "General Smuts will have nothing to do with you. You may do as you please." On the morning of November 6, 1913, Gandhi recalled. "We offered prayers and commenced the march in the name of God." There were 2,037 men, 127 women, and 57 children making the illegal cross-border eight day march to Leo Tolstoy farm.

Gandhi was arrested on the first day of the march, but since he was a lawyer and familiar with the system, he convinced the magistrate to release him on bail under the law. He was arrested again on the second day, only to be released again with bail. The third time he was arrested, he was kept in prison. The marchers went on, following Gandhi's instructions. The government had thought the marchers would be demoralized, but such was not the case. They weren't led personally by Gandhi, but by the principles that Gandhi had taught them. The government had imprisoned Gandhi, but they could not imprison his principles. The South African government then decided to arrest all the strikers. Special trains were sent and all the strikers were placed on board and sent back to Natal. Having several thousand prisoners on hand and not knowing what to do with them, the government sentenced the strikers to hard labor in the same mines that they had left previously.

The prisoners were told not to object their arrest, but they objected to this cruel joke of being sentenced to hard labor in the very mines they had left and refused to obey the order. Their refusal was met by severe whippings and beatings. Word of this cruelty began to spread in Natal and soon other miners in the north and west of the region went on strike and Indians began to walk off the plantations where they worked as laborers. In response, the government adopted a policy of 'blood and iron'. Military police was called in and Indians were literally beaten back to work. Meanwhile Gandhi was isolated in a cell ten feet by seven feet. He was refused a bench, a light, and was not allowed to walk in the cell. But the movement lead by the principles of Satyagraha was spreading like wildfire and soon over 50,000 laborers were on strike.[567] The news of the march and subsequent beatings and ill-treatment of Indians sent shockwaves throughout India and reverberated in London. Two hundred million in India were watching tens of thousands of Indians in South Africa using principles of nonviolence for the first time and the nervous authorities in India began to criticize the South African government. Bishop Lefroy, the Metropolitan of India, sent an outspoken letter to the press while more and more Christians began to question the conduct of their Christian government. India's Viceroy, Lord Hardinge, claimed "...the most recent developments have taken a very serious turn and we have seen the widest publicity given to allegations that this movement of passive resistance has been dealt with by measures which would not for one moment be tolerated by any country that calls itself civilized."[568]

The South African government, now under pressure, suddenly released Gandhi from prison on December 13 and General Smuts offered to create a commission of inquiry. But this time Gandhi refused, on the grounds that the racist background of some of those nominated as members of commission would prejudice its recommendations and announced he would again march across the border to be arrested again and sent to prison. As these turbulent days passed, another critical event was about to take place in South Africa. Twenty thousand mostly white railroad workers in South Africa, in a dispute separate from the protest of the Satyagrahis, threatened to go on strike, a move that surely would have broken the South African government's back. Given the potential impact of a second strike, Gandhi made a decision that only a man with principles as firm as his could have made. He called off his march and announced that it was not part of the Satyagraha tactics or principles to "destroy, hurt, humble, or embitter the adversary, or to win a victory by weakening him. Civil resisters hope, by sincerity, chivalry, and self-suffering, to convince the opponent's brain and conquer his heart. They never take advantage of the government's difficulty or form unnatural alliances."[569] In an unprecedented act, the entire Satyagraha campaign taking the attention of England and all her colonies was called off to allow the government to meet the demands of the white railroad workers.

Gandhi's friends warned against canceling the march and reminded him of the deceitful behavior of General Smuts in 1908. Gandhi replied by quoting in Sanskrit: "Forgiveness, is the ornament of the brave."[570] This time, General Smuts realizing the incredible power of nonviolence at Gandhi's side accepted the principles of negotiation. Congratulations poured in from all over the world to Gandhi for his chivalrous action.

Over the next several weeks, General Smuts and Gandhi worked on the agreement sentence by sentence and word for word. Finally, on June 30, the term of a complete agreement were reached. Under the terms of the agreement, Parsi, Hindu and Muslim marriages were valid and legal. The three pound tax was abolished and the humiliating registration act was annulled. Indians obtained everything they had fought for. Satyagrahis had achieved a major victory and a new hero was born in South Africa. This was the first time in history that a nonviolent movement had won such a great and decisive victory. Gandhi had created a practical force for struggle out of the wisdom he had acquired from reading what had been written throughout history about the power of humanity and love.

Having won this great battle, he decided to say farewell to South Africa forever. He had come to this country as a young man for a one year term for the salary of 105 pounds. At one point he was making over 5,000 pounds from his law practice. Yet, he had given up all this in search of his principles of justice and for Satyagraha. In the journey, he had transformed himself from a young, confused Indian wearing European clothing and struggling with his beliefs in Hinduism and vegetarianism to a firm believer in humanity, in love, in God, and his principles of nonviolence. After saying farewell to a large crowd gathered in Johannesburg, Gandhi, along with his wife and Herman Kallenbach, said farewell to South Africa. Gandhi, having achieved victory for thousands of Indians in South Africa, set a new goal for himself— securing social justice for two hundred million in India. The same principles of Satyagaraha were now to be applied in a much larger theatre in India and a much larger battle for the next thirty years.

CHAPTER 7 – CIVIL DISOBEDIENCE IN INDIA

"Nothing but organized nonviolence can check the organized violence of the British government..."

~M.K Gandhi

Gandhi in India

Upon arriving in India, professor Gokhale, Gandhi's mentor, advised him to spend the first year in India with "his ears open and his mouth shut." Gandhi spent a year traveling across the country and did not always heed his mentor's advice. He continued to build on the principles of India's right to independence, which he had set forth and published in a booklet in 1909. In response to the anarchist philosophy of Indian movement for self-rule, he had written, "if we act justly, India will be freer sooner. You will see, too, that if we shun every Englishman as an enemy, Home Rule will be delayed. But if we are just to them, we shall receive their support...". The booklet titled *Hind Swaraj* or Indian Home Rule received mixed response from Indians. Gokhale called it "crude and hastily conceived". Yet not everyone had dismissed it as such. The old philosopher of love in Russia, Leo Tolstoy, had read the booklet in his last year of life and praised its philosophy. Gandhi had written "Some Englishman state that they took and hold India by the sword. Both statements are wrong. The sword is entirely useless for holding India. We alone keep them... We like their commerce; they please us by their subtle methods and get what they want from us... We further strengthen their hold by quarreling amongst ourselves."[571] If one reads these sentences and is not familiar with Gandhi and history of India, one could mistakenly think that the author was writing not about British in India at the beginning of 20th-century but perhaps about the Islamic regime in Iran at the beginning of 21st century. In fact, Gandhi's observation was prophetic at the time. This statement comprises one of the principles of nonviolence— that the rule and force of a despotic regime is only the result of cooperation and participation of the people within that system. Having reached this conclusion, Gandhi knew that

CHAPTER 8

the secret to his success was the empowerment and enlightenment of the people which would lead to the defeat of the British.

Just like Iranians of today, Gandhi's struggles were not just against the politics of violence, but also against the engrained culture of violence and discrimination in India's society as well. The form of injustice known as caste system—dividing citizens into four different castes—was, in effect, a violent offense against human rights. In this system, the *Brahmans* or the priests were considered the highest caste in India. The second caste, known as *Kshatriya*, constituted the Warriors and their families. The merchants and the farmers were the third caste or *Vaisya*. The fourth caste was comprised of craftsmen and their families. This system had been in place for thousands of years, so Hindus considered it religious and the will of God. There were others who did not belong to any of the castes. They were referred to as *Panchama*, or the fifth caste, and were mostly confined to doing work that the other four castes would consider dirty, tasks like cleaning toilets and collecting garbage. Because of such work, the members of other four castes would avoid any contact with *Panchamas*. These people were not allowed to touch an object, food or water not meant for them. Any contact with a *Panchama* required the Hindu to immediately take a bath and wash away what he considered the filth of humanity. For this reason, the members of the fifth caste were called the 'Untouchables'. Gandhi did not believe such a practice belonged in his religion and his culture. Over the next few decades, his struggle was thus aimed not just against the political violence of the British, but also against the greater culture of violence manifesting itself as discrimination and injustice in India.

In 1918, in his newly formed Ashram near Ahmadabad, an Untouchable couple with their daughter Lakshmi, approached Gandhi and asked that they be admitted as permanent members. Gandhi agreed. His acceptance of them created a storm. Gandhi's ashram was considered polluted. The wealthy Hindus who were funding Gandhi's ashram withdrew their support. Gandhi's wife was revolted by the idea of an untouchable woman in the kitchen cooking with others and washing dishes. Gandhi tried to appeal to his wife's reason and listened patiently to her concerns. He tried to make her understand that untouchability did not exist in early Hinduism. But the prejudice against the Untouchables was so deep-rooted in the unconscious mind of his wife, members of his ashram, and India that reason could not prevail and Gandhi was subjected to increasing pressure. When his Ashram's bookkeeper informed him that donors are refusing further help because of the Untouchables and they are facing severe financial problems, Gandhi announced that he would live in the Untouchables quarters of the city if necessary. In response to his wife's disagreement and in order to send a message to others, he adopted Lakshmi as his own daughter. Gandhi spent the rest of his life preaching against this ancient inhumane prejudice. Fanatic Hindus never forgave Gandhi for his love of the Untouchables. Throughout his political career he encountered great resistance to his position on this issue.

While attending the annual convention of Indian national Congress in 1916, a poor peasant approached Gandhi and asked him to come to Champaran, the man's native district near the foothills of Himalaya, to help advance a legal case against the British. Gandhi had never heard of the place and told the peasant that he had other commitments to meet during his scheduled tour of India. The peasant followed Gandhi for weeks, constantly requesting him to come to his aid. When Gandhi returned to Ahmadabad, the peasant followed. Finally Gandhi agreed to go and hear the grievances of the villagers in the region against the British.

When Gandhi investigated the situation he found that the peasants in those villages were mistreated and compensated unfairly. The British were the large landowners in the district. The peasants who worked on the farms were required to plant indigo for industrial dye in at least 15% of their crop yield, which would be turned over to the British as rent. But in recent years, as part of their achievements in industrial chemistry, the Germans had developed synthetic indigo and the price of indigo had plummeted. In return, the British landowners had required the peasants to pay a lump sum in exchange for their freedom from indentured laboring. The peasants had hired lawyers; the landowners had responded by hiring thugs. Gandhi began investigating the situation in the village and advocated the peasants not to cooperate with the British and refuse to pay an unjust tax. He was soon served with a notice to appear in district court.

The peasants did not know who Gandhi was. In the morning when Gandhi was to appear in court, thousands of peasants spontaneously gathered in front of the courthouse. The British soldiers in the district were terrified and felt helpless. Gandhi stood on the steps of the courthouse and helped the British direct and regulate the crowd while being polite and friendly to the authorities. The prosecutor and the judge decided to reconsider their case against Gandhi and announced postponement of the trial. Gandhi objected and read a statement pleading guilty to breaking the law. The judge announced that he needed time to pronounce the sentence, and asked Gandhi to furnish bail. When Gandhi again refused, the judge released him without bail. All the peasants in the district were moved by Gandhi's action.

Here was an Indian from hundreds of miles away willing to break an unjust law and go to prison in order for justice to be obtained for these poor peasants. This was a great symbolic act from a man spending his whole life fighting injustice as the voice of poor in India. Soon the lieutenant governor of the province ordered the case to be dropped and Gandhi was victorious. This was the first act of civil disobedience in India and the first victory for Satyagraha. Soon after, a commission was formed to investigate the claims of peasants. Gandhi was their legal representative. He spent a year of his life on this case and at the end he announced "what I did was a very ordinary thing. I declared that the British could not order me around in my own country."[572]

Soon after, he was occupied by another case of ill-treatment of workers. This time it was grievance of textile workers against the Indian owners of the factories in which they were employed. The wealthy Indian owners were friends and supporters of Gandhi. Gandhi encouraged the workers to go on strike and vow not to return to work until their demands were met. Yet as the strike dragged on, the attendance of striking laborers at meetings dropped. The workers morale was extremely low and Gandhi increasingly feared that violence would break out. One morning as he was addressing the strikers' assembly, in a spontaneous moment without previous thought, as he was witnessing the workers giving up on their demands, he announced that if the strikers could not continue with their pledge, "I will not touch any food."[573]. His words shocked the audience and some began to cry. Some strikers announced that they were willing to fast along with Gandhi. But Gandhi objected and told him they just needed to stay with the strike. He told the mill owners that his fast was not directed at them but at the workers, to encourage them to remain on strike. This posed a dilemma for the owners, who respected Gandhi and were committed to supporting Satyagraha. They did not want to be responsible for Gandhi's death; yet Gandhi did not want to coerce the owners. He just wanted to stiffen the resolve of the strikers. The pressure on the mill owners became overwhelming. On the third day of the fast, they accepted arbitration.

It is said that in a hunger strike, if one is fasting as an act of nonviolent resistance to reform an enemy, a violent and brutal enemy is very likely to allow fast to continue until the death of the resister. "Let him die", a tyrant would say. Gandhi acknowledged this. He later said "I fasted to reform those who loved me... You cannot fast against a tyrant."[574] This is an important lesson on hunger strikes which is a very common form of nonviolent resistant. A fast or a hunger strike is a symbolic nonviolent act of defiance and suffering. Although it has been used successfully in the past against tyrants, it is really intended to raise the consciousness of the people and to influence them for action. A tyrant, in response to a hunger strike, can easily shrug and say, "let him die!". But dying is not the desired outcome of such a nonviolent act of resistance. Gandhi's objective was not to kill himself, he wanted to raise the consciousness of those around to create a system of arbitration in which the disputes between workers and factory owners could be settled in a peaceful matter. He had performed his fast directed at those who cared for him and he was highly successful through this act of nonviolence.

The system of conflict-resolution for laborers adopted after his fast is still in existence today in India.

Adoption of Nonviolence in the Path for *Swaraj*

Gandhi's nationwide struggle against the British did not take shape until 1919, when he was 50 years old. During World War I, Gandhi had traveled across India advocating loyalty to the British Empire and recruiting Indians to go fight against Germany. In many cities and towns across India, he and his companions were boycotted by the population—at times people even refused to feed Gandhi and his followers because of his loyalty to the British during the war. The onset of World War I coincided with heightened rebellion against the British. Bal Gandahar Tilak, known as 'Lokamanya' had waged a war of violence and terror against the British for nearly 20 years. He and his followers were constantly imprisoned by the British because of assassination attempts and acts of terror against the authorities reminding us that the Indian struggle for independence, before Gandhi came on the scene, was mostly a struggle of violence and unsuccessful use of terror.

Jawaharlal Nehru, in his autobiography, wrote that in 1907, when he went to Cambridge as a student, "almost all without exception were either Tilakites or extremists."[575] In 1917, Edwin Montagu, the Secretary of State for India had written in his diary that Tilak was "at the moment probably the most powerful man in India."[576] Tilak's views and those of the Indian activists for independence were completely opposed to Gandhi's principles. Tilak preferred violence, Gandhi advocated Satyagraha. Tilak preached Hindu supremacy, Gandhi advocated Hindu-Muslim unity. Gandhi believed the means and the journey would ultimately lead to the end, Tilak believe that the end justified the means.[577] Gandhi, in his 1909 booklet '*Hind Swaraj*' (Indian Self-Rule) had strongly condemned violence; he had argued that Satyagraha, or Soul-Force, was superior to violence.

Indians, like the Europeans and Iranians, had thousands of years of experience with wars, rebellions, despotism, and violence and knew its potential and its application. Violence was the only weapon they knew, the only means they regarded as effective. Indians had just a violent past as any other country and Hinduism had inculcated as much prejudice and violence as any other religion. To assume that the philosophy of nonviolence was conveniently available to Gandhi because of his culture is a fallacy. In addition, to assume that nonviolence if adopted by people can automatically be maintained during the heat of the battle is even a greater mistake. As Gandhi learned, in nonviolence people require education, discipline and courage. They also require self-cleansing, love and kindness.

A journey for nonviolence without education and self-cleansing can become a 'Himalayan Mistake'. This is how he characterized his defeat when he asked Indians to embark on a struggle for freedom without a firm belief in love and nonviolence. Gandhi learned that travelers on a journey of nonviolence, carrying luggage filled with hate and anger, will soon encounter violence and defeat. This was a painful lesson through defeat for Gandhi. The next chapter in the story of nonviolence and one of its first greatest defeats, what Gandhi called the 'Himalayan Mistake', begins with the end of the great World War of 1914-1918.

'Himalayan mistake'

In response to terrorism and acts of violence during the Great War, the British enacted wartime measures for censorship and further suppression of the population. Secret tribunals were set up across the country to deal with Indian activists. Newspapers were censored or closed. The Indians expected the measures to end with the end of war, but on March 18th, 1919, the measures enacted during the war became permanent. This action of the British sent shock waves across India. Over 500,000 Indians had volunteered for the British army during the war and the new permanent law of the land was an insult that outraged them.

The insult was only a part of the larger story of Indians beings subjects of a foreign nation. For one hundred years, their leaders had offered only the tools of violence as weapons. Indians had rioted, engaged in assassinations and sabotage, and tried to terrorize the British, but to no avail. Such petty use of violence was directed at the greatest imperial power since ancient Rome and the British were defending a civilization and way of life that depended on owning its colonies.

In the morning of the day after the passage of the law, as Gandhi walked into a prearranged meeting, he announced that an idea had come to him during his dream the night before— "that we should call on the country to observe a general *hartal*."[578] *Hartal* was an Indian term for a general strike by the population. In the *hartal*, stores were to remain closed, factories shut, loading and unloading of the ships halted as a weapon in this battle against the British. '*Hartal*' was not new to Indians and their culture. It wasn't a foreign concept. Indians knew it as a symbolic act of both mourning and protest. But a '*hartal*' as a symbol of independence and freedom was a new invention.

It had been only several years since Gandhi returned to India from long absence in South Africa. Upon return, he had immediately been called 'Mahatma' or 'Great Soul'. Within few years, the 'Great Soul' of India was more and more the voice of over two hundred million citizens of a proud and ancient civilization.

Gandhi had spontaneously become the spokesperson for the soul of millions mothers, fathers, children, and lovers who did not care for violence, yet did not know of any other way to fight their war. Thus, they had become passive and silent, preferring to remain as subjects. Gandhi was now expressing what they could not express themselves and had given them a symbolic act or expression in the form of a '*hartal*' whereby they could express their desires for freedom. Gandhi's call for a '*hartal*' "united vast multitudes in common action; it gave people a sense of power. They loved Gandhi for it. The *hartal* paralyzed economic life; the dead cities and towns were tangible proof that Indians could be effective. What the Indian people needed most, and lacked most, was faith in themselves. Gandhi gave it to them."[579] People soon began to take vows of Satyagraha throughout India.

Gandhi declared: "Even such a mighty government as the government of India, will have to yield if we are true to our pledge. For the pledge is no small thing. It means a change of heart. It is an attempt to introduce the religious spirits into politics. We may no longer believe in the doctrine of 'tit

CHAPTER 8

for tat'; we may not meet hatred with hatred, violence with violence, evil with evil; but we have to make a continuous and persistent effort to return good for evil...Nothing is impossible."

The *'hartal'* was observed for a day in Delhi on March 30, 1919. It was repeated in other cities and towns across India on April 6. It was spectacular. Delhi had come to a standstill; this was followed by the paralysis of all commerce in Bombay. Yet, despite the success of the *hartal* in Delhi, riots had also broken out. Local leaders in Delhi asked Gandhi, who was in Bombay, to come and help calm the situation. On April 9, on his way to Delhi, the authorities removed him from his train, released him in Bombay, and banned him from traveling outside the city.

Meanwhile, he learned that violence has taken place in Bombay. His heart was broken when he further learned of other towns in which people had resorted to violence, especially his hometown of Ahmadabad, a place in which he thought nonviolence would prevail. He had underestimated the power of violence and the extent of hatred. The news of violence reached him when he was about to get on the train again to break the law and be arrested. After hearing the news, he gave up on the idea.

He had realized his mistake. He had attempted to change the system politically, while his attempt was defeated by the engrained culture of violence. Gandhi began to retrace his steps and evaluate the situation. Back home at a huge gathering in Ahmadabad he told his people: "We have burnt down buildings, forcibly captured weapons, extorted money, stopped trains, cut off telegraphs, wires, killed innocent people, and plundered shops and private homes." Meanwhile, the situation in Punjab province, in which Delhi was located, reached a climax. In the city of Amritsar with a population of 150,000, after the successful hartal, the British authorities deported the two main Indian leaders from the city. As the anger of population grew, the two people who could have controlled the crowd were absent from the city. A mob burned down the one bank and then beat the British manager and assistant manager to death. At another bank, the manager had tried to defend himself using a revolver, but he was also killed and the bank burnt. This form of violence had been exactly what the British needed to defeat nonviolence. The British did not know how to respond to a large nonviolent event, but they were very familiar with responding to violence. The British army's response was so horrifying that the shock waves reached all the way to London.

On April 13, in midst of violence breaking out in their city, a large number people in Amritsar who still believed in Satyagraha gathered in a square called 'Jallianwalla Bagh'. The word *'bagh'* to Persians and perhaps to Indians conjures up images of an exotic garden with trees, fruits, and flowers. Although this place may have been such a paradise centuries before, at the time it was a large flat square bordered by high walls with only a single, narrow entrance. On that morning, an estimated ten to twenty thousand peaceful Indians gathered to hear speeches on nonviolence. As speeches were taking place, Brigadier General Reginald Dyer, with two armored vehicles accompanied by fifty Indian soldiers, approached the *'bagh'* and ordered his troops to enter the cordoned off square. When the armored vehicles were unable to get into the square, Dyer's soldiers entered the square and lined up on each side of the entrance. Meanwhile, the thousands of men, women, and children who had assembled there to listen to speeches and carry out a nonviolent symbolic gathering watched as, without any warning to disperse and without leaving an exit point through which the people could flee, General Dyer ordered his troops to fire.

For ten minutes the troops continued firing round after round into the terrorized crowd. When the firing ended, the square was carpeted with dead bodies. A total of 1,650 bullets were fired at the crowd. As the result, there were 379 dead and 1,137 wounded; an incredible 1,516 casualties out of 1,650 bullets. [580] The British had resorted to an incredible use of violence, yet Satyagraha was defeated because the Indians had made the fatal mistake of using violence first.

On April 18th, Gandhi characterized his premature campaign of nonviolence as a 'Himalayan Mistake'. He called off the national movement and announced that he would fast for three days and nights to atone for his mistake. Gandhi realized that Indians first had to be trained in principles of nonviolence before they could undertake an act of civil disobedience. "I am sorry", Gandhi said "that when I embarked upon a mass movement I underrated the forces of evil, and I must now pause and consider how best to meet the situation."[581]

Yet despite this setback, Gandhi continued to advocate independence and never retreated from his goal of a free, independent, democratic, and secular India. In October of that year, he was elected the President of All-India Home Rule League, which demanded an India ruled by Indians. Meanwhile, London began placing pressure on the Viceroy to arrest Gandhi and send him to prison, but the Viceroy was reluctant to take action until the right opportunity presented itself.

The Viceroy was afraid of consequences of imprisoning Gandhi without sufficient justification. Gandhi had become ever more popular after the defeat of the 'hartal'. His visits to towns and cities would bring out tens of thousands. On many occasions he had almost been crushed by the crowds. At times, his legs would bleed when thousands of people swarmed him to rub their hands on his legs or feet. He would travel third class amongst the poor, eating a handful of nuts and fruit during the day. At one village, the population threatened to lie on the tracks if Gandhi's train did not stop for them.

In November of 1919, along with many other Hindus, he was invited to a Muslim Conference in Delhi. Despite the rising animosity, anger and hatred between the Hindus and the Muslims that had been driven by a culture of divide and rule instituted by the British, Hindus and Muslims were standing peacefully, side by side. Speaker after speaker debated what to do and many suggestions were made. Some talked about boycotting British textiles, some advocated boycotting all imported textiles. Gandhi sat on the platform, searching for a word that would describe their plan of action, a word that would symbolize all that they wanted to accomplish. As he sat there pondering, he was called on to speak. He sat there for a moment, paused, and then the word 'noncooperation' came out of his mouth.

To the leaders sitting there and waiting for him to speak, 'noncooperation' symbolized everything they wanted to do. Gandhi didn't want Indians to just boycott British textiles, he wanted them to boycott everything British: British clothes, British food, British schools, British courts, and British commerce. He asked for all who had been given special honors and medals to reject them. He called for complete 'noncooperation' against the British.[582]

One of Gandhi's biographers, Louis Fischer wrote: "'Non-cooperation' became the name of an epoch in the life of India and of Gandhi. Noncooperation was negative enough to be peaceful but positive enough to be effective. It entailed denial, renunciation, and self-discipline. It was training for self-rule.[583]

Thousands of students and teachers from English schools left the cities and went to villages to teach and educate the illiterate. Hundreds of British-trained lawyers left their lucrative practices in order to join the movement of 'noncooperation', including Motilal Nehru, the father of Jawaharlal Nehru, the future leader of independent India. Villagers began to boycott the alcoholic beverages sold by British companies. Meanwhile, Gandhi traveled for months in uncomfortable trains, crammed in with thousands of his fellow Indians. He often traveled with Mohammad Ali, the younger brother of two of the most influential Muslim leaders in India.

In each town and village, tens of thousands would show up to hear Gandhi speak. Since he addressed the crowds without benefit of a microphone and loudspeakers, many of those who were not close enough to hear him were content to stand and merely get a glimpse of the man who had given them strength and confidence. At the end of his speeches, Gandhi would ask everyone to take off all foreign clothes and throw them into a mound of clothing that would be burned. As Gandhi lit those fires in town after town, thousands would scream and cheer in moments of ecstasy that India had not felt for centuries.

Gandhi also told everyone that they needed to learn to spin and weave their own cotton which India had an abundance of. He spent half an hour a day spinning and required each of his associates to do the same. Gandhi emphasized daily spinning as a form of meditation and prayer. He would say that spinning made the mind 'Godward'. The *charka* or the spinning wheel had become the new symbol of resistance, a way of symbolic communication to fellow Indians of their desire for independence and freedom. Later, *Charka* would become the symbol representing India on its national flag. In 1921 Gandhi, in a further symbolic gesture, forever shed his clothing of the sleeveless vest and his homespun cap and adopted the Indian loincloth called *dhoti* as his only garment.

Around the same period, his spiritual transformation was also complete. He had reached a state where his ego no longer mattered. Nonviolence, kindness and humanity mattered. His family was India, and his life was dedicated to India's freedom, independence, nonviolence, and democracy.

In October 1921, the Congress Working Committee, now representing India's struggle for freedom, asked all Indian soldiers in the British army to resign and urged civilians working for the British to sever all ties. The British warned the population that such desertion was against the law and reminded Indians of the imprisonment of the Ali brothers, who had previously advocated noncooperation with the British army. Despite the threat of imprisonment and coercive violence, the Indians joined in this next stage of nonviolent struggle resigning from their British posts and duties.

In December 1921 alone, over twenty thousand Indians were imprisoned for civil disobedience. In January 1922, ten thousand more were jailed. The

CHAPTER 8

crisis was reaching a climax that the British Empire could not afford. Volunteer organizations were banned and routine nightly raids of activist offices and meeting places were taking place across India. The treatment of political prisoners also grew worse. India was the British Empire's most prized and precious colony—the Jewel in the Crown. The wealth acquired from the country had helped the British become a world power in 19th century and England was now even more powerful than ever. It had just defeated Germany and the Austro-Hungarian Empire and subjected them to the humiliation, indemnities, and dismemberment imposed by the peace treaties. The Ottoman Empire had been carved up by the British as if they owned Middle East. They had coerced and bribed corrupt Iranian officials to obtain long-term rights to Iran's oil fields for practically nothing. The British, along with the rest of the Allied Powers, had been given control of 'mandates' in many parts of the globe—notably, among others, Palestine. Yet, amongst all its possessions, India remained the most precious.

As the year 1921 came to a close, the British would not budge. Some nationalists began to call for rebellion, but Gandhi believed in nonviolence. For him, independence was inevitable and a matter of time; the only weapon postponing Indians independence was violence. In his nonviolent struggle against the British, he had won the hearts of thousands of British citizens who were supporting Indians and their struggle for liberation through nonviolence. For him, it was just a matter of time until the British government recognized India's right to independence. Yet even as he advocated nonviolence and preached against violence, he despised cowardice. He was willing to accept defeat in order to maintain peace, but was not willing to accept cowardice in order to maintain nonviolence. "Where there is only a choice between cowardice and violence, I would advise violence," he wrote. He kept reminding the population that nonviolence required far greater bravery than violence, and in nonviolence, forgiveness was the most difficult task. Gandhi kept reminding Indians that the ability to forgive was the path for peace within oneself and within the society. It took far more courage to forgive than to resort to hatred, anger and violence. For in forgiveness, one had to place one's trust in humanity and the love of people, which required courage. Violence did not.[584]

Yet as much as Gandhi was fighting the British, his struggle against the engrained culture of violence in India was even more difficult. In November 1921, during a royal visit by the Prince of Wales, riots broke out in Bombay, where 58 people were killed and an additional 381 injured. Upon hearing the news, an eyewitness described Gandhi as 'Thrown into a stage of utter despondency, he began to indulge in such words of grief and bitter self-reproach as would melt even the stoniest-hearted men."' But Gandhi continued to believe in love, and in the goodness of India's people, and maintained his high hopes for the triumph of nonviolence.

In November of 1921, the All-India Congress Committee passed a resolution to launch a campaign of civil disobedience throughout India in order to paralyze the British. Gandhi asked the leaders to allow him to make an experiment on a small scale in the province of Bardoli, near Bombay, in order to gauge India's readiness. Bardoli had a population of 87,000 and contained 137 villages. It was small enough for Gandhi to supervise the experiment there personally. In addition, a successful mass civil disobedience in one small province could energize all of India.

On February 1, 1922, Gandhi informed the Viceroy of India of his plan for civil disobedience. He did not believe the British arms could defeat a nonviolent army. But within four days after the limited nonviolent campaign, on February 5, Indians of Bardoli defeated their own nonviolent movement.

As a procession of Satyagrahis was passing through a street at night, police began to hassle some of the stragglers. The stragglers called on the procession for help and a mob returned to their aid. One policeman began to fire his weapon but soon ran out of ammunition and fled to city hall. The mob followed him and set the building on fire. When the policeman exited and surrendered, the mob beat him to death and threw his body into the fire.

Gandhi was sickened by the violence and his heart was broken. He wrote: "No provocation can possibly justify brutal murder of men who had been rendered defenseless and who had virtually thrown themselves on the mercy of the mob."[585] "Suppose, the non-violent disobedience of Bardoli was permitted by God to succeed and the government had abdicated in favor of the victors of Bardoli, who would control the unruly elements that must be expected to perpetrate inhumanity upon due provocation?"[586] What would be the cost of destruction, violence, murder, and insult he thought, if such an experiment was carried out not just within a small province with a population of no more than 87,000, but amongst two hundred and fifty million Indians across thousands of provinces. Does murdering innocent men, women and children justify freedom? Does murdering the enablers of this colonization, those who are using violence in order to maintain Indians as subjects, serve the cause of freedom? Can one gain the 'ends' of freedom through the 'means' of violence? Gandhi did not believe in violence and did not believe that ends justify the means. He believed freedom obtained through violence would only hand the power of violence to another group of people who would, in turn, subjugate the population. Thus he believed any violence in a revolution is an evil which cannot be justified.

The violence and killing at Bardoli was more intense than Gandhi could handle on a larger theatre of India. He expected more from India. He thus not only canceled the planned noncooperation in Bardoli, but he also canceled noncooperation in all of India. "Let the opponents glory in our humiliation or so-called defeat", he said. "It is better to be charged with cowardice and weakness than to be guilty of denial of our oath and to sin against God. It is a million times better to *appear* untrue before the world than to *be* untrue to ourselves."[587] The incident in Bardoli he said "shows the way India may easily go, if drastic precautions be not taken." Writing to Jawaharlal Nehru, he said "I assure you, that if the thing [noncooperation] had not been suspended we would have been leading not a nonviolent struggle but essentially a violent struggle."[588] As for himself, "I must undergo personal cleansing. I must become a fitter instrument able to register the slightest variation in the moral atmosphere about me."[589] Gandhi then undertook a fast lasting five days and nights only drinking water when needed with a pinch of salt.

Shortly after in March, the British Empire decided it could no longer tolerate the risk Gandhi represented to them and ordered his arrest. At 10:30 in the evening on March 10, 1922, a police officer stopped by Gandhi's Ashram and announced that Gandhi was under arrest. Surrounded by his Ashramites, he led a prayer and joined them in singing a hymn. He then walked with the officer to prison, awaiting one of the most famous trials of the 20th century.

Anticipating his arrest, he had written an article titled "If I Am Arrested".:

"Rivers of blood shed by the government cannot frighten me, but I should be deeply pained even if the people did so much as abuse the government for my sake or in my name. It would be disgracing me if the people lost their equilibrium on my arrest."[590]

Upon his arrest, India took a deep breath and remained at peace. Prior to his arrest, Gandhi, in a series of articles had declared that the "noncooperaters are at war with the government. They have declared rebellion against it… Noncooperation, though a religious and strictly moral movement, deliberately aims at the overthrow of the government, and is therefore legally seditious …The fight that was commenced on 1920 is a fight to the finish, whether it lasts one month, or one year or many months or many years … No empire intoxicated with the red wine of power and plunder of weaker races has yet lived long in the world."[591]

The trial took place on March 18th and took no more than 100 minutes. The government used evidence from the series of articles Gandhi had recently written. But they didn't need to make much of a strong case. Gandhi pleaded guilty for deliberately breaking the law and asked for the harshest sentence possible. And then he went ahead to read the emotional and eloquent statement he had prepared.

He had seen and felt the pain and poverty of India he said. His people had endured the humiliation of their proud civilization. He had witnessed tens of thousands of his countrymen sent as slaves in name of indentured labor to the mines of South Africa. In his statement, he did not defend himself, but merely pleaded his case and his reasons for his noncooperation and the deliberate breaking of the law in the form of civil disobedience. "I discovered that as a man and as an Indian I had no rights. On the contrary, I discovered that I had no rights as a man because I was an Indian."[592] He told the judge that he had once regarded the British presence as good. He had worked as a British trained lawyer defending its laws, he had volunteered as a medic in the British army during the Boer wars in South Africa, and during World War I he had encouraged thousands of his countrymen to serve in the British army. "I gave the government my voluntary and hearty co-operation, criticizing it fully where I felt it was faulty, but never wishing its destruction."[593]

Gandhi's activism had transformed over the decades from a reformer, initially supporting the British and advocating humane and just laws under British rule to a revolutionary, adamant about the necessity of India's complete self-rule, independence, and freedom. As a reformer, he had believed in the goodness of the British in allowing Indian freedom with continued British presence. He had dreamed of reforms under the British and a symbolic presence of the British monarchy in a free India. He described how circumstance had changed his views. His principles on human rights, freedom, and independence of India had also matured to one that he now believed in.

The lessons Iranians learned from the failure of the reformist movement were similar to lessons Gandhi learned prior to 1920. The young Gandhi believed that India could be free and independent yet function with conditional presence of symbolic British institutions. But, the more mature Gandhi had learned that freedom, justice, and democracy cannot be conditional. In order for one to secure justice, one must emphasize justice and opportunity for every single citizen regardless of their sex, religion, beliefs, and culture. This belief in equal rights for every single human being must come above all else. Gandhi had realized that even a symbolic presence of Great Britain was a threat to justice in future India.

Learning from Gandhi's experience, it is important for Iranians to remind themselves that people have the right to choose and interpret their religion the way they wish. But the interpretation of religion cannot be accomplished through a reformist movement aiming to maintain the laws of Islamic Republic yet in a more reformed and humane way. In such a case, it is only a matter of time, perhaps several decades or several generations, when the religious institutions will attempt to overpower the democratically elected institutions of the country. The reformist philosophy of Gandhi failed and the reformist movement of Iran failed because, in both cases, they attempted to incorporate and justify undemocratic institutions against the principles of democracy and human rights.

Gandhi's transformation from a youth sympathetic to the British to a man leading India towards democracy, independence, and human rights was a change from a person with broken principles to principles incorporating what Gandhi believed to be the 'truth'. In his statement, Gandhi maintained that his faith in the British system had failed and thus his principles were altered. From then on, he had called for the unconditional independence and freedom for India.

Gandhi had learned that the principles of a struggle for freedom require freedom to be unconditional. Freedom with conditions is no longer freedom. Gandhi then told the court how he reluctantly came to the conclusion that the "British connection had made India more helpless than she ever was before, politically and economically...She has become so poor that she has little power of resisting famines... No sophistry, no jugglery in figures can explain away the evidence the skeletons in many villages present to the naked eye. I have no doubt whatsoever that both England and the town dwellers of India will have to answer, if there is a God above, for this crime against humanity. [594]

He ended the court session by addressing the judge "The only course open to you, ... is either to resign your post or inflict on me the severest penalty if you believe that the system and law you are assisting to administer are good for the people."[595] The judge was placed in a difficult situation. He was well aware of the immense respect in which this fifty-three year-old was held, not just in India and but also by thousands of British citizens including himself. Yet, having no choice, he sentenced him to six years in prison. Gandhi was seen wearing his trademark smile as he always had as he was led away from the court.

Appendectomy

On the evening of January 12, 1924, in his second year in prison, Gandhi developed acute appendicitis, which in the pre-antibiotic era was a life-threatening condition. As they were waiting for Indian doctors who were three hours away, the British surgeon warned Gandhi that if he did not operate immediately, his life would be in jeopardy. This was a serious problem for England. If Gandhi died in prison, especially under the care of British doctors, the English would be blamed for his death. Gandhi signed a statement in the presence of several Indians that he was voluntarily allowing the British surgeons to operate and he had the utmost confidence in them. The operation went well, but on February 24, 1924, just over a month after his surgery, the British released Gandhi on medical grounds, fearing that he might die while in their custody.

Gandhi was released to an India that had greatly changed during his two-year absence. While in prison, the cohesiveness of the independence movement fell apart. Various factions began to form in the Indian National Congress, some advocating violence. But worst of all, the peace between Muslims and Hindus that Gandhi had worked so hard to achieve had broken down. There was religious violence all over India, and that violence was fueling more and more hatred, which was followed by more violence. In Gandhi's absence, Indians had given up on the noncooperation strategy because of the tremendous amount of courage and energy it required and which Gandhi had previously supplied.

Gandhi had been ill for months in prison prior to his appendectomy and the surgery itself took a great toll on his body. Following the surgery, because he had not fully recovered, touring the country further weakened him. He was down to 102 pounds. Yet physically he was not as wounded as he was spiritually and this spiritual pain and wounding hurt him the most. Witnessing renewed violence between the Hindus and Muslims was too much for him to bear. In addition, some of his most staunch supporters were now advocating violence as a tool to fight the British. At an All-India Congress Committee meeting in June of 1924, when he was told by so many of his associates that

CHAPTER 8

they no longer believed and lacked confidence in nonviolence, Gandhi began to weep openly in the meeting. Unable to unite India for nonviolence against the British, he made the Hindu-Muslim unity and friendship his highest priority. "The only question for immediate solution before the country is the Hindu-Muslim question", he said, "I agree ... that Hindu-Muslim unity means *swaraj* [self-rule]".[596]

Gandhi's struggles were previously focused on the British and *swaraj*. It was a political fight for a political solution, but he had soon realized how the engrained culture of violence in India could destroy his hopes. His attention was then turned to a war against violence and his main focus became healing and treating the culture of India from its affliction with its disease of violence. This again is not unlike the struggle in Iran, in which a political struggle lies ahead, yet that struggle needs cultural healing and forswearing of violence.

Once released from prison, Gandhi discovered the reason behind the increase in the culture of enmity and violence between the Hindu's and Muslims. The British had been instigating and promoting hatred between the two religions in order to increase violence and further justify their presence in India. In the seven hundred thousand villages of India, Muslims and Hindus had been living side by side and in peace for centuries. This relative peace had continued until the 20th century when the British needed to encourage a division between the two religions in order to maintain their grip, the classic imperial strategy of 'divide and rule'. In order to achieve this, they passed a series of laws designed to alienate the Muslims from the Hindus. In 1904, Lord Curzon, the Viceroy of India, divided India into two halves along religious divides and decreed the partition of the province of Bengal. Indians had never been divided based on religion. India had always been religiously diverse nation and Indians always had respected the many religions of the country. This move to divide India greatly angered the Hindus but their anger was directed not at the British but towards Muslims, who they regarded as advocating such a religious and social division in their country. Subsequently, the cancelation of the division inflamed the anger of Muslims toward the Hindus, who they blamed for failure of the plan. In 1906, Lord Morley, assistant to secretary of State in India, devised another plan to further inflame enmity between the Muslims and Hindus. Under his direction, a prominent Muslim named Agha Khan was to urge the government to decree that in all future elections in India, Muslims could only vote for Muslims and Hindus vote for Hindus. Such division is one of greatest evils in pseudo-democracies.

It gives those uneducated about the principles of democracy a false sense of equal rights, yet separates people along religious divides.

This is also the case in Iran where such a system has been in place since 1906. In the Iranian system, Christians, Jews and Zoroastrians are allowed to only vote for their own candidates in the parliament. They are then told that this is a democratic way of elections, by means of which there will always be two dedicated religious minority candidates representing them in parliament. But these candidates are no more than symbolic participants in the nation's affairs. In a democratic and secular Iran, this symbolic division amongst Iranians must end. Religious minorities must be allowed to vote for candidates of their choice in parliament or city councils regardless of their religion. And they must be allowed to declare themselves candidates in any future elections without any prejudice or discrimination by the law or any undemocratic institution. Every Iranian must have the right to declare himself or herself a candidate on any ballot regardless of their sex, religion, or ethnicity.

Similar laws of division enacted by the British were an important source of anger between the Hindus and the Muslims. Gandhi had now realized that the political system of British rule was instigating and creating further violence in society. In September of 1924, he felt it his duty to fast in order to focus the heart and minds of Indians on peace between the two great religions. He went to Mohammad Ali's house, the younger of the two Ali brothers who had continued to advocate peace and friendship between Muslims and Hindus. In his house, the weakened and exhausted Gandhi announced that he would fast for twenty-one days and nights, drinking only water when necessary.

Such a long fast in the home of Mohammad Ali came as shock to disillusioned and disheartened India. The 'Mahatma' of India would surely die if he refused to eat for twenty-one days. But Gandhi was adamant; he felt it was his religious duty. In addition, Gandhi did not believe in suicide. Even though he acknowledged the possibility that such a fast could be fatal, the concept of suicide was repugnant to him. He had too much unfinished business to kill himself at such a crucial moment. His belief in God and humanity was so immense that he believed he would find the strength to undergo this ordeal. He believed no other action could refocus India in her struggle for independence after the loss of hope and disillusionment engulfing the country since his imprisonment. He thought that such a fast was necessary for him and for India spiritually.

CHAPTER 8

When Gandhi made a decision based on religion, the whole world could not dissuade him. Despite the objections of numerous Indian leaders, the fast was to take place for twenty-one days and the focus of India was to be placed on Mohammad Ali's house and Hindu-Muslim friendship and peace. Muslims and Hindus were all to watch as the 'Mahatma' of India effectively put his life in the hands of Mohammad Ali's brothers, the most respected Muslims in India.

Gandhi's highest weight after his surgery had been 112 pounds. He was down to 102 pounds when he started the fast. During the first few days, Gandhi received visitors and wrote several articles to be published. But he became weaker as each day passed. In the first seven days, he lost nine additional pounds. On the sixth day, he wrote several paragraphs with a total of 112 words in which he claimed "… The change has still to come. But the struggle must for the moment be transferred to a change of heart among the Hindus and the Mussulmans. Before they dare think of freedom they must be brave enough to love one another, to tolerate one another's religion, even prejudices and superstitions, and to trust one another. This requires faith in oneself. And faith in oneself is faith in God. If we have that faith we shall cease to fear one another. "[597]

He grew weaker and weaker each day. At nights, he would sleep under the open sky under moonlight. At times, his voice was so weak that he could be heard only by those nearest to him. On the twentieth day, he called his fast as days of "grace, privilege, and peace". On the twenty-first day, he called Imam Sahib and asked him to recite the opening verses of Koran, then asked C.F Andrews, his nurse and a Christian missionary whom he called the 'good Samaritan,' to sing his favorite Christian hymn and finally asked the Vaishnava hymn to be recited from Upanishads. He then asked all those Hindu and Muslim leaders present to "lay down their lives if need be for the cause of brotherhood." For twenty-one days, India had been given a powerful lesson in meditation and power of nonviolence.

His fast had an immense effect on India. It focused the will of now nearly three hundred million Indians back on nonviolence and prepared them for a new struggle for freedom. Yet the fast, the earlier surgery, and illness had taken their toll on Gandhi. He was exhausted and no longer able to travel from city to city and town to town to tell people about Satyagraha, self-respect and nonviolence. He needed rest for his body and mind. In January of 1926, Gandhi announced that he would engage in a year of political silence. He needed rest so he was not to travel outside his Ashram and certainly not beyond Ahmadabad. This year of rest for Gandhi is referred to as the year of silence.

He greatly enjoyed the year of silence, during which he rested his body and his spirit. He would spend long hours playing with the children of his Ashram, who called him Bapu. After the year of rest, Gandhi again began to travel through the country. Five years had passed since India's failed attempt in Bardoli and the outbreak of violence. He went from town to town reiterating his message of nonviolence and Hindu-Muslim friendship. Violence between the two great religions was still sporadically occurring in India. There were reports of Hindus and Muslims abducting each other's women and children and forcibly converting them to their religion. Leaders of Hindu and Muslim nationalist movement were also being assassinated by fanatic Muslim and Hindus. In this poisonous atmosphere Gandhi called any attempt at or announcement of independence as empty words.

His arrival in cities sometimes drew up to two hundred thousand. Without the aid of microphones or loudspeakers, Gandhi would often raise his right hand for the crowd and point to his thumb, announcing that the thumb symbolized 'equality for Untouchables', then he would point to the forefinger and say 'spinning'. As thousands in the crowd could not hear him, his message was relayed from person to person imitating him and his message. The third finger symbolized 'sobriety', cleansing of body, soul and India from alcohol and opium. He would point to the forth finger and announce, Hindu-Muslim friendship. And when he pointed to his fifth finger, he would announce it symbolizes 'equal rights for women'.[598] The wrist connecting all the fingers together stood for 'nonviolence'.

These five acts together with nonviolence, Gandhi believed were the keys for a future independent, democratic, secular and free India. The largely illiterate Indians in thousands of towns and villages would often just watch Gandhi as he progressed through the steps of pointing to his fingers and wrist while reciting their symbolic significance.

For Gandhi, it was not just a matter of making speeches. He was a general, gathering and training an army, an army that could become as large as three hundred million. For his battle, he was constantly searching for new ways. War against the British meant civil disobedience, and civil disobedience meant proper training in nonviolence and discipline. Without absolute discipline, any effort at nonviolence would fail.

After two years of traveling throughout India and focusing the population's attention on nonviolence, Gandhi felt India was ready for

CHAPTER 8

another battle. For this, he had to find the proper time, place, and form of civil disobedience or breaking of the law. On February 28, 1928, six years after the retreat from civil disobedience following the violence in Bardoli, Gandhi gave the signal and announced the battle with the British was to resume. Civil disobedience was again to take place. As his battlefield, Gandhi chose the same place where he had been defeated previously, Bardoli.

This small province with its 137 villages and 87,000 citizens was again to be the test ground for the battle and the focus of India for months to come. The British had passed a law increasing the tax on the villagers by 22 percent. Gandhi directed the population to boycott the tax. In the campaign led by Vallabhbhai Patel, the mayor of Ahmadabad and Abbas Tyebji, a Muslim, the villagers responded and boycotted the tax. Hundreds were arrested. Soldiers would attack people's homes and walk away with pots and pans as payment for taxes, but people refused to turn to violence. They were driven off their farms, their animals and carts were confiscated, yet disobedience persisted and this time Indians remained nonviolent. They had learned an important lesson in 1922; violence had led to their defeat. This time, they were disciplined in nonviolence. For months the Indians of Bardoli persistently disobeyed, while all of India watched and supported them. When the peasants asked Patel if they could block the roads and place spikes to burst the officials' tires, he replied, "Your fight is not for a few hundred rupees, but for a principle…You are fighting for self-respect which ultimately leads to *swaraj*."[599]

On June 12th, Gandhi announced a nationwide 'hartal' in support of the peasants in Bardoli. On July 23rd, in response to the widening crisis, the government invited the Satyagraha leaders to a conference. As part of culture of nonviolence now in use, the leaders of Satyagraha were open to negotiations. Yet, compromise did not mean the abandonment of demands and principles which set the nonviolent movement into action. Thus, a compromise with the British could not be reached and Bardoli villagers continued their disobedience against the tax. On August 6th, the British finally accepted defeat. All the prisoners were released. All the property confiscated was returned and the rise in tax was canceled. A small battle had been won and Satyagraha had achieved victory. But, India had passed a major test. India had matured to the degree where now it collectively had renounced violence in a province in which nonviolence had been defeated six years before.

At the annual congress session in December of 1928, the young men of the committee led by Jawaharlal Nehru, now empowered after the victory in

Bardoli, lobbied for declaration of immediate independence. Gandhi suggested a two-year warning to the British. They finally agreed on a year's warning. It was decided that if India had not achieved freedom under Dominion Status by December 31st, 1929, India would take action on its own through civil disobedience.

In 1929, the Viceroy found the situation in India "bordering on a state of alarm."[600] Thus in October 1929, he released a statement inviting Indian leaders to a Round Table conference to discuss the "natural issue of India's constitutional progress...the attainment of Dominion Status."[601] The leaders of independence movement, including Gandhi, in return released a statement calling Viceroy's announcement as 'favorable'.

But the British Empire was not ready to give its most precious jewel that easily. Back in London, the House of Lords and House of Commons began heavily attacking the Viceroy. The idea of a Dominion Status could not be tolerated by a nation that saw itself as the most powerful empire the world had ever seen. In 1930, the British ruled a large part of the world and in the words of Winston Churchill, "the nauseating and humiliating spectacle of this one-time Inner Temple lawyer, now seditious *fakir*, striding half-naked up the steps of the Viceroy's palace, there to negotiate and to parley on equal terms with the representatives of the King-Emperor" could not be tolerated.[602] Any possibility of reforms through negotiations with the Viceroy granting Dominion Status to India was rejected by London. The stage was set for major civil disobedience.

Salt Act

A symbolic act of courage is transformative. For an individual, it can change a human being. At societal level, it can change a nation. As the year 1929 came to a close, the Indian National Congress ratified a resolution in favor of unabridged independence and secession. '*Swaraj*' Gandhi declared, "is now to mean complete independence."[603] The British had left no more room for negotiations. The struggle for Dominion Status in India with elections and self-rule under British sovereignty, much like the negotiated path of Iranian Reformist attempt for free elections within the Islamic Republic, had failed. India, like Iranians 70 years later, was met with a violent power unwilling to cede control. India's National Congress urged its members to withdraw from legislatures and sanctioned the non-payment of taxes imposed by the British. The Congress was responsible for beginning the civil disobedience campaign, but from January 1st 1930, all eyes were on Gandhi.

Everyone knew Gandhi was the country's general and the nation awaited his signal. The world had never seen an army of three hundred million in a war where one side refused to use violence. Gandhi as the natural leader would choose the time, the place, and method of civil disobedience. Indians wanted to know what they were to do and when to start. But Gandhi was not content with a simple announcement.

The British Empire was also paralyzed. If they arrested Gandhi, it would do considerable harm to their status and quite likely lead to a nationwide war against all of India. They had no choice but to see what Gandhi's next move was. In January 1930, the British continued to watch Gandhi as India waited for the signal. Gandhi was going to announce to the world the commencement of a campaign of civil disobedience in the most dramatic fashion.

Gandhi believed in the inner voice of the unconscious and the wisdom of a life time where an individual, through meditation and prayer, could find God and insight. He spent weeks on his charka spinning cotton and praying, waiting for that inner voice to guide him Perhaps it would come in a dream, perhaps in a moment of peace, while playing with children, or praying. He was like a prophet waiting for a signal from God. On January 18th, when a colleague asked what he has planned for the country he replied, "I am furiously thinking night and day, and I do not see any light coming out of the surrounding darkness."[604]

Finally, on February 27th, nearly two months after the decision by the Indian National Congress to start disobedience, clues came through a series of articles written by Gandhi in *Young India*. The first was titled "If I am arrested." The next several articles referred to the penal sections of the Salt Act. The Salt Act was England's monopoly on one of the most important and vital commodities of India. Salt is as important to the body as air and water. And especially in hot, humid climates like India's, in which people lose large amount of salt per day, the intake of salt is vital. As part of colonization, the English had banned any Indian from possessing or using salt not produced by an English manufacturer. It was a humiliating symbol of colonialism and the mastery of the English over their subjects. But Gandhi's articles just talked about the Salt Act, and not how he was to signal the commencement of civil obedience to the people of India.

On March 2, Gandhi sent a letter to the Viceroy in India warning that in nine days he would give the signal. Gandhi addressed the letter, "Dear Friend," which perhaps can be considered the most unique letter ever written from the representative of one nation to another about to go to war. In it, he reiterated his position and gave the reasons for this journey. "My personal faith is absolutely clear. I cannot intentionally hurt anything that lives, much less human beings, even though they may do the greatest wrong to me and mine. Whilst, therefore, I hold the British rule to be a curse, I do not intend harm to a single Englishman or to any legitimate interest he may have in India…"

Gandhi was about to use the strangest weapon the world had ever seen. The British of 1930, who considered themselves masters of warfare on the ground and at sea, were faced with an opponent who refused to step into their battlefield of violence, yet refused to step aside. Gandhi's battlefield was in the conscience of humanity. He was inviting the Viceroy to step into humanity's conscience and meet Gandhi on his turf. "My ambition is no less than to convert the British people through nonviolence, and thus make them see the wrong they have done to India. I do not seek to harm your people. I want to serve them as I want to serve my own."

Of all the weapons invented in the 20th century, none was as unique and powerful as what Gandhi was proposing -- to disarm the British through conversion using nonviolence. He wanted Indians to have self-respect, and at the same time get the British to respect them as equals and grant freedom to India. Only then was freedom and hence democracy possible. If violence led to success, it only meant the creation of a more violent army to overcome the enemy. Gandhi was well aware of the cycle of violence in history. For Gandhi, the problem and the enemy itself was violence. To overcome violence, he had to eliminate it. This could only be achieved through the conversion of the British from imperialists intent on retaining their hold on a colony, to recognizing India as an equal partner in dialogue and trade. "I respectfully invite you to pave the way for the immediate removal of those evils, and thus open a way for a real conference between equals…I have too great a regard for you as a man to wish to hurt your feelings…" Gandhi wrote, but he continued, "Nothing but organized non-violence can check the organized violence of the British government…"[605]

Without telling the Viceroy exactly what he intended to do, he informed him, "if you cannot see your way to deal with these evils and if my letter makes no appeal to your heart, on the eleventh day of this month, I shall proceed with such co-workers of the Ashram as I can take, to disregard the provisions of the Salt Laws....It is I know, open to you to frustrate my design by arresting me. I hope that there will be tens of thousands ready, in a disciplined manner, to take up the work after me. "[606] The letter was signed "I remain … Your sincere friend, M.K Gandhi. "

No declaration of war had ever been made in such a form. During most wars, a nation is aroused by orators, writers, poets, and leaders who ignite anger, and fear. In a nation under attack, those same people mobilize their population by reminding them of the death, destruction, and slavery that would occur by a victorious enemy. Any tool is used to nurture the anger needed to take an active stance in a war. Yet in a nonviolent struggle, a declaration of war free of hate and anger was needed. The strangest war in history was about to begin, in which the death of a single Englishman meant the defeat of India.

In the ten years since Gandhi had first convinced the leaders of Indian National Congress in 1919 of the potential of nonviolence, he had disciplined an army of three hundred million on the principles of nonviolence. At a time when radio and mass media were unavailable he had converted the hearts of the people in over seven hundred thousand villages. This was one of the greatest accomplishment by a general in such a short period of time in the history of humanity.

Thus the Viceroy of India was informed that Gandhi would signal the commencement of a war of nonviolence on March 11, 1930. Gandhi soon received a reply not dissimilar from the message given over and over to Iranians as a tool to encourage their silence. "His Excellency", replied the office of the Viceroy "regrets to learn that you contemplate a course of action which is clearly bound to involve violation of the law and danger to the pubic peace."[607] The commandment not to break the law or disturb the peace has been the same message given by regimes who want to maintain a culture and a political system built on inequality and violence, yet want to do so in relative peace, thus encouraging pacifism. Like the British who had envisioned special privileges secured through fear and violence, the Islamic Republic envisions privileges for the religious class through the same means. Thus, the message given to Gandhi is the same given to those wanting democracy and human rights in today's Iran. When Gandhi read Viceroy's reply, he said "On bended knee, I asked for bread and I received a stone instead."[608]

As days went by, more and more journalists gathered in front of Gandhi's Ashram waiting for the announcement. Thousands of Indians gathered around his village waiting but Gandhi continued to keep his silence. Finally on March 12th, Gandhi appeared from his Ashram together with seventy-eight of his followers. They sang prayers, and as the British and all of India was watching, they began to walk south.

For twenty four days, and two hundred and forty miles, they walked from village to village and town to town, still without any sign for civil disobedience. As they marched, more and more Indians joined their ranks. Tens of thousands of people were lined up along the road throwing flowers and cheering. Everywhere they went, the national colors of India could be seen. The British could do nothing. Gandhi had not insulted them, nor threatened violence; just a promise of a signal for civil disobedience.

By the time they reached the village of Dandi on the shores of the Indian Ocean, his army of seventy eight swelled to thousands. On the evening of April 5, Gandhi spent the night praying with his Satyagraha army. In early morning, he took a dip in the sea and as he came out, he walked on the sand a few feet and then picked up a pinch of crystallized salt from the sand. Under British rule, possession of salt by an Indian, not manufactured through a British affiliate, was against the law. In defiance, Gandhi held the salt high, signaling the nation that he has broken the law and his disobedience to British rule.

One of his biographers, Louis Fischer wrote:

"Had Gandhi gone by train or automobile to make salt, the effect would have been considerable. But to walk for twenty-four days and rivet the attention of India, to trek across a countryside saying, 'Watch, I am about to give a signal to the nation,' and then pick up a pinch of salt in publicized defiance of the mighty government and thus become a criminal, that required imagination, dignity, and the sense of showmanship of a great artist. It appealed to the illiterate peasant and it appealed to a sophisticated critic and sometime fierce opponent of Gandhi..."[609]

One cannot change a subjugated culture accepting its occupation as *fait accompli* to a culture of self-rule without introducing acts of courage symbolizing freedom. Within days millions in villages across India were walking to the sea and taking salt as a symbolic gesture of freedom. It was an act symbolizing cultural transformation, noncooperation against British rule and a referendum for self-governance. Participation in it meant the expression of freedom and its significance relied on a principle of humanity dictating that a freed spirit of a human being, tasting the joy of participation in a free act, can never be enslaved again.

CHAPTER 8

The British had thought Gandhi's performance at the sea would cause some Indians to follow, resulting in arrests. The reaction of the people of India was nothing like they had predicted. In village after village, Indians were making salt from the sea, at home or on the street, breaking British law. Indian National Congress also took action, distributing literature on salt-making techniques. Members of the Indian National Congress were making salt on the roof of their headquarters. A crowd of sixty thousand gathered at the headquarters in Bombay as the police tried to arrest the leaders of the Indian National Congress.

In Karachi, fifty thousand went to the seashore to perform this symbolic act. The policemen faced with a tsunami of disobedience found themselves at a loss. Still, thousands were arrested across India, including Jawaharlal Nehru,- in Allahabad. In Delhi, a crowd of fifteen thousand listened to speakers urging people to boycott foreign clothes. The crowd cheered as the speakers bought illegal salt as a symbol of defiance. Throughout India, people began to picket liquor shops and foreign clothes shops.

In Bihar, thousands marched down the highway to the place where salt was manufactured. When the police blocked the road , the marchers laid on the ground for forty hours. The British warned they would launch a cavalry charge against the protestors. The marchers remained on the road. As the cavalry charged, the protester stayed where they were. When the horses reached them, the British cavalry horses stopped, refusing to trample them. There was a contagious sense of courage spreading across India expressing the dream of freedom. The defeat of the invincible British army through nonviolence was now a possibility. Freedom, a dream only a few years before, could now be tasted. The spirit of self-rule knew no bounds.

In Bengal, peasants refused to pay taxes. Teachers, students, and professors also joined the civil disobedience movement. In the northwest province of Peshawar, a British armored car opened fire on a peaceful crowd, killing seventy and wounding a hundred others. The British pressured the local Indian legislatures and officials to handle the civil disobedience. Local officials resigned in protest. The industrial town of Sholapur in Bombay completely surrendered to Indians and national flags were raised all over the town.

In Peshawar, Khan Abdul Ghaffar Khan, a Pashtun known as the 'Frontier Gandhi' had organized an army of Muslims committed to nonviolence. The *Khuda Khedmatkars,* known as the 'Red Shirts' for the red uniforms they wore, were regarded as the most disciplined army of nonviolence in India. During a demonstration, British soldiers opened fired and continued shooting for three hours; two hundred people died and hundreds were injured. The news horrified the Pashtuns, the Muslims, and all of India. Yet the 'Red Shirt' army of Ghaffar Khan refused to use violence.

Within three months of Gandhi's signal, nearly all of India was participating in the civil disobedience. British rule was broken. Even though the British still occupied India, India was free. The British had arrested approximately sixty thousand people, including nearly every member of the Indian National Congress. On May 4th, 1930., thirty soldiers marched into Gandhi's Ashram and arrested him. This time, there was no trial, no sentence and no fixed term of imprisonment. Gandhi was taken straight to prison indefinitely.

Even with Gandhi and nearly every Indian leader in prison, civil disobedience and *satyagraha* continued. Before his arrest, Gandhi had planned to march to Dharasana Salt Works to nonviolently take over the facility, an act later categorized as-'Nonviolent Change through Intervention,' and seen in 20th century in many variations from peaceful occupation of lunch counters and televisions stations to forceful closure of roads to the heroic efforts of Egyptians to take over and hold onto Tahrir Square. Nonviolent takeover of a facility or symbolic location is the most dangerous form of nonviolent struggle and often with the most casualties.-

On the morning of May 21st, twenty five hundred volunteers gathered 150 miles north of Bombay in front of the salt manufacturer for a daring and most dangerous act in a nonviolent struggle. The volunteers marched in a column toward the police guarding the facility. As the Satyagrahis reached the gates, the native policemen attacked them with steel-shod lathis, smashing their skulls and bones. As those struck fell unconscious, others would step forth to take their place. Even though the Indians were unable to nonviolently take over the facility, their bravery and unwillingness to respond with savagery of violence had remarkable effects as a form of protest. It was an incredible act of courage by Indians, which reverberated in newspapers across Europe and America, forcing many in the colonial culture of England to look upon their continued occupation of India as an act of brutality incompatible with modern times.

By August 1930, over one hundred thousand Indians were imprisoned. The Viceroy's government was barely functioning; civil disobedience had taken root in every town and village across India and continued, despite the imprisonment of Gandhi and nearly every first, second and third tier leader of the National Congress. And above all, after all the beatings and killings carried out by the colonial government, with the exception of one act of isolated terrorism and murder in north-west India by some revolutionaries, no act of violence had taken place.

The British government approached Gandhi, Motilal, and Jawaharlal Nehru in search of a way to reach a truce. After two days of discussion, a joint statement was released stating "an unbridgeable gulf" between their position and that of the British. The British then convened the first Round Table Conference in London. Gandhi and the Indian National Congress did not participate. On closing the Conference on January 19, the Prime Minister of Britain, Ramsey McDonald, made conciliatory statements towards India and ordered the Viceroy to take a similar stance. On January 26, the Viceroy unconditionally released Gandhi, the Nehrus and twenty other top Congress leaders.

On March 5th, nearly one year after Gandhi's signal to India, a Pact known as Irwin-Gandhi or Delhi Pact was signed. Weeks of negotiation and debate had taken place. The Pact called for the civil disobedience to be suspended, all political prisoners released, confiscated properties returned, salt manufacturing permitted, and specified that the Indian National Congress would attend a Round Table Conference in London with the purpose of 'constitution building' for a free India. [610] Victory was achieved at a colossus level and humanity had been taught a crucial lesson in the use of nonviolence.

Yet the British, as masters of conquest, were not done. Their army was no match for the disciplined army of nonviolence, yet any army, with the right moves, can be defeated and most armies are vulnerable when divided. The colonial empire was the master at dividing and conquering and they still had a trick up their sleeves. Through the nonviolent struggle, India was freed spiritually. The details had now to be figured out with the hopeful cooperation of the British in a conference in London.

London Roundtable Conference

Gandhi went to London in September of 1931 to attend the conference. Because the Indian National Congress needed its leaders to stay in India and maintain the order and spirit of the pact, Gandhi was sent as the sole representative of the Congress. Within two weeks of his arrival in London however, Gandhi realized that the British had a well-planned strategy to derail the conference and had no intention of granting independence to India. The British had organized a conference that turned out to be exactly what they had planned. A conference that was "worse than failure".

There were 112 delegates at the conference. Except for Gandhi, every single delegate was picked by the British. There were 20 delegates representing United Kingdom, 23 delegates representing Indian Princes, Rajas, Maharajas, and their subordinates, and 64 representing British India. The delegates of British India included representatives of merchants, landlords, Muslims, Christians, Hindus, women, labor, Untouchables, Anglo-Indians and Parsis. The English had chosen such representatives because they thought that these delegates would not see themselves as representatives of India, but representatives of their particular group. Gandhi, the sole representative of the Congress, was the only delegate who saw himself as Indian and not as a Muslim or a Hindu, a Parsi, a Christian or a Raja. In addition, the British who were running the Conference encouraged each minority group represented to lobby for the number of seats in future legislature and the electorates given to each minority group. The British did not intend to give independence to India. What they wanted to do was to divide parts of India into many different states, each ruled by a prince while maintaining rule over a third of India which would be known as British India. The British plan worked perfectly. As long as Indians saw themselves as Muslims or Hindus, they could never agree on the principles of democracy, thus they could never find the will to attain and the path to independence. The British plan was to divide and rule, which they achieved through separating Indians based on religious, ethnic, or economic lines.

The Conference turned out to be just what the British wanted, a 'magnificent failure'. Gandhi was isolated and Indians divided. Muslims wanted designated seats in the legislature for Muslims themselves, landlords for themselves, Untouchables for themselves. Before achieving independence and freedom, these delegates were fighting over the spoils. They were arguing over how to cut the cake, one that they did not actually possess. Prime Minister McDonald even joined the game, calling Gandhi on the last day of meeting in December a 'Hindu'. Gandhi exclaimed, 'Not Hindu!', perhaps annoyed at the British attempts to divide India based on religion, ethnicity and caste.

The concept of democracy requires every citizen of the state to have equal rights and equal opportunity before the law. The law cannot give one group special interests or rights based on their religion, ethnicity, or economic position. A concept with special privileges to a group is no longer a democracy. Any such a system is inherently wrong even if it calls itself a democracy. Similar to the undemocratic demands of representatives in London, the concepts of 'Islamic Democracy' or 'Islamic Republic' advocated by reformists in Iran are also concepts that divide people based on their ideologies or religious preferences and must be considered undemocratic.

The only representatives at the Conference in India who refused to divide India along religious or minority lines and who stood by Gandhi were the women. They maintained their demands for equal rights as human beings like every other Indian and refused to ask for special electorates or privileges. When Ramsey McDonald, who had created a 'Minorities Pact' of Indians that included the minority religious groups and castes, commented that this group represented 115 million Indians, Gandhi interrupted him and said "You have had on behalf of the women of India a complete repudiation of special representation, as they happen to be one half of the population of India."[611] But the British could now proclaim that India was not ready for Independence since the parties demanding self-interests as opposed to 'human rights' were irreconcilable. Gandhi was defeated the second time—not through violence, but because of the delegates refusal to embrace human rights and democracy. Gandhi believed in a secular, democratic India in which every single person is free to vote for whomever he or she chooses regardless of religion, caste, or economic standing.

The British had two weapons at their disposal in order to crush the aspirations of India for freedom. The first was violence. Gandhi had defeated them on this battlefield. The second weapon at their disposal was to convince Indians of their inability to compromise on democracy and thus justify the British rule as better than the alternative. These are also the same two weapons at the disposal of the Islamic Republic of Iran. The Islamic Republic in power is master of violence and any form of violence or threat of violence is returned with powerful show of force and crackdown by the security forces. The second strategy is to present and promote alternatives to the population which will have no appeal to the population. Such alternatives will present themselves as democratic, yet, when it comes to democratic and human rights principles, such alternatives advocate systems with flaws and undemocratic principles.

Gandhi returned to India on December 28th as a defeated leader. Over two hundred thousand came out to listen to their beloved Mahatma even in defeat. This time, with the help of a loudspeaker, Gandhi addressed the crowd and stated, "I have come back empty-handed, but I have not compromised the honor of my country."[612] The British had achieved a victory through the division created along religious and cultural lines. A united India they could not fight, but a divided India was easy to defeat. He soon learned that Nehru and Abdul Ghaffar Khan, the nonviolent Muslim leader in Northwest province, had been arrested. The British had authorized emergency measures prior to Gandhi's arrival in order to seize buildings, impound bank balances, confiscate properties, arrest without warrant, suspend court trials, deny bail and habeas corpus, disband political organizations, and prohibit picketing and boycotting.[613] Gandhi landed in India on December 28; he was arrested without trial on January 3. That month 14,800 Indians were jailed for political reasons; in February, 17,800 more were imprisoned. The British had declared a total war against India. The crown jewel of the British Empire was not to be allowed to win its freedom. Winston Churchill proudly declared in the House of Commons that the repressive measures were more drastic than any since the 1857 mutiny.[614] The freedom of the press was curtailed and Indian National Congress was outlawed. Over 98 newspapers were either closed or their security deposits with the government confiscated. Meanwhile, Gandhi was isolated in prison and unable to talk to other leaders or to citizens of India. The government in England was drafting a constitution without the input of Gandhi or Congress Leaders with the aim of providing some limited rights to Indians while maintaining its hold on Britain's precious colony. Indian leaders did not expect much from the new constitution.

While reading some newspapers given to him in prison, Gandhi learned that the British were not only granting separate electorate to Muslims and other religious minorities, they were going to treat the Untouchables as a separate class and grant them separate electorate as well. Gandhi had been overpowered by the minority sects of India at the Round Table conference demanding separate electorates. He considered such practice inhumane and undemocratic. But the separation of Untouchables as a 'Depressed Class' by the British and making such division law of the land was a dagger aimed at the heart of his beliefs in religion and humanity. In order to raise consciousness of India about this four-thousand year-old inhumane practice of division and hatred, he continuously called the Untouchables '*harijans*', or children of God, and had named his newspaper '*harijan*' as well. The cruel and deceptive tactic of making a law that partitioned Untouchables into a separate electorate was more than he could tolerate. Perhaps just as painful was the belief by the Untouchable community that such an arrangement was to their benefit and required to protect their democratic rights.

While in prison, he wrote to the Secretary of State for India "A separate electorate for the Depressed Classes is harmful for them and for Hinduism … So far as Hinduism is concerned, separate electorates would simply vivisect and disrupt it…The political aspect, important though it is, dwindles into insignificance compared to the moral and religious issue."[615] He then announced his decision, one that reverberated throughout India. He wrote that if the government continued with its decision to grant separate electorates to Untouchables, "I must fast unto death." "For me the contemplated step is not a method" he wrote, "it is part of my being."[616] He then wrote to Prime Minister McDonald "I have to resist your decision with my life, The only way I can do it is by declaring a perpetual fast unto death from food of any kind save water with or without salt." He announced to India that the fast would begin on September 20th of that year, 1932.

Gandhi never fasted in order to convince his enemies. He fasted to convince those who loved him. This method of nonviolent struggle for change is now classified as 'Nonviolent change through Protest and Persuasion'. It is one of three classes of nonviolent methods and perhaps the most long-lasting and significant. Gandhi did not intend to change the British viewpoint on the rights of the Untouchables to a separate electorate, he wanted to change a 4,000–year-old culture of India in which artificial division was imposed on humanity. The British had convinced the Untouchables of India of the merits of separate electorates. India and Untouchables were convinced that such a system is just. Gandhi did not intend to convince and persuade the British; he wanted to convince India.

Much discussion took place between Gandhi, the British officials, and the leaders of Untouchables in order to convince him not to fast. The British and Untouchables leadership attempted to persuade Gandhi that the provision for a separate electorate was proper way of protecting their rights in a highly divisive culture. On September 9, in a letter to the Prime Minister, Gandhi wrote, "I should not be against even over-representation of the Depressed Classes. What I am against is their statutory separation, even in a limited form."[617] He then again announced that if this British written constitution creating separate electorates for Depressed Classes were to be enacted into law, he would commence his fast until death in 11 days, on September 20th. Gandhi again reiterated that he had sacrificed everything he had for India, but he was going to give his life for the Untouchables.

Nehru writes of his experience while in prison in hearing of Gandhi's decision to take his life. "I felt angry with him...felt annoyed with him for choosing a side issue for his final sacrifice...then a strange thing happened to me, I had quite an emotional crisis, and at the end of it I felt calmer, and the future seemed not so dark. Bapu had a curious knack of doing the right thing at the psychological moment, and it might be that his action--impossible as it was from my point of view--would lead to great results not only in the narrow field which it was confined, but in the wider aspects of our national struggle...Then came the news of tremendous upheaval all over the country...What a magician, I thought, was this little man sitting in Yeravda Prison, and how well he knew how to pull the strings that move people's hearts."[618]

His attempt to change India at a time when today's mass media was nonexistent, when over 90% of India's three hundred and fifty million citizens were illiterate, and when in all of India there were no more than 5,000 radios. A single individual, weighing no more than 100 pounds yet with a heart as great as India, isolated and seemingly defeated in a prison cell had managed to arouse India once again to fight for justice. The news of Mahatma's fast until death on behalf of the Untouchables began to travel across India with the wind.

Within days, 4,000–year-old forms of injustice and discrimination, engrained cultural forms of violence, were crumbling across India. On September 20th, in solidarity with Gandhi, millions of Indians fasted for 24 hours. Across India, the news of Mahatmas fast had caused great change in the soul of the nation. Hundreds of millions of India's Hindu's now began to question the inhumane act of division within their religion, where one group of Hindu's was given lesser rights in the society as others. Within a week after the fast began, the great orthodox temples of Hinduism, Kalighat Temple in Calcutta and Ram Mandir or Benares for the first time in history opened their doors to Untouchables.[619] With this act, a great taboo of Hinduism was broken. In Bombay, women organized a poll in front of seven big temples for people to cast their votes in admission of Untouchables. There were 24,797 votes in favor, 445 against.[620] Spontaneously, across the country, temples, wells, and public places for the first time in history were opened to the Untouchables. Nearly two weeks later, on October 2, Gandhi's birthday was commemorated by the creation of Anti-Untouchability Week. Newspapers began publishing the names of hundreds of temples across the country every week that were opening their doors for the first time to Untouchables. The very orthodox mother of Nehru accepted food from an Untouchable hand in public and further publicized it. This was followed by thousands of women across India doing the same and breaking this ancient cultural taboo. "In villages, small towns, and big cities, congregations, organizations, citizens' unions, etc. adopted resolutions which formed a man-high in heap in Gandhi's prison yard."[621]

He had announced that his fast was based on his faith in the cause, faith in the Hindu community, and faith in humanity. His faith was well founded. After a week of fasting and a great many discussions and negotiations between Gandhi and the leaders of Untouchables, who were demanding these separate electorates, an agreement referred to as Poona Act was reached. A separate electorate for the Untouchables was to be abolished. But the political ramifications of this settlement are insignificant in comparison to the social and cultural. Through nonviolence, one of the most deeply rooted cultural discriminations in India was torn down. Gandhi broke his fast after a week without food on September 26th.

Gandhi was released from prison in February 1933 on the day after he announced he was planning on a 21 day fast for self-purification. The British were again afraid he might die in prison. In July, he proposed to march from Yeravada to Ras. The British arrested him, but released him three days later and ordered him not to leave the city of Poona. Within half an hour, Gandhi broke the law again and set out to march. The British arrested him again and sentenced him to a year of imprisonment. Gandhi again began to fast. Shortly after he began, he was rushed to the hospital in critical condition. The British, again terrified of Gandhi dying in prison, released him. Gandhi, who possessed the sort of chivalrous respect for the enemy one finds in mythological tales, respected his one-year sentence even though he was freed from prison. He did not resume civil disobedience for the duration of his sentence while traveling across India.

He nevertheless continued his message of nonviolence. In an incredible month's tour for Untouchable welfare, he visited every province of India. For the next several years, Gandhi spent most of his time educating India on social responsibilities, humanity, and democracy. When approached by Marxists attempting to sway him to their persuasion, he spoke and wrote of how repelled he was by the Bolshevik movement in Russia, in which violence was justified as a form of class warfare. He could not justify violence under any circumstances. When an American journalist visited him, he noticed the pictures of only two individuals in his room, Leo Tolstoy and Jesus Christ.

The journalist, surprised at the pictures, had asked him why he had a picture of Jesus Christ in his room, "I am a Christian," he replied, "I am a Christian, and a Hindu, a Muslim, and a Jew."[622]

In 1937, the new constitution of India went into effect, granting Indians elections to the provincial and central legislature. The Indian National Congress with support of Gandhi participated in the elections. India had come a long way in twenty years of Gandhi's struggle towards independence. Yet the British continued to maintain their grip on India.

In September 1938, Gandhi was deeply disturbed by Chamberlain and Daladier's betrayal of Czechoslovakia to Hitler and called it "… a triumph of violence". "It is also a defeat" he said, "[Britain and France] quailed before the combined violence of Germany and Italy. But what have Germany and Italy gained? Have they added anything to the moral wealth of mankind?"[623] In an article called "If I were a Czech", Gandhi advised them to choose the path of nonviolence against the dictatorship. "They can lose nothing by trying the way of non-violence." he wrote, "Democracy dreads to spill blood…the philosophy for which the two dictators stand calls it cowardice to shrink from carnage … Science of war leads one to dictatorship pure and simple. Science of non-violence can alone lead one to pure democracy."[624] These words may have been intended for the Czechs, but they are of as much value for Iranians as if they had been written for my generation's struggle for democracy. The path towards democracy can only go through nonviolence Gandhi reminded the world. Victory achieved through violence will only place the tools of violence in the hands of those who will ultimately suppress the voice of opposition.

He had a keen sense of sensing injustice to humanity far more quickly than others. In November of 1938, when the world was still ignorant of the plight of the Jews in Germany, Gandhi realized the catastrophic act of inhumanity that was taking place. In an article he wrote:

"The German persecution of the Jews seems to have no parallel in history. The tyrants of old never went so mad as Hitler seems to have done. If there ever could be a justifiable war in the name of and for humanity, war against Germany to prevent the wanton persecution of a whole race would be completely justified. But I do not believe in any war…If I were a Jew and were born in Germany and earned my livelihood there, I would claim Germany as my home even at the tallest gentile German might, and challenge him to shoot me or cast me in the dungeon … And for doing this I should not wait for the fellow Jews to join me in civil resistance, but would have confidence that in the end the rest were bound to follow my example. If one Jew or all the Jews were to accept the prescription here offered, he or they cannot be worse off than now…The German Jews will score a lasting victory over the German gentiles in the sense that they will have converted the latter to an appreciation of human dignity."[625] He wrote these words before the start of World War II and long before the world had realized the tragedy of Holocaust inflicted on the Jews, the Gypsies and others in Europe.

On September 1st, 1939, the German army invaded Poland. The British took India to war against the Nazi's without any input from the Indians. Gandhi and the Indian National Congress resented the fascist regimes of Germany and Italy. They were sympathetic to the plight of the Poles enslaved by the Soviets in the East and the Nazi's in the west. Yet the Indian National Congress had a problem with the principles of allying itself with Britain. How could Britain ask India to fight for the freedom of the Poles, when it did not shed itself of its imperialistic culture in India. In a statement released by the executive committee they announced "A free democratic India will gladly associate herself with other free nations for mutual defense against aggression and for economic cooperation…"[626] Gandhi rejected this criteria and stated as a principle, "whatever support was to be given to the British should be given unconditionally". But he also believed support should be only through nonviolence. He did not believe India should have an army. Yet, after voicing his opinion, he voiced his support for the National Congress's position regardless of his own position.

The Viceroy of England rejected the call for freedom for India and postponed the matter until after the war. Five days later, the Indian national Congress voted against aiding the British in war. The next two years were the dark years in Great Britain's history. In a flash of military might, Hitler overtook Denmark, Belgium, Norway, Holland and France. By 1942, Japan had sunk two great British battleships in the Pacific and were marching towards India from the East. Some in India were calling for the final battle to free themselves of England. Yet Gandhi refused. "We do not seek our independence out of England's ruin. This is not the way of nonviolence."[627] When National Congress wanted to help Britain, he kept quiet and silently approved. When some asked to take action against Britain, he would object.

In July of 1940, the Viceroy promised India of more freedom in return for aid in the war against Germany and Japan. In a resolution, Indians announced their full assistance to Great Britain if given complete independence and central government. The government in London headed by Winston

Churchill, however, could not even contemplate granting complete independence to England's most prized possession. In November of 1942, Churchill announced "I have not become the King's First Minister in order to preside at the liquidation of the British Empire."[628] In order to sidetrack the independence movement, the British announced that no move towards independence could take place without the approval of the Muslims.

Thus, the British stipulated that Muslims of India were to be given veto power over any future government of India. Despite the fact that Indian National Congress was made up of both Muslims and Hindu's, the British decided to strengthen another organization, the 'Muslim League' to force the National Congress to submit. In 1942, the British made an official offer to Gandhi and India. The offer was for full-fledged Dominion—but with the proviso that one-third of the constituent assembly in India were to be appointees of Indian Princes, over whom the British had considerable influence. In addition, the offer was to lead to breakup of India into many different provinces; a Hindu India, a Muslim India, a Princely India, and possibly a Sikh India. Gandhi rejected this proposal and told the representative from England "If this is your entire proposal, I would advise you to take the next plane home."[629] Soon, the situation of war became even more dire. The Japanese, having control over much of China, captured Hong Kong in December of 1941, and then Singapore in February 1942. In March of 1942, the Japanese occupied Java, Sumatra, and islands of the Dutch East Indies. On March 9th, Burma, India's neighbor to the east, was taken by the Japanese. India was to be next.

Gandhi, however, still refused to openly advocate economic and non-violent aid for the British. He wanted a united, free, and democratic India. Churchill was offering the breakup of India into many different pieces, with England maintaining control over a British India and Princely India. In order for this division to take place, Muslims were encouraged more and given more voice by the British to oppose Gandhi and National Congress' concept of United India and to demand their own Muslim India. The British, in order to gain political hegemony over future India were planting the seeds of division and hatred between the Muslims and Hindu within the politics of India which eventually led to one of the great tragedies of humanity and acts of violence in the twentieth century. We must be reminded again that ultimately the roots of violence lie in the division of human beings. It is through division that hatred can form. Hatred that then leads to violence.

CHAPTER 8

In 1942, despite the advance of Nazis in Europe and Japanese in Asia, Gandhi again reiterated his desire for a free India and began to prepare for a mass civil disobedience to force England to 'Quit India'. He wanted the world's democracies to defeat fascism and believed that India, as a democracy, could help them achieve this task, but he wanted India to help in the war effort as a free nation. He wanted self-government and freedom during the war and not postponed to after the war. In 1942, in addressing the Americans, he declared "Your President talks about the Four Freedoms. Do they include the Freedom to be free?"[630] Yet, despite all this, despite the defeat of the British in Asia and possible conquest of India by Japanese now in Burma, Churchill refused to let go of India. A major battle was shaping up between Gandhi and Churchill. With England reeling under attacks by Germany, Gandhi could have taken hold of India with a mere suggestion. Britain, did not have the will to fight 400 million nonviolent Indians and Gandhi was again planning a nationwide civil disobedience campaign to convince the British of their desire to be free.

On August 8, 1942, after a meeting of several hundred members of Indian National Congress, a resolution was passed stating "British rule over India must end immediately" which was followed with a national civil disobedience campaign under Gandhi's leadership.[631] That evening, Gandhi, Nehru, and other leaders of the National Congress were arrested. When Kasturbai, Gandhi's wife, announced she would speak in place of her husband, she was arrested as well.

With Gandhi in prison, the hope and discipline requisite for nonviolence was devastated and the nonviolent army of India exploded into violence. Fires erupted at police stations, telegraph offices, government buildings, railroads, a variety of British institutions and buildings in city after city. The British, shocked at the situation, blamed Gandhi for the outbreak of violence. British officials began a propaganda campaign accusing Gandhi of secretly siding with the Japanese and blaming him for the violence. But, in London, in front of British press, an old adversary came to his aid. Field Marshal Smuts, who Gandhi had fought in South Africa, held a press conference in London denouncing the propaganda against Gandhi and calling it "sheer nonsense". "He is one of the great men of the world," Smuts insisted.[632]

Gandhi, along with Kasturbai, was imprisoned in Agha Khan's palace. In February of 1944, Kasturbai fell ill. After sixty two years of marriage, the journey of these two seventy-five year-olds was coming to an end. She died in his lap on February 22, 1944. Her last words to Gandhi were "I am going now…We have known many joys and many sorrows."[633] Her last wish was to be cremated in a sari from a yarn spun by him. In response to condolences from the Viceroy, Gandhi replied that, "we were a couple outside of ordinary."[634] Earlier in Agha Khan's palace, Gandhi had lost Mahdev Desai, his closest associate, secretary, and disciple, a man who was more like a son to him. While in this last prison, Gandhi's health began to deteriorate. His seventy-five year-old body had led a life of struggle. He contracted malaria in May and began having fevers that spiked up to 105 degrees. He was then found to be inflicted with Hookworm (ankylostamiasis) and amoebiasis of the intestine. His blood pressure was often about 170/110 and at times reached 220mmHg. Despite his stubborn belief against taking medications and his faith in the curative power of nature, doctors persuaded him to take quinine for his malaria.

Gandhi was released, for the last time, from prison on May 6, 1944. During his lifetime, he had spent a total of 2,089 days in prison in India and 249 day of imprisonment in South Africa.

Within weeks after his release, Gandhi regained his strength and began his work all over again. He would need all of his strength during the next several years as the future of India was decided.

The British foment division between Muslims and Hindus

Since the end of 19th-century, the British had planted the seeds of division between the Muslims and the Hindus. The Muslims, who comprised one fourth of India's population, had lived in relative peace with the Hindus for centuries. But as demands for independence grew at the turn-of-the-century, the British began to remind Muslims of their potential status as second-class citizens in the majority Hindu India. Syed Ahmad Khan supported and knighted by England raised fears amongst Muslims that a democratic India with a Hindu majority would subjugate Muslims and encouraged Muslims to stay away from the Indian National Congress. The repeated assurances, by those in the National Congress that in a secular and democratic India religion would be a personal matter and not a matter for politics, was unpersuasive. In a British report that led to the drafting of the British Reform act of 1919, Lord Chelmsford stated: "division by creeds and classes means the creation of political camps organized against each other, and teaches men to think as partisans and not as citizens."[635]

CHAPTER 8

By 1938 this hatred had reached such an extent that a simple quarrel of three drunk Hindus and a Muslim over a game of cards in a park led to "rumors of Hindu-Muslim disturbance" that spread through the city like wildfire and caused panic, stabbings, stone-throwing, and arson. Troops had to be called in. 14 people were killed, 98 injured, and over 2,000 people arrested.[636] This violence from British-promoted political divisions was, however, insignificant in comparison to the violence which was to come when the Muslim League announced it insisted on a separate Islamic country that would be called Pakistan. Two separate Muslim countries were envisioned, one in the Northwest and the other in the Northeast provinces of India.

The architect of such national division was Muhammad Ali Jinnah. Jinnah was a Muslim activist and leader who came into prominence before the First World War. His name, Jinnah, was a Hindu name indicating his family's relative recent conversion to Islam. He drank alcohol and seldom prayed at a mosque. Like Gandhi, he was British educated, but favored extravagance in his home and lifestyle. After the round table conference of 1932, at which Jinnah lobbied for a separate electorate for Muslims, he decided to retire in London. But in 1935, in response to the insistence of some friends in England, he had decided to return to India.

In 1945, the Labour Party in London had a major victory and the party, after decades of influence from Gandhi and Satyagrahis, was disposed to allow India its independence. The British no longer could hold onto their imperial hegemony after six years of war against fascism, racism, and the attempts to enslave the world by the Axis powers.

The new Viceroy of India, Lord Mountbatten, summoned the Indian leaders to a conference in Simla in May of 1945 in order to go over the details of possible Indian independence. The Viceroy's plan provided for equal number of Muslims and Hindus in a newly built executive counsel. But Jinnah rejected the plan. He did not object to equal seats with the Hindus, but he wanted every single Muslim on the Council to be selected by him only. This, of course could not be accepted by the Indian National Congress. The National Congress was not a Hindu body and did not wish to be a religious council. There were many Muslims in the Congress who believed in a secular and democratic India in which people could freely choose their representatives regardless of the representative's religious belief. Jinnah considered himself the only leader of Muslims in India and he wanted the Muslim League to represent all Muslims regardless of their political beliefs. In the 1937 elections, the representatives of Muslim League had received no more than 5% of the Muslim vote[637]. Yet Jinnah, with the support of the British positioned himself a few years later to have complete veto power over any decisions on the future of India.

Since 1939, Jinnah had continuously demanded to safeguard Muslim rights and had repeatedly questioned the merits of a democracy in such a vast and pluralistic country with a Hindu majority. At the same time, Jinnah began to develop his two-nation theory, one that was later accepted by the All-India Muslim League.

"Vivisect me before you vivisect India" was Gandhi's comment on hearing the two nation theory. Gandhi considered the potential religious governments in India and Pakistan as two "...lands flowing in poison."[638] He was terrified by the prospect of what would follow the creation of states dominated and defined by any one religion. For him, such a state would be essentially against God, against religion, against humanity and human rights. "I do not believe in state religion even though the whole community has one religion." said Gandhi, "religion is purity a personal matter". [639] Gandhi considered nationalism, the love for one's country, essential to both democracy and internationalism, and he was a deeply religious Hindu who lived every moment of his life following what he believed was the path of God, love and nonviolence. Yet, above all, he considered himself a human being and what he advocated for India was what he believed was best for humanity— a democracy without the overarching authority of any religious laws or institutions.

The demand for a separate Muslim India called Pakistan surprised everyone including the British. Through division and hatred, the British had created a monster which they could no longer control. On August 12, 1946, the Viceroy commissioned Nehru to form a government. Nehru went to Jinnah and offered him choices of places in the government for the Muslim League. Jinnah was not interested and refused. Nehru then formed his cabinet with 5 caste Hindus, one Untouchable, one Christian, one Sikh and two Muslims. The Viceroy then asked Jinnah to also name five Muslims to the cabinet. Jinnah again refused. Instead, Jinnah chose violence and proclaimed August 16th as the 'Direct Action Day' for Muslims.

Throughout negotiations, Jinnah had never ruled out violence as a possibility. For him, nonviolence was a policy that should sometimes be followed but, if necessary, ignored. The 'Direct Action Day' proclaimed by Jinnah was a tragic day in history of India. Hundreds of Muslim hooligans

CHAPTER 8

began roaming the streets of Calcutta, burning buildings, and then injuring and killing of civilians. This was followed by retaliatory violence by the Hindus. Neighborhood after neighborhood was attacked and burnt. According to official British estimates, 5,000 were killed and 15,000 were injured. Unofficial estimates of casualties were much higher. Over 100,000 people were left homeless on this day.

The events in Calcutta inflamed further hatred in other parts of India. In the predominantly Muslim Province of Noakhali in East Bengal, widespread attacks occurred against the Hindus. Noakhali was a densely populated rural area comprised of many small villages. The violence in Noakhali led the neighboring mainly Hindu province of Bihar to declare 'Noakhali Day', a declaration followed by sensational newspaper articles and speeches filled with hatred against Muslims. Bihar had a population of 31 million Hindus and 5 million Muslims. These messages of hatred led to slogans of "Blood for Blood" by the Hindus, followed by thousands of Hindus rioting in the streets, in turn followed by burning of Muslim homes or injuring and killing of Muslims in the streets. The *London Times* reported nearly 5,000 killed. Gandhi's estimate of those killed was closer to 10,000. Hatred and violence was spreading like wildfire across India.

In order to quell the violence, Gandhi decided to go to Noakhali and help bring peace and calm to the region. "My present mission is the most difficult and complicated one of my life...I am prepared for any eventuality. 'Do' or 'Die' has to be put to test here. 'Do' here means Hindus and Mussulmans should learn to live together in peace and amity. Otherwise, I should die in the attempt."[640]

In Noakhali, Gandhi would spend his day in each village calming the population and asking for peace. At four in the morning, he and his few disciples would rise and walk miles in their bare feet to the next village where they would begin to calm the population and ask for peace. For four months, the 76 year old walked, aided by his bamboo stick from village to village trying to calm the population. After he reached a village, fighting Muslims and Hindus would weep in his presence and ask for forgiveness. He never failed to forgive. Gandhi spent his 77th birthday in this turmoil.

Over 10,000 Hindus were forced to convert to Islam in Noakhali alone. Hindu women and children were abducted and forcefully married to Muslims against their will and were forced to remove the 'happiness mark' on their forehead. Men were forced to grow beards. Hindu temples were destroyed and their religious relics condemned as idols and smashed. Gandhi declared that he would stay in Noakhali as long as it takes for peace to return. But while in Noakhali, the news of Hindu atrocities against Muslims in Bihar reached him.

In January 1946, at conference in London between Nehru, Jinnah, and other Indian leaders, the decision was made to divide India into three federal states. Gandhi begged the Indian leaders to reject any such plans and warned them of the great human tragedy such a partition would cause in India. But an India engulfed in hatred and violence was no longer listening to Gandhi. The Hindus wanted independence from Great Britain, and the Muslims wanted a separate and independent Pakistan. The decision to divide India made in London led to one of the great 20th century tragedies of humanity. Over 15 million Hindus and Muslims were forcibly ejected from their homes in India and Pakistan and forced to walk across the treacherous plains of India in time of war. Along the way, in moment of societal madness and hysteria, Hindus were raping and murdering Muslims and Muslims were doing the same.

Many Muslims who refused to leave India and wanted to stay as Indian citizens had their properties taken from them by force by Hindus arriving from Pakistan. Many other Hindus and Muslims were not as fortunate, they were killed throughout India. Muslim and Hindu women were kidnapped and children killed. Horror stories of atrocities committed by Hindus and Muslims spread throughout in India.

Gandhi headed to Bihar, where great atrocities were being committed by Hindus against Muslims. In every locality, before addressing the population, he would visit the ruined homes of Muslims or homes of families who had suffered death in the hands of Hindus. Each evening at his prayer they would first read from the Koran before Hindu prayers. He insisted Hindus should help Muslims rebuild their homes and reestablish their businesses. In March 1947, Jinnah again reiterated his demands and threatened that without legal and political partition there would be "terrific disasters".[641] To Gandhi, the division of India was "absolute evil"[642] and he considered such talk by Jinnah "blasphemy".

On August 9, 1947, Gandhi arrived in Calcutta. Since Jinnah's 'Direct Action Day' a year earlier, Calcutta had been in constant rioting and turmoil. With the former minister of Bengal, Gandhi drove in an automobile and went from one city neighborhood to another. In every neighborhood he visited, rioting and violence would stop and Muslim and Hindu's would begin shouting joyously "Long Live Mahatma Gandhi", "Long Live Hindu-Muslim Unity". Within five days of arriving in Calcutta, complete peace and order returned to the city. In order to maintain peace in Calcutta, Gandhi decided to stay in the city in a prominent Muslim's house.

On August 31, a group of Hindus stormed into this man's home and threw a brick at Gandhi. The brick missed Mahatma, but injured his Muslim host. The Muslims of Calcutta were outraged; riots again broke out in Calcutta. The next day, Gandhi announced that he would fast in Calcutta until death or until order was restored in the city. Within three days, complete order and peace returned to the city while riot leaders and those who had committed murders came to Gandhi's bedside to ask for forgiveness. On September 4th, after three days of not eating, the seventy-eight year-old had a glass of lime juice and broke his fast. After his three day fast in Calcutta, even as riots, murders, rapes, arson and kidnapping raged across towns and cities in India, the city of Calcutta and the province of Bengal remained riot free. He had not convinced India, but Calcutta was convinced.

Gandhi then went to Delhi where a great deal of violence had been inflicted on the Muslims. 137 mosques had been either damaged or destroyed, or had been converted to Hindu temples. Many mosques were used as camps for Hindu refugees fleeing Pakistan. Near Delhi, there was an Islamic academy in Okla, one very dear to Muslims. For days, the Muslim students had watched from their rooftops as Muslim villages and homes went up in flames. The circle of fire was getting nearer and nearer to the academy. When Gandhi heard of the threat to the academy, he went to Okla, where his presence saved the academy from attack.

Gandhi increasingly realized the futility of his efforts to turn India away from the madness that had overtaken it. The sheer horror and scale of killing and destruction across India is almost beyond description. Millions either were killed or made homeless and forced to flee. Muslims in India were fleeing their ancestral homes, desperately heading towards Pakistan, and Hindus in Pakistan were fleeing their ancestral towns and villages for India. Near the border between India and Pakistan, the caravan of those fleeing their homes was 57 miles long. Along the way, people suffered from hunger, cholera, small pox and thirst. But these elements were secondary compared to the horrors the refugees would experience as Muslims and Hindus encountered each other. Those wounded or sick were left to die along the path by their families. Vultures hovered over the caravans of fleeing refugees and then swept down to feed on the tens of thousands of corpses left behind.

Of the 15 million people who fled their homes across the border between what became India and Pakistan, more one million never made it to a destination; others who reached cities across the border were forced to live in the streets.

Gandhi walked across India trying to bring hope wherever he went. In the midst of the carnage and violence he would often recall a poem by one of his favorite Indian poets:

Walk alone.
If they answered not to thy call, walk alone;
If they are afraid and cower mutely facing the wall,
O thou of evil luck,
Open thy mind and speak out alone.

If they turn away and desert you when crossing the wilderness,
O thou of evil luck,
Trample the thorns under thy tread,
And along the blood-lined track travel alone.

If they do not hold up the light when the night is troubled with storm,
O thou of evil luck,
With the thunder-flame of pain ignite thine own heart,
And let it burn alone. [643]

Gandhi felt helpless, yet he was not hopeless. His belief in nonviolence stemmed from his belief in love, his belief in love was derived from his belief in God, and he had lived every moment of his life for God. A world without love for Gandhi was a world without God. He believed that capturing the attention of four hundred million people required an act powerful enough to inspire them in turn towards meditation and prayer. He needed a tool. He had to stop the madness. He had to make India refocus on nonviolence again, if only for a moment. For Gandhi, capturing the attention of now four hundred million people required an act of meditation powerful enough to demand their attention and inspire them in turn to meditate and pray. For him, this instrument for meditation and prayer was fasting. Throughout his life, Gandhi had fasted in order to purify himself and purify others.

But this time he was not helping individuals or cities to cleanse themselves of anger and hatred but an entire nation gone mad, a quarter of which were Muslims and no longer considered themselves Indians. Of all the fasts he had done in his life, this was to be the most difficult and the greatest. He had never been as weak as he was now physically, yet he had lived every moment of his life preparing his soul for this final challenge.

Gandhi was the only hope that remained for India. If there were few spots of sanity within the madness, they were due to his presence. Amongst the thousands of Hindus and Muslims hoping for sanity, the possibility of old and weak Gandhi embarking on a fast, risking his life and, possibly, dying was horrifying. The possibility of Gandhi's death was even more real since Gandhi had repeated many times that his life as a witness to such carnage was not worth living. He no longer had the physical strength to undertake the kind of fast that he had done when he was younger. Now, he was seventy-eight years old and weighed 107 pounds. On his previous fast he had developed pericarditis, the inflammation of the sac lining the heart. He had then developed acute renal (kidney) failure. He was since weakened from malaria and parasites and had dangerously high blood pressure sometimes reaching 220mmHg. At best his body could tolerate a few days or a week of fasting, precious little time to calm four hundred million. His physicians, Nehru, and everyone around him knew that any sort of fast put at great jeopardy the life of the man considered the soul of his country. He would probably die from fasting well before any sort of calm and peace returned to India and this may cause disaster and violence for decades to come. His death would instigate further violence with no hope of an end in sight. In the most optimistic estimates, it would take weeks and even months for calm and sanity to return to India. Given his frailty, Nehru and other leaders implored Gandhi not to fast and reminded him of the critical importance of his presence in India.

On January 13, 1948, without consulting Nehru or other leaders and without consulting his doctors, Gandhi began what he called 'my greatest fast'. He had decided that death, "would be a glorious deliverance rather than I should be a helpless witness to the destruction of India, Hinduism, Sikhism and Islam."[644] When those around begged him to reconsider, "I am in God's hands" he replied "turn the searchlight inward; this is essentially a testing time for all of us."[645]

Fasting for him was a process of self-purification in a step closer to God. Those who were concerned, he asked them to do the same and purify themselves. When Muslims in Pakistan asked what they could do, he invited them to take part in self-purification. "Supposing there is the wave of self-purification throughout both parts of India", he said, "Pakistan will become *pak*, pure…Such a Pakistan can never die. Then, and only then, shall I repent that I ever called partition a sin…"[646]

By the second day of the fast, Gandhi had weakened considerably. He could no longer drink water because it made him nauseous. He refused to add drops of citrus juice or honey in water to prevent nausea. Meanwhile, his kidneys failed from dehydration. On the third day, he dictated a letter to the Indian Union asking them to pay the government of Pakistan 550,000,000 rupees, or $180,000,000, the Pakistan government's share of the pre-partitioned treasury of India. The Indians had delayed payment, which caused additional animosity between the two countries. Nehru reiterated the demand of 'Bapu' and the Indian government immediately released the funds. By this third day of fast, news of Gandhi's fast unto death, word of his request for self-purification and friendship between Hindus and the Muslims was spreading from town to town across India and Pakistan. Yet his health deteriorated considerably since he remained unable to take any water. His body had still the capacity to go without food, but not without water.

On the fourth day, while severely dehydrated, he spent the day with eyes closed and half-conscious, curled up in the fetal position. Thousands of Indians lined up for miles to walk pass his bed and see the Mahatma for perhaps the last time. His kidneys had already failed the day before and he was too weak to talk. Yet with his eyes closed he could sense the passing of the crowds by this bed. "I am happy" he whispered to an associate. He was making a difference and this was the first time in months when he did not feel helpless. It was the first time in months that he was happy.

At the 5pm prayer, he was fully awake, but could not walk to the prayer ground. He spoke through a microphone from his bed to the crowd. He was so weak that he could only speak a few words. He said "each of us should turn the searchlight inward and purify his or her heart as much as possible. I am convinced that if you purify yourself sufficiently, you will help India and shorten the period of my fast…you should think how best to improve yourselves and work for the good of the country…"[647] Later, Gandhi's pulse became irregular and doctors were very concerned that he had not passed any urine. By the end of his fourth day of fast, both India and Pakistan had heard his voice. After months of killing and violence, the two countries were quiet. The news of peace in the hearts of 400 million people cheered him. "I have not felt so well on the fourth day of a fast" he said. [648]

He was given a colonic irrigation by the doctors, which helped him absorb some water. He was still too nauseous to drink. Nehru came to his bedside and wept. Gandhi received hundreds of telegrams from every corner of India and Pakistan informing him of the restoration of peace between the Hindus and Muslims. On January 18th, the fifth day of the fast, over a hundred delegates from nearly every community, organization, sect, and dominion in Delhi including Delhi's Chief of Police and his deputies, prominent Hindus, Muslims, Sikhs, Parsis, Christians, and Jews signed a pledge of peace. Pakistan's ambassador in Delhi also came to Gandhi and made the pledge.

Those present read the pledge to Gandhi: "We take a pledge and wish to protect the life, the property and faith of the Muslims and that the incidents which have taken place in Delhi will not happen again." Gandhi listened and nodded. They continued to make their pledge and promised protection for movement of Muslims and their religious celebrations. All the mosques that had been taken over by the Hindus were to be returned to Muslims. Muslims forced to flee would be allowed to return. They then told Gandhi about incidents where Muslims had been helped by Hindus and an incident in which "150 Muslims of Subzimandi were given an ovation and then feted by the Hindu's of the locality."[649]

Barely having the strength to utter words, he could no longer control his emotions. He broke down and began sobbing in front of all those present. Many of those delegates wept as they watched the Mahatma weeping his last ounces of energy as he neared his death. When he regained control, he was too weak to speak. All he could do was whisper to his doctor. His doctor would then repeat aloud his questions as he and the audience were in tears:

"Were they deceiving him?"

"Were they merely trying to save his life? "

"Would they guarantee peace in Delhi and allow him to go to Pakistan and plead for peace there?"

"Did Muslims regard Hindus as infidels who worshipped idols and who should therefore be exterminated?"

Maula Azad and some other prominent Muslims who were present and in tears, assured Gandhi that in Islam all mankind are brethren, irrespective of race or religion. The Pakistani ambassador also reassured Gandhi. The Sikh delegate also reaffirmed his pledge for peace.[650]

After a long silence, he announced that he would break his fast. A Japanese prayer was read, followed by a Quranic prayer, followed by a Zoroastrian hymn. Then those assembled sang the Hindu verse:

Lead me from untruth to truth,
From darkness to light,
From death to immortality. [651]

Children of his ashram then came and sang his favorite Christian hymn, "When I survey the wondrous Cross."

At the evening prayer, when speaking of the pledge, Gandhi said, "Come what may, there will be complete friendship between the Hindus, Muslims, Sikhs, Christians, and Jews, a friendship not to be broken."[652] The Foreign Minister of Pakistan in the newly created U.N Security Council announced that "a new and tremendous wave of feeling and desire for friendship between the two dominions is sweeping the subcontinent in response to the fast."[653] On the day after the fast, Gandhi was recuperating. He planned to go to Pakistan in order to cement the friendship between the two nations. On January 30th, twelve days after the fast, the Deputy Prime Minister Patel, his old friend came to see him. There was much friction between him and the Prime Minister of the new India, Jawaharlal Nehru, which troubled Gandhi. They met at 4:30pm. At 5:05pm, Gandhi excused himself; he was five minutes late for the evening prayer. Over 500 people were waiting for him in the prayer ground. Gandhi, still too weak to walk was helped by companions outside. Out of the crowd came a Hindu named Godse. He had been forced out of his home in Pakistan, fled across the border to Delhi, and had found refuge in a mosque taken over by the Hindus. But Gandhi's fast and the pledge to return all the mosques to Muslims had forced him and many others onto the streets. On the streets, he had joined an extremist Hindu gang that aimed at reuniting India and Pakistan through violence. As Gandhi reached him, Godse touched his palms together showing the Hindu sign of respect. Gandhi, still very weak from his 'greatest fast' twelve days before, removed his arms from the shoulders of the two companions helping him walk, and returned the gesture, the Hindu symbolic act for peace. Godse then pulled out a pistol from his sleeve and shot three bullets into Gandhi's chest. Within seconds, Gandhi's white cloth, woven by his own hands turned red while simultaneously, his now famous dark facial complexion turned white. As he was about to lose consciousness, he uttered his last words "oh God".

For thousands of years, great human beings had surfaced who spoke of inner love. Yet, in midst of violence, their message, and those who believed in it, had encountered persecution, suppression, and destruction by political violence. Human beings were told of love by the great poets, oracles, and prophets of the past. Yet, the message of love, without tools to implement its promise, was always in the retreat and hidden. Gandhi, through the development of principles, theories and strategies of nonviolence had shown humanity that love, if used properly, can be a tool for society and that nonviolence, with the right principles, well thought out strategies, and the courage and discipline of an army can defeat the culture and armies of violence. Gandhi had shown the world for the first time that society did not need to either submit to violence or return violence with violence. One can fight violence with nonviolence. His contribution of nonviolence as a tool and strategy to overcome tyranny may perhaps be one of the greatest accomplishments of human beings in their violent history. He had given the world a lesson in use of societal love through nonviolence, a lesson that did not belong to India only but to all humanity.

The next day, as his body was taken from Birla house for the five-mile journey to Jumna River, a million and half people marched inch by inch alongside the body. The journey of the immense ocean of humanity took five hours. Repeatedly amongst the sea of people, silence and sobbing was broken by shouts of Hindus, Muslims, Parsis and Anglo-Indians in the crowd crying "Long live Gandhiji". Another million people had waited since early morning by the holy waters of the Jumna River where the cremation of Gandhi's body was to take place. Nearly everyone was wearing white. For the cremation, his body was placed on sandalwood with its head facing north and feet facing south, the same manner and position in which the body of the Buddha was placed when India had said farewell to him more than 2,500 years ago. The leaders of nearly every nation and religion sent their delegates or messages of condolence to India.[654]

At 4:45pm, his son set fire to the funeral pyre as a sudden wail went up from the immense crowd. It burnt for fourteen hours as people performed continuous prayers.

No one had the courage to announce his death on the radio, so Prime Minister Nehru, was given this task. In tears and choking he told the country "Our beloved leader, Bapu as we call him, the father of our nation, is no more. Perhaps I'm wrong to say that. Nevertheless, we will not see him again as we have seen him these many years."[655] Nehru struggled on, continuously interrupted by his tears "The light has gone out, I said, and yet I was wrong…The light that has illuminated this country for these many years will illuminate this country for many more years, and a thousand years later that light will still be seen in this country and the world will see it and it will give solace to innumerable hearts. For that light represented the living truth, and the eternal man was with us with his eternal truth reminding us of the right path, drawing us from error, taking this ancient country to freedom. "[656]

When the news of his death reached the UN Security Council, the meeting was interrupted while the delegates paid tribute to Gandhi. The UN lowered its flag as a gesture of respect. General George Catlett Marshall, the United States Secretary of State, called Gandhi the "Conscience of all mankind."[657] Amongst those who paid tribute were the President of United States, France and the heads of states of nearly all the European countries, including the King of England, head of state of his long-time adversary. Others including Pope Pius, the Dalai Lama of Tibet, the Archbishop of Canterbury and the Chief Rabi of London publically expressed grief. The last Viceroy of England, Lord Mountbatten, said that Gandhi's life might "inspire our troubled world to save itself by following his noble example."[658] In a century which created some noteworthy human beings, the British Attorney General, Sir Hartley Shawcross, called Gandhi the "most remarkable man of the century."[659]

Remarkable indeed he was. At the time when the world plunged into two world wars and managed to invent and use the atom bomb, he taught the world of the new weapon of nonviolence to fight tyranny. Upon his death, nonviolence was still at its infancy and no one knew whether it can be applied without his presence or against oppression outside of India. Yet, he showed human beings that this weapon could be even more powerful and longer lasting than the atom bomb. He thought humanity to fight without hate and to use love as a weapon against injustice. Humanity, with these lessons in hand, was not going to be the same.

CHAPTER 8 - NONVIOLENCE IS REBORN IN AMERICA

"I became convinced that noncooperation with evil is as much a moral obligation as is cooperation with good."

~Martin Luther King

Civil Rights Movement in the United States

By 1930's, Gandhi's example of success through nonviolence and love had inspired people across the world; they saw it as a way to guide them on their own struggles for freedom. In the southern states in America, the oppression against the African Americans continued in the form of segregation. Three generations before, slavery had been abolished, yet the southern states continued to separate blacks as citizens with lesser rights than whites. A violent and secret organization called the Klu Klux Klan had its members infiltrated as city council members, policemen, mayors, governors and Congressman. The society in southern state was physically divided into two in order to separate the whites from the descendants of the freed slaves. In public places, water fountains were designated for whites and blacks had to use their own water fountains. Blacks were not allowed into white public restrooms, schools, and many other public places and institutions. In most downtowns, Blacks were not allowed to eat at the lunch counters where whites dined. They were allowed to buy food but had to go to the sidewalk or somewhere else outside to eat. In movie theaters, African-Americans were not allowed to enter through the main entrances and were only allowed to come in through side doors at the back. On city buses, the front seats on the bus were reserved for the whites and African-Americans were forced to stand in the back even if there was plenty of room in the front. When getting on the bus, they had to come in through the front door first, buy their ticket and then exit and reenter the bus through the back. At times, the racist white drivers would speed away while there were still paid black riders waiting to get aboard. They were constantly insulted, humiliated and disrespected. The whites used violence or the threat of violence as an instrument to enforce such apartheid. In addition to violence, segregation had been written as law into city ordinances and state laws. The fact that an African-American could not sit in the front of the bus was not because the driver was telling him to do so, but because the law required him to sit in the back. Refusal to go in the back or leave a 'whites only' lunch counter first meant possible violent reaction by hooligans or white supremacists present at the scene followed by arrest, insults, fines and possible incarceration in black prisons, which were notorious for their abusive treatment of African-Americans.

With the end of slavery, African Americans in the South had repeatedly tried fighting segregation only to be faced with violent reaction through beatings, torture, rape, and murder by such organizations as Ku Klux Klan. In 1930's, several black intellectuals traveled to India to meet Gandhi, the man who, through his philosophy of nonviolence, had brought the world's most powerful empire to its knees. Amongst these travelers to India was Howard Thurman, whose illiterate former slave grandmother had insisted on him getting an education. He was the first black in his city to gain an eighth grade education. But the grandmother had not been satisfied and had encouraged him to get a high school diploma eventually graduating from Morehouse College.

Morehouse College was first founded as the Augusta Institute in the basement of Springfield Baptist Church in Atlanta, the oldest African American church in America. In 1913, it was renamed Morehouse College and was the foremost African American institution in creating leaders of African American clergy. After high school, Thurman had attended Colgate-Rochester Theological Seminary where he was the only black student in his class and where he had finished at the top of his class. For a summer he had rented a room for 55 cents a day in New York City's Harlem neighborhood in order to go to Columbia and study philosophy where he was introduced to Plato, Spinoza, Kant, and Hegel. He was then introduced to the nonviolent philosophy of Christian Quakers through Dr. Rufus Jones. He spent one year studying with Jones, during which, for the first time, he was introduced to the history and study of mysticism. In 1932, he was called to Howard University in Washington, D.C., to be Dean of the Chapel and Professor of Systematic Theology.

In 1935, while he was on a trip to India and Burma, Gandhi had sent him an invitation to meet, stating "If you cannot come to me, I will take the train with my doctor and come to you."[660] In a three hour meeting, Dr. Thurman was introduced to Gandhi, his philosophy, and Gandhi's view of Christianity.

CHAPTER 8

Thurman would become one of the first African American intellectuals who introduced Gandhi's philosophy of nonviolence as a tool for social change in America.

There were other African American intellectuals who were looking at the events in India with interest. Benjamin E. Mays, who was to be the longtime president of Morehouse College from 1940 until his retirement in 1967, was among them. In 1936, he also traveled around the world and, in what was to be a significant trip for him, he visited India and met Gandhi. Others were also influenced by Gandhi's philosophy of nonviolence, includingCed. Mordecai Johnson, who was to become the first African American president of Howard University in Washington, DC. He also had traveled to India where he had met with Gandhi.

But nonviolence as tool for social change was still nonexistent amongst the thousands of African American students in various colleges much less millions of African-Americans across the United States who would not even have the opportunity to attend college.

In 1944, in this atmosphere of social injustice and need for change, 15-year-old son of a well-respected minister in Atlanta enrolled at Morehouse College only after completing his 11th grade and without finishing his senior year in high school. The college life was to be very difficult for this young man. He not only had skipped one grade but also later admitted his reading skills were no more than at eight grade level on his admission to college.[661] The name of this fifteen year old was Martin Luther King Jr. In college, he found the atmosphere and freedom at Morehouse refreshing and invigorating. Not only there was academic freedom to learn, but the professors also had academic freedom to teach. As a freshman, like every other African American of his generation, he was concerned about racial inequality and injustice. In his first year at Morehouse College, he read Henry David Thoreau's essay 'On Civil Disobedience' and learned about that New England sage and mystic who told the world and humanity to listen to its conscience and not to blindly obey unjust and inhumane laws. He read how Thoreau chose to go to jail and not pay his tax to a government that was justifying the use of violence for slavery and in war with Mexico. Through Thoreau, for the first time, the 15-year-old King was introduced to the theory of non-violent resistance. "I became convinced that non-cooperation with evil is as much a moral obligation as is cooperation with good," wrote Martin Luther King when speaking of Thoreau and what he learned.

In 1948, he finished Morehouse College and enrolled in Crozer Theological Seminary. There he began a more serious and deeper study of humanity, injustice and embarked on a philosophical journey for discovering methods of eliminating social evil. He studied Plato and Aristotle. He then read Rousseau, Hobbes, Bentham, Mill, and Locke. Yet, he was still lost and without direction. In 1949, he read the works of Karl Marx in order to understand the appeal of communism worldwide. Still he did not find the answers that he was searching for. He rejected Marxism based on three main principles. First, Marx's materialistic interpretation of history did not leave room for religion or God, elements of which Martin Luther King, as a Christian could not live without. He believed in God and God was an important aspect of his life. But there were two other major issues with Marxism. Marx spoke of 'ethical relativism' where violence was a justified tool for struggle. This use of violence by the Marxists meant murder, terrorism and even torture as justifiable means of attaining the end. Lying was even a justifiable means for the end. "This type of relativism was abhorrent to me," wrote King, "constructive ends can never give absolute moral justification to destructive means, because in the final analysis the end is preexistent in the means."[662] The third reason for his rejection of Marxism was its belief in political totalitarianism. In a Marxists-Socialist state, the individual was the subject of the state. There was the promise of a classless society, but the path towards this utopian society meant enslavement of the individual and elimination of his rights and freedoms. "And if any man's so-called rights or liberties stand in the way of that end, they are simply swept aside," wrote King in his critique of Marxism. "His liberties of expression, his freedom to vote, his freedom to listen to what news he likes or to choose his books were all restricted. Man becomes hardly more, in communism, than a depersonalized cog in the turning wheel of the state."[663]

Despite his rejection of Marxism, like many other African-Americans of this time, he believed that the solution to social problem of segregation was an 'armed revolt'. The concept of Christian love he was familiar with, but, like others, he believed that such love was personal and individual. All this, however, was about to change on one Sunday afternoon as he drove up to Philadelphia to hear a sermon by Dr. Mordecai Johnson, the president of Howard University. Dr. Johnson, who had visited India, spoke of the life and the teachings of Gandhi. He spoke of how 'love' was used as an instrument in fighting evil. King listened as the speaker told of the great Salt March to the sea where a single man, armed with the power of nonviolence had defied the dominance of the British Empire. Everyone had heard of Gandhi, but few knew who Gandhi really was, what he stood for, how he fought and what he fought for. Martin Luther King was so moved that he immediately purchased half a dozen books on Gandhi and began studying him. He learned that 'satyagraha', Gandhi's concept of force, was derived from love, the truth, and the soul. He began to believe in 'love' as a powerful force for social change. "The 'turn the other cheek' philosophy and the 'love your enemies' philosophy were only valid, I felt, when individuals were in conflict with other individuals; when racial groups and nations were in conflict a more realistic approach seemed necessary. But after reading Gandhi, I saw how utterly mistaken I was."[664]

King wrote:

"Love, for Gandhi, was a potent instrument for social and collective transformation. It was in this Gandhian emphasis on love and nonviolence that I discovered the method of social reform that I had been seeking. The intellectual and moral satisfaction that I failed to gain from the utilitarianism of Bentham and Mill, the revolutionary methods of Marx and Lenin, the social contract theory of Hobbes, the 'back to nature' optimism of Rousseau, the superman philosophy of Nietzsche, I found in the nonviolent resistance philosophy of Gandhi."[665]

In 1951, King headed to Boston University School of Theology for his doctorate. There, King also studied Hegel's *Phenomenology of Mind*, *Philosophy of History* and *Philosophy of Right*. While in Boston, he met a beautiful young aspiring singer named Coretta Scott. Coretta had worked her way through the New England Conservatory in Boston with the aid of a scholarship. She was a mezzo-soprano and she aspired to be a concert singer. In Coretta, King found that she shared the same concerns for justice and humanity as he did. They were both from the South and were very familiar with the culture of racism and segregation prevalent in society. She was strong, passionate and caring.

In describing Coretta years later, King wrote "in the midst of the most tragic experiences, she never became panicky or overemotional. I have come to see the real meaning of that rather trite statement: a wife can either make or break a husband. My wife was always stronger than I was through the struggle. While she had certain natural fears and anxieties concerning my welfare, she never allowed them to hamper my active participation in the movement."[666] They were wedded on June 18, 1953 in Marion, Alabama in a ceremony performed by Martin Luther King Sr.

Upon graduation from Boston University, King was offered positions at several churches including one in Massachusetts and one in New York. In addition he was offered various academic positions in different colleges, including a teaching post, a deanship, and an administrative position. But the offer that caught his attention was the position of a preacher at Dexter Avenue Baptist Church in Montgomery, Alabama.

Montgomery was the heart and soul of the Confederate South. A few blocks down the street from Dexter Avenue was the historic state capital of Alabama. It was in this building that nearly a hundred years before, Alabama had voted to secede from the United States, in order to preserve slavery and tear the nation apart through the most violent war in country's history. It was on the steps of this building that Jefferson Davis took the oath of office of the president of the Confederate South. It was here that people of the South decided they would rather die than abolish slavery. And even after the humiliating violent defeat in the hands of Northern Yankees, their descendants continued to use violence in order to keep the racist ideology of the South alive in the form of segregation. A position here as opposed to one in New York or Massachusetts meant resubmitting oneself to the humiliation and disrespect of racism. Raising kids in Montgomery meant exposing them to segregation as children. Coretta was from Alabama and the prospect of going back to the segregated world was not appealing. In addition, Northern cities offered much better opportunities for an aspiring singer.

"Finally we agreed," King wrote, "that despite of the disadvantages and inevitable sacrifices, our greatest service could be rendered in our native South."[667] In September of 1954, the newlyweds, married for just over a year, moved to Montgomery, Alabama. On November 17, 1955, Yolanda Denise, their first daughter was born. Two weeks later, on December 1st. a proud and courageous 42-year-old seamstress named Rosa Parks performed an act that changed King's life forever

Montgomery bus boycott

One of the great humiliating and symbolic aspects of segregation in Alabama was the treatment of African-Americans on public buses, as described above. This was a constant source of irritation and reminder of inequality they faced every day. In between the two sections of the bus, there were seats within a gray zone where blacks could sit as long as there were no white passengers waiting. On March 2, 1955, a high school student named

CHAPTER 8

Claudette Colvin had refused to give up that grey seat for a white woman. When confronted by the driver and later by the police, she had become angry and had used language which was disapproved of by both the white passengers as well as the black passengers. The local chapter of NAACP decided not to take on her case. Leaders of the influential Women's Political Council in Montgomery criticized and pressured the leadership of NAACP to no avail. Colvin was reported as being "immature - prone to breakdowns and outbursts of profanity."[668] In October of that year, another woman named Mary Louise Smith again refused to vacate her seat on the city bus. She was arrested, convicted, and fined for her disobedience. But again, the local chapter of NAACP decided not to make a case. Smith's father was an alcoholic and they lived in a shack outside the city. NAACP leaders were afraid that if reporters went out to visit her, the credibility of their fight would be in jeopardy. Once again, the leadership of Women's Political Council complained that "Smith's shortcomings were irrelevant to the principles of the case."[669] But Smith paid her fine and NAACP did not appeal on her behalf.

On Thursday December 1st, when Martin Luther King's daughter Yolanda had turned two weeks old, a tired Rosa Parks left her job as a seamstress at Montgomery Fair department store. She was 42 years old, wore rimless spectacles, spoke quietly, and wrote and typed excellent letters. In addition to her full-time job, she did seamstress work on the side for extra money. She was also the secretary to the local chapter of NAACP. In fact, the letter of appointment for Martin Luther King to the local executive committee came from her. She was a devout churchgoer and one of those "rare people of whom everyone agreed that she gave more than she got."[670]

As she took her usual bus ride that afternoon, she was forced to sit with three other African-American women in the middle row, which separated whites from the blacks. She was in that grey zone where blacks were allowed to sit only if there were no white passengers waiting. When additional white passengers arrived, the driver ordered Mrs. Parks and the other African Americans to move to the back. The women sitting next to Rosa Parks complied. But Rosa Parks responded that she was not in the white section and did not need to move. Driver responded that the white section is where he said it was and now he was telling her she was in the white section. He then threatened to have her arrested. Rosa replied that he could have her arrested if he chose to. The entire bus was silent. Rosa was speaking so softly that people could barely hear what she was saying. She was calm and respectful. She had no anger or hatred towards the driver, yet would not disrespect by moving herself either. Everyone was listening to see what would happen. The driver told her not to move until he came back with the police in order to arrest her. Rosa Parks was not planning on moving.

After being taken to jail, she first called her mother. The first question her mother asked was "did they beat you?"[671] Soon, the president of local chapter of NAACP was there to see her and asked her the important question; would she be willing to fight the case, the way she knew they had wanted to fight earlier on behalf of Colvin and Smith?

This meant that Rosa had to stay in the city's jail voluntarily, a place notorious for its treatment of blacks and where she could face insults and possible physical harm. When she asked the opinion of her husband, he was terrified and became emotional. "The white folks," he told her, "will kill you, Rosa." He pleaded for her to just pay the fine and not make a political issue out of it. Rosa Parks became silent and thoughtful. And then she said "If you think it will mean something to Montgomery and do some good, I'll be happy to go along with it."[672] She had sounded the horn of battle and given the signal of noncooperation with evil. The battle for justice in Montgomery was about to begin.

One of the first people to be called was a volunteer member in the Women's Political Council named Jo Ann Robinson. The group had built a powerful network of concerned women who gave their time and effort for justice. Jo Ann Robinson then began calling other women in the group and women began responding as if an alarm had rang out across the city. Jo Ann Robinson, who was a teacher at Alabama State University, called for a meeting of women in her office on campus. They did not have access to newspapers, radio, or television so they decided the best way to notify everyone in Montgomery's African American community was to write a letter, make copies of it, and pass it around the city. In the letter they notified the citizens that "Another Negro woman has been arrested and thrown into jail because she refused to get up out of her seat on the bus...the next time it may be you... we are, therefore, asking every Negro to stay off the buses on Monday in protest of the arrest and trial."[673] It was a nonviolent plan for noncooperation. Thousands of copies were made using the mimeograph machines on campus. At three in the morning, they called the president of local NAACP and told him of the plan. He told the women that he would hold a meeting tomorrow for the prominent African-Americans in the community to notify them of the boycott and obtain their support.

CHAPTER 8

The weekend before the Monday boycott, an army of women walked around Montgomery, distributing 7,000 fliers asking people to boycott the buses on Monday. They were hoping at least 50-60% of the people would participate in the boycott. That evening, everyone went to bed anxiously awaiting the response of the African American community to the bus boycott. This boycott would symbolize the community's stance against injustice. If people continued to ride the bus, the symbolic act would have been defeated and the case against injustice lost.

At 5:30 Monday morning, Martin Luther King and Coretta Scott were fully dressed, ready to see if the boycott had gone forward. As the first bus went by their house, Coretta called out "Martin, Martin, come quickly!" They could not believe their eyes, the bus on one of the busiest lines in Montgomery, one usually filled with African American laborers, was completely empty. 15 minutes later, the second bus rolled down the street; it was also completely empty. In the third bus to pass by, there were only two white passengers. King got in his car to go around town and see what was happening on other buses. Everywhere he looked, buses were empty and people were walking to work. He saw a total of only eight African-Americans on buses that morning. Sidewalks were filled with thousands of workers walking to work, some walking as much as 12 miles. It was a bitterly cold winter in Alabama and walking such long distances was a difficult task for laborers going to jobs that mostly required physical labor all day long. Yet for the tens of thousands of African-Americans in Montgomery, this was about their dignity and self-respect. No amount of relative comfort in a city bus could've been exchanged for their dignity.

That afternoon, fifty prominent African American leaders gathered at the Baptist church where they created a new organization called the Montgomery Improvement Association. When it came to choosing a president, Reverend Martin Luther King Jr, the 27 year old, the most eloquent and intelligent preacher in town was nominated and unanimously selected.

Some then suggested that in the mass meeting which had been planned for 7pm that Monday evening, people should only sing and pray and if any decisions were to be made, they should be done in secret, away from the ears of reporters. In addition, the names of the leadership should be kept secret. E.D Nixon, the president of NAACP then got up and said "Somebody's name will have to be known, and if we are afraid we might just as well fold up right now. We must be man enough to discuss our recommendations in the open; this idea of secretly passing something around on paper is a lot of bunk.

The white folks are eventually going to find out anyway. We'd better decide now if we are going to be fearless men or scared boys."[674] From then on, it was decided that nothing would be done in secret. This transparency and openness in a nonviolent struggle is one of the important principals of nonviolence that this movement in Montgomery had just adopted.

In a nonviolent struggle, everything has to be out in the open. Everyone must have the option of questioning and scrutinizing every decision. The moment there is secrecy there will be conspiracy. Gandhi always wrote a letter to the Viceroy and told him about his intentions prior to taking up any action against the British. It is just as important for decisions to be transparent and communicated to the enemy as it was for them to be transparent for the participants. There cannot be any surprises in a nonviolent struggle. A surprise for the enemy is an invitation for the possible use of violence by its soldiers. The enemy in a nonviolent struggle must always be aware of your plans and must always be reminded constantly that under no circumstances will you or your supporters use violence. A complete transparency in a nonviolent struggle is the first step towards dialogue and debate, and the foundations of a democratic movement and, ultimately, a democratic end.

In a nonviolent struggle, openness, transparency and truthfulness are principles that cannot be violated. Secrecy not only leaves people out of the decision making and outside full participation in the struggle, it will also make it more likely that the adversary will use violence and torture to obtain that secret. The Iranians, in their nonviolent struggle, must accept openness and transparency as principles of the struggle. In this path, there cannot be secret negotiations, secret decisions, or secret organizations. Everything must be open and transparent. This was a great step the African Americans took on that evening.

The meeting of African Americans in which they decided on transparency as a principle ended at 6pm, an hour before the mass meeting was scheduled at the church. King rushed home and notified his wife of his responsibility as the president of the newly formed Montgomery Improvement Association. Coretta was supportive. He then had 20 minutes to prepare the most important speech of his life.

When he was heading back to the church, he noticed traffic jam 5 blocks from it. Thousands of people were coming that night to participate in the meeting. Every single seat in the church was filled and people were standing along the isles. Television cameras were there, as well as a number of reporters. Several people spoke before King and then he delivered his speech to a totally silent crowd waiting to hear this young preacher. He told the story of Rosa Parks and then in words not directed toward the crowd but at human beings irrespective of time and place, he made African Americans' case for them.

"We are here", he said "…because…we are American citizens and we are determined to apply our citizenship to the fullest of its meaning. We are here also because of our love for democracy; because of our deep seated belief for democracy transformed from thin paper to thick action is the greatest form of government on earth… There comes a time when people get tired of being trampled over by the iron feet of oppression. There comes a time, my friends, when people get tired of being plunged across the abyss of humiliation…. we, the disinherited of this land, we who had been oppressed so long, are tired of going through the long night of captivity. And now we are reaching out for the daybreak of freedom and justice and equality… but I want to tell you this evening that it is not enough for us to talk about love. Love is one of the pivotal points of the Christian faith. There is another side called justice. Not only are we using the tools of persuasion but we've come to see that we've got to use the tools of coercion."[675]

These words may have been spoken that evening to an audience of thousand African-Americans, but these words were meant for the ears of all humanity and all those fighting for injustice. These words are as relevant today in the Iranian struggle for democracy as they were for the African-Americans of Alabama. After he spoke, there came time for the most important decision. They had successfully completed the boycott city buses for a day. They needed to decide whether to continue until their demands were met or begin negotiations while they had successfully shown their unity. The motion was read for African-Americans to continue to boycott until all demands are met. The speaker then asked for those in favor to stand. Every single person in that packed church stood and those already standing in the isles raised their hands in favor. The African-American community had unanimously supported the continued boycott of city buses as a symbolic act of nonviolence.

Martin Luther King later wrote:

"The unity of purpose and esprit de corps of these people had been indescribably moving. No historian would be ever be able to fully describe this meeting and no sociologist will ever be able to interpret adequately…. the real victory was in the mass meeting, where thousands of black people stood revealed with a new sense of dignity and destiny. That night we were starting a movement that would gain national recognition; whose echoes would ring in the ears of people of every nation; a movement that would astound oppressors, and bring new hope to the oppressed. That night was Montgomery's moment in history."[676]

The complete boycott of city buses continued all week, with buses remaining empty and tens of thousands of African Americans walking miles to work. Eighteen African-American taxi companies volunteered to give rides for charges equal to city bus fares. By Friday of that week the Police Commissioner issued an order to taxi companies stating their reduced fare was illegal. The taxi service aiding the bus boycott came to an end. The leaders of the boycott then began a campaign to find volunteers who would drive and carpool people to their work. Over 300 people with cars volunteered— including several white women. With the carpool, the boycott continued and the empty city buses continued to roam the city streets. Many white housewives who depended on their African-American maids also began to drive them back and forth to work. When rain began to pour down, the leaders worried that the boycott would collapse, but rain came and went and African-Americans valued their dignity above wet feet. Weeks went by and the boycott continued.

The white city leadership began spreading false rumors about King that he had purchased a brand new Cadillac for himself and Buick for his wife. Their integrity was questioned and attempts were made to divide the leadership. Older African-American leaders were approached and encouraged to take over the leadership from the young preacher, but they refused. On January 22nd, nearly two months after the boycott began, local newspaper falsely announced that a settlement had been reached with several prominent African-American ministers. It was an attempt to get African-Americans back on city buses. King and other leaders went from church to church and to nightclubs and taverns to inform everyone that no such settlement had been reached. The three African-Americans mentioned by the white segregationists were neither prominent nor members of Montgomery Improvement Association, which had taken the lead in the boycott.

King and his family were receiving threatening phone calls every day. Abduction, beatings, lynching, and murder of African-Americans were a common occurrence in heavily racist south of the time. In the evening of January 27, while Coretta and baby had fallen asleep, King's telephone rang and the caller, in an angry voice, told him "Listen, nigger... before next week you'll be sorry you ever came to Montgomery."[677] King had received many threatening calls, but this somehow bothered him deeply. He couldn't sleep that night and began walking around in his house. He doubted himself, his courage, his tactics, and his end goal. He went over by the bed of his young daughter and watched his beautiful young wife as she lay sleeping. Fear began to take over him. As he sat on the kitchen table in the early morning hours of that evening, he began to pray. "Lord, I'm down here trying to do what's right. I think them right. I am here taking a stand for what I believe is right. But Lord, I must confess that I'm weak now, I'm faltering. I'm losing my courage. Now, I'm afraid. And I can't let the people see me like this because if they see me weak and losing my courage, they will begin to get weak. The people are looking to me for leadership, and if I stand for them without strength and courage, they too will falter. I am at the end of my powers. Have nothing left. I've come to the point where I can't face it alone."[678]

There comes a time at every nonviolent movement when the participants go through the doubts and the entire movement begins to question itself. These are the moments when history is made, when a battle turns to victory or defeat. Before a nonviolent movement begins to ask these questions of itself, such questions go through the minds of its leadership. If they're not resolved in those minds of individuals whom others reach for help in time of crisis, they will not be resolved in the mind of the movement. In these moments, such leaders no longer can take comfort in the love of their mothers or advice of their fathers. Even though their own lives may not matter, they still fear for the lives and hardship on their wives, children and those who look at them for leadership. These are the moments when leaders come face-to-face with those deepest beliefs in the deepest corners of their hearts. In that early morning, sitting alone and in fear in his kitchen, when doubt and uncertainty had taken over Martin Luther King and he could no longer find the courage to risk the pain and suffering he might place on his wife and child, he heard a voice deep within: "Martin Luther, stand up for righteousness. Stand up for justice. Stand up for the truth. And lo, they will be with you. Even until the end of the world."[679] At once his fear began to leave and a sense of calmness overpowered him. He had reached what Gandhi described as the Truth and in that Truth, he found courage, faith, and belief in his purpose.

Three nights later, on January 30th, as he was addressing a gathering in his church, he began to notice commotion and uncertainty. He noticed that while he was talking, people had begun to stop listening and instead were whispering to each other. People were looking at him but as his eyes would turn toward them, they would look away. News had reached everyone in the church and no one had the courage to tell this young preacher of an evil act of terror. Several attempted to approach him, but could not muster the courage. King then called three of his closest associates and demanded that they tell him what has happened.

While he was in the church, several young white supremacists had gone to his house and bombed his house while his wife and young child were inside. In a calm manner from his experience several nights before, he asked if his wife and child were OK. "We are checking on that now,"[680] he was told. Again in a calm manner he left the church and went home to find out for himself. In front of his house, several hundred angry African-Americans were standing and threatening to return violence with violence. He walked into the house and saw Coretta holding their child. The courageous young woman was neither angry nor panicky. She had an unbelievable composure and calmness and had accepted the event with unbelievable strength. King was even calmer and, after he witnessed the calmness in Coretta, he immediately began to realize that outside, the nonviolence movement might at any moment turn into violence. He immediately went outside and addressed the crowd:

"We believe in law and order. Don't get panicky. Don't do anything panicky at all. Don't get your weapons. He who lives by the sword will perish by the sword. Remember that is what God said. We are not advocating violence. We want to love our enemies. I want you to love our enemies. Be good to them. Love them and let them know you love them."[681]

The bus boycott had just passed one of its most important tests of strength. In face of an act of hatred and terror, the African-Americans had refused to turn to hatred and the use of violence. The bombing and the act of hatred responded without violence brought unbelievable further strength and courage to African-Americans. They were no longer in fear. They now believed in themselves and believed they had the strength to carry on this task to the end.

Nearly a month later, as the boycott continued and thousands of African-Americans continued to walk for miles in show of dignity and self-respect, the Montgomery grand jury used an old anti-boycott law to indict King and other leaders of the movement. When the list of those indicted was announced, people enthusiastically went to Sheriff's office to see if their names were on the list and were even disappointed if they were not indicted. They were no longer afraid. King was found guilty and sentenced to $500 fine or 386 days of hard labor. He appealed his case and as he left the courtroom he was faced with hundreds of African-Americans who began to sing "We ain't gonna ride the bus no more."[682]

When the insurance companies refused insurance to those providing car pool and helping the boycott, African-Americans found an insurance company in London to insure them. Month after month, the city buses continued to roam the streets empty. Regardless of the outcome, African-Americans had claimed one of the biggest symbolic victories for unity, freedom and justice since the Civil War. When the city lost the battle to have the driver's insurance taken away, they took legal action to call the car pool itself illegal. On November 13, nearly a year after the boycott as King and his associates were sitting in the courtroom waiting for the judge to rule that the car pool was illegal and trying to figure out how to continue the boycott into second-year, news reached the courthouse that the Supreme Court of United States has ruled that Alabama's state and local laws requiring segregation on buses were unconstitutional. Victory had been achieved.

Within a month, the African-Americans were to sit next to whites on city buses as equal citizens. The desegregation of city buses itself was not the victory. The victory was for nonviolence. Gandhi's method of love and nonviolence and social change had produced profound effects across the globe for another group of oppressed people. Martin Luther King wrote that, before the boycott, most had heard of Gandhi but few were aware of his tactics. But by the time the boycott ended and victory was reached, "the name of Mahatma Gandhi was well known in Montgomery. People who had never heard of the little brown saint of India were now saying his name with an air of familiarity. Nonviolent resistance had emerged as the technique of the movement, while love stood as the regulating ideal. In other words, Christ furnished the spirit and motivation while Gandhi furnished the method."[683]

Those who had advocated violence, however, also continued to support segregation and inequality. The day after Supreme Court ruling went into effect, a 15-year-old African-American girl standing at a bus stop was beaten by five white men. This was followed by shotgun fire aimed at integrated city buses. Two days later another series of shootings at an integrated bus sent a pregnant African-American to the hospital with bullet wounds in both legs. But the worst was yet to come. On January 9, the home of Ralph Abernathy was bombed. Ralph Abernathy was a minister at the First Baptist Church. His wife and baby were at home at the time of the bombing, but fortunately had escaped injury. The bombing of his home was immediately followed by the bombing of his church. Within minutes of the bombings, three or four other explosions were heard in Montgomery. Abernathy and King soon found out that Bell Street Church and Mt Olive Baptist Church had also been targeted. Two other churches had been bombed but were less damaged. African-Americans in Montgomery after such dignified victory were now victims of violence. At a Monday evening meeting, Martin Luther King, while addressing the crowd, for the first time broke down and cried. "Lord, I hope no one will have to die as a result of our struggle for freedom in Montgomery. Certainly I don't want to die. But if anyone has to die, let it be me."[684]

During the next few days, Montgomery remained quiet but, once again, on January 28 another series of bombings began, this time at People's Service Station and Cab Stand and another at the home of a sixty-year-old African-American hospital worker. The next morning, an unexploded bomb was found on the porch of Martin Luther King's home. To the crowd that had gathered in front of his home King announced, "We must not return violence under any condition. I know this is difficult advice to follow, especially since we have been the victims of no less than 10 bombings. But this is the way of Christ; it is the way of the cross. We must somehow believe that unearned suffering is redemptive."[685]

Again throughout the violence, the African-Americans in Montgomery refused to return evil with evil. They never showed anger or hate and continued to advocate love and nonviolence. Their courage and belief in the use of nonviolence finally convinced the city officials and on January 31st, seven white men were arrested in connection with the bombings. The real victory had now been won. *Time* magazine published a cover story on the Montgomery movement in February of 1957 and Dr. Martin Luther King Jr. was now a nationally recognized leader of nonviolence. In fact, Martin Luther King was not just a leader of nonviolence, he had become a symbol for nonviolence. The movement in Montgomery also gave strength and courage to African-Americans in every town and city in the South. Soon the boycotts, sit-ins, and other forms of non-cooperation and non-violent intervention were everyday occurrences throughout the South.

On February 3, 1959, Martin Luther King, accompanied by his wife Coretta, set out on a journey to India to see the land and culture that had produced that 'little brown saint of India'. Martin Luther King was now the voice of the old man of India in a land far away and to people now touched and guided by his philosophy and methods. The tactics and philosophy of Gandhi had now been proved effective in an experiment by another set of oppressed human beings who also had found the strength and power in nonviolence.

In India, he found a land where they were looked upon as brothers. Because of their struggle against racism, there was a strong bond of understanding between them and the Indians who had just overcome the oppression of imperialism. Indians particularly liked the hymns and songs— spirituals— of African-Americans and, while Martin Luther King was touring India lecturing on the movement, Coretta spent the time singing spirituals for them. Prime Minister Nehru greeted them in New Delhi, wearing his famous white jacket with a rose pinned on it. King was so enthusiastic and so eager to learn as much as he could about Gandhi that at one point Nehru had to remind him of the surprisingly pragmatic ways of that old saint and the impossibility of guessing what he would have advised King if he were still alive.

The Kings visited the home in Bombay that Gandhi used to stay at; the home with no furniture, no heat, no water or shower and only two Indian style toilets, which were holes in the floor. On March 1st, Martin Luther King and Coretta reached Gandhi's Ashram in Ahmadabad and stood on the same ground where Gandhi had stood on March of 1930 with 78 of his followers and had begun the historic 218 mile walk to take salt illegally from the sea and to signal noncooperation to India. It was the journey that brought the British Empire to its knees. India's journey through nonviolence had begun on that spot. Here Martin Luther King recalled Gandhi telling his people "if you're hit, don't hit back; even if they shoot at you, don't shoot back. If they curse at you, don't curse back. Just keep moving. Some of us might have to die before we get there. Some of us might be thrown in jail before we get there, but let's just keep moving."[686] King recalled Gandhi's nonviolent struggle for independence as "one of the most significant things that ever happened in the history of the world. More than 390 million people achieved their freedom, and they achieved it nonviolently."[687]

King recalls leaving India more determined than ever to follow the path of nonviolence. He was now convinced more than ever that nonviolent resistance "was the most potent weapon available to oppressed people in their struggle for freedom."[688] After his trip to India, King wrote: "the aftermath of hatred and bitterness that usually follows a violent campaign was found nowhere in India. The way of acquiescence leads to moral and spiritual suicide. The way of violence leads to bitterness in the survivors and brutality in the destroyers. But the way of nonviolence leads to redemption and the creation of the beloved community."[689]

James Lawson

There were many other African-Americans in the 1950s who were influenced by Gandhi's writings. One was James Lawson, a Methodist minister and graduate student at Vanderbilt school of Divinity. At a visit to A. J Muste of the Fellowship of Reconciliation (FOR) - an interfaith group dedicated to peace and justice, Lawson was introduced to Gandhi's writings and history of nonviolence. He also subscribed to FOR Magazine, which recounted the story about Howard Thurman, the minister who had visited Gandhi in 1936. During the Korean War, he had openly refused cooperation with military draft because of his beliefs in nonviolence and was imprisoned for a little more than a year because of his refusal. After his prison sentence, he finished his degree at Baldwin-Wallace, in Ohio, and left for India for three years. There he intensely studied Gandhi's life and work and met with many of his disciples. As a Christian he came to believe that Gandhi's path was the practice in real life of the spirit and teachings of Christ. He returned to Ohio in 1956 to enroll in a master's degree program at Oberlin College with the intention of obtaining a Ph.D. in theology. In 1957, on a visit by Martin Luther King, Lawson told King of his trip to India and his great interest and admiration for Gandhi. He told King how he wanted to go down South after his studies, but Martin Luther King told him that his knowledge of Gandhi's method was invaluable and that the movement needed him immediately. There were very few black leaders in the South who truly understood the philosophy and teachings of Gandhi. His presence, leadership, and knowledge about nonviolence learned from his years with Gandhi's disciples in India were much needed. In 1958 James Lawson went to Nashville, Tennessee to organize a nonviolent movement against segregation.

In fall of 1959, Lawson began holding workshops at Clark Memorial Methodist Church for students willing to challenge the status quo and participate in a nonviolent struggle. Lawson taught them lessons of Gandhi's movement in South Africa and in India. Nonviolence was repeatedly stressed, with Gandhi and Jesus Christ being the central figures providing the philosophical backbone for their struggles ahead. He told the students about Gandhi's 'Satyagraha' or 'soul force' as a weapon for fighting and justice. When he asked the members of community what bothered them most about the injustices in their city, some women pointed to white-only lunch counters in downtown stores.

White-only lunch counters were a common feature of downtown department stores across much of Southern towns and cities of mid-20th century. Prior to the advent and popularity of fast food restaurants, these lunch counters were the most popular and desirable means of obtaining lunch while out shopping or at work in downtown areas. African-Americans were allowed to shop at the stores but if they wanted to sit and rest their feet, they were not allowed to sit at counters and if they wanted to eat, they had to purchase their food and take it to the sidewalk. In addition, they were not allowed to use the restrooms in the stores. African-American women, who often made up a considerable portion of their business, were humiliated by having to eat their food outside and having to wait on their feet often while holding their tired and hungry babies.

Lawson decided that he and his students would focus on these lunch counters as symbols and undertake a nonviolent struggle in order to obtain justice at these counters as symbols of a greater struggle for civil rights. He had learned that in the Gandhi's method of nonviolent struggle, these symbolic gains can be equivalent to obtaining strategic geographic positions in a military battlefield. Lawson knew that a victory at these downtown lunch counters in Nashville, Tennessee would have effects far beyond. In fall of 1959, he began training students for this nonviolent confrontation. The method Lawson chose was a formal protest where the students would occupy the counters and deliberately break the law.

There are three basic classes of nonviolent methods. There is nonviolent change through protest and persuasion, in which, through symbolic acts, the participants attempt to show their unity in their struggle for justice to convince the enemy of their humanity and rights. The Salt March of Gandhi and his fasts were examples of this. The second class of methods in nonviolent struggle are the methods of noncooperation. Labor strikes and boycotts are examples of this form of campaign. The third class of nonviolent struggle are methods of change through intervention, most of which are popularly known as 'occupy' methods where participants physically and nonviolently prevent the execution of injustice. This method is the most dangerous form of nonviolent resistance and one which requires the most training. It also requires the participants to be completely free of fear and be willing to suffer physical and psychological punishment. Nonviolent intervention as a form of resistance requires far more courage than nonviolent change through noncooperation or nonviolent change through protest and persuasion.

Lawson began holding workshops for the students on non-violent intervention and direct action in November and December of that year. Students would learn how to react when threatened with physical injury. Lawson would practice yelling at them, insulting them, and cursing in order to try to create anger and then would teach them how not to become angry and never become disrespectful. Sitting at an all-white lunch counters was both culturally not allowed and legally not permitted. Students sitting at these counters would face the threats and violence of hooligans, followed by arrests by the police. Jim Lawson taught them how to curl up and protect their vital organs when being beaten and how to help those being beaten by spreading the beating to number of individuals instead of allowing beating to be concentrated on one person. One group of students would sit in a row of chairs while another group would pretend to be angry hooligans calling them 'niggers' and then pushing and shoving them to the floor. Lawson taught the students to always keep eye contact with the assailant since this can check the attackers rage. These sessions taught the students how not to hit back and not to get angry when provoked.[690] Before the Christmas break, a decision was made to begin the sit-ins in February of 1960. By the time students came back from vacation and January rolled around, word of their nonviolent campaign in February was circulating throughout local black colleges. The number of those now volunteering to participate rose to several hundred. On February 13, Lawson held a meeting at an auditorium where hundreds of volunteers showed up. News suddenly came that in North Carolina, two African-Americans had walked into Woolworth's lunch counter and had refused to get up. Soon, sporadic episodes of this symbolic act of nonviolent resistance were occurring in neighboring states.

With hundreds of new untrained volunteers, Lawson held workshops, stressing to the newcomers that under no circumstances should they retaliate in any way. Any form of retaliation, anger, or insult by one of the volunteer participants would mean the defeat of the struggle. Lawson needed to move quickly, but they were not willing to send an untrained army to the battlefield. The volunteers were told to dress well, talk quietly, and wait patiently for hours if need be at the lunch counters. Most important, they had to be willing to be insulted, beaten, and sent to jail.[691]

On the morning of Saturday, February 13th, a hundred neatly dressed African-American students showed up at first Baptist Church ready to undergo this historic journey. It was a cold winter morning. Half a foot of fresh snow had carpeted the street of Nashville. People were assigned at the church to monitor the upcoming events in downtown lunch counters. Some were assigned to take instructions to downtown from the church and bring back information from the events downtown. The participants were calling themselves the Nashville Student Movement.

When signal was given, the students began walking two at a time down the sidewalk for several blocks until they reached the city's main shopping district. The white Nashville residents witnessing the event did not know what was happening. The students, neatly dressed and polite walked into downtown stores, bought a few items and then sat down at lunch counters. The stores' owners, waitresses and customers did not know what to do. Several customers began cursing at the students sitting on the counters, but since they did not respond, they grew tired and left. When a student attempted to order lunch, he was told 'niggars' are not served here. [692]

The stunned waitresses, not knowing what to do put up a sign 'Counter Closed'. Students continued sitting there for hours until the lights were turned off. Then messengers arrived from First Baptist Church bearing the instruction for students to head back. When they got back to church, they knew they had made history. The students were screaming and cheering with joy. They had successfully carried out a powerful nonviolent symbolic act. In nonviolence, symbolism and such symbolic acts are victories, just as capture of land and cities are in war. "It was like New Year's eve - whooping, cheering, hugging, laughing, singing."[693]

The white citizens of Nashville were confused and perplexed. They had no idea what had just happened. The events had taken them completely by surprise. In a moment of confusion, they had closed their lunch counters in order to prevent such a symbolic act of desegregation from taking place. Above all, as a great sign of victory for the students, there was no violence by the nonviolent army. Two more sit-ins were held on the following Thursday and Saturday. Both events occurred under similar circumstances, and on both occasions, the white establishment was confused and just closed the counters in retaliation. The next sit-in was planned for February 27th.

Three days before the next event, the black leaders of the community received information that the white establishment would be dealing differently with the students on the next occasion. The plan was for the police to move out of downtown areas and allow hooligans and violent segregationist and supremacist organizations to come in and physically beat the students. Then the police would come back in and arrest those students still present. Every black student growing up in the South was well aware of horror stories told by those taken to prison. The culture of segregation and racism was built on violence. Violence was the weapon of the choice for division, hate, and anger and the white segregationist were now ready to use their weapon.

Lawson and other leaders now planned for a more coordinated effort in reprising this symbolic act. It was planned that for every student arrested and every seat emptied, another student would walk up and fill that seat. This required great communication and teamwork between every single volunteer and leadership in first Baptist Church and those downtown. But in the early morning of the event, Lawson had another worry. What if students were intimidated by the prospect of violence and possible imprisonment and decide not to show up. These are the moments when the strength of a movement is tested and, in a nonviolent struggle, this strength comes from the principles of such a movement and belief in the movement. If principals are based on the sound and humanistic principles of nonviolence taught by those who walked along the same path in history, such a movement will survive and prosper. But if the principles of a movement are flawed, then the struggle will fail. That evening Lawson made copies of simple instructions that anyone still showing up in the morning had to follow. The flyer read:

Do Not:
1. Strike back nor curse if abused.
2. Laugh out.
3. Hold conversations with floor walker.
4. Leave your seat until leader has given you permission to do so.
5. Block entrances to stores nor the isles inside.

Do:
1. Show yourself friendly and courteous at all times.
2. Sit straight; always face the counter.
3. Report all serious incidents to your leaders.
4. Refer information seekers to your leaders in a polite manner.
5. Remember the teachings of Jesus Christ, Mahatma Gandhi and Martin Luther King.

Love and nonviolence is the way.

CHAPTER 8

MAY GOD BLESS EACH OF YOU. [694]

These instructions are not unlike instructions given to an army platoon before a major battle. In fact, nonviolent warfare is itself a form of battle. But in this battle, it is nonviolence fighting violence and love overcoming hate. To Lawson's great surprise that morning, more than 300 brave and courageous soldiers of nonviolence showed up for the event.

At the lunch-counters, the police evacuated from the area and thugs rushed in. Students were cursed and insulted. Some were beaten. One had a lit cigarette thrust against his back. Throughout all this, no volunteer fought back. Not one person cursed or insulted the thugs. Then police came in and began arresting the students. For every student arrested, cheers of joy were heard. And for every seat emptied, another student was sent to fill it again. "The kind of power we felt", said one student, "was more forceful than all their police force... and all of their dogs, or billy clubs or jails."[695] The power students felt was the power of nonviolence and the potential for human struggle for freedom through nonviolence on the societal level. In such a struggle, the victory comes through self-respect and respect for the adversary. The victory comes when the participants do not turn to violence or insults. It comes when the participants refuse to become angry in face of great anger. Saturday the 27th was called the 'Big Saturday'. After arresting more than 80 students, the police asked the managers of the stores to close down. The mayor of Nashville either could step up the violence or a make a concession and end this situation. When the students refused to pay bail, the mayor asked the judge to reduce bail to $5. Students again refused to pay. Not knowing what to do, the authorities released them that night without bail. The judge then levied a $50 fine on each student. Once again, students refused to pay. He then sentenced them to 30 days in prison. But a couple of days later, the mayor stepped in and released the students.

As a concession, the mayor created a biracial committee to look into the matter of segregation at the lunch counters. Meanwhile, he asked the students not to resume the sit-ins. The students agreed and for three weeks they waited. But when they found that the committee would be dividing the lunch counters into two sections of all-white and all-black counters, they resumed their sit-in on the following Saturday. The segregationists now decided to go after Lawson. Under pressure, Lawson was expelled from the University and then arrested on March 3rd.

Lawson and the students were now heroes in Nashville's African American community. At a jam-packed meeting in First Baptist Church, a call went out to undertake the second form of nonviolent struggle—noncooperation. Noncooperation was less threatening and less provocative. It was decided that the African-Americans would boycott downtown stores until owners agreed to desegregation. The women were the main shoppers at these stores and they began a campaign of notifying each other and members of the community of this form of nonviolence. Through flyers and phone calls, word was spread. Volunteers were placed out by downtown stores to notify African-Americans entering and leaving the stores. The downtown stores soon turned into 'ghost towns'. Not only African-Americans were staying away, many white customers were also avoiding the stores because of the demonstrations and tumultuous events.

The stores' owners were now coerced into justice through the use of nonviolence and agreed to desegregation. But this wasn't their decision, it was also a cultural and legal decision and any such decision had to come from city leadership.

On Monday, April 19, a bomb blew up at the home of one of Nashville's African-American leading activists. By noon, the students decided they would walk out of class and march downtown to the courthouse. A thousand students left class and silently began walking downtown. By the time they reached the courthouse, their numbers had grown to several thousand. Amongst the students was a young white man named Guy Cawaran who had brought his guitar to the march. He was influenced by James Lawson, but he was also a collector of folk songs which he had gathered from many different African American churches and communities in the South. There, amongst the crowd, he decided to sing one of the songs he had learned at the Highlander Folk School. When he began to sing, most people did not know the words to the song, but it was familiar to them and the words were easy to learn. "We Shall Overcome" he sang, "We shall overcome, someday". The song was to become one of the greatest symbols of nonviolence. Decades later, in Prague, people sang this song in their moment of freedom. The song was sung in the far away streets of Jakarta, Indonesia and Cape Town, South Africa.[696]

The mayor came out and spoke to the students. He was first interviewed by a young minister who accused the mayor of silence in face of bombing and violence. The mayor was becoming defensive and agitated. Then a young 22-year-old student named Dianne Nash spoke and appealed to the Mayor's sense of fairness. She asked if it was right for people to be discriminated against based on skin color, then she asked if he thought lunch counters should be desegregated. The Mayor paused, and then finally said 'Yes'. The crowd erupted in cheers and applause. Everyone was hugging each other. Nonviolence had prevailed. Next day's headline in newspapers read 'INTEGRATE COUNTERS-MAYOR'.[697] Throughout the struggle, Lawson, who had spent years studying Gandhi, had kept insisting that victory would come when "we changed enemies heart through the show of love, self-sacrifice and awakening the sense of justice and humanity."[698] Victory had come.

By spring of that year, 1960, the philosophy of nonviolent struggle preached by those like Martin Luther King and Jim Lawson and learned from the practices of Gandhi was well known throughout America. By the end of April, there were sit-ins at 78 cities across southern United States. Over 70,000 individuals participated in such non-violent form of resistance and over 3,000 were arrested. By the end of 1961, over 100 towns and cities across United States were integrated. [699]

Freedom Ride

In 1961, activists organized a 'Freedom Ride' on which a group of African American's would ride the bus from Washington D. C. to New Orleans and test compliance with recent Supreme Court ruling that required desegregation of interstate buses and terminals. But when the group reached South Carolina, the bus was forced off the road and firebombed. The Freedom Riders were beaten and clubbed by local gangs. The riders secured another bus and continued their journey. Once again, in Birmingham, Alabama, they were beaten by the white mob with the consent of local police. The incident of these nonviolent activists riding the bus south now became a national headline and the Kennedy administration was forced to act. Robert Kennedy, the Attorney General of the United States, decided to help the riders get out of Birmingham. But as soon as he convinced the riders to leave under federal protection, another group of students volunteered to continue to journey. This time Robert Kennedy sent a deputy and police escort for the students. At Montgomery, the local police was supposed to take over the responsibility of protection, but once the bus got into town, the local police were absent. The riders were again beaten badly. Amongst those beaten was Robert Kennedy's deputy, who was hit in the head with a lead pipe and fell unconscious. The Attorney General petitioned the Interstate Commerce Commission to desegregate all interstate bus terminals. In 1961, Supreme Court finally also gave ruling to integrate all terminals.

Separately, in a mass nonviolent campaign in Albany, Georgia hundreds were imprisoned, including Martin Luther King. The campaign in Albany eventually failed and King learned an important lesson from that failure. The campaign failed because in King's opinion, the demands were too broad and not specific. The leadership of the Albany movement wanted desegregation everywhere. Their campaign involved sit-ins at bus stations, libraries and restaurants. Albany's chief of police mass arrested participants, including Martin Luther King. At one point, nearly 5% of Albany's African-American citizens were in prison for noncooperation. Over 95% of African Americans participated in the boycotts. The boycotts were extremely effective, with bus transportation brought to a halt and merchants deeply hurt economically for their practice of segregation.

Here in Albany, the chief of police also had a new strategy. He also refused to use violence. The local authorities realized that violence against protesters backfired, since it resulted in increasing sympathy, both local and national, for the demonstrators. In fact, in a nonviolence struggle, although initially the reaction of the violent adversary is the use of all forms of violence, as time goes on and nonviolent movement continues, regimes who also depend on the support of their people or the international community realize that violence will only hasten their own defeat. In addition, once the enemy realizes that the participants will not turn to violence under any circumstances, it then finds it harder and harder to use violence itself. This is true even at times of the most brutal regimes.

After nearly a year of nonviolent struggle in Albany, the white leadership refused to back down. The demands of the Albany movement were too broad and difficult to fulfill. The movement began to lose composure and discipline. On July 24, the city leadership unleashed a storm of violence on protesters. Many peaceful protesters were beaten, including a pregnant woman who was beaten by a cane. In retaliation, the protesters, heretofore nonviolent, began hurling rocks and bottles at the police. Because of retaliation and violence by the protesters, Martin Luther King called off the protest in Albany, much as Gandhi had called off his nonviolent struggle in Bardoli in 1920's after use of violence by Indians. In order to show his followers his determination for using only the tactics of nonviolence, King called for a 'Day of Penance'. He invited everyone to pray for nonviolence.

CHAPTER 8

After months of boycott, the movement in Albany lost its momentum. "We lost an initiative that we never regained." wrote Martin Luther King, "the mistake I made there was to protest against segregation generally rather than against a single and distinct facet of it. Our protest was so vague that we got nothing, and the people were left very depressed and in despair. It would have been much better to have concentrated upon integrating the buses or the lunch counters."[700] From then on, King never made broad and unspecific demands. He was more specific in search of more symbolic objectives. But the movement in Albany was not a complete defeat. Afterwards, the city commission appealed the entire section of the city code that carried segregation ordinances.[701] The public libraries were then integrated. In addition, the nonviolent movement in Albany convinced thousands of African Americans to participate in upcoming elections. In the local elections, in which segregationists were running against moderates, these voters propelled moderates to power and, as a result, Georgia had its first governor who pledged to respect the rights of all citizens equally. Even in face of defeat, the movement had given the African Americans in Albany the strength and courage to stand up for their rights. They took pride in going into jail. They took pride in standing up for justice and equality. King wrote:

"To the Negro in the South, staggering under the burden of centuries of inferiority, to have faced his oppressor squarely, absorbed his violence, filled the jails, driven his segregated buses off the streets, worshiped in a few white churches, rendered inoperative parks, libraries, and the pools, shrunken his trade, revealed his inhumanity to the nation and the world, and sung, lectured, and prayed publicly for freedom and equality - these were the deeds of a giant. No one would silence him up again. That was the victory which could not be undone. Albany would never be the same again. We had won a partial victory in Albany, and a partial victory to us was not an end but a beginning."[702]

King then moved on to Birmingham, Alabama and began a nonviolent struggle to desegregate the downtown merchants' stores. Meetings were held in Birmingham at which King gave a series of talks on the philosophy and practice of nonviolence. He planned to hold sit-ins at lunch counters like those done previously in other cities. They called between 250-350 people for a meeting at the church.

Only 65 showed up and on April 3, began marching out of church towards five downtown stores. The waitresses at the lunch closed the stores and police dragged 21 demonstrators to paddy wagon. With a disappointing effort, the leadership decided to march to City Hall. Dozens of people marched on April 6 and were arrested.[703] The number of arrests was larger than the arrests made three days before but still disappointing to King and other organizers. Volunteers were scarce. Enthusiasm was low. The movement had little energy and the masses could not be mobilized. Yet the leadership persisted and believed that they could fill up the jails in Birmingham and find new courage in overcoming the injustice. In the eight days after the start of the movement, only a disappointing 150 had been taken to prison. In comparison in Albany, twice as many had been jailed on just the first day, yet in Albany, they had achieved only a partial victory.[704] In addition, the movement had run out of funds and there was no more bail money available to get poverty-stricken African Americans out of prison and back home.

On April 12th, King held a meeting at his motel suite with 24 African-American leaders of the nonviolent movement including his father. He was told by the leadership that they needed money and, since King was the only person with national contacts who could raise the money for them, King's going to prison was out of the question. They believed that King going to prison would mean the end of the struggle. Those at the meeting were disappointed and looking for ways to reorganize. The most dedicated leaders of nonviolence were filled with feelings of 'hopelessness'[705] King remained silent as these 24 men tried to figure out a way to move forward. As he was listening, he whispered to himself "I must go". He did not know what would happen and where the money would come from, but he knew he had to go to prison. His announcement that he was going to purposely break the law through civil disobedience and go to prison shocked everyone—yet there was no arguing. He had made his decision. The only person who spoke up against Martin was his father, who asked him to obey the laws "at this time".[706] "I have to go" Martin replied, "I am going to march if I have to march by myself." His father realizing the immense courage and determination in his son replied "Well, you didn't get this nonviolence from me, you must have got it from your Mama."[707] There was silence in the room and as 25 of them stood up, they held hands and sang 'We Shall Overcome'. Within days, King was to march out of the Baptist Church with the intention of breaking the law and getting arrested.

When King began his march from 16th Street's Baptist Church nearly three hours behind schedule, crowds of African Americans had lined up on the sidewalks to watch him take on this journey. There was excitement in the air; they were expecting their hero to walk up and face the injustice of the white leadership all by himself. When King finally showed up, cheers went up and people began singing and following him. By the time they reached the police blockade, more than a thousand singing, jubilant African Americans were walking with King. Without warning, a police officer grabbed King and threw him in a paddy wagon. Without allowing him to call his wife, who had just given birth to their fourth child, or a lawyer, he was thrown into solitary confinement and held incommunicado. There was no word of him; no one knew of his condition.

On Sunday, Coretta Scott, not knowing what else to do, called the White House and asked for President Kennedy to intervene. The President, called her back and assured her he would do everything he could. Within half an hour, King was allowed to call Coretta. And later, two attorneys were allowed to come and visit King. He was informed that Harry Belafonte had raised $50,000 for the movement and had sent word that whatever else Dr. King needed, he would see that it was provided. While in solitary confinement, King was given a newspaper and in the paper he found an article attacking their movement by eight leading white clergyman in Birmingham calling on King to accept a reformist path of negotiations and a peaceful outcome of limited victory by King in a form that would be acceptable to the white racist community. Angered at this letter, King wrote a response on the pages of the newspaper. This response, now known as 'Letter From Birmingham Jail' is considered one of his most famous letters.

The clergymen were calling King and the demonstrators, extremists, lawbreakers, and believers in anarchy. In his 21 page reply, King wrote "I cannot sit idly by in Atlanta and not be concerned about what happens in Birmingham." He continues with the words that are now the one of the most famous quotes in 20th century America. "Injustice anywhere", he tells them, "is a threat to justice everywhere."[708] These are important words for Iranians to remember, since they are often told by those who justify injustice in Iran for the sake of peace and security and who claim that the cruelty and violence in Iran is a matter only for those Iranians within the country; the path for democracy and human rights in Iran is an issue only to be dealt with by those in Iran they tell the world. Those Iranians outside of the country should remain silent and mind their own business. The leadership in Birmingham was telling Martin Luther to go back to Atlanta and not concern himself with injustice in Birmingham. This is, essentially, the same message repeatedly given to Iranian expatriates. For believers in democracy and nonviolence, injustice done to a woman in Isfahan is just as much a concern as injustice in one's own neighborhood. The struggle for justice in Iran is not only a concern by those facing injustice; it is a concern for all the people in the world, regardless of where they live or what language they speak.

Martin Luther King in his famous letter states that there are four basic steps to a nonviolent campaign, a lesson that Iranians can greatly appreciate and benefit from. First is the "collection of the facts to determine whether injustices exist". I believe the facts of injustice, despotism, and violence are well-known to Iranians in their struggle and path towards democracy. The second step in the nonviolent campaign he calls 'negotiations'. Negotiation is always the first attempt in the nonviolent struggle, but it often leads to failure since few, if any, tyrants and enemies of justice are willing to give up their power through negotiation alone. The period of negotiations in Iran's path towards democracy was the reform movement before the 2009 elections. The reform movement in Iran was an attempt to negotiate with dictatorship. People were asked by the reformists to be patient, abide by the law and allow the reformists to carry out negotiations on their behalf, an attempt that led to failure. Thus the reform movement may be considered the second natural step in the path towards maturity of a non-violent movement. The third step in the nonviolent campaign King called 'self-purification'. This is the moment when those embarking on the journey for nonviolence announce their beliefs in the principles of nonviolence and declare that under no circumstances they will allow feelings of anger, hatred or vengeance to dictate their actions. This is the attempt to find love in one's heart and free one's self from violence. Without this process of 'self-purification', the struggle for nonviolence is a dangerous path that can easily turn to chaos and violence. The last step in a nonviolent campaign Martin Luther King called 'Direct Action'. It is only after taking the first three steps that people are ready to sacrifice for nonviolence.

To those critics of Martin Luther King saying "Why direct action? Why sit-ins, marches, and so forth? Isn't negotiation a better path?", King replied "Indeed, this is the very purpose of direct action. Nonviolent direct action seeks to create such a crisis and foster such a tension that a community which has constantly refused to negotiate is forced to confront the issue. It seeks to dramatize the issue so that it can no longer be ignored."[709] As opposed to the philosophy of nonviolent action, the leaders of the reform movement in Iran repeatedly attempt to diffuse the tension and create a peaceful atmosphere with the hopes of negotiations within the institutions and constitution of the Islamic Republic. In a nonviolent struggle, negotiations with a stubborn,

CHAPTER 8

unjust, and power-hungry tyrant are only for the exit and the surrender of the tyrant and can come only after direct action. "We know through painful experience that freedom is never voluntarily given by the oppressors," Martin Luther King wrote. "It must be demanded by the oppressed."[710]

With the funds now available for bail, King was released after nine days of solitary confinement. Once he was free, plans were made for another march downtown to occupy lunch counters and intentionally break the law. This time, the volunteers began recruiting students in local high schools. They first started with basketball stars and other well-known students. Workshops were held on nonviolence, its philosophy, techniques, and the power of symbolic act as a way of defiance as opposed to insults, threats, or violence. Every day, more and more students were showing up at the workshops and every day, there were younger and younger children. Leaflets began circulating in high schools asking all students to leave at noon on Thursday, May 2nd.

In response to the shifting of the movement's recruiting to younger kids, the city was becoming tense. The parents were nervous and worried. Those African Americans against the march argued against it and reminded King and the community of notorious dangers of jailhouses for teenage blacks, including dangers of rape and beatings. They pleaded not to allow children to go on the march because of long term scars such exposure can bring to a child. The FBI notified the local police of leaflets distributed at local high schools. The night before the march, anxiety filled the air as two armies, which had been facing each other for weeks and preparing for battle, knew that tomorrow the battle would begin. This battle was going to be fought eight years after the Rosa Parks incident. A general had led an army of nonviolent soldiers across America for eight years and he was giving signal for a new fight in the morning. Eight years ago in Montgomery, someone had asked an elderly woman why she was involved in the struggle. "I'm doing it for my children and grandchildren" she had said. The next morning, after eight years of struggle, it was now time for the children to stand. In the morning, the young soldiers of this nonviolent army were to march out of 16th Street Baptist Church to downtown lunch counters and commit civil disobedience.

On the morning of May 2nd, called D-Day by the organizers, police placed roadblocks along the route from the church to downtown. A crowd of people had gathered around the church to watch the events about to unfold. At one o'clock, as everyone was watching, the doors to the church opened and 50 teenagers, singing "We Shall Overcome" began marching out two abreast. The police gave several warnings and then began to arrest the students and placed them in paddy wagons. It seemed a routine act of nonviolence and imprisonment. Birmingham police looked at it as a victory. But moments later, the church doors opened again and another group of fifty began to march outside. Then another, and another and another. Paddy wagons were all filled and officers on the police radio were anxiously calling for additional paddy wagons for further arrests. The police department then called the sheriff and pleaded for additional help. Meanwhile, more and more groups of teenagers were marching out the church until they overwhelmed the police. A group of twenty slipped by the barricades and headed downtown. When police asked how many more were in the church, "At least a thousand!" was the reply. "God Almighty," was the police response. [711]

At one point, thirty-eight elementary school children marched out. When police tried to intimidate them, they told the police they knew what they were doing. An elderly woman was seen breaking away from the bystanders, running to the children and saying "sing, children, sing".[712] A policeman asked an eight year old girl, "What do you want?" Looking into the policeman's eyes and unafraid, "F'eedom" she responded.[713] Another little girl while being arrested and placed in the paddy wagon was asked "How old are you?" "I am six years old", she responded.[714] Four blocks away, the police was able to catch the twenty who had slipped by the barricades. Police eventually called for school buses to hold the arrested children. By four o'clock, all the children were arrested. In prison, as many as 75 children were placed in jail cells built for eight.

That evening, a thousand people, including most of the high school and elementary school parents gathered at the church. Martin Luther King announced, "I have been inspired and moved today, I have never seen anything like it." A total of 985 students had signed up for jail and 600 were imprisoned. In church, they spoke of the courage of these children and the inspiration they had given the community. Crowds of people stood up in the church with the intent of marching on to prison. As they began singing freedom songs, another 300 people were marching up and down the aisles in a symbolic gesture of the march, which was to take place in the morning.

Next morning, a crowd again formed outside the Sixteenth Street Baptist Church. Anxious parents waited to see if their child was to march out of church. At noon, a group of sixty students began to march. But, this time, the police had already filled the jails and could not arrest any more children. The strategy of police this time was to contain and disperse the children. In order to achieve this, the police department had obtained a very powerful type of fire hose from the fire department. This new type of hose was called a miracle in long-range firefighting. It could knock bricks loose from mortar and strip bark from trees at a distance of one hundred feet. When the group of sixty students came close to the police line, a warning was given and then water lines were opened. Immediately fifty of the children were swept off their feet and the crowd that had gathered began to disperse. But ten of the students held their ground and with all their might began to sing one word, 'Freedom' to the tune of 'Amen'. The bystanders, who were horrified by the scene and were not trained in nonviolence, lost their composure and threw bricks and rocks at the police. Songs of freedom turned to screams.

As soon as the crowd was pushed back, the doors to the church opened again and another group of children marched out. The children kept coming and soon outflanked the fire hoses and continued to march downtown. The police, unable to hold the children back with water, deployed eight K-9 units. Many fled instantly at the sight of angry German Shepherds. Some threw rocks at the dogs. On command, the officers and the dogs attacked students. Three students were severely bitten and had to be rushed to the hospital. Others fled in terror and confusion. Some retreated back into the church. An AP photographer caught a photo of a policeman holding a leash in one hand and grabbing an African-American teenager by the other while the dog was biting the student in the abdomen. That photo went on the front page of many major newspapers, including the *New York Times*.

President Kennedy, on seeing the photo the next day, declared it made him 'sick', yet a statement came only from his brother, stating "the timing of the demonstrations is open to question. School children participating in street demonstrations is a dangerous business. An injured, or maimed child is a price that none of us can afford to pay." Yet he added that the injustices in Birmingham were a local matter and not a federal responsibility and stressed that such injustice must be resolved through good faith negotiations and not on the streets. [715] The boy being bitten had his arms relaxed on his sides, his chin high in self-respect and his back straight with no intention of insulting the police or striking back. His demeanor in the photo was symbolic of the entire nonviolent movement.

By three o'clock, the remaining students were back in the church and police had surrounded the building. Only half of the volunteers had yet stepped off on their jail march, and of those, 250 were arrested. [716]. King and other leaders were not fazed by the political attacks questioning the use of children. These people never cared for the miserable school and societal conditions these children were raised in and now, all of sudden, they were expressing concern about their health and well-being. The Kennedy administration's envoy urged King to halt the demonstration. King regarded Kennedy's involvement as a success, proof that their symbolic nonviolent action had sent tremors across the country and into nation's capital. Knowing that he had achieved the desired victory, he accepted a truce for the day. In the two days of marching, nearly a thousand children had been jailed.

That evening the Sixteenth Street Baptist Church was packed with concerned parents and citizens. Andrew Young, who spoke before King told the crowd: "We have a nonviolent movement, but it is not nonviolent enough." He condemned stone-throwing and reactionary violence by the participants. "We must not boo the police when they bring up the dogs... we must praise them. The police don't know how to handle the situation governed by love, and the power of God."[717] When it was time for King to speak, he told the parents, "Your daughters and sons are in jail... they are suffering for what they believe, and they are suffering to make this nation a better nation." Hundreds of children were placed in prison yards due to lack of space indoors.[718]

Parents were seen outside of jail yards throwing blankets and food over the fence to their rain- drenched children.[719] King announced that the march would go on. "Yesterday was D-Day," he announced, "and tomorrow will be Double D-Day." To this announcement, deafening cheers went up from the crowd.[720] King and his advisers were up until midnight on Friday devising the strategy for the next morning.

On Saturday afternoon, a tense and nervous police line surrounded the 16th Street Baptist church. But King and his advisers had a surprise ready. Five blocks away, a group of ordinary looking African-American students were walking down the street when all of a sudden a little girl in between them took out a banner stating "Love God and Thy Neighbor". The panicking police rushed in and arrested them. Immediately, a report came in that a woman and a little girl had knelt on the steps of City Hall to pray. These were symbolic acts of nonviolence. In nonviolent struggle, such symbolic acts are weapons of war and tools for expression and freedom. Such an act of prayer or marching without symbolism is solely personal, but when carried out with symbolic intent, these acts are as powerful as those of people marching down the street and shouting slogans of freedom. The police had to rush another unit to City Hall in order to arrest the woman and the girl. Then word came that young students were stepping out at two different churches and many of the police units had to be rushed to those locations in order to surround those churches and arrest those students. Over 150 were arrested. The police surrounding the 16th Street Baptist Church approached all the exits and trapped the young demonstrators inside. The hundreds of parents and spectators watching outside were enraged at this sight. They were not trained in nonviolence like the students and, once again, began throwing rocks at the police. All of a sudden the situation became dangerous. All those trained in nonviolence were locked up inside the church, while spectators, among them hooligans armed with rocks, knives, and guns were becoming more and more angry at the police outside. One of the nonviolent leaders, James Bevel, realizing the danger and the possibility of a riot, managed to convince a policeman to lend him his bullhorn and announced. "Everybody get off this corner! If you're not going to demonstrate in a nonviolent way, then leave!"[721] The use of violence in a nonviolent movement is prescription for defeat. Everything King and the nonviolent army had achieved in the last several days could easily have been washed away by one police officer getting hurt by a bystander. One police officer being stabbed or shot would have put an end to the nonviolent struggle nationally. Bevel suspended all marches and activities. Martin Luther King announced a one-day moratorium on all activities and called Sunday a day of prayer and purification.

On Monday morning, Robert Kennedy's representative, Deputy Attorney General Burke Marshall, spent over two hours trying to convince King to cancel the afternoon demonstrations in order for negotiations to take place. But King refused to shut down the nonviolent movement in Birmingham when he had only a promise of negotiations. That morning, 2,000 spectators were across the street from 16th Street Baptist Church waiting for events to unfold. Rows of school buses were made ready for arrests. Inside the church, King was preaching nonviolence to his army. On his signal, 19 students marched out of the church, singing songs of freedom. As police began arresting them, they were seen singing and dancing as they were directed into the buses, while another group began to march outside. The arrests had become so routine that the police were merrily directing and waving the marchers into buses and paddy wagons. For the first time, many older people were seen amongst the children. For nearly two hours, African-Americans were walking out the church at a rate of ten per minute.[722] Over 800 were arrested, while hundreds managed to get by the police line and walked downtown to occupy lunch counters and sidewalks. At 2:40pm, bystanders again began to throw rocks at the police. Fearing the outbreak of a riot, King's aides rushed outside and announced "That's it for today!" and urged everyone to go home. Again, at the moment when they felt the impact of violence and the fear of defeat, King's army called for a strategic truce and withdrawal.

That evening, between 5,000 to 10,000 African-Americans crammed themselves into four churches across the city. To a packed audience, King announced, "I don't know how many of you would be able to write history books. But you are certainly making history, and you are experiencing history. And you will make it possible for historians of the future to write a marvelous chapter. Never in the history of this nation have so many people been arrested for the cause of freedom and human dignity!"[723] Then he continued to speak on the subject of love. "Now we say in this nonviolent movement that's you've got to love this white man." To this, a collective response of "Yes!" was heard from the crowd, "And when you rise to love on *this* level, you love those who don't move you. You love those that you don't like. You love those whose ways are distasteful to you. You love every man because God loves him!"[724]

That night, King and his aides changed strategies. They had learned that downtown business district had become a ghost town since the start of their nonviolent movement. Not only were African-American shoppers staying away, white shoppers were staying away as well. Before noon on the next day, several dozen students left 16th Street Baptist Church as decoys. The police officers, who had surrounded the church, focused on those students. Meanwhile hundreds of other students from all corners of the city began marching downtown. Soon over 600 were occupying downtown, lunch counters, and in the streets. Police commanders continued to expect students to march out of 16th Street Baptist Church. Reports of African-Americans all over the city carrying signs and banners indicating their pledge to nonviolence were heard on police radios. More and more police units were asked to leave the church and head to various parts of the city. As the police line thinned out more and more, all of a sudden the church doors opened and an endless stream of African-Americans marched right past the greatly outnumbered police. Soon the march turned into a sprint as if freedom was at hand. In the downtown area, scattered police officers were seen walking in between thousands of African-Americans. Lost in the sea of nonviolence, policemen were observed merely grabbing and ripping signs or tearing a banner.

CHAPTER 8

That morning, 75 white businessmen and city officials were meeting across the street from the stores with Burke Marshall. Throughout the morning they remained adamant about their position and refused to negotiate. When discussions were halted for lunch, these white leaders found themselves outside amongst a sea of African-Americans and unable to buy food at any lunch counters. African-Americans had jammed the sidewalks and streets in wild celebrations. Newspapers estimated as many as 3,000 people were demonstrating. Police commanders informed city leaders that they were no longer making arrests because the jails were full. Persuaded, hungry, and defeated, the civic leaders came back after lunch and agreed to King's demands.

When Martin Luther King was informed of the city leaders' announcement of compromise, he was filled with joy—like a great commander who's been told that his army has just captured the enemy flag. Yet he was very cautious and nervous. Mostly students were trained in nonviolence and without the police presence and with thousands of people on the streets, the situation could easily turn into violence and riots. If he called for people to leave, his followers would listen, but those who remained would be the hooligans and troublemakers. Despite the fears of chaos and violence that could be, counterproductively, sparked by joy and celebration, all those in the streets honored the principles of the nonviolent movement and not a single act of violence took place.

On Friday, May 10, eight days after the start of Birmingham campaign, a pledge of desegregation and agreements between Martin Luther King and the city's leaders was announced to Birmingham and the world. In one week, a marvelous chapter in history of nonviolence was written. America would no longer be the same. The campaign in Birmingham sent shock waves across America and emboldened 20 million African-Americans all over the nation. On June 11, a month after the agreement in Birmingham, President Kennedy announced a new civil rights proposal. Martin Luther King met with President Kennedy on June 22 and, on August 28 of that same year, over 250,000 Americans, most of whom were African-Americans, gathered in front of the Lincoln Memorial in Washington DC, where Martin Luther King delivered one of the most famous speeches in American history. For the first time, millions of Americans watched on television as hundreds of thousands marched in love and nonviolence for their rights and freedom. In less than eight years, from the time Rosa Parks refused to move from her seat on the bus in Montgomery, one of the most spectacular nonviolent movements in history had unfolded. "A social movement that only moves people is merely a revolt," Martin Luther King wrote. "A movement that changes both people and institutions is a revolution."[725] A great revolution in the hearts and minds of Americans took place in those years. King and other civil rights leaders again met with President Kennedy on September 19th. Two months later Kennedy was assassinated.

On July 2nd, the monumental Civil Rights Act of 1964, which was first proposed by John F. Kennedy was passed by both houses of Congress. Martin Luther King was present when Lyndon Johnson signed it into law. On December 10, 1964, Dr. Martin Luther King received the Nobel Peace Prize. He spent the next several years traveling tens of thousands of miles per month and making countless speeches advocating nonviolence and rights of the underprivileged and the poor. In one estimate, King traveled up to 780,000 miles per year, while giving speeches on and preaching nonviolence.[726] When riots broke out in the Watts neighborhood of Los Angeles in August of 1965, King flew out to urge calm and nonviolence. On August 12, 1965, he became one of the first people to condemn violence in Vietnam. He repeatedly called for peace in Vietnam through negotiations, admitting Communist China to the UN, and halting the bombing of North Vietnam.

His stance on Vietnam soon brought criticism from his own camp from some of his old friends. He was criticized for "not sticking to the business of civil-rights."[727] His criticism and opposition to the war in Vietnam was an important turning point for King.

He began to ask the question: who is Martin Luther King and what does he stand for? Is he a civil rights advocate or is he an advocate of nonviolence and love. If he stood for non-violence and love, could he remain silent about the war in Vietnam? The constant criticism soon engulfed him— until he decided to get away from all issues and better understand himself, his values, and principles. He moved away from politics for two months, during which time he meditated, prayed, and spent his time thinking about the issues of civil rights, the bombings of North Vietnam, and humanity. At the end of two months, he read an article on 'Children of Vietnam'. After reading it, his position was solidified and he announced to himself, "Never again will I be silent on an issue that is destroying the soul of our nation and destroying thousands and thousands of little children in Vietnam. I came to the conclusion that there is an existential moment in your life when you must decide to speak for yourself; nobody else can speak for you."[728] King was announcing that one cannot believe in nonviolence and love of his own

CHAPTER 8

people, yet be ignorant of suffering and violence of those thousands of miles away. A person who believes in nonviolence believes in humanity, he had concluded. This person cannot remain silent about violence under any circumstances.

On April 4, 1967, he delivered his first public antiwar speech in New York. In the speech, King declared, "there is... a very obvious and almost facile connection between the war in Vietnam and the struggle I and others have been waging in America." He then continued to tell of how the war in Vietnam had taken the focus of the country from his struggle on poverty towards "a society gone mad on war," and how America was taking "the black young men who had been crippled by our society and sending them eight thousand miles away to guarantee liberties in South East Asia which they had not found in southwest Georgia and East Harlem... I knew that I could never again raise my voice against the violence of the oppressed in the ghettos without having first spoken clearly to the greatest purveyor of violence in the world today: My own government. For the sake of those boys, for the sake of this government, for the sake of hundreds of thousands trembling under our violence, I cannot be silent."[729] [730]

"I am convinced that if we are to get on the right side of the world revolution, we as a nation must undergo a radical revolution of values. We must rapidly begin to shift from a thing-oriented society to a person-oriented society. When machines and computers, profit motives and property rights, are considered more important than people, the giant triplets of racism, extreme materialism, and militarism are incapable of being conquered... true compassion is more than flinging a coin to a beggar. It comes to see that an edifice which produces beggars needs restructuring."[731]

After taking his stance against the war in Vietnam, nearly every newspaper criticized it. He was attacked by blacks and whites alike. People threatened to withdrew their support of the Southern Christian Leadership Conference. A journalist once asked him, "Dr. King, don't you think you're going to have to change your position now because so many people are criticizing you?"[732] In a speech, he declared, "I do not believe our nation can be a moral leader of justice, equality, and democracy if it is trapped in the role of a self-appointed world policeman", then he again repeated his now famous line, "... injustice anywhere is a threat to justice everywhere."[733]

He later declared:

"I wish I was of draft age. I wish I did not have my ministerial exemption. I tell you this morning, I would not fight in the war in Vietnam. I'd go to jail before I do it... they can just as well get ready to convict me, because I'm going to say to young men, that if you feel it in your heart that this war is wrong, unjust, and objectionable, don't go and fight in it. Follow the path of Jesus Christ."[734]

King continued to travel the country and give speeches on nonviolence, compassion for the poor, peace in Vietnam, and love for humanity. In one week alone, in March of 1968, King delivered 35 speeches.

By the winter of 1968, King's focus, in addition to civil rights and the war in Vietnam, was on the poor. A mass rally was planned in Washington, as great as the civil rights rally of 1963 in order to raise awareness on the issue of poverty. King wrote:

"We have moved into an era where we are called upon to raise certain basic questions about the whole society. We are still called upon to give aid to the beggar who finds himself in misery and agony on life's highway. But one day, we must ask the question of whether an edifice which produces beggars must not be reconstructed and refurbish. That is where we are now."[735]

On March 1968, King went to Memphis in order to help the campaign of the Sanitation Department workers in that city who were trying to unionize. This small effort in Memphis was to be a testing ground for a larger scale national movement for the poor. But the protest march led by King soon turned to failure as participants turned violent, breaking store windows and looting merchandise. The march soon turned to riot. Police used tear gas to suppress the riots. More than fifty were injured and one black youth was fatally shot. Members of the National Guard were called in to impose a curfew on the city and over 120 were arrested.

Much like Gandhi's failed campaign in Bardoli more than 45 years earlier, the movement in Memphis failed when the participants turned to violence. King was devastated. He was depressed and heartbroken. A few days later, on April 3rd, he was scheduled to give a speech at the Masonic Temple in Memphis, but when the day of speech came, he was too heartbroken and did not see himself up to addressing the crowd. He asked Ralph Abernathy, his longtime friend and associate, to go the temple in his place. When Abernathy reached the Temple, he was moved by the presence of thousands of enthusiastic supporters of King and nonviolence who had not given up. He called King back and begged him to come. That evening, the jubilant crowd cheered and sang for King as the oratory genius and the greatest American speaker for and advocate of love and nonviolence delivered his last address.

CHAPTER 8

The speech is now famously known as 'I've Been to the Mountaintop'. It's as if he was aware of his impending death. He opened the speech by saying "I guess one of the great agonies of life is that we are constantly trying to finish that which is unfinishable." He then recalled the dream of Gandhi and how he was killed before he could realize his dream of a democratic, secular, and independent united India. He cited Woodrow Wilson and his dream of League of Nations before he died. He recalled Apostle Paul's dream of going to Spain and preaching Christianity, only to have been executed in Rome. He then told the crowd not to be discouraged. It is not the end goal that matters but our attempt to change ourselves and take a step towards the path that matters.

"Get somebody to be able to say about you: 'he may not have reached the highest height, he may not have realized all of his dreams, but he tried.'", he told the crowd, "isn't that a wonderful thing for somebody to say about you?"[736]

He reminded the crowd of the role of nonviolence in today's world.

"Men for years now have been talking about war and peace. But now, no longer can they just talk about it. It is no longer a choice between violence and nonviolence in this world; its nonviolence or nonexistence. That is where we are today. "[737]

That is perhaps also where Iran and Middle East is today.

He recalled his life and his memories of nonviolence. He reminded the crowd of those brave teenagers in Birmingham, proudly walking out of the Sixteenth Street Baptist Church day after day, and faced with police dogs and fire hoses. He recalled how they would sing, 'We shall overcome' as police arrested them by the hundreds. He recalled the great sit-ins at the lunch counters as tens of thousands of African-Americans across the South mobilized in a spectacular nonviolent movement to occupy lunch counters in so many cities. "And I knew that as they were sitting in," he told the crowd, "they were really standing up to for the best in the American Dream and taking the whole nation back to those great wells of democracy which were dug deep by the founding fathers in the Declaration of Independence and the Constitution."[738] He recalled the great gathering at Washington DC in 1963 where he was given the opportunity to tell America of his dream.

"Well, I don't know what will happen now; we've got some difficult days ahead. But it really doesn't matter with me now, because I've been to the mountaintop. And I don't mind. Like anybody, I would like to live a long life - longevity has its place. But I'm not concerned about that now. I just want to do God's will. And he's allowed me to go up to the mountain. And I've looked over, and I've seen the promised land. I may not get there with you. But I want you to know tonight, that we, as a people, will get to the promised land. And I'm happy tonight. I'm not worried about anything. I'm not fearing any man."[739]

When the desired result is conquest through violence, the goal must be achieved in one's lifetime. But when the goal is to serve humanity and the means of achieving that are through nonviolence, then conquest or victory for a person is meaningless; it is victory for one's people that becomes paramount. It is because of this principle of nonviolence that people like Gandhi and Martin Luther King never die. They change the human perception of victory from conquest to humanity, from enslavement to human rights. They don't look at personal achievements or personal victories in nonviolence. For them, human rights, nonviolence, and love are not end goals, but paths in a way of life to live every day. Their success does not come from their ability to disarm their enemy, but in their ability to disarm themselves and to find love within their own hearts.

When they do reach the moment when they no longer view their enemy with hatred and when they find the power of love inside them, they then become immortal. They no longer fear anyone or anything. Death becomes as beautiful as birth. They are like a scientist who has just made an immense discovery that he knows will change humanity. For that person, life is that discovery, love is that discovery, humanity is that discovery. Those throughout history who, through chance, have stumbled across the discovery of love, have had such immense transformations that they've spent their lives trying to teach others and the world of that greatest and the oldest of all discoveries. In thousands of different languages and, through tens of thousands of symbols and words, they've promised those around them heaven and earth, of moments of euphoria and eternity. Through pleadings, cries, pain, and suffering they have tried to tell us of their discovery. In speeches, in books, in poems, and in movies, they have told us about the power of love.

Martin Luther King was introduced to the power of love as a Southern Baptist, but, like countless others, this love, he was told, was personal, to be practiced only at certain venues and through certain rituals. At the age of 26 when he first learned about Gandhi, he found that this love is most powerful when it is applied as a pillar for social justice. Within 12 years, through this message, he changed America like no other person in the 20th-century. This message of love caused a tremendous social revolution, unimagined when

Rosa Parks first refused to give up her seat in Alabama. King touched the hearts of millions of Americans who heard him through the power of mass media. Now, the night before his death, while giving his last speech, like a prophet who has witnessed his own death, he finished his speech by reminding the audience of "life's final common denominator - that something we call death".[740] He told the crowd that he sometimes thought of his own death and his own funeral and told the audience what he would like to be said at his funeral.

"I'd like somebody to mention that day, that Martin Luther King Jr.. tried to give his life serving others.

I'd like somebody to mention that day, that Martin Luther King Jr., tried to love somebody.

I want you to say that day, that I tried to be right on the war question.

I want you to be able to say that day, that I did try to feed the hungry.

And I want you to be able to say that day, that I did try, in my life, to clothe those who were naked.

I want you to say, on that day, that I did try, in my life, to visit those who were in prison.

I want you to say that I tried to love and to serve humanity."[741]

That evening, in his hotel room, on a piece of torn paper, King had written out this quote and put it in his briefcase:

"Gandhi speaks to us: 'In the midst of death, life persists. In the midst of darkness, light persists.'" King then had written: "We're today in the midst of death and darkness. We can strengthen life and live by our personal acts by saying 'no' to violence, by saying 'yes' to life."[742]

On another piece of paper, he had written:

"The major problem of life is learning how to handle the costly interruptions, the door that slams shut, the plan that got sidetracked, the marriage that failed or that lovely poem that didn't get written because someone knocked on the door."[743]

Death of Martin Luther King

The next day, as he was standing on the second-floor balcony of his motel in Memphis, a convict with history of racist tendencies named James Earl Ray had spotted him from across the street through the telescopic lens of the powerful Remington Gamemaster Model 760 hunting rifle, one able to knock down a deer at a distance of more than 300 yards. This powerful, advanced, and precise tool of violence was the same type of rifle James Earl Ray had trained on during his time in the army. It was loaded with 150-grain bullet that could exert 2370 foot-pound of force at 100 yards.

While on balcony, King's driver told him to bring an overcoat because of the cold. Before King could turn around, a sound was heard; it sounded much like a firecracker. The powerful bullet that hit King on the right side of the neck lifted him off the ground and pinned him against the wall. His arms were spread wide from the impact as if he were placed on a cross. The bullet broke his lower cervical and upper thoracic spine and smashed his mandible (jaw) to pieces. It severed his right subclavian and carotid arteries as well as his jugular vein. It was the type of bullet, gun, and accuracy needed to bring down superman—and it did. Reverend Abernathy, who was King's confidant, associate and close friend since the Montgomery bus boycott, rushed out the motel room and held King's face in his hands. In that moment, King looked him in the eyes and tried to say a word, but couldn't.

He didn't need to. At 39 years of age, he had said more to the world than any other American in the 20th century. He told the world of the predicament of hundreds of millions of his ancestors enslaved for 300 years and the continued injustice of racism for a hundred years after. He had told the world of the power of love and nonviolence and was America's moral leader through one of the greatest social revolution in American history.

Gandhi had dreamed that his message of nonviolence and love would perhaps be reborn through the efforts of the 'American Negro'. Martin Luther King Jr. fulfilled that dream. At no other time in history was the Christian message of love as spoken by Jesus fulfilled at a societal level the way it was done under Martin Luther King Jr.'s leadership. For millions of Americans raised in racist families and indoctrinated with the belief in the superiority of whites over blacks, the eloquence, wisdom, and intelligence of King was the proof of that fallacy. He spoke for the millions of African-Americans who did not have the opportunity to get the schooling he did. He spoke of the injustice done to them, the ongoing racism and disrespect, their poverty, their pain, and their suffering. He told America of their desires, their hopes, their dreams— and their love. After his famous speech at the Lincoln Memorial in 1963, when he told America of his dream, President Kennedy, who had initially opposed the tremendous march on Washington, repeated to King, "I have a dream". His dream, the dream of the President's Irish ancestors, the dream of twenty million Americans, became the American dream, a country free of racism and injustice. It is still the dream of America

CHAPTER 8

and will continue to be the American dream for generations to come. Martin Luther King thought that this dream of justice, human rights, and democracy can only be found through love for life, humanity and a commitment to nonviolence. Today, we now know that it is no longer Martin Luther King Jr.'s dream or Gandhi's dream. It is not an American dream, a European dream, or an Indian dream. It is not a dream of philosophers, artists or athletes. It is the human dream. This dream is as alive today as it was during Martin Luther King's or Gandhi's lifetime. As long as this dream is alive in human hearts, those like Gandhi and Martin Luther King Jr. who told us of this dream are alive as well. Like Gandhi, Martin Luther King Jr., was not killed by an assassin, he found immortality long before the bullet shed his blood.

CHAPTER 9 NONVIOLENCE AS SCIENCE

"Gene Sharp begins his study with a simple premise that the means of maintaining power by an authoritarian regime is dependent on the obedience of the population."

Gene Sharp

After learning the lessons of Gandhi and Martin Luther King on nonviolent resistance for human rights, what can we say about the Iranian struggle? Where can Iranians start? How does a nonviolent movement and ultimately a nonviolent revolution take form? What tactics does it incorporate?

Where did countries like Ukraine, Czechoslovakia, and Poland begin? What strategies were used by the Serbs to overcome Milosevic and the Pilipino against Marcos? What were the formulas used by Lithuanians and Estonians?

Nonviolence in practice would have been difficult if each of these countries had to reread the numerous biographies of Gandhi or the many eyewitness accounts of the Civil Rights movement led by Martin Luther King. If scattered accounts such as these were all that was available, formulating and strategizing each country's nonviolent movement would have been an enormous task requiring ingenious minds such as those of Gandhi or Martin Luther King. But in 1973, the story of nonviolence forever changed. In a three volume set called *The Politics of Nonviolent Action,* Professor Gene Sharp of University of Massachusetts Dartmouth and Harvard University changed the art of nonviolence to the science of nonviolence.

Starting in 1949, Sharp began writing books on Gandhi, nonviolent defense, and dictatorships. He was perhaps most influenced by Gandhi's views on nonviolent strategy and struggle. In the three volume set published in 1973, professor Sharp formulated a theory of nonviolent struggle derived from nearly a century of collective experience of participants in nonviolent resistance. From then on, the science of nonviolent struggle was clearly presented, enabling a student of nonviolence to easily become familiar with the basics without having to go through volumes of anecdotal experience in the 20th-century. The works of Gene Sharp are perhaps one of the most important texts for any nonviolent activist. Nearly every nonviolent movement in the 1980's and 90's was somehow influenced by his writings, whether it was the successful Solidarity movement in Poland or the failed nonviolent attempt at Tiananmen Square. His formulas on nonviolent struggle were instrumental in the movements of Latvia, Estonia and Lithuania to secede from the failing Soviet Empire. Those same concepts were also used in the Velvet Revolution of Czechoslovakia, the Orange Revolution in Ukraine, the Rose Revolution in Georgia and the student led movement against Slobodan Milosevic. His books have been translated to over 27 languages.

In devising and formulating a strategy for Iran's nonviolent struggle, one needs to have a firm and deep understanding of history and philosophy as taught to us by Gandhi and Martin Luther King, but one also has to learn the science behind the philosophy through the study of Gene Sharp. Only through such a systematic study can one find a nonviolent solution to the current Iranian predicament, which fits both with developed theories of nonviolence as well as the current realities of confronting the extremely ruthless regime of today's Iran.

The opportunity to study the formulas of Gene Sharp gives Iranians the opportunity to formulate their own path.

The Politics of Nonviolent Action

Gene Sharp begins his study with a simple premise that the means of maintaining power by an authoritarian regime is dependent on the obedience of the population.[744] Every nonviolent movement against dictatorships must begin with understanding the roots of obedience in the population. Without this obedience in society, authoritarian regimes are powerless.

There are multiple reasons why people obey their authoritarian rulers. Sharp divides these reasons into seven. The first he calls obedience out of habit— people are in the habit of obeying their authoritarian rulers as generation after generation before them having done. This is not the sole cause of obedience, but an important one. The habit of obedience was an important element in the explanation of why Iranians jumped from one authoritarian regime in 1979 revolution into another. If it weren't for Khomeini, the same tendency, or conditioning to, habitual obedience may have been exploited by Rajavi's MKO party or Kianoori's Tudeh party. It just so happened that more people were in the habit of obeying a religious figure than other figures who were vying for power after the fall of the Shah.

Sharp identifies the second cause of obedience by the population as 'fear of sanctions', i.e. the fear of punishment. Fear of punishment is perhaps one of the most important causes of obedience by Iranians today. Punishment usually comes in the form of physical violence but can also can come in the form of economic deprivation or psychological pressure.

The third factor that he cites as a cause of obedience by the population is 'moral obligation'. Moral obligation is divided into various factors, including the belief that obeying the ruler is for the 'common good of society'. Moral obligation can also include the "identification of the law giver or the ruler with superhuman qualities, powers, or principles which make disobedience inconceivable."[745] This was an important element for millions who blindly obeyed Khomeini because they believed he possessed superhuman qualities and religious purity.

Other elements of obedience due to 'moral obligation' include 'legitimacy of the command'. This includes the belief that an order given must be obeyed because "it is seen as being in accordance with tradition, established law and constitution" and that "the ruler has obtained his position through the established procedure."[746] This is perhaps the most important cause of obedience by much of the reformist movement, including former President Mohammad Khatami, who has repeatedly declared that the laws of Islamic Republic must be obeyed in their struggle for reform and any action must be taken through legal procedures. The population is constantly told by the reformists that the regime and its constitution are not inhumane and in fact, those breaking the law of the Islamic Republic are at fault and need to be addressed. If people want to obtain freedom and democracy, the reformist have kept repeating, they must learn to obey the law first. This method of maintaining the population's obedience to the current regime continues to represent an important pillar for the support of the Islamic Republic.

The fourth important cause of obedience Gene Sharp states is for 'self – interest'. Individuals give their obedience to an authoritative regime because of the incentives offered by universities, nongovernmental institutions, scientific institutions, businesses, and government ministries. Promising money, positions, and prestige are important elements of securing obedience by the population.

The fifth explanation for obedience Sharp calls 'psychological identification with the ruler'. This means that people believe they share a common purpose with the authoritarian leadership and give their obedience because of this commonality. In Iran today, many former leftist activists support the anti-Western agenda of the regime because of their own deeply rooted hatred for United States and Western imperialism. In 1979, the various Marxist organizations were instrumental in advocating the population to vote 'yes' in the national referendum for the Islamic Republic because of this 'psychological identification with the ruler'. Similarly, after the post-revolutionary hostage crisis in Iran, many leftist political organizations directly or indirectly supported the hostage taking and gave their support to Khomeini because of their common goal of damaging United States interests in Iran and the Middle East.

The sixth explanation for obedience Gene Sharp labels as 'zones of indifference'. This is similar to obeying an authoritarian regime out of habit. In a "zone of indifference...each individual will accept orders without consciously questioning their authority".[747]

The last explanation for obedience amongst the population is the "absence of self-confidence among subjects". This is perhaps another important reason why the majority of Iranians continue to maintain their obedience even though those who are part of regime's forces are far outnumbered by the population. Any attempt to disobey will automatically raise the question "what next?" If this regime leaves, who will replace it? Another authoritarian regime handpicked and supported by the west? A leftist-Islamic group like the MKO, which tortures and imprisons even its own members? Certainly not the Iranian people! Iranians can't rule themselves! One often hears ordinary Iranians who are devout enemies of the regime claim that Iranians are not civilized enough to hold elections like those in the west. We are not civilized enough they claim to have free speech without tearing each other apart. Iranians, they say, are not civilized enough to respect each other's religion and have mature societal debates without insulting one another's beliefs. Since people living under such authoritarian regimes have "no strong will of their own, they accept that of their rulers, and sometimes prefer rulers who will direct their lives and relieve them of the task of making decisions." Furthermore, Gene Sharp points out, "the subjects may be disillusioned, exhausted [or] apathetic."[748]

These words were not written by a current scholar evaluating the situation in Iran; these are laws of humanity for any group of people imprisoned and subjugated for long period of time. The concepts of nonviolent action against dictatorships presented by Sharp in 1973 applies to any nationality, any dictatorship, any authoritarian regime, whether a religious dictatorship like the one today in Iran, a racially based dictatorship like that of South Africa, or one of numerous military dictatorships throughout history. Humanity is all the same anywhere in the world. Thus one can easily learn from other struggles across history and apply the lessons learned to Iran today. "The most important single quality of any government," wrote Gene Sharp, "without which it would not exist, must be the obedience and submission of its subjects."[749]

To understand this concept is to understand the roots of how nonviolent struggle works. In a nonviolence struggle, the theory relies on the basic premise that such obedience is not absolute. Ultimately, obedience is a decision. The decision to obey could be the result of threat of sanctions, such as fear of violence, imprisonment, loss of job, career, home, or respect. Or it could be due to any of the other six reasons given above. But ultimately, the decision to obey rests with the citizens. Even when a person is dragged off to prison, that person still has the capability to disobey. While in prison, the last option left to the individual to show his disobedience is a hunger strike. Hunger strikes by political prisoners are the ultimate symbolic acts to tell the ruling regime: You may pull me into a dungeon by physical force but I will not obey you voluntarily. You may imprison me by force but I refuse for people to believe that my imprisonment was an order which I obeyed. And I will not obey your orders even if your order is for me to eat. Such symbolic acts are the ultimate acts of disobedience. The essential concept of obedience that Gene Sharp points to is the fact that obedience is ultimately a decision made by an individual and thus is voluntary.

In a way, many of the five million Iranians who fled the country were carrying out an act of civil disobedience by announcing, "I will leave my home and my country because I refuse to stay and take orders from an authoritarian regime that I don't respect." There were millions of others who also would have left if given the means and opportunity to do so. For many of the five million who left the country, their immigration itself was an act of nonviolence. It was a symbolic gesture of defiance.

Gene Sharp tells us that, ultimately, one goal of nonviolent struggle is to help put an end to the voluntary obedience of the population. This change of will is considered a cornerstone of nonviolent struggle. Gene Sharp credits Gandhi for formulating this concept and summarizes Gandhi's strategy as a need for 1)a psychological change away from passive submission to self-respect and courage; 2)recognition by the subject that his assistance makes the regime possible; and 3)the building of a determination to withdraw cooperation and obedience.[750] "The change in the subjects' will may lead to their withdrawing from the ruler their service, cooperation, submission, and obedience." And, Sharp adds, "this withdrawal may occur among both the ordinary subjects and the ruler's agents and administrators."[751] "My speeches", Gandhi had said, "are intended to create 'disaffection' as such, that people might consider it a shame to assist or cooperate with a government that had forfeited all title to respect and support."[752]

Gene Sharp also emphasizes that nonviolent struggle does not mean inaction. Nonviolence is not passivity, submission, or cowardice.[753] Nonviolent struggle also differs from conciliation, verbal appeal to the opponent, compromise, or negotiation. "Conciliation and appeals are likely to consist of rational or emotional verbal efforts to bring about an opponent's agreement to something," writes Sharp, "while nonviolent action is not verbal--it consists of social, economic, and political activity of special types".[754] He gives an example of a worker asking for a pay raise. This verbal attempt to obtain increased wages is not nonviolent action. A worker refusing to work and going on strike is a form of nonviolent struggle. In practice, negotiation and verbal attempt at persuasion often precede a nonviolent struggle. The worker does not just walk off his job without first attempting to ask for a raise. Similarly, in a political struggle against an authoritarian regime, the opposition first attempts verbal persuasion and negotiation, but because such verbal attempt often do not bend the will of an authoritarian regime, compromise and negotiation turns into a nonviolent struggle. The reformist movement in Iran was an attempt at negotiation and compromise with the authoritarian regime. During the eight years of President Khatami's rule, people were repeatedly told by the reformist leadership not to undertake civil disobedience, to obey the laws of the Islamic Republic, and allow the leadership to negotiate a compromise with the Supreme Leader and the Revolutionary Guards. Every nonviolent movement undergoes this predictable route. Quite often, of course, this process does not go on for as long as it has in Iran's case, but nevertheless, an arduous nonviolent struggle could not be sustained unless people believe that an attempt at negotiations took place prior to the costly nonviolent struggle.

Sharp repeatedly emphasizes what Gandhi and others emphasized. "Nonviolent action is a means of combat, as is war," writes Sharp, "it involves the matching of forces and the waging of battles, requires wise strategy and tactics, and demands of its soldiers courage, discipline, and sacrifice."[755] Nonviolent action is not peaceful action. In a nonviolent struggle, the participants are not demanding peace, they are demanding their rights. Peace activists demand an end to violence regardless of whether one party continues to suppress the rights of another while a nonviolent activist struggles for human rights and not for peace.

In addition, Sharp reminds us of several other important principles of nonviolence taught by Gandhi and Martin Luther King. First, a nonviolent movement must avoid exaggerations, distortions, and falsehoods. In addition, feelings of hatred and intolerance should not be aroused.[756] Nonviolent movements also cannot act in secrecy. Truthfulness and openness are prerequisites. Sharp also tells us that nonviolent action in severely repressive regimes often employs political *jiu-jitsu*, where the violence of the opponent is used against itself. Through political *jiu-jitsu*, the brutality of the opponent is exposed to the largest degree and as tools available to the opposition.

With this knowledge in hand, how does a strategy for a nonviolent movement begin to form? What are the mechanisms and methods of a nonviolent strategy? Where does one even start when thinking about a nonviolent movement?

Sources of Power

Sharp identifies the power to rule by an authoritarian state as residing in sources within the society. In other words, the people themselves provide the consent and cooperation or the sources of power needed by the regime to rule. This cooperation can arise from the population's obedience or indifference, but it is a decision which can be reversed and one of the main strategic goals of a nonviolent struggle is the identification and elimination of 'sources of power' in a dictatorship. Later in 1990's, Robert Helvey described how these 'sources of power' find expression in a dictatorship through organizations and institutions called the 'Pillars of Support'.

Gene Sharp's sources of power include 1) 'authority' or the legitimacy to rule. This legitimacy can often be obtained through elections and referendums within the dictatorship. In Iran, the popular support for the 1979 revolution and the immediate referendum for the Islamic Republic are the main source of authority and legitimacy for the regime. Popular participation in elections in 1997 and 2009 are further instruments used as a source of authority and legitimacy for the Islamic Republic. 2) 'Human resources' is the second source of power for a dictatorship. These are the people, civil servants and soldiers providing support and cooperation to the Islamic Republic.

3) 'Skills and knowledge', Gene Sharp identifies as the third source of power. Skills and knowledge of the people allow the regime to function for its survival. Gene Sharp labeled the fourth source power for a dictatorship as the 4) 'Intangible factors'. In Iran, these factors include elements such as exploitation of religion, promotion of revolutionary values, cultural and religious habits, Iranian attitudes towards obedience and submission. 5) 'Material resources' which in Iran's case is gained mostly from the oil and less from taxes on the economy is the fifth source of power and 6) 'punishments or sanctions' against the population for unacceptable behavior is the sixth source of power according to Sharp's classification.

Robert Helvey described how Sharp's 'sources of power' find expression in organizations and institutions that are necessary for the day to day survival of the dictatorship and called these the 'pillars of support'.[757] Identification, neutralization and deactivation of 'pillars of support' of a dictatorship thus becomes the centerpiece of strategy for a nonviolent revolution. Helvey described institutions and organizations such as the police, military, civil servants, media, business community, youth, labor, religious organizations and NGOs as potential pillars of support for a dictatorship.

Pillars of support are often fluid and sometimes disguised and a detailed evaluation of Islamic Republic's 'pillars of support' is beyond the scope and intention of this book. But a cursory look at the Islamic Republic will show half a dozen institutions or sources of power that are easily identified as pillars for the regime and should become the focus for activists in search of Nowruz Revolution. The most important pillar of support for the regime and one of the main sources of brutality and fear in society is the institution of the Revolutionary Guards of the Islamic Republic. This institution whose mission and bylaws dictate using any violence necessary in defense of the Islamic Republic has become the greatest source of power within Iran and the main pillar of support for the regime. The *basij* whose hundreds of thousands of members are often recruited from mosques, schools and community centers across the country is another institution that serves as a pillar of support for the Islamic Republic.

The clergy and religious institutions across Iran including religious schools, religious community centers (*Husseiniye-ershad*) and Friday prayers are the third pillar of support for the Islamic Republic. Ironically, of the more than 300,000-500,000 clerics in Iran, only less than 10,000 are thought to be in Tehran and active political supporters of the regime. Remaining majority of clerics live under fear like the rest of society and provide their cooperation and obedience as a pillar for the regime.

Another pillar of support for the Islamic Republic is the reformist faction which includes powerful political parties, newspapers, former ministers and former presidents. The reformists who are a well-known opposition to Khamenei's system of repression in the Islamic Republic are on the other hand devout believers in the constitution as well as the revolutionary values of the Islamic Republic. The reformists are highly experienced in Iranian politics, are well financed with dozens of newspapers and even television stations. They advocate noncooperation with seculars and liberals in Iranian politics and refuse to participate in conferences and seminars with those advocating the dissolution (*enhelal*) of the Constitution of the Islamic Republic and the adoption of a Constitution based on Declaration of Human Rights. Reformists advocate obedience to the system and the laws of the Islamic Republic, disapprove of acts of noncooperation that can weaken the Islamic Republic and are one of the most important causes of division within the pro-democracy movement and perhaps one of the more important yet under recognized 'pillars of support' for the Islamic Republic.

Economically, there are three main 'pillars of support' which allow the functioning of the Islamic Republic. The most important is the National Iranian Oil Company whose thousands of engineers and technocrats, often unsympathetic to the current system, continue to do their duties because of fear of punishment or the fear of unknown consequences of their noncooperation. The second pillar of economic support is the '*bazaar*' whose tens of thousands of merchants include many that are close associates and families of the ruling clergy and who have benefited greatly from the Islamic Republic. Widespread noncooperation in the Iranian *bazaar* may be a difficult task and will probably not occur until the later neutralization of other pillars of support.

The third pillar of economic support for the system is the transportation industry. Billions of dollars worth of cargo are unloaded every month in the southern ports of Bandar Abbas, Bushehr, Bandar Mahshahr and Abadan and transported via trucks and railways to Tehran and other cities across Iran. The regime relies on this economic 'pillar of support' for its day-to-day functioning. Because of concentration of both the oil industry and the transportation industry in southern ports, politicization of society in the south leading to noncooperation can be the centerpiece of a successful strategy for Nowruz Revolution.

CHAPTER 9

Mechanisms of Nonviolent Action

Gene Sharp calls 'casting off fear' as one of the prerequisites of a nonviolent movement. As long as people are afraid, they cannot participate in a nonviolent struggle. In return, the ultimate goal of a despotic regime is to maintain a continued presence of fear in the hearts of its citizens. This is also the case in a military campaign. A great general first makes his army unafraid. An army in fear is an army bound for defeat. With fear, a soldier cannot enter the battlefield and face the possibility of death and injury. "Cowardice and ahimsa [nonviolence] do not go together any more than water and fire," wrote Gandhi.[758]

It is important for us to remember the psychological state of Iran today. Millions of Iranians are traumatized, perhaps suffering from post-traumatic stress disorder and live in constant state of fear and anxiety. There are enough parents and grandparents living in fear to dampen any effort of attempted nonviolent struggle that may possibly place them, their family or friends in a path of violence or lead to societal uncertainty. Thus an important first goal of Iran today is not to overcome the despotic regime; the first goal is to overcome fear. In addressing the millions of Indians living with fear, Gandhi wrote "we have to dispel fear from their hearts. On the day they shed all fear, India's fetters shall fall and she will be free."[759] Gandhi often argued that the use of nonviolence requires more bravery than the use of violence.[760]

Just as a soldier of violence is familiar with aims of victory, a soldier of nonviolence must also be familiar with the end goal of a nonviolent army. In a war waged through violence, victory comes when every single enemy soldier has succumbed to one of three end results. There are those who surrender, those who are wounded, and those who are killed. In nonviolence, the end results for the enemy is far different. You don't intend to kill the enemy, injure them or harm them in any form. Gene Sharp categorizes the mechanisms of nonviolent action into one of four means.

The first mechanism of nonviolent action is through 'conversion' where a pillar of support in the enemy camp changes its view and ceases support for the dictatorship. Reformists who struggle for and advocate the survival of the Islamic Republic are perhaps the most easily identified group who can potentially be 'converted' into supporters of democracy and human rights. Reformists who often believe that a religious government is *fait accompli* of Iran, are an important group who represent hurdles and challenges against the Islamic Republic and represent an important pillar of support for the regime.

More often however, it is ordinary and average Iranians who need to be inwardly changed. They need to be converted into individuals who believe in human rights above all other rights. They need to believe that they are not subjects of any religious figures or institutions. They need to be converted and persuaded that they were born free and they must always be free, that their rights as a woman must be equal to that of a man, that their rights as a Sunni, Christian, Jew, Atheist, Bahai, Gay or Lesbian must be equal to a an Ayatollah. In this process, ordinary Iranians must be persuaded that human rights, freedom of expression and separation of religious institutions from government are the pillars of any democracy and the basic tenets for the goals of a nonviolent revolution.

Those who fall in the category of 'conversion' also include Iranians who oppose the regime, yet who've (mistakenly) learned through Iran's legacy of violence that bloodshed is the only solution to their predicaments. The greatest challenge is to convert and persuade this group of Iranians to believe in nonviolence, human rights and democracy as the solution to their predicaments.

The second mechanism of nonviolent action is through 'accommodation'. Through 'accommodation', a pillar of support realizes that your intentions are not threatening to them and in turn, their economic and social demands will be met after the victory of nonviolent forces. "In accommodation", write Gene Sharp, "the opponent is neither converted nor nonviolently coerced; yet there are elements of both involved in his decision to grant concessions to the nonviolence actionists."[761] In 'accommodation', the opponent has not necessarily changed his mind, but now believes that it's best to yield to demands of a nonviolent army than to continue their fight. "The main reason for this willingness to yield", writes Sharp, "is the changed social situation produced by the nonviolent action."[762] One of the main dynamics of this change in point of view is the realization by members of this group that violent repression is no longer appropriate and is not to their benefit. To get to this point, the nonviolent movement has proven its willingness not to harm or hurt such individuals in the democratic society of tomorrow. The members of this group will then join the nonviolent movement when their fears are met. These fears often mean guaranteeing their economic and social security in face of change.

Such individuals may include members and families of the armed forces and those who have respectable and prestigious jobs in various governmental institutions. In addition, there are many, including the powerful economic force of Iranian bazaar, who have gained economic strength and wealth under the current system and who fear reprisals and loss of those economic gains in the event of a nonviolent revolution. In the nonviolent struggle, they must be reassured that the intended changes are not vindictive. Iranians do not intend to punish or take revenge on people who have benefited in the past. For this group of Iranians, their beliefs in the survival of the Islamic Republic, in the office of Supreme Leader or the Guardian Council is not as great as their interest in their social and economic security.

Then there is that small minority which will never 'convert' or 'accommodate'. Gene Sharp categorizes them as those who are 'coerced' into your position through nonviolent pressure. In this group, the opponent has not changed his mind and will refuse to surrender. In a nonviolent struggle, the end goal is to make them unable to fight by converting or accommodating all those who were previously supporting them followed by overwhelming nonviolent action. Gene Sharp describes nonviolent 'coercion' taking place through one of three ways. 1) the defiance of the nonviolent movement may become too widespread and massive to be controlled by the opponent's repression; 2) the noncooperation and defiance may make it impossible for the social, economic, and political systems to operate unless the actionists' demands are achieved; 3) even the opponent's ability to apply repression may be undermined and may at times dissolve.[763] In 'nonviolent change through coercion', the opponent continues to believe in his ideology but no longer has the power to defeat the forces of nonviolence. Such individuals who comprise the families and relatives of those ideologically sworn to principles of the Islamic Republic form the main ideological pillar for the system and are often the last and the most difficult challenge to a nonviolent revolution.

Lastly, when the balance of power has shifted with large number of population 'converted' or 'accommodated' and others 'coerced', the mechanism of 'disintegration' takes place.

Methods of Nonviolent Action

In his 1973 work, Gene Sharp also researched and detailed all the methods of nonviolent struggle invented throughout history ranging from the peasants of Sicily to those invented in tribes of Africa to the tremendous wealth of knowledge learned through the labor movements of nineteenth and twentieth century to those invented by Gandhi and King into 198 different groups, classified under three broad categories. This classification serves as a categorized 'toolkit'—a compilation of methods from which Iranians and any other nonviolent movement can look through on the path for nonviolent revolution. In order for Iranians to understand what methods are available to them, they must be familiar how methods of nonviolent action are classified.

Methods of Nonviolent Intervention

Of the 198 different methods in three major classes, 41 of the methods Sharp labeled as 'Methods of Nonviolent Intervention'. This group comprises the most dangerous methods of nonviolent action and some of them are popularly known as 'occupy' methods. In this group of actions, nonviolent participants directly intervene and interrupt the opponent's plan without the use of violence. The lunch counter sit-ins in the American South, in which participants would sit and refused to move are an example of a method that falls into this category. In that example, the students faced imprisonment and beating while they attempted to directly intervene in face of severe repression. These methods are more offensively directed and require the greatest courage and the participation of the most psychologically healthy members of a nonviolent struggle. The participant in these forms of nonviolent struggle must be free of fear.

Gene Sharp separates these 41 methods of 'Nonviolent Intervention' into five subclasses of psychological, physical, social, economic and political. The more famous and well-known case of psychological intervention is through self-suffering, such as the hunger strikes or Satyagrahic fasts of Gandhi where he would place tremendous psychological pressure on society. Other types of 'Nonviolent Intervention' include physical interventions such as 'sit-ins', 'stand-ins' and 'occupy' methods. In this group of methods, the participants occupy a building or other forbidden spaces as a form of protest. The nonviolent takeover of Tahrir Square in Cairo will perhaps become a classic example of this method as well as the world-wide 'occupy movement' for economic justice. Another form is a nonviolent raid, in which the participants attempt to invade a strategic or symbolic place through sheer nonviolent physical force. A more famous example of this was the attempt by the Indians to take over the British-run salt factory, which led to one of the more violent reactions by the British-led soldiers. Such attempts at nonviolent physical interventions are futile against a regime that will not hesitate to use the most violent methods of repression. Another category within 'Nonviolent Intervention' is nonviolent social intervention. This requires a nonviolent action that breaks a symbolic social norm. As an example, Gene Sharp offers the case of American abolitionists in 1830's who deliberately associated with black Americans. An Antislavery Convention of American Women in 1838 adopted a resolution which encouraged women to identify with these oppressed Americans by inviting them to participate in services in their churches, walking with them in the streets, visiting them in their homes, and encouraging them to visit with the participants. They were encouraging the participants to accept the blacks as they did their 'fellow white citizens'.[764] Such direct defiance of social norms and nonviolent intervention risked a severe violent backlash against women by white slave owners and the overall racist establishment. This form of intervention again carries with it great risks for violent reprisal. An example of this would be if the women in Iran were to remove their symbolic mandatory head scarves as a symbolic nonviolent social intervention. Such an action would elicit a violent reprisal by the vigilantes and security forces and risks the infliction of considerable violence on those women. If however carried out, such a nonviolent action by the women would fall into this category.

Another form of nonviolent 'social intervention' is the 'overloading of facilities' as a form of protest. In this method, the population demands services from an institution or government facility far beyond the institution's capacity in an attempt to cripple the system.

'Economic Intervention' also belongs in this category. 'Stay-in strike' falls into this category, in instances in which the workers not only refuse to work, but also refuse to leave the factory or their workplace. Their refusal to work is not a method of intervention, but their refusal to leave the factory is a form of intervention that is included in this category. Another method that Gene Sharp mentions as part of this group is 'Nonviolent Land Seizure' in which people, through nonviolent means, occupy and take over a piece of land not owned by them. Sharp cites examples of nonviolent land seizure by the peasants in Southern Italy and Sicily in 1919 and 1920. Many other examples are also cited of nonviolent land seizures by peasants in South America. Other forms of 'Nonviolent Economic Intervention' include deliberate defiance of an economic blockade or sanctions. All these methods carry great risks for the participants.

The last group of methods within nonviolent intervention include 'Nonviolent Political Intervention'. Gene Sharp places six different methods in this sub-category. One of these methods is 'seeking imprisonment' by a large number of participants, with the intent of overloading the prison system. This method was used by both Gandhi and Martin Luther King as a method of nonviolent action. The Islamic Republic has learned to use terrorizing methods of imprisonment such as solitary confinement, torture, rape, secret locations, and even executions in order to dissuade such an attempt by the population. Iranian prisons are notoriously frightening for a population already steeped in fear and trauma from violence. Disclosing the identities of secret agents also falls into this category of nonviolent political intervention. This method is successfully carried out today on the internet and Facebook with number of sites posting the names, identity and addresses of Iranian security officers responsible for beatings and torture. Other methods include creating a dual or parallel government within the regime.

The category of 'Nonviolent Intervention' with six different sub-categories and forty-one methods, overall, carry tremendous risk for violent reprisal by a regime that will not hesitate to prolong the prevailing state of fear and anxiety through the most ruthless forms of violence.

Nonviolent Methods through Noncooperation

The second category of nonviolent action consists of all those actions of nonviolence that stem from an act of 'noncooperation'. This category of 'noncooperation' is the largest category of selected methods for a nonviolent movement. Gene Sharp divides these actions into four groups. The first he calls 'Methods of Social Noncooperation'. This category includes acts of noncooperation with social events, customs and institutions as well as withdrawal from participation in social systems. The next two categories are both forms of 'Economic Noncooperation'. The first category includes methods of economic boycotts and the second category includes the methods of economic strikes. The last category of 'noncooperation' consists of the methods of Political Noncooperation.

Methods of Social Noncooperation include 'Ostracism of Persons'. In this form of noncooperation, those persons deemed supporters or collaborators of the regime are socially boycotted. The term Ostracism comes from ancient Greece where individuals were banished from Athens through a form of voting by citizens. During the American Revolution, royalists who supported the continued British occupation were socially boycotted and were called 'infamous Betrayers of Their Country'.[765] During the 1901 occupation of Finland by czarist Russia, the Finn opposition issued declarations against those accommodating the Russians and instructed people to treat them in "daily life like carriers of the plague or violent criminals." According to a published opposition bulletin, "Contacts between relatives and friends were broken off if they happened to take opposite sides in the conflict; they did their shopping in different stores... in one town, a new secondary school was founded because families belonging to opposite political camps did not want their children to attend the same institution."[766] In the Indian national movement, social noncooperation was used constantly to remind the Indian supporters of the British of their shameful anti-Indian behavior. In the 1930 campaign in India, the All-India Working Committee of the Congress issued a statement advocating a social boycott of all government officials. [767]

In social noncooperation, great care must be taken not to induce feelings of hatred and resentment against persons being boycotted. Inevitably, and unfortunately, this form of boycott leads to feelings of hatred and resentment, emotions that may lead to violence. Gandhi spoke of social noncooperation as an act that may be performed depending on the spirit and the manner it is carried out. He was concerned about feelings of hatred and vindictiveness in this form of noncooperation. Unfortunately, such emotions are inevitable when there's so much pain. If carried out by Iranians today, such a method of nonviolence is highly likely to arouse feelings of vindictiveness.

Other forms of Social Noncooperation categorized by Sharp include refusal to engage in sexual relationships. This is when women decide to boycott any form of sexual relationship with their husbands until their demands are met. Around the year 1600, in response to continued warfare by the tribal men, women of Iroquois Native American tribe decided to undertake this form of noncooperation and to boycott lovemaking and childbearing until "men conceded to them the power to decide upon war and peace." The movement was instantly successful and women obtained a great victory through a completely nonviolent method. [768] In December of 1963, the African women of Southern Rhodesia won another victory through this form of social noncooperation by refusing sexual relations with their husbands until outbreak of bombings and explosions had ceased.

In the sad societal and cultural state of Iran today, sexual relation by countless women is no longer a pleasurable act of choice, but a forced act of economic or legal necessity. Far too many Iranian women are forced into sexual relationships against their will in marriages solely out of economic necessity; others are forced into sexual relations out of wedlock or forced into sexual relations in the form of prostitution. Such a form of social boycott by women, when the threat of violence is readily used to compel sexual acts is not feasible for the current environment of Iranians.

Other category of social non-cooperation includes the suspension of social and sports activities. This form of noncooperation will close the doors to the only forms of recreation and methods of psychological healing available to the young. In fact, the regime struggles to extirpate many forms of cultural and social events. In addition, the regime, through indirect psychological pressures, attempts to ensure that certain sport activities such as soccer do not become popular enough to be used as symbolic gestures of antigovernment sentiment. In today's Iranian predicament, such methods of social noncooperation can hurt the population more than the regime.

Methods of Economic Noncooperation: Economic Boycott

Economic boycott is perhaps one of the most widely used forms of noncooperation. Gandhi's insistence that Indians should boycott British-made textiles was a great example of this form of noncooperation. The great Iranian boycott of tobacco in 1890 after Nasser-al- Din Shah granted tobacco concessions to the British is a well-known case of economic boycott in Iranian history. During this tobacco boycott against Shah's concession, even the women of his haram refused to smoke their hookas. In 1892, the Shah was forced to repeal the concession.

There are countless examples and various forms of economic noncooperation. These include boycotting of single consumer good to boycott of consumer goods from a particular nation. In addition, this category includes the refusal of workers to use particular supplies from a particular manufacturer. Refusal of the producer to sell or deliver a certain product is also within this category. Withdrawal of bank deposits and boycotting of banking institutions, refusal to pay fees, dues, or debt, and even refusal to handle a government's money are all within this category.

All these forms of boycott have the potential to hurt the Iranian citizens far more than their potential to make a difference as an economic force or as symbolic gesture. Iranians will have a difficult time advocating any form of economic noncooperation that has the potential to cause economic suffering on a population already in profound financial despair and resisting a regime that depends on oil exports and not on the economic support of the population for its survival.

CHAPTER 9

Methods of Economic Noncooperation : The Strike

The refusal to continue economic cooperation, known as 'the strike' is perhaps the most widely form of nonviolent struggle in the 20th-century. Sharp segments this group into agricultural strikes by the peasants and farm laborers, strikes by special groups such as prisoners, professionals or forced laborers, strikes within particular industries such as mining, printing, or petrochemical, sympathetic strikes of some workers in support of other fellow workers, 'slow-down' strikes by the workers in which laborers continue to work, but at a much slower pace or 'working-to-rule' strike, in which laborers meticulously follow every detail and every rule in the workplace to such an extent that it paralyzes production. This category also includes multi-industry strikes through which economic life in a given area is brought to a halt. It also includes Gandhi's practice of *'hartal'* as a category in which economic life is brought to a standstill for a limited duration such as 24 or 48 hours through a voluntary strike by merchants and shopkeepers.

These forms of economic noncooperation also place great financial pressure on the participants. In addition, when labor strikes are used as political tools, laborers lose an important form of protest, one traditionally used to file grievances and seek redress for their salary or their conditions. In this environment, any form of strike intended to improve the work conditions of the workers is violently and harshly suppressed by the regime. In 2005, the regime violently suppressed the labor strike by The Syndicate of Workers of Tehran and Suburbs Bus Company (*Sherkat-e Vahed*) after the regime perceived the strike as a political move and not a demand for wage increase. Dozens of bus drivers were subsequently arrested, severely beaten, and tortured. Hassan Osonlu, the labor leader was severely tortured and is still in prison.

Methods of Political Noncooperation

The last category within 'noncooperation' is Political Noncooperation. Thirty-eight different methods were categorized by Gene Sharp in this category. Most notable of these is the 'Boycott of Legislative Bodies'. "In undemocratic systems," Sharp writes, "legislative bodies may be used to bolster the regime's prestige and influence and to offer the appearance of democracy."[769] It's as if Sharp, in 1973, was writing about how the *Majles* and Presidencies of Islamic Republic function. The opposition to a regime may then decide to temporarily or permanently boycott such legislative bodies and elections. This can come through the population boycotting the election process and refusing to participate or the opposition groups refusing to field candidates in order to publicize the undemocratic nature of the elections.

The false appearance of democracy within the Islamic Republic, through undemocratic elections, where thousands of candidates are vetted by the Supreme Leader and Guardian Councils are well known. The secular-democratic groups and organizations have nearly always used this form of nonviolent action through their repeated boycott of elections in the Islamic Republic.

Citizens have also widely boycotted elections in the Islamic Republic. Most famous of such form of noncooperation was the near universal boycott of March 2012 parliamentary elections. Again, this call for a boycott of elections is a form of nonviolent struggle that falls within this category.

Other forms of political noncooperation include refusing to assist the government by serving as a government official or employee. In this method, the individual decides not to hold any government assigned position, whether administrative, political, or technocratic. This method has been used since the 1979 revolution by hundreds of thousands of Iranians. There are a large number of Iranians who decided to leave the country and not work for the government.

Other forms of Political Noncooperation include the boycott of government agencies, ministries and educational institutions. Such a boycott can also be limited in its effect in Iran because of the often dependency of the population on such institutions and not the dependence of these institutions on the people.

Another form of political noncooperation that is perhaps most well known is civil disobedience of 'illegitimate laws'. This form, which was the main argument for Thoreau and a major weapon for Gandhi and Martin Luther King, requires the active breaking of illegitimate laws by the population. The justification of civil disobedience is based on "a conviction that obedience would make one an accomplice to an immoral or unjust act or one which is seen to be, in the last analysis, itself illegal."[770] In Gandhi's view, Civil Disobedience could be used to 1) Redress a local wrong 2) As a means of self-sacrifice to arouse people's awareness and conscience about some particular wrong or 3) Focus on a particular issue as a contribution to a wider political struggle.[771] Gandhi regarded civil disobedience as an "inherent right of a citizen and any attempt to put it down was an 'attempt to imprison the conscience'".[772] In Gandhi's view, civil disobedience is dangerous to an autocratic state, but harmless in a democracy that is willing to submit to the will of public opinion. [773]

Other forms of political noncooperation by other nations include the withholding of diplomatic recognition, cancelation of diplomatic events, and expulsion from international organizations.

The Methods of Nonviolent Protest and Persuasion

The third great category, which comprises the remaining methods of nonviolent methods, is called 'Nonviolent Change through Protest and Persuasion". Gene Sharp defines this category as a "class which includes a large number of methods which are mainly symbolic acts of peaceful opposition or of attempted persuasion, extending beyond verbal expressions but stopping short of noncooperation or nonviolent intervention."[774] He further defines an act of protest or persuasion as one "intended primarily to influence the *opponent*- by arousing attention and publicity for the issue and thereby, it is hoped, support, which may convince him to accept the change; or by warning him of the depth or extent of feeling on the issue which is likely to lead to more severe action if a change is not made."[775] The two key components for these methods of nonviolent action are the symbolic acts and the communication of those acts to others. A key element to note is that such acts go beyond 'personal verbal expressions of opinion' and become symbolic corporate expressions of opinion of a group of people. Sharp presents case histories of 54 different methods within this category and groups them into 10 subclasses.

The first subclass within this category is acts of 'Formal Statement'. Within this subclass are methods that have been widely used by Iranians in the last 100 years and with which Iranians are most familiar. Letters of opposition or support signed by groups of individuals, 'open letters' intended to influence the general public or the supporters of the regime, declarations by organizations and institutions, signed public statements, public speeches, and group or mass petitions fall within this category.

Other methods of nonviolent change through 'protest and persuasion' include 'picketing' which is a familiar sight in many countries in which workers are on strike. A worker going on a strike is applying pressure through economic noncooperation, but is also using methods of persuasion by holding up placards and signs outside the factory or business location in order to influence the opinions of his employer or the public. In severely repressive regimes, a laborer may choose to go on strike to apply economic noncooperation and may choose to avoid 'picketing' to minimize regime's dangerous retaliation. Other symbolic acts within this category are processions of individuals and groups in the form of marches, parades, religious processions, and motorcades. Assemblies of protest or support, protest meetings, walkouts, and even turning one's back have been historically used as methods which fall in this category.

Nonviolent change using 'symbolic acts'

Within the category of 'nonviolent change through protest and persuasion', there are a group of actions that were used to a limited extent by Iranians in the last several years which while incurring minimal psychological risk for the participants, are powerful enough for cultural and political transformation.

This last category involves using 'symbolic acts'. In categorizing the various methods in this group, in addition to use of symbolic flags and wearing symbolic colors, Gene Sharp includes other acts of protest and persuasion, including symbolic prayer and worship, symbolic lights such as torches and candles and symbolic displays of portraits. There are many variations—symbolic displaying of signs, symbolic sounds, symbolic visuals, humorous skits and pranks by artists and comedians, symbolic performances of music and plays by actors and musicians singing songs of symbolic connotation, mourning the death of an individual as a symbolic gesture, and even creating mock funerals. The essence of this category lies in the use of symbolic acts.

National celebrations, in particular Nowruz celebrations would fall within this category. In addition to their potential as a acts of protest, celebrations which contain symbolic acts of kindness, charity, and rebirth are also societal tools which can help shape and transform human cultures. Furthermore, as we will learn in the next chapter, a celebration can also have a psychological function as a powerful instrument of psychological healing for families and communities and as a tool creating a space where fear is reduced. As symbolic acts, Nowruz and other Iranian celebrations can become instruments against the multifaceted challenge of cultural, political and psychological violence facing Iranians.

Before that, there were still several other important developments in nonviolence which we still need to review.

CHAPTER 9

***

The Birth of Leaderless Revolutions - Philippines

As this generation's activist interested in nonviolent struggle in Iran explores the history of nonviolence and heroism under Gandhi and Martin Luther King, he or she will wonder who will be the leader of Iran's nonviolent struggle. How and where will a Gandhi or a Martin Luther King arise for Iranians? What is the nature and theory of leadership in modern nonviolent struggles for democracy?

Some people see Gandhi and King as natural born charismatic leaders, who are the coincidences of history and are not seen in today's Iranian struggle. They see such individuals as once-in-a-century exceptions from the rest of humanity, heroes who become the necessary leaders of a generation. Aside from the absence of such a figure, even if a Gandhi is born in Iran, Iranians are so terrified of the possibility that this Gandhi may turn into a Khomeini that they automatically shun such a figure. With this cultural skepticism of leadership for Iranians, where will the necessary leadership arise to lead Iranians in their struggle?

The story of nonviolent struggle in Philippines perhaps provides one answer. In reviewing those events, we learn of the first successful nonviolent revolution without a charismatic leader like Gandhi or Martin Luther King, a revolution which opened the door for other leaderless revolutions in the last few decades. The Filipinos thought the world that modern nonviolent movements for democracy are not led by individuals, but are led by principles of nonviolence, democracy and human rights, which act as guiding lights for such movement. In such revolutions, it is the concept of 'Principle Based Leadership' that forms the core of decision-making. In this form of leadership, no single leader gives birth to a movement; tens of thousands of leaders arise, each of whom is led by the principles inspiring the movement. The notion of Principal Based Leadership is a concept that Iranians must understand, because they cannot expect one individual or political party to guide them on the path of nonviolence for Iran; tens of thousands of ordinary Iranians, led by principles, must each become the leaders in the struggle.

The world is accustomed to having a leader direct an army in war; this traditional concept of leadership demands that people put their faith and trust in this leader and do what he or she tells them to do. This is the military concept of leadership, born out of centuries of warfare. Orders are given from above, and soldiers carry out these orders. Unfortunately, most Iranians, when striving for democracy, look for this form of military leadership. In their efforts to mount a campaign for democracy, Iranians evaluate major figures in the country's political spectrum and try, unsuccessfully, to identify those who have the potential to lead them away from the current despotic regime. In other words, they hope for a charismatic leader to come along, hoping this new leader will somehow be more like Gandhi and show them the way out of the darkness of oppression. But a modern nonviolent struggle for democracy cannot put its faith in one person or political party.

What Gandhi did was merely introduce the people of India to the *principles* of nonviolence. Martin Luther King did the same for African-Americans in the United States. Their greatness was due to their fervent belief that it is through these principles of nonviolence which truth is sought, from which justice is found, giving rise to human rights and democracy. These leaders thought humanity that the end goals of achieving democracy can be derived from the truth while the mechanisms and methods of a nonviolent struggle are also born from the same truth. For them, the ends of achieving democracy by other than non-violent means could not justify the means. The means of a nonviolent struggle and ends were based on principles and one and the same.

In opposing the military form of leadership and taking action in a way similar to a nonviolent movement, democracies don't depend on individuals leading their citizens; but on principles of democracy as guiding lights for the society. Individuals and political parties, in turn, each present platforms and plans that offer ways to achieve a more perfect society based on these guiding principles. Thus, in a democracy, presidents and prime ministers are expected to carry out certain duties while following the principles of democracy set forth in their nation's constitution. Similarly, campaigns for nonviolence, human rights or democracy are led by their respective principles, while individuals, groups, and political parties each attempt to present various ideas and techniques that are in accord with those beliefs and principles.

In Principle-Led democracies, ultimately the principles of democracy prevail, and those who are in positions of trust and authority are just as subject to the restraints of democratic principles as any other citizen. Sooner or later, those who betray the trust reposed in them will be sanctioned or voted out of office. Similarly, in a nonviolent struggle, those who betray the principles of nonviolence, democracy, or human rights will lose the trust placed in them and will be discredited as central figures of the movement by the movement itself.

In the Philippines, the world was taught a lesson in the use of 'Principle Based Leadership' in a nonviolent revolution. We can perhaps learn more about this form of leadership when we study the story of 'People's Power' revolution in Philippines in more detail.

***

In 1907, Filipinos voted for the first time for their representatives. Yet, much like many other elections at the turn-of-the-century, these elections did not really signify that the country was a true democracy. The Philippines, after the Spanish-American war, was, in effect, together with Puerto Rico a territory of the United States and these elections were largely symbolic and gave a limited measure of local decision-making to the Filipinos. Filipinos continued their dependent relationship with the United States for the next several decades until after World War II when they obtained their independence. Yet this independence did not mean freedom or democracy. The postwar regimes in the Philippines were mostly ruthless, violent dictators, who controlled the population with the support of the United States, while waging continuous wars against violent rebels, separatists, Marxist militias, and guerillas. In 1965, Ferdinand Marcos won the presidency and began major infrastructure development projects. He built more roads and schools than any of his predecessors and, with the economic aid from the United States, brought more prosperity to the Filipinos than ever before .

In 1969, Marcos was elected for a second term and further consolidated his grasp on the military and the power structure. The corruption within his administration and the legislature was rampant in 1970s and the government ruthlessly suppressed discontented farmers and workers. Marcos and his close associates amassed billions of dollars that were extracted, in large measure, from poor and underprivileged Filipinos and parked the money in various offshore banks. His political opponents were brutally crushed. Between September 1972 when martial law was proclaimed and 1977, over 60,000 political arrests were made in the Philippines.[776] The corruption and the gap between his and the small group of elite families' wealth and the poor population served to enhance the power and appeal of extremist, revolutionary groups, most of which had Communist orientations.

In early 1970s, violent disobedience and resistance in Philippines grew at a rapid pace. The Communist Party of Philippines formed the New People's Army. The separationist Moro National Liberation Front was waging a violent struggle for a Muslim state in Mindanao. Faced with spreading lawlessness and violence, Marcos declared martial law on September 21, 1972. He closed down the Congress, brought the media under his control, and began a campaign of arrests and imprisonment of his opponents. One of them was a leading Senator and opposition activist, Benigno 'Ninoy' Aquino Jr.

***

Born into a wealthy Filipino family, at the age of 17 Aquino was the youngest correspondent to cover the Korean War for the *Manila Times*. Because of his brilliant journalism and war coverage, he became the youngest person to be given the Philippines Legion of Honor award by the president when he was 18. At the age of 21, he became a close adviser to then Secretary of Defense in Philippines; Aquino was the youngest person ever to hold this position. He had briefly studied law then switched to journalism. In 1954, he was assigned to act as a personal emissary for the President during negotiations with Luis Taruc, the leader of the militant arm of the Philippines Marxist resistance. After four months of negotiations, the 22-year-old Aquino was credited for Taruc's unconditional surrender signifying his brilliance at such a young age. He became the mayor of Concepcion in the same year, the youngest person ever to hold such a position in Philippines. He also married his wife, Corazon, in the same year.

In 1961, at the age of 29, he became the governor of Tarlac, again the youngest person ever to hold such a position. In 1967, at the age of 34 he became the youngest elected senator in Philippine history. As a young senator, he became the most ardent critic of the Marcos regime. Because of his courage and his brilliant critique of the Marcos regime, he was named the most outstanding senator by *Philippines Free Press* magazine. At the time, he was the most popular candidate for the presidency in Philippines and the most likely successor to Marcos, who was serving his second and last term.

On August 21, 1971, thousands gathered for Ninoy Aquino's nighttime liberation party rally at Plaza Miranda across from a historic Spanish church. There, Aquino was planning to speak out candidly about and offer proof of the graft and corruption of Marcos. At 9:13pm, just minutes after the party leader began to speak, two bombs exploded. Three seconds later, another

CHAPTER 9

bomb hurled dozens of chairs and people into the air. [777] Nine people were dead. More than a hundred were wounded. Chaos followed as the participants and the candidates ran for safety. The violence, which was probably organized by Marcos, was used as an excuse by the regime to clamp down on its opponents. A wave of arrests began in 1972 and Marcos declared martial law. One of the first people to be arrested on trumped up charges of murder, illegal possession of firearms, and subversion was Benigno 'Ninoy' Aquino.[778]

In 1975, after four years of imprisonment while undergoing his trial, Aquino went on a hunger strike to protest the injustice of his military trial. During the first ten days of fasting, he was forced to come to court every morning and sit throughout the day's proceedings. No mention of his fast was allowed in the press, yet he was visibly getting weaker as the country watched the proceedings.[779] Disturbed by the tremendous pain and suffering he was causing his wife and family, he wrote to Cory "my dear beloved wife…there comes a time in a man's life when he must prefer a meaningful death to a meaningless life." He then asked her to forgive him for the "immeasurable anguish and sorrow."[780] On the tenth day of drinking two glasses of water per day, in addition to taking salt tablets and some amino acids, Aquino asked his lawyers to withdraw all motions submitted for his trial to the supreme court since he intended to let fasting determine his destiny. The fast continued day after day; Aquino's weight dropped from 180 pounds to 120. On the fortieth day, some priests, close friends, and family finally convinced him to break his fast, reminding him that even Jesus fasted for only forty days.

In 1977, the military court found Aquino guilty of all charges and sentenced him to death by firing squad.[781] In 1980, after 7 years of imprisonment, mostly in solitary confinement, Aquino suffered a heart attack. Marcos, who was afraid his death would make Aquino a martyr, reluctantly allowed him to go to the United States for bypass surgery on the condition that he did not speak out publically against the Marcos regime. [782]

He spent most of his three years of exile in the United States in Boston, on a grant from Harvard University. In the United States, he spent most of his time on telephone, speaking to the many anti-Marcos activists and leaders. His commitment to the opposition and his focus made him the defacto leader of the opposition. Yet many of his visitors and associates were still part of anti-Marcos groups that advocated violence. [783] . While in prison, Aquino had read a great deal about Gandhi and Martin Luther King. Yet his understanding of the principles and practice of nonviolence was limited and he believed nonviolence to be a method of struggle that could somehow be employed in concert with violent opposition. He still associated himself with radical violent groups like the April 6th Liberation Movement, which carried out terrorist operations. In 1980, this group was responsible for nine bombings in the Philippines, killing two people. [784][785] In a letter to an associate, Aquino called the violence a 'triumph' and praised the terrorist group as "pulling off its biggest coup"[786] In Aquino's three years outside of Philippines, he travelled to Middle East, South East Asia, and Central America to interview and talk to leaders of nonviolent revolutions. His travels, the speeches of Gandhi and Martin Luther King, and the Bible helped him shape his ideas on nonviolence. Cory Aquino later said that "It was after the Nicaraguan visit that he realized that violence was not the answer either. That's when he realized that the killers of today become the leaders of tomorrow."[787] Finally, watching Richard Attenborough's 1982 movie on Gandhi, which was released while he was living in America, helped to solidify his position. For Aquino, nonviolence became first and foremost in his struggle for freedom, with human rights and democracy as its central principle.

In a statement to the subcommittee on Asian and Pacific Affairs of the House of Representatives, on June 23, 1983 he said:

"...I have concluded that revolution and violence exact the highest price in terms of human values and human lives in the struggle for freedom. In the end there are really no victors, only victims...I have decided to pursue my freedom struggle through the path of nonviolence, fully cognizant that this may be the longer and more arduous road...I have chosen to return to the silence of my solitary confinement and from there to work for a peaceful solution to our problems rather than go back triumphant to the blare of trumpets and cymbals seeking to drown the wailing and sad lamentations of mothers whose sons and daughters have been sacrificed to the gods of violent revolution. Can the killers of today be leaders of tomorrow? Must we destroy in order to build? I refuse to believe that it is necessary for a nation to build its foundation on the bones of its youth." [788]

After declaring his commitment to nonviolence, he spent the following month preparing to return to Philippines. Many family members and friends were opposed to his returning and feared for his life. Yet he was adamant. Many inside the Philippines were calling him 'Steak Commando' and claimed he was enjoying the hospitality of the United States while his comrades were suffering in prisons. The democratic opposition was weakening and political activists were calling for his return. After the Philippine government refused to grant him a passport, he obtained forged identification and announced that no one could keep him away from his native country. When warned that he was risking his life, he replied, "according to Gandhi the willing sacrifice of the innocent is the most powerful answer to insolent tyranny." [789] [790] With his life on the line, in August 1983, he boarded a China Airlines flight bound for Manila. For Filipinos, it was a moment of joy. After three years in exile, despite Marcos' refusal to admit him into the country, their revered political prisoner and the most determined and outspoken opponent of the Marcos regime was coming home.

As the plane was approaching the airport, over 20,000 Filipinos gathered at the terminal, awaiting his arrival. Over 1,200 soldiers lined up as the jetliner was taxing down the runway. As soon as the doors to the plane opened, several soldiers went inside and took Aquino out a side door. And within minutes, to the horror and shock of everyone present, gunshots rang out. There were screams and cries from the crowd as they witnessed Benigno 'Ninoy' Aquino, lifeless and face down on the tarmac with blood streaming from his body. When the 20,000 horrified supporters of Aquino were dispersed by the police, what was left behind were dozens of leaflets bearing words from his homecoming speech: "I have returned to join the ranks of those struggling to restore our rights and freedom through nonviolence." [791]

The story of Philippines teaches us that those who sacrifice their lives to follow the path of nonviolence are not *leading* the population; they are led and motivated by their principles. One person, or even a few, are not leaders in the struggle; their principles of nonviolence are the essential guidance for a nation's citizens on their path to freedom.

The nonviolent struggle in Philippines began with Aquino's death. It created a consensus in a majority of the population on the necessity to adhere to nonviolence and democracy as guiding principles of their struggle. The death of Aquino did not mean the death of nonviolent leadership or the death of a struggle for democracy. Millions of Filipinos, the ultimate 'leaders', chose to follow the same path as Aquino and voluntarily accepted the principles of nonviolence. The story of what happened in the Philippines' struggle for freedom is an inspiring and practical lesson in Principle-Based leadership within a modern nonviolent movement.

***

Aquino's mother asked her son's body to be laid out wearing his bloodstained shirt as mourners came to pay their respects. For days after his death, thousands of Filipinos lined up to see him as his body reposed first in his home and later in a church. Cab drivers would line up first, before 6 a.m. when their shift would start. A farmer coming to see his body cried "He was our best bet. Why did he die?" The poorest Filipinos as well as the wealthy, ruling elite families were lined up to pay their last respects.[792] As his body was taken on a truck through the vast urban sprawl of Manila, over 2 million Filipinos came out for a glimpse of that courageous man. Banners on the streets read "Justice for all victims of political repression and military terrorism."[793]

Fists were raised high, with the thumb and the forefinger held out in the shape of the letter 'L' the symbol for Aquino's political party, LABAN, which meant 'to fight'. This was a powerful yet simple symbol used to show the commitment of Filipinos to the principles and path of Benigno Aquino. Aside from this, another powerful symbol emerged and unified the supporters of nonviolence. In the fall and winter of 1983, the color yellow became the symbol of nonviolence in the Philippines. Week after week, yellow pages of phonebooks were turned into confetti and scattered out of the windows of office buildings in the heart of Philippines financial center. Color is the most powerful and simplest method of communication when all other forms of communication are banned. Colors are somehow more powerful than slogans; those in authority have a hard time stigmatizing the use of color and those in opposition to authority send a message to their oppressor that is both clear and difficult to deal with. The adoption of yellow as a banner of opposition was a collective, not an individual, decision. Principles of nonviolence were leading Filipinos to show their colors.

On September 21, 1983, a month after Aquino's death, his wife Corazon held a rally outside the *Malacañang* Palace, the seat of government. A crowd of 15,000 people, who were each now acting as leaders of the struggle, marched away and were faced with a solid wall of soldiers, firemen, and riot police[794]. Unfortunately, some of those in the crowd were not disciplined enough to adhere to nonviolence. Two explosions killed two firemen. This provoked violent reaction; the military fired on the demonstrators. Riots ensued. Eleven people were killed and hundreds injured. Yet, when the principles of nonviolence are leading a nation, a nation ultimately stands up for those principles. When guided by the principles of nonviolence, acts of violence are only brief interruptions in the movement, after which, those tens of thousands remind others of the effectiveness of acting according to the principles of nonviolence. No matter how many individuals the despotic regime eliminates, the principles of nonviolence that are leading the struggle continue to lead.

In July 1984, 20,000 demonstrators staged a symbolic rally. Two months later, 3,000 others staged a candlelight vigil throughout the night. [795] On the following morning, when they refused to move, the police used tear gas and water cannons to disperse them. As the struggle for nonviolence gained momentum, more and more veterans of nonviolence joined the ranks of Filipinos in their efforts. In summer of 1984, Hildegard and Jean Goss-Myer, who had worked for decades promoting nonviolence in Europe and Latin America, travelled to Philippines and held seminars on the practice and discipline of nonviolence for six weeks.[796] Six months before, on their visit to Philippines, Butz Aquino, the brother of slain Benigno Aquino, had expressed his ambivalence about the use of nonviolence as a means to pressure an oppressive regime or ferment a revolution. Butz Aquino had told them: "A few days ago, the arms merchants visited us and said to us ' Do you think that with a few demonstrations you will be able to overthrow this regime? Don't you think you need better weapons than that? We offer them to you... make up your mind."[797]

Those unfamiliar with the history and power of nonviolence always emphasize that violence is the most effective tool in overcoming tyranny. But what they don't realize is that whenever violence is used to overcome a regime, the ensuing regime will invariably continue to use violence and will itself become a tyranny.

The visit by these nonviolent activists and the belief in principles of nonviolent struggle soon turned the tide and convinced the country that nonviolence was the only method through which democracy can be won. The veterans of nonviolence who were visiting the Philippines kept repeating the same principle over and over: "Nonviolent opposition to the structural violence in Marcos' economic and political system, and abandonment of the inner violence in one's own heart." [798] The message of Gandhi given generations before was now being repeated in the back streets of Manila.

Meanwhile, political uncertainty was putting severe economic pressure on Marcos. Over $500 million was withdrawn from Filipino banks and moved to the United States, Switzerland and Hong Kong. The Philippines national debt rose $6 billion in 1983.

Marcos, who was confident of his position and power, decided to hold elections in order to prove to Filipinos that the opposition represented only a minority of Filipinos. In a surprise announcement in November 1985, he proclaimed that he had decided to hold a snap presidential election within three months. Marcos' hold on power through rigged elections and his method of maintaining power through those elections was not much different than the strategies of the Islamic Republic of today. In the Islamic Republic, opposition candidates are vetted prior to the elections. Those who are allowed to remain as candidates in elections are sworn to support the regime, its undemocratic constitution, and it's institutions of Supreme Leader and Guardian Council.

Marcos did not have such a system. He allowed everyone to run, but then he controlled the ballot boxes and, through election fraud, only allowed candidates who had sworn allegiance to him to win.

Marcos' system wasn't always effective. In the 1984 national assembly, when the opposition decided to participate, gains were made by the opposition camp and the number of representatives loyal to Marcos decreased from 90% to 70%. Pulling off election fraud in every single parliamentary constituency was a difficult task, but fraud when it came to the election for the office of presidency was much simpler. All Marcos needed to do was hold elections, cook the results, and proclaim himself the winner. Through such sham elections, he could maintain his status in the eyes of the world and the majority of Filipinos. In his opinion, such a victory would end the endless stream of yellow banners and confetti symbolizing nonviolence and democracy and littering the streets of Manila.

Corazon Aquino who was now herself being led by the principles of nonviolence and democracy, agreed to run only if a million signatures could be collected. [799] In a short period of time, 1.2 million signatures were collected. The other main opposition to Marcos, Salvador Laurel, also agreed to join Aquino as her vice president. He was now also being led by the principles of democracy. This was a major blow to Marcos. He was counting on the opposition to field multiple candidates, which would enable him to divide and conquer.

While the Marxists and other ideological leftists decided to boycott the elections, the nonviolent opposition to Marcos began a campaign focused on three activities: 1) encouraging people to vote, 2) putting poll-watchers in place, and 3) organizing the gathering of voters in prayer tents.[800] Over half a million volunteers were trained to be present at the polls on election day and conduct themselves in accordance with the principles and imperatives of nonviolence.

Prayer tents were set up in 10 densely populated areas; each night from mid-January until Election Day, streams of Filipinos came to these tents for prayers and fasting. Hilgard Goss-Myer, who again came to Philippines to train Filipinos in the principles and practices of nonviolence, emphasized the importance of these prayer tents:

"We cannot emphasize enough the deep spirituality that gave the people the strength to stand against the tanks later on. People prayed every day for all those who suffered in the process of changing of the regime, even for the military, even for Marcos. It makes a great difference in a revolutionary process where people are highly emotional state whether you promote hatred and revenge or help the people stand firmly for justice without becoming like the oppressor. You want to love your enemy, to liberate rather than destroy him."[801]

During the elections, there was massive fraud throughout the Philippines. Opposition supporters were told by the regime "they knew where they lived and where their children went to school and what time they left the house. A man might be willing to die for the cause, but he is not ready to risk the lives of his children." [802] As expected in any regime built on violence, Marcos was using the power of fear and terror to silence the opposition.

When the elections took place, in Manila alone, 600,000 people could not vote because Marcos' agents had scrambled the voters' lists.[803] Out of every 10 voters in Philippines complained that his or her name had been removed from the voting list.[804] Tens of thousands of poll watchers stationed across Philippines, each a leader of nonviolence, reported intimidation and violence by the military at their sites. Two days after the elections, when Marcos was about to announce his victory, thirty-one computer technicians in the government-controlled commission on elections, now acting as one of the thousands of leaders and each led by the principles of nonviolence, walked out in a symbolic gesture. The bishops in the Philippines Catholic Bishops conference, who were also some of thousands of leaders in the Philippines, announced that there had been "widespread vote buying, intimidation of voters, dishonest tabulation of the returns, harassment, terrorism and murder." And, on February 13, less than a week after the elections, the bishops had denounced the elections as fraudulent and encouraged the people to resist Marcos with peaceful nonviolence.[805]

The powerful Catholic body, which was being led by principles of nonviolence, then issued a statement:

"The way indicated to us now is the way of nonviolent struggle for justice. This means active resistance of evil by peaceful means - in the manner of Christ ... now is the time to speak up. Now is the time to repair the wrong...but we insist: Our acting must always be according to the Gospel of Christ, that is, in a peaceful, nonviolent way." [806]

Meanwhile, Cory Aquino, who was also being led by the principles of nonviolence and democracy, was meeting with 350 key advisers, including Goss-Myers and Cardinal Jaime Sin, all of whom were each led by the principles of nonviolence and democracy. Principles of nonviolence were being embraced spontaneously across Philippines in the hearts and minds of millions of Filipinos. On February 16, when Cory Aquino launched a campaign of civil disobedience, a crowd of one million gathered to applaud and support her nonviolent path. People were, once again, making the symbol 'L' on their thumbs and forefingers as a gesture of solidarity and support for Aquino and nonviolence. Marcos responded that he intended to meet force with force and condemned his opposition as "foreign funded and out to cheat him of his votes"[807]. His threat was followed by the assassination of Evelio Javier, one of the leaders of opposition and a good friend of Benigno 'Ninoy' Aquino. Javier's death brought the total number of election-related murders to 264.[808] Marcos was reminding the world of one of the principles of violence—that tyrants never relinquish their power without struggle. As Gandhi and Martin Luther King had realized decades before, love itself does not uproot such regimes; only the force of love through nonviolence can shake the foundations of tyranny.

On February 15th, the official count of the vote was announced, with Marcos winning by 10,807,197 votes to Aquino 9,292,761.[809] But people were resilient and an estimated 1.5 million Filipinos gathered at Luneta Park in Manila where Corazon Aquino announced "I am not asking for a violent revolution. This is not the time for that. I always indicated that now is the way of nonviolent struggle for justice. This means active resistance of evil by peaceful means."[810]

A nationwide form of noncooperation was chosen as the method of nonviolence. Banks, schools, newspapers, beverage stores, and movies were picked as instruments of nonviolent struggle. People were urged to withdraw their funds from banks associated with Marcos. Schools nationwide were

CHAPTER 9

encouraged to shut down. Readers were urged to boycott Marcos's newspapers, not purchase popular beverages made by companies owned by Marcos or with close ties to Marcos, and no one should go to see movies starring pro-Marcos actors. People were to delay paying utility bills until electric and phone companies threatened to cut off service.

But the main opposition was about to come through Marcos' own military. A nonviolent struggle, following its principles, will continuously create new leaders. Disgruntled junior officers with ties to former defense minister Juan Ponce Enrile had formed a secret opposition movement within the military called Reform the Armed Forces of Philippines Movement (RAM). Four officers with ties to RAM had been arrested earlier and plans had been divulged. Enrile resigned from Marcos' government and announced "I have served him for twenty years. I must now serve my country." [811]

On morning of February 22, 1986, two officers from RAM rushed to Enrile's home and warned him of imminent arrest. Enrile ordered 400 of his troops to report at Defense Ministry headquarters in downtown Manila. He then contacted General Ramos for support, one of his allies who were in charge of two battalions stationed at the national police headquarters directly across the street. Ramos responded "I'm with you all the way..."[812] and ordered his battalions to make their stand at Camp Cramer, the national police headquarters directly across from where Enrile's officers had convened.

The situation was now tense. Several hundred military officers dedicated to nonviolence and democracy had now locked themselves up inside the Defense Ministry awaiting a bloody confrontation with Marcos' army. Violent confrontation could have easily derailed the nonviolent movement and even if that opposition had claimed victory through violence, the resulting government in power would not be democratic but another regime determined to rule through violence— and not the power of the people.

By that evening, several hundred other military personnel joined the rebels. Enrile and Ramos held a press conference at which Enrile announced "As of now, I cannot in conscience recognize the president as the commander in chief of the Armed Forces... I believe that the mandate of the people does not belong to the present regime."[813] Knowing that they could not withstand a violent confrontation with Marcos' military, they called Cardinal Sin who told them "Alright... just wait, in 15 minutes your place will be filled with people." [814] The Cardinal then made a statement over Catholic Radio Veritas "calling on our people to support our two good friends at the camp... show your solidarity with them in the crucial period... I wish that bloodshed will be avoided." [815]

Catholic seminarians were the first ones to arrive and began to form a human chain around the headquarters. Volunteers offered free rides to those wanting to augment this human chain. Trucks and buses, each driven by a leader in this nonviolent struggle, were being filled by volunteers, each of whom was another leader—among many. Cab drivers were filling their cars and taking people free of charge. Anticipating attacks, the volunteers barricaded the main routes; one was comprised of six empty buses spread across a multilane avenue. Others brought food and coffee for the rebel soldiers. Soon, an estimated 50,000 Filipinos had gathered around the headquarters, singing, dancing and horn-blowing. Enrile later said: "It was funny; we in the defense and military organization who should be protecting the people were being protected by them." [816] "It was the first time in history", said a lieutenant colonel "that so many civilians went to protect the military."[817] The Filipinos were joyous, but the situation was tense. Marcos was planning a violent frontal assault on the people and the rebel soldiers. Several hundred rebel soldiers put up barricades in the streets of downtown Manila .Protected by a sea of nonviolent leaders, the non-violent opposition was up against a violent army of 250,000 at Marcos' disposal.

Wealthy and poor alike were in the crowd. There were grandparents, children, teachers and workers, and priests— each a leader committed to nonviolence. Pregnant women were seen next to mothers with babies in their arms. The festive and celebratory mood became more and more tense the next day as Marcos threatened to unleash an army artillery barrage and the bombing by the air force to flatten the compounds. The next day, the moment of battle arrived as Marcos ordered two armored battalions to crush the rebels. At 3PM, a large force led by tanks and followed by marines and armored personnel carriers, began rolling down the streets of Manila towards the rebels. A modern army, equipped with the latest and most powerful weapons, was going up against a nonviolent army handing out sweets, flowers, and cigarettes as their weapons. On the way to the compound, a kilometer away from the rebel soldiers, the great weapons of steel were blocked by the nonviolent army of tens of thousands, individuals ready to die but not to kill. The general in charge of the army ordered the citizens to disperse and to allow the tanks through. People in return were offering sweets and flowers to the soldiers and had spontaneously gone on their knees for prayers. Some were holding a statue of Virgin Mary to summon the resolution needed for this confrontation. Butz Aquino, the brother of the murdered hero, 'Ninoy' Aquino, was seen climbing up on an armored vehicle and instructing people not to use violence under any circumstances. He reminded the crowd that this is what 'People Power' was all about.

This is how leadership comes about in a nonviolent movement— spontaneously from the masses. People are effectively guided by principles of nonviolence, democracy, and human rights. Those who understand these concepts continue to rise from the crowds to remind others of these principles. It is unlike military confrontations, in which a leader gives orders to his army and the soldiers in that army follow orders given from above. In nonviolence, following orders is democratic—there is room for the dictates of conscience and ethical precepts. People are free to choose the path they wish to go— based on their principles. No leader can order them to do something if it violates their moral values. Hundreds of individuals spontaneously rise and suggest various paths to justice and democracy. People then follow those paths if they believe those paths abide by their principles. This is Principle Based Leadership, and it is only through this form of leadership that Iranians can find themselves on the path to nonviolence and ultimately attain democracy. Any other form of leadership, whether by individuals, leadership council, or political party, will lead to the fatal paradigm—the members of an army getting its unquestionable orders from commanders, and an unquestioning citizenry obeying the dictates of leaders. This military or authoritarian form of what comes down to dictatorship can produce effective leaders for a time, but upon victory in war or political struggle, those leaders, drunk with power, will continue to use their authority to order their nominal fellow citizens, who become subjects rather than free citizens, to obey their commands. Meanwhile these leaders live lives of privilege, luxury, and indifference to the welfare of the people who placed them the authority that they now abuse. The leadership for Iran's nonviolent struggle does not reside in Tehran, Tabriz, Isfahan, London or Los Angeles. The leadership is in the hearts of seventy million Iranians and within the principles of nonviolence.

***

As Butz Aquino was pushed off a tank, engines began to roar and the army prepared to annihilate those who stood in its path. The gentle sound of prayers was replaced by weeping and cries for mercy. In front of the lead tank stood three nuns, kneeling at an arm's distance from the machines. Behind them, row after row of thousands of Filipinos stood, prepared to die. An eyewitness recalled: "young people in their late teens, early twenties, with their entire lives stretched before them…a young mother with a baby in her arms and another in her womb… I saw one doctor who was beyond seventy … I saw no one leave. I saw no one yield to fear."[818] People had linked arms in a human chain in front of the tanks. "I looked at the faces of the people around me", said an eyewitness, "and especially at the man to my right was holding on tightly to my arm. My big concern was, I am going to die with this man and I don't know his name."[819]

The general on the tank used a megaphone to warn those in the crowd that he had orders to kill anyone who obstructed the movement of his force. Shouts of "Go on, kill us!" were heard from the crowd. He then ordered his tanks forward. The engines of the heavy armored vehicles roared and belched a cloud of black smoke. Tanks inched forward— but the people were not moving. One tank moved forward, again, but stopped. There was a moment of silence, uncertainty, and anxiety, which was then followed by wild cheers and applause from the thousands of people in the crowd. Marcos' general looked at them, turned, and shook his head. But even as the general hesitated, a Marine jumped on top of one of the tanks and ordered the rest forward. Thousands were chanting "Cory, Cory", the popular variant of the name of Corazon Aquino, and showing the symbol 'L' with their hands. Those kneeling in front of the tanks were prepared to be ground up under their treads. The tanks inched forward—but, once again, came to a halt. Eighty-one-year-old Mrs. Monzon of Arellano University, who had stayed in the street all night on her wheelchair, managed to push her way to the tanks and, as they were about to crush the crowds, the old lady, armed only with a crucifix and love, called out to the soldiers. "Stop. I am an old woman. You can kill me, but you shouldn't kill your fellow Filipinos." The soldier on the tank, overcome by the power of love emanating from this old woman jumped off the tank and embraced her. "I cannot kill you", he told her "you are just like my mother."[820] The marines and tanks withdrew without firing a shot.

What weapon is more powerful than a tank? What weapon other than love could have pushed that army away? What weapon other than love could have made that soldier climb down from his tank and for the General to halt his advance? Nonviolence, summoned through love for life and humanity, are the most powerful weapon developed in the 20th century. Violence

CHAPTER 9

crushes and enslaves the enemy. Love frees both the individual and his enemy. In nonviolence, love is the weapon of choice. And in order to arm thousands of citizens with this weapon, it is crucial that they banish the hatred, fear and anger that lurks in every human heart. The battle for nonviolence is a battle that begins in every person's heart. It is the discovery of love and humanity within oneself. It is the ability to overcome fear and find courage. When love replaces hatred, then that special kindness derived only through love will replace violence.

***

On that night of confrontation in 1986, Filipinos in Manila continued to sit and protect the rebel soldiers until dawn, when, Marcos ordered three thousand marines to use tear gas and disperse the crowd. He also ordered seven helicopter gunships to fire on and flatten the buildings where rebel troops had gathered. The helicopters had sufficient ammunition and firepower to obliterate those buildings. The commander of the helicopter unit circled the rebel camp once and on the second turn, instead of firing on the buildings and the crowd, ordered his helicopters to land peacefully within the compound. "Pandemonium broke loose. The rotor blades were still turning and the people were swarming all over us. They were shouting and jumping and hugging," said the commander, "all I wanted to say was we followed our conscience. I have not really done much in my life and for once I wanted to make a decision for my country." The commander of the helicopters was now also one of the leaders of nonviolence. [821]

The helicopters were then used to seize television Channel 4 headquarters. While Marcos was defiantly addressing the nation, he was abruptly cut off and his image disappeared from the screen. The rebels now had the TV station in their control. Marcos ordered several platoons of loyalist Scout Rangers to retake control of the station. A priest, now also another leader in the movement of nonviolence, brought statues of crucified Christ and Virgin Mary and began singing and praying in front of the soldiers. The soldiers, who were sporadically shooting off their weapons, stopped. Crowds of people, led by the priest, approached the soldiers and offered them doughnuts, orange juice, and hamburgers. Armed with deadly weapons, soldiers of violence were peacefully defeated by soldiers of nonviolence.

On afternoon of that day, 48 hours after the rebel soldiers had barricaded themselves in the headquarters, Cory Aquino decided to meet with those in the vast crowd over the security objections of her guards. Hundreds of thousands had now come out into the streets.

Finally, Marcos' longtime ally, the United States, held a top level meeting at the White House; it included President Reagan, his chief of staff, Donald Regan, and Secretary of State George Shultz. After the meeting, the White House issued a statement that urged Marcos to avoid all bloodshed or face immediate cutoff of all aid and offered him safe passage out of Philippines. A few days later, Marcos and his wife were airlifted by US helicopters and taken to Hawaii.

What happened in the Philippines offers a moral, spiritual, and practical example for Iranians. When hundreds of thousands came onto the streets of Manila to renounce their dictator, the outpouring was not unlike the 1979 Iranian revolution. But in 1979, instead of 'Principle Based Leadership', leadership was placed in the hands of a single individual, Khomeini, who gave orders to citizens much in the way a military general issues orders to an army. A nonviolent revolution begins in the hearts of a population who adopt the principles of nonviolence who then each become leaders of nonviolence. In the nonviolent struggle for human rights and democracy, thousands at first, later tens and even hundreds of thousands of leaders are made as they each strive to teach others of the principles of nonviolence, human rights and democracy. Such was the story of 'People's Power' revolution in Philippines and such will be the story of nonviolence in Iran.

***

Truth and Reconciliation

In the waning years of the 20th century, the final chapter in the story of nonviolence was written. Much had been achieved in theory and principles of nonviolence, but there was an unresolved dilemma in the practice of nonviolence not properly addressed by either Gandhi or Martin Luther King. Many nations and people struggling for nonviolence were asking how a country transitioning into a pluralistic democracy should deal with past injustice. What happens when the injustice and violence against the population is so deep and painful and hatred so ingrained that a transition to democracy may open the wounds leading to mass violence and perhaps civil war.

In India, the British, responsible for so much violence, left the country after the independence. After the bloody partition, there was also relative separation of Muslims and Hindu's into the countries of Pakistan, India, and (some years later,) Bangladesh, thus minimizing further hatred and violence. Some South American and Central American nations had created commissions to deal with past crimes. But these commissions were regarded as failures for granting amnesty to persons such as General Pinochet of Chile without any inquiries of what had happened and any statements of regret on behalf of those who had murdered and tortured. The failure of these commissions due to uncertainties and unknowns about those missing or killed was a source of continued resentment amongst the population, leaving seeds of hatred and possible violence within society. In addition, as such countries had moved forward, not only the pain of previous injustice and violence was not healed; the acts of violence by those regimes were not properly condemned by society to prevent their repeat.

In addition, what if the number of victims to injustice and violence was not hundreds or thousands but tens or hundreds of thousands of human beings? How can a country overcome the trauma of violence not just from dictators in power for several years but from a regime's systemic use of terror and violence for decades? How can a country overcome its hatred and its potential for violence when the human rights of the majority were violated to an extent that any freedom given to the population might entail mass bloodshed and violent retaliation by the people?

By mid-1990s, South Africa had endured more than 40 years of the one of the most ruthless and unjust systems of the modern era; it was called 'Apartheid'. In 1948, the national party of South Africa, which had ideological ties to Hitler's Nazi party, passed legislation separating human beings into separate biological categories of Africans, Coloured (mixed races), Asians and Whites. The laws made it illegal for members of different human categories to live in the same neighborhood, marry, or have sex with members of another group. Over the following decades, blacks were forced to live in neighborhoods outside the cities and needed special permission to travel within white areas. If the white government wanted a certain area reserved for white citizens, entire communities were uprooted, their homes destroyed, and its population scattered outside the cities and forced to live in shantytowns. Blacks were not allowed to have representatives in the parliament or any say in the government. The black original inhabitants of South Africa were forced to work in mines or other industries thriving on cheap labor. Protesters were beaten, tortured, and killed. The population was continuously terrorized by the apartheid regime. This mixture of terror, insult, and disrespect was perhaps equal or even more traumatic than the one endured by Iranians under the Islamic Republic.

With the international economic and political pressure on South Africa and the notion of eventual end to Apartheid, there was fear of mass violence and acts of vengeance against the whites. Toward the end of the Apartheid regime, the greatest resistance against pluralistic democracy was the fear of civil war, which might well erupt shortly after the collapse of the regime. In order to transition to democracy and avoid mass bloodshed, South Africans embarked on a plan for societal reconciliation in order to overcome the hatred between whites and blacks and even the animosity between different factions of blacks. But in order for this reconciliation to be effective, it could not be just a process of hollow symbolism, one that gave a free pass to those who had committed horrendous crimes during the apartheid era. The commission had to dig deep into the soul of the nation and find the strength to heal the wounds of decades and even centuries. It had to find the means to restore dignity and a sense of humanity to a population shattered by walls of racism and find a sense of justice for a generation embarking on a path that would lead to former enemies becoming neighbors. The commission was given the task of providing amnesty to those meeting the qualification and demands set forth by the nation and to also identify those who could not be forgiven and were to be tried in criminal courts for crimes during the apartheid era.

In order to meet this challenge, the commission engaged in a process in which healing, reconciliation, and justice were achieved through a ritual heard on the radio, witnessed on television, and documented in newspapers and books. The Truth and Reconciliation Commission, whose 17 members were chosen from all of walks of life in South Africa, was given the unbelievable task of national healing and the greater and more difficult task of national forgiveness. They were charged with the task of transitioning South Africa from an apartheid country to a 'Rainbow Country'. In a country as divided and as wounded as South Africa, this task might well have been an impossible dream. Yet the country was able to overcome its past and transition to a pluralistic democracy under the leadership and guidance of two ambassadors of forgiveness and reconciliation. The first was a Nobel laureate, Bishop

CHAPTER 9

Desmond Tutu, who was charged with leading the Truth and Reconciliation Commission.

During the commission's sessions, when perpetrators of apartheid crimes spoke of their crimes, torture and murder, and while the nation watched on national television as their history was documented in front of their eyes, Bishop Tutu wept with the victims as mothers told of murders of their children, laughed as they embraced their former enemies, danced with them when they needed to dance, sang with them as they tried to heal, and prayed with them as they asked for forgiveness. Through his leadership in the Truth and Reconciliation Commission, Bishop Tutu became a symbol of healing and forgiveness. In addition, while the country was struggling to overcome decades of apartheid and while the Truth and Reconciliation Commission was under relentless attacks by those refusing to forgive, the unbelievable charisma, wisdom, and power of forgiveness of the new president of South Africa, Nelson Mandela, guided them towards the 'Rainbow Nation'.

This grand struggle of national healing and reconciliation in South Africa was undertaken by this commission whose task was to find and document the truth, provide amnesty to those apologizing to the country and showing remorse, identify those not meeting the standards for amnesty and most important of all, guiding the victims and the nation through a process of forgiveness which was to become a model for other nations and people attempting to overcome a similar history of violence. For Iranians, understanding the process of reconciliation and forgiveness during transition from an autocratic, violent regime toward a pluralistic democracy is as important as understanding the principles of nonviolence leading a country to such a transition.

In order for Iranians not to repeat the same cycle of violence repeatedly experienced by 100 generations of their ancestors, they must adopt not just the principles of nonviolence, but also the techniques and models developed as tools for transitioning nations into democracies. The success and failures of South Africa provide essential lessons for any nation attempting to overcome its history of violence.

Hundreds of books and articles have been written about the experiences of the Truth and Reconciliation Commission and a review of the comprehensive work of the commission, eventually published in five volumes, is beyond the scope and purpose of this book. The lessons in South Africa were analyzed, structured, and formulated by many scholars watching the events unfold. One such scholar, Russell Daye, formulated the task of the

Truth and Reconciliation into five acts that are extremely useful for Iranians to learn and apply as they envision a transitional justice system breaking the repeated cycle of violence in their history. The transition to democracy in Iran cannot pass through a period of vengeful violence against tens and maybe hundreds of thousands of soldiers, bureaucrats, clerics, businessmen, and others responsible for the crimes and injustice of the Islamic Republic. The structure of five acts observed in the Truth and Reconciliation of South Africa and formulated by Russell Daye are a useful blueprints for a similar such a commission in the democratic Iran of tomorrow.

Five Acts of Russell Daye

For Russell Daye, the drama in the reconciliation process takes place in five acts. The first act is the 'Truth Telling' by the victims and perpetrators of the crimes. Act two becomes the 'Apology and the Claiming of Responsibility' by the perpetrators. Once these two acts are performed, act three deals with the 'Transitional Justice Framework' which involves the option of 'Amnesty' versus 'Retributive Justice' against the perpetrators as well as 'Restorative Justice' for the victims. Act four involves 'Finding Ways to Heal' and, finally, the last act of the reconciliation process and perhaps the most difficult becomes 'Embracing Forgiveness'.

Act One

In the first act in South Africa, the truth had to be told. The process of truth telling involved the victims, their families and the perpetrators of the crimes. The stories of terror, torture and, murder related before the commission were broadcast live on the media and heard, seen, and read about throughout the nation. In addition to crimes performed by whites against blacks, acts of political murder by black anti-apartheid groups against others were also brought before the commission. Any form of political violence whether pro-apartheid or anti-apartheid was within the domain of the Truth Commission.

This point cannot be overlooked by Iranians as they attempt to trek down a path of nonviolence towards democracy. Various organizations struggling against the Islamic Republic of Iran have also turned to violence and terrorism over the last few decades. Most important of these organizations is the MKO (Mujahedin Khalq Organization), which includes members who continue to embrace murder as an appropriate method of resistance. In addition, there are some who committed torture and political violence during the previous regime in Iran. Holding everyone who has committed a political crime before a national truth and reconciliation commission in Iran is as integral and important as including the political crimes performed solely in the name of the Islamic Republic.

In the five-volume final report of the commission, four kinds of truths were acknowledged and documented. The first kind of truth was a forensic or the objective truth where the investigative arm of the commission was deeply involved in the report. The second kind of truth was the personal or the narrative truth. In this form of truth, victims, their families, and the perpetrators of the crime told the stories of the criminal acts. They were allowed to express their emotions as well as their motivations for crimes. The third kind of truth was a social or dialogical truth obtained through exhaustive debate on the national level. The last kind of truth was the restorative truth that attempted to heal the wounds of the past through acknowledging the pain people have suffered as well as the acceptance of responsibility by the perpetrators. [822]

"In sum, a society recovering from the trauma of state violence needs as much truth as possible", wrote Walter Wink, "Truth is medicine. Without it, a society remains infected with past evils that will inevitably break out in the future."[823] Another scholar, Priscilla B. Hayner wrote: "the most straightforward objective of a truth commission is sanctioned fact-finding: to establish an accurate record of the country's past, clarify uncertain events, and lift the lid of silence and denial from a contentious and painful period of history."[824]

Within the truth and reconciliation commission, comprised of 17 commissioners, a committee on human rights violations was created, led by eight of the commissioners. This committee took charge of uncovering the truth of 40 years of apartheid and providing a comprehensive account of human rights violations both by the apartheid regime and anti-apartheid activists between 1960 and 1993. Each victim was to be named and human rights violation against them, whether murder, kidnapping, or torture, was to be documented for the country, the world, and history.[825] Victims of apartheid or their families were invited to submit statements or reports of violations of their human rights. Over 21,000 victims or their family put forward statements to document their case and take part in the truth and reconciliation commission. Many who were unable to write were forced to recount their statements for their application orally, making the submission process long and laborious. In addition to individuals, businesses, labor unions, religious institutions, the legal community, representatives of the health sector, political parties, and NGOs were also invited to come forth and take part in the truth telling process for the country.

Hearings on the apartheid police and security services allowed the uncovering of a complicated bureaucracy terrorizing the population in order to uphold the apartheid regime. Special hearings were also undertaken regarding the compulsory military service as well as human rights abuses against children and women. [826]

Millions of South Africans watched the drama every day on their televisions as horrific acts of terrorism and human rights violations were broadcast, often showing victims in tears or perpetrators asking for forgiveness. There were anti-apartheid activists who, under torture, had been forced to name the location of their comrades. One such a victim on the verge of physical and psychological collapse a dozen years after leading security forces to the home of his comrade was urged by his therapist to attend a truth commission. His statements were so excruciating that he would often break down during his story. For a long time after his statement, he was unable to interact with anyone except members of his close family and had a breakdown. But later, after this truth telling, he found a sense of hope and said "[the experience] convinced me that it is possible to create a space where we are able to face each other as human beings."[827]

Act Two

The second act in the truth and reconciliation commission, as categorized by Russell Daye, is 'Apology and the Claiming of Responsibility.' Here, Daye invokes the sociological description of apology by Nicholas Tavuchi's in 'Mea Culpa: A Sociology of Apology and Reconciliation.' As such, apology was defined as "acknowledgement and painful embracement of our deeds, coupled with a declaration of regret."[828] The two important components of apology are thus the "acknowledgment of deeds" and "declaration of regret".

"Unlike accounts, explanations, or appeals to special circumstances, which rationalize the offenders actions and seek to distance the offender from them," writes Daye, "an apology requires an unqualified acknowledgment and a painful embracing of the deeds."[829]

Central to the act of apology is the naming of the offense and its identification as an 'apologizeable' action. This is followed by the apology itself. Apology is different than recounting the truth, and certainty different than justifying the criminal act. Central to an act of apology is the expression of sorrow and regret. "The sincere expression of sorrow," writes Daye, "is of central import."[830]

Although apology often takes place between the offender and the victim on a personal level, apologies between groups, institutions, and even religions function in a similar manner. "In an apology from 'the many to the many" writes Daye, "individuals do not figure as principles but as official attendants or representatives. The weight of their words comes from their position of speaking and acting on behalf of a larger body."[831]

During the truth commission, there were many difficult expressions of apology by former members of the security police, who, because of their nature, psychological predisposition, training, and experience were unemotional and unsympathetic. In the presence of victims and their families, such apologies would often turn to anger instead of forgiveness. On one occasion, after a white policeman offered an apology on live national TV for the death of a young activist while in custody twenty years before, the victim's mother and father listened patiently. The victim's son, who was now in his 20s and who had lost his father when he was an infant, was also seen listening to the account of his father's death. The policeman asked for forgiveness but the mother, who was gracious and patient, wanted to know the whole truth, which meant the details of his son's murder and the kinds of torture he had suffered. The policeman responded that he was not present during the torture or his death but would not name the perpetrators who were present. When pushed further, he showed no remorse and no sorrow and simply stated that he had come to apologize and expected forgiveness.

Completely lacking in emotional understanding of this act, his apology was only a procedural act needed for amnesty and forgiveness. At this point, the victim's son, as he was listening to the story, instead of finding forgiveness was becoming more and more enraged and did not possess the patience and kindness of his grandmother. While the nation was watching on TV, he picked up a vase and smashed it on the policeman's head, fracturing his skull.[832]

Apology is not just a procedure that can be performed by a computer; it is an instrument from the soul, which only a human being can express and only a human being can understand. If performed without sorrow and remorse, not only it may fail to accomplish its task, it may also backfire and cause even more anger and resentment.

Act III

The third act in the process of political forgiveness is characterized by Russell Daye as 'Building a Transitional-Justice Framework'. In the path to democracy, Iranians must realize that the nature of the justice system during the time of transition to democracy requires a different framework for punishment than what they expect based on past models of punishment and revenge and perhaps what they should expect in a democratic future.

No society in the world has a judicial system in which a murderer or a person who has participated in numerous acts of torture is able to complete a process of truth telling, apology and reconciliation, be given amnesty, and be forgiven. The mere mention of such a judicial system in the United States or any European country would immediately cause uproar from the population. Similarly, for Iranians the concept of a political forgiveness is one that is hard to swallow. In the anger and resentment against those responsible for torture and murder, there will be uproar against a 'Transitional Justice Framework'. But Iranians must realize the creation of a 'Transitional Justice Framework' is a necessary tool to disarm the brutal regime in power, a tool for the healing of society and a necessary step in overcoming the nation's horrifying past.

There are thousands who believe that murderers of innocent political activists should be executed, and that torturers must serve a lifetime in inhospitable prison systems built by the torturers themselves and in which life within them, by itself, amounts to torture. They ask, how can a nation forgive the likes of Khamenei, Fallahian, or Rafsanjani? They ask "would you forgive and give amnesty to someone like Khomeini or Khalkhali if they were alive today?" Then I have to remind them and asked them "How many people did Khomeini murder? "This question always begins a hotly debate on the number of Iranians killed in 1980's. Often the response is in "tens of thousands". Then I have to remind them that tens of thousands of young Iranian boys and girls tortured and murdered tens of thousands of other Iranians. In the last 30 years, millions of young boys drafted into compulsory military service patrolled the streets and parks of Tehran and other cities harassing, threatening, and beating citizens who they now must live next to as neighbors and as citizens of the same country. Those who've committed acts of political violence are not a few at the top as many Iranians may imagine. Hundreds of thousands are guilty of violence and millions are enraged with anger, resentment, and hatred; fuels for violence.

There are many leaders in the Islamic Republic whose actions amount to crimes against humanity and who should be handed to an international court for prosecution, but these may be a few hundred individuals at the top who conspired and planned the tortures and murders of a generation. But there are tens of thousands of soldiers who often regret their action and want to join the side of the people for freedom, if only they are allowed an option for amnesty. In South Africa, it was this option for amnesty which was considered an important step in bringing the 'dawn of freedom'.

Justice during a transitional period in the nation's history requires different standards than the framework of justice in other times in the nation's history. In transitional political justice, there is also an option of 'Amnesty'. Without this option, those guilty of crimes that may number in the tens of thousands will continue fighting and will struggle to maintain power with every ounce of their energy. Without a 'Transitional Justice Framework', these individuals, groups, and institutions will kill and torture even larger numbers in order to stay in power. Without the option of amnesty, a powerful weapon is removed from the arsenal of those struggling for democracy. Act three in the drama of political forgiveness is a difficult pill to swallow for many, but a necessary medicine.

The debate on 'Transitional Justice framework' in South Africa began in the apartheid era. In 1988, long before the fall of apartheid, in a conference outside the country discussing the possible constitution of a post-apartheid South Africa, the chair of the conference declared that those who had committed human rights violations such as murder, bombing, and torture in name of apartheid must be tried in a Nuremberg-style tribunal to deal with crimes similar to those of the Nazis. He insisted that such criminals cannot be pardoned and no compromise was acceptable. Amongst the crowd in the conference was a lawyer who had opposed apartheid and defended anti-apartheid activists. Living as a dissident outside his country in Mozambique, his car had been bombed, causing the loss of one arm and serious injury to his upper body. Amongst the many attendants raising up their arms and requesting to speak, his raised arm was noticeable and the chair of the conference allowed him to speak. He argued that "calls for vengeance would delay the dawn of freedom," and announced to the chairperson, "comrades, if I can forgive them, I am sure many more will do so."[833]

The question of amnesty was a difficult one for South Africans. The human rights of the vast majority of the population had been curtailed and abused for decades. Examples of amnesty, even by other nations such as

Chile, where General Augusto Pinochet and his officers were given freedom without a proper framework, was not encouraging and certainly not effective models for the healing of a country. The example of Pinochet was even more discouraging for South Africans, since the man who perpetrated horrendous crimes in Chile was allowed to maintain power over the armed forces.

Nearing the collapse of the apartheid regime, the Nationalist Party responsible for apartheid and the Inkantha Freedom Party (IFP) of black South Africans, responsible for many acts of murder against both whites and blacks, requested 'blanket amnesty' for political crimes during the apartheid era. This request meant everyone was to be forgiven. The African National Congress, with many of its leaders also responsible for acts of violence, was a proponent of amnesty for its leaders but rejected a blanket amnesty for everyone.

Ultimately, South Africans argued that amnesty could not be unconditionally given to everyone; amnesty in South Africa had to be granted through a process. Those requesting amnesty had to apply to the Truth and Reconciliation Commission. Their application had to be accepted, after which they had to participate in a truth commission and amnesty hearing. Depending on their participation, the commission would decide whether to grant amnesty or to reject their application. If rejected by the amnesty commission because of the gravity of their crimes, they were to be tried later in criminal courts.

Desmond Tutu later explained:

"For all these reasons, a nation, through those who negotiated the transition from apartheid to democracy, chose the option of individual and not blanket amnesty. And we believe that this individual amnesty has demonstrated its value. One of the criteria to be satisfied before amnesty could be granted was full disclosure of the truth. Freedom was granted in exchange for truth. We have, through these means, been able to uncover much of what happened in the past."[834]

Russell Daye explains that during the HRV (Human Rights Violations) hearings and investigations, tremendous amounts of information about killings, beatings and torture were uncovered. But more information was uncovered later during the 'Amnesty' hearing when those who had committed crimes gave verbal and written testimonies about the apartheid years.[835] In the amnesty hearings, those committing torture and execution would often name their superiors and persons ordering the crimes, those seniors in turn named their own superiors, uncovering the pyramid of conspiracy leading to the terror and violence of apartheid. The wealth of information uncovered could not have been secured without the amnesty hearings.

The decision on the amnesty process was not an easy one and required much painful negotiation and lobbying. In the end, amnesty was to be granted only if the members of the committee "were satisfied that applicants fully disclose their role in and knowledge of the act or event [for] which they were making application."[836] Amnesty was offered for "the violation of human rights through a) the killing, abduction, torture, or severe ill-treatment of any person; or b) any attempt, conspiracy, incitement, instigation, command or procurement to commit an act referred to in paragraph (a)."

The committee allowed amnesty only for crimes committed between March 1960 and 10th of May, 1994. In addition, amnesty was offered only for crimes committed out of a 'political motive'. Human rights violations for personal gain, economic gain, theft, vengeance, or nonpolitical ends were not offered the opportunity for amnesty. [837]

December 14, 1996 was set as the deadline on application for amnesty, but the large number of applicants forced the committee to extend the deadline until May 10, 1997. 7,112 applications were submitted to the Amnesty Committee. 5,392 were refused because they did not fit the definition of crimes set forth for the amnesty process. The vast majority of those refused by the commission did not fit the criteria of crimes committed out of a 'political motive'. [838] Thousands offered to tell the truth, apologize to the nation, and help create the 'Rainbow Nation' of the future.

Just before midnight on the last hour before the deadline for amnesty was to expire, six black youths walked into the Truth Commission offices in Cape Town and filled out the last and perhaps the more powerful symbolic applications for amnesty. In their application, they requested forgiveness and amnesty for what they called 'apathy'. The truth commission official was puzzled and asked, "but where does apathy fit into the act?" The official wanted to know what were their crime and the essence of the human rights violation. The young people responded that "we decided to ask for amnesty because we had done nothing...And that's what we did: we neglected to take part in the liberation struggle. So, here we stand as a small group representative of millions of apathetic people who didn't do the right thing."[839] It was a symbolic last application for a historic process of national reconciliation.

The hearings were painful for South Africa. Witnessing agents of apartheid recount the horrific acts of torture and murder on television was devastating. Many called for those applying for amnesty to be imprisoned and even executed. Not all the applications accepted by the committee were given amnesty. One famous case of amnesty refused by the commission was against Joe Verster, the director of a secret agency responsible for acts of murder and torture. During his hearings, he presented himself wearing a wig and a false beard to limit his recognition in society. Information he was presenting was also limited to much of the already known facts regarding cases of murder and torture. He revealed as little as possible about his role in the agency and the extent of his agency's participation in acts of violence. He also refused to show sympathy towards his victims and their families. He was refused amnesty by the commission. Other applicants from the same secret governmental agency also showed limited cooperation in truth telling and sympathy for the victims. Some were seen laughing and joking in the hallways of the committee during the breaks. They were also refused amnesty and were later tried as criminals [840]

Another important component of Act III of the reconciliation process is Restorative Justice for the victims of past political crimes. In Restorative Justice the focus is not on the extent of punishment for the offenders or their qualification for amnesty but on the creation of a post-conflict society with equal opportunities for the victims and the offenders. This requires the society to provide appropriate compensation to victims of past crimes, providing educational opportunities for the victims to regain their dignified place in society, appropriate health and mental care for the victims and their families, and appropriate economic opportunities and appropriate social networks to guarantee the rights of victims and their family. In order to meet this challenge in South Africa, the Truth and Reconciliation Commission created the Committee on Reparations and Rehabilitation, which was charged with this task.

As important as the amnesty process in Iran will be, the process of compensation for the victims of violence under Islamic Republic is equally important. In addition to victims of torture and imprisonment, Iranians as a society must also address the needs of the victim's families, including their spouses, children, mothers and fathers. Those who have lost a son, daughter, husband, wife, father, or a mother to torture or execution have suffered terrible psychological consequences and as a result are often suffering tremendous economic hardship. In addition to this group of victims, Iranians, in creation of a Committee for Reparation and Rehabilitation, must also take into account other groups who are not direct victims of human rights violation, yet need urgent attention. The largest number of victims of violence in the era of the Islamic Republic is comprised of those hundreds of thousands of veterans of Iran-Iraq war suffering greatly from physical and psychological ailments related to their duties. They are economically and educationally disadvantaged because of the difficulty in meeting their psychological and physical needs. Providing adequate health care, mental care, and educational and economic opportunities for the veterans of Iran-Iraq war must be one of the most important challenges of a future democratic Iranian society.

Act IV

Russell Daye designates 'Finding Ways to Heal' as the fourth act in the process of reconciliation. Here the attention turns to healing for the nation, which is suffering from trauma not unlike that of an individual suffering from Post-Traumatic Stress Disorder. He turns to the work of Judith Herman on trauma in addressing the three stages through which recovery from trauma takes shape, stages also considered in the evaluation of trauma in Iranian society. The first step is the creation of a safe environment in which the victim is no longer threatened and the human rights of citizens are guaranteed and upheld. The second stage in the recovery is remembrance and mourning for the victims and their families. Creation of memorials is an important and powerful component for this second stage in the healing process. During this stage, the painful memory of the past is acknowledged, documented, and remembered. In addition, during this painful process of remembering, attention is placed to ensure that the victims do not fall into the trap of fantasizing revenge. [841] In the last stage of the healing process as described by Dr. Herman, the victim reconnects with ordinary life. This requires the victim to shift from the past to the future and to renew social connections. In this stage, the victim attempts to overcome the isolation that is often a side effect of the traumatized state.[842] The Committee on Reparations and Rehabilitation recommended providing health care, mental health, housing, education, and conflict resolution for the victims of apartheid as important means to help heal the nation from the violence of the past. In South Africa, those who had suffered from human rights violations were allowed to make claims for reparations and compensation. These claims were investigated by the Committee on Human Rights Violation, which in turn determined which individuals were to be compensated.[843] Five categories of compensation were determined; these included addressing emotional suffering and pain, as well as providing medical care, economic and educational assistance, and the creation of memorials.[844]

Act V

The last act in the process of reconciliation, and perhaps most difficult and the most important, is forgiveness. In an interpersonal relationship between two people, forgiveness is the third act after 1) process of truth telling and naming of the harm done followed by 2) apology in which the offender claims and accepts responsibility, and then, finally, 3) forgiveness. In societal forgiving and reconciliation, Russell Daye added two additional essentials— 'Act III : Building a Transitional Justice Framework' as well as 'Act IV: Finding Ways to Heal'. In societal reconciliation and healing, 'forgiveness' becomes act five of the drama. In South Africa, Desmond Tutu and Nelson Mandela led the struggle for forgiveness and used both the elements of Christian philosophy as well as the African philosophy, tradition, and folklore of *'ubuntu'* or 'humanity'. [845]

Regardless of culture or religion, in nearly every society there is strong resistance to forgiveness. There are several reasons for this resistance, all of which are important and need to be addressed. Some associate forgiving with forgetting. While forgiving is important in process of reconciliation and creation of a post-conflict society, forgetting is extremely dangerous and can reignite violence of the past in a new form under new names. Building memorials, documenting violence, and creating rituals of remembrance are important elements helping a country to forgive without forgetting. Another resistance to forgiveness comes out of the urge to forgive without proper truth telling, or the documentation of crimes and acts of apology. In other words, resistance to forgiving comes when the first four acts of reconciliation are not performed appropriately and the people are merely told to 'forgive'. Another resistance to forgiveness is the ingrained cultural belief that vengeance is an appropriate response to an offense. Here, Restorative Justice for the victims is an important step in overcoming this hurdle. Reestablishing the victim's dignity as well as his or her societal status is an important step in overcoming the thirst for vengeance. In addition, some believe that forgiving and granting freedom for perpetrators of crimes can allow that person to freely repeat the acts of violence. Here, the sincere expression of regret and sorrow as discussed in Act II is an important component for the truth commissioners before granting amnesty and forgiveness so that the perpetrators of violence are no longer dangerous to society.

There have been many calls in the last few years for Iranians to forgive the crimes of the past in the hope of a new post-conflict democratic society. These calls have failed because of lack of proper attention to the process of reconciliation while placing undue emphasis on the most difficult and challenging component, 'forgiveness'. These calls for forgiveness were made without the call for the essential acts of truth telling, apology, creation of transitional justice system, and finding ways to heal. Calls for forgiveness without the framework of reconciliation and without a proper belief in the principles and theories of nonviolence can be inadequate, insufficient, and ineffective for society. In the last decade of the 20th century, South Africa made an important contribution to the path of nonviolence. There, the framework of reconciliation was created. It may and should serve as the means of overcoming the effects of political violence for centuries to come. Certainly, it may serve as a framework for the current generation of Iranians to overcome the violence of their past.

"The solitary Mexican loves fiestas and public gatherings. Any occasion for getting together will serve, any pretext to stop the flow of time and commemorate men and events with festivals and ceremonies. We are a ritual people, and this characteristic enriches both our imaginations and our sensibilities, which are equally sharp and alert."[846]
~Octavio Paz, 1990 winner of Nobel Prize in Literature

Part III

Celebrations as Civil Disobedience

CHAPTER 10 – RITUALS AND CELEBRATIONS THROUGH ANTHROPOLOGIC AND PSYCHOLOGICAL VIEWS

"Performance of rituals likewise heightens awareness of the common system of sentiments."

~ Clyde Kluckhohn

Celebrations and Rituals as Psychological Tools for Healing

It is widely known how Iranians live in fear and as we discussed in the first chapter, it is plausible to assume that vast numbers of Iranians are suffering from Post-Traumatic Stress Disorder and exhibiting its symptoms on a societal level. Because of this suffering and the continued use of threat and violence by the regime, when individuals in families or at schools attempt to speak up, they are often faced with blank stares or are ignored by their peers. They are constantly reminded by others of a regime that is too ruthless for them to overcome and the consequences of speaking out— prison, torture, and even death. In addition to fearing the regime, Iranians fear change as well. They are reminded of what their parents' generation experienced during revolution and radical change, which led to devastating, violent consequences. Thus they are paralyzed politically, fearful of taking the necessary steps toward democracy and only hoping for minor changes within the regime through what they call 'reforms'.

The situation in Iran reminds me of a patient suffering from anxiety disorder and in need of treatment but is so terrified of the treatment's possible side effects and consequences that he completely gives up on therapy. This is the state of affairs for Iranians. They know that their nation must adopt not just a democratic regime free of violence, but also a democratic culture free of violence. Yet the citizens of this nation, suffering from a terrible anxiety disorder brought on by violence, fear the possible consequences of treatment to such an extent that they fear the attempt to bring about change.

With all the advances in science today, psychologists and psychiatrists have come a long way in treating people with Post Traumatic Stress Disorder. But these are treatments for individuals and not communities or societies. In addition, even if there were an established modern medical method for treatment of hundreds of thousands of people suffering from trauma, the regime itself would not allow such a treatment. Intuitively, the regime is well aware of dangers of a psychologically healthy and capable population.

As one learns more and more about post-traumatic stress disorder and its therapy, one realizes that the essence of the Islamic Republic and its control over the population is the battle between the force which wants to keep its citizens in a continued traumatic state and the struggle of the population to overcome their fears. In this battle, terror and violence are fundamental tools for the regime, which attempts to continuously create anxiety and uncertainty through creation of crisis after crisis. Thus the psychological healing of the nation is one of the more important components of the Iranian battle for democracy.

What tools are available for Iranians to go through the process of healing and therapy at a societal level? In addition, how can they engage on this path of healing while at the same time voicing their desire for democracy and human rights, thus ridding themselves of the culture and politics of violence?

In order to answer these questions, we must acquire a better understanding of the components of therapy for Post-Traumatic Stress Disorder and then look at the potential of rituals and celebrations as tools to overcome fear and trauma at the societal level.

***

Rituals

With the new science of anthropology in the beginning of 20th century, a world of new cultures, languages, and practices was opened up to Europeans. For the first-time, Europeans were sent to Africa, North and South America, Asia and Australia, not as conquerors, traders, or missionaries, but as scientists eager to learn of the thousands of fascinating cultures across the world. The science of anthropology dictated that in order for someone to study a culture, that person must at least learn the language and live amongst its people for a period of time in order to gain a deeper understanding of that particular culture. Within a culture, the anthropologists would document and study the language of the people, their mythology, stories, beliefs, customs, and rituals. In other words, the new wave of scientists would travel to forests and deserts and live amongst tribes and cultures to collectively study the symbolic acts, symbolic words, and symbolic images of cultures.

In this gigantic 20th century effort to study local tribes and customs of more than 4,000 world cultures, anthropologists discovered that some of celebrations or rituals that are commonly practiced were found to be functioning as tools for overcoming the fears and anxieties of society.

Kluckhohn

Studying each culture's rituals was part of the new field of anthropology. By mid-20th century, scholars no longer looked at rituals as only religious symbolic acts and recognized the importance of ritual in everyday life of human beings separate from their religious purpose. Thus, with systematic study of rituals, new theories arose on the function of ritual in society. A theory that is important for us to examine was one developed by Clyde Kluckhohn (1905-1960), a professor of anthropology at Harvard University.

Kluckhohn suggested that a ritual can function to alleviate anxiety both at the individual level and at the societal level. His main focus of study was the culture of Navajo Indians. In his studies of rituals and mythology of Native Americans, he wanted to go beyond simple explanations of human activity. "It is easy to understand why organisms eat. It is easy to understand why a defenseless man will run to escape a charging tiger. The physiological basis of the activities presented by myths and rituals are less obvious."[847]. Thus, Kluckhohn searched for psychological explanations of rituals and myths. He stated that in every society there are two types of anxieties. First, he categorized some anxieties as "those that may be understood in terms of 'reality principle' of psychoanalysis: Life is hard - and unseasonable temperature, a vagary of rainfall does bring hunger or actual starvation; people are organically ill." In other words, there are natural threats to life and humanity from sources outside the control of the society and which are nearly universally felt. The threat of prolonged drought is a reality in every farming society and nearly every farming society has rituals in which the society collectively participates in activities that they believe will help them bring rainfall. These activities are rituals that help deal with the anxiety of possible drought or famine. In addition to this 'reality based' anxiety, there are various forms of what Kluckhohn called 'neurotic' anxieties. These anxieties are society-specific. Each culture, because of its restrictions or limitations, creates anxieties within its population. Kluckhohn described sexual anxiety as the main type of 'neurotic' anxiety prevalent in the American and European societies of 1950s. In today's Iran, an important form of 'neurotic' anxiety, or anxiety which is society specific and brought about by the man-made restrictions on the population, is the fear of violence from the Islamic Republic as described in Chapter One. The inability of Iranians to take charge of their future and their country is mainly due to this form of anxiety. The regime, through violence and the creation of various social and economic crises, tries to keep the population in this state of psychological paralysis.

Kluckhohn described how rituals are a form of therapy both for populations and individuals. In his study of Navajo Indians, he learned that the major societal anxiety of Navajo tribes had to do with illness and disease. Navajo Indians were mainly hunters and gatherers, which meant the forced periodic migration from one region to another. Without the use of horses or other tools for transport, a member's illness was very burdensome on the population. It was difficult to transport a sick individual to a new location, and if illness was prevalent, moving to new lands could become impossible for the tribe. Widespread illness thus could place the tribe and society in danger of running out of game and food in the nearby region. Thus for Navajo Indians, the threat of illness and anxiety generated from this threat was the major societal form of anxiety.

Through his studies, Kluckhohn found that nearly all the rituals used by Navajo Indians were designed to help individuals and families psychologically deal with potential disease and illness in the tribe. He then looked at Pueblo Indians. Pueblo Indians were Native tribes related to Navajos but had settled into towns and villages and were mainly farmers, even though they lived in the same type of physical environment as the Navajo Indians. The main societal anxiety of Pueblo Indians was no longer illness, but mainly dealt with concerns about rainfall and the fertility of the land.

Even though the Pueblo Indians lived in towns and cities, which meant that the threat of endemic disease was more severe than for the Navajo, their anxiety about illness was less prevalent and their rituals were geared for coping with anxieties of drought and crop failure as opposed to illness.

Kluckhohn also observed that: "Performance of rituals likewise heightens awareness of the common system of sentiments. The ceremonials also bring individuals together in a situation where quarreling is forbidden. Preparation for and carrying out of a chant demands intricately ramified cooperation, economic and otherwise, and doubtless this reinforces the sense of mutual dependency."[848] Through the study of Navajo mythology, he claimed "certain passages in the myths indicate that the Navajo have a somewhat conscious realization that the ceremonials act as a cure, not only for physical illness, but also for antisocial tendencies."[849].

"Myths and rituals are adaptive from the point of view of the society in that they promote social solidarity, enhance the integration of the society by providing a formalized statement of its ultimate value attitudes, and afford a means for the transmission of much of the culture with little loss of content- thus protecting cultural continuity and stabilizing the society."[850]

Rituals are routines that create a sense of stability and constancy in face of fear arising from change. Deaths in the family, loss of employment, divorce, or children moving away are all understood by societies around the world as sources of anxiety. But the real cause of anxiety in these events is not death or divorce; it is change. Human beings are creatures of habit. We take comfort in the life that is both routine and predictable. What we fear most is change and uncertainty. When we lose a family member to death, anxiety associated with this is not the death itself, it is the arrival of a new life where that family member no longer exists. Divorce itself is not traumatic; it is the change to a divorced state that brings about anxiety. With change comes uncertainty and with uncertainty comes anxiety. Rituals are routines that help us deal with this change. In the moment that an individual has lost a parent or child, the psychological chaos itself may be the most painful experience. Thus every culture creates a set of rituals called funerals or memorials to deal with this anxiety. Many cultures have ceremonies and rituals designed for when children move away and start a life of their own. In addition, rituals not only help individuals and societies deal with anxieties associated with fear and uncertainty, they are also tools used in dealing with the near anticipation of change.

Looking at Iran at the societal level, we not only have the great anxiety from the current fear, threat, or use of violence of the regime, the mere anticipation of a major political and cultural change can be a highly anxiety provoking threat that Iran's society has a difficult time dealing with. One of the important reasons for resisting elimination of the current Islamic Republic regime structure and adoption of a democratic constitution by many Iranians is the state of anxiety, fear, and uncertainty that such a political change can bring about psychologically. It is not a surprise then that most democracy activists have a fear of the mere mention of the word 'revolution', even when speaking of nonviolent revolutions of late 20th century. The word revolution for them is associated with change and uncertainty. This change and uncertainty, together with the experience of 103 generations of Iranians having violence determine their fate, can be very anxiety provoking.

Milan Psychiatric Group and the use of Rituals in Psychotherapy

In 1960's, independent of the work on rituals by anthropologists, a group of psychiatrists in Milan began to study the role of rituals in psychotherapy. This group, which became known as the Milan Group, began publishing a series of articles in Italian in 1960s on the role of rituals in psychotherapy. These psychiatrists described ritual as "an action, or a series of actions, accompanied by verbal formulae and involving the entire family… it must consist of a regular sequence of steps taken at the right time and in the right place."[851] This group of psychiatrists found rituals to be very effective in the treatment of families and especially dysfunctional families. A regular routine given to families in psychological chaos was an important step in bringing the family together and creating communication channels. A dysfunctional family can greatly benefit from a regular ritual of everyone eating dinner together each night at 7 p.m. Such an act creates channels for communication between family members in a setting where quarreling and fighting is forbidden. The Milan Group tells the story of a little girl who had not spoken at all since the death of her younger brother. After the death of the little boy, the family had refused to talk about the incident and the young girl had refused to talk at all. The Milan Group suggested a ritual in which all the family members get together and take the clothes and toys of the little boy for a burial and funeral service, while explaining to the young girl what had happened to her brother.[852] This burial ritual was very important to help the little girl understand what had happened and see the tragedy shared by other members of her family. The little girl soon began to speak again after the performance of the symbolic ritual of burial.

Van Der Hart

The Milan Group continued its work and published a book 'Paradox and Counter Paradox' in 1978 to further describe its work on rituals and their use in psychiatry.[853] The work on rituals by the Milan Group influenced other psychiatrists around the world, particularly a Dutch psychiatrist named Van der Hart, who published a book in 1978 called *Rituals in Psychotherapy: Transition and Continuity*. [854]

Van der Hart improved on the use of rituals in psychiatry by incorporating lessons learned through the study of rituals by anthropologists. Like the anthropologists, Van der Hart emphasized ritual as a symbolic act and not just a routine. He emphasized that, when performing a ritual as a symbolic act, the participants must understand and actively involve themselves in the symbolic meaning of the act. Without such involvement, the ritual becomes a 'hollow' or an 'empty' ritual with limited therapeutic effects. [855]

He stated that "certain rituals are repeatedly performed throughout the lives of those concerned; others, on the contrary, are performed only once."[856] In addition, Van der Hart introduced additional concepts in the study of rituals. He discussed how rituals have opened parts and closed parts.

"Open parts provide enough fluidity so that participants can invest the experience with their own involving and idiosyncratic meaning. Closed parts provide enough structure to give safety to strong emotional components, pass on new cultural information, and give form to the actions."[857] In describing the open parts and closed parts of rituals, he was creating a framework for ritual as an act where individuals are free to use their creativity to form their own personal meaning for the ritual, while at the same time allowing the closed parts to provide structure for psychological stability.

The study of rituals by psychiatrists was in effect in general agreement with the anthropologists. Clyde Kluckhohn had come to this conclusion when studying rituals:

"Rituals constitute a guarantee that … people can count upon the repetitive nature of the phenomena…The personal sorrow of the devout Christian is in some measure mitigated by anticipation of the great feasts of Christmas and Easter. Perhaps the even turn of the week and its Sunday services and midweek prayer meetings gave a dependable regularity which the Christian clung to even more in disaster and sorrow. For some individuals, daily prayer and the confessional gave the needed sense of security… Rituals and myths supply, then, fixed points in a world of bewildering change and disappointment."[858]

Celebrations as form of ritual can help individuals in societies come together and focus on overcoming their terror. Even in today's world, celebrations are the most powerful tool in bringing people together and creating new relationships. The great sport rituals and celebrations of the

Olympics and the World Cup are important events in helping to spread peace around the world. Families have rituals and celebrations of visiting parents and grandparents on Mother's day, Father's day and birthdays. Celebrations are used in weddings and graduations as rites of passage in lifting individuals to a higher state of spiritual understanding. Many countries have a celebration for their Independence Day, a ritual that unifies people in celebrating their country.

***

Rituals and Celebrations as Frameworks for Recovery after Trauma

How does a celebration function as a tool for psychological therapy? In order to better understand how a ritual achieves its healing power, it is important to understand the steps required for the treatment of a patient suffering from trauma. Dr. Judith Herman in her book *Trauma and Recovery* describes the "core experience of psychological trauma [as] disempowerment and disconnection from others. Recovery, therefore, is based upon the empowerment of the survivor and the creation of new connections"[859]. This statement very well describes the societal state of Iranians across the world. Iranians feel disconnected from each other and their most difficult challenge has been to unify themselves through creation of new connections. In addition, Iranians feel disempowered.

Most have the notion that Iranians suffering from trauma are hidden, forgotten in their solitude because of their psychological challenges. Yet, when one discusses democracy with ordinary, well to do Iranians, the most common response of seemingly psychologically healthy individuals is their tremendous fears and anxiety during a transition to democracy, fear of greater and greater violence by the regime or statement in regards to the immense power of the regime and Iranian people's inability to do anything about it. Post-Traumatic Stress Disorder at the societal level is not only found in millions of Iranians suffering from addiction and poverty and living outside the discourse for democracy as anxiety-stricken individuals suffering in solitude. This lack of empowerment, fear and anxiety for change is seen in the most functional Iranian university professors and businessmen. They feel defeated and paralyzed in confronting the Islamic Republic, a psychological phenomenon which was mostly absent during the workup to the 1979 revolution where a psychologically healthy population had no fears for uncertainty when calling for the Shah to leave. Today, Iranians are afraid of possible uncertainties arising from the regime's collapse and are too fearful to believe that Iranians can reconnect with each other to build a democratic society.

Dr. Herman, in describing the therapeutic path for a traumatized individual continues: "Recovery therefore is based upon the empowerment of the survivor and the creation of new connections."[860] Empowerment takes place at a personal level, allowing every Iranian to participate and feel they are participating in a process that leads to societal and national healing. This participation cannot place the individual in possible harm's way and should not be physically or psychologically demanding. One cannot expect Iranians to go into the streets so they can feel they are empowering themselves. A mere threat of violence by the regime can trigger traumatic memories and severe anxiety. Empowerment has to come from within and in relative safety from possible threats of violence. Thus, empowerment of individual and creation of new connections are the goals of therapy. But if such are the goals of therapy, what is the process of therapy?

Herman describes the process of recovery unfolding in three stages. "the central task of the first stage is the establishment of safety. The central task of the second stage is remembrance and mourning. The central task of third stage of therapy is reconnection with ordinary life."[861] Iranian national celebrations can fulfill the requirements of all three stages of therapy.

"The central task of the first stage is the establishment of safety."

Safety is extremely important in treatment. The woman or child suffering from Post-Traumatic Stress Disorder because of domestic abuse cannot be treated and placed in therapy while she remains in the environment in which the abuse is repeated. A political prisoner cannot be treated for Post-Traumatic Stress Disorder in face of repeated threats and the use of violence and torture. Iranians cannot be treated for their traumatized state while performing tasks that can lead to fear, terror and further risks of psychological trauma. The regime, without knowing the psychology and science behind Post-Traumatic Stress Disorder, continuously aims to destroy the relative safety Iranians possess. Safety is eliminated even in the comfort of one's living room with security forces raiding family gathering and parties at will. Nighttime raids at parties are common occurrence in Iran. These raids are psychological tools the regime uses to destroy the relative safety people attempt to create and through which they can find comfort and perhaps set out on the path to free themselves from fear. The regime is well aware that Iranians must continuously be subjected to one crisis after another. If a crisis does not occur on its own on the world stage, the regime must create such a crisis either domestically or attempt to instigate a crisis internationally. In the course of treatment, creation of relative safety for the population is an important step towards therapy.

In Iran today, celebrations can create the space where a person can find a relative refuge for safety. It is the potential for this stage of therapy which a celebration provides in which the regime intuitively fears and it is because of this potential for empowerment which causes the regime to ban most forms of celebration in Iran thus making celebrations not only instruments for overcoming fear, but also as instruments for civil disobedience.

"The central task of the second stage is remembrance and mourning."

Today, nations who want to overcome their painful past create rituals, celebrations, museums, memorials and monuments to achieve the central task of this second stage. Celebrations, whether a day long or a month long, can play an important role as tools for remembrance and for public education. In America, there are day long and month long celebrations for Women, African-Americans, Veterans of Wars, Native-Americans, Gay and Lesbians and nearly every other group who is trying to overcome a form of painful past and needs a celebration as a vehicle.

But again, without knowing the psychology and science behind this, the regime, using its own intuition for staying in power, refuses to allow free nationals celebrations for the people and only tolerates the minimum of Nowruz, Souri and Yalda which it was not able to eliminate through ridicule or fear. The regime realizes that any form of celebration may serve as remembrance of the pain Iranians go through every day and can become powerful vehicles for empowering the population. Their intuition is right on.

Celebrations, as tools of remembering and recollecting the past can also play an important role in fulfilling the second stage of treatment for trauma while again serving as instruments of civil disobedience.

"The central task of the third stage [of therapy] is reconnection with ordinary life."

Reconnection to ordinary life involves the right to joy and happiness as the basic right of every human being. The love one can experience from family, children, and friends is a component of an ordinary life and reconnection to family and loved ones is a step in the healing process. At a societal level, such loss of connection can result in loss of basic trust in society with the feeling that everyone is trying to cheat you and you should cheat everyone else.

Young people in Iran continuously attempt to reconnect with ordinary life. In this attempt, they strive to be more active in sports, recreations, arts, and culture. Weekly hiking and mountain climbing is a ritual amongst the youth in many cities of Iran. Recreational participation in sports and watching soccer matches has become more and more important for young people attempting to cope with the hopeless and traumatic situation of their economic and societal security. Underground musicians, painters, writers, and artists having weekly and monthly gathering are seen in nearly every family in Iran. These are all natural attempts to overcome the third stage in recovery.

In a society suffering from trauma, celebrations can be used as powerful bridges reconnecting Iranians to each other regardless of the village, town, or city they live in and regardless of ethnicity, religion, sex or age. In this process, no group, council, assembly or organization can create the necessary bridges for connections for Iranians quite like celebrations. The symbolic act of reconnection can take place within the safety and security of one's family and on the individual level through participation in shared national acts. The incredible power of a celebration allows participants to be instantaneously connected spiritually and psychologically to millions of other in other cities, villages and towns who are simultaneously undergoing the same celebration and symbolic act. Celebrations thus also serve as powerful vehicles for the third stage of therapy from trauma and since they are banned or detested by the regime, they also serve as vehicles for civil disobedience.

***

CHAPTER 10

Far more than their healing function and as tools to overcome fear, terror and trauma, Nowruz and other celebrations are symbols of Iranian national identity. In addition, Nowruz and other Iranian celebrations are symbolic acts for popular joy and hope, elements that are not tolerated by the current regime. Furthermore, a religious regime must rely on religious acts and rituals to continuously legitimize its rule. Symbolic acts and rituals outside the realm of religion are thus acts which can ultimately undermine the religious regime's legitimacy. Thus it is not surprising that the Islamic Republic abhors non-religious national celebrations of Iran which are centered on festivities, joy and celebration.

CHAPTER 11 – CELEBRATIONS OF RESISTANCE AGAINST WINTER

"Such fires, which can function as symbolic acts of civil disobedience will serve as beacons of hope and courage for a generation desperately trying to overcome the darkness of fear, terror and violence of the Islamic Republic."

Introduction to Iranian Celebrations

In 1960's and early 70's, a group of Iranian volunteers headed by Mr. Anjavi-Shirazi set out to hundreds of towns and villages across Iran to document the ancient celebrations, traditions and folklore of far off towns and villages and the variations in their customs and rituals. One autumn, in the village of Jilard, near the volcanic peak of Damavand, they documented women hand-picking apples, oranges and pears for a special burial just outside the village. Such burial of fruit required great care and it wasn't done at any particular location. Grandmothers guided their daughters and granddaughters and instructed them on the proper soil, depth and care. The fruit had to be placed away from water and moisture and the earth had to be free of pests. As far as they knew, this practice had been passed down from grandmother to granddaughter for centuries.

The fruits weren't buried for a special sacrifice to gods. It wasn't gesture and ritual to thank Mother Earth. Fruits weren't placed to provide nourishment to the soil or nearby trees. The practice of burying the fruit in autumn by the women in the village of Jilard was the first act for one of the oldest rituals and celebrations of human beings still practiced today.

Months from now, the coming of winter would remind the villagers of the oldest natural fear of human beings. Before humanity feared terrorism and war, prior to fear of atomic holocaust, Nazism and fascism, prior to fear of colonization and slavery, fear of religious wars, invasions from afar, fear of King-Gods of Babylon and Egypt and the fires of hell, there was the fear of winter. In the cold winter, the plants shed their leaves, the animals slumber to conserve their energy and human beings all over the world witness the months of darkness and death. Winter would place the fear of hunger, cold,

CHAPTER 11

and disease back in the hearts of mothers and fathers. It was in winter when grandparents would die after respiratory infections. The close quarters required to conserve heat would serve as conduit to pass infectious diseases from the elderly to children. Mothers would place their infants close to their bodies at nights to provide the vital heat needed to survive. Fire was a precious commodity and a necessity for survival.

The landscape of Iran and much of the world conjures images of heat and desert for Europeans and Americans. Many mistakenly picture sand dunes and palm trees interspersed with Iranians cities as images of what Iran is like. Yet, although much of Iran is covered by desert land, most of the population does not live in these regions. The majority of Iranians live in cities, towns, and villages that are atop or near its mountains.

Winter months in Iranian mountains could be far more treacherous than the desert. Iran's winters are harsh and Iranian mountains are not forested mountains like in Americas or Europe with their unlimited supply of firewood. Snow begins to fall in late October in much of Azarbaijan and Kurdistan and much of work in summer and autumn is spent in preparation for winter. Many of the elderly in Iran can die in winter. Children are at great risk as well. The food gathered and stored by farmers often barely feeds the population through the cold months, which means a lengthening of winter cold would mean possible shortages and hunger.

Humanity's experience with winter does not encompass several centuries or several millennia. The witnessing of seasons and the coming of winter predates the advent of farming 10,000 years. In fact, the experience of winter dates back to our origins as human beings.

During episodic global warmings over 200,000 years ago, tribe after tribe of early human beings continuously headed north from Africa and repeatedly challenged themselves and tested their survival in the most northern hospitable climates. As human beings tested their limits each winter and each generation, those who survived the cold would teach the younger generations of their skills. For thousands of winters, such skills were tested and retested in order to optimally adapt human beings with the fear and violence of winter.

Those cultures more prominently affected by winter managed to turn the cold and dark months to occasions for celebration as a remedy to overcome wintertime's great anxiety and fear of cold. Iranians in particular created an elaborate set of celebrations to overcome their psychological pain and anxiety. The harsh winters in Iran were turned to great occasions for celebration through the practice of such ancient rituals. The women burying fruits in the villages outside Damavand were merely using an ancient technique of refrigeration to ensure the presence of fresh fruit for one of the most important celebrations and nights of the year. The Night of *Yalda*, or *Chelleh* on the first night of winter and the longest night of the year has been a special night throughout Iranian history. For thousands of years in Iran, the great violence of winter has been challenged through this celebration marking the beginning winter. Yet, this celebration is only the opening drama for an intricate set of celebrations which for Iranians continue through the harsh months of winter, the amazing renewal and rebirth of life in spring, the long and hot months of summer and the flowing of rivers and the shedding of leaves in autumn. In order to understand these intricate cultural rituals of Iranian, one must first understand the Iranian calendar.

***

Iranians today, like their ancestors, still divide their year into twelve months beginning with *farvardin*, the first month of Spring. Each month is named after one of the god-elements of nature seen in beliefs and practices of ancient Persia. *Esfand*, the third month of winter, is so named because it was in this time of the year when plants and animals were again nurtured by the earth, so the month was named after goddess *Esfandarmaz* or Mother Earth and held a special place in the calendar of Iranians as a symbol of femininity, thus making it a celebration of women. *Farvardin*, the first month of spring is named after the kind spirit of those who passed away, perhaps during the harsh winter or during the previous year. *Khordad*, the last month in spring, is named for goddess of water, a vitally important element for plants and animals in the coming harsh summer months.

What is different on today's calendar for Iranians is the naming of the days. As opposed to the seven names of Monday, Tuesday, etc. creating a week, which is used across the globe, ancient Iranians had each of the thirty days uniquely named. Like the names of the months, the names of days were named after god-elements of Iranian culture. The names of twelve of these days were also the names of each of the twelve months. In other words, just as there was a month called *Farvardin*, once a month there was a day named *Farvardin*.

On the Iranian calendar, when the name of the day in a month fell in that particular month, the suffix *'gan'* was added to the name and the day was marked as occasion for great celebration all over Iran. These celebrations helped Iranians socialize, organize, communicate, and heal. As an example, the fifth day of every month in Iran was named *Esfand* day. When *Esfand* day fell in the month of *Esfand* in the last month of winter, the celebration of *Esfand*gan, or the celebration of women, would ensue. The 16th of every month was day of *Mehr*. Thus, on the day of *Mehr*, in the month of *Mehr*, *Mehregan* was the great Iranian celebration. This intricate Iranian calendar thus created a culture where a different celebration was held every month.

The warmth and sense of love on these celebrations helped Iranians overcome the fear and anxiety of winter and the occasional harsh droughts of summer. Today, this societal tool for healing can be greatly appreciated by a population living in constant fear, anxiety and violence of another kind.

Today, such celebrations can be tools needed for Iran's societal psychological healing. In addition, because of how they symbolize kindness, charity and harmony with nature and with other human beings, these rituals of Iranian culture are symbolic tools to help change from culture of political violence to a new culture of respect, tolerance, and human rights. In addition, these rituals are symbolic acts that can serve as tools for Iranians to express themselves politically at a time when all other avenues are closed. The current regime will interfere with any attempt at political campaigns or a movement seeking to secure a mass referendum towards democracy. An attempt to hold such a referendum through a ballot box will either be crushed or will be tampered. In such an atmosphere and at this particular time in Iranian history, these monthly celebrations could provide a platform for Iranians to express themselves in a referendum for political change. A color or another symbol on such days of celebration can serve the same function as a vote dropped in a ballot box. These deeply rooted rituals for healing are tools created and handed to Iranians by their ancestors for times of fear and need. Now is one of those times.

***

The Evening of December 21st – *Yalda*

For Iranians, the first month of winter is called *Dei* meaning God. In Pahlavi, the language of Iranians during the Sassanid era, it was called *Deiv*. In Avesta, it is called Daeva. In Sanskrit, it is Deva, what we now call Diva. Those ancient Indo-European tribes who came to Europe continued to incorporate this word for God as Deus which in Greek language and culture was changed to Zeus.[862] The English word 'Theo' was derived from the word

Dei, meaning God, creating words such as 'theology', the study of God. In Irish, it is referred to as 'Dia', in French 'Dieu'. The word 'deity' in English language is derived from this prehistoric word for God which for Iranians still represents the first month of winter. 'Divine' also has the same root. 'Diurnal', the opposite of 'nocturnal', actually refers to the part of the day when God is present.

Ancient Iranians naming each day of the month, called the first day of every month '*Dei*', which meant the first day of each month was a day of rest, reflection, and prayer. The 8th, 15th and 23rd of every month also incorporated '*Dei*' within their names, giving Iranians a day of rest approximately every seven days, similar to the Semitic concept of rest once a week later adopted in Iran.

The first month of winter in Iranian calendar was called and is still called '*Dei*' which meant that for Iranians, the first day of winter as the day of '*Dei*' in the month of '*Dei*' or what some called '*Deigan*'. Throughout Iranian history, the evening before this day has been a special night for them. The celebration and ritual of '*Yalda*' or 'Birth' or what Iranians also call the celebration of '*chelleh*' is held the evening before '*Deigan*'.

For Iranians, the longest night of the year, when earth prepares for the cold, pain and suffering of winter, is a time which may seem most removed from a celebration. Yet perhaps it is because of this darkness and the coming of the unknown winter that people needed a healing celebration at such a time and had the most need for kindness of *Dei* for their families. Yalda, one of the most cherished of Iranian celebrations was created and passed from generation to generation until today to perhaps serve as a tool to remind Iranians of courage, strength and patience needed against the violence of winter.

The celebration often involves gathering at a grandparent's house and eating fruits and food prepared for this night. The memory of the longest night of the year enfolded in the warmth of love, family, and stories in hundreds of thousands of towns and villages across Iran is the first of a series of elaborate national celebrations journeying Iranians through the cold of winter, rebirth of life in spring, the joy of water and rain in heat of summer and the brilliance of autumn.

***

In order to understand the healing powers of the ritual and celebration of *Yalda*, one must become familiar with the atmosphere in the home of an

CHAPTER 11

Iranian family on this night. Although it is called a celebration, *Yalda* is more like a joyous ritual for family. On *Yalda*, the cold and dark of the night is suddenly transformed on the occasion to warmth and light of food and stories. Thus, suddenly, one may forget that one is experiencing the longest night of the year and is lost in an artificial space created by human beings, a space in which only kindness and joy is allowed. There are no words of pain, hatred, or anger. Animosities between in-laws are forgotten and the cold harsh *zemestan* or winter begins for Iranians in this setting.

It is through thousands of symbolic words and images that a culture is formed. It is easy to translate the word 'winter' from English to *zemestan* in Persian. Both words essentially describe the cold months of the year. Yet the same word conjures up very different images for a European or a North American than the images conjured up for an Iranian. European and American winters conjure up images of woods covered with snow, families gathered around their hearths, which provide them with the warmth of winter.

None of these images are evident in a winter in Iran. The altitude of the Iranian plateau brings about a winter just as harsh as that in northern and even temperate zone countries, but it is the abundance of wood in Europe and North America which helps create their rituals of winter. The hearth and chimney, which are essential symbols of winter and a gathering point for families and their rituals in many countries, is absent in Iranian towns and villages. You find a *tanour* in Iranian homes—which may look like a chimney—– but a *tanour* is solely for the baking of bread and cooking of food and plays little part in providing warmth in wintertime. The lack of wood as a natural resource for providing heat in Iran has helped create another tool for warmth that requires much less in the way of natural resources. The tool for warmth in wintertime and one which forms the centerpiece of *Yalda* celebration in Iran is *korsi*.

About 2 feet high and 4 feet wide, a *korsi* looks like a coffee table made out of wood. In wintertime, it is placed in middle of the family room and is covered with a large comforter that not only covers the *korsi*, but also extends well beyond to cover family members' torsos while they lie with their feet under the *korsi* itself. A source for heat is then place underneath the *korsi*. In the cold winters of my childhood in Tehran, the source of heat was a small electrical heater big enough to heat a closet yet, with the *korsi*, warm enough for the entire family. Without electricity in some of Iran's villages, *korsi* is done the old fashion way. If the floor of the room is dirt, a little hole about one foot deep is dug in and reinforced with bricks. If the floor is stone or wood, a metallic pan is placed in the middle. The hole is then filled with ashes and then glowing charcoal is brought in and placed in the pan or the hole. The charcoal is covered with ash, except for a two-inch opening on the top to allow oxygen to flow in and heat to escape. Thus, in the cold of winter, only several pieces of charcoal are enough to warm an entire family.

Korsi is one of those words that cannot be translated into another language. It is the device around which the night of *Yalda* is formed. It is around the *korsi* that families gather for their feasts and celebrations. The children, parents, and grandparents gather around *korsi* and use its warmth as they sleep under its covering during the cold night. It is difficult for an Iranian to think of this night and not recall the nights of listening to stories of parents and grandparents under the *korsi*. The age of petroleum has helped make the *korsi* more or less obsolete. Most homes in Iran are now heated with natural gas or heating oil. But even as the *korsi* may have become obsolete in many homes, the symbolism and healing power of *Yalda* is desperately needed in a culture of distrust, hatred, and anger of today. This healing power has kept Yalda alive for Iranians.

Food

In many villages, a colorful handmade quilt is placed on top of the *Korsi* and decorated with food and fruits specially prepared for *Yalda*. Weeks of preparation and planning are involved in this celebration. The women in far off villages near Damavand were storing and refrigerating fruit for use on this night. In most villages, yogurt and butter are made and placed in clay jars to be used on this night and in winter. Watermelons placed in nets and hung in cools basements in summer especially for this night are brought out for the family. In town of Azar-shahr, in Azarbaijan and in village after village in Iran, people believe that eating watermelons on this night will help them overcome the cold and disease in winter.[863] Pomegranate is also a traditional fruit on this night. In towns near Damavand, a large dish filled with all kinds of fruits and vegetables including apples, pears, carrots, walnuts, watermelons, and apricots are placed on *korsi* and families believe that a person should eat each one of these fruits in order to stay healthy during winter.[864] If a family cannot afford all these fruits, watermelon and carrots are a must and should be prepared for this night at all costs. In Arak, Qazvin, and many other towns, they believe watermelon is not only important in helping overcome disease and illness during wintertime, but also believe the effect of watermelon eaten on this night will continue past winter unto summer heat and will help their livers stay healthy and will keep them cool in the warmth of summer. Watermelon, the traditional fruit of summertime, aside from the likely nutritional value needed for the family, was perhaps also important psychologically as reminder of the warmth of sun in the summer. In town of Taleqan and many other towns, it is customary to eat the thick Iranian noodle and bean soup known as *ash-reshteh* on this night. In the village of Jeyyid, a local dish called *khashil* made of flour and sugar and mixed with herbs is served on this night. It is then topped with butter. In the town of Nahavand, a special dish is made by placing grain in the juice from feta cheese until the grain is wet and has absorbed the fluid. The mixture is then cooked. Almonds and walnuts are then added.[865]

The traditional dinner served in Ardebil on this night is usually rice with chicken and a local *khoresh* (stew) named *mosanba*.[866] After dinner, yogurt prepared for this night is brought out. They believe that eating yogurt on this night will keep them healthy all winter. Each member of family is given a bowl of yogurt and a bowl of fruit and sits around *korsi*.

Traditionally, in many towns and villages, night begins with the oldest members of family reminiscing the coldest winters they remember and stories and memories of those winter nights decades ago. The night is then spent listening to stories or music. Mothers with brides send their daughters gifts on this night. In addition, those engaged send their fiancés gifts as well.

Customs

Children of Taleqan go to neighbors and in a ritual reminiscent of European rituals of Christmas carols or Halloween sing outside their doors until owners hand out sweets.[867] In Anzeha, near Firouz-Kouh, story of Rostam from the epic of Ferdowsi is a popular tale told by the elders. In the city of Nahavand, those who are literate and have good voices also recite stories from Ferdowsi's *shahnameh* for the family to enjoy.[868]

In most towns in Gilan, telling fortunes by reading Hafez is a popular and old tradition.[869] The first *ghazal* from Hafez is recited for the oldest member of the family followed by a poem for each other member moving to the youngest. In homes where they do not have a copy of Hafez or do not have a literate member in house, fortune is read using walnuts.[870] Another form of fortune telling for children on this night is called *falgoosh*. In this form, participants take a mirror and a key and stand at crossroads, randomly listening to conversations of pedestrians. The random words heard by the children are in turn interpreted as their fortunes.[871] Singing and dancing are popular activities.[872] Gathering at towns and villages of Gilan and most other cities lasts through early hours of morning.

Spoon-beating is another tradition on this night popular in Mazandaran and much of Iran. In this tradition, women holding a large wooden spoon cover and hide themselves with *Chador* and go from house to house knocking on the doors. Owners place food or other necessities in the spoon. Gathered items are then given to the poor.[873]

In some towns and villages of Mazandaran, children have a tradition of taking a hand knitted large red sock. In a ritual strangely similar to Christmas ritual of placing gifts in large red socks, children go from house to house and neighbors place gifts or nuts in their socks. Some children jump from rooftop to rooftop and with a string lower their socks to the neighbor's window. This again is reminiscent of Santa Claus visiting rooftops and with the Europeans placing their large red socks next to their fireplaces as opposed to children lowering them on the window. Neighbors then fill-up the socks with gifts or snacks before children pull them back up again. It is very likely that both the Christmas version of this ritual and this version performed on December 21st in far off villages of Iran are both variations of a pre-historic human ritual for the start of winter practiced by common Indo-European ancestors thousands of years ago.[874]

In the town of Azar-shahr in Azarbaijan, few days before *Yalda*, in an Iranian ritual called *khooneh-takani*, the home is thoroughly cleaned from corner to corner, furniture are removed to clean all the crevices, the sheets are washed, and the rugs cleaned.[875] Four walnuts are broken under the four legs of *korsi* and kept all night. Night is usually spent listening to old Azari stories told by the elders.

Tale of Old Woman and Her Cat

An old tale told in villages of Azerbaijan on this night is the story of an old woman who lived with her daughter and a cat. The elderly who tell the story speak of how one summer people were reminding the old woman to prepare for winter. The old woman replies that she does not need to prepare as she is going to die before the cold. The old woman's daughter replies that she will marry before winter and the cat replies that she will go to live with another family when the old woman and her daughter are gone. When winter came, the old woman had not died, her daughter had not married, and the cat did not go to live with another family. The family survived the cold winter with great difficulty.[876] The story tells us a great deal about the psychology of an ancient culture still alive in the towns and villages across Iran. Nothing is certain in this uncertain world except for winter the story tells us. Even the moment of death is uncertain, yet cold and darkness of winter arrives every year with certainty.

Joy, Kindness and Celebration as Essence of the Night

One of the more universal traditions for this night is the emphasis that previous enmities, hatred and anger must be set aside and gotten rid of. People in villages of Azerbaijan believe that the more hatred and anger exists on this night, the more winter skies will be covered with clouds and storms, and the less sunshine will people see.[877] People in the towns and villages use this night as an extremely powerful traditional tool of peacemaking. If there are two families in town with unresolved issues, friends and neighbors will use this night to gather those two families at each others' or a third person's home in order for them to resolve their differences. Even if two mortal enemies exist, in the spirit of goodwill for this night and goodwill for their village, they kiss each other on the cheek and make peace. In the town of Alamdar in Azerbaijan, locals believe that if your most hated enemy comes to your house on this night, even if they have blood on their hands, the host is to forgive and make peace.[878] People believe that if there is hatred and anger in their town during this ritual, their prayers are not answered by God.[879] For the people, to forgive when that person has come to your house to ask for your forgiveness is a long tradition attributed to ancient Iranian concept of chivalry or what is called *javanmardi*.[880]

Natanz

In Natanz, now world famous for its source of tension and fear from its billion dollar underground centrifuge facility, life for people still revolves around the ancient rituals of Iran. On the night of *Yalda*, families spend weeks preparing food for the ritual. Traditionally in Natanz, doors to all homes were open for visitors who usually spend all night around *korsi* telling stories and reminiscing on the past. In 1960's and 1970's, before the fear and terror of the Islamic Republic and the fear of bombing of Natanz, locals told that a family usually had to be invited to come for dinner, but after-dinner activities and socialization required no invitation. After dinner, one of the children was usually sent to another person's home and was told to come back if they are not home. If the child took long to come back, the family would know the other family is home and waiting for guests. Many times, plans were made during the day while shopping and preparations were done in the bazaar.

Across Iran, when a family visits for *Yalda* gathering, everyone is invited, including the children and elderly. No one stays behind unless they are sick. The homes are left empty. These stories of villages and in particular Natanz are not stories of forgotten celebrations performed in ancient times. They are rituals of an ancient city still kept alive by the people. In the atmosphere of international competition, threats of war, and military strikes, the customs, the culture, and the human beings living in the city are often forgotten, while achievements are measured in terms of the number of centrifuges underground. The celebrations of the people in this city, like every other city in Iran, helped people survive psychologically and kept alive a society in harmony with itself and nature through the fear and anxiety of winter.

Today, without any input or permission from people of this ancient city, billions of dollars are spent building an elaborate underground facility filled with radioactive uranium. No citizen of Natanz was asked for their opinion about such a project in their town and no parliament of Iran approved such a project. Like one hundred generations before them, the people of Iran are again pawns in elaborate schemes of their rulers, who are attempting to prolong the primacy of their power. This time, the rulers believe creating a nuclear capability can extend their rule. The danger which faces Natanz by this underground uranium enrichment facility is symbolic of the threat of violence against this generation of Iranians and Iranian culture itself.

One must view Yalda and other Iranian celebrations in the context of their function for society. Celebrations are powerful rituals of healing. Despite violent and horrific history, through such rituals, in village after village, town after town and city after city, people used these rituals as tools for kindness, hope and rebirth. Celebrations can be tools of psychological healing for those suffering from traumas of loss, illness, natural disasters, and death. Celebrations are tools that allow families to come together, overcome their anger, forgive their neighbors for offenses and mistakes, and bond in a more powerful unit better shaped to meet their psychological and societal needs. Celebrations are tools for a culture to remind itself of benefits of celebration and peace as opposed to enmity and violence. It is partly because of these celebrations of kindness, respect, and societal love that Iran has managed to endure as a culture and as a nation.

Perhaps these celebrations serve as one of the pillars of Iranian civilization. Repeatedly in their history, Iranians have changed their language and their religion yet their identity has remained the same partly because of such national Iranian rituals. Yet this Iranian identity seen through such celebrations is often concealed because of the overwhelming pervasiveness of violence for political gain. An important challenge of this generation is to revive these celebrations of Iran as symbols of Iranian pride as opposed to current political violence of the Islamic Republic attempting to use military prowess and number of centrifuges as essence of national pride.

Today, these powerful rituals can be effective tools for a traumatized society suffering from anxiety, fear, and hopelessness; a society filled with anger, hatred, and ill-will, a society perhaps suffering from post-traumatic stress disorder, but because of their inherent message of kindness, charity and nonviolence, these celebrations can also help Iranians heal culturally, and move us away from the culture of political violence, despotism, and patriarchy to a culture of human rights, democracy, and egalitarianism. But change for Iranians cannot be restricted solely to psychological and cultural healing while maintaining a regime and a system which uses the law to foment discrimination, violence, and patriarchy through unjust and undemocratic laws and institutions. These celebrations of Iran are not only tools for people to heal psychologically and culturally, they are also symbolic acts which can allow the expression of a political belief as seen in the philosophy and theory of nonviolence. Iranian participation in such rituals can be a form of expression and in a regime which abhors and detests such celebrations as incompatible with its revolutionary values, such acts can be expressions of disobedience and ultimately a referendum for democracy.

How can Iranians express themselves politically while taking part in such a ritual? Does the expression need to be verbal? Is the mere participation in such a celebration a form of expression when millions of Iranians are already participating without any awareness of the symbolic value of this ritual?

Expressions of support for a culture free of violence, a psychological state free of fear, and a political system free of inhumanity need not be verbal. Celebration itself is often the only tool for expression Iranians need. The power of a celebration can be even greater when a symbolic color or candle or an image is added to the celebration. The first and the most important audience for Iran's path to nonviolence is the people themselves. The referendum for political change cannot take place on a national level unless the referendum takes place in people's homes and within their family and then ultimately is expressed on the societal and national stage.

**

Sadeh

10th of *Bahman*. January 30th

In the Iranian calendar, winter is divided into the three months of *Dei*, *Bahman* and *Esfand*. Yet even though the winter calendar is so structured, the villagers and townspeople across Iran often have a slightly different division system for winter. In many towns and villages in Iran, the first forty days are called the greater winter, the next twenty days are the lesser winter. The day between the greater and lesser winter, or the fortieth day of winter they call '*Sadeh*', the next celebration in Iranian calendar.

Sadeh, the name of this ancient celebration, means one hundredth in today's Persian, but spelled with a different letter for 's' than today's Persian word for 'one hundredth'. Some believe that *Sadeh*, even with its variant in spelling, came from the word 'one hundredth' for two main reasons.[881] From this night on, there are fifty nights and fifty days left of winter until Nowruz. But in addition, this night was also the 100th night of the great winter in the Iranian mythological calendar and perhaps the more ancient calendar of Iranians.

The clue to the more ancient way of calendar again lies in the history of Iranians as a people dating back to their mythological era. Iranian mythology tells us of the great migration of Iranians southward, led by the mythological king Jamshid across sixteen countries. This mythology tells us that Iranians came from the cold lands far to the north, which Iranians historically thought meant Russia's steppes. In fact, genetic anthropology of Iranians and other people of Indo-European family extending from Ireland in the west to India in the east has mostly confirmed this pre-historic migration.[882] How does the celebration of *Sadeh* involve this ancient history?

Iranian mythology also tells us that those people divided the year into the great winter followed by the great summer and not divided into four seasons as it is in Iran today. The greater summer, began on Nowruz (March 21st) and lasted until *Aban* 1st (October 21s). Then began the cold and dark greater winter on the first of *Aban* (October 21st) and lasting until Nowruz. '*Sadeh*' was the 100th day of this dark, cold and long winter. It also marked fifty days and nights until the arrival of Nowruz.

Today, the memory of greater winter of prehistoric Indo-Europeans, beginning on October 21st (*Aban* 1st), is lost in Iran. Yet, the celebration of the start of that long, dark and cold winter which, no doubt had important pagan religious functions, was kept alive by the Irish into the 20th century, as 'All-Hallow's Eve' celebration. It's possible that this celebration was also performed on October 21st, and shifted ten days on the calendar through the thousands of years of human history as January 24th, Christmas eve shifted to January 6th on the orthodox Christian Church calendar. Today, 'All Hallow's Eve' celebration, as remembered by the Irish, is one of the most famous celebrations on earth and known as Halloween and celebrated on October 31st.

In the towns and villages near Damavand, the greater winter (first forty days) and lesser winters (next twenty days) who meet on night of *Sadeh* are referred to as two brothers. Ahman is the name of greater winter lasting forty days, Bahman, named after another god of ancient Iran, is the god of lesser winter, which lasts for twenty days. People in these villages believe that these two brothers engage in warfare in the last four days of greater winter and the first four days of lesser winter. These eight days are thus called *'char-char'*. The word *'char'*, is derived from the word *chahar*, meaning 'four'. Thunder and lightning on these days and nights are the sounds of war between these two gods. The villagers will tell you of Bahman, the god of lesser winter, asking his brother Ahman, "What did you do in your forty days?" Ahman, taking pride in the bitter cold delivered during his reign replies, "I broke many clay jars and vases, and I destroyed many homes." He then asks his younger brother, "What will you do during your reign?", Bahman replies "I will freeze the old women under their *korsi* and the infants in their cribs." [883] The older brother then laughs and tells the younger, "you are all talk; you live next to Spring and there is not much you can do."[884]

Likewise in Sanard, near Garmsar, these two brothers are also referred to as Ahman and Bahman and their stories are similar to those from Damavand.[885] In the town of Takestan, the locals say the lesser winter, Bahman, asks his brother "what will you do this winter?", the brother replies, "I will break the clay jars next to infants cribs." The taunting and threats of two winters on

Sadeh always ends the same by the greater winter reminding the lesser that his back is against Nowruz and Spring and thus he will fail. [886]

In Qazvin where the lesser winter is very harsh, it is said that younger brother tells his older brother "Oh brother, I wish my life was as long as yours, if the forty days were given to me, I would freeze children in their mothers bellies, but regret and a thousand regrets that my life is only twenty days."[887] Some old women in this region, will make a concoction made of opium in the size of a pill. Each night they take one of these pills to help them through the cold of night. They apply oil made of animal fat to their skin to protect it from the cold. [888]

In town of Taleqan, children go up to adults and from house to house to get candies and sweets in a ritual which seems as reminder of *Sadeh*'s pre-historic ties with Halloween. In this ritual, children say, "Mister, I have news for you, the younger brother [Bahman] came and told us, 'my older brother came and went and did not do much, I will freeze the infants in their cribs, the crows in their nests, water in the bucket, and old man in his sleep.' Give us candy and we will share it with the younger brother and will ask him not to be harsh this winter."[889]

In Khomein, people believe the coldest days and nights of winter begin on the 35th day or 5th of *Bahman* and last for ten days until the 15th of *Bahman*.[890] Sadeh they believe is on the coldest night of the year.[891]

In town of Mokhles-Abad, near Arak, and in many other towns and villages across Iran, they say once upon a time, there lived an old lady who had forty sons. On the thirty-seventh day of winter, one of the sons named Kordak went to the mountains and was trapped by the cold of '*char-char*' in a cave. When the old lady was handing out forty spoons for his sons, she realized a boy was missing.[892] This story of the old lady is retold in many variations across the villages of Iran. Many villages believe that once the old lady realized her son was missing, she went to the rooftop, set her spinning wheel on fire, and began singing a song in hope that it would help her son find his way back. The fire from the spinning wheel made the earth warm on that night and in the morning, when Kordak came out of his hiding hole, he noticed steam rising from the snow and realized it was warm enough to head back. The old lady's spinning wheel was lit on night of *Sadeh*. Kordak they believe found his village on the forty-fifth day of winter. Snow falling on this day is thus called in many places in Iran as *Kordak's* snow.[893]

Many towns and villages of Azarbaijan date this celebration back to time of Abraham, others to time of Moses which in Iranian culture usually means ancient times.[894] In the village of Abhar, elderly call it the 'ancient celebration' and say that one year, when there were fifty days left until the end of winter, Moses, while returning for his lambs, noticed they have all given birth to twins. Out of joy, he ran to his wife and began to sing and dance. Since that time, a celebration is done on this night in honor of that event.

In the ancient city and nearby villages of Hamedan, formerly known as Ekbatana, and in much of Azarbaijan and Fars provinces, the celebration of *Sadeh* involves a dancing party bringing the good news of only fifty days and nights left until spring. A group of men in each village, mostly sheepherders who are jobless at this time of year because of cold of winter, create the '*Kooseh*' party led by the main actor called '*Kooseh*'. The group of women, usually those running the bathhouses, also jobless because of cold of winter, create the women's party called '*Zan Khani*' (Women Singing) and are led by the main actor called '*Gol Khanoom*' (Flower Lady). In Arak and nearby villages, the dancing parties are also made up of the less fortunate and those jobless because of cold of winter and are called '*Reshki* and *Masi*'.[895] The gifts given them by the villagers and townspeople help their families carry on until the end of winter.[896]

In many towns and villages, these dance parties begin the celebration of Sadeh in the morning by each group walking from house to house during the day and handing out a single fruit to each family. Families who look forward to this dance accept the fruit as a sign of good fortune. The fruit is cut by the family into as many pieces as there are members in the house with each member having to take a bite no matter how small. The giving of fruit is an indication of the dance party coming to that house later in the day.[897] The family in return prepares some flour, rice, vegetable oil, raisins, or nuts for dance party to arrive.

Each party is usually made of 5-6 actors with two in '*Kooseh*' dance playing roles of bride and groom. The actors of '*Reshki* and *Masi*' parties usually wear red shirts and hang little bells all over their clothing. In a tradition again strangely resembling the clothing of Santa Clause and perhaps pointing to the common ancient origin of these two rituals, '*Reshki* and *Masi*' wear a cone shaped red hat similar to the one worn by Santa. Others following the actors carry tambourines and other instruments. As they enter the house, music begins. Fire is often lit by the host and the family, children, and neighbors sing and dance as they watch the actors put on a show around the warmth of fire on the coldest night of winter. The main actor's role is to keep everyone entertained. If the host forgets to bring their gifts at the end of the dance, the *kooseh* or *gol-khanoom* throw themselves on the ground pretending to have passed out and will not wake until gifts are given.[898] The lady of the house usually brings forth gifts on a platter and as she carries the plate, she performs a dance with the music of the guests.[899] After receiving their gifts, the party gives prayers to the family and leaves for the next house. People believe that music and dance on this night will take away all the pain, anger and sorrow from their home. The prayers of dance party on *Sadeh* are also believed to help avoid draught in the upcoming year. Others believe this ritual of dance by sheepherders must take place on *Sadeh* to protect their herd from disease and death in the coming year.[900]

At the end of the night, the group of men and women who were performing separately all gather with members of the community in the biggest house in town usually owned by the largest landowner and continue the celebration.[901] Not long ago, during my parents' and grandparents' childhood and prior to the Islamic Republic, on *Sadeh*, the coldest night of winter, the fear and anxiety of harsh and dark winter was turned into the joy of groups of dancing and singing children and adults walking the snow filled streets of villages and towns of Iran.[902]

Fire on Sadeh

Although much of the song and dance may have local variations and differences, the ritual of making fire and people gathering around it, is one of the most important acts of *Sadeh* and has near universal presence across Iran and written about by chroniclers since ancient times. Some light fire on their rooftops, others on their streets or main squares.

Ferdowsi, the 9th century author of Shahnameh, the mythological epic story of Iranians tells of *Sadeh* as a celebration dating to Iranian people's earliest history, during the hunter-gatherer period of mythological Shah, Houshang. The celebration of *Sadeh* in Iranian mythology, Ferdowsi tells us, is the celebration of the most important discovery in human history, the discovery of fire.

Shahnameh tells the story of mythological king Houshang and his companions setting off to the mountains on this coldest night of the year for a hunt. During their hunt, a great black snake appears on their path. Houshang attempts to ward off the snake by hurling a rock. The rock misses the snake but lands on another rock, which sets off sparks to nearby bushes. The small fire causes great excitement amongst the hunters. They collect the fire and keep it alight for use. Houshang and his companions regard fire as a great gift from God. They spend all night keeping it alight while celebrating its discovery. A great celebration was held on that night for this discovery and every year after that, people celebrated that great discovery of fire by lighting fires in their homes in the evening of that anniversary on *Sadeh*. [903]

Abu Rayhan Biruni, the great Iranian scholar of 11th century in his collection of ancient Iranian rituals and practices, "*Asar-ol-baghieh al Qoroon-ol-khalieh*"('Remnants of Lost Centuries'), tells us that on the night of *Sadeh* or fortieth night of winter, the cold reaches its extreme. People celebrated this night as reminder for them to expect the end of winter soon. [904] Biruni in his book '*al-tafhim*' and Gardizi in his book, '*Zin-al-akhbar*' tell another story related to *Sadeh* which occurs in much later time in Iranian mythology, during rule of the evil king, Zahhak.

The story of Zahhak is one of the most important mythological stories of Iranians. Every Iranian learns this story as a child. In fact, it is one of the most important stories of Iranian culture. In the story, Devil befriends a prince called Zahhak who had overthrown the previous king, the illustrious *Jamshid*, who had fallen from favor of the people after nine hundred years of rule. The Devil appearing as a chef fools Zahhak into allowing him to kiss the prince's shoulders and from each shoulder, a snake grows and bites at Zahhak's face and head. Every time they cut a snake's head, a new one would grow more vicious. In order to keep the snakes satisfied, the Devil reappears to Zahhak and tells him that these snakes only rest when fed the brain of a youth each day. Thus the serpent king is forced to kill two youths each day and feed their brains to each snake. For Iranians, this mythological era lasting one thousand years is a time of darkness, fear and terror and symbolic of every dark and evil regime ruling over Iran. Biruni and Gardizi tell us of a Vizier called Ermael who is in charge of gathering two youths each day which are to be sacrificed for the snakes. Although people view the Vizier as an evil person aiding Zahhak, in fact, Ermael the story continues, was freeing one of the two prisoners each night and sending them to the mountains as freed citizens. He would then add the brain of a sheep to the stew for the snakes. At the end of this mythological story, when people and Kaveh are finally victorious over Zahhak, the Vizier falls into disfavor. People don't believe the Vizier's story, so in order for the discredited Vizier to prove the existence of these freed citizens, he asks those who were freed to light fires on the mountains on *Sadeh* to show they exist. On the night of Sadeh, fires were seen across the mountains and all the people looked upon the fires as a reminder of each citizen freed by Ermael. The king and the people were then convinced of Vizier's efforts in freeing those people. [905] Ferdowsi tells us that these freed people who continued to live freely in the mountains became the people of Kurdistan. From then on in the mythological history, the lighting of fire and the celebration of *Sadeh* was a reminder of those freed from Zahhak and the beginning of a new day in Iranian history.

Omar Khayyam, the 11th century poet, mathematician, astronomer and scholar in his book *Nowruz-nameh* and Mulla Mozafar, the astronomer of Shah Abbas in 16th century also tell of *Sadeh* Celebration as the day Iranians were victorious against the evil regime of Zahhak. They tell us that Fereydoon and all the citizens who had suffered greatly under Zahhak's rule celebrated *Sadeh*. Khayyam tells us that each year Iranians continued to celebrate *Sadeh* in memory of that victory. [906][907]

One of the characteristics of this night as recorded in towns and villages of Iran prior to the 1979 Islamic Revolution was the emphasis on the community coming together and working together to prepare for this celebration. Firewood was often gathered from nearby deserts and valleys through a community-wide effort involving all citizens.

A contemporary Iranian scholar of celebrations and rituals in late 1960's wrote:

"The gathering of firewood was like a religious duty with its religious rewards. Each person in his or her own capacity would set off to gather wood. The wealthy, aristocrats and their children would pay others to carry on the task for them in their name. This act unified the citizens and they believed such teamwork is essential in weakening and warding off evil. The remains of this practice, way of life and way of thought to ward off evil can still be seen in many villages and towns in Iran such as in Kerman."[908]

Such rituals had deeply meaningful functions for a society striving to survive and prosper. In the cold of winter, when food and work was scarce, a ritual such as this functioned to remind the citizens of their common predicament. Paying the poor to carry on the task of gathering firewood functioned to help the poor make money at a time of winter when often no other means of work was available to them. In effect, the poor were in charge of gathering the wood and preparing for the celebration or entertaining the families while the rich were forced to pay a cultural tax to pay for the costs. This was justified on mythological and traditional grounds. Nevertheless, it had a special function to unify the community and society and to remind the families they were a part of a larger society.

CHAPTER 11

During the Arab invasion and occupation, Iranians tried to keep much of their earlier celebrations alive, yet century after century, these celebrations were under constant attack by religious fundamentalists who called them pagan rituals, rituals of fire-worshippers, sun-worshippers and only allowed their limited practice in Zoroastrian communities and strictly as a Zoroastrian celebration. Five centuries after the Arab occupation of Iran, the 11th century religious fundamentalist scholar, Imam Mohammad Qazali, who shaped much of the fundamentalist view of religion in the Middle East, mentions *Sadeh* as a celebration of infidels. He writes of the shopkeepers selling masks, wooden swords, and wooden shields on this night for a celebration that appears to have been an event with costumes. He gives a fatwa against the celebration and tells the Muslims that selling of costumes is not haram, but since these items are to be used on night of *Sadeh* as masks and costumes and as symbols of infidels, selling of such merchandise for this night should be haram.[909] Interestingly, from this fatwa, we learn that *Sadeh* was a night in which people bought masks in the bazaar in a celebration that must have created a carnival-like atmosphere.

At times, Sadeh turned into a symbolic statement, the most famous example of which was the tale of how Mardavich Dailami, son of Ziar, organized Sadeh in Isfahan in the winter of 935 C.E. as he was preparing to march to Baghdad to unseat the Abbasid Caliphate. He ordered much firewood to be gathered from the valleys and mountains around Isfahan. Atop the hills and mountains around the city, huge piles of wood were placed and prepared for *Sadeh*.

"And when they set fire upon the mounts, it was as if entire mountains were on fire. All around the city were mounts of firewood...great date trees were hollowed and filled with oil and tar and were wrapped together using metal wires...atop these grand palms, candle like pillars were formed...all across Isfahan and across Zayandeh River valley, there was not a single hilltop not burning with firewood, or such palms...When the sun set, sounds of music and dance were heard in all neighborhoods of Isfahan and Zayandeh River valley."[910]

Badi-al-Zaman Hamedani 11th century fundamentalist Muslim scholar, also called *Sadeh* a celebration of *kafers* or infidels and issued a fatwa against holding such festivities.[911] Yet, despite the propaganda against *Sadeh* in early centuries after Islam, *Sadeh* was kept alive in Iran, sometimes as traditions but other times as political statements. Some of the Caliphates in Baghdad were sympathetic to such celebrations. In the year 1091CE, Malek Shah of Saljuqi, on his visit to Baghdad celebrated this night. The historian Ibn Hasir writes:

"In the month of Ramadan, in the year 484 (1091CE), when Malek Shah reached Baghdad…followed by his friends and allies including his brothers…he celebrated *Sadeh* in such a way which the people of Baghdad had never seen before and later most poets [of Baghdad] wrote poems about that night and those celebrations."[912]

This historical anecdote tells us that despite the constant attack against such practices by the religious fundamentalists, even in Baghdad, the capital of Caliphate and Islamic Empire and even on the month of Ramadan, the holiest month of the year for Muslims, such a celebration was permitted and tolerated. This practice is not tolerated today in the privacy of the rooftops of homes in Tehran.

***

In the modern world, the celebration of midwinter has lost its significance and function. When homes are heated with petroleum and food is refrigerated months at a time, a celebration counting the days until spring no longer has a purpose in society; therefore, unless such a celebration finds a proper function in the modern world, its utility is limited and its life unnatural.

Today, there is a need for such a celebration for Iranians, whether in London or Los Angeles or in the far off villages of Azarbaijan, Kurdistan and Khurasan. Like Nowruz and Yalda, Sadeh is one of the celebrations of Iranian identity. But more than just expressions of identity, such celebrations are symbols of a culture of kindness for families and communities. They are symbols of hope and pursuit of happiness. They are cultural symbolic acts that can form the pillars of a new culture of nonviolence in Iran. Iranian celebrations containing symbolic acts of charity and kindness can ultimately help create cultures of tolerance and human rights for Iranians, just as symbolic rituals of militarism, hatred, and anger will ultimately form cultures of violence. Dictatorships create the cultures of fear and terror through the parades and rituals of violence. If Iranians are to create the culture of nonviolence and human rights of tomorrow, it can come through the creation and participation in celebrations of nonviolence.

Participation in a celebration such as *Sadeh* can transform an individual from a passive witness of culture and politics to an active citizen shaping and reforming the culture and society. Participation in such a celebration can not only help Iranians heal psychologically from their struggles with terror, fear and violence but it can also express, create, and shape a culture of nonviolence, tolerance, and democracy. Furthermore, in a regime which bans such celebrations, Sadeh can also serve as a symbolic act of civil disobedience and ultimately a vote and a voice for democracy and human rights.

Celebratory fires on *Sadeh*, in city squares, sidewalks and rooftops across Iran can send a message of hope and resistance more powerful and effective than tens of thousands of people filling the streets and shouting slogans. Such bonfires in yards and homes will allow Iranians who have no other way of expressing their desires to find the strength and courage to celebrate what is their right in their streets and city squares. Such fires, which can function as symbolic acts of civil disobedience will serve as beacons of hope and courage for a generation desperately trying to overcome the darkness of fear, terror and violence of the Islamic Republic.

***

Esfand

Celebration of Women's Month
February 21st-March 21st

"It can safely be affirmed that every woman, without exception, was subordinate to the authority of and under the restraint of a particular man (i.e. father, brother, husband, son), and that her material well-being and personal happiness were entirely dependent upon…whatever male happened to be exercising that authority over her at any given time."[913]

This statement was intended to describe the status of women in Iran five centuries ago. But it can easily be a description of the plight of women in this or any other century in Iran's long existence. Thus you can imagine the importance of this next celebration in the struggle for human rights and democracy in Iran.

How joyous must have been the signs of spring for ancient Iranians. With the end of *Bahman*, the second month in winter, the worst of cold and snow was over. The last month of Iranian winter, *Esfand*, is the month when earth begins to impregnate itself with life again. The green leaf buds and grass now sprouting across the land must have always painted a picture of life and joy for ancient populations counting the days of winter. In *Esfand*, nature again comes to life and mother earth will again feed its children and provide an environment for life, pleasure, and kindness.

For ancient humanity, including Iranians, the spirits in heavenly skies were often of both feminine and masculine nature. Their behavior was unpredictable and not always kind. One could predict the path of Sun across the heavens, but Sun could bring drought one year, followed by floods the next. The goddess of rain was not always present for farmers much in need of water.

But of all the gods and goddesses of humanity, Earth was always kind. Earth always provided when cared for. Because of it, for many cultures, the kindness of earth was similar to the unconditional love of a mother; thus it is not surprising that in many cultures, Earth was symbolized as feminine. *Esfandarmaz*, which the goddess of the third month of winter in Iranian calendar is named, was a symbol of Earth, as well as a symbol of femininity and women. For ancient humanity, including Iranians, Earth would impregnate itself in this month and ultimately was human being's source of life, metaphorically, much like a woman was a source of life in society.

In the Iranian calendar, where each day of the month had a special name and meaning. The fifth day of every month was called *Esfand*-day for this goddess of Earth, and when in the month of *Esfand*, *Esfand*-day, the fifth day of the month would arrive, it signaled one of the monthly celebrations of ancient Iran, *Esfand*gan. For ancient Iranians, *Esfand*gan was a celebration of and for women. It was customary on this day to give gifts to women and celebrate the day in their honor.

Biruni, in his 11th century account of ancient Iranian practices writes:

"The [celebration] of *esfandarmaz* [*Esfandgan*] is due to the falling of *Esfand*-day, fifth day of the month in the month of *Esfand*…and in the old days, this month and in particular this day was the celebration for women; and on this day men give women presents and this tradition is still practiced in the cities of Isfahan, Rey and other towns where Pahlavi [Sassanid] culture is still alive."[914]

The rituals a society create and adhere to ultimately dictate what that society considers to be of importance. If Americans create a ritual for 4th of July and celebrate it year after year, they are placing importance on their identity as a nation, their freedom, constitution, and independence. Creating a Memorial Day or a Veterans Day ultimately serves to remind the population of the importance of their soldier's sacrifice, Labor Day is intended to remind people of the importance of workers and labor in society.

CHAPTER 11

In Iran today, a ritual reminding us of the importance of women in society is of utmost priority for a culture where women are not only culturally discriminated against, but are also legally given significantly less rights and opportunities than men. The issue of women's rights in Iran is not a side issue against the backdrop of a larger struggle for democracy; it is one of the central issues of human rights in Iran. No other group of Iranians have been systematically discriminated against and for as long of a time as women in Iran.

The systematic placement of women as citizens with lesser rights is not a process dating back decades. It is not a phenomenon dating back centuries or since Islamicization of Iran. It is a process dating back thousands of years, perhaps to the dawn of civilization. The discrimination against women coincides with and parallels the culture of rule through violence. The ultimate freedom for women must then parallel the society's path in ridding itself of violence and adopting a culture of nonviolence.

When trying to revive *Esfand*gan as a celebration of women, it is important to remember that, symbolic acts of violence such as discrimination are likely present in any cultural ritual dating from pre-modern eras. Thus when one studies a ritual of the past, one must continuously be aware that such a ritual was practiced in a world where such elements of violence and inequality were tolerated and even sometimes advocated.

One of the rituals practiced on *Esfand*gan in ancient Persia was a celebration where the society would shift from a patriarchy to matriarchy on this day. In ancient Iran, men and women would completely change roles in society on this celebration. Women were made heads of households and men had to obey everything women ordered them to do that day. On this celebration, women were kings and rulers of society.

On the surface, such a celebration and ritual may seem innocent and even beneficial for helping women obtain their rights in society. But the importance of a ritual lies in its symbolic act. When a ritual chooses to make women rulers in homes and society one day out of the year, it points towards a culture where men are the rulers and heads of families the other 364 days of the year. Not only it doesn't help the cause of women to win their rights in society, such an innocent ritual may even help emphasize the chauvinistic culture one is trying to correct.

A nonviolent look at such a ritual does not mean to suppress and destroy such a celebration for women. It means to create a ritual for 21st century of Iran, inspired through nonviolence with the function to address the significance of women in society. Thus, in the effort to recreate the ritual of women's' day on *Esfand*gan, our aim should be to recreate *Esfand*gan itself.

In 1960's, the nonviolent efforts of African-Americans led by Martin Luther King convinced America that major efforts need to be done to undo the systemic centuries old injustices against African-Americans. In time, it was decided that a ritual and a celebration is needed which can help undo the inequality. Yet, the inequality and injustice was so culturally deep that a ritual, one day of the year was too insignificant against the systemic culture of discrimination. For this effort, a month-long ritual, as opposed to a daylong ritual, was needed and thus in 1976, the month of February was chosen as 'Black History Month', as a celebration of African-American contribution to American society and culture and a ritual for healing, growth, and reconciliation.

During this month, everyone in America is reminded of the important contributions of African Americans to music, painting, photography and cinema. There are celebrations reminding people of the sacrifices of African Americans as soldiers in previous wars, as doctors, lawyers, scientists, and engineers. Children are taught about the contribution of African-American authors, screenwriters, and poets. The great cultural discrimination against African Americans required a month long ritual of celebration and education.

Similarly, in Iran, the women's rights issue is not one to which Iranians can dedicate one day of the year and expect any significant cultural changes. Thus Iranians, instead of *Esfand*gan as celebration of Women, need to delegate the entire month of *Esfand* as Women's Month Celebration.

And what would such a month-long ritual entail?

On each day of *Esfand* month, Iranians can celebrate the achievement of women as writers, poets, painters, and directors as well as engineers, scholars, doctors, lawyers, teachers and leaders. *Esfand* month could be the celebration of the will of Iranian women playing soccer and polo despite systematic discrimination against them as well as the accomplishments of Iranian women on the world stage as directors, astronauts, and Nobel Prize winners. If Iranians dedicate every day of *Esfand* as a ritual and reminder for women's right in Iran, the 17th of *Esfand*, the eighth of March, now universally referred to as the International Day for Women's Rights can also serve as a ritual reminding Iranians of discrimination against women in all parts of the world. It is a beautiful and powerful coincidence that March 8th, International Women's Day falls in the month that historically symbolized women for ancient Iranians. Even better, the month of March has been designated in much of the world as Women's History Month or the International Women's Month roughly corresponding to the month of Esfand on Iranian calendar.

Celebrations in Esfand can each send powerful messages of the desire for elimination of all forms of violence in society including discrimination, the most widespread and accepted form of violence. We must also be cognizant that our greatest challenge to democracy in Iran is not a system that believes in violence; it is a society that tolerates violence and even advocates violence as a solution to ridding itself of injustice. In a constitution and religious regime that systematically institutionalizes violence against women, this celebration can be a symbolic act rejecting that violence. And like every other symbolic Iranian celebration, *Esfand* Month, the celebration of women can also function as an act of civil disobedience and a ritual reminding Iranians of their desire for nonviolence, democracy and human rights.

***

Chahar-Shanbeh Souri

Festival of Fire
The evening before the last Wednesday of winter.

There is no Iranian today who is unfamiliar with this celebration. As the sun is about to set before the last Wednesday of winter, countless piles of firewood are being readied on street corners of Iran and in city squares. This celebration of the end of winter takes place in lands as far east as Tajikistan, Uzbekistan, and Afghanistan to isolated Kurdish villages in mountains of Syria, Iraq, Turkey and to places as far north as Chechnya. When the sun sets on this evening, fires are lit in streets and city squares.

Grandparents and children jump over the fires as they sing *"Zardi-e-man az to, Sorkhi-e-to az man."* The song symbolically asks the fire to take the yellow, jaundiced, diseased look of winter from the people and give them the warmth, red color, energy and life of fire.

Bonfires are made in rows of three, five or seven and, as children and adults jump over them going in one direction, they walk and dance past the fire coming back. Sounds of spoon beating is heard in neighborhoods as people go door to door banging on pots with their spoons while homeowners place specially made nuts and dried fruits in their pans. This celebration is widely held despite the discouragement, intolerance and disapproval of the

Islamic Republic. No celebration in Iran today symbolizes people's desire for political freedom than this festival of fire and no celebration is feared by the regime as much as this. Across the Islamic Republic of Iran, there is one night when regime's ruthless control over the population is lost, when people are free to celebrate and rejoice, when the propaganda of calling this celebration fire-worshipping, sun-worshipping, Pagan worshipping, Zoroastrian, a celebration for 'idiots and donkeys' as influential Ayatollah Motahari famously told Iranians on state television after the Islamic Revolution bears no weight, when young girls lost in the euphoria of celebration dare to take their headscarfs off and hold their boyfriends' hands. No other night symbolizes the desire of Iranians to keep a dying culture alive and no other celebration has historically symbolized a political expression as powerfully as this night.

In the pre-Islamic Iran, people did not have a seven day week calendar and if one were to tell an ancient Iranian about a celebration of fire on the eve before the last Wednesday of the year, that person may have been puzzled about the meaning of Wednesday and perhaps would have responded: "Do you mean the *Souri* celebration before *panjeh*?" The thirty days of the month each had a name as days of the week do today. For ancient Iranians, the year was divided into twelve months of thirty days each adding up to 360 days. This calendar system would leave five days after the end of winter and start of Nowruz called *panjeh* to complete the 365 day calendar. This celebration with fire was on the eve of the last night of winter and the start of *panjeh*, five days before Nowruz, the Iranian New Year.

It is not known why, after the Islamic period, the celebration was changed from five days before New Years to the evening before the last Wednesday of the month. The oldest document mentioning this celebration dates back to the mid fourth century of the Islamic period. Abu-Jafar Narshahi in his book, 'History of Bukhara', tells of a 'Celebration of *Souri*':

"And when Mansour-ibn-Noah [Samanid] came to power in the year 961CE, he ordered the *saray* to be rebuilt. The *amir* then took his seat at the throne and the year was just ending when festival of *Souri* as was the custom of old was celebrated. A grand fire was made, then suddenly a flame escaped and caught the roof of the *saray* and soon rest of *saray* was in flames."[915]

This unfortunate incident allowed this celebration to be documented historically and serves as the oldest mention of this festival. What is important of this document is the referral of this celebration as '*Souri*' and not '*Chahar-shanbeh Souri*' as is called today. *Chahar-shanbeh* means Wednesday, so it makes sense to mention the celebration only as *Souri*, irrespective of the day of the week on which it fell. *Souri* is thought to come from the word *Suric* meaning red in pre-Islamic Pahlavi language of Iran. In many places in Iran, people still sometimes call a red flower as '*souri*' flower.[916] In this document, we also see the author call it a celebration of the old which, at that time, nearly always referred to the pre-Islamic celebrations and festivals of Iran.

Even though there are very few historical documents describing how this festival was celebrated in ancient Iran, the widespread celebration on this night across the region today provides plenty of cultural customs and rituals associated with this night. This celebration in many regions of Iran today is one of the most important celebrations of the year. It is one of the few remaining public rituals that survived the intolerance of the Islamic fundamentalists over the centuries.

***

In many towns and villages, preparations for this night begin 15 days before the event. After a long year and a cold winter, this night signals the end of the calendar cycle and the coming of Nowruz. On this night, Iranians believed that the kind spirits of those who died in the previous year would come to visit them for the upcoming new-year celebration. These spirits were called *farvardegan* or *foruhars* or *faravashis* after which the first month of spring and the new year is named. People believed that these *faravashis* or kind spirits visiting them would remain amongst them for 10 days. In order to guide the kind spirits to their homes, fires were lit in city squares, on rooftops, and on the hills. These fires were the guiding lights for the spirits to find their way home.

In addition to the religious function this ritual may have played for Zoroastrians and pre-Zoroastrian Iranians, this ritual perhaps also had an important psychological function for the society. Mothers who had lost a child during the year would celebrate the end of winter with the memory of their loved one, children who had lost a parent would smile into the sky as they lit the fires on their streets, grandparents were remembered, and a family that may have lost hope and fallen apart was given a structure and ritual in which they could come together again and celebrate renewal and rebirth with the memory of their loved ones. Such a ritual is a powerful societal tool for healing, developed through thousands of years of human experience of death, fear and loss. It is a psychological tool available to individuals, families, community, and the country as a whole.

In the state of Gilan, on the southwest shore of Caspian Sea, this celebration is considered one of the most important and the oldest of them all. The locals believe that spirits coming home on this night come for guidance and to fulfill their hopes and dreams. Prior to this night, the *korsi's* are usually removed and the homes are cleansed from corner to corner.

In a ritual called *khaneh-tekani*, every piece of furniture and every rug is moved and the crevices in the homes are thoroughly cleaned. All clothes, linen, and rugs are washed and cleaned. People believed that this housecleaning is important to rid homes of dirt and disease, and that such cleanliness is necessary for the arrival of *faravashis*. One can easily see the immense function this ritual plays for families and societies in thoroughly cleaning homes from the dust, dirt, and allergens gathered after a long winter. People in Gilan traditionally prepare seven different foods for *farvardegan* on this night.

Since ancient times, in preparation for this night, elderly in the towns of Fumen and Masouleh in Gilan province pick several youths and assign them the task of going to the hills and mountains in the south, in an area called *tatal-chai*, to obtain special clay, which is often blue but also can be yellow in color. This clay, which is called *tatal* or *foush*, is then brought to the village and, in a ceremony, the elderly and young people share the clay amongst all families.

The clay is then mixed with large amount of water and is applied to the walls in the homes across the village. When the mixture is dried, it turns to a beautiful sky blue color decorating the homes across towns and villages in the region. For the ceilings in the homes, white clay is mixed with water and applied. On the floors, red clay is mixed with water and bran from rice plants. As the mixture is applied to the floors and prior to it drying, women use their fingers to draw designs in the forms of flowers and leaves onto the red clay.[917]

Once everything is dried, the embellished red floors are decorated with the families' rugs and other belongings. The mothers then take empty trash bins to nearby streams and rivers outside the village and in a ritual symbolizing the complete cleanliness of their homes go through motions of emptying their trash bins in nature. This final act symbolizes the complete cleanliness of their homes, which have been readied for the arrival of very special guests.[918] The homes are now ready for *farvardegan* to arrive.

On this night in Gilan, on a tablecloth in the main room of the house, it is customary to place a mirror, a bowl of newly sprouting seeds, mixture of nuts and cereal, hard-boiled painted eggs, a bowl of water, flowers, candles and

CHAPTER 11

seven types of food. These items, except for the food, will remain on the tablecloth until Nowruz when the seven symbolic items of Nowruz are added.

The mixture of nuts and cereal is made two days prior to the celebration by the lady of the house and in Gilan it is made up of rice, lentil, chickpea, sunflower seeds, dried squash seeds, raisins and walnuts. Because this mixture is prepared for the health of *farvardegan*, people believe it possesses exceptional nutritional benefits. In each home, portions of such mixtures are placed in clay jars for several months and are given to workers in the fields later on during the farming season. [919]

A special dish called *torsheh-tareh* is prepared in Gilan; it is made up of forty different herbs that grow simultaneously in that region and at that particular time of the year. The lady of the house takes a portion of this herbal dish and places it in a special jar that will hang by the door of the house.[920] Fish is often served with *torsheh-tareh* on this night. Mothers trim their daughters' hair and several strands of hair are then blown with the wind.

During the day, dry wood is readied in piles of three or seven. The moment the sun sets, fires are lit. Children, parents and grandparents come together with neighbors and other families in the community, and watch as people leap over the fire while singing. A mother in a town of Sangachin, near the city of Bandar Anzali (Pahlavi) in Gilan told of how her mother used to look in the stars and tell the locals whether they should have three or seven fires lit for that year. How the stars were used for this task is thought to be forgotten.[921]

In Tajikistan and Uzbekistan, after the ritual of cleaning, men shave their heads before participating in this celebration as further symbols of purity and rebirth. For them, the three fires set on this night are symbols "kind thoughts, kind words and kind deeds", the ancient Iranian trio of virtue and citizenship.

In many towns and villages in Azerbaijan and Kurdistan, this celebration not only takes place before the last Wednesday of the year, but before every Wednesday in the last month of the year.[922] In towns and villages of Kurdistan and Lorestan and in central area of Farahan, celebration with fire on this night is again repeated on the eve of the New Year.[923] In the town of Shah-abad, in Kermanshah, people believe this night as the anniversary of Kaveh's victory over Zahhak ending the thousand-year rule of evil in Iran. [924]

Another common ritual on this night is spoon-beating performed mostly by children. In this ritual, groups holding spoons and pans go from door to door banging their pots with their spoons. Homeowners place sweets or

457

specially prepared nuts in their pots. In a custom local to Tehran of old, a special dish is cooked with nuts and cereal gathered by the spoon-beaters called '*abu-dard*' which is believed to be a cure to many illnesses and pains. [925] In towns and villages around Herat and Balkh, in Afghanistan, the ash from these fires is gathered by a young woman and is carried to the countryside outside the village and scattered in the wind.[926]

In Kurdistan, the youth lit fires on the rooftops, in the hills and mountains with celebrations continuing all night. The Kurds believe that such fires should not be set out until dawn. Kurds believe that dinners on this night should be elaborate and consumed in celebratory atmosphere filled with love. This is believed to provide joy to spirits visiting on this night. Poorer families who cannot provide such meals are helped by neighbors and others in the community. Water from springs on this night is collected in clay jars and is believed to have a special purity that wards off illness and disease. Throughout the year, family members stricken with illness are given water from such jars.[927]

***

No other Iranian celebration has come to symbolize people's political desires as much as this night. Participation in this festival against the wish of the regime has come to symbolize people's expression of discontent. It is the only public celebration that has survived centuries of fatwas, ridicule, and violent oppression. On the eve of the 1979 revolution, many influential clerics who came to power repeatedly called this celebration and all other similar Iranian celebrations as celebrations for devil-worshippers, fire-worshipers, sun-worshipping, superstition, un-Islamic, dangerous and immoral. Nearly every Iranian celebration that required public's participation in the streets and city squares has been suppressed and eliminated from the culture over the centuries. This last remaining public ritual still practiced was seen by the Islamic Republic as the next battle for elimination of Iranian rituals considered un-Islamic from society. Thus, this celebration of fire had to be eliminated.

It is perhaps because of this strong attack against this celebration that forced the people to symbolize participation in this particular ritual as an expression of disobedience. Yet because of Iran's violent history and the culture of political violence prevalent in society, the celebratory atmosphere of this night, which included the participation of parents and grandparents, has turned today into a dangerous game of fireworks, firecrackers, and use of explosives in a society driven to extremes. Several years ago, when preparations for this night were taking shape, I was speaking to an uncle in Iran. During the conversation I asked if he would be going out that evening to enjoy the celebration with fire. "No way!" was his response. "I'll get a heart-attack from those firecrackers and explosives the young use now-a-days. This stuff is no longer for us; it's become a dangerous game for the young."

A society that believes that violence is an option to rid itself of this regime will show its discontent through tools symbolic of violence and will create rituals symbolizing violence. Use of firecrackers and explosives expressions of discontent is symbolic of an outlook on how a struggle is carried out. People who believe violence is the way to engage in a struggle will symbolize their discontent by acts that have violence hidden in their meaning. The celebration of *Chahar-shanbeh Souri*, which symbolized the end of winter, the memory and spirit of loved ones and the arrival of Nowruz, has turn today into an expression of anger, rage, hurt, and violence by many youths.

Every year on this night dozens of children lose their hands, their eyesight, and even their lives while playing with dangerous explosives. The children have come to use such explosives out of habit and custom on this night, just like the society that now turns to violence out of habit and custom.

Iranian's silence about the use of such explosives is a silence directed against violence and the threat of violence against the youth. The continued use of such explosives is the continued belief in violence. The absence of families and grandparents participating in such rituals is the beginning of the death of such Iranian celebrations.

Every ritual has a function for the society and the ritual is kept alive as long as it continues to provide that function for individuals, families, and communities. If the ritual is beneficial physically and psychologically, it is strengthened and practiced by more people. If it is detrimental or harmful to physical or psychological health of the participants, it is eliminated from the culture. The use of explosives instead of song, dance and fires has detrimental physical and even psychological effect on the people and is the key to eliminating this ritual from Iranian culture. Those who trek along the path of nonviolence must continuously remind others that Iran's struggle is not just against the regime, their struggle is against violence.

This night is a cultural battleground against violence. Iran's identity as a nation is formed through collective actions of Iranians on such a celebration. The Iranian struggle for a culture filled with kindness and nonviolence is a struggle to teach children, families, and neighbors about violence, how it is manifested, how it is symbolized, and how it destroys hopes and dreams. Nationwide participation in this festival has come to symbolize people's discontent, yet Iranians must change its symbolic meaning from a ritual symbolizing anger, hate and rage to a celebration symbolizing hope and joy and ultimately an expression for freedom and human rights.

Chahar-shanbeh Souri, the ancient Iranian festival of fire and the celebration of the end of winter is a tool which today has come to represent civil disobedience more than any other Iranian celebration. This celebration is pivotal in helping to transform every other Iranian celebration into monthly acts of civil disobedience. Yet, it must be rid of explosives and other dangerous symbols which prevent widespread participation of grandparents and children on this night and it must come to symbolize Iranian desire for nonviolence, democracy and human rights as opposed to general expression of anger.

CHAPTER 11

CHAPTER 12 - CELEBRATIONS OF REBIRTH AND RENEWAL IN SPRING

"*Har roozetan* Nowruz." May Your Everyday be Nowruz.

NOWRUZ

First Day of Spring – March 21st

No other word defines the hopes, desires and dreams of Iranians quite like Nowruz. No other word in the Persian language invokes memories and expressions of love, kindness and good will as much as Nowruz. No other symbol is as inherent to Iranian culture as this symbol of rebirth and renewal. And no other celebration is as cherished by Iranians.

Nowruz which literally means New-Day begins on the exact moment when the tilt of the earth's axis is aligned with the sun, marking the end of winter and the start of new Iranian year. Celebrated over thirteen days, the festivities culminate on the thirteenth with a day spent in nature. In a country where everything seems ancient, this historic celebration seems to outdate everything and people often refer to it simply as the 'the ancient celebration.' Celebrated from Tajikistan in the east and across the mighty mountains of Afghanistan to Kurdish villages of northern Syria and eastern Turkey in the west and as far north as Chechnya, overextending artificial political boundaries and religious beliefs, Nowruz universally is celebrated as a symbolic act of renewal and rebirth. More than any other ritual and celebration, the commemoration of Nowruz has helped shape and form the Iranian cultural identity.

Over the course of countless centuries, Iran's language has morphed and changed many times. Even today, many Iranians do not speak Persian, preferring Azari, Kurdish, or one of the many other local dialects and languages of Iran. Iran's religion has also undergone many changes and metamorphosis. Yet, despite all the diversity of language and religion in Iran, the collective cultural identity of Iranians is held together in large part through the celebration of the rebirth of nature on Nowruz.

Despite uprisings, foreign and civil wars, massacres, even genocides, Iranians observed the coming of spring with Nowruz as a time of charity, hope, and peace. Throughout their history Iranians have used the ritual of Nowruz as a tool for rebuilding and recreating their communities, their environment, and their society. For a society repeatedly suffering from violence, trauma, and anxiety, Nowruz was the societal psychological therapy. Today it continues to perform an important function for Iranians, providing hope in an era of violence and despair.

Throughout generations of Islamic fundamentalism, when nearly all public national celebrations were banned and suppressed, Nowruz survived. In the privacy of people's homes and away from the violence and animosity of religious fundamentalists, Iranians continued to revive it year after year. One of Khomeini's first attempts to crush secular Iranian traditions was his effort to destroy and denigrate the significance of Nowruz by labeling it and other Iranian festivals as fire and sun-worshiping, un-Islamic for pagans and infidels. It was one of Khomeini's few failures and defeats during his violent and nearly decade long rule. It was in Nowruz, where Iranians found that fear could not crush their spirit for resistance.

The Rituals and Symbols of Nowruz

Any European or American who has experienced the wonder and grandeur of Christmas can relate to the joy and excitement, the kindness and generosity of spirit felt in Iranian towns and cities with the nearing of spring. Winter's end is marked by the sprouting of green plants on the hillsides. Colorful wildflowers during Nowruz blanket the deserts like exquisite handmade rugs. Thousands of mountain streams of melted snow give life to trees and bushes that were dormant for months. The ancient underground *qanats* of villages are gushing with fresh water. Across Iranian towns and villages just before Nowruz, groups of young laborers are seen walking in the streets, singing in a melodic tone "*aab hozi – aab hozi*" (pool-water, pool-water) with an offer to clean the ponds and pools of homes for the coming of spring. All across Iran, the courtyards of people's homes are scrubbed, their pools and ponds filled with fresh water, streets are swept, rugs are washed, and homes decorated with flowers and greens.

Several weeks before Nowruz, Iranian bazaars are bustling with activity and families can be found shopping for new clothes. Banks, jewelers and money exchangers are busy as grandparents, uncles and aunts gather brand new minted currency and coins to be given as gifts to children. No matter how poor, freshly minted coins are obtained by the elderly, even if pennies, and given as gifts to children or those in need. Shopkeepers light their storefronts with green and red light bulbs, colors of spring as well as the Iranian flag. Candy stores decorate their shops with colorful sweets. Pastries are especially popular and an important part of the ritual. Iranians believe that eating pastries on Nowruz will sweeten their tongues as well as give them a year of sweet words.

Abdullah Mastoufi, who wrote about his life and his era at the end of 19th century, the Qajar era, tells us of the preparations for the ritual of Nowruz at the dawn of modernity in Iran:

"For the shopping of Nowruz, crowds gather in the bazaar particularly in fabric stores, shoe stores and hat makers. Each person within his own capacity is in thought of providing new Nowruz clothing for their family. Tailors no longer accept new orders two weeks before Nowruz. From ten days before the celebration, stores begin to decorate their shops…Grocers hang sorb fruit (*senjed*). Colored candles of green and red decorate these fruits. Piles of food and nuts which were half empty are filled and replenished. The brass plates in the shops are cleaned and filled with beans and nuts…piles of soap are placed like small pyramids in the shops with the tips decorated with paper flowers. Newly cleaned jars of vinegar, which often were on the highest shelf in the stores, are shining this time of year and are decorated with colored papers…Nut sellers decorate their shops with piles of chestnuts, peanuts, pistachios, and dried, roasted watermelon or squash seeds… fruit sellers, aside from decorating their shops with fresh fruit, place fresh flowers for decoration."[928]

Several weeks before Nowruz, in each Iranian house, a bowl of seed, usually of wheat, barley or lentil is placed in water for two days, then removed and placed on a round plate atop a wet cloth. As Nowruz approaches, the seeds give rise to green sprouts of grass and the plate containing the grass called *sabzeh* is then placed on *sofreh*.

Sofreh is the tablecloth placed on the family rug or dining table and serves as the centerpiece for the Nowruz items. The sprouting green grass symbolizes life and nature's rejuvenation during Spring. The green sprouting wheat called *sabzeh* is the first and the most important symbolic item of Nowruz in each Iranian home. The green grass is tied with a red ribbon giving rise to the green and red colors of Nowruz and Iranian flag.

When the grain first sprouts its silver buds, a portion of it is removed and used for a ritual involving the baking *Samanou*, the second item on *sofreh* symbolizing affluence. Wheat, the single most important dietary staple for

CHAPTER 12

Iranians, has always been the most important gauge of prosperity versus poverty for them throughout their history. For the making of *Samanou*, the silver sprouting grain is crushed, its juice extracted and mixed with flour and cooked on medium heat as family members take turns churning it. Slowly, the mixture acquires its brownish color and its distinctive sweet taste. Almonds with their skin still on (*badam mengha*) are added to the dish. A bowl is given to all those present and placed on *sofreh* next to the green sprouting *sabzeh*.

The making of *samanou* is not performed in every home. If a family is busy with other preparations, they might visit a bazaar or shopping center to hear the melodic voice of merchants singing "*samanou*, ay, *samanou*.." Where you hear the singing of *samanou*, you can find fresh bowls for sale, ready for your *sofreh*.

Next to *samanou* and *sabzeh*, two other items are added, each beginning with the letter 's.' A bowl of *sir* (garlic), or *sumaq*,(a purple and reddish, grounded herb) known for their medicinal properties and one of the essential ingredients of many Iranian dishes are the third and sometimes fourth objects. Both symbolize health.

Senjed, the dried fruit of the oleaster tree is the fifth element to be added to *sofreh* and encircles the sprouting green *sabzeh*. A bowl of *sib* (apples), the heavenly fruit, symbolizing beauty, is added. *Sekkeh* (coins), symbolizing prosperity is often included. Lastly, *sonbol* flower is placed. Called hyacinths in the west, these white aromatic blooms of Spring, native to Iran, are responsible for the fragrance in Iranian homes during Nowruz and complete the seven symbolic items which begin with the letter 's' and are known as *haftsin*.[929]

Next to these items is a bowl of goldfish, symbolizing life. Candles are placed as the representation of enlightment, and spirituality. The family's holy book or a copy of Hafez's collective works called *Divan* or Ferdowsi's *Shahnameh* is then placed on the *sofreh*.

Hard boiled eggs painted with colors are arranged on *sofreh* and represent rebirth of nature and life in spring. Next to it, a bowl of water containing a floating *narenj*, a type of orange-citrus fruit native to Iran. Grandparents tell children it represents the earth. The fruit floats with only one third of it above water like an island in a vast ocean, much like how ancients saw earth peeking out of the endless sea.

The last item on the *sofreh* is a mirror representing self-reflection and self-discovery and when one approaches the *sofreh* with all the colorful, aromatic and symbolic items, one catches a glimpse of self. Thus, with the aid of a mirror, the participant, together with the family, become the last symbolic item of Nowruz.

Children, still joyful after their participation in the Festival of Fire, are now given new clothing and the promise of thirteen more days of pleasure and peace. As the exact hour, minute and second of the spring equinox approaches, the rush to finish preparations for the celebration intensifies. Television and radio are filled with well wishes of Nowruz by celebrities and politicians. Phone lines are jammed with calls to grandparents and families. In the last hours mothers can be seen running with children and shopping bags in hand. Bus drivers and taxis are serving their last route. Merchants close shops and Iranians worldwide turn to television and radio to count the final minutes until Nowruz.

As the New Year approaches, streets often become empty. Nearly everyone is gathered around *sofreh* waiting for the countdown and eating the sweets. As families hear the familiar 10, 9, 8…, members kiss and congratulate each other. As the seconds tick away, cheers are heard and each television station, radio and home is filled with the traditional music of Nowruz heralding the start of spring and New Year.

In the following two weeks, the nation takes a deep breath while Iran's focus becomes the national ritual of rebirth, kindness, and nonviolence. Stores and offices remain closed. Families don't quarrel, old enemies become friends, neighbors greet each other warmly, and communities take part in a societal form of psychological therapy more powerful than any medicine or technique for overcoming trauma and loss the modern world could offer. Just as the societal ritual of Christmas helped the Europeans cope with centuries of violence, plague, and warfare, Nowruz has helped Iranians survive through a history no less violent and no less traumatic.

In the Sassanid era, during the last pre-Islamic Persian Empire, 224 to 651 CE, twelve clay pillars were built in the Shah's court 25 days before Nowruz. On top of each pillar, the seeds for different crops were planted. On the sixth day of Nowruz, people would examine the sprouts of each crop and predict the yield for the subsequent year.[930] Fortune-tellers and readers of these *sabzehs* would notify the people of the each crop's relative growth. In every home across ancient Iran, it is said that families repeated the ritual of planting *sabzeh* in clay bowls. While the Shah's court planted twelve crops across the palace, the people planted the seven crops or *sabzehs* in their homes.

Participation in the ritual of Nowruz in the Sassanid court was an important duty, one which could not be neglected. In the year 565CE, the

CHAPTER 12

Eastern Roman Emperor Justinian, sent an ambassador to Anushirvan, the Shah of Iran. No doubt such an emissary between two world powers must have been an important event in the ancient time. Yet the arrival of this ambassador coincided with the celebration of Nowruz. Because of the culture's emphasis on this celebration, the Shah did not greet the newly arrived ambassador until the end of the celebration. For historians, this coincidental arrival of the ambassador on Nowruz has served to document the importance of this ritual in ancient times. [931]

Some believe that over centuries, the ritual of planting seven different *sabzeh* changed into planting just one. In its place, people used the seven symbolic items in their homes all starting with the letter 's', a version of the tradition with which contemporary Iranians practice. *Sabzeh*, or the sprouting green itself remains the centerpiece of the modern Iranian Nowruz table.

The ritual of Nowruz encourages generosity, charity, and philanthropy. Those who can afford it are encouraged to give gifts. Children usually receive money from the adults and elderly in the family. The rich provide clothing, food, and money to the poor and those in need. Similar to the custom during Christmas, extra tips or gifts are given to cabdrivers, garbage collectors, postmen, housekeepers, laborers, and employees. The spirit of charity and kindness prevails in nearly every neighborhood and city square.

Centuries ago, in addition to giving gifts to those in need, the wealthy gave gifts to the Shah, providing a considerable additional source of revenue. During the Umayyad regime (661CE-750CE), all Iranian festivals, including Nowruz, were banned as un-Islamic. Yet Iranians continued to celebrate Nowruz in their homes and through the practice of gift giving towards their Umayyad ruler's, created an incentive for the Islamic Caliphs to tolerate this celebration and keep it alive in society. One of the reasons nearly every other Iranian celebration except for Nowruz, was forgotten, was due to the newly found source of revenue enjoyed by the Umayyad Caliph and later by the Caliphs of Abbasid family in Baghdad. This voluntary gifting on Nowruz helped the celebration survive but the Caliphs soon turned it into an opportunity for a mandatory taxation, reportedly amounting to as much as 10 million dirhams during the Umayyad reign of Mo'awieh.[932]

In the fifth century of Islamic era, the Iranian finance minister of Fars province, Ibn-Balkhi, was compiling a book on Iranian heritage and history in his region. He was told of the ruins of an old palace near the city of Shiraz. On the northern steps of this grand palace now referred to in the West as Persepolis were images of citizens giving gifts to the Shah.[933] For the Iranians, this ritual of gift giving was a well-known practice of Nowruz still prevalent at the time.

At the time Iranians were familiar with the mythology on the origins of Nowruz, believing the celebration dates back to Jamshid, the third mythological king of Iran. It was on Nowruz during the reign of Jamshid that a new era in Iranian history begins and it is thought that because of what it was thought as depiction of Nowruz on the palace of Persepolis that Iranians called this palace *takht-e-Jamshid* (Palace of Jamshid). It is said that during this era, Jamshid returns home victorious from foreign wars and establishes an era of peace and prosperity for the citizens. Iranians believed the end of war and Jamshid's victory occurred on Nowruz and from then on Iranians celebrated the rebirth and renewal of their country year after year. The practice of giving gifts to rulers and the Shah was abandoned with the destruction of Iranian culture and society after the Mongol invasion. Yet the celebration of Nowruz survived as an important ritual of healing for centuries.

Today, Nowruz serves as the cornerstone ritual of the Iranian national identity. Iranians of every religion and ethnicity celebrate the coming of spring and dawn of the New Year as a symbol of hope, and rebirth, nonviolence and healing. No matter the extent of quarreling in families, when Nowruz arrives, members overlook their animosities and gather around *sofreh*. Growing up, it was only on Nowruz and around *sofreh* where we could see relatives with leftist, Islamist, or monarchist views, mortal enemies of each other at any other time, laugh as they enjoyed the celebratory atmosphere and the cooking of a great aunt or grandmother.

The first day of spring is usually spent in the home of the oldest member of the family. As a child, we would visit both grandparents. The second and third days were often reserved for great aunts and uncles, later visits to older relatives and friends. In each home, harmful or hurtful language was forbidden and the ancient Iranian trio of kind thoughts, kind words and kind deeds were brought to life.

In Iranian homes, the universal greeting becomes '*har roozetan* Nowruz' (May your everyday be Nowruz), a fleeting wish for the unrealized potential of Iranians to live in a society of nonviolence, hope and rebirth 'every day' as opposed to only a few during Nowruz. Yet, through generations, these words have become so routine that their meaning is overlooked and their message unheard. Nowruz is now the excuse for escape from the 'every day' of pain in a society where violence is believed to be *fait accompli*, a momentary getaway from the despairing thought of living in a never ending totalitarian state. For

CHAPTER 12

Iranians, Nowruz offers a brief respite from this dark winter era of Islamic Republic, and perhaps a glimpse of an unforeseeable future in which Nowruz will be lived 'every day'.

Yet dreams are often envisioned in moments of pleasure and lives altered in quiet moments of bliss. Celebrations, a society's break from 'every day', can become occasions for hope, and potential powerful tools for societal transformation. In a regime that abhors and forbids joy and festivity, a celebration can not only be an escape but a symbolic act of defiance against the laws and commands of the totalitarian state. For a government that survives on use of violence to continuously maintain fear, trauma and terror in society, Nowruz is the momentary reminder of a life free of violence, and prohibition and censorship, a life of hope and peace and joy and prosperity for each and every citizen, 'every day' of the year.

***

Sizdah Bedar

13th of *Farvardin* - April 2nd

During the celebrations of Nowruz, visiting family and friends starting with the elderly to the youngest members of family is repeated day after day. After twelve days of vising homes comes '*sizdeh-bedar*' celebrating the 13th day of spring. On this day, Iranians no longer visit families and neighbors in each other's homes. The celebration is now taken outdoors to parks, fields, gardens, by the streams and lakes and in nature. Food is prepared for a grand picnic with participation of millions of Iranians across Iran and across the world.

As Nowruz symbolizes the renewal and rebirth of life, the celebration of '*sizdeh-bedar*' on the 13th is a reminder of human beings place amongst nature. The fields are now green, trees are blossoming and streams are filled with fresh melted snow. One of the important symbolic acts on this day is the placement of sprouting '*sabzeh*' grass, taken from the Nowruz table into running streams as symbol of humanity in harmony and helping the rebirth of nature.

With this ritual of '*sizdeh bedar*', thirteen days of healing, rebirth, and kindness come to an end. From the next day on, school is back in session, laborers go back to work, the bazaars reopen, and people head back to their jobs, reenergized and with new outlook and appreciation for life.

Today, in Islamic Republic that dislikes national symbols of Iranian identity, hosts on Iran's national television and radio are instructed not to refer to the gathering of Iranians across the fields and parks of Iran as 'sizdeh bedar'. If they need to, the hosts are instructed to simply mention celebration 'outdoors' or in 'nature' in the hopes that Iranians will somehow forget their ancient rituals. As children, purposefully, we were given tremendous amount of homework to ensure that we are unable to finish on time and will be forced to stay home on this celebration in the effort that the Islamic regime will succeed in eliminating children and families from parks and fields. Yet, Iranians continue to defy their totalitarian regime and continue to celebrate '*sizdeh bedar*' as their ancestors have done for centuries. Celebrating '*sizdeh bedar*' with nature on the 13th and last day of Nowruz celebrations is again a tool not only for psychological healing and cultural transformation towards nonviolence, but a symbolic act which again can be turned into an act of civil disobedience for human rights against a regime that abhors celebrations.

***

Farvardegan – Memorial Day

19th of *Farvardin* – April 8th

Today, the celebration of *Farvardegan* on the 19th day of spring is mostly forgotten as a national celebration and only practiced by the Zoroastrian communities of Iran. *Farvardin*, the first month of spring and Iranian calendar year which forms the basis for this celebration is named after *foruhars* or *faravahars* or *faravashis,* the kind spirits of friends, family and loved ones no longer alive. For ancient Iranians, the memory of loved ones during the joyous festival of Nowruz was a tool for healing and coping with loss. The Festival of Fire, a few nights before Nowruz, was a celebration where bonfires served as guides for these kind spirits visiting their homes.

Therefore, celebration of *Farvardegan* like all Iranian celebrations of ancient Iran, including Nowruz, at one time had important religious functions. It is not known whether these Iranian rituals were Zoroastrian rituals incorporated into the Iranian calendar or were rituals of pre-Zoroastrian Iranians incorporated into the religious beliefs of Zoroastrians. What we do know is that these rituals took on a very religious, Zoroastrian function during the

CHAPTER 12

Sassanid era of religious government. Thus, with the demise of Zoroastrianism in Iran, many of the celebrations that were considered religious rituals like *Farvardegan* were eliminated as national rituals. Others like Nowruz, the Festival of Fire, and *Yalda* shed themselves of their religious beliefs and survived into the modern era as secular national celebrations.

The origin of these rituals and their religious function in the past however is not as important as evaluating the role and function these rituals can play for this generation of Iranians. Celebrations like Farvardegan can only have widespread appeal, if like Nowruz and Yalda, they shed themselves of their religious past and are reborn as secular national celebrations for the 21st century. Reinterpretation of the forgotten healing rituals and celebrations of Iran requires us to reinterpret these celebrations with a new lens for the modern cosmopolitan, pluralistic, and democratic society of tomorrow.

Therefore, we must readjust our view of such rituals, regarding them as secular and pluralistic national rituals of healing, kindness, community, and nonviolence as opposed to religious rituals of the past with little significance today. A national ritual remembering the spirit of loved ones may have been inspired by the religions of ancient Iran, but it belongs to Iranian culture and not to any particular religion. Thus, recreation of such a ritual can be performed by anyone, speaking any tongue, and practicing any religion.

For ancient Iranians, the 19th day of *Farvardin* month, like the 19th of every month, was called *Farvardin*-day, the same name as the name of the first month. As was the custom in Iran, when the name of day on the calendar coincided with name of the month, special rituals or celebrations were performed. Meanwhile, rituals of Iranian calendar were always referred to as celebrations, even though many of them lacked the music or dancing often one associates with a celebration. It is important for us to understand that Iranians regarded such days as celebrations because they were occasions for joy. In the ancient culture of Iran in which these rituals were shaped and structured, mourning, sorrow and grief were considered undesirable emotions, unfit for a national ritual and celebration. The celebration of *foruhars* or *faravashis*, the kind spirits of loved ones in this month was not considered an occasion for mourning and sorrow, but a memorial celebration and an occasion for joy.

The celebration of *Farvardegan* on 19th day of *Farvardin* was a celebration of thanksgiving for the kind spirits who visited people's homes during Nowruz. For this celebration, Iranians would visit cemeteries and memorials of loved ones and place flowers and food there. Rosewater would be used to wash the tombstones and the day was spent with the memory of *foruhars*, this time not in one's own home, but in the symbolic resting place of loved ones.

The practice of creating memorials of loved ones is a powerful tool of psychological healing. Such memorials are created through symbolic places and images, symbolic words in form of poems or prayers, or symbolic acts in form of funerals. The celebration of *Farvardegan* was such a symbolic act of memorial meant for healing of families, communities, and the society.

Outside of Iran today, meetings and conferences remembering and celebrating the lives and spirits of important national figures lost the previous year, can be a powerful symbolic tool helping Iranians come together in an atmosphere free of rage, anger and violence.

The celebration of *Farvardegan*, performed today in cemeteries of Iran next to memorials of national figures, national poets, national writers, and other symbolic figures can be a tool for psychological healing of a nation. In addition, it can be a symbolic cultural tool expressing Iranian population's desire for the secular culture of Nowruz and other Iranian celebrations. In addition to the psychological and cultural healing such a gathering may provide, the intolerance of the regime for such gatherings will again turn these events into acts of civil disobedience.

Iranians cannot have a secular-democratic regime free of violence unless millions of individuals are able to express their desire for such a culture and political system. National rituals are tools allowing expression of a population's desires. Yalda, Sadeh, Nowruz are all such occasion when people can express themselves in a united fashion. *Farvardegan* on the 19th day of *Farvardin* is also such an occasion. While some rituals are performed at home, some on rooftops, some on streets, *Farvardegan* is performed in cemeteries, next to memorials and places of remembering. Regardless of location, such a ritual can be performed as a symbolic act of civil disobedience and as a referendum for democracy in Iran.

***

Ordibeheshtgan – Earth Day

3rd of Ordibehesht – April 23rd

Ordibehesht is the second month in spring and thus the second month on Iranian calendar. If a European asks what the word '*Ordibehesht*' means, an average Iranian will likely guess that it may mean: 'Like-Heaven'. Their response is perhaps natural since the second part of the word '*behesht*' means 'heaven' in modern Persian and also because of the beauty of earth in mid-spring. No other time of year is closer to humanity's vision of heaven on earth than this time of year. In *Ordibehesht*, the flowers are blooming. The countryside is green. Streams, creeks and rivers are filled with melting snow. Fresh fruit is found in nearly every garden around town. The herbal aromas of colorful dishes made with fresh spring ingredient are savored in nearly every home. In the villages of Iran, young and old alike are working in the farms. Local songs and music is heard on the fields and in homes.

Throughout Iranian history, the heavenly environment of *Ordibehesht*, in mid-spring was an inspiration to poets, writers and musicians. Iranian art was thus often a reflection of this vision of heavenly life on earth. The blooming fields of mid spring for Iranians were the canvas on which nature was reflected at this time of year; *Ordibehesht* for Iranians was thus art and beauty in its natural form. For the citizens enduring the long winter and concerned about the hot and dry coming summer, the earth in *Ordibehesht* inspired the joy, love and pleasure of life free of the threats and fears of the climate.

Europeans are familiar with Omar Khayyam as the 12th century Iranian poet. But for Iranians, Omar Khayyam is foremost the mathematician, astronomer, and scholar who revived the modern Iranian calendar. Much of Omar Khayyam's work while recreating this calendar is covered in his book 'Nowruz-nameh'.

This is how he describes *Ordibehesht*: "They call this month *behesht* (heaven) because in this month, world and nature is like heaven, filled with pleasure, green and life."[934] Others have also interpreted the name of this month as a reflection of heaven on earth. Yet, the word '*Ordibehesht*' is far older and unrelated to the conception of heaven. Like other months of Iranian calendar, it was inspired by the most ancient religious beliefs of early Iranians.

In Avesta and in Zoroastrian religion, *Ordibehesht* is the second *Spenta*. The seven *Spentas* were the primary protectorate gods and goddesses of ancient Persia and aids to Ahura-Mazda, the God of creation.

The first part of the word, '*ordi*' is derived from the ancient word '*Arta*', which in turn is derived from even more ancient word which in Sanskrit we know as 'Rta'. The ancient Indo-Europeans traveling south into Iran and India brought this word with them where in ancient Persian languages, it was eventually turned to 'ordi' as in the name of this month, '*arta*', and later '*raast*' as seen today by words such as '*doros*t' (correctness) and '*raastin*' (righteousness). Those traveling west to Europe also carried this concept of '*rta*' with them where in English it was modified to 'right' and 'righteous'. The second part of the word '*Vahishta*' means 'the most'. Thus 'ordi-behesht' means the 'most-righteous'.

As you recall, for Iranians, each day of the month had a special name. The third day of each month was called *ordibehesht*. As was the custom of ancient Iranians, when *Ordibehesht* day fell in the month of *Ordibehesht*, special rituals and celebrations were held called *Ordibeheshtgan*. Today, except for few Zoroastrian faithful performing religious ceremonies on this day, this celebration is nearly completely forgotten.

For Iranians, *Ordibehesht*, the protectorate of righteousness was also assigned as the keeper of fire. Fire in ancient Iran signified purity and cleanliness. It seems one of the important components of this ritual was its religious significance as a celebration for people attending temples, lighting candles, and as occasions for prayers. Yet the function of this celebration was more than a religious ceremony. There are also many references that the celebration of *Ordibeheshtgan*, in addition to its religious component, also had an 'earthly', secular component which was an obligation to attend the court of local governors and to volunteer ones time and effort for the community.

From the few references, it seems that Iranians in ancient times would go to their local governors and ask "How can we volunteer our time today to help the city, town or village?"[935] Thus, *Ordibeheshtgan* was a community wide ritual for improving the world people lived in. In effect, it was also a day of volunteerism.

This day of 'volunteerism' or '*Ordibeheshtgan*' was possibly an important ritual in an undemocratic era when rulers needed routines and rituals to demonstrate their legitimacy to the people. It's very plausible that any time people participated in this ritual, not only they were helping their community and society, but by approaching their rulers and volunteering their time for them, they were also indirectly giving a vote of confidence to their unelected governors.

After the Arab invasion of Iran and in the Umayyad and Abbasid eras, weekly and yearly Islamic prayers and rituals which praised the Umayyad and Abbasid caliphates provided the necessary structure for praising the rulers and thus replaced this more ancient Iranian and Zoroastrian practices. The loss of this ancient ritual thus had more to do with lack of function it played in people's lives and society which was using the new Islamic rituals for its purposes. In effect, this celebration's function as a religious tool for prayer and meditation was lost for those converting to Islam. The community, 'earthly' function it played as a 'day of volunteerism' for local governors was also lost as people no longer associated with foreign speaking governors and rulers treating them as their new found colony. In addition, this ritual was also under attack by those opposing to Abbasid courts, included Shi'ites who were attacking ancient Persian celebrations as un-Islamic and saw this ritual of volunteerism as a potential tool providing legitimacy to the caliphate in Baghdad.

Imam Jaffar Sadegh, the fourth Shi'ite Imam and one of the leading Shi'ite scholars in his fatwa against this celebration writes:

"On this day, *Ordibeheshtgan* ... stay away from all needs, works and do not refer to Sultan's court. Do not buy, sell or socialize on this day. Don't seek help for your desires. On this day hold your desires and stay away from Sultans work and action. Instead, give charity to religious causes as much as you can afford."[936]

While at the same time, this Shi'ite leader was attacking this celebration and sending a fatwa against it, he did not forget the humanitarian use of this ritual and at the end of his statement while he is discouraging any social, secular work of charity for the community, he encourages charity for religious causes.

What function can the ritual of *Ordibeheshtgan* play for the modern generation of Iranians? How can it serve as a tool for psychological healing of today's society? How can it be used as a tool to introduce a new culture of nonviolence, kindness and democracy to Iran? And, how can it be used as a political statement for civil disobedience?

The essence of *Ordibeheshtgan* which involves the call for volunteerism is evident from the ancient texts, but also today '*Ordibehesht*' recalls its modern Persian meaning of '*behesht*' as a time of heaven on earth. If we utilize 'volunteerism' for public service, one of the ancient functions of this celebration, we will again face the same questions and dilemmas as in the Umayyad and Abbasid eras where volunteering ones effort for the government was a form of praising and legitimizing the regime and counterproductive in today's undemocratic and authoritarian atmosphere. Despite this, the modern recreation of this ritual for 21st century should not sway far from the essence of 'volunteerism' practiced centuries ago.

In a broader look, volunteerism does not need to be only for one's government. Governments are only tools and vehicles guiding the efforts of the population for specific tasks. These public tasks then function to serve the community and the environment. Thus, volunteerism does not need to be for one's government or regime, it needs to ultimately serve the community and the environment people live in. If we realize the beauty and significance of this month as the month in the year when earth is much like heaven, one then realizes the importance of earth and environment for the splendor of this month. Thus, this ritual could focus on volunteerism for earth and environment and this ancient celebration could be resurrected for the 21st century needs in the same manner as today's celebration and ritual of Earth Day.

A ritual devoted to the well-being of the environment and the earth is not just a way to meet the modern Iranian need for psychological, cultural and political healing, it is a human need of modern society; without it, little care is given to forests, streams, and natural habitats. No other organism has destroyed as much of the earth, has driven as many species into extinction, has enslaved and abused as many animals and plants for production and has jeopardized its own existence as much as humanity. For much of human history, the use of environment, whether the hunting of animals, destroying trees and forests, or cultivating tracts of land for farming were acts of survival necessary for a species battling the forces of nature. But today, human beings unending appetite for growth is itself threatening the survival of humanity.

Farming, city planning and economic production are performed for short term gains with little regard for the environment. Through our disregard for the earth, we are poisoning the ground and underwater aquifers with millions of gallons of chemical herbicides, pesticides and heavy metals. Trees function only as tools of shade and instruments propping up home values. Mountains are obstacles for eight lane highways, while streams and rivers are beneficial and protected if only serving a purpose for human beings. More than eighty million barrels of oil per day are extracted from the deepest caverns of earth, and then burned as fuel, pouring tons of pollutants, mainly carbon dioxide, into the skies and oceans. Fish are poisoned with mercury leached into the sea while whales, elephants and tigers are hunted for profit. Sheep and cows are genetically engineered for more meat and milk, horses engineered for racetracks, while corn engineered with built-in genes that produce pesticides.

Iranians, like people in every other culture and nation, need a ritual that provides a way to face the challenges of the environment in 21st, 22nd century and beyond. In the last several decades, April 22nd has grown to become the internationally recognized 'Earth Day', a day of volunteerism for the environment. The ancient Iranian ritual and celebration of *Ordibeheshtgan* on April 23rd a day that follows the international Earth day is not a coincidence that should be ignored. If there is to be a national, secular day of volunteerism for protecting and enhancing the environment in Iran, it is appropriate for it to be on *Ordibeheshtgan*.

In addition to the benefits this day of 'heaven on earth' will provide for the environment, volunteering one's time for the community is also one of the more powerful tools for healing the community. Care for the environment, planting of trees, saving the forests, mountains, streams and caring for animals are some of the most powerful forms of societal healing. For a country suffering from fear, anxiety, trauma, the simple act of picking up garbage from streets, streams, fields or beaches can serve as a powerful tool, transforming the participants from passive spectators of violence to an active individual taking strides in psychologically healing themselves and others around them. It is a symbolic act which can not only heal a psychologically traumatized nation, by can also serve as a symbol of kindness and nonviolence helping to forge the culture of Iran of tomorrow. Such a celebration can transform not only individuals, but also communities and ultimately, the society.

And because it is performed as a yearly ritual of *Ordibeheshtgan*, another celebration abhorred by the Islamic Republic, it will take on a symbolic value as another ritual and celebration of Iranian national identity. It can become a national ritual symbolizing Iranians' desire for a country free of violence, discrimination, and fear. Like all other rituals of Nowruz, participation in this ritual can become a symbolic act of civil disobedience.

***

Khordadgan – Lover's Day Celebration

6th of *Khordad* - May 27th

Iranian calendar's sixth day of every month was named *Khordad* day, named for *Havr-vatat*, the goddess and protector of water. If one walks into an Iranian jewelry store today and asks for a pendant of *Khordad*, one is often shown an image of a beautiful woman sitting and pouring over a jug of water as the goddess of this month. On the sixth of every month, *Khordad* was celebrated as the protectorate of water or the symbol of life. Abu Reyhan Biruni in his 11th century account of ancient practices writes : "… on this day, people wake at dawn and wash themselves with water from *houz* (pools) or *qanat* (underground streams) and at times they pure water on themselves as a symbol of cleansing, health and good-fortune."[937]

The ritual of cleansing with water played an important role in ancient Middle Eastern cultures. In the desert lands of Middle East, water was a symbol of life, health, and prosperity. Thus the ritual of cleansing with water on *Khordad* (sixth) day of each month was a spiritual and psychological renewal for the participants, the families and communities. Across Middle East, one can see numerous rituals of psychological and spiritual cleansing with water, one form of which still exists today in the form of Baptism in the Christian church.

While respect, attention, and importance of water was emphasized on *Khordad* day (sixth day) of every month of the year, the last month in spring, was also called *Khordad* and thus on the sixth day of this month, when the day of *Khordad* fell within the month of *Khordad*, the celebration of *Khordadgan* was performed by people spending the day next to streams, rivers and lakes.

In the agricultural desert world of the ancient Middle East, water was the source of life. Gods and goddesses of water can be found in the history of nearly every culture since the dawn of farming. Kindness from the goddess of water meant plentiful harvest, prosperity, and health for the community. The anger of this goddess meant drought, famine and disease. For human beings and Iranians in particular, the need for rain was especially acute at the end of spring and beginning of summer, which is why in the Iranian calendar, the last month of spring is named after this goddess.

The celebration with water and praising of the goddess of water played an important function for human societies of past as tools for easing people's fear, terror, and anxiety caused by an unpredictable climate. The pattern of weather, which could not be accurately forecasted, was a great source of societal fear for human beings in nearly every culture dependent on rain. Accordingly community and societal prayers and rituals were performed in order to alleviate this anxiety.

Yet, in the modern world, the needs of human beings are different. We now know that rain doesn't come because we pray or are good. Disease and drought are not due to societal misbehaving. Because of our modern understanding of weather patterns and our ability to alter the environment by building water dams and canals, the rituals of water have lost their value and function in most cultures. In addition, today's world is also mostly urbanized which again reduces the significance of water and rain as a source of fear and anxiety for citizens. Because of this lack of function for a water ritual in today's world and lack of this rituals Zoroastrian function for Iranians today, the ritual of *Khordadgan* is no longer seen in Iran unless practiced as a religious ritual by the small Zoroastrian communities of Iran.

Any ritual whose function is no longer necessary disappears from the culture and society. And if a ritual or celebration of *Khordadgan* is to be brought back to life, it must play an important function in meeting the needs of today's generation and not an attempt to revive practices meeting ancient needs. Attempts to revive *khordadgan* like its ancient past next to Iranian streams, lakes, and rivers, would only result in creating a dysfunctional modern ritual with millions of urban citizens attempting to find a spot next to the few remaining natural sources of water around their city. Such a dysfunctional ritual would result in experiencing traffic jams, headaches, and pollution, likely a one-time event without any psychological, spiritual or societal function. In addition, the few remaining natural water resources around Iranian cities would soon be destroyed by countless families trashing such treasures in the name of celebrations.

The attempt to use Iran's own ancient culture of past as an inspiration for making the 21st century culture of tomorrow cannot be a dogmatic attempt at reinvigorating every belief and practice of ancient Persia. Such a foolish attempt is no different than the Islamic, Christian or Jewish fundamentalists' attempting to recreate the exact practices and laws of 1300, 2000 or 5000 years ago. Our past should inspire us, but it cannot dictate the practices of today. The celebration of *Khordadgan*, like other ancient celebrations, can be an inspiration for us as we try to recreate the essential elements of Iranian culture in the 21st century globalized world. A traditionalist view at attempting to recreate such rituals based on ancient needs is a fruitless attempt for a short-lived practice.

If the celebration of water, as it was done centuries ago, is not a practical or functional ritual for today's Iran, then what is an alternate societal need of today's Iran which *Khordadgan* can represent? Where else can we find inspiration for *Khordadgan* celebration?

In addition to history books, traces of the Iranian past are sometimes found in the country's villages and communities. Communities most vulnerable to forgetting the past are those in the major metropolitan centers whose cultures, practices, and rituals are often manipulated and influenced through constant struggles of violence and rule. To find traces of ancient practices untouched through the millennia, one needs to travel outside the cities to villages, particularly villages more free from the influence of violence, wars, and persecutions. In Iran, many such villages exist in the mountains, still protecting and preserving enduring cultural practices tested and retested over centuries of village and community work to ensure they are practical and useful.

The village of Savad-Kuh, situated on the northern face of Alborz Mountains, near the borders of Gilan and Mazandaran, is one such place. It is a beautiful natural treasure from the past, with citizens still practicing the beliefs of their ancestors at times dating back thousands of years. The mountains have protected these villagers from perhaps most of the 103 generations of violence experienced by most. In this mountainous region on the southern shores of Caspian Sea, people have a celebration at the end of spring they today call *Khordad-Eid*. This celebration at the end of *Khordad*, as opposed to the sixth day, marks the end of spring.

What does the celebration of *Khordad-Eid* entail for the people of Savad-Kooh?

People there believe it is good fortune to be married in Khordad and especially on Khordad-Eid, so it is often filled with joy and celebration of local weddings. This day, which could perhaps be labeled the day of love, marks the end of spring, which can be called season of love.

It is easy to see why these ancient people labeled this time of year as a time of marriage. The end of spring is one the more beautiful times of the year. After three months of working the fields and farms, lovers have had the opportunity and time to court each other and make proper expressions of love. Food is plentiful and people joyous.

The expression of love is one of the more important societal needs of human beings; countless rituals have been created in response to this need. It may come as a surprise to an American or a European to see flower shops in today's Tehran under the Islamic Republic bustling with activity on February 14th, Valentine's Day. The stores often run out of flowers by sunset. On February 14th of every year, because of the need and desire to express love, countless young Iranians rush to buy flowers for their lovers, a practice much disliked by the Islamic Republic. This adoption of Valentine's Day as day of love by this generation of Iranians is evidence of cultural identity crises for a people who have lost the symbolic tools and practices of their own for the expression of love. A culture with an identity crisis in a globalized world is a culture bound for extinction.

Meanwhile, a ritual in which young and old can symbolically express love for others is important and perhaps necessary for society. If Iranians are to adopt and create a ritual for love similar to the European and American ritual of Valentine's day, *Khordadgan*, inspired through the *Khordad-Eid* of Savad Kooh is a natural candidate for this occasion. The beauty of nature in spring has always served as a source of inspiration and love for countless generations across many cultures. The Iranian belief of good fortune to be married in *Khordad* by people of Savad-Kooh is not a mere coincidence. The world is filled with life at this time of year. Citizens are cheerful and inspired by nature.

Such a simple ritual where people are allowed to express their love by giving one another a flower or another symbolic item can serve as a tool for overcoming people's fear of such expressions. Such a healing ritual, like all other monthly rituals can serve as instruments for healing in a society suffering from terror and violence. A society living in fear and traumatized by violence is thus given a channel to express its love for those close to them. But in addition, such a new symbolic expression in homes and communities will surely be followed by references to other Iranian celebrations. The expression of love on *Khordadgan* will also serve as a symbolic act in favor of the healing culture of Nowruz for Iranians. It can be a tool for cultural change.

Just as in other monthly healing rituals of Iran based on the spirit of Nowruz, the symbolic words and acts expressed on this day will send messages of hope across the countless communities, towns, and villages of Iran. Such an expression will be another example of a nonviolent method of struggle for democracy against a regime that detests love and romance. In a nonviolent way, it will serve as an act of defiance against the regime, a referendum for democracy and a powerful weapon that questions the legitimacy of the Islamic Republic.

CHAPTER 13 –SUMMER AND AUTUMN CELEBRATIONS AND THE CYCLE OF LIFE

"The religious regime in Iran may not permit the celebration of Mehregan in the streets of Tehran, Isfahan, or Tabriz, but one day Mehregan will be celebrated freely on those same streets."

Tirgan - Tir, Tishtar (Tishtrya in Avesta)

13th of *Tir* - July 4th
While the month of *Khordad* and sixth of every month was named for goddess of water, 13th day of every month as well as the first month of summer was named after *Tir*, the goddess of rain. The word is derived from the Pahlavi word *Tishtar*, which in Avesta is referred to as *Tishtrya*. This ancient goddess was seen in the heavens as a constellation of stars known to Europeans as Sirius. The celebration of *Tirgan* occurred on the day of *Tir* (13th), in the month of *Tir*.

The repeat of water theme again, this time in form of rain, points to the importance of this precious liquid and the dependence of ancient farmers, communities, and society on water and rain. Just as Kluckhohn saw the creation of rain rituals by Pueblo Indians as a therapy for their societal anxiety, another ancient Persian ritual involving water reflects the ancient fears of draught and thus famine.

Zoroastrians today continue to celebrate *Tirgan* with a celebration involving water, one that includes symbolic acts of cleansing and renewal. With the Islamisation of Iran, rituals and prayers of Islam served to replace rituals serving to overcome the fear and anxiety from natural forces. With this loss of its religious function for Iranians as well as the constant attack against Iranians celebrations by Islamic fundamentalists, except for the Zoroastrian faithful, most Iranians naturally stopped participating in this celebration.

Tirgan was known as one of the more important celebrations of ancient Iran. It was also referred to as one of the most joyous celebrations of the past. The reason for the significance and joyous occasion of this celebration did not just involve the importance of rain in summer for the population. *Tirgan* happened to also mark one of the most significant mythological events for ancient Iranians. This event must have been as real to ancient Persians as any documented historical event of today. It was on this day of *Tirgan* in Iranian mythology when the long war between the mythological neighbors, Turan and Iran, came to an end marking the beginning of an era of peace. The celebration of *Tirgan* marked the start of the celebration of peace.

It is also important to note that this proclamation of peace was not achieved through victory in war or peace after tragedy of defeat. The celebration of *Tirgan* marks one of few mythological stories in human cultures where peace was achieved through negotiation, dialogue and a treaty.

The story of great wars between the mythological nations of Iran and Turan is engrained in every Iranians' psyche since their childhood, in a way not unlike the great Trojan Wars of ancient Greece are to Europeans. The deeds of many of the archetypal hero figures of Iranian culture, including the story of Rostam, take place against this setting. Such mythological stories often form foundations of cultures and at times civilizations.

In the Iranian mythology, the generations-long great war of Iran and Turan led to Turan's surrounding the Iranian army in Tabarestan. Without supplies, Iranians began to cook the fruit available to them and to bake wheat, even though they did not have the means to grind the wheat into flour. One of the rituals of *Tirgan* still involves baking of wheat, a symbolic act referring back to the time when they were unable to make flour.

The events in the story occur during the reign of mythological king Manouchehr, who was at war with Afrasiab, the king of Turan. In the story, realizing the defeat of Iranians, Manouchehr suggests peace. In order for the two countries to establish their national boundaries, Manouchehr negotiates a way of settling the matter; an Iranian will be allowed to shoot an arrow into the air and where that arrow lands, the borders of Iran and Turan were to be formed. In the story, *Esfand*, the Goddess of Earth, sends Iranians a message about how to make the proper bow and also names the soldier who is shoot it. The soldier named Arash was found and was given the task.

In the story, Arash, who knew the significance of this arrow, is said to have taken his clothes off and announced, "Look, my body is free of scars and wounds, and I will cast this arrow with all my strength, knowing it will tear my muscles apart and I will die of wounds. But I will undertake the task at hand". In the story, on that day which was *Tirgan*, he climbs the Damavand peak and with all the strength in his body and spirit draws back the bowstring and sends the arrow towards the farthest reaches of Khurasan. As he predicted, the effort tears his muscles apart and he dies when the arrow is let go.

In the story, a goddess instructs the wind to carry the arrow, taking it thousands of miles away, and landing on a great walnut tree in Central Asia marking the borders of Iran and Turan. Peace was proclaimed and from that day on, and every year after on *Tirgan*, Iranians celebrated peace between two neighbors. The 13th is often referred to as the lesser *Tirgan*. People believed the arrow traveled for a whole day and landed on the 14th, which was celebrated with more joy and is sometimes referred to as the greater *Tirgan*.

The story of Arash and his bow is repeated numerous times in Iranian literature. Today in Iran, the name Arash is one of the most common Iranian names. Yet, despite the collective memory of Arash and this event, centuries of societal focus on violence and warfare forced *Tirgan*, the celebration of peace, to be forgotten. Iranians remember and retell the story, but they fail to celebrate it and they fail to learn from it.

If we are to change Iranian culture from one of violence and war to a culture of nonviolence and peace, we must learn to practice and celebrate peace. Not being violent does not mean that an individual is actually nonviolent. One adopts the culture of nonviolence only when one learns to practice nonviolence through action and symbolic acts. Iranian celebrations of Nowruz and all other Iranian celebrations are such symbolic acts, and bringing a celebration for peace back to life will be one of the more important of such symbolic gestures. Yet, like Nowruz and all other national celebrations of Iran, *Tirgan* needs to also shed itself of its ancient religious functions and become a tool for all Iranians regardless of their religious beliefs.

What kind of a celebration can be performed on *Tirgan* meeting the needs of the 21st century Iranians? How can *Tirgan* function as a tool for healing and therapy? What is the function that this ritual can perform for individuals, families, communities, and the nation as a whole? How can Tirgan become an act of civil disobedience?

Tirgan represents peace between two neighbors. Two neighbors could represent two nations, but they may also represent two communities or two families. In today's urbanized world in which millions of citizens are crammed in apartment complexes and living wall-to-wall from each other, a ritual of peace between neighbors is a necessity. Without the enactment of rituals of peace for neighbors in today's urbanized world, neighbors living wall-to-wall may not see each other for months at a time and may not have worthwhile conversations for years at a time. A ritual of peace between neighbors is perhaps required in today's complex world.

CHAPTER 13

In the preindustrial rural cultures, neighbors were families. They would greet each other at bazaars, farms, bathhouses, and on the streets. Community dances and festivals would bring neighbors closer to each other as rituals of healing. Neighbors were invited to weddings and treated as if they were family. Neighbors were the first people at hand when an animal or a child was ill. A sense of community, interest in affairs of the village, town, and society began with neighbors. Such a connection between neighbors is lost in today's world. The frightening speed of modern world allows enough time for only a quick 'hello' when greeting neighbors in stairwells or on sidewalks. The random chance of seeing one's neighbor in the market or bazaar is insignificant. Rarely do two neighbors work in the same field.

The industrialization and urbanization of life has created a world without the proper rituals of community. Lack of such rituals of friendship and kindness has created societies in which neighbors have a good chance of greeting each other in courthouses, where they are joined out of anger. In much of the world in 21st century, two families living wall-to-wall are strangers to each other. A knock on each other's door is often followed with warnings to keep the noise down or to perform an overdue task. A good neighbor in today's world is one not seen, not heard, and not bothersome. We'd rather have no neighbors than the current strangers living next door to us.

21st century urbanized human beings desperately need a ritual through which, once a year, neighbors can invite each other over for tea or snacks, a symbolic act of peace, friendship, and nonviolence. For a few hours, such a ritual allows two estranged neighbors to sit with each other and share their common burdens and common dreams. How many countless misunderstandings are due to lack of such simple yet immensely important rituals? How many neighbors have turned to anger, lawsuits, and even violence because of the lack of such a ritual?

The invitation of a neighbor over for tea on *Tirgan* can be a powerful symbolic act. Ultimately, such a ritual can serve as a healing tool for communities and the nation. Communication between two neighbors through a ritual of peace will stir interest in their environment, in their schools, in their local governments, and ultimately create a desire for democracy. In addition, the atmosphere of kindness fashioned during Nowruz can again be rekindled on *Tirgan*. Politically, like Nowruz and other Iranian celebrations, it can symbolize nonviolence and ultimately the desire for human rights and democracy.

Outside of Iran, expatriate Iranians can also celebrate *Tirgan* as a ritual for peace. While the current Iranian regime is sponsoring hatred, anger and enmity in various countries in Middle East, Iranian people and the expatriates in particular, can send a message to the world of the Iranian desire of nonviolence and peace with neighbors in the region.

When faced with an authoritarian regime bent on the use of violence and feeding on the spread of hatred, a ritual for peace is a weapon and a threat to the legitimacy of that regime. It is, in effect, a national referendum calling for a change in culture. It is a symbolic act with messages far deeper and more powerful than votes cast in a ballot box. It is a ritual transforming a passive defeated individual into an active citizen.

Yet, how can Tirgan function as an act of civil disobedience? It already has.

In July of 2011, some youth in Tehran created a Facebook page inviting people to come to a park in central Tehran for one of the more popular acts in this celebration, the splashing of water. On that hot summer day, hundreds of people together with young children showed up with water guns and water balloons for what they expected was a joyous celebration of Iranian heritage. But they soon realized that in a regime which abhors joys and Iranian heritage, celebrations of ancient Iran are automatic acts of disobedience. Dozens were arrested and later humiliated on national television for their participation in this celebration. Overnight, Tirgan was turned into another future occasion for civil disobedience.

Tirgan, like other celebrations of ancient Iran, is one of the many gifts given to Iranians which each can be treasure houses of collective wisdom for use at times of desperation when an entire nation is suffering from fear, violence, and trauma. This is one of those times— and *Tirgan* is another of those tools.

***

Amordadgan – Celebration for the Elderly

7th of *Mordad* – July 29th

The second month of summer in Iranian calendar is *Mordad*. This word, which in its current form includes the word 'death' in its meaning, is derived from the more ancient word '*Amordad*'. This word in Avesta is referred to as '*amertat*'.

A characteristic of ancient Indo-European languages which is still commonly seen in English and sometimes in Persian is the prefix of 'a-' in front of a word as a form of negation of the word. As an example, 'apolitical' in English-language means without politics. Similarly, the word '*Amordad*' means life, longevity, and, literally, 'without-death'.

Amordad in ancient Iran was the name of another Spenta, the god and goddess companions of Ahura-Mazda, the God of creation. In Avesta, *Amordad* is sometimes used as an adjective describing the everlasting life of Ahura Mazda. She is also referred to as the goddess of plants. In the Iranian calendar, the seventh day of every month was called *Amordad*-day and when *Amordad*-day arrived in the month of *Amordad*, Iranians celebrated *Amordadgan*.

The content and the ceremonies involved on this ancient ritual are not clear today. For Zoroastrians, this celebration has a religious connotation and functions as a spiritual ritual. Perhaps it is because of this spiritual and religious function, which was fulfilled by Islamic rituals for Iranians, that this ritual is now forgotten as a national celebration. Like all other rituals, bringing this ritual back to life requires this celebration to shed itself of its religious function and serve as a national celebration for Iranians to meet the needs of 21st century society. It must also function as a tool for healing of families, communities, and the nation. It must also serve as a tool for communicating the national desire for a nonviolent, democratic, and secular Iran. Above all, like other rituals, it must derive inspiration from its own roots and history.

Longevity and life 'without death' is the wish and dream of any healthy individual. Iranian children often hear elders tell them '*pir shi javan*' (may you get old). This may sound strange to a modern culture that abhors aging, yet a long life is a beautiful wish not often fulfilled in the past as it is today. Science is pushing the life expectancy of human beings more and more to its limits and the dream of longevity is now a reality for most people in developed nations. Yet without proper rituals, the role, function, and place of elders in society is often not well-defined. Lack of proper rituals accompanying 21st century's advancement in medical sciences has created societies and cultures in which the emphasis for the elderly is not on quality of life but on living longer. Elderly often feel shunned by families that do not have the proper rituals to celebrate their lives. Their wisdom on happiness, love, diet, sleep, war, death, and disease is dismissed and ignored in favor of sometimes unscientific, 'scientific' studies proclaiming their own findings. In the modern world, old age is shunned as weak and ugly while emphasis is placed on physical strength and beauty. Because of the lack of proper rituals that celebrate the elderly in modern cultures and societies, the elderly's position and importance in society has diminished. In return, the elderly feel unimportant and, at times, a burden for their families which serves as causes of depression and anxiety for them.

Modern science allows us to live a long life. Scientists and physicians are given freedom to create new drugs and therapies to keep us alive. But the traditionalist view of culture shuns the creation of new rituals celebrating that long life. This traditionalist resistance to change in a culture and emphasis on keeping rituals the same as they were practiced in ancient times creates societies without proper rituals meeting the challenges of today.

In every ancient culture, one can find many sources of inspiration for creating and forming the modern cultures of today. Without the use of such inspiration, modern societies are forced to abandon their cultural roots in favor of globalized and generic rituals that are at times misunderstood by more traditional cultures. This cultural abandonment in a globalized world will ultimately lead to death of hundreds of cultures around the world in favor of few global cultures. This lack of diversity for humanity is a dangerous phenomenon that gives rise to the hegemony of one culture that will ultimately eliminate diversity in art, education, and even politics. The solution for this cultural loss is a continued effort by cultures to redefine themselves in order to meet the challenges of modern world. Creating a functioning ritual for *Amordadgan* suitable for needs of 21st century and inspired by the culture of ancient Iran is a way of meeting this challenge and keeping Iranian culture functional and alive in the future.

Creation of a functional '*Amordadgan*' requires realizing the need for a ritual celebrating the lives of the elderly and emphasizing their value as human beings and sources of wisdom in society. The participation in such a ritual will focus the attention of society and enable it to meet the demands of the elderly in the modern age. *Amordadgan*, which celebrates longevity, can be a celebration of their lives. A family, community, and national ritual celebrating the elderly will create time and space for families to show their love and respect for their grandparents, great uncles, and great aunts.

A community ritual celebrating the elderly will also help communities tackle the challenges of the elderly by creating proper homes, activity centers, and social events. A national ritual celebrating the elderly will help the nation focus on the needs of the elderly for health care, retirement benefits, transportation, and elderly rights. *Amordadgan*, celebrating life 'without-death' can function as such a ritual.

Without support of any governmental or international organization, Iranians can begin celebrating *Amordadgan* by visiting the eldest member of the family. Such a celebration of a grandparent or a great aunt or uncle does not require any national preparation or government support. It is possible that a regime that abhors pre-Islamic Iranian culture will do everything it can to discourage such a celebration, yet the celebration of *Amordadgan* is a healing tool for families estranged from their elderly members. It is a tool by which grandchildren, by focusing on the lives of their grandparents, can learn of their experiences in life. Children can learn of life prior to the modern age and memories of playing in the fields, experiences with love and loss, memories of violence and death, and the elderly's dreams for children. For a society living in fear and suffering from posttraumatic stress disorder, this ritual can be a form of therapy. Bringing to life another ritual of Nowruz will also help change a culture focused on violence towards a culture of Nowruz. Politically, participation in such a ritual will again be a symbolic act of nonviolence which this time will focus on the support of grandparents in the path for democracy. Thus, creating and celebrating this ritual is a tool not just for psychological or cultural healing, it is also a political tool that can be used to send a message of democracy to family members, within communities, and ultimately nationally and internationally. It is a tool helping the gain the support of the elderly for the struggle for democracy, more powerful than flooding the streets with slogans of anger.

Amordadgan is again an inspiration from the past, yet a celebration for tomorrow. It is a tool that helps the elderly find their proper place and function in the modern world, and it can ultimately pave the way for understanding our proper place and function in our own old age.

***

Shahrivargan - Veteran's Day

4th of *Shahrivar* – August 6th

The last month of summer in Iranian calendar is named *Shahrivar*. In the ancient Iranian calendar, the fourth day of every month was also called

Shahrivar-day. Thus the celebration of *Shahrivargan* occurred on the fourth day in the last month of summer. In the Zoroastrian religion, *Shahrivar* is another of the seven Spentas, the companions of Ahura-Mazda. The first portion of the word *shahr* means city and state as well as Shah or the king. *Shahrivar*, like other spentas had both a spiritual place in the universe as well as a material place. In the spiritual world, she was the protector of Ahura Mazda, the great God of ancient Iran. In the material world, she was the protector of the nation, metals, and also, weapons of war.[938] Omar Khayyam writes in the 12th century that the name *Shahrivar* was given to this month because it marked the time, at the end of summer, when farmers were due to pay taxes to their kings from their crops.

Shahrivargan was categorized as one of the celebrations involving fire. In the Zoroastrian tradition, this celebration is a religious ceremony and functions as a ritual for meditation and prayer. It is thought that in ancient times on this day, Iranians would visit their temples and light a candle or fire in honor of this Spenta. In the Islamic era, Iranians turned to Islamic rituals for prayer and, over time, this celebration was forgotten nationally except for the small remaining minority of Zoroastrians.

Like all other rituals, it is the societal function of a ritual that allows it to survive over centuries. And, as in the case of other rituals, the key to bringing this ritual back to life lies in creating the proper place and function for *Shahrivargan* for the needs of 21st century. While respecting the ceremony of Zoroastrians on this day, Iranians can adopt a national celebration of *Shahrivargan*, inspired by Iran's ancient culture yet relevant to today's psychological, cultural, and political needs.

Today, *Shahrivar* as the protector of the nation is perhaps symbolic of soldiers who fought and died while attempting to protect their country. War is one of great tragedies of humanity and the psychological trauma from war, destruction, and death is always a great challenge for a society to overcome. In the 20th century, people across the world realized that the greatest way to overcome grief, sorrow, and sense of loss occasioned by death in war is through creation of rituals memorializing lives lost. In nearly every country today, there are days in the year during which the population reflects on the tragedy of war and great loss of life associated with it. In the United States, celebrations of Veterans Day and Memorial Day are national rituals established to remember those who served their country. The great Vietnam Memorial in Washington, DC, inscribed with the names of 58,000 Americans has served as one of the most important and valuable healing tools for thousands of soldiers who served in that war.

The great loss of life during the Iran-Iraq war is thought to number greater than 300,000 with hundreds of thousands of others physically and psychologically wounded. Such trauma requires the creation of numerous memorials and rituals to serve as instruments of healing for families, communities and the nation as a whole. In reaction to this need, in the 1980's, thousands of street names were named after the lost veterans of war. In nearly every village in Iran there are monuments built for lost soldiers that help surviving parents, wives, and children cope with the deaths of their loved ones. Creating a ritual memorializing the heroism of a country's soldiers is a necessary tool of psychological, family, and community healing for any society.

Yet, despite the countless memorials and reminders of the hundreds of thousands of soldiers who lost their lives during the war with Saddam, a national ritual inspired by the ancient Iranian culture memorializing and remembering their lives is still necessary. In addition, there are absolutely no memorials in Iran for the countless heroes and soldiers who died in prison for their country while fighting and struggling against the Islamic Republic. *Shahrivargan*, the ritual for the Spenta symbolizing the protector of the nation can serve as an inspiration for such a national ritual. Creation of such a national ritual will also give Iranians a tool to truly celebrate their soldiers as national heroes, as opposed to heroes of the Islamic Republic.

Expatriate Iranians living in Europe and United States can celebrate *Shahrivargan* through organizing conferences and seminars to memorialize the lives and heroism of the soldiers in war and in prison. Through these conferences they can invite former soldiers and former political prisoners to speak about their experiences, their memories of violence, trauma and war, and of friends lost. Their stories about the tragedy of violence will serve as an important healing tool, first and foremost for those veterans themselves, and then for their families, and finally for the country. By recording and printing stories and memories of war, such acts of violence forever remain fresh in the minds of generations to come as reminders of the pain, loss, and suffering resulting from such tragedies. Such conferences can also raise awareness on the suffering of hundreds of thousands of former war veterans disabled physically and psychologically from trauma. These veterans are neglected by the Islamic Republic and left without adequate governmental support. Iranians are responsible for their health, their comfort, and their well-being.

Iranians have a responsibility to aid and comfort their grieving mothers and fathers, their brothers and sisters, and their children.

In addition, on this celebration, a simple thanking of soldiers standing on street corners by citizens can serve as powerful symbolic tool of nonviolence. Such a simple act of kindness towards a soldier of Islamic Republic can leave a lasting impression of kindness for that soldier. A flower given to a soldier on this day will have a more powerful and lasting symbolic meaning than hundreds of angry protesters marching the streets. Such an act towards a soldier will send shivers down the spine of a regime fearful of its soldiers turning against it. Such a simple act out of kindness and nonviolence will forever remain in the heart of that soldier and remind him of the desire of people for a country built on pillars of kindness and charity Iranians learn on Nowruz. Donation of a meal, money, clothing, or other supplies to veterans and their families on this celebration will also function as an important societal tool for healing and reconciliation.

A symbolic act towards soldiers of Islamic Republic inspired by a celebration of Iranian heritage will undoubtedly be seen as a threat to the security of the system and will be discouraged at first. If people persist, it will be banned followed by punishments against participants allowing this celebration to become another act for civil disobedience.

***

Mehregan

16th of Mehr - October 8th

One of the more important divinities of pre-Zoroastrian ancient Iran was *Mehr*. In Avesta, she is called Mithra and in Pahlavi, she is referred to as Mitr. In Hindu Sanskrit texts, she is referred to as Mitra.[939]

In 1907, when archaeologists were searching through a region called Kapatuka in northwest Anatolia, in the land of ancient Hittites, they came across a clay tablet dating to 1400BCE. This tablet sets out the details of a peace treaty between the Hittites and neighboring Mitanniens, both of Aryan or Indo-European origin. This tablet of peace names the goddesses Mitra and Veruna as witnesses to their pact. This is known as the oldest archaeological find mentioning this goddess.[940] The last archaeological mention of *Mehr* or Mitra was found in Europe, dating to fifth century CE.

CHAPTER 13

In the ancient Hindu text of Veda, Mitra meaning 'pact' appears a number of times. In Avesta, the ancient Iranian religious text, a chapter named '*Mehr-yasht*' is dedicated to this divinity.[941] This chapter in Avesta contains some text that appears to be far older than some additions made to the chapter.[942] In Avesta, the names of Ahura Mitra and Ahura Veruna often accompany the God of creation, Ahura Mazda.[943]

Many Iranians and Indians believe that Mitra represented the goddess of 'sun'. Yet, Sun in Avesta is referred to as *hvare-khshaeta* and *Mehr* appears to represent 'sunlight'.[944] The second verse of *Mehr-Yasht* in Avesta, mentions Mitra as the goddess who will punish those who break a pact sworn in her name. It maintains that a social or political pact made in the name of Mitra is sacred, whether it is made between Mazda worshippers or Div worshipers (likely Diva worshipers).[945] Thus often social, tribal, and political pacts were agreed under her name. More important, as the protector of such pacts, *Mehr* symbolized friendship and kindness.[946]

The first month of autumn in Iranian calendar is named after this divinity of sunlight, friendship, and kindness. In ancient Iran, the 16th of every month was also named *Mehr*-day. And as in every other month when the name of the day fell within that month, a celebration was held. The celebration of *Mehregan*, on the 16th of *Mehr* and lasting six days, is one of the biggest celebrations of Iranian heritage.

Before the Sassanid era, the Greek and Roman chroniclers writing about Persia refer to the great celebration of Iranians not at start of spring, as was the case during the Sassanid period, but 'Mitrakana', at the start of autumn which likely represented *Mehregan*.[947] During the Parthian era, the rituals and beliefs associated with Mitraism were introduced to Europeans by tens of thousands of Iranian soldiers, who found their way to Europe, often as enslaved captives in Persian-Roman wars. By the first century BCE, the Iranian beliefs and religion of Mitraism had spread across the Black Sea and into all the Roman territories. By the fourth century, this religion was the most prevalent of all religions practiced by the Romans and even after their conversion to Christianity, many practices, beliefs and rituals of Mitraism were incorporated into Christianity. The most important was the adoption of 'Sunday', the day of Mitra and *Mehr*, as the Christian day of religious services, prayer, and meditation.[948] With Zoroastrianism becoming the official religion of Iran in the Sassanid era, the importance of *Mehregan* was diminished and Nowruz took its current place as the most important Iranian celebration.

It's easy to speculate about the function of *Mehregan* in ancient times. At the end of summer, work on farms and fields had come to an end. Farmers and herders had spent the spring and summer collecting crops and stocking supplies. With the end of summer, taxes were paid and people were beginning to prepare for the long winter. In this setting, one can easily see the immense function of a grand celebration for exchange of commodities and purchase of supplies for winter as well as a celebration of thanksgiving for the triumph of life and rebirth in spring and summer. One can also easily imagine the significance of Mehregan as a forum for the artisans to sell their craftwork and prepare supplies for winter. The usual trade and exchange of goods that took place in marketplaces and bazaars during spring and summer was given a psychological lift through the creation of a celebratory mood across Iran, where people created one last push for exchange of goods and commodities through a giant party and bazaar.

Tezias, who wrote of this celebration in 390 BCE, tells us that Achaemenid kings were not allowed to get drunk and were cautious in their drinking except during Mitrakana, when they would join the people in drinking and celebration.[949] Strabo, tells us that for this celebration, the king of Armenia would give a thousand horses in a special ceremony as gifts to Shah of Iran.[950] Each day of celebration had its own style and rhythm of music traditionally used for Mehregan. Except for the names of some of these styles mentioned in the books as the *Mehregani* scale, greater *Mehregan* scale, and lesser *Mehregan* scale, the music itself is thought to be lost.

After the Arab invasion and during the Taliban-like Umayyad period, *Mehregan* celebration was banned much in the same way as *Sadeh*, Nowruz, *Tirgan* and remainder of Iranian celebrations. Despite this, and in order to keep the tradition and ritual of these celebrations alive, Iranians began restoring the ritual of gift-giving to their rulers on these occasions in hopes of influencing their foreign caliphs. These attempts initially backfired, because the gifts given were turned into mandatory taxes on these occasions during the Umayyad regimes. But eventually, in the Abbasid era, the Iranian influence in Baghdad turned Nowruz and *Mehregan* into accepted celebrations and the practice of gifts given to the caliphs was restored as a voluntary practice.[951]

During the reigns of the Samanid and Ghaznavid families in eastern Iran, the celebrations of Nowruz and *Mehregan* were again revived. Gifts given to the Kings on these occasions were often accompanied by poems written for such occasions and the extent of literature from this era of speaking of

CHAPTER 13

Nowruz and *Mehregan* is testimony to their popularity.[952] Ferdowsi, the great poet also writes of this celebration in his epic tale of Iranian mythology. [953]

Mehregan, like *Tirgan* and *Sadeh*, had a mythological root in addition to its social, entertainment, religious, spiritual, and meditative functions for society. The emphasis on the mythological origins of *Mehregan* is seen repeatedly in works by Iranian writers and poets including Ferdowsi writing in the 10th century as well as Biruni, speaking of Iranian celebrations in his 11th century collection of the forgotten rituals and practices of the past.

Like *Sadeh*, the celebration of *Mehregan* is also a celebration related to the mythological victory of people over the evil serpent king, Zahhak. His thousand-year mythological rule is remembered and transmitted orally from generation to generation as the symbol of ruthless and dark eras for Iranians. The fact that this story is also told in ancient Hindu literature tells us of the ancient roots of this story.[954] As mentioned earlier, the serpent shouldered Zahhak was in misery because of the snakes biting at his head and was forced to kill two youths each day for their brains to be fed to the snakes. This powerful symbolic mythological story has been the constant reminder of the extent of evil and darkness that can overcome a nation and drain the minds of its youth. The snakes striking at the king are symbols of the madness that comes from greed and power and the brains of the young fed to snakes are symbolic of youth giving their lives and their minds in service of despotic, evil regimes. As this one thousand year period of darkness continued, a blacksmith named Kaveh was ordered to surrender his two children to the king. Kaveh refused to surrender them and used his smith's apron made of lion-skin as a flag and a symbol of resistance. In this Iranian mythological story of people revolting against their evil king, his apron, named '*derafsh-e-kaviani*' becomes a symbol of the people and later adopted with colors of purple and gold as the flag of Iran until being destroyed at the battle of Qadesieh.

Kaveh's revolution helped the mythological king Fereydoon to gain his seat. Sa'abeli, an 11th century scholar, tells us that Fereydoon imprisoned Zahhak on the day of *Mehr* in the month of *Mehr* and a great celebration was held across the land for six days on this joyous occasion which we now know as *Mehregan*.[955]

Abu Reyhan Biruni, writing in the 11th century, tells us that the revolt against Zahhak began on day of *Mehr* in the month of *Mehr*, with Kaveh holding up his apron as the symbol of the people. Later, when he is speaking of *Raam*-day, the 21st of the month, he explains why the celebration lasted six days, with the last day nominated as the Greater *Mehregan* :

"The 21st day of *Mehr*, *Raam*-day was the celebration of greater *Mehregan*. The origin of the celebration dates back to the victory of Fereydoon over Zahhak and imprisonment of Zahhak. When they brought Zahhak to the new king, Zahhak asked to spare his life in the name of their ancestors...Fereydoon then ordered him to be imprisoned in the mountain of Damavand such that the people will be spared of his evil. This day was then celebrated as a joyous occasion."[956]

Borhan Qateh (in 17th century) writes of *Mehregan* :

"On this day [*Mehregan*], Gods came to Kaveh's aid and Fereydoon regained the throne. On this day, Zahhak was imprisoned and sent to Damavand and the people because of this occasion held a great celebration and feast. From then on *Mehr* and kindness was shared between the people and their rulers. And since *Mehregan* means kindness and bonding, it remained as such on this occasion."[957]

It is important to remember one of the important and forgotten messages of this mythological story. The great evil king Zahhak, after a thousand years of murder and torture, was imprisoned. He was not tortured, he was not beaten, he was not humiliated, and he was not executed.

Prior to the Mongol invasion, very little remained of the grandeur of *Mehregan*. Six centuries of fundamentalist attack on symbols deemed un-Islamic had taken its toll on this public celebration. And if that wasn't enough, the Mongol invasion wiped off any hope of its revival and eventually almost completely wiped away any memory of its existence. In the dark ages of Iranian history after the Mongol invasion, there was no room for celebrations. Later, Shah-Abbas's astronomer and historian, Mullah Mozafar. He writes of *Mehregan* as the occasion for celebrating the defeat of Zahhak and his imprisonment in Damavand.[958]

Despite this apparent loss of its cultural symbolism, *Mehregan*, like many other ancient Iranian celebrations, remained in the cultural psyche of Iranians who were waiting for the opportunity to freely express themselves without fear of violence and backlash. In early 1990s, a group of Iranian-American professionals in Orange County, California again revived this ancient celebration. It is now a cornerstone celebration of Iranian heritage in Orange County, CA where more than 20,000 attend the festivities each year. In recent years, similar celebrations for *Mehregan* were also held in Los Angeles, drawing similar enthusiasm from Iranian-Americans.

CHAPTER 13

The revival of this event with such enthusiasm is not just an excuse for further celebration in America where people are free to celebrate every day. It is the revival of a cultural symbol. It is an outburst of the unconscious desire of a displaced people to proclaim themselves free of fear and to join together in a cultural celebration symbolizing kindness and their heritage. It is an instrument for societal psychological healing, one more powerful than any prescription modern medicine can offer and a chance to participate in celebration, dancing, and songs regardless of one's religion, ethnicity, or language.

Participation in this celebration requires only the desire for joy and kindness, elements which, if people are given the freedom to express them, are the desires, hopes, and dreams of every human being. Participation in this celebration is more powerful and more symbolic than the chaotic expressions and communications through street protests. It is a referendum for change away from violence, fear, and intolerance towards culture of kindness, love, and nonviolence.

The coming together of a community on this occasion is a powerful psychological tool for healing. For a population suffering from anxiety caused by fear and trauma, *Mehregan* offers an opportunity to create a space free of fear and censorship, one in which music and dance are used as instruments for healing. Politically, participation in this celebration anywhere in the world will send a powerful message to Iranians everywhere of the desire for turning away from the politics of violence to politics of nonviolence, from the politics of fear, discrimination and intolerance to the politics of tolerance and human rights. It expresses a desire for change from an authoritarian regime intolerant of people's opinions to a democracy with full participation of every single citizen. It is also a symbol of change from a religious government using people's religious beliefs as instruments of rule to a secular government that respects the religious beliefs, traditions, and rituals of every citizen.

Mehregan cannot be as elaborately celebrated everywhere as it is in California, yet it is not the size of the celebration that is important, but the power of its symbol. Anywhere there is an opportunity to play music and dance is an opportunity to celebrate *Mehregan*, whether this is done in one's living room or atop the Alborz Mountain. It is the power of symbolism that will transform the participants from passive individuals suffering from a legacy of violence to free human beings taking active and symbolic stance against fear. *Mehregan* is a symbolic act, denouncing violence and violent rule while embracing kindness and charity. Moreover, it is a symbol of nation's mythological past, the grand Iranian celebration of victory over Zahhak's regime of darkness, fear and terror and the dawn of freedom in Iran.

The religious regime in Iran may not permit the celebration of *Mehregan* in the streets of Tehran, Isfahan, or Tabriz, but one day Mehregan will be celebrated freely on those same streets. And as long as a religious regime detesting Iranian secular heritage is in power in Iran, any form of celebration on Mehregan will automatically become an act of civil disobedience.

***

Abangan

10th of *Aban* – November 1st

Aban, also known as Nahid and Anahid was the goddess of water, rivers and fertility. Christian theologian, Titus Flavius Clements, known as Clement of Alexandria, who lived in the second century BCE cites the third century BC Greek Brossus on his remarks about this goddess. He tells us that it was Artaxerxes II, the Achaemenid king who built temples in honor of Anahita in Susa, Ekbatana, and Babylon and who taught the Persians about this goddess.[959]

Archaeological finds also confirm the importance this Achaemenid king placed on Anahita. It was during his reign that the importance of Anahita was again emphasized and her name, together with Mitra was mentioned as equals to Ahura Mazda.[960] The temples of Anahita in ancient Iran were some of the most elaborate structures of the time. Some of these structures, including the Temple of Anahita in Hamedan, date to the pre-Achaemenid era and are believed to have been built by the Medes.[961]

Anahita, like Mitra, was likely another of the ancient pre-Zoroastrian goddesses whose importance was likely reduced within the structured Zoroastrian religion. In the ancient Hindu scripture Rig Veda, there is mention of two goddesses, Sinivali and Sarasvati, who resemble Anahita and are likely of the same origin. In Avesta, we are told that it is this goddess of fertility and life who palliates the pain of childbirth for mothers and helps mothers make the nourishing milk in their breasts.[962]

In the dry land of the Middle East, water has always been associated with fertility and life, thus making Anahita one of the more important goddesses of ancient Iran. The 10th of each month in Iranian calendar was named *Aban*-day in honor of this goddess. The 10th day of Nowruz was marked by a special celebration involving water. Rain on this 10th day of Nowruz was thought of as good fortune and regarded as a forecast of additional rain during spring and summer. The 10th day of *Aban* month was the celebration of *Abangan* in honor of Anahita. This celebration involved spending the day next to streams and rivers as part of a ritual of thanksgiving to Anahita. Special precautions were always taken to keep the waters clean and pure.

Iranians believed that the origin of this celebration date back to mythological times during Iran's war with Turan. It is said that during these wars the enemy-king Afrasiab orders the destruction of rivers and canals. The Iranian mythic king Tahmasb then orders the rebuilding of the canals followed by the resumption of the flow of water and the celebration of *Abangan* marks this occasion. It was also believed that on this day, the news of Zahhak's imprisonment in Damavand finally reached every corner of the country. Another tale speaks of droughts lasting eight years, with many dying and many farms abandoned. After eight years, people said it was on *Abangan* when it finally rained and from then on people celebrated Abangan every year. [963]

As was the case for *Khordadgan*, a modern celebration of water next to streams and rivers today in this urbanized world may have negative environmental effects. Yet if we see the symbolic function of Anahita as the protector of mothers in childbirth and as the nourisher of milk in their breasts, one realizes this celebration's potential as a national Mother's day celebration.

Today, the religious regime of Iran attempting to rid the country of any un-Islamic symbol spends millions of dollars every year promoting the birth of Prophet Mohammed's daughter and the mother of the second and third Shiite imams as the national Mother's Day. There's nothing wrong with people celebrating her birth as a ritual for Mother's Day, except that not all Iranians are Muslims and not all Iranian Muslims are Shiites. This attempt at using religious figures and dates for the survival of the Islamic Republic is often seen by Iranians as another attempt of an authoritarian regime to use Shi'ism as a tool for its legitimacy. In the Pahlavi regime, resources were spent promoting birthday of Shah's mother as the national Mother's Day, another attempt by an authoritarian regime to create a ritual to serve as a tool to bolster its legitimacy. Iranians need a Mother's Day ritual free of religious and political beliefs and one that is rooted in their own culture and history. *Abangan* can serve as this ritual. Participation in this ritual through gift giving to our mothers and informing mothers of *Abangan* can help create and strengthen a new culture in Iran based on the principles of kindness of

Nowruz resurrected on *Abangan*. This celebration can also serve as a tool for informing and recruiting mothers across the country for civil disobedience and a nonviolent culture of tomorrow. In addition, such a celebration for mothers rooted in nonviolence can ultimately serve as reminder of this generation's desires for the protection of families and mothers not just from political violence, but also from domestic violence.

Participation in this symbolic celebration will be just as empowering as tens of thousands rushing into the streets and will create a momentary space of safety where reconnection to ordinary life can be celebrated next to mothers and in the safety of one's home. It can help rally mothers for the cause of human rights and can send a powerful message against the strongest defenders of violence.

***

Azargan

Azar 9th - November 30th

Evidence of controlled flames is found in campsites in South Africa dating back to 1.5 million years. Ashes and remains of fires are also found in caves in China from around the same time.[964] These fires were not used by us, species of human beings called Homo sapiens. They were fires created in campsites by Homo erectus, earlier human-like creatures who roamed the earth for close to 2 million years and who survived until the evolutionary advent of modern human beings more than two hundred thousand years ago. Throughout all this time, fire was a source of light and an instrument for protection from wild beasts. It was while sitting around campfires night after night, year after year, generation after generation for hundreds of thousands of years that human beings learned to speak, communicate, socialize, and create cultures. Incredibly, fire may have played an important role in enabling human beings to evolve into their current form. Fire was the first great discovery of humans and their greatest asset in their wild and hostile world.

Over tens of thousands of years, fire as the source of light turned into symbol of light which for human beings across the world adopted a spiritual meaning. For early human, who believed daytime were the hours when God was present, the darkness of night symbolized death, evil, and disease. Fire at night was the reminder of God's presence amongst them. Any time a flame was present, our ancient ancestors perhaps felt and sensed the security and warmth which they associated with presence and kindness of God. Over time, in many cultures, fire became no longer a tool of protection against wild animals, but the symbol of higher powers and often God itself.

In nearly every major religion today, light, candles, and fire continue to serve as symbols of God, spirituality, and peace. Such is the case in the world religions of Judaism, Christianity, and Islam. Respect for this symbol of spirituality can be seen in the easternmost borders of Asia as well as the southern tips of African and South America. In the dawn of nearly every civilization, one can find the traces of respect for and importance placed on fire. In the ancient Indo-European text of Rig Veda, considered the oldest book in Sanskrit. Agni, the god of fire, was considered one of the most important divinities. There, fire is referred to as a gift from gods, a gift that first came in the form of lightning. One of the sons of lightning in Sanskrit was named Adhravan, meaning 'holder of fire'. In the Hindu tradition, a class of people called *adhravan* was in charge of fires at temples. Similar classes of individuals in charge of fires at temples were also prevalent in ancient Greece and Rome. In Iran this class was known as *adhorban* or *azarban*. In Avesta they are referred to as *Athravan*. In Sanskrit, Adri refers to 'flame', which in the Iranian languages was changed to *Azar*. The ancient text of Rig Veda begins with a prayer for Agni, the god of fire, a prayer in which the rhythm and style is much like the prayers in the ancient Iranian text of Gatha.[965] The origins of these two texts are probably connected, much in the way that the origins of Indian and Iranian cultures are intertwined.

In ancient Persia, the significance of fire was maintained and heightened in culture and religious practices. Fire was incorporated into people's daily, monthly, and yearly religious rituals for Zoroastrians as a symbol of God and a tool for facilitating meditation and prayer. In an era without lighters and matches, temples became guardians of fire. A family that needed fire for prayer, for cooking, or for heating in winter would approach the temple and obtain fire with the blessings of the priest.

Aside from the Iranian culture and its symbolic relation to fire, the lighting of candles still symbolizes the presence of God for Christians in a church, Jews light candles during their rituals, and Muslims consider light as symbolic of God. During the Sassanid era, with the Sassanid religious class strengthening the function and importance of temples within the society, the importance of fire as a symbol of God further increased. Fires were religiously categorized and differentiated, based on their use and their origin. Fire used for cooking was obtained differently than fire used for warming of homes or fire used for religious rituals. This categorization and differentiation of fire forced the population to depend on the temple and the priest for their daily fire need but more importantly for performing religious rituals and their communication with God. Thus, temples and their priests, by taking on the role of distributing fire to people were in actuality in control of peoples' relation to God.

In much of the world today, temples and religious institutions have lost the monopoly over human beings' relationship with God. Such institutions today often serve as guidance and are optional for those seeking more or differently guided intervention. In the democratic world, people are free to pray, meditate, and go their preferred church, temple, or mosque without fear of persecution or discrimination. No one is punished for not believing in the same God or for not practicing the same religion as others. In the democratic world based on principles of human rights, religion is a matter of free choice for everyone and the government is not allowed to influence, misuse, or persecute religious figures or institutions.

There were many rituals and celebrations in ancient Iran that involved fire. Some of these rituals developed a more nationalistic symbolism such as *Sadeh* (the mid-winter festival of fire) and *Chahar-shanbeh Souri* (the end of winter celebration with fire). In the ancient Iranian calendar, the 9th day of every month was called *Azar*-day. The last month of autumn was called *Azar* and on the ninth day of this month, when the day of *Azar* fell in the month of *Azar*, *Azargan* was celebrated.

The celebration of *Azargan* which had a purely religious and spiritual function was lost as a national celebration for Iranians as they changed their religion to Islam. In ancient Persia, Iranians would visit their temples and obtain the sacred fire that would warm their homes and perhaps their *korsis* in the cold months ahead. Religious rituals were performed consecrating this fire. Today's Zoroastrians continue to hold this day sacred because of its spiritual and religious function but, for the majority of Iranians who satisfy their spiritual and religious needs through their own beliefs, this celebration and symbol of ancient Iranian culture is no longer relevant. And just like every other ritual, if it does not perform a useful and proper function for today's society, any attempt at bringing this celebration back to life will be a short-term waste of effort.

In order to create a modern functioning celebration on this occasion, one must again evaluate both the symbolic meaning of this day in the context of ancient Iranian culture as well as the psychological, cultural, and political needs of today's modern society. This day functioned as a day of prayer and meditation in ancient times. Rituals of prayer and meditation are some of the most powerful healing tools for societal anxiety. But when religion becomes a tool of violence in the hands of a religious government, religion can no longer function as a tool for healing. In Iran, Islam has lost its power as a tool for spirituality for tens of millions of citizens, who associate their religion with terror and violence.

Azargan provides the opportunity of creating a national celebration which like Nowruz can be free of personal religious beliefs, yet can function to celebrate spirituality and religious thought. Today, such a celebration based on the same philosophy of religious inclusiveness and freedom seen in Nowruz can function as a tool for Iranians demanding the freedom of religion from violence and terror. Inspired from Iran's ancient past, it can serve as a national celebration for spirituality and God irrespective of a person's religious beliefs.

This desire for a secular government and religion free of violence is not just an Iranian desire, it is humanity's desire. It is the desire for one of the most basic human rights—the freedom of belief and worship. Any form of religious government or populist promise of a religious democracy inevitably leads to infringements of human rights. Thus, religious freedom and the separation of religious institutions from the government must be on the agenda of every nonviolent activist.

On this national celebration inspired from the message of nonviolence on Nowruz, Iranians lighting candles will be reminded of the importance of religious freedom in human life. Lighting a candle on *Azargan* will be a reminder of the symbolic meaning of fire and light throughout human history and in many different religions. A moment of prayer and meditation in front of a candle on this celebration will spiritually connect that individual to others meditating and praying at the same moment for the same dream. *Azargan* can connect millions of Iranians simultaneously and create that relative space of safety where empowerment can be born. This ritual can serve as an event in which Iranians can invite neighbors and friends of other religions into their homes and celebrate each other's religious heritage in an atmosphere of kindness.

Iranians in Europe and United States on *Azargan* can focus the world's attention on the plight of Iranian religious minorities, particularly the Baha'is who have been forced to live under the most difficult conditions over the last 150 years. They can raise awareness of hatred and persecution against Yazidis, worshipers of one of the most ancient Middle Eastern religions, believers who are labeled as 'devil-worshipers' by religious extremists in Iran and Iraq. They can challenge the outlook of some who view Iran not as a nation for all Iranians, but a nation for Muslims in which Jews and Christians are tolerated with different rights. They can challenge the misconception of extremists who demonize Zoroastrians as fire worshipers and protest the restrictions imposed on newly converted Iranian Christians who seek to practice their religion freely. The religious persecution and discrimination in Iran is also not only limited to non-Muslims. Sunni Muslims are greatly persecuted, especially in majority Sunni regions of Kurdistan and Baluchistan. Sunni's in Tehran, Isfahan, Tabriz, and other major cities are either silent or are forced to change to Shi'ism because of the atmosphere of fear and terror created by the regime. Tehran is the only capital in the world without a Sunni mosque or Islamic center, an incredible fact that an American will find hard to believe. In addition to religious minorities, atheists in Iran are afraid to voice their opinion or are forced to leave the country.

A moment of meditation and prayer in candlelight on *Azargan* can be a reminder of religious persecution and discrimination and the dream of religious freedom for millions of Iranians. It is an instrument of nonviolent change meant to raise awareness of family members, neighbors, and friends. Such a change in awareness brings about the transformation of passive individuals into active citizens, empowering them for further action for their human rights.

More than its message of protest against a regime which severely limits religious freedom, because of *Azargan's* connection to other pre-Islamic celebrations of Iran, the regime will no doubt ban any form of celebration on this day which will automatically turn this celebration for religious freedom into another act of civil disobedience.

***

Bahmangan

Bahman 2nd - January 22nd

Not much is known about this celebration. The section talking about this day in Biruni's book is incomplete. But we do know that the celebration was prevalent during the Islamic Abbasid caliphate and its name was changed to its Arabic form *Bahmanjaneh* by the Abbasid court. *Bahman*, and it's more ancient form in Avesta called Vahumana was one of the more important spentas or sacred gods and goddesses for Iranians. This word is comprised of two components, 'vohu' meaning kindness and goodness and 'mana' meaning thought. Thus *Bahman* or *Vohumana* can be thought of as the spenta of kindness and kind thoughts.[966] This god was also known as the protector of animals on earth. The second day of every month on Iranian calendar was named *Bahman* as well as the second month in winter, thus the celebration of *Bahmangan* fell on the second day of the second month in winter.

Bahmangan involved people inviting neighbors and friends over for celebration in their homes. An important component of the celebration was the gathering of a flower named *Bahman*, which blooms in the hillsides in red and white colors around this time. Ancient Iranians considered this flower as an herbal medicine that protects the mind and enhances memory. On the morning of *Bahmangan*, family members often drank a mixture of this flower mixed with milk. On the celebration of *Bahmangan*, a popular Iranian soup (*aash*) called *'sholghalamkar'* was cooked. It included all the various herbs, beans, and meats available in household. Often, the red and white *Bahman* flowers were added to this meal, either cooked with the soup, steamed or added to milk or other products. Thus, one of the rituals of *Bahmangan* involved going to hillsides and collecting medicinal herbs and flowers blooming at this time of year. [967]

Although the celebration of *Bahmangan* survived during the Islamic era in the form of *Bahmanjaneh*, it was lost with the Mongol invasion. Renewal of such a celebration in its ancient form would likely not have much of a function in today's society and unless the current generation can find a symbolic value for this ritual, the meanings and function of the celebration cannot be fulfilled.

Many Iranians today advocate the celebration of *Bahmangan* as a celebration of kindness to animals and pets based on *Bahman* or *Vohumana's* role as the protector of animals on earth. Certainly, such a celebration would be beneficial for society as a tool for education. The politics of violence in the region have turned Iranian society into one that is often not tolerant towards other human beings, much less animals. Many species in the northern forests of Iran are on the verge of extinction, farm animals often live in despicable quarters and are maltreated by their owners and stray dogs are hunted and shot in the streets by revolutionary guards. Iranians have lost their harmony with nature and as a result are estranged to animals.

How can *Bahmangan* be turned into civil disobedience? In a regime that detests Iranian celebrations, any symbolic act to protect animals on this day will not be tolerated and can potentially turn into civil disobedience. One time can tell how Iranians will use the tools of celebrations available to them and how the regime will react. Through this interaction, new symbols will be formed and new cultures will be created.

***

When one reviews all the monthly celebrations available to Iranians as tools of therapy, cultural change, and political protest, one can easily pinpoint one important celebration missing. This ritual involves the celebration of the father's role in life or Father's Day celebration. Where can Father's Day be celebrated on Iranian calendar?

In order to answer this question, we must take a look at the symbolic father figure of Iranian identity and culture. Some Iranians may consider Cyrus the Great as the father figure of the nation. Yet Cyrus did not give birth to Iranian culture but was a product of the culture. He created the political establishment of the country, but short term national borders and political establishments are often artificial boundaries maintained through diplomacy, violence, or common needs. Iran as a nation did not exist for a thousand years after the Arab invasion, yet after centuries of dormancy, it again took shape in its current form. This renewal and rebirth of Iranian nation was not the work of Cyrus the Great. It was accomplished through the will and the genius of Ferdowsi, who lived in the 10th century and recreated the Iranian culture, identity, and language in its current form through his epic tale of *Shahnameh*. This grand book is one of the pillars of Iranian cultural identity.

In his epic, Ferdowsi rarely talks about himself and his personal life, but on few occasions he makes references to his age and the number of years and even decades spent working on his masterpiece. On one such occasion, he makes a reference to himself turning sixty-three years old and in the line just before that writes of his birthday in the month of *Bahman*, on the day of Hormoz. He tells us that he was born on 1st of *Bahman*, the day before the celebration of *Bahmangan*.[968]

It is only appropriate for Iranians to also create a national symbolic Father's Day to complete their national celebrations. While Iranians want to overcome the culture of patriarchy prevalent in today's society, they cannot understate or devalue the role and function of a father in society. Iran's struggle in overcoming patriarchy is not a struggle against fathers or father figures; it is the struggle against violence and forced acceptance of belief and laws from more powerful figures in society.

Creating a celebration of Father's Day, along with all other modern Iranian festivals celebrating life, renewal, rebirth, and spirit of Nowruz is an important step in completing the cycle of life symbolically expressed in the monthly national celebrations of Iran.

Celebrating the life of our fathers in Bahman is a valuable psychological tool of healing for millions of families torn apart by unresolved conflicts. Father's Day celebration is another ritual for psychological healing desperately needed by a society suffering from traumatic effects of violence and living in cycles of anxiety, depression, or addiction. It is also an important symbolic tool for cultural change away from political violence and patriarchy to culture of nonviolence created in spirit of Nowruz. Such grand cultural change in a society filled with anger, mistrust, hatred, and violence can only be accomplished through the active participation of citizens through symbolic gestures and rituals, which celebrations are one powerful form. Celebrations can also be symbolic political tools of protest and expression against despotism and patriarchy in Iran's culture and political institutions. Nonviolent change through protest and persuasion does not begin against the dogmatic adversary in power, but begins with persuading millions of fathers, mothers, friends, and neighbors to work for democracy and human rights. Only through the power of persuasion of other citizens can Iranians ultimately use these rituals as a form of referendum for human rights and as acts of civil disobedience. Celebrations are tools given to Iranians by their ancestors for use in moments of fear, anxiety and desperation. They are gifts for societal psychological therapy, and instruments for cultural transformation from culture of fear to culture of Nowruz, and can ultimately serve as acts of disobedience against a regime that detests ancient Iranian symbols and celebrations.

EPILOGUE

Nowruz Revolution in this game of *Shogi*

No other tool in history has been used as extensively to discuss strategy in conflicts as the game of chess. In chess, the opening game has its own requirements, tactics and foresight which are useful teaching tools for a general in any classroom with officers. The psychology and planning in the middle game has its own characteristics and a brilliant end game strategy is what separates masters from others.

The two sides in a game of chess are intent on eliminating as many pieces of the enemy force as possible to ultimately check mate the other. This is true of any classic military battle and conflict. To a casual observer, a nonviolent revolution may ultimately seem like a game of chess where the two sides systematically eliminate each other's pieces until the check mate is forced on the enemy leader. Yet, a nonviolent revolution is much more like *shogi*, the Japanese chess than the game of chess we all grew up with.

There is one significant difference between *shogi*, meaning general's board game in Japanese and classic game of chess which allows *shogi* to be used for discussing strategy in a nonviolent conflict where chess has its shortcomings. *Shogi* has a board slightly larger than chess, 9x9 as opposed to the classic 8x8 chess board. There are some additional pieces in *shogi* such as the gold generals and the silver generals who have movement abilities different than bishops and knights and the lance which can only move up and down like the rook without the ability for lateral movement. Yet these differences are not what makes strategy in *shogi* relevant to Nowruz Revolution.

The significant difference in *shogi* from chess is in what is called the 'drop rule' which was incorporated by the Japanese into the game in the 16th century. With this rule, an enemy piece captured in battle is not killed or eliminated from the game like in war, but is converted to your side and can be placed back on the board as your own piece. It is thought that this rule was developed for circumstances where the enemy soldiers switched loyalties upon capture to avoid execution.

Unlike chess where the ultimate goal is to eliminate enemy pieces one by one until check mate is reached, in *shogi* and in a nonviolent conflict, converting enemy soldiers to your side is an important strategic consideration without which battle against AK-47 and the baton would be impossible. Yet conversion can only play one part of the strategy in Nowruz Revolution and ultimately, like chess and *shogi*, there are considerations for the opening, the middle game and the end game which need to come together for Nowruz.

Opening Game: Gaining Moral Legitimacy

One characteristic of a successful nonviolent revolution is its need for massive popular support. This is ultimately seen in mass rallies and occupy methods in later stages of the conflict, but later steps require more preliminary tasks without which popular support cannot be achieved. One of the most important steps in a nonviolent revolution and perhaps in any movement for social change is the need to develop and gain 'moral legitimacy' not only against the dictatorship, but also in relation to all other philosophies and strategies.

A closer look at the struggle of liberals who want the dissolution (*enhelal*) of the constitution of the Islamic Republic and the adoption of a constitution based on Declaration of Human Rights, shows constant attack, ridicule, and condemnation against them by reformists who claim them to be 'out of touch' with popular support for Islamic Republic, 'out of touch' with popular love and affection for Khomeini and the 'revolutionary values' of Islamic Republic and out of touch with the peaceful methods and mechanisms the reformists envision for a struggle.

Activists who want a constitution based on human rights, in the same stroke as being called 'out of touch' are then quickly labeled as supporters of monarchists, terrorist groups, Kurdish and Baluchi separatists, are called supporters of bombings or war against Iran or agents of CIA or American pawns hoping to bring American influence back to Iran.

Repeatedly, during the course of writing this manuscript, I was asked and told by reformists in Los Angeles and abroad to change the title and avoid use of the word 'revolution' as something undesirable by the people. Reformists repeatedly express in media and articles that there are two strategies against the Islamic Republic, 'reform' strategy which they consider the peaceful strategy which we should all support and which attempts to recreate the Islamic Republic in a new more humane form versus the 'revolution' strategy which the reformists claim leads to a bloody overthrow of the regime and will lead to chaos. In this simplistic breakdown of strategies, anyone not a reformist is then associated with 'revolutionaries' advocating violent overthrow which allows the reformists to maintain the 'moral legitimacy' which ultimately is the opening game in any successful strategy.

After gaining the 'moral legitimacy' in public, the reformists then advocate reforms through the established procedures and institutions of the Islamic Republic and aim for peace within the Islamic Republic and survival of the Islamic Republic in a more democratic vision.

It is incredible how quickly the 'moral legitimacy' of a reformist melts as they realize they are speaking to someone advocating nonviolence and a nonviolent revolution. I quickly remind them that a nonviolent activist is against any form of violence whether violence inflicted by a foreign power or legal, religious or cultural discrimination instituted into law. I remind them that I consider constitution of the Islamic Republic which in its first and most important opening line establishes Shi'ism as the official religion of Iran as a form of discrimination against non-Shi'ites and thus a form of violence and I consider the reformism as a philosophy which rejects one form of violence but is a pillar of support for another kind.

Adoption of the principles of nonviolence is the first and perhaps the most important step in Nowruz Revolution and in any movement for human rights seeking popular support. In this epic battle for the fate of a generation, 'nonviolence' is the invincible weapon that can open eyes and can allow the conscience of humanity to come to the side of the Iranian people. Nothing can be more powerful than the courage of an enlightened human being supported by the voice of conscience.

Green movement may seem to an outside observer to have been a united movement facing incredible brutality, but on the ground, it was a broken movement in constant turmoil, confusion, quarrel and dispute. The reformists wanted to focus on Ahmadinejad and dispel him from power while maintaining the two pillars of *nezam (*system*)*, the Constitution of the Islamic Republic and the 'revolutionary values of the Islamic Republic'. While, hundreds of thousands of activists of my generation on Facebook and on city streets were trying to seize the opportunity for *enhelal* (dissolution) of the constitution of the Islamic Republic, free elections and the adoption of a constitution based on the Declaration of Human Rights.

Throughout those turbulent months, the reformists asserted 'moral legitimacy'. They would claim it was their election, their candidates, their slogans and their peaceful strategy of reforms within the pillars of the Islamic Republic which my generation on Facebook , seculars and liberals were challenging. The reformists needed the support of liberals and the Iranian public on radios and satellite televisions, on blogs, on Twitter, on Facebook and on the streets. Yet, millions of Iranians would march on the streets, disobeying the 'red lines' of the reformists with calls for an 'Iranian Republic' as opposed to 'Islamic Republic'.

In response to crossing of 'red lines', the frustrated reformist leadership would reaffirm their loyalty to path of 'Imam' (Ayatollah Khomeini), 'Constitution of the Islamic Republic' and 'revolutionary values of the Islamic Republic', further dividing the Green movement and Iranians. Their attempt to win 'moral legitimacy' through claiming ownership on the Green Movement was the tool in trying to guide the movement within a reformist strategy and within the boundaries of *'nezam'* (system).

On January 1st, 2010, after the brutal crackdown on *ashura*, when the activists were still recovering from the psychological trauma of the previous days, the statement issued by Mir Hussein Mousavi again reiterated his loyalty to revolutionary values of the Islamic Republic, the 'righteous' path of Ayatollah Khomeini, the founder of the Islamic Republic and the Constitution of the Islamic Republic.[969]

Those words were a final dagger in the hearts of many activists like me. I lost hope and withdrew my support for a movement resting on those 'revolutionary values of Islamic Republic' and I watched countless other secular activists do the same. As we withdrew our support, we saw the movement take a deep breath and slumber for a long winter.

A social movement can only exist as long as its philosophy provides moral legitimacy for its participants. Since the arrest of the reformist leadership, no group has been able to claim 'moral legitimacy' for the movement. The movement is no longer about the 2009 elections and the political desires of Iranians are much more focused on democracy and human rights. Reformists today have a hard time claiming that this movement is about their elections and their candidates. Yet the liberals have not been able to claim 'moral legitimacy' in the struggle partly because of the sensitivities of my generation to violence. Many liberal activists, particularly of the previous generation outright reject nonviolence, while many others see nonviolence as a tool for pacifism for activists of my generation or even as a tool for reforms within the Islamic Republic.

It is imperative for those who advocate nonviolence to express themselves publicly by not only denouncing any mechanisms or methods of violence but also dissociate themselves from reformists and other groups who advocate survival of the Islamic Republic or survival of any form of injustice or discrimination in Iran. The first and the most important step in Nowruz Revolution is this expression of existence through raising the flag of nonviolence and grasping the 'moral legitimacy' necessary for popular support. As long as the reformists preserve their desires for 'revolutionary values' and 'struggle in the path of Imam Khomeini' and within the constitution of the Islamic Republic, they cannot gain the undivided moral legitimacy necessary for this generation's epic battle. These calls are evident that reformists are lingering remains of Iran's legacy of violence and cannot have a role in the leadership of a future nonviolent revolution.

Nowruz Revolution is ultimately a path of nonviolence resting on principles. In today's world, it is in the Declaration of Human Rights which activists often find the closest legal interpretation of a society built on pillar and the principle of 'do no harm'. In this view, an advantage given to one religious group in the law is a disadvantage to another group and ultimately a form of violence. Nowruz Revolution must separate itself from the reformist strategy first through a moral challenge. This moral challenge is a process which can only lead to good and which may end up recreating a more cohesive Iranian opposition built on the principles of nonviolence and human rights. Through sound principles, eyes can be opened and hope can be rekindled in the hearts of millions. Such a challenge is the necessary opening move in this game of *shogi*.

Opening Game: Politicization of Society

In my lifetime, I've witnessed Iranian society politicized on three occasions. As a six year old I witnessed the politicization of everyone around me in Autumn and Winter of 1979 which continued for couple of years after the revolution. The terror and horror of events in 1980 and 1981 soon forced Iranians to turn their backs on politics and mind their own business.

In Spring of 1997, I again witnessed Iranian society becoming politicized through the presidential campaign while the victory of the people allowed this politicization of society to dominate culture in the following 3 years. This societal change created an atmosphere where most were actively involved and opinionated in one way or another in politics and political discourse. This politicization of society led to the student uprising in the Summer of 1998 which was brutally crushed. Couple of years later, the closing of newspapers, jailing, torture and beatings of students, activists and journalist against forced the society to disengage from politics and for people to mind their own business.

EPILOGUE

During the course of 2009 presidential campaign, and especially as elections got closer, the society again became more and more politicized. The election coup was a spark which ignited political will in millions more, even politicizing those who had not taken part in the election process. During those months of political struggle, elderly were seen in the streets next to their grandchildren.

Again, this political state of the society which is the opening game in any conflict against dictatorship was the threat to the system which had to be brutally destroyed. Through violence and terror, fear was ignited in the hearts of millions and because of the divided nature of the Green Movement, hope was lost in millions others. Soon apathy took over and people again began to mind their own business and stay out of politics.

No movement can form and no nonviolent revolution can succeed without activism of ordinary citizens. The massive popular support which is the requirement of a successful movement requires a politicized society. Iranians are disgruntled, unhappy, and angry at their current predicament. Those who follow Iranian events often refer to Iranian societal situation as 'fire under the ash'. It seems everyone knows that society will soon ignite and will become political again, but they don't know when, how and for what purpose.

There are three ways which the Iranian society can become politicized. One is if it is done again within the political institutions and procedures of the Islamic Republic such as was done during the 1997 and 2009 elections. Such path will again create a strategy created within the red lines of the system and which will likely be controlled and directed by the reformists intent on saving the Islamic Republic. People will again be used as instruments of pressure during negotiations with hardliners and if people's demands cross the red lines of the Islamic Republic, they will be shunned and de-politicized by either the reformists or hardliners in power.

Society can also become politicized through a random act of courage, an act of terror or even an accident. The beating, torture and death of Khaled Said in Egypt created widespread condemnation followed by politicization of ordinary people on Facebook and eventually led to civil disobedience and uprisings across the country. Self-immolation of Mohammad Bouazizi in Tunisia was the precipitating factor which politicized Tunisian society and gave rise to Arab Spring. In Iran, many consider the state of terror after Cinema Rex as the precipitating factor giving rise to the political state of the society in the following Autumn and Winter.

The spark that ignites passion in the hearts of millions plays an incredibly important role throughout the movement. Throughout the struggle, people often recall the spark as their inspiration. Whenever the movement becomes divided, people remind themselves of the message and passion of that initial spark that led them down this path. If the spark is inspired by hatred, anger and violence, then the movement often takes on a violent path of revenge and punishment. If the spark is inspired through the institutions of the dictatorships and with the support of the dictator, often the outcome is a reform movement intent on survival of at least some components of the dictatorship. And if the spark has symbolic meanings of nonviolence inherent in it, it is likely that the movement will take on a nonviolent path and will have the best chance of achieving a nonviolent revolution.

Iranian celebrations are tools with inherent message of nonviolence ingrained within them. If the spark occurs during nonviolent action on an Iranian celebration such as Tirgan, Mehregan, Yalda or Sadeh, it will have tremendous value as a constant reminder throughout the movement of the intention of nonviolence inherent in that first step. Such a movement will be united and determined to stick to the path of nonviolence in defeat or victory. It is not important how large the initial spark is, whether it occurs on a winter celebration or in the summer, it does not even matter if the spark occurs inside or outside of Iran. As long as the spark gives rise to politicization of society, it will be remembered and will continuously provide the energy and passion for the struggle.

The politicization of Iran requires a spark and Iranian national celebrations of peace and nonviolence are tools available to the society for such an action. My generation cannot fail to disregard and overlook the significance and value of Nowruz and other celebrations. If Iranians of next-generation are to build a country built on nonviolence, it must start with our generation turning those cultural values of nonviolence into acts of nonviolent action and ultimately as inspirations for a nonviolent revolution.

The Middle Game: Islamic Republic's Sources of Power and it's Pillars of Support. The Mechanisms and Methods of Nowruz Revolution.

Gene Sharp identifies six sources of power in society that are fundamental for the survival of a pluralistic model of dictatorship. Robert Helvey, shows how these sources of power are expressed as 'pillars or support' in organizations and institutions of the dictatorship.

Gene Sharp's sources of power include 1) 'authority' or the legitimacy to rule. 2) 'Human resources' 3) 'Skills and knowledge' 4) 'Intangible factors' such as exploitation of religion, promotion of revolutionary values, cultural and religious habits, Iranian attitudes towards obedience and submission. 5) 'Material resources' and 6) 'punishments or sanctions' against the population.

Robert Helvey describes how Sharp's 'sources of power' find expression in organizations and institutions called the 'pillars of support' that are necessary for the day to day survival of the dictatorship.[970] As mentioned earlier, these 'pillars or support' include: police, military, civil servants, media, business community, youth, workers, religious organizations, and nongovernmental organizations (NGOs).

The ultimate strategy of Nowruz Revolution and every nonviolent revolution is the conversion, accommodation, coercion or disintegration of each pillar of support. Depending on whether one is pulling on a pillar such as the struggle against the reformists or attempting to eliminate an economic support through politicization of oil industry, or disarming the revolutionary guards, different mechanisms and methods are appropriate. Methods of a nonviolent conflict were detailed earlier and fall within the three categories of protest and persuasion, noncooperation and intervention.

As an example in a strategy for Nowruz Revolution, a celebration such as *Ordibehesht-gan* can be a tool to politicize society in poor southern ports Bandar Abbas, Bushehr, Abadan and Mahshahr in the hopes of political and economic noncooperation by laborers, engineers and truck drivers working in the ports, oil wells and refineries of the south. Such a movement using celebrations as tools can ignite political will amongst tens of thousands of oil industry workers often living side-by-side and as neighbors with those working in the transportation industry and can be an instrument in a nonviolent revolution.

Aside from the 'pillars of support', evaluation of the roots of obedience in society is an important element which needs to be taken into account in a strategy for Nowruz Revolution. A dictatorship survives because of the obedience of the population and the ultimate centerpiece of the strategy often involves creating the will for disobedience. Sharp divides the reasons for obedience into obedience out of habit, fear of punishment and sanctions, self-interest, moral obligation of those who believe obedience is for the good of society, obedience towards a ruler for his perceived superhuman, all-powerful or godlike characteristic, psychological identification with the ruler, indifference towards obedience and obedience due to absence of self-confidence. All these need to be taken into account by strategists and leaders in the course of active nonviolent struggle for democracy. Helvey summarizes obedience as "primarily a combination of habits, fears and interests", he then continues: "--and habits and interests can be changed and fear can be overcome."[971]

Ultimately, the Iranian opposition needs a strategic estimate to include all the elements of the above. Creating and executing a strategy for a movement is classically the work of the leadership in a struggle and the absence of visionary and creative leadership for Iranians is one of the most important elements for the status quo. Yet, leadership does not need to be realized in its classic form. In a contemporary nonviolent movement, led by tens of thousands of nonviolent activists, each activist is a visionary and the creator of ideas. Each activist is in charge of executing the strategy while the strategy is formed based on principles and through collective consciousness of society.

Nowruz Revolution must base itself on the philosophy of nonviolence which ultimately is reliance on what Gandhi called the 'truth'. In truth, a movement finds justice. Most activists in nonviolence today consider the United Nations Declaration for Human Rights as the closest legal representation of justice and thus truth and nonviolence. Nowruz Revolution thus must consider a constitution based on human rights as the centerpiece of its strategy and must consider any constitution based on the values of a particular religion as ultimately a restriction on the rights of non-believers, a threat against their human rights and ultimately a form of violence. A united movement can arise based on sound principles and these principles cannot be negotiated away or disregarded based on short term influence or pressure from the reformists advocating human rights in an Islamic Republic.

United on strategy, a successful movement will employ conversion and accommodation in its initial stages to undermine many pillars of support. These mechanisms may include symbolic nonviolent acts targeted at the reformists in Tehran or the clergy in Qom or laborers in southern port with the intention of using conversion as a mechanism against these pillars of support. Mechanisms of accommodation can be employed against soldiers looking to join and support the people. Ultimately, against a brutal regime like the Islamic Republic, conversions and accommodations lead to mechanisms of nonviolent coercion which may involve occupy (intervention) techniques and which can have high casualty rates. Soldiers should be asked to abandon their loyalty and defend the people in their occupation. Such defense which may involve use of weapons however should solely be for defense of the people and should avoid unnecessary harm or injury to pillars of support of the Islamic Republic.

No one can predict or plan what the middle game in the Nowruz Revolution may look like. Just as the details in every game of chess is different, so are the details in every nonviolent revolution. A successful struggle, like a military struggle must constantly improvise, adapt and overcome. But as long as the movement adheres to its principles of nonviolence, then hope and dream for its success will live. Whether it will take five months, five years or fifty years, as long as there is inequality in Iran, there will be a need for a Nowruz Revolution and as long as this revolution is led by the principles of humanity and peace seen in Nowruz, it will shine as a beacon of hope in the hearts of tens of thousands of Iranian dreamers for generations to come.

The End Game: The Political Solution

Just as check mate is the ultimate objective of any game of chess, a political solution involving the adoption of a constitution based on human rights and the adoption of the rule of law in society are the ultimate objectives of any nonviolent revolution.

The great divide in Iranian politics today is not between those who believe in armed resistance versus those who believe in nonviolence. Iranians are nearly completely disarmed and because of the experience with violence in 1980's, there is little appetite for violence in my generation. The great divide today in Iranian politics is between seculars who want a constitution based on principles of human rights and the Islamists(reformists) who want a constitution based on sharia law. The reformists, while jailed and suppressed by the dictatorship hope to recreate the constitution of the Islamic Republic in a more democratic way under the supervision of a more open theocracy. They insist that Shi'ism should be declared the official religion of Iran and insist that the clergy should have final say on all legislature and even some executive decisions. Seculars who advocate nonviolence see a constitution declaring Shi'ism or Islam as the official religion of the people as ultimately a form of discrimination against nonbelievers and ultimately a form of violence. This division amongst seculars and the reformists is the main division today within Iranian opposition.

If Iranians are to rally for a nonviolent revolution, the ultimate objective cannot be anything but a constitution drafted on the principles of nonviolence which today are best expressed as the Universal Declaration of Human Rights. In this path for a constitution based on human rights, cooperation, assistance and support for the reformists who want to maintain the Islamic Republic and who ultimately serve as a pillar of support for the Islamic Republic, is cooperation and assistance to a form of discrimination and ultimately a violent path.

In addition to the division between the seculars and Islamists(reformists) within the democracy movement, there is also division amongst seculars between those who want a republic form of government versus those who want a constitutional monarchy. Both these groups want a constitution based on human rights and the rule of law, yet the division between these two secular camps is sometimes very intense. This division often dates back three or four generations, far longer than the division amongst Islamists and seculars which dates back two generations to 1979.

Some Iranian seculars advocating a republic refuse to cooperate and support any movement that may leave the door open for a future referendum that can potentially reestablish constitutional monarchy. Because of this ingrained fear, many seculars in the last 20 years have allied themselves with the Islamists (reformists) and are willing to accept more tolerant forms of an Islamic Republic only if this republic continues to censor and eliminate monarchists from Iranian political spectrum. This fear of potential return of constitutional monarchy by some and the alliance of this group with the reformists since mid-1990s has given the upper hand of political power to the Islamists (reformists) and has helped create a strong pillar of support for the Islamic Republic.

In addition to the division in the secular camp between advocates of the republic versus those advocating constitutional monarchy, there is also division with ethnic minorities, especially the Kurds, who advocate a federal form of government. The Kurds who are mostly Sunnis are strong adversaries against the Constitution of the Islamic Republic which bases

Shi'ism as the official religion of Iran. They are a proud and ancient Iranian ethnic group with and fought bravely and courageously against the Islamic Republic in early 1980s and were massacred indiscriminately by the regime.. Many seculars advocating constitutional monarchy or republican form of government fear calls for federalism as a threat against national integrity of Iran and refuse to cooperate or assist movements which have federalism as their basis. Thus one sees another great political division in the opposition camp.

The unsuccessful Iranian opposition strategy since 1979 has been the failed attempt for all these varied viewpoints to work together with the aim of the overthrow of the Islamic Republic followed by a public referendum on the form of government. An obvious flaw of the Iranian opposition strategy, which has prevented the Iranians from cooperating with each other, is the ultimate need for the various groups to compete and ultimately eliminate each other in the hypothetical referendum of the future after the overthrow. This strategic flaw arising from the ultimate need to eliminate one group or another through a future referendum is the source of much division and distrust amongst the opposition. Kurds cannot work with groups who want to make sure the word federalism is eliminated from political discourse in the future and their rights potentially curtailed. Monarchists can't get the cooperation of the republicans and those republicans allied with the Islamists (reformists) are not trusted by the seculars, Kurds or the monarchists. All of this arises from the failed and flawed Iranian opposition strategy that a public referendum should be called in the hypothetical future of Iran for the elimination of one viewpoint or another from politics.

To make matters even more complicated, the Islamists (reformists) disgruntled by the current makeup of the Islamic Republic have argued successfully and justly that if people are to choose between a constitutional monarchy, republic and a federal state, they should also have the choice of picking an Islamic Republic in the future referendum. This argument has been accepted even by monarchists and some of them insist that people should have the right to choose a theocracy if it is the will of the majority. In this strategic mess, Iranian communists and socialists who still maintain a powerful political voice have also interjected and have added socialism as another obvious choice on that hypothetical referendum further dividing the opposition. Thus the failed Iranian opposition strategy has become a coalition of opponents who try unsuccessfully to unite with the intention of democratically eliminating one another in a future referendum. All these groups meanwhile advocate human rights while supporting a failed referendum strategy which can potentially create forms of governments which can curtail the human rights of many.

This strategic mess cannot serve as a successful political solution for tens of thousands of Iranian activists expected to risk their safety and lives for a cause. If a strategy is a failure on paper, it will likely be a failure in action. A nonviolent revolution needs massive popular support and this support can only come through shared understandings and beliefs that the strategy is sound on paper, it is fair to all and will not lead to curtailment or restrictions on human rights of any group or elimination of any political view in the future.

***

There is another solution which is far simpler and potentially far more effective in helping the Iranian opposition to cooperate with one another. This solution which can be referred to as 'one nation, one constitution', involves the strategy of drafting the constitution of Iran based solely on the Universal Declaration of Human Rights and the elimination of popular decision making (referendum) on the nature of the constitution from the opposition strategy. In 'one nation, one constitution' strategy, Iran's constitution is drafted free of any prejudices and desires of one political party or another and free of concepts such as monarchy, religion, socialism or federalism. The constitution of the country solely guarantees the human rights of the citizens and establishes rules, responsibilities and independence of the three branches of government.

The desires for a decentralized decision making by the ethnic minorities, respect for religious values of the Muslims, calls for more socialist programs and agendas and the issue of monarchy are then constantly presented, debated and decided through bills and legislation in the Iranian parliament or even through popular referendums without changes to the constitution of the country. As long as any legislation does not curtail the human rights of a particular group, as expressed in the constitution, and does not change the constitution itself, it can function to allow expression of political desires of opposing views for generations to come without the need for elimination of one viewpoint or another.

Similar to presenting legislation regarding Islamic institutions and values in the parliament, or legislation presented by ethnic groups for more decentralized decision making or legislation for socialist programs, advocates of the institution of monarchy must have the right to present their legislation freely in the parliament like others and if their legislation for an institution of monarchy does not curtail the human rights of others, does not allow special legal privileges for a family or a person and does not change the constitution of Iran, it must be allowed to be expressed and presented freely within the parliament like any other legislation or form of speech.

In such a strategy where the constitution based on human rights is the law of the land, the right to create an institution of kingship, separate from the government, should be no different legally than the right to create a religious institution for a grand Ayatollah separate from government. In such a democratic system where people are free to create their non-government institutions as they choose, there cannot be any restrictions on freedom of speech as long as that speech is not harmful or hurtful to others. And just as some have the right to financially support a grand ayatollah and maintain his institution, others should have the right to financially support a shah of their choosing and maintain his institution. Furthermore, while people have the right to support multiple grand ayatollahs and their institutions, no family can have monopoly on royalty and people should have the right to establish and support multiple institutions of royalty within the rules of law.

A successful strategy for Nowruz Revolution must ultimately have a successful political strategy as the end game. Such a strategy can only be successful if it relies on the principles of human rights, democracy and nonviolence. The unity in Iranian opposition for a nonviolent revolution cannot be achieved based on short term coalitions with expiration dates. Unity must be based on principles and must aim for the collective rights of all Iranians regardless of ethnicity, religion, political view, education level or economic means.

***

Iranians are in a dark winter of religious totalitarian state. Iran seems like a never ending prison sentence to some and a strange and unfamiliar occupied country to others. There seems to be a complete loss of moral fabric in society with rampant prostitution and addictions seen in the streets in 12 and 13 year olds. Corruption has penetrated every facet of economy and violence dominates politics. Many feel as if living in captivity and hyperfocused on escape, others are numbed and withdrawn from politics and society.

Celebrations are banned, concerts closed, cinema curtailed, the streets polluted, lakes disappearing, and environment neglected. Courage is imprisoned, voices are silenced, and hope is crushed. Religion is turned to a weapon and spirituality has become a strange and unseen phenomenon. The darkness and violence of this unforgiving winter is crushing, its forces all too powerful and this winter's intention of maintaining power seems never-ending. It seems that this winter has the power to manipulate itself and elude spring.

I was born in 1973 which in Iranian society is one of the first years of a tremendous population boom which continued into late 1980's. More than 80% of Iranians worldwide are younger than me and are mostly in their 20's and 30's. Our memory of pre-revolutionary Iran seems at times like a colorful 8mm movie. During brief moments of courage in the last few decades, we've fantasized what a free Iran would look like, how colorful our universities could be, how diverse our arts and our culture can become and the hospitality we can show to tourists and travelers from across the globe. We've dreamt of entrepreneurship in a free country with an educated and tremendously creative workforce, have dreamt of cinema and music without censorship and football without politics. Our generation is still alive and will continue to dream and even if we are not able to create the colorful nation which we dream of, we will teach that dream to our children and will teach them not to lose hope. For as long as there is hope for spring, there is preparation and a countdown to Nowruz.

During the green movement, for a few brief months, we felt the possibility of waking from this recurring nightmare and living a normal life, yet the fear and violence of this winter was overpowering. In those turbulent months, any attempt at freedom would lead to traumatic deaths of individuals who looked, dressed and believed like everyone else in our generation, making each of their deaths traumatic and as intense as the horrible death of a brother or a sister. The struggle for freedom was painful, the defeat was emotionally crushing, yet even if hope was lost in some, it lived in others.

Despite our crushing defeat, if you ask any Iranian democracy activist what happened to the green movement, they will respond that it is alive and waiting for the next chapter. It is silent, but as if resting and not afraid. The movement does not see the way out, but does not seem hopeless.

***

Yet one cannot forget that the green movement was divided, broken and in turmoil even without the violence of the regime. The reformists who saw themselves as the inspirations of the movement and by far were the most organized group wanted the survival of the Islamic Republic. They were rightly upset at the election coup, but were agitated at the presence of seculars and liberals within the movement, crossing the red lines of the Islamic Republic. Those who called for the dissolution (*enhelal*) of the Islamic Republic were shunned and avoided. In rallies in Los Angeles, New York and Washington D.C. organized by reformists, signs and flags crossing the red lines of the Islamic Republic, especially the 1906 constitutional flag of Iran, were banned, speech against the system of the Islamic Republic banned and the participants threatened with reformist security officers and even threatened with arrest. Inside Iran, as hundreds of thousands would change the revolutionary slogans of 'Islamic Republic' to 'Iranian Republic', meaning desires for a secular state, the reformists would publish statements shunning calls for abolition of the Islamic Republic and would refer to them as reactionaries, hijackers of the reformist green movement, trouble makers, monarchists, and even agent provocateurs instigating violence and terrorism. The reformists continuously reminded our generation that the green movement aims for the path of 'Imam Khomeini', the founder of the revolution and his revolutionary values. Those questioning the Islamic state were shunned and rejected by the reformists without realizing the tremendous unseen and unorganized social power of Iranian seculars and without realizing the distaste for the survival of the Islamic Republic in Iranian society. The green movement was divided between those who wanted to focus the movement on the election dispute and those who wanted to rid themselves of the Islamic Republic all together.

In the next chapter of the struggle for Iranian democracy, the reformists will again call for a struggle within the institutions and the red lines of the Islamic Republic while the seculars will focus on the dissolution of the constitution and establishment of rule of law under a constitution based on principles of human rights. It is noteworthy that the reformists also call for the rule of law and human rights, but they want the rule of law and human rights within a theocracy and under Islamic laws and guidance.

It is a very reasonable assumption that those enlightened on the injustices within a religious regime, the potential harm of an Islamic Republic against religion and spirituality, and the grave threat against freedom and human rights within an Islamic Republic can never shut their eyes once more on their principles and support groups and individuals advocating populist and superficial calls for more humane (*rahmani*) versions of Islamic Republic. The inability to form a coalition in Iranian politics between the reformists and the seculars who fundamentally disagree on the nature of government is a forgone conclusion. Yet, while the seculars insisting on a constitution based on human rights cannot join forces with the reformists, more and more reformists are seeing the error and potential threat to God, Islam and Shi'ism inherent in a religious state, the discrimination against non-Shi'ites in a constitution which declares Shi'ism as the official religion of the state, are shunning calls for reforming and recreating the Islamic Republic, and are joining the seculars in their demands for a constitution based on human rights.

A powerful coalition for a nonviolent revolution against the Islamic Republic must be based on sound principles of nonviolence as the basis of its strategy. These principles include adoption of human rights as the basis for the constitutional law of Iran. Nowruz Revolution must rest on principles and those principles cannot be curtailed or ignored for short term coalitions with more organized and powerful reformist groups.

***

To many, democracy and human rights in Iran may seem like an impossible dream, but I see Iranians closer to it than ever in their history. Iran is one event, one instigation, one spark away from a societal explosion. Whether that explosion will lead to violence and civil war or to a Nowruz Revolution, one cannot predict. But we can become activists for one or the other. We can believe in the power of nonviolence and can change our future. We can believe in the improbable and be prepared for the 'black swan' which at any unexpected moment can alter Iranian and perhaps Middle Eastern psyche. In that moment, perhaps chaotic, euphoric and unpredictable, Iranians will need principles which every grandmother and grandchild can relate to and can be employed to give order within the chaos and unpredictability. Nowruz for Iranians provides that source of structure, identity and civility. Nowruz is a pillar of stability for Iranians and a tremendous cultural resource for kindness and humanity; elements so absent from the corruption and violence of today and needed in the time of chaos and unpredictability during the disintegration of the Islamic Republic.

If Iranians can turn one moment of their struggle into Nowruz, they can be reminded of their ancient wish of every day becoming Nowruz. That

EPILOGUE

reminder is sometimes all a movement needs, a reminder of hope, peace, and of life free of fear, trauma and terror. Such reminders can at times be life altering for individuals and even for societies. Just as a scent of rose can reawaken hope in a prisoner in solitude, Nowruz can reawaken hope in hearts of Iranians. That reawakening is the revolution, that reawakening is the step towards democracy and freedom and human rights. That reawakening can undo the fear from the deepest hollows of despair and perhaps can be the solution to the immense Iranian dilemma. Nowruz can provide the philosophy, principles and symbols which Iranians can unite around and can be the source of hope and courage much needed in Iranian politics. The foundation for the fondest memories of every Iranian childhood regardless of war or revolution is intertwined with spring and at the start of every spring, there is Nowruz.

#Nowruz

~ Farvardin ~

	1 Nowruz	2	3	4	5	6
7	8	9	10	11	12	13 Sizdeh-bedar
14	15	16	17	18	19 Farvardegan	20
21	22	23	24	25	26	27
28	29	30	31			

~ Ordibehesht ~

	1	2	3 Ordibehesht-gan	4	5	6
7	8	9	10	11	12	13
14	15	16	17	18	19	20
21	22	23	24	25	26	27
28	29	30	31			

CALENDAR OF CELEBRATIONS

~ Khordad ~

	1	2	3	4	5	6 Khordadgan
7	8	9	10	11	12	13
14	15	16	17	18	19	20
21	22	23	24	25	26	27
28	29	30	31			

~ Tir ~

	1	2	3	4	5	6
7	8	9	10	11	12	13 Tirgan
14	15	16	17	18	19	20
21	22	23	24	25	26	27
28	29	30	31			

~ Amordad ~

	1	2	3	4	5	6
7 Amordadgan	8	9	10	11	12	13
14	15	16	17	18	19	20
21	22	23	24	25	26	27
28	29	30	31			

~ Shahrivar ~

	1	2	3	4 Shahrivargan	5	6
7	8	9	10	11	12	13
14	15	16	17	18	19	20
21	22	23	24	25	26	27
28	29	30	31			

CALENDAR OF CELEBRATIONS

~ Mehr ~

	1	2	3	4	5	6
7	8	9	10	11	12	13
14	15	16 Mehregan	17	18	19	20
21	22	23	24	25	26	27
28	29	30				

~ Aban ~

	1	2	3	4	5	6
7	8	9	10 Abangan	11	12	13
14	15	16	17	18	19	20
21	22	23	24	25	26	27
28	29	30				

~ Azar ~

	1	2	3	4	5	6
7	8	9 Azargan	10	11	12	13
14	15	16	17	18	19	20
21	22	23	24	25	26	27
28	29	30 Yalda/Chelleh				

~ Dei ~

	1 Deigan	2	3	4	5	6
7	8	9	10	11	12	13
14	15	16	17	18	19	20
21	22	23	24	25	26	27
28	29	30				

CALENDAR OF CELEBRATIONS

~ Bahman ~

	1	2 Bahmangan	3	4	5	6
7	8	9	10 Sadeh	11	12	13
14	15	16	17	18	19	20
21	22	23	24	25	26	27
28	29	30				

~ Esfand ~

	1	2	3	4	5 Esfandgan	6
7	8	9	10	11	12	13
14	15	16	17	18	19	20
21	22	23	24	25	26	27
28	29	30 Chaharshanbeh-Souri				

Bibliography

Ackerman, P., & Duvall, J. (2000). *A Force More Powerful, A Century of Nonviolent Conflict*. New York: Palgrave.

al, S. e. (1998, 12 December). Prospective study of post-traumatic stress disorder in children involved in road traffic accidents. *British Medical Journal*, 317:1619-1623.

Amir Mokri, M. (2003). *Nowruz, ostureha va digar jashnhaye irani dar gozargahe zaman (Nowruz, Mythology and other Iranian Celebrations through Time)*. Los Angeles: Dehkhoda Publishing.

Anjavi Shirazi, A. (1973). *Jashn'hā va ādāb va mu'taqidāt-i zamistān [Celebrations, Costumes and Beliefs of Winter]*. Tehran: Amir Kabir Publications.

Ashtiani, A. E. (2003). *History of Iran in Islamic Period*. Tehran: Namak Publishing.

Avery, P. (., Hambly, G. R., & Melville, C. (. (1968-1991). *The Cambridge History of Iran, Vol. 7: From Nadir Shah to the Islamic Republic (Volume 7)*. Cambridge: University Press.

Axworthy, M. (2006). *The Sword of Persia : Nader Shah, from Tribal Warrior to Conquering Tyrant*. London ; New York: I.B. Tauris ; New York : Distributed by Palgrave Macmillan.

Ayers S, P. A. (2001). Do women get posttraumatic stress disorder as a result of childbirth? A prospective study of incidence. *Birth*, 28(2): 111-8. .

Backash, S. (1991). *The Reign of the Ayatollahs : Iran and the Islamic Revolution*. Millefleurs.

Bamforth, D. B. (Mar., 1994). Indigenous People, Indigenous Violence: Precontact Warfare on the North American Great. *Man, New Series, Vol. 29, No. 1*, pp. 95-115.

Biruni, A. R. (1974). *al-āthār al-bāqiyah an al-qurūn al-khāliyah [vestiges of the past]*. Tehran: Ibn Sina Publishing.

Bock, P. (1969). *Modern Cultural Anthropology*. Borzoi Book Publishing.

Branch, T. (1988). *America in the King Years 1954-63, Parting the Waters*. New York-London-Toronto-Sydney: Simon and Schuster Paperbacks.

Briant, P. t. (2001). *Histoire de L'Empire Perse de Cyrus a Alexander*. Tehran,Iran: Nashr-e-Ghatreh.

Brown, M. H. (1991). *The Search for Eve*. Harpercollins.

Burton, S. (1989). *Impossible Dream: The Marcoses, the Acquinos, and the Unfinished Revolution*. New York: Warner Books.

Calyborne, C. (. (1998). *The Autobiography of Martin Luther King, Jr*. New York: Warner Book Group.
Chinnock, E. J. (2011). *The Anabasis of Alexander . Translated, with a commentary*. British Library, Historical Print Editions .
Christiansen, A. (. (1991). *Īrān dar zamān-i Sāsāniyān : tārīkh-i Īrān-i Sāsānī tā ḥamlah-i 'Arab va vaẓ'-i dawlat va-millat dar zamān-i Sāsāniyāh*. Tehran, Iran: Dunyā-yi Kitāb,.
Cook, J. (1983). *The Persian Empire*. London: J.M Dent and Sons.
Cordesman, A. H., & Wagner, A. (1990). *The Lessons Of Modern War, Vol. 2: The Iran-Iraq War*. Westview Press.
Cortright, D. (2006). *Gandhi and Beyond, Nonviolence for an Age of Terrorism*. Boulder-London: Paradigm Publishers.
Cottrell, A. J. (n.d.). *Iran's Anned Forces Under the Pahlavi Dynasty*. Elwell-Sutton.
Curtin, J. (1908). *The Mongols; a History*. Boston: Little, Brown.
Daly, M., & Wilson, M. (1988). *Homicide*. New York: A. de Gruyte.
Darnell, R. (1974). *Readings in History of Anthropology*. Harper & Row.
Daryaee, T. (2003). *The Sassanian Empire*. Tehran: Ghoghnus Publishing.
Daye, R. (2004). *Political forgiveness: Lessons from South Africa*. Orbis Books.
de Waal Malefijt, A. (1974). *Images of Man; A History of Anthropological Thought*. Knopf.
Dehkhoda, A. A. (1998). *Loghatname [Encyclopedic Dictionary]* . Tehran: University of Tehran Publications.
Eghbal Ashtiani, A. (1997). *tarikh-e-moghul va avayel ayam-e teimuri (Mongol History and Beginning of Teimurid Period)*. Tehran: Namak Publishing.
Ehrlich, P. R. (2002). *Human Natures : Genes, Cultures, and the Human prospect*. New York: Penguin Books.
Ellenberger, H. F. (1970). *The Discovery of Unconscious- The History and Evolution of Dynamic Psychiatry*. United States of America: BasicBooks.
Ember, C. R. (Vol. 17, No. 4 (Oct., 1978)). Myths About Hunter-Gatherers. *Ethnology*, pp. 439-448.
Ferdowsi, A. a. (2007). *Shahnameh, The Persian Book of Kings*. Penguin Group.
Fischer, L. (1950). *The Life of Mahatma Gandhi*. New York: Harper & Row.
Fox, R. (1962). *Genghis Khan*. Castle Hedingham, Essex : Daimon Press.
Frye, R. N. (1968-c1991). *The Cambridge History of Iran, Vol. 4: From the Arab Invasion to the Saljuqs (Volume 4)*. Cambridge: University Press.
Frye, R. N. (1975). *The Golden Age of Persia : the Arabs in the East*. New York: Barnes & Noble Books.

BIBLIOGRAPHY

Gandhi, M. K. (C1948 (1983)). *Autobiography, The Story of My Experiment with Truth.* New York: Dover Publications.

Gibbons, A. (Vol. 290, No. 5494 (Nov. 10, 2000)). Europeans Trace Ancestry to Paleolithic People. *Science*, pp. 1080-1081.

Ḥāfiẓ, & Ladinsky, D. J. (1999). *The gift: poems by the great Sufi master.* Penguin Books.

Haq, M. (1960). *A History of Early Islam. Study of the Rise, Expansion, and Development of the Islamic Society, State and Culture from 570 A.D. to 661 A.D.* Peshawar: University Book Agency.

Harris, M. (2011). *The Rise of Anthropological Theory: A History of Theories of Culture*. Altamira Press.

Hegel, G. (1991). *The Philosophy of History.* Buffalo,: Sibree.

Helvey, R. L. (2004). *On Strategic Nonviolent Conflict: Thinking About the Fundementals.* East Boston, MA: Albert Einstein Institute.

Herman, J. (1992). *Trauma and Recovery. The Aftermath of Violence from Domestic Abuse to Political Terror.* New York: BasicBooks.

Herodotus. (n.d.). *The Histories.* New York: Barnes and Noble Classics.

Holmes, R., & Gan, B. L. (2005). *Nonviolence in Theory and Practice.* Long Grove, Illinois: Waveland Press Inc.

Homer, J. A. (1951, 2005). *The Wit and Wisdom of Gandhi.* Mineola, NY: Dover Publications.

Homer, J. A. (1956 (revised 1994)). *The Gandhi Reader.* New York: Grove Press.

Honigmann, J. J. (1976). *The Development of Anthropological Ideas.* Homewood, Ill.: Dorsey Press.

Imbe-Black, E., Roberts, J., & Whiting, R. A. (1988). *Rituals in Families and Family Therapy.* New York: Norton.

Irving, A. (1976). *Contributions to Anthropology.* University of Chicago Press Hallowell.

Jackson, P., & Lockhart, L. (1968-1991). *The Cambridge History of Iran, Vol. 6: The Timurid and Safavid Periods (Volume 6).* Cambridge: University Press.

Keeley, L. H. (1996). *War before civilization.* New York: Oxford University Press.

Kennedy, H. (2005). *When Baghdad Ruled the Muslim World: The Rise and Fall of Islam's Greatest Dynasty.* Cambridge, MA: Da Capo Press.

Kennedy, H. (2007). *The Great Arab Conquests : How the Spread of Islam Changed the World We Live In.* London: Weidenfeld & Nicolson.

Khodadadian, A. (2002). *Sassasian*. Tehran: Nashr-e-Behdid.

Kingdon, J. (1993). *Self-Made Man : Human Evolution from Eden to Extinction*. New York: Wiley.

Kinross, P. B. (1977). *The Ottoman Centuries : the Rise and Fall of the Turkish Empire*. New York: Morrow.

Kinzer, S. (2003). *All the Shah's men : an American Coup and the Roots of Middle East Terror*. Hoboken, N.J.: John Wiley & Sons.

Knauft, B. M., Daly, M., Wilson, M., Donald, L., & Morren, G. E. (Vol. 28, No. 4 (Aug. - Oct., 1987)). Reconsidering Violence in Simple Human Societies: Homicide among the Gebusi of New Guinea. *Current Anthropology*, pp. 457-500.

Knauft, T., Abler, S., Betzig, L., Boehm, C., & Knox, R. (Vol. 32, No. 4 (Aug. - Oct., 1991)). Violence and Sociality in Human Evolution [and Comments and Replies]. *Current Anthropology*, pp. 391-428.

Krech, S. I. (1999). *The Ecological Indian : Myth and History*. New York: W.W. Norton & Co.

Krech, S. I. (Vol 371 , 1 September 1994). Genocide in Tribal Society. *Nature*, 14-15.

Kuper, A. (1999). *Culture. The Anthropologists' Account*. Cambridge, Massachusetts/London England: Harvard University Press.

Ladinzky, D. J. (1999). *The Gift: Poems by the Great Sufi Master*. Penguin Books.

Layard, S. A. (1923 (2001)). *Early adventures in Persia, Susiana, and Babylonia, including a residence among the Bakhtiyari and other wild tribes before the discovery of Nineveh*. Nabu Press .

Leakey, R. (1992). *Origins Reconsidered - In Search of What Makes Us Human*. New York: Bantam Doubleday Dell Publishing Group.

Lockhart, R. L., & Denison, W. a. (1938). *Nadir Shah; a Critical Study Based Nainly Upon Contemporary Sources*. London: Luzac.

Magli, I. (2001). *Cultural Anthropology : an Introduction; translated by Janet Sethre*. Jefferson, N.C.: McFarland.

Mair, L. (1965). *An Introduction to Social Anthropology*. Oxford: Clarendon Press.

Man, J. (2004). *Genghis Khan : Life, Death and Resurrection*. London New York: Bantam.

Mandela, N. (1995). *Long Walk to Freedom*. Boston-London-New York: Little, Brown and Company.

Marozzi, J. (2006). *Tamerlane: Sword of Islam, Conqueror of the World* . Da Capo Press.

BIBLIOGRAPHY

Masson, J. (1984). *The Assault on Truth. Freud's Suppression of the Seduction Theory.* New York: Farrar, Straus and Giroux.

May, R. (1996). *The Meaning of Anxiety.* New York: W.W. Norton and Co.

Mercado, M. A. (1986). *An Eyewitness History, People Power-The Phillippine Revolution of 1986.* Manila, Philippines: James B. Reuter, S.J Foundation.

Mertin P, M. P. (2002 Oct). Incidence and correlates of posttrauma symptoms in children from backgrounds of domestic violence. *Violence and Victims,* 17(5):555-67.

Merton, T. (1965). *Gandhi on Nonviolence, A Selection from the Writings of Mahatma Gandhi.* New York: New Directions Books.

Mokri, M. A. (2003). *Nowruz - Mythology and Iranian Celebrations Through the Ages.* Los Angeles: Dehkhoda Publishing.

Muir, S. W. (1878 (2009)). *The Life of Mohammad From Original Sources.* Cornell University Library.

Nagler, M. N. (2004). *The Search for a Nonviolent Future.* Maui, Hawaii; San Francisco, California: Inner Ocean Publishing.

Nanda, B. (2004). *Mahatma Gandhi: A Biography.* Oxford Paperbacks.

Nanda, B. R. (1997). *Mahatma Gandhi, A Biography.* Delhi: Oxford University Press.

O'Brien, J. M. (1994). *Alexander the Great: The Invisible Enemy : a biography.* Routledge; Reprint edition .

Olmstead, A. (1948). *History of the Persian Empire.* Chicago: The University of Chicago Press.

Otterbein, K. F. (1989). *The Evolution of War; a Cross-Cultural Study.* New Haven Conn: HRAF Press.

Paz, O. (1994). *The Labyrinth of Solitude: The Other Mexico, Return to the Labyrinth of Solitude, Mexico and the United States, the Philanthropic Ogre.* Grove Press.

Pinker, S. (2002). *The Blank Slate : the Modern Denial of Human Nature.* New York: Viking.

Pinker, S. (2011). *The Better Angels of Our Nature: Why Violence Has Declined.* Viking Adult .

Pollack, K. M. (2004). *The Persian Puzzle- The Conflict Between Iran and America.* New York: Random House.

Prawdin, M. (1940). *The Mongol Empire : Its Rise and Legacy.* New York: Macmillan.

Pritchard, D. B. (1994). *The Encyclopedia of Chess Variants.* Surrey,UK: Games and Puzzles Publications.

Puri, R.-S. (1987). *Gandhi on War and Peace.* New York: Praeger Publishing.

Rafizadeh, F. (2003). *chahar shanbeh souri, pajuhesh mardom shenasi dar zamineh jashnhay atash dar sarzamin irani [Suri Festival of Fire Celebration: Anthropological Study of Fire Festivals in Iranian Lands].* Tehran: Novid Shiraz Publications.

Razi, H. (2000). *gah-shomari va jashnhay iran-e-bastan [Chronology and Ancient Iranian Festivals].* Tehran: Behjat Publications.

Razi, H. (2003). *din va farhang irani pish az asr-e zartosht [Pre-Zoroastrian Religion and Culture of Ancient Iran].* Tehran, Iran: Entesharate-Sokhan.

Ring, T., Salkin, R. M., Watson, N., La Boda, S., & Schellinger, P. (1995). *International Dictionary of Historic Places.* Taylor & Francis.

Roberts, M. (1996). *Khomeini's Incorporation of the Iranian Military.* National Defense University .

Ross. (1983; 179, 182-83). Political Decision Making and Conflict: Additional Cross-Cultrual Evidence and a new Analysis. *Journal of Conflict Resolution,* 29: 547-79.

Rothschild, B. (2000). *The Body Remembers. The Psychophysiology of Trauma and Trauma Treatment.* New York: W.W. Norton and Co.

Russell, D. (1984). *Sexual Exploitation: Rape, Child Sexual Abuse, and Sexual Harassment.* Beverly Hills: Sage.

Savory, R. (1980). *Iran Under the Safavids.* Cambridge ; New York: Cambridge University Press.

Segal, R. A. (1998). *The Myth and Ritual Theory : an Anthology.* Malden, Mass.: Blackwell Publishers.

Sharp, G. (1973). *The Politics of Nonviolent Action, Part I Power and Struggle.* Boston, MA: Porter Sargent Publishing.

Sharp, G. (1973). *The Politics of Nonviolent Action, Part II The Methods of Nonviolent Action.* Boston, MA: Porter Sargent Publishers.

Sharp, G. (1973). *The Politics of Nonviolent Action, Part III The Dynamics of Nonviolent Action.* Boston, MA: Porter Sargent Publishing.

Sharp, G. (1979). *Gandhi as a Political Strategist.* Boston, MA: Porter Sargent Publishing.

Sharp, G. (2005). *Waging Nonviolent Struggle, 20th Century Practice 21st Century Potential.* Boston: Extending Horizons Books.

Sider, R. J. (1989). *Nonviolence, The Invincible Weapon?* Dallas-London-Sydney-Singapore: Word Publishing.

BIBLIOGRAPHY

Siegel, D. J. (2003). *Healing Trauma: Attachment, Mind, Body, and Brain*. W. W. Norton & Company.

Siegel, E. b. (2003). *Healing Trauma. Attachment, Mind, Body and Brain*. New York: W. W. Norton and Company.

Sinha, R. (1992). *Gandhian Nonviolence and The Indian National Struggle*. Delhi: H.K Publications.

Smith, W. (n.d.). *A Smaller History of Greece: From the Earliest Times to the Roman Conquest*.

Strange, G. (2004 (1900)). *Baghdad During the Abbasid Caliphate*. Published by Kessinger Publishing,.

Sykes, P. (1951). *A History of Persia*. London: Macmillan and Co.

Tavuchis, N. (n.d.). *Mea Culpa: A Sociology of Apology and Reconciliation*. Stanford: Stanford University Press.

Tolstoy, L. (1984). *The Kingdom of God is Within You*. Lincoln, Neberaska; London, England: University of Neberaska Press.

Ulrich, W., Borza, E., & Richards, G. (1967). *Alexander the Great*. W. W. Norton & Company.

Voget, F. W. (n.d.). *A History of Ethnology*.

Walker, P. L. (Vol. 30 (2001),). A Bioarchaeological Perspective on the History of Violence. *Annual Review of Anthropology*, , pp. 573-596.

Wells, S. (2002). *A Journey of Man, A Genetic Odyssey*. London: Penguin Books.

Wells, S. (2002). *The Journey of Man - A Genetic Odyssey*. New Jersey: Princeton University Press.

West, E. W. (n.d.). *The Bundahishn ("Creation"), or Knowledge from the Zand, from Sacred Books of the East, volume 5*. 1897: Oxford University Press,.

Worthington, I. (2003). *Alexander the Great*. Routledge.

Wrangham, R., & Peterson, D. (1996). *Demonic Males : Apes and the Origins of Human Violence*. Boston: Houghton Mifflin.

Yarshater, E. (1968-c1991). *The Cambridge History of Iran, The Seleucid, Parthian and Sasanian Periods / (Volume 2)*. Cambridge: University Press.

Zarrinkub, A. (1976). *Do Gharn Sokoot [Two Centuries of Silence]*. Tehran: Entesharate Javidan.

References

Introduction
[1] Sider p 1

Chapter 1
[2] Nazila Fathi "Spate of Executions and Amputations in Iran" New York Time , . January 11, 2008

[3] Herman p 11
[4] Siegel p 174
[5] Herman pp. 10-11
[6] Herman pp.13-14
[7] Herman pp. 13-14.
[8] Herman p 14. See also: F. Rush "The Freudian Coverup," (1977): 31-47; J.L Herman, Father-Daughter Incest (Cambridge: Harvard University Press, 1981); J.M. Masson, The Assault on Truth. Freud's Suppression of the Seduction Theory (New York: Farrar, Straus and Giroux, 1984)
[9] Herman p 20
[10] Herman p 20
[11] Herman p 21
[12] Herman p 21, quoted from Show Walter, The Female Malady, 177
[13] Herman pp. 21-22
[14] Herman p 27
[15] Herman p 30 quoted from D.E.H Russell, Sexual Exploitation: Rape, Child Sexual Abuse, and Sexual Harassment (Beverly Hills, CA: Sage, 1984)
[16] Siegel p 169
[17] Herman p 28
[18] Herman p 33
[19] Siegel p 169
[20] Siegel p 169
[21] Siegel p 168
[22] Mertin pp. 555-67

[23] Stallard et al. pp.1619-1623
[24] Ayers pp. 111-118.
[25] David Satcher et al. (1999).

REFERENCES

"Chapter 4.2", Mental Health: A Report of the Surgeon General
[26] Rothschild
[27] May p 55
[28] Rothschild p 20
[29] Herman pp. 35-36
[30] Herman pp. 37-42
[31] Herman pp. 42-47
[32] Herman
[33] Herman p 43
[34] Herman p 74
[35] Herman p 43
[36] Herman p 75
[37] Pollack p 186 (Bakhash p 113; Cordsmam pp. 57-67; Cottrell pp. 419-422; Roberts pp. 36-50; Wright. In the Name of God pp. 84; Zabih, "The Iranian military in Revolution and War, pp115-161; Pollacks interview with former senior Iraqi military officers Nov 1998, June 1999, Sept 1999
[38] Pollack pp. 186
[39] Pollack pp. 186
[40] Pollack pp. 194
[41] Pollack pp. 197-198
[42] Pollack pp. 228 from Cordsman and Wagner, "The Lessons of Modern War, Vol 2 pp 363-368; Palmer "Gaurdians of the Gulf p 138; Pollack "Arabs at war" p 229; Pollack "The Threatening Storm pp. 23-24
[43] Pollack p 228

Chapter 2
[44] Daye p 22
[45] Herodotus p 108
[46] Herodotus pp. 109-113
[47] Herodotus p 114
[48] Herodotus pp. 115-122
[49] Herodotus p 119
[50] Herodotus pp. 124-125
[51] Bryant p 49
[52] Herodotus p 130
[53] Bryant p 50
[54] Bryant p 50
[55] Bryant pp. 50-51
[56] Sykes p 146
[57] Sykes p 156
[58] Herodotus
[59] Olmstead p 49 from Isaiah chapter 35, 40-55
[60] Cook p 31
[61] Cook p 30
[62] Omstead p 53
[63] Olmstead 51
[64] Olmstead 51
[65] Olmstead 52 from Cyrus' cylinder, 11. 30-32
[66] Olmstead 52- from Ezra chapter 1, Aramain decree of Cyrus 6:3-5
[67] Herodotus pp. 209-210
[68] Archeology Volume 53 Number 5, September/October 2000. Newsbrief by Salima Ikram
[69] Bryant p 85
[70] Bryant
[71] Bryant p 148
[72] Bryant p 94
[73] Bryant p 161
[74] Bryant pp. 175-176
[75] Bryant p 183
[76] Bryant p 187 from tablet DB bab &25 and DB bab 32
[77] Bryant p 187
[78] Cook p 87
[79] Herodotus p 445
[80] Cook p 65 from her II-58
[81] Bryant p 895
[82] Bryant pp. 899-900)
[83] Sykes p 228
[84] Sykes p 229
[85] Sykes p 229
[86] Sykes p 231
[87] Sykes p 231
[88] Sykes p 232
[89] Sykes p 242
[90] Arrian pp. 7-16
[91] Wilcken p 146
[92] Smith p 194
[93] O'Brien

[94] O' Brien p 101
[95] O'Brien from estimate of Donald W Engels based on Curtius
[96] O'Brien p101
[97] Worthington p 314
[98] Sykes pp. 287-288
[99] Sykes p 290
[100] Sykes p 331
[101] Sykes p 331
[102] Sykes p 331
[103] Sykes 334
[104] Sykes 335
[105] Sykes 335
[106] Sykes 335
[107] Sykes p 351
[108] Sykes p 360
[109] Sykes p 377
[110] Sykes 379
[111] Sykes p 382
[112] Sykes p 382
[113] Sykes pp. 382-383
[114] Sykes p 383
[115] Sykes pp. 383-384
[116] Sykes p 384
[117] Sykes p 387
[118] Sykes p 387
[119] Sykes p 396
[120] Sykes p 400
[121] Sykes p 403
[122] Christensen 177
[123] Christenesen 178
[124] Christensen p 181
[125] Christensen p 182
[126] Christensen p 182
[127] Christensen p 181
[128] Christensen pp. 206-207
[129] Christiansen p 260
[130] Sykes p 415
[131] Sykes p 415
[132] Sykes p 423
[133] Sykes p 431
[134] Sykes p 438
[135] Sykes p 442
[136] Sykes p 443
[137] Sykes p 446
[138] Sykes p 449
[139] Sykes p 450
[140] Sykes p 450
[141] Sykes p 451
[142] Sykes p 451
[143] Sykes pp. 455-456
[144] Sykes p 456
[145] Christiansen p 507
[146] Christiansen p 512
[147] Christiansen p 517
[148] Christiansen p 517
[149] Sykes p 465
[150] Sykes pp. 472-475
[151] Yarshater pp. 162-164
[152] Sykes p 481
[153] Sykes p 481
[154] Yarshater p 168
[155] Yarshater p 169
[156] Christiansen p 586
[157] Christiansen p 586
[158] Christiansen pp. 590-591
[159] Yarshater p 170
[160] Sykes p 489

Chapter 3
[161] Ashtiani p 50
[162] Haq p 313
[163] Zarrinkub p 48
[164] Haq p 318
[165] Haq p 319
[166] Kennedy p 108
[167] Haq p 321
[168] Zarrinkub p 50
[169] Zarrinkub p 50
[170] Zarrinkub p 51
[171] Christensen p 656
[172] Haq p 324
[173] Zarrinkub pp. 52-53 (from Akhbar-al-Taval)
[174] Frye p 61 (from Baladhuri)
[175] Zarrinkub 55
[176] Zarrinkub 55
[177] Zarrinkub p 57
[178] Zarrinkub p 57, Muir p 173
[179] Zarrinkub p57
[180] Muir p 174, Ashtiani p56, Zarrinkub pp. 57-58
[181] Frye p 60

REFERENCES

[182] Muir p 175
[183] Frye p 60
[184] Muir p 176
[185] Zarrinkub p 67
[186] Zarrinkub p 67 (from Farsnameh Ibn Balkhi 116)
[187] Zarrinkub p 67 (from Majma-al-tavarikh 283)
[188] Zarrinkub p 67 (from Kamel incidents in year 29)
[189] Zarrinkub p 67 (from Balazary 326)
[190] Zarrinkub p 97
[191] Zarrinkub p 69
[192] Muir p 194
[193] Muir p 201
[194] Muir p 201
[195] Christiansen pp. 658-659
[196] Muir p 209
[197] Muir p 209
[198] Muir p 209 from Masudi
[199] Al-Tusi (al Mabsut VII:279) from Rebellion and Violence in Islamic Law By Khaled Abou El Fadl
[200] Muir p 267
[201] Muir p 302
[202] Muir p 307
[203] Muir p 309
[204] Muir p 311
[205] Muir p 296
[206] Frye p 95
[207] Frye p 96
[208] Frye p 96
[209] Frye p 95
[210] Zarrinkub p 112
[211] Zarrinkub p 112
[212] Zarrinkub p 115
[213] Zarrinkub p 115
[214] Zarrinkub p 115
[215] Zarrinkub p 116
[216] Zarrinkub p 117
[217] Zarrinkub p 119
[218] Zarrinkub p 121
[219] Baghdad during the Abassid caliphate – G Le Strange- 1900 p 16

[220] Kennedy p 137
[221] Le Strange p 22
[222] Le Strange p 20
[223] Le Strange p 31
[224] Zarrinkub p 156
[225] Zarrinkub pp. 125-130
[226] Zarrinkub p 131
[227] Zarrinkub pp. 133-134
[228] Zarrinkub p 187 Zarrinkub p 135
[229] Zarrinkub p 123
[230] Zarrinkub p 135
[231] Zarrinkub p 188
[232] Encyclopedia Iranica, 'Babak Khorrami' by G.H. Yusofi
[233] Zarrinkub p 193
[234] Zarrinkub p 206
[235] Frye 1968 p 71
[236] Frye 1968 p 72
[237] Frye 1968 p 95
[238] Frye 1968 p 95
[239] Frye 1968 p 95
[240] Frye 1968 p 96
[241] Frye 1968 p 76
[242] Frye 1968 p 100
[243] Frye 1968 p 100
[244] Frye 1968 p 103
[245] Frye 1968 p 103
[246] Frye 1968 p 111
[247] Frye 1968 p 112
[248] Frye 1968 p 113
[249] Frye 1968 pp. 118-119
[250] Frye 1968 p 136
[251] Frye 1968 pp. 139-140
[252] Frye 1968 p 212
[253] Frye 1968 p 213
[254] Frye 1968 p 217
[255] Frye 1968 p 253
[256] Frye 1968 p 255
[257] Frye 1968 p 625
[258] Frye 1968 p 625
[259] Frye 1968 p 153
[260] Frye 1968 p 170
[261] Frye 1968 p 170
[262] International Dictionary of Historic Places By Trudy Ring,

Robert M. Salkin, Noelle Watson, Sharon La Boda, Paul Schellinger p764 Published by Taylor & Francis, 1995

[263] Frye 1968 p 179
[264] Frye 1975 p 224
[265] Frye 1975 p 227 (from Ibn-Athir pp. 266-273)
[266] Fox p 153
[267] Eghbal p 20
[268] Eghbal p 20
[269] Fox p 195

Chapter 4
[270] Weatherford p 111
[271] Fox p 161
[272] Fox p 145
[273] Fox p 161
[274] Fox p 156
[275] Fox p 163
[276] Fox p 163
[277] Fox p 163
[278] Eghbal p 20
[279] Fox p 168
[280] Fox p 180
[281] Man p 169
[282] Man p 169
[283] Man p 171
[284] Curtin p 110
[285] Eghbal p 30
[286] Fox p 179
[287] Fox p 178
[288] Fox p 178
[289] Curtin p 111
[290] Curtin p 112
[291] Quoted from Weatherford p 113
[292] Curtin p 114
[293] Curtin p 114
[294] Eghbal p 39
[295] Eghbal p 39
[296] Eghbal p 39
[297] Eghbal p 40
[298] Curtin p 118, Eghbal
[299] Man p 174
[300] Man p 175
[301] Man p 177
[302] Fox p 182
[303] Curtin p 125
[304] Curtin p 125
[305] Eghbal p 65
[306] Curtin p 129
[307] Curtin 132
[308] Curtin 132
[309] Eghbal pp. 135-145)
[310] Eghbal p 173)
[311] Eghbal p 184
[312] Curtin p 253
[313] Eghbal p 195
[314] Jackson
[315] The gift: poems by the great Sufi master By Hafiz, Daniel James Ladinsky. Penguin Books 1999
[316] Prawdin p 414
[317] Marozzi p 7
[318] Prawdin
[319] Marozzi
[320] Marozzi 43
[321] Marozzi 32
[322] Prawdin 433
[323] Marozzi 115
[324] Marozzi 116
[325] Marozzi 116
[326] Marozzi 116
[327] Marozzi 132
[328] Maroozi 132
[329] Marozzi 132
[330] Marozzi 133
[331] Marozzi 142
[332] Prawdin 443
[333] Prawdin 447
[334] Marozzi 148
[335] Marozzi 149
[336] Marozzi 149
[337] Marozzi 153
[338] Marozzi 153
[339] Marozzi 154
[340] Marozzi 267
[341] Marozzi 269
[342] Marozzi 271
[343] Prawdin
[344] Marozzi 272
[345] Prawdin

REFERENCES

346 Marozzi p 309
347 Prawdin p 493
348 Marozzi 154
349 Marozzi p 154
350 Los Angeles Times (23 Aug.1994
351 Christian Science Monitor (3 June 1997
352 Taheri p 112
353 Taheri p 103
354 Taheri p 77
355 Taheri p 79
356 Taheri p 131
357 Taheri p 131
358 Taheri p 132
359 Taheri p 176
360 Taheri p 180
361 Taheri p 182
362 Taheri p 195
363 Taheri p 196
364 Taheri pp. 188-189
365 Kinross p 167
366 Taheri p 195
367 Taheri p 198
368 Savory p 55
369 Savory p 60
370 Taheri p 228
371 Savory p 62
372 Savory pp. 69-70
373 Savory pp. 69-70
374 Savory p 83
375 Savory p 86
376 Savory p 83
377 Savory pp. 86-88
378 Savory p 145
379 Savory p 145 from Pope Introduction pp95
380 Savory p 145
381 Savory p 148
382 Savory p 133
383 Savory p 187
384 Savory p 233
385 Savory p 182
386 Savory p 182
387 Savory p 182
388 Savory p 183

389 Savory p 183
390 Savory 195-196
391 Savory 197
392 Savory p 155
393 Savory p 169
394 Savory p 170 from Curzon Vol II, p 38
395 Savory p 171 quoted from Curzon v.II pp45
396 Savory pp. 172-173 from Curzon V.II 47
397 Taheri p 392
398 Savory p 176
399 Savory p 176 from Stevens p 174
400 Savory p 176
401 Savory p 163 from Pope. Survey Vol III pp 1185
402 Savory p 165 Blunt and Swaan p71
403 Savory p 166 from Iranian Studies. VII (1974) Studies on Isfahan Part I pp320-347 by Ali Bakhtiar
404 Savory p 158
405 Taheri p 393
406 Savory p 159
407 Savory
408 Savory p 170 quoted in Curzon Vii pp39
409 Savory p 166
410 Taheri p 395
411 Savory p 95
412 Savory
413 Savory p 103 - from Lt-Col P.M Sykes A History of Persia, 2 vols London 1915 vol2-p 268)
414 Savory p 231
415 Savory p 229- Quotes of Jesuit Fr Krusinski and Joans Hanway and E.G Browne, A Literary History of Persia, 4 vols (cambridge 1925-1928), cols 4, p 111-112
416 Savory p 231
417 Savory p 232
418 Ashtiani -tarikh Iran pas az Islam p 601

[419] Savory p 237
[420] Savory p 238
[421] Savory p 241
[422] Savory p 241
[423] Savory p 244
[424] Savory p 246
[425] Savory pp. 248-249
[426] Savory p 249
[427] Savory p 250
[428] Savory p 250
[429] Lockhart p 23
[430] Lockhart p 32
[431] Lockhart pp. 36-39
[432] Lockhart p 39
[433] Lockhart p 39 from Ahwal p 205
[434] Lockhart p 42
[435] Lockhart p 43
[436] Lockhart p 43
[437] Lockhart p 47
[438] Lockhart p 46
[439] Lockhart p 49
[440] Lockhart p 50
[441] Lockhart p 54
[442] Lockhart p 57
[443] Lockhart p 59
[444] Lockhart p 62
[445] Lockhart p 63
[446] Lockhart p 70
[447] Lockhart p 71
[448] Lockhart p 71
[449] Lockhart p 72
[450] Lockhart p 75
[451] Lockhart p 104
[452] Lockhart p 120
[453] Axworthy p 6
[454] Axworthy p 7
[455] Axworthy p 8
[456] Axworthy p 9
[457] Axworthy p 10, Lockhart p 152, Cambridge history Vol VII edited by Peter Avery
[458] Axworthy p 11
459 Avery p 45
[460] Avery p 50
461 Nadir Shah. Stanhope essay for 1885. pp52 By Herbert John Maynard (sir.), Nâdir (shah of Persia.) Oxford, B. H. Blackwell. 50 Broad Street. London. Simpkin, Marshal and Co 1885
[462] Avery p 77
[463] Avery p 77
[464] Avery p 78
[465] Avery p 82
[466] Avery p 97
[467] Avery p 98
[468] Avery p 99
[469] Avery p 100
[470] Avery p 103
[471] Avery p 92
[472] Avery p 93
[473] Avery p 93
[474] Avery p 115
[475] Avery p 115
[476] Avery p 116
[477] Avery p 116
[478] Avery p 118
[479] Avery p 125
[480] Avery p 128 from Artemi 'Memoirs' p 228-229
[481] Avery pp. 130-131
[482] Avery p 149
[483] Avery p 132
[484] Avery p 133
[485] Avery p 336
[486] Avery p 338
[487] Avery p 168
[488] Avery p 169
[489] Avery p 580
[490] Avery p 581

Chapter 5
[491] Keeley p 18
[492] Keeley p 18
[493] Keeley p 28 from (Otterbein 1989: 21, 143-144, 148 "The evolution of War: A Cross-Cultural Study", New Haven Conn: HRAF Press
[494] Keeley p 28 from Ross 1983: 179, 182-83 "Political Decision Making and Conflict: Additional

REFERENCES

Cross-Cultrual Evidence and a new Analysis."Journal of Conflict Resolution 29: 547-79)
[495] Keeley p 28 from Jorgensen 1980: 503-6, 509-15, 613-14)
[496] Keeley p 29 from Harris 1989:288-289; Meggitt 1962:38,42,246)
[497] Keeley p 29
[498] Keeley p 29
[499] Keeley p 29
[500] Keeley p 29
[501] Keeley p 30 from Knauft 1987: 464
[502] Keeley pp. 32-33
[503] Keeley p 33
[504] Man, N.S 29, 95-115
[505] Bamforth p 105
[506] Bamforth p 106
[507] Bamforth p 107
[508] Bamforth p 107
[509] Keeley p 38
[510] Keeley p 38
[511] Keeley p 37
[512] Keeley p 37
[513] Keeley
[514] Keeley p 37
[515] Ehlrich p 207
[516] Ehlrich p 207
[517] Ehlrich p 208 quoted from Goodall 1986 p 530
[518] Ehlrich p 208
[519] Ehlrich p 205 from Waal 1983
[520] Ehlrich p 205 from Waal 1989
[521] Wrangham

Chapter 6

[522] Thoreau p 133
[523] Thoreau p 136
[524] Thoreau p 137
[525] Thoreau p 141
[526] Thoreau p 142
[527] Thoreau p 145
[528] Tolstoy p viii
[529] Tolstoy, Quote from 'Confessions'
[530] Tolstoy p viii
[531] Mathew 5 King James Bible
[532] Tolstoy p ix
[533] Tolstoy p ix
[534] Matt 5:39, King James Bible
[535] Tolstoy p 32
[536] Tolstoy p 32
[537] Tolstoy p 33
[538] Tolstoy p 33
[539] Tolstoy p 33
[540] Tolstoy p 36
[541] Tolstoy p 35
[542] Tolstoy p 44
[543] Tolstoy p 44
[544] Tolstoy p 50
[545] Homer p 37
[546] Intro to Letter to a Hindu
[547] Vladamir Chertkov - Translated into English by Benjamin Sher "Road to Terror Yale Univ. Press 1999
[548] (Carrie Taylor : On Tolstoy's Death : A Young Student's Memoir)
[549] Ibid.
[550] Tolstoy p xi
[551] Homer p 6
[552] Homer p 6
[553] Gandhi p 18
[554] Gandhi p 120
[555] Gandhi p 121
[556] Gandhi p 166
[557] Fischer p74
[558] Homer pp. 63-64
[559] Fischer p 77
[560] Fischer p 80
[561] Fischer pp. 80-81
[562] Fischer p 82
[563] Fischer p 87
[564] Fischer p 89
[565] Fischer p 108
[566] Nanda p 113
[567] Fischer p 113
[568] Nanda p 117 (quoted from Hardinge of Penhurst: My Indian Years, London, 1948, p91
[569] Fischer p 115
[570] Fischer p 115

Chapter 7

[571] Fischer p 125
[572] Fischer p 153
[573] Fischer p 155
[574] Fischer p 156
[575] Fischer p 172
[576] Nanda p 153
[577] Fischer p 173
[578] Fischer p 174
[579] Fischer p 177
[580] Fischer p 182
[581] Fischer p 179
[582] Fischer p 187
[583] Fischer p 187
[584] Fischer p 194
[585] Fischer p 197
[586] Fischer p 198
[587] Fischer p 198
[588] Nanda p 236
[589] Fischer p 198
[590] Fischer pp. 200-201
[591] Fischer p 201
[592] Nanda p 238
[593] Nanda p 239

[594] Nanda p 239
[595] Nanda p 240
[596] Fischer p 218
[597] Fischer p 223
[598] Fischer p 245
[599] Fischer p 254
[600] Fischer p 260
[601] Fischer p 261
[602] Fischer p 277
[603] Fischer p 262
[604] Fischer p 265
[605] Fischer p 266
[606] Fischer p 266
[607] Fischer p 267
[608] Fischer p 266
[609] Fischer p 268
[610] Fischer p 287

[611] Nanda p 315
[612] Fischer p 297
[613] Fischer p 298
[614] Fischer p 300
[615] Fischer p 306
[616] Fischer p 306
[617] Fischer p 308
[618] Fischer p 308
[619] Fischer p 318
[620] Fischer p 319
[621] Fischer p 319
[622] Fischer p 333
[623] Fischer p 344
[624] Fischer p 345
[625] Fischer p 34
[626] Fischer p 351
[627] Fischer p 352
[628] Fischer p 354
[629] Fischer p 358
[630] Fischer p 376
[631] Nanda p 461
[632] Nanda p 468
[633] Nanda p 473
[634] Nanda p 473
[635] Nanda p 401
[636] Fischer p 476
[637] Nanda p 406
[638] Fischer p 466
[639] Fischer p 456
[640] Fischer p 449
[641] Fischer p 462
[642] Fischer p 463
[643] Nanda p 496
[644] Fischer p 495
[645] Fischer p 495
[646] Fischer p 496
[647] Fischer p 497
[648] Fischer p 498
[649] Fischer p 500
[650] Fischer p 461
[651] Homer p 462
[652] Fischer 502
[653] Fischer p 502
[654] Fischer p 7
[655] Fischer p 9
[656] Fischer p 9
[657] Fischer p 10
[658] Fischer p 11
[659] Fischer p 11

REFERENCES

Chapter 8
660

http://www.nathanielturner.com/howardthurman.htm
661 King p 13
662 King p 20
663 King p 20
664 King p 24
665 King p 24
666 King p 37
667 King p 44
668 Branch p 123
669 Branch p 127
670 Branch p 125
671 Branch p 129
672 Branch p 131
673 Branch p 131
674 King p 57
675 King p 61
676 King p 62
677 King p 77
678 King p 77
679 King p 78
680 King p 79
681 King p 80
682 King p 87
683 King p 67
684 King p 102
685 King p 103
686 King p 129
687 King p 129
688 King p 134
689 King p 134
690 Ackerman p 315
691 Ackerman p 316
692 Ackerman p 318
693 Ackerman p 318
694 Ackerman p 321
695 Ackerman p 322
696 Ackerman p 332
697 Ackerman p 327
698 Ackerman p 327
699 Ackerman p 328-329
700 King pp. 167-168
701 King p 168
702 King p 169
703 Branch p 708
704 Branch p 726
705 Branch p 729
706 Branch p 730
707 Branch p 730
708 King p 189
709 King p 190
710 King p 190
711 Branch p 757
712 Branch p 757
713 King p 207
714 Branch p 757
715 Branch p 762
716 Branch p 761
717 Branch p 763
718 Branch p 763
719 Branch p 772
720 Branch p 763
721 Branch p 765
722 Branch p 770
723 Branch p 773
724 Branch pp. 773-774
725 King p 220
726 Branch p 225
727 King p 334
728 King p 335
729 King p 338
730 King p 337
731 King p 340
732 King p 342
733 King p 343
734 King p 345
735 King p 346
736 King p 358
737 King p 360
738 King p 364
739 King p 365
740 King p 365
741 King p 366
742 CNN: Special Investigations Unit. The Life of Dr. Martin Luther King Jr.

743 Ibid

Chapter 9
744 Sharp p 12

[745] Sharp p 21
[746] Sharp p 21
[747] Sharp p 23
[748] Sharp p 23
[749] Sharp p 16
[750] Sharp p 31
[751] Sharp p 31
[752] Sharp p 32
[753] Sharp p 65
[754] Sharp p 65
[755] Sharp p 67
[756] Sharp p 474
[757] Helvey p.9
[758] Sharp p 456
[759] Sharp p 457
[760] Sharp p 457
[761] Sharp p 733
[762] Sharp p 733
[763] Sharp p 741
[764] Sharp p 391
[765] Sharp p 186
[766] Sharp p 186
[767] Sharp p 187
[768] Sharp p 191
[769] Sharp p 289
[770] Sharp p 316
[771] Sharp p 316
[772] Sharp p 316
[773] Sharp p 316
[774] Sharp p 117
[775] Sharp p 118
[776] Ackerman p 374
[777] Burton p 79
[778] Burton p 94
[779] Burton p 96
[780] Burton p 96
[781] Burton p 100
[782] Burton pp. 104-108
[783] Burton p 108
[784] Burton p 109
[785] Ackerman p 375
[786] Burton p 109
[787] Burton p 111
[788] Sider p 57
[789] Ackerman p 370
[790] Burton p 113
[791] Burton p 120
[792] Ackerman p 370
[793] Ackerman p 371
[794] Ackerman p 377
[795] Ackerman p 377
[796] Sider p 59
[797] Sider p 59
[798] Sider p 59
[799] Burton p 299
[800] Sider p 60
[801] Sider p 61 quoted from (Hildegard Goss-Mayr "When Prayer and Revolution Became…" p 9)
[802] Ackerman p 381
[803] Sider p 62
[804] Ackerman p 381
[805] Sider pp. 61-62
[806] Sider p 63
[807] Mercado p 67
[808] Ackerman p 384
[809] Ackerman p 384
[810] Ackerman p 384
[811] Ackerman p 386
[812] Burton p 378
[813] Ackerman p 386
[814] Ackerman p 387
[815] Ackerman p 387
[816] Ackerman p 388
[817] Sider p 65
[818] Ackerman p 388
[819] Ackerman p 389
[820] Sider p 67
[821] Ackerman p 390
[822] Daye p 41
[823] Daye p 43
[824] Daye p 44
[825] Daye p 48
[826] Daye p 50
[827] Daye p 53

[828] Daye from Nicholas Tavuchis, Mea Culpa: A Sociology of Apology and Reconciliation (Stanford: Stanford University Press, p.19)
[829] Daye p 65

REFERENCES

[830] Daye p 65
[831] Daye p 65
[832] Daye pp. 71-72
[833] Daye p 80
[834] Daye p 85
[835] Daye p 85
[836] Daye p 87
[837] Daye p 87
[838] Daye p 95
[839] Daye p 90
[840] Daye p 105
[841] Herman pp. 175-195
[842] Herman p 155
[843] Daye p 141-142
[844] Daye p 142
[845] See Daye pp. 152-165
[846] Paz p 47

Chapter 10
[847] Segal p 332
[848] Segal p 336
[849] Segal p 337
[850] Segal p 329
[851] Imbe-Black p 3
[852] Imbe-Black p 4
[853] Imbe-Black p 5
[854] Imbe-Black p 5

[855] Imbe-Black p 6
[856] Imbe-Black p 5
[857] Imbe-Black pp. 5-6
[858] Segal p 332
[859] Herman p 133
[860] Herman p 133
[861] Herman p 155

Chapter 11
[862] Razi 2003 p 180
[863] Anjavi-Shirazi v.1 pp. 2-28
[864] Anjavi-Shirazi v.1 p 20
[865] Anjavi-Shirazi v.2 p 156
[866] Anjavi-Shirazi v.2 p 30
[867] Anjavi-Shirazi v.1 p
[868] Anjavi-Shirazi v.2 p 157
[869] Anjavi-Shirazi v.1 p 109)
[870] Anjavi-Shirazi v.1 p 126
[871] Anjavi-Shirazi v.1 p 126

[872] Anjavi-Shirazi v.1 p 108
[873] Anjavi-Shirazi v.1 p 127
[874] Anjavi-Shirazi v.1 p 127
[875] Anjavi-Shirazi v.2
[876] Anjavi-Shirazi v.2 p 14
[877] Anjavi-Shirazi v.2 p 54
[878] Anjavi-Shirazi v.2 p 54
[879] Anjavi-Shirazi v.2 p 54
[880] Anjavi-Shirazi v.2 p 54
[881] Razi 2000 p 575
[882] See Wells, The Journey of Man, A Genetic Odyssey
[883] Anjavi-Shirazi v.1 p 3
[884] Anjavi-Shirazi v.1 p 3
[885] Anjavi-Shirazi v.1 p 3
[886] Anjavi-Shirazi v.1 p 3
[887] Anjavi-Shirazi v.1 p 3
[888] Anjavi-Shirazi v.1 p 5
[889] Anjavi-Shirazi v.1 p 27
[890] Anjavi-Shirazi v.1 p 4
[891] Anjavi-Shirazi v.1 p 4
[892] Anjavi-Shirazi v.1 pp. 7-8
[893] Anjavi-Shirazi v.1 p 8
[894] Anjavi-Shirazi v.2 p 102
[895] Anjavi-Shirazi v.1 p 67
[896] Anjavi-Shirazi v.2 p 92
[897] Anjavi-Shirazi v.2 p 93
[898] Anjavi-Shirazi v.2 p 99
[899] Anjavi-Shirazi v.2 p 106
[900] Anjavi-Shirazi v.2 p 100
[901] Anjavi-Shirazi v.2 p 106
[902] Anjavi-Shirazi v.1 p 67
[903] Razi 2000 p 574
[904] Razi 2000 p 576
[905] Razi 2000 p 579
[906] Razi 2000 p 586
[907] Razi 2000 p 588
[908] Razi 2000 p 577
[909] Razi 2000 p 604
[910] Razi 2000 p 624
[911] Razi 2000 p 606
[912] Razi 2000 p 607
[913] Avery p 586
[914] Biruni p 302
[915] Razi 2000 p 231
[916] Razi 2000 p 235

[917] Rafizadeh p 19
[918] Rafizadeh p 19
[919] Rafizadeh p 20
[920] Rafizadeh p 21
[921] Rafizadeh p 22
[922] Rafizadeh p 31
[923] Rafizadeh p 33
[924] Rafizadeh p 34
[925] Rafizadeh p 36
[926] Rafizadeh p 36
[927] Razi 2000 pp. 243-247 (from Nowruz miane kords-ha, Sadigh Safih Zadeh)

Chapter 12
[928] Amir Mokri p 336
[929] Some replace serkeh (vinegar) as an item on the table. *Sabzeh* is also counted as one of the seven items.
[930] Razi 2000 p 211
[931] Razi 2000 p 211
[932] Razi 2000 p 252
[933] Amir Mokri p 216
[934] Razi 2000 p 129
[935] Dehkhoda Volume 2
[936] Dehkhoda volume 2
[937] Razi 2000 p 379

Chapter 13
[938] Razi 2000 p 638
[939] Razi 2000 p 511
[940] (Ayeen-e-Mitra Martin Vermaseren- transleted into Persian Bozorg Naderzad)-p 15
[941] Vermaseren p 16
[942] Razi 2000 p,Vermaseren p 16
[943] Vermaseren p p16
[944] Razi 2000 p 511
[945] Razi 2000 p 513
[946] Razi 2000 p 517
[947] Razi 2000 p 522
[948] Razi 2000 p 521
[949] Razi 2000 p 522
[950] Razi 2000 p 523
[951] Razi 2000 p 542
[952] Razi 2000 p 543
[953] Razi 2000 p 544
[954] Razi 2000 p 537
[955] Razi 2000 p 540
[956] Razi 2000 p 539
[957] Razi 2000 p 540
[958] Razi 2000 p 535
[959] Razi 2003 p 267
[960] Razi 2003 p 267
[961] Razi 2003 p 269
[962] Razi 2003 p 272
[963] Razi 2000 pp. 671-672
[964] Brown p 181
[965] Razi 2003 pp. 125-126
[966] Razi 2000 p 682
[967] Razi 2000 p 682
[968] Shahnemeh – Reign of Shapur Zu'l Aktaf, Section 16, lines 56-69

Epilogue
[969] Public Statement #17 by Mir Hussein Mousavi. January 10, 2010
[970] Helvey p.9
[971] Helvey p.23